THE ARCHAEOLOGY OF SOUTH ASIA

This book offers a critical synthesis of the archaeology of South Asia from the Neolithic period (c. 6500 BCE), when domestication began, to the spread of Buddhism accompanying the Mauryan Emperor Asoka's reign (third century BCE). The authors examine the growth and character of the Indus civilisation, with its town planning, sophisticated drainage systems, vast cities and international trade. They also consider the strong cultural links between the Indus civilisation and the second, later period of South Asian urbanism which began in the first millennium BCE and developed through the early first millennium CE. In addition to comparing the evidence for emerging urban complexity, this book gives equal weight to interactions between rural and urban communities across South Asia and considers the critical roles played by rural areas in social and economic development. The authors explore how narratives of continuity and transformation have been formulated in analyses of South Asia's Prehistoric and Early Historic archaeological record.

Robin Coningham is UNESCO Chair in Archaeological Ethics and Practice in Cultural Heritage at Durham University. He has participated in more than twenty UNESCO missions and currently codirects UNESCO's excavations in Nepal at Tilaurakot and Lumbini, the birthplace of the Buddha. He has published eight books and more than eighty papers and chapters.

Ruth Young is Senior Lecturer in the School of Archaeology and Ancient History at the University of Leicester. She has published in journals such as *Antiquity, International Journal of Heritage Studies, International Journal of Historical Archaeology, Historical Archaeology* and *World Archaeology*. She is also writing a monograph on her work in northern Pakistan.

CAMBRIDGE WORLD ARCHAEOLOGY

SERIES EDITOR
NORMAN YOFFEE, *University of Michigan*

EDITORIAL BOARD
SUSAN ALCOCK, *Brown University*
TOM DILLEHAY, *Vanderbilt University*
TIM PAUKETAT, *University of Illinois*
STEPHEN SHENNAN, *University College London*
CARLA SINOPOLI, *University of Michigan*
DAVID WENGROW, *University College London*

The *Cambridge World Archaeology* series is addressed to students and professional archaeologists, and to academics in related disciplines. Most volumes present a survey of the archaeology of a region of the world, providing an up-to-date account of research and integrating recent findings with new concerns of interpretation. While the focus is on a specific region, broader cultural trends are discussed and the implications of regional findings for cross-cultural interpretations considered. The authors also bring anthropological and historical expertise to bear on archaeological problems and show how both new data and changing intellectual trends in archaeology shape inferences about the past. More recently, the series has expanded to include thematic volumes.

RECENT BOOKS IN THE SERIES

THE ARCHAEOLOGY OF SOUTH ASIA

From the Indus to Asoka, c. 6500 BCE–200 CE

ROBIN CONINGHAM

Durham University

RUTH YOUNG

University of Leicester

CAMBRIDGE
UNIVERSITY PRESS

CAMBRIDGE
UNIVERSITY PRESS

32 Avenue of the Americas, New York, NY 10013-2473, USA

Cambridge University Press is part of the University of Cambridge.

It furthers the University's mission by disseminating knowledge in the pursuit of
education, learning and research at the highest international levels of excellence.

www.cambridge.org
Information on this title: www.cambridge.org/9780521846974

First published 2015

Printed in the United States of America

A catalog record for this publication is available from the British Library.

Library of Congress Cataloging in Publication Data
Coningham, Robin.
The archaeology of South Asia : from the Indus to Asoka, c. 6500 BCE–200 CE / Robin Coningham
(Durham University), Ruth Young (University of Leicester).
    pages   cm. – (Cambridge world archaeology)
Includes bibliographical references and index.
ISBN 978-0-521-84697-4 (hardback)
1. South Asia – Antiquities.   2. Antiquities, Prehistoric – South Asia.   3. Archaeology and history –
South Asia.   4. Excavations (Archaeology) – South Asia.   5. Cities and towns, Ancient – South Asia.
6. Indus civilization.   7. Indus River Valley – Antiquities.   8. Social archaeology – South Asia.
9. Social change – South Asia – History – To 1500.   I. Young, Ruth, 1963–   II. Title.
DS338.C64   2015
934–dc23   2015016107

ISBN 978-0-521-84697-4 Hardback

CONTENTS

ILLUSTRATIONS, TIMELINES AND BOXES

ILLUSTRATIONS

TIMELINES

BOXES

ACKNOWLEDGEMENTS

We are both extremely grateful to the many individuals and institutions who have contributed to the research and scholarship which underpins this volume. Much of our writing has also been informed by long seasons of fieldwork with colleagues and friends across South Asia and Iran.

In the field and in conferences, seminars and lectures, we have particularly benefitted from contributions and feedback from Kosh Prasad Acharya, Gamini Adikari, D. P. Agrawal, P. Ajithprasad, M. S. Alam, Ihsan Ali, Taj Ali, Bridget Allchin, the late Raymond Allchin, Alessandra Avanzini, the late Massoud Azarnoush, Hossein Azizi, the late Senake Bandaranayake, Nicholas Barrington, Nabha Basnyat-Thapa, Kuldeep Bhan, Mokammal H. Bhuiyan, Basanta Bidari, Ravindra Singh Bisht, Irina Bokova, Osmund Bopearachchi, Crispin Branfoot, Charlotte Cable, Pierfrancesco Callieri, Dilip Chakrabarti, Ranabir Chakravarti, P. J. Cherian, James Cormick, Bhesh Narayan Dahal, the late George Dales, Mahinda Deegalle, Siran Deraniyagala, M. K. Dhavalikar, Senarath Dissanayake, R. Dittmann, the late Fazand Ali Durrani, Mukhtar Ali Durrani, Roland Fletcher, Dorian Fuller, Krista Gilliland, Gavin Gillmore, Ian Glover, Prishanta Gunawardhana, Sunil Gupta, Norman Hammond, U Nyunt Han, Jason Hawkes, K. Hemachandran, Hengameh Ilkmani, Shahnaj Husne Jahan, Rukshan Jayewardhana, Peter Johansen, J. P. Joshi, Maiya Kaiti, Hassan Karimian, Mangala Katugampola, Steven Kemper, Jonathan Mark Kenoyer, Farid Khan, Gul Rahim Khan, Muhammad Ashraf Khan, Shakir Ullah Khan, Ravi Korisettar, Krishna Bahadur KC, K. Krishnan Nampoothiri, Ram Kunwar, Takefumi Kurose, Win Kyaing, Nayanjot Lahiri, Sirinimal Lakdusinghe, Shanti Limbu, Roland Lin, Lisa Lucero, U Kyaw Oo Lwin, U Thein Lwin, John MacGinnis, Mehran Maghsoudi, R. Mahalakshmi, Mala Malla, Christian Manhart, B. R. Mani, K. S. Mathew, Richard Meadow, Costantino Meucci, David Michelmore, V. N. Misra, Mats Mogren, Rabindra Mohanty, Elizabeth Moore, Kathleen Morrison, Mehdi Mortazavi, Mohammed Rafique Mughal, the Rev. Toshun Murakami, Ohnmar Myo, Muhammad Naeem, Maryam Naeemi, S. Nagaraju, Kalum Nalinda, Harendralal Namalgamuwa,

Hassan Fazeli Nashli, Lotika Nehru, Yukio Nishimura, Wannasarn Noonsuk, Pashupati Nyaupane, K. Paddayya, S. K. Pandey, Asko Parpola, Beena Paudyal, Cameron Petrie, the late Gregory Possehl, Saubhagya Pradhanang, Sheikh Sultan bin Mohammed Al Qasimi, Gyanin Rai, K. Rajan, Umanga Roshani Rammungoda, Colin Renfrew, Poori Saeedi, Minoo Salimi, Jean-Francois Salles, Vern Scarborough, V. Selvakumar, Swadhin Sen, Jayampath Senanayake, Sudharshan Seneviratne, S. Settar, Sri Acharya Karma Sangbo Sherpa, Vasant Shinde, B. B. Shrestha, H. Shrestha, Sudhir Bhakta Shrestha, Steven Sidebotham, Ian Simpson, Upinder Singh, Prakash Sinha, Monica Smith, Janice Stargardt, Bharat Subedi, A. Sundara, Farooq Swati, Romila Thappar, Chris Thornton, Rakesh Tiwari, Roberta Tomber, Maurizio Tosi, Himal Kumar Upreti, Supriya Varma, Massimo Vidale, Willem Vogelsang, Jagath Weerasinghe, Kai Weise, Michael Willis, Rita Wright, Mumtaz Yattoo and Muhammad Zahir.

We are also very grateful to a number of our former and current colleagues for their continued support and advice, including Janet Ambers, Ian Bailiff, Graeme Barker, Cathy Batt, Julie Bond, Julie Bone, Mary Brooks, Chris Caple, Mike Church, Christopher Davis, Steve Dockrill, Randy Donahue, Dave Edwards, Lin Foxhall, Christopher Gerrard, Mark Gillings, Tony Gouldwell, Colin Haselgrove, Carl Heron, Rob Janaway, Chris Knusel, Anna Leone, Nick Lewer, Paul Luft, Mark Manuel, Armineh Marghussian, David Mattingly, Terry O'Connor, Deirdre O'Sullivan, Marilyn Palmer, Graham Philip, Mark Pollard, Charlotte Roberts, Chris and Judith Scarre, Geoffrey Scarre, Armin Schmidt, Sarah Semple, Jo Shoebridge, Ben Stern, Keir Strickland, Jill Thompson, Jen Tremblay-Fitton, and the late Tony Wilkinson. These lists are not exhaustive and the authors extend their apologies to anyone inadvertently omitted.

We are also indebted to the following individuals for allowing us to reproduce their images within this volume: Bridget Allchin and William Allchin; Jo Shoebridge; Peter Johansen; Chris Thornton for the Bat Archaeological Project; K. Krishnan for the Department of Archaeology and Ancient History, MS University of Baroda, India; Luca Maria Olivieri for the Italian Archaeological Mission to Pakistan; Armineh Marghussian and Warwick Ball. Craig Barclay of Durham University's Oriental Museum facilitated access to the photographic archive of John Marshall and we are grateful to him for allowing the reproduction of some of Marshall's images. Mark Manuel, Chris Davis, Armineh Marghussian and Keir Strickland kindly prepared the line drawings and scanned many of the images. Jen Tremblay-Fitton kindly assisted with the creation of the index, Chris Davis with the preparation of a number of boxes, and Jeff Veitch provided invaluable help by scanning many of the original slides.

Finally, we should like to acknowledge the highly professional assistance of the Cambridge production and editorial team as well as the invaluable prompts and recommendations from Professor Norman Yoffee of the University of

Michigan, the Series Editor, who guided our way through to the current volume. We also benefitted from the close reading of earlier versions of the text by Professor Carla Sinopoli of the University of Michigan, two anonymous Cambridge readers, Professor K. Krishnan of MS University of Baroda, Professor Prishanta Gunawardana of the University of Kelaniya and Director-General of Sri Lanka's Central Cultural Fund, Professor Hassan Fazeli Nashli of Tehran University and Kosh Prasad Acharya, former Director-General of Archaeology, Government of Nepal.

PART ONE

THE CONTEXT

CHAPTER I

INTRODUCTION AND DEFINITIONS

SCOPE AND THEMES

South Asia, also known as the Indian Subcontinent, covers 4.5 million square kilometres and contains 109 of the world's mountains that rise over 7,000 metres (Figure 1.1). This region is home to one-third of the world's population and encompasses several hundred local languages and dialects and is the site of the emergence of four major world religions and one of the four Old World Civilisations. It now accounts for a massive US$ 1.854 trillion of the world's gross domestic product and is the source of a diaspora of some 30 million people. Given the economic and political significance of contemporary South Asia, it is no surprise that this vast geographical region has a matching richness within its archaeological and historical record. It is so vast and rich that it is correct to question whether it is even possible to present a volume which draws together such disparate topics as hunter-gathers from western India, the major urban forms of the Indus Civilisation, the Iron Age megaliths of Peninsular India and the imperial ideology of the Mauryans. We believe that this is possible but also believe that in order to do so, it is important to present this information through the medium of a major narrative theme in order to structure our material. Rather than just pursuing a route of describing site sequences and moving from one chronological building block to another, encyclopaedically detailing all the different cultures that have been identified across the region or focusing on technical descriptions of pottery or stone tools in an attempt to define archaeological cultures, we have chosen to take a site and regional-based themed approach structured within a distinct developmental framework.

Whilst fully conscious of the multiplicity of narratives, identities, approaches and paradigms present within contemporary South Asian archaeology, or rather archaeologies, our selected theme involves the direct comparison of South Asia's two largely urban-focused developments, generally termed the Indus or Harappan civilisation and the Early Historic or Indo-Gangetic civilisation. We will also undertake a detailed consideration of the people and

Figure 1.1. Map of South Asia showing modern nation states.

settlements belonging to the period between the two, which has frequently
been presented and interpreted as a distinct cultural, political and social transformation. We have chosen to do this for two main reasons. The first is that
there were many similarities in the internal sequences and cycles of both these
developments and the time lapse between them has now been reduced to a
matter of centuries. The second reason is that research now establishes clearly
that the origins of both the Indus and the Early Historic urban-focused developments were much older and that both developed far more slowly than has
often been presented in the past and, as such, have formed distinct traditions.
Within this volume, we will also explore a range of different theories about
state formation and social organisation in relation to South Asia, and then test
them against a range of archaeological and, where appropriate, historical evidence. This process will serve to demonstrate how much our understanding

and perspectives have changed archaeological theory and fieldwork in South Asia since Cambridge University Press's foundation publication of Raymond and Bridget Allchin's *The Rise of Civilization in India and Pakistan* in 1982 in the Cambridge World Archaeology series.

Whilst we will closely examine the dynamics of both of these urban-focused populations in turn and consider issues such as continuity and transformation, similarity and difference, it is also important to remember that few regions have ever existed in a vacuum. South Asia has always influenced and been influenced by its near neighbours and more distant trading partners. Recognising this perspective is critical for understanding questions of diffusion and indigenous development as these two fundamental issues of continuity and transformation dominate discussions of archaeological explanation in South Asian archaeology. By exploring the development, character and ultimate transformation of each of the two main urban-focused sequences in depth, we will present a range of past and current theoretical explanations. We will also demonstrate how these have influenced the development of past and contemporary archaeological and historical interpretations, which in turn have resulted in a number of enduring social and political narratives. We would also stress that this volume is not focused solely on urban forms or urbanism but on settlements and communities more broadly and their networks and connections. Although, of course, chapters and debates on the urban-focused development of the Indus and Early Historic societies receive considerable coverage. As such, we believe that the title of the volume reflects its contents, which consider the archaeologies of urban development and their spheres of influence as well as non-urban communities and non-urbanised regions and their populations between the Indus and Asoka.

Traditional synthetic archaeological studies of South Asia have tended to either follow a chronological narrative introducing the main events and developments across the whole region, or present the developmental sequence of either the Indus or the Early Historic civilisations. Whilst some of these general chronological or synthetic narratives provide invaluable sources of evidence, such as Settar and Korrisettar (2002) and Singh (2008), they remain largely separate from theoretical concerns or explanations of change. Eltsov has recently contributed to this cohort of scholarship with a volume exploring concepts of the ancient South Asian city as gleaned from heavily edited textual sources but remains largely urban-focused and controversial in his application of later texts to the third millennium BCE (2008). Some of the works that have explored either the Indus or the Early Historic urban and rural sequences have provided innovative approaches for the analysis of those complex societies, for example Shaffer's (1992) concept of an 'Indus Valley Tradition' to which we return later. However, most have focused on either one tradition or the other, thus continuing the long-standing division between the Indus and Early Historic, for example Wright (2010), Sengupta and Chakraborty

(2008), McIntosh (2002) and Kenoyer (1998). This division can be broadly traced back to the later years of European colonial influence in South Asia and the impact of individuals such as Mortimer Wheeler (1950), Gordon Childe (1934) and Stuart Piggott (1950) with their claims that a distinct cultural, linguistic and social transformation lay between the Indus Civilisation and the Early Historic. This is not to suggest that this was purely a colonial concept as a number of post-Independence South Asian scholars also adopted and adapted it, including Dani (1967), Banerjee (1965) and Lal (1955). Furthermore, some scholars have viewed the Indus through a prism influenced by the archaeology of Mesopotamia, such as Wright 2010. As this volume considers merchant populations within the Arabian Sea and Indo-Iranian Plateau, we also feel justified in citing relevant comparative models and concepts associated with those regions and beyond if they help us advance our understanding of the sequences and processes under discussion (Trigger 2003).

Archaeological research in South Asia has of course moved far beyond these simplistic models, but the influence that such early interpretations of key sites and materials had on the development of archaeological explanation has been immense, and one which we will explore, along with other archaeological discussions and theories throughout this volume. Although elements of continuity between the two periods have been recognised by an increasing number of scholars (e.g. Agrawal 2007; Upadhyay 2008; Eltsov 2008; Coningham 1995a; Shaffer 1993; Kenoyer 1991b; Chakrabarti 1999), the techniques, theories and methodologies for studying these two urban-focused developments have tended to remain separate – as indeed do most of the archaeologists working on them. Indeed, one recent comparative study of South Asian cities from 2500 BCE until after the ninth century CE has even stated that their configurations appear to have been quite separate: "The Indus, Early Historic and Medieval urban phases were independent developments" (Smith 2006a: 130). It is not the intention of this volume to lionise the contributions of colonial scholars but to join other scholars in acknowledging that their theoretical and methodological influences are still distinctly traceable (Basant 2008: 191); therefore addressing this artificial divide is one of the cornerstones of the present volume.

CHRONOLOGICAL AND GEOGRAPHICAL SPAN

Bridget and Raymond Allchin presented three major synthetic texts to South Asian archaeologists; *The Birth of Indian Civilisation* (1968), which began with the Early Stone Age, continued through the Indus Civilisation and terminated with the Iron Age and what the Allchins called the beginnings of history. In parallel, *The Rise of Civilisation in India and Pakistan* (1982) began with a discussion of hunter-gathers and nomadic pastoralists, moved through early sedentary, agricultural populations to the main focus of the book, the Indus

Civilisation. Finally, Raymond Allchin's edited *The Archaeology of Early Historic South Asia* (1995a) revisited the transitional end of the Indus Civilisation, and then concentrated on the emergence and regional development of the second urban period, concluding with the Mauryan Empire. Sharing a similar title with Allchin's edited volume, Gautam Sengupta and Sharmi Chakraborty's book contains a number of contributors who question the usage and very definition of the term 'Early Historic' (2008). Dilip Chakrabarti's text *India: An Archaeological History: Palaeolithic Beginnings to Early Historic Foundations* (1999) primarily covered the archaeology of the modern state of India from the Palaeolithic to AD 300, and Upinder Singh's *A History of Ancient and Early Medieval India*, up to the twelfth century AD (2008). Our own text falls between these approaches; we aim to be less wide ranging chronologically than Chakrabarti and Singh's volumes, which allows us to look in greater detail at sites and issues, and we draw together the two main urban-focused South Asian developments which formed the subject of separate Allchin volumes (Timeline 1.1).

The very term 'South Asian' as a description of people from the geographical region of South Asia is contested by some, and there is current debate surrounding the suitability of this term to describe people or groups of people who have originated from the countries of Bangladesh, India, Nepal, Pakistan, Sri Lanka and associated states, or are descended from citizens of these places. To many, 'South Asia' is considered a colonial construct, a blanket term that oversimplifies the geographical and cultural complexity of the region, and thus reduces the people so described to a uniform ethnicity. In place of 'South Asian', it has sometimes been proposed that people and groups of people are better referred to by their religion, such as Sikh, Muslim, Hindu or Buddhist. While there are clearly many issues with this (and other) suggested classificatory and descriptive system, the main point here is that many of the archaeological and cultural terms that we use within South Asia have been developed externally and may not always be appropriate. In many cases, it is important to realise that forcing the fit of such terms and names is not only inappropriate but may also have been a means of masking internal or indigenous activity. There are also a number of terms and related issues that are used commonly in South Asian archaeology, about which we need to make our own position and understanding clear. Notwithstanding these points, we will continue to use 'South Asia/n' as a geographically descriptive term, a form of shorthand, for the nation states outlined in Chapter 2. However, as we make clear in Chapter 2, this is not intended to mask differences, whether physical or cultural, as these differences are integral to our understanding of the prehistory and early history in this region. Rather, it is intended as an overview term, which we feel is relatively free from ethnic, religious or other content whilst reflecting the strong cultural and historical connections of this region and distinguishing it from West and South East Asia.

The Archaeology of South Asia - Timeline

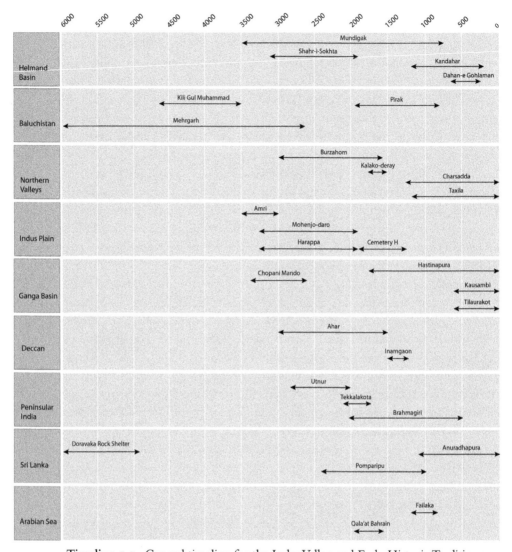

Timeline 1.1. General timeline for the Indus Valley and Early Historic Traditions.

   South Asia today is a highly complex region with multiple religions, ideologies and belief systems, languages, ethnic groups and social identities, and this was also true in the past. As a result, we cannot offer a 'one size fits all' approach to understanding the past here because very different processes were running at the same time in different parts of the region. For example, when the first iron-using farmers sailed from Peninsula India to Sri Lanka they appear to have coexisted for a while alongside lithic tool-using hunter-gatherering populations, apparently bypassing Neolithic and copper artefact-using phases. Rather than starting this volume by presenting the earliest evidence for human activity within South Asia, and moving chronologically through each region, we will draw out core themes and processes and follow a comparative approach. For this reason, rather than beginning with early communities of hunter-gatherer-foragers, we will begin by considering South Asia's first food producers and analysing their material culture, in order to both understand change and organisation within these populations, and to present them as the roots of increasing complexity and incipient urbanism. We are also aware of the great contrasts between available data sets, primarily chronometric dates ranges and published sites, across South Asia. While it is clear that there are foci of excellence, such as the pioneering work of Siran Deraniyagala (1992) exploring microlithic tool-using populations within the tropical rainforests of central Sri Lanka, comparative perspectives from elsewhere are not yet available. Until such data are more systematically investigated and approached across South Asia as a whole, it is unlikely to be systematically synthesised and presented. This situation is changing, as seen in publications such as those of Robin Dennell (2009), Sheila Mishra (1995; Mishra et al. 2013) and Ravi Korisettar and Mike Petraglia's teams in the Deccan (1999), so we may anticipate a greater degree of knowledge and information in the near future.

Similarly, the decision about where to finish the narratives within this volume was as difficult as determining the starting point, and we debated whether we should end with the opening of the Gupta 'Golden Age' or the era of Kanishka or possibly even as early as the movement of the Macedonians into the far west of the South Asian region. However, we have chosen to end it with the reign of Asoka (r. 269–232 BCE), the great Mauryan Emperor who had details of his life and ideology recorded in a variety of sources, including primary historical texts, and inscribed stone pillars and boulders. We have chosen this point to finish as we suggest that the Mauryan Empire brought together for the first time much of South Asia under a single hegemony, one which formed the basis of the state traditions which held sway for the next two millennia. Modern South Asia draws heavily on the time period covered in this book for many of its economic, social and cultural narratives, and these issues of identity and recognition will be discussed in our next chapters, where we consider the role of archaeology, identity and nationalism within the modern nation states of South Asia.

Given the great range of people and cultural markers within a single country such as India, Nepal or Sri Lanka, it is reasonable to ask how we consider it possible to explore the prehistory and early history of a number of countries over a six thousand year timescale. We argue that it is precisely because of this time depth that we can consider the countries of South Asia as a larger entity existing beyond modern geopolitical boundaries. By exploring the development of the two major urban-focused traditions in this region, we are able to examine both similarities and differences across a wide range of environmental, social, ideological and cultural groupings. In Chapter 2, we will discuss the geographic boundaries which both unite and define the modern states of

South Asia, and we will also situate the study region within its wider setting of the Indian Ocean and the Himalayan and Hindu Kush mountain barriers. In so doing, we will ensure that modern geo-political boundaries do not artificially constrain our discussion.

Whilst there are a number of convincing geographical and cultural elements that make this region a coherent whole for the purposes of long-term study, there are of course many links with regions outside the immediate boundaries of study that can be elucidated through archaeological analysis. Historical and art historical sources inform us about contact with the Classical Mediterranean, the Red Sea and the Near East, Eurasia and, of course, Achaemenid Persia to the west. Indeed, we have accounts of Megasthenes, the Seleucid Ambassador to the Mauryan court, and the later records of the Chinese Buddhist pilgrims with records of contact with China and Central Asia, as well as South East Asia. However, in order to understand the nature and dynamics of such contact in earlier periods, we need to turn to archaeology, and we will explore these contacts in greater depth in relevant sections. For example, we will examine the evidence for the reported presence of Indus merchants and entrepots in Mesopotamia, northern Afghanistan and along the Persian Gulf, along with evidence from Indus sites in South Asia indicating external contact in Chapter 7. The impact of South Asia itself on surrounding regions is also important, not only with respect to trade and exchange, but also in the spread of ideologies such as Hinduism and Buddhism to various parts of South-east and Central Asia. In turn, pilgrims from these areas to South Asia have also had impact on developments in the region (e.g. Bellina and Glover 2004; Indrawooth 2004).

KEY CONCEPTS AND THEIR ARCHAEOLOGICAL INDICATORS

There are many concepts in modern archaeology which are frequently used, although different scholars may attach somewhat different understandings as to their exact meanings and applications. For example, differing definitions of urbanism in South Asia have hindered comparisons between the Indus and Early Historic Traditions and, as a result, we believe that it is important to provide definitive explanations of potentially controversial terms and concepts from the outset. This section will therefore present and consider a wide range of different archaeological concepts relevant to our broader discussions, and offer definitions or outlines which will be of value to readers as well as helping to ensure that misunderstandings and misinterpretations do not arise. We will also draw on the definitions presented here to underpin current understanding (and misunderstandings) of the main chronological and cultural events within the region.

Many of the following terms and concepts are closely linked, and there is often a degree of overlap between definitions, but they are all part of our search for greater understanding of the origins of urban-focused communities and their populations. We have also explicitly engaged with the concept and definition of 'civilisation' as it is frequently identified as one of the fundamental questions to be addressed by archaeology (Gamble 2001: 157), albeit one of the most debated and contested. Just as important as understanding the origins of any archaeological phenomenon, is an understanding of the dynamics and processes which carried that phenomenon forward giving rise to tangible evidence which we as archaeologists have recovered in the present. Indeed, understanding and explaining issues of cultural resilience and stability may also shed light on differing trajectories of adaptation.

Differentiation and Social Inequality

Exploring and recognising the advent and development of inequality within a cultural sequence is one of the fundamental questions and challenges that concerns archaeologists and ancient historians (Price and Feinman 2010). Concepts of differentiation and social inequality are closely tied to the emergence of social and economic complexity itself, making it important to understand what we mean by these terms and processes. Traditionally, many archaeologists accepted a definition of a 'simple' society as one with few formal layers of decision-making, whether these represent hierarchies of power or social and economic organisation (e.g. Renfrew and Bahn 2010; Stein 1994). For example, a group which belongs to the social anthropology category of 'band' is frequently defined as having a small number of members, fewer than 100; with an egalitarian approach to power, decision making and leadership; a subsistence strategy based on mobility with little, if any, emphasis on storage or the production of surplus (Service 1971). In direct contrast with this category, a complex society is traditionally referred to as a state or civilisation and is frequently defined through its possession of a large population, often greater than 20,000 individuals; a clear hierarchy with many social classes or groupings; the production and redistribution of agricultural surplus which allows the maintenance of a large section of the population who are not engaged in food production; the presence of a centralised bureaucracy; the emergence of a shared religious ideology; and the creation of differentiated groups of specialised craft-workers (Childe 1950; Trigger 2003). We are also aware that such terms, including chiefdoms, are continually interrogated, developed and redeveloped (Earle 1991; Stein and Rothman 1994). Indeed, some scholars strongly question the uncritical usefulness of such categories, particularly band and chiefdom, and stress that we must acknowledge that even 'archaic' states followed extremely different trajectories (Yoffee 2005). We must stress, however, that we wish to avoid the judgements which are frequently associated with the use of the terms 'simple' and 'complex' or 'core' and 'periphery', and that we are not judging lifeways in terms of sophistication and adaptation, or pursuing Eurocentric or Orientalist dichotomies of value. However, we do recognise that we need terms which will allow us to consider, compare and contrast different forms of social organisation and transformation within our two major urban-focused traditions.

We will also refer to concepts of social inequality as an analytical approach, which enables us to begin to explore the differing social classes and groupings which began to emerge with increasing levels of social complexity (Chapman 2003). In less complex societies, where every individual is involved in food production and building domestic structures, every person may be expected to have more or less similar access to resources. However, in more complex societies, the emergence of specialised classes such as priests and officials would alter this balance, as these smaller groups with specialist functions may have greater social influence or power and be privileged in their access to resources (Yoffee 2005). Various archaeologists have applied these concepts to their interpretations of the archaeological record. For example, B. B. Lal (1955 and 2003) suggested that the plan of the Indus city of Kalibangan was designed to reflect the social and spatial differentiation of its disparate population, and other scholars have suggested that historic examples of such deliberate town planning may be traced back to the work of treatises such as the *Arthashastra*, an Early Historic text which contained advice on the 'ideal' city, such as advocating the settlement of different groups of people within different parts of the city (Wheatley 1971).

Urban Form

As suggested earlier, the task of finding a single definition for urban form or state-level societies has eluded archaeologists for more than seventy years (Cowgill 2004). One of the earliest comprehensive definitions was proposed by Vere Gordon Childe (1950: 15), and the influence of Childe's work is still clearly visible in almost all definitions and descriptions of 'urban' that have been developed since (Smith 2006a: 103). Box 1.1 presents an outline and discussion of Childe's urban trait list and although Childe's work has been heavily criticised as descriptive rather than explanatory, it nevertheless offered a number of key criteria which have allowed archaeologists to recognise urban sites as distinct from other forms (Gates 2003: 3; Smith 2003: 9). However, defining urban forms is considerably easier than defining and modelling the processes which led to the development of urbanism and complexity, which remains an area of great debate. Various models and theories have been proposed to account for a move to complexity, usually arising from a study of one of the major Old World state-level societies, but are we right to look for one model with main driving factors to account for the development of all complex societies? Surely, the unique nature of each different urban society or state-level society should be modelled in its own right, that is, if archaeologists themselves can agree on the definition of a state (Smith 2006b). This lies at the heart of the comparative debate and, indeed, at the heart of our own analysis and discussion of the development of urban-focused, complex societies in South Asia (Trigger 2003). In support of this approach, we will demonstrate in this volume the emergence of a number of alternative adaptations of urbanism within South Asia, including a form of low density urbanism within the tropical dry zone of Sri Lanka at Anuradhapura (Fletcher 2009; Coningham and Gunawardhana 2013). We also explore the nature of Indus urban forms, and consider arguments for classifying them as cities or towns, or whether alternative regional definitions are valid, such as Dhavalikar's suggestion that sites like Lothal were actually fortified trading factories and not urban forms (1995). It should also be noted that whilst urban forms usually stand at the peak of a number of settlement tiers, it is not always the case that the largest settlement is the most important. Evidence for alternative explanations, such as heterarchy, whereby "a system in which elements are unranked relative to one another or ranked in a variety of ways depending on conditions" (Crumley 1995: 30) should also be considered. Put more simply by Yoffee as "the existence of many hierarchies in the same society" (2005: 178), such patterns have been identified within the hinterland of Early Historic Anuradhapura in Sri Lanka where the settlements surrounding the royal city core were either secular or religious and thus formed two separate hierarchies (Coningham and Gunawardhana 2013). It is possible that similar heterarchies may have been present in other parts of South Asia at different times. We should also recognise that the process of urbanisation affects both city populations and those people living in the hinterland, as Yoffee has observed: "the social evolutionary trend that we normally call "urbanization" has often an equally important counterpart: "ruralisation"" (2005: 60). Finally, we should acknowledge the phenomenon of 'city-states', reflecting the hegemony which may emanate from such urban forms. A number of comparative studies have defined them as "small, territorially based, politically independent state systems, characterised by a capital city or town, with an economically and socially integrated adjacent hinterland…. City-states frequently, but not inevitably, occur in groups of fairly evenly spaced units of approximately equivalent size" (Nichols and Charlton 1997: 1). Moreover, it has been recognised that such early urban forms were arenas: "the earliest states are mostly city-states, the scene of new struggles for power and authority, the battlegrounds for independence and dominion." (Yoffee 1997: 263).

Box 1.1. Childe and Urban Forms

Professor Vere Gordon Childe (1892–1957) was one of the most influential archaeologists of the early twentieth century, perhaps best known for his descriptions of two of the most significant human transitions to have occurred in prehistory – the 'Neolithic Revolution' and the 'Urban

(continued)

Revolution' (1936). The first involved the domestication of plants and animals, and the fundamental changes that this brought to human populations who had lived entirely through hunting-gathering-foraging until then, and the second involved the emergence of urbanised, state-level civilisations. Whilst we may not necessarily adopt Childe's terminology or approach, most archaeologists today would agree that these are major transformations worthy of engagement (Gamble 2001, Kintigh et al. 2014: 880, Zeder 2006) and that Childe's impact on succeeding studies has been immense. In view of the coverage of this volume, it makes sense to consider Childe's contribution to definitions of the urban form.

Gordon Childe's 'Urban Revolution' theory was developed between the 1930s and 1950s and followed on in many ways from his 'Neolithic Revolution' (1936 and 1950). He proposed that the same region that produced the first farmers, Mesopotamia's Fertile Crescent, was also the location where the first urbanised societies emerged. Indeed, he identified this area as the birthplace of civilisation. Just as Childe's model for the domestication of plants and animals was based on environmental changes, so his model of urbanisation was based on the ability of farmers to produce agricultural surplus. Manipulation of the land, particularly through irrigation and the diversification of farming strategies, meant that food could be produced, stored and redistributed, allowing the support of non-food producing sectors of the population and their activities. This, Childe argued, was one of the key factors which facilitated the transition to urbanisation along with the emergence of a class of specialist craft-workers, in particular those involved in metallurgy, which he saw as a key element in the emergence of social stratification. From this base, Childe developed a list of traits which he believed were essential for an urban society, and it is easy to see from the list how Childe envisaged the development of this type of complex organisation. Childe's ten major traits were (Childe 1950: 15–16):

- large urban centres
- craft workers, merchants, officials, priests (supported by an agricultural surplus)
- the production of agricultural surpluses expressly for a (divine or secular) ruler
- monumental architecture
- ruling class not participating in food or other production
- recording systems (both written and numeric)
- exact practical and predictive sciences
- realistic art
- evidence for regular long-distance trade
- social organisation based on residence rather than kinship.

Childe's list was never universally accepted, and early critics of his work pointed out that it was descriptive and added little to an understanding of processes or changes involved; that script was not a necessary trait; and perhaps most concerning, that the list was overwhelmingly based on knowledge of early states in the Near East and Egypt. Despite focusing on these well-known examples, the utility of his list has even been questioned with respect to the urban nature of Old and Middle Kingdom Egypt although Trigger has noted that some scholars have disputed the urban status of Egypt and also the Maya, suggesting that they lacked 'real' cities according to a strict definition but also recorded that "yet no anthropologist was prepared on that account to deny these two particular literate societies the status of civilizations" (Trigger 2003: 44). Childe's emphasis on the need for craft specialisation has also been criticised with a number of researchers demonstrating that Chiefdoms, or less complex, more egalitarian societies, also have clear archaeological evidence for craft specialisation and production (Earle 1991). These examples illustrate the problems which archaeologists encounter when trying to fit evidence into monothetic models of social organisation and change, and also touch on some of the challenges that arise when a simplistic equation between people and material culture is made. However, Childe was without doubt a pioneer in the comparative study of state-level societies and complexity, and many later researchers, including those working in South Asia (Sengupta and Chakraborty 2008; Chakrabarti 1995; Smith 2006a), owe an immense debt to his early work.

Craft Specialisation

Humans create and modify objects for a whole range of purposes from the strictly utilitarian to the highly symbolic and, as archaeologists; these objects are often our only means of reconstructing aspects of past human activities and intentions (Brumfiel and Earle 1987; Sinopoli 1991). Craft specialisation is the focus of individuals, or of individual communities, on a single type of craft or material, rather than engagement with a whole range of craft activity. The production of tools and the production of ceramic vessels are two of the most ubiquitous craft categories, found on a wide range of sites in most parts of the world and from many periods. Specialisation can occur with the selection of certain types of materials, the production of certain standardised shapes and forms, and the application of certain decorations or embellishments; and the greater the degree of specialisation, the greater the skill required (Hurcombe 2007). Rarity also plays an important role in craft specialisation with regard to both skills and material, and these elements are likely to increase the value of an artefact. Control of materials and craft production also allows the control of wealth and authority, and it is probable that limiting access to rare craft goods and the control of production within early populations contributed to increasing differentiation and social complexity (Trigger 2003; Yoffee 2005). We will return to issues of craft production and specialisation again in this volume in relation to the Regionalisation and Integration Eras of the Indus, the Localisation Era of the Indus and the Early Historic urban developments.

Indo-Aryan/Indo-European

The Indo-Aryan or Indo-European debate is one that continues to be current within South Asian archaeology despite an absence of convincing evidence to support the mass movement of a group of people into the region during the second or first (or third) millennium BCE (Thapar 2006a). At relevant points throughout this volume, we shall also consider the evidence for major discontinuities in the archaeological record, but hold that there are few (if any) ways of linking the prehistoric or protohistoric material culture record to a specific linguistic group. The linguistic evidence, however, indisputably defines the existence of a broad language family which covers a vast geographical area from western Europe across to South Asia (Renfrew 1987). This language family, known as Indo-European or Indo-Aryan, includes modern English, Urdu and Sinhalese, as well as ritual languages like Sanskrit and extinct languages like Latin. The term Aryan or *Arya* is derived from Sanskrit and refers to a people as 'the Noble' and was used by people who identified themselves as Aryans in early Vedic hymns to differentiate themselves from another people known as *Dasyu* or *Dasa* – a phrase which later was used to refer to attendants or slaves. From the middle of the twentieth century onwards, many linguists, historians and archaeologists suggested that the *Dasas* inhabited the cities of the Indus and that they were defeated by the warlike Aryans from Central Asia, who later established the 'Indo-Gangetic Civilisation' (Thapar 2006a). In contrast, many Indian scholars have argued for continuity, claiming that the Indus Civilisation was already Aryan in character and that attempts to define Aryans as outsiders were part of a colonial policy of alienation of the South Asian past from its inhabitants at the time of contact (Sharma 2010). Aryan was also the term used by speakers of Old Persian to describe themselves, and the name of the modern nation state of 'Iran' is derived from '*Ariana*' or '*Aryanam*' meaning 'land of the Aryans' (Trautmann 1997: 13). Inextricably linked to racial justification and activity in twentieth-century Europe, we will not use it as a descriptive term when referring to language groups and their analyses, preferring the term Indo-European. We do recognise, however, that many South Asian scholars continue to use the term, for example, B. B. Lal recently referred to 'Vedic Aryans' and utilised floral and faunal evidence in an attempt to locate their homeland within South Asia (2005), whilst N. C. Beohar (2010: 61) suggested that "Unarmed peace-loving ancients of the Indus Valley Civilization might have found themselves to be an easy victim before the more sophisticated warrior Aryans. Therefore this might be the much more plausible cause of the destruction of the Indus Valley Civilization". We hope that as the various arguments and claims surrounding the presence and actions of 'Indo-Aryans' are challenged and explored through careful analysis of archaeological material, the time will soon come when there is an end to 'Indo-Aryans' being produced as a reality in order to easily satisfy particular archaeological questions.

Complexity

As noted earlier, complex societies are those considered to demonstrate a marked degree of inequality or hierarchy within their social organisation (Chapman 2003). Matthews has offered a discussion of complexity in Mesopotamia (2003), and has drawn out a number of areas which can be identified within the archaeological record that may confirm the presence of social complexity. These include some elements of monumental architecture and prestige items, selectively placed and recovered; a tiered settlement hierarchy; evidence of distinct craft specialisation as well as the means to produce and store surplus; a distinct ideology presented by temples or similar buildings, and "cultic paraphernalia" (Matthews 2003: 96). Thus far, there are distinct similarities with Childe's early urban trait list (see Box 1.1) but Matthews has also provided the need for evidence of the development, expansion and finally demise of complexity. At the core of this definition of complexity is the concept of representing the contribution of many connected parts and, of course, as archaeologists we are interested in changes in complexity, both as it increases and decreases or simplifies. Matthews' list therefore offers a way to begin an exploration of complex societies (although it is by no means exhaustive), and also gives us a framework from which to begin comparing our two major urban developments. We will return to elements on this list as we examine the development, expansion and transformation of complexity in South Asia as well as consider the impact of scholars like Chapman (2003), Yoffee (2005), and Price and Feinman (2010). When we consider change and causes of change we wish to avoid settling into, or relying on, monocausal explanations or those explanations that require evidence to take certain forms.

Alongside the emergence of complexity, the emergence of a dominant ideology is also a common feature and we will examine the evidence for this development in both Indus and Early Historic cityscapes and landscapes. While the acknowledgement of the presence of a single ideology of authority throughout the Indus is still contested by scholars, the spread and eventual imperialisation of Buddhism during the Early Historic period, for example, resulted in the emergence of a broadly shared common cosmography shared throughout the region. This pattern appears to match closely to the scenarios described by Colin Renfrew and John Cherry in the process that they called Peer Polity Interaction (1986). In this model, Renfrew suggested that it was possible to recognise "in a given region several autonomous political centres which, initially at least, are not brought within a single, unified jurisdiction" (Renfrew 1986: 1). Noting that they frequently shared similar political institutions, weights and measures, recording and "essentially the same structure of religious beliefs" (ibid.: 2), he suggested that they formed Early State Modules (ESMs) which were brought closer together (even unified) through a process of "competition (including warfare), and competitive emulation; symbolic entrainment, and the transition of innovations; and increased flow in the exchange of goods" (ibid.: 8). Readapted in part by subsequent studies of the city-state (Yoffee 1997), Norman Yoffee has referred to the development of territorially small "city-states (or micro-states)" which emerge sharing a civilisation or "social order and set of shared values" (2005: 17). However an attractive fit, it is important to reflect on the presence of examples of complexity reached through models of alternative means. For example, Jenne-jeno in the inland Niger Delta has been identified as a large-scale urban cluster of more than eighty hectares with "aggregation, population growth, increasing scale, and specialisation" but not with the normative traits of "subsistence intensification, highly visible ranking or stratification, [or] imposing public monuments" (McIntosh and McIntosh 2003: 104). The result of a clustering of manufacturing and exchange specialists for a larger market, and for stability and safety, the McIntoshs suggested that the clustered spatial organisation allowed those specialists to retain a physical distinctiveness. In this way, complexity and urbanism were achieved, but through a very different pathway driven by mercantile activities.

Collapse and Transformation

What happened to the people who inhabited the urban forms and cities of the Indus Valley in South Asia after circa 1900 BCE? Studies of the archaeological record of this period point strongly to the demise of Indus state-level societies and the contraction of many of its urban and rural sites. However, there was no single shared trajectory of change which may be applied across the region deemed to be Indus or Harappan in nature on the basis of material culture. Just as there were many differences in the 'Mature Period' or Integrated Era of the civilisation, there were also many differences in the organisation and structure of sites and areas in the period following circa 1900 BCE. Traditionally, early scholars considered this period a distinct transformation, when the urban culture rapidly dispersed and disappeared and was replaced by a social, economic and cultural vacuum (Wheeler 1959: 114). More recent explorations of sites assigned to the period between the 'end' of the Indus and the 'beginning' of the Early Historic, however, have greatly altered our understanding (Sengupta and Chakraborty 2008; Shaffer 1993; Coningham 1995a; Coningham and Ali 2007a; Young 2003). We can now observe that while there were significant changes and transformations in social and economic organisation during the

500 years or so between, there was also a great deal of continuity. It is precisely this continuity and the need for further understanding of the links between the two urban-focused developments that has encouraged us to take a comparative approach to the archaeologies of South Asia, and the concept of this apparent discontinuity is still acknowledged by a number of contemporary scholars (Chattopadhyaya 2008: 8).

What actually constitutes the collapse or transformation of an urban, state-level society? Discussions of the collapse and transformation of the Indus cities and settlements have focused on the loss of markers such as monumental architecture and large urban settlements, or long-distance trade and highly developed, specialised craft industries, and there is certainly evidence that the urban way of life, well established by circa 1900 BCE changed distinctly in form (Kenoyer 1998; Agrawal 2007; Wright 2010). At some sites, this transformation appeared to have occurred quickly, even dramatically, but at others the change was more gradual, and many aspects of the former, urban Indus organisation remained over a number of years. This concept of collapse and transformation as a rapid and all-encompassing change is of course closely linked to that of a major social transformation between the two urban-focused developments. However, if it can be shown that there was a high degree of continuity between the two, then it becomes necessary to re-evaluate evidence for the collapse of the Indus, and offer new interpretations in light of the much longer time frame that archaeologists such as Shaffer have proposed (1992). According to early pioneers of archaeology, the demise of the Indus Civilisation was at least in part the result of incoming Aryan invaders from the north-west and this invasion was followed by a period of social decline so rapid and complete that it warranted the term 'Dark Age' (Wheeler 1968: 132). However, Wheeler was also later adamant that having a single cause for the collapse of a civilisation was highly unlikely, and that archaeologists needed to embrace multiple causes, which is now the accepted approach in the analysis of the causes of both complexity and collapse. Elsewhere, scholars have attempted to codify collapse as the outcome of increasingly 'marginal returns' for extended societal complexity (Tainter 1988; 2006), in other simpler words, "the center is no longer able to secure resources from the periphery, usually having lost the 'legitimacy' through which it could 'disembed' goods and services. ... The process of collapse entails the dissolution of those centralized institutions that had facilitated the transmission" (Yoffee 2005: 139). In this volume, we will explore the ways in which the explanatory debate has shifted from monocausal to polycausal and from invasion to environmental catastrophe, and on to human agency – and consider the alternative explanations for the transformations which occurred. As will be noted in Chapter 7, some scholars still refer to the disappearance of the Indus cities in this way, with Kohl describing it as "an 'eclipse in the East' in terms of overall collapse in urbanism and social complexity" (2007: 215).

NOMENCLATURE AND TERMINOLOGIES

The purpose of this section is to establish a number of key definitions for the terminologies and chronologies used in this book, so that readers are aware of how and why we use particular terms and phrases, and the basis for our dating of sites and events across South Asia. Although it might seem self-evident, we believe that it is worth stating that language is not only very powerful, but is also evolving and changing. Terms become fashionable or unfashionable and they can take on positive or negative meanings of their own, often largely dependent on context. A good example of this can be found in discussions of neo-evolutionary language associated with the development of complex or state-level societies (see e.g. Chapman 2003; Yoffee 2005). As we shall see in Chapter 3, the British antiquarian movement and early British archaeological activity had a great influence on the practice of archaeology in South Asia, therefore it is not really surprising that British and European terms and concepts were imported to describe and explain South Asian material culture and cultural developments, although many of these early models are no longer credible. An example of this is the ways in which chronologies and time in South Asia have been dealt with by colonial archaeologists, and then later challenged by South Asian archaeologists after Independence. The standard European 'Three Age' system of dividing prehistory into progressive chronological sequences based on materials (i.e. stone, bronze, iron) was enthusiastically adopted by early archaeologists such as Robert Bruce Foote (Pappu 2008), Wheeler (1948), Piggott (1950), and Gordon (1960) for application across South Asia. Of course, the Three Age system has since been challenged across the globe and South Asia is no exception – the presence of microlithic stone tools alongside evidence for settlements, domestication, and other craft working at numerous sites shows how difficult it is to categorise past human activity according to a very narrow material culture definition (Box 1.2). Challenges to the European understanding of time have come from a number of scholars, with analyses of the ways in which precolonial Indian time has been understood as cyclic, unchanging and ahistoric and European time has been understood as linear and progressive (Sen 2002: 349; Thapar 2002: 27–28). New analyses of Early Historic texts has allowed the argument that 'traditional' time was (and is) both cyclic and linear. These types of challenges to pervasive Colonial scholarship and interpretation are very important for highlighting the layers and nuances of South Asian prehistory and early history.

Box 1.2. What Are Microliths?

Microliths, literally small stone tools, are frequently characterised as tools which generally measure less than five centimetres long. In South Asia, some of the most common materials used for microlith manufacture were chert, chalcedony, crystal, jasper and agate, and the range of tool types includes what Dilip Chakrabarti has termed "pigmy versions of the upper Palaeolithic types, such as points, scrapers, burins, awls etc." (1999: 91) as well as new types such as crescent shaped tools and geometric microliths. The availability of raw materials varied according to region, but most stone is thought to have been gathered from river gravels or even quarries, and transported over long distances. The recovery of stone tools from areas lacking natural resources strongly suggests that some form of trade or exchange network was in place at this time and that the value of particular types of stone was both well known and shared. The important issue is that we can observe the clear development of a new set of stone tools, in general much smaller than the Upper Palaeolithic tool set, although the continuation of the styles and types strongly suggests continuation across what we now perceive of as a major cultural boundary, and which is now also supported by stratigraphic relationships from a number of sites.

Tools that are smaller than five centimetres in size are small indeed; try holding a piece of paper that measures five centimetres in your hand and think about how you would use it as a tool – you will probably conclude that it would be very difficult to use on its own. It might perhaps be used as a small scraper or similar, but the general consensus is that microliths were almost certainly hafted in numbers into bone or wood, and used as arrowheads, spears or perhaps sickles for harvesting.

One of the best-known Mesolithic sites in India is Bagor in Rajasthan, where three occupational levels or periods have been identified and dated as: Period I circa 5000–2800 BCE (Mesolithic); Period II circa 2800–600 BCE ('Chalcolithic'); Period III circa 600–200 BCE (Iron) (Kennedy 2000: 210–211; Singh 2008: 87). Microliths were recovered from both Periods I and II. The occupation evidence uncovered included stone paved house floors and other possible circular stone structures, and some paved places where large numbers of animal bones were found were thought to be slaughter or butchering areas. Wild animals such as wild cattle, deer, jackals, turtles and monitor lizards have been identified, as well as bones from domesticated species such as cattle, sheep and goat from Mesolithic layers. Querns and rubbing stones have also been recovered from the early layers and indicate the processing of food plants. The presence of structures with paved floors, as well as domesticated animals, and possibly even pottery from Mesolithic layers raises many interesting questions about the lifeways of the people at Bagor.

Kennedy has argued that the presence of copper tools, handmade pottery and three human burials in Period II "Strongly suggest the communication of the hunting-gathering Bagorians with early agricultural peoples of the region" (2000: 211). Rather than the simple equation of Mesolithic people equalling mobile hunter-gatherer-fisher lifeways, it is therefore clear that

(continued)

not only was there considerable investment in building domestic structures at some sites and evidence for animal husbandry (as at Bagor), but also that mobile strategies would have continued at other sites and periods alongside settled even urban societies (see for example Rafique Mughal's work in Cholistan discussed in Chapters 5 and 6). Although often useful for archaeologists to broadly categorise periods according to dominant subsistence strategies and lifeways, this often masks the great variability and fluidity that the archaeological record indicates for much of South Asia.

Another example of the way in which traditional, European archaeological classification, description, analysis and ultimately interpretation are neither useful nor appropriate within South Asia is centred on the lifeways of hunter-gatherer-foragers. There was demonstrably a great diversity of population and communities present within the Indus or Harappan civilisation, traditionally characterised as urban-focused and literate with a uniform material culture spread over an area of almost 3,133,886 square kilometres (Wright 2010). The nature of many early finds and their comparison with Mesopotamian material culture placed the whole discovery firmly within the category of Old World Civilisation (Marshall 1931a: Wheeler 1953), and that is how the civilisation is still presented in much of popular culture and some academic writing today (Kenoyer 1994). However, it is becoming increasingly clear that the Indus cities closely interacted with sizable populations reliant on technology that would traditionally be associated with 'Neolithic' or even 'Mesolithic' lifeways (Mughal 1997; Possehl 1979). At the site of Bagor in Rajasthan, for example, we can see this duality in the archaeological remains, where characteristically Indus artefacts, such as bronze fishing hooks and drilled carnelian beads, have been recovered alongside microlithic tool assemblages. Langhnaj appears to mark a similar site as it yielded burials, a copper knife and microlithic tools (Wright 2010: 175). In order to articulate these populations with those of the cities, M. K. Dhavalikar (1995) has suggested that the inhabitants of such sites may have co-ordinated the collection of nodules of semi-precious stones and exchanged these at sophisticated processing centres, such as Kuntasi or Lothal, and Possehl (2002a, 2002b) and Morrison (2006) have both stressed the potential of such symbiotic exchanges.

A further example is the impact of the appearance of iron within the sequences of sites across South Asia. Across Europe, early archaeologists assumed a major social and economic transformation to have accompanied this innovation. However, in South Asia, iron working appeared within the sequence at the site of Pirak in Baluchistan where it was not accompanied by other fundamental changes in material culture. Indeed, this new metal technology was practiced immediately adjacent to the already established copper and bone-working areas (Jarrige and Santoni 1979). A further example is provided by the transition from the production and use of only stone tools ('Mesolithic') to the production and use of iron ('Iron Age') in Sri Lanka. Unlike the sequences across the Palk Straits in South India, where it is possible to trace a series of cultural transformations from a 'Neolithic' to a phase of using copper tools and then to an 'Iron Age', Sri Lanka's sequence appears to have shifted from an established 'Mesolithic' to the abrupt appearance of iron tools and associated ceramic types at the beginning of the first millennium BC (Deraniyagala 1992, 1990). Finally, it is worth noting the difficulty of using the term 'Bronze Age' to refer to the Indus Civilisation and 'Chalcolithic' to discuss some of the contemporary and later farming communities in the Deccan and Peninsular India. This is because although copper and bronze objects were utilised in both regions and during both phases, stone tools were also utilised and appear to have retained an important position. For this reason, we shall refer to both the Indus Civilisation and the later farming communities of the Deccan and Peninsular India as 'Chalcolithic'. This list is by no means exhaustive, and there are many other examples which demonstrate that South Asian cultures and people did not always adopt or select linear progressions in technological and social change.

This complex picture suggests that models derived from Europe may not always be applicable to the diversity of South Asia, parts of which did not become 'historic' until recent times. This is not to advocate the presence of residual Pleistocene populations as some scholars have attempted to do based on comparisons of modern distributions of tribal languages with scatters of microlithic tools (Parpola 1994). Nor should it be suggested that such communities may be viewed as conservative or unchanging; rather that some groups of people have made choices to exploit the lucrative resources of forest and jungle and, like the Veddas of Sri Lanka, such groups have often been in contact with literate, state-level populations for centuries (Fox 1969). This inability to categorise archaeological sequences on the basis of monothetic classificatory schemes is a theme to which we will return.

CHRONOLOGIES IN SOUTH ASIA

Chronologies and dating, two of the pivotal axes of archaeological analysis and interpretation, are also far from straightforward in South Asia, and we will examine the impact of early historical geography on the development of relative chronologies and the way they became entrenched in archaeological practice. Clearly this position owes much to the personalities and interests of the influential early British antiquarians such as Cunningham and Prinsep, as discussed in more detail in the following chapter. Radiocarbon date estimates have been exploited by archaeologists with increasing frequency in many parts of the world throughout the second half of the twentieth century, and samples suitable for processing are now routinely collected. We will look at scientific dating across the different regions of South Asia and discuss the dearth of radiocarbon dates from archaeologically crucial periods, such as that between the two major urban-focused developments. As discussed earlier, this period has often been designated a transformation, and we suggest that this commonly accepted concept (and others, such as diffusion) is in many ways the product of lack of research, archaeological visibility and poor relative and scientific dating. This problem is illustrated very clearly when we examine the Indus cities, where despite nearly 150 years of archaeological exploration and research on various sites by numerous archaeological teams, there is still no absolute agreement about dates, and even within a single key site such as Harappa, there remain gaps in the radiocarbon chronologies (Kenoyer 1997a). Despite this, Kenoyer has correctly described Harappa as one of the most important sources of information about the whole Indus Civilisation and it has been the focus of numerous collaborative research projects.

The point we wish to make here is that although scientific dates for specific sites and different cultures in South Asia do exist, they often stand in isolation, and even when dealing with one of the most studied sites in South Asia, there are gaps and uncertainties. While Kenoyer has been able to draw on more than 70 radiocarbon date estimates, along with stratigraphy, architectural analysis and diagnostic artefacts in order to construct this chronology for Harappa (1997a: 266), few other Indus sites have been sampled so intensively. For example, Sonawane has presented radiocarbon date estimates from ten sites in Gujarat, which are believed to fall into what is termed the 'post-urban' Indus, or the period falling between circa 1900 and 1400 BCE (2002: 168). Yet of the ten sites covered, only one (Rojdi) had more than five date estimates, while three sites had only a single date estimate (Sonawane 2002). Similarly, a synthesis of 'pre-Indus' cultures in Gujarat has presented material from eight sites, of which one has four date estimates, while five sites have two or only a single date estimate (Ajithprasad 2002: 133). Using a single date to evaluate the sequence of an entire site is always challenging but there are ways of mitigating the risk. For example, evaluations of the radiocarbon measurement 'chronological hygiene' have been developed in other parts of the world in order to separate more reliable dates (e.g. Pettitt et al. 2003), but such studies have not been adopted broadly within South Asia. Moreover, it is possible to apply OxCal to sequences of radiocarbon measurements from single sites to obtain a greater chronological resolution through the application of Bayesian statistics, but few projects have chosen this route. While radiocarbon measurements and Optically Stimulated Luminescence dating remain so expensive, and thus out of the range of many projects within South Asia with notable exceptions (Haricharan et al. 2013), more traditional techniques of typologies will continue to be used to develop relative dating frameworks. We will return to specific chronologies for sites, regions and cultural developments in following chapters, but these examples serve to illustrate some of the difficulties archaeologists face when there is an absence or scarcity of scientific dates around which to construct a chronological framework. We will also consider the problems which can arise when archaeologists attempt to link material culture to known historical dates and sites identified through historical geography.

TRADITIONS, ERAS AND PHASES

One of the tasks archaeologists frequently undertake is the subdivision and differentiation of the past, and within South Asia this is no different. As noted previously, many of the pioneering archaeologists and antiquarians to work within South Asia brought with them existing systems from elsewhere, such as the Three Age System. Additionally, archaeologists have often adopted the application of a tripartite division to the civilisations of the world, and this includes the Indus. In the mid-twentieth century, Wheeler divided the Indus Civilisation into three main periods: the Early, the Mature, and the Late Indus. The highly influential British archaeologists Raymond and Bridget Allchin used similar subdivisions in their work (1982), and this largely cemented the chronological nomenclature in common use (Singh 2008). We believe that the continued use of these descriptive, limited chronological terms has contributed to the restricted approaches to understanding the development and decline of the major urban-focused developments in South Asia, and we hope that by moving beyond these traditional chronologies we may begin to provide a framework to enable us to look at alternative ways of exploring and discussing key events and processes.

As noted earlier, many works on South Asian archaeology have either followed a broad narrative concentrating on India and Pakistan to the large exclusion of neighbouring territories or have studied the developmental sequence of only the Indus or that of the Early Historic. Reinforcing a division between the two which dates back to the early years of archaeology in South Asia, and despite evidence of continuity to the contrary (Sengupta and Chakraborty 2008; Agrawal 2007; Shaffer 1993; Coningham 1995a; Kenoyer 1991b), the techniques, theories and methodologies for studying the two traditions continue to remain separate – as do most the majority of their practitioners. A good example of this dichotomy is illustrated by a comparison of Shaffer's 1992 study of the Indus Valley, Baluchistan and the Helmand chronologies with the chronologies of Possehl and Rissman's 1992 study for the Early Historic period of the same region. Although both of these chronologies were presented within the same volume, the *'Chronologies in Old World Archaeology'* (Ehrich 1992), and despite sharing the same geographical region, they followed entirely separate frameworks and therefore there were no links between the two. Whilst significantly different from Possehl's more traditional approach,

Shaffer utilised his chapter to pioneer the establishment of an innovative developmental framework for the north-western areas of South Asia which drew on
three general archaeological structures: Tradition, Era and Phase (1992: 411).

Rather than restricting focus to the Indus cities or even the 'Early Harappan
period', Shaffer and Lichtenstein argued that it was possible to perceive a
broader 'Indus Valley Cultural Tradition'; identifiable as "persistent configurations of economic adaptations, basic technologies and other cultural systems
within the context of temporal and geographical continuity" (1989: 119). This
definition allowed these scholars to argue for the "integration of both stylisti-
cally similar and diverse patterned sets of archaeological assemblages into a
single analytical unit which implies the existence of cultural and chronological
relationships" (Shaffer and Lichtenstein 1989). This larger analytical unit was
made up of Phases grouped within a number of Eras, in which the Phase
represented "the smallest analytical unit; and its main feature is a diagnostic
ceramic style located at one or more sites during a particular time" (Shaffer
1992: 442). The Era was, in turn, defined as forming "a sequential series pro-
ceeding in the same order and connoting changes in general cultural organisation within the areal traditions" (Shaffer 1992: 442). He further identified
the presence of four major Eras within the Indus Valley Tradition: Early Food
Producing, Regionalisation, Integration and Localisation. The first of these was
defined as an Era characterised by "an economy based on food production and
an absence of ceramics" and the second as an Era of "distinct artefact styles,
essentially ceramics, which cluster in time and space, and interaction networks
which link dispersed social groups" (Shaffer 1992: 442). The third, Integration,
was defined as "pronounced homogeneity in material culture distributed over
a large area reflecting an intense level of interaction between social groups" and
the fourth, Localisation, as being "comparable to regionalisation except that
there is a more generalised similarity in artefact styles, including continued,
but altered, presence of interaction networks" (Shaffer 1992: 442). We recognise that other scholars have used 'Integration' to denote "the political process
in which differentiated social groups come to exist within an institutionalised
framework" and that "States have the power to disembed resources from the
differentiated groups for their own ends and glorification, not least because
symbols of incorporation are so critical in establishing the legitimacy of societies." (Yoffee 2005: 32–3). However, it is important to note that at no stage
did Shaffer suggest that integration implied a complete social, economic and
political consolidation within a single state, and we follow this understanding.

Associated with the concept of interaction systems with avenues of social
communication within and between social groups across traditions and phases,
the framework was developed to examine longer-term sociocultural developments, and Shaffer suggested that the exploration of these structures "not only
may adumbrate social interrelationships for which we have no specific information as to their nature, but they are also highly important in establishing

relative chronologies when radiocarbon determinations are inadequate and in reinforcing those dates that do exist" (1992: 442). A critical feature of Shaffer's developmental framework was replacing the traditional Mesolithic/Neolithic, 'Chalcolithic'/Early Harappan, Mature Harappan and Late Harappan terminology with Eras which were intended to reflect the longer-term changes or processes which provided the platform for eventual complexity and urbanisation. Thus, in Shaffer's scheme, there was a development from the Food Producing Era to the Regionalisation Era, then to the Integration Era and finally the Localisation Era (1992). Notably, Shaffer's categorisation also allowed scholars to frame sites such as Mehrgarh, accepted by all as partly ancestral to the Indus cities within a distinctly pervasive Indus Tradition rather than lying outside a Pre-Urban or incipient urban phase.

Shaffer's chronological framework has been successfully adapted and adopted by a number of scholars, such as Mark Kenoyer in his 1997 chapter on *Early City-States in South Asia* and his 1998 book *Ancient Cities of the Indus Valley Civilisation,* and by one of the present authors in his 2005 chapter on the archaeology of South Asia in Thames, and Hudson's *The Human Past.* Other scholars, whilst not adopting it entirely, have developed parallel themes, and Rita Wright's recent volume on the ancient Indus followed a similar framework with an Early Food Producing Phase, followed by a Pre-Urban Phase, an Urban Phase and a Post-Urban/Late Harappan Period (2010: 22). It is equally important to note that not all archaeologists have, by any means, adopted Shaffer's framework. For example, the late Greg Possehl grouped archaeological phases into a seven stage development sequence from: Beginnings of Village Farming Communities and Pastoral camps (Stage One), Developed Village Farming Communities and Pastoral Societies, the Early Harappan, the Early Harappan-Mature Harappan Transition into the Mature Harappan. From the Mature Harappan, the sequence travelled through the Posturban Harappan, and the Early Iron Age of Northern India and Pakistan (Stage Seven) (2002a: 29). Possehl's mixture of older periodisation (Mature Harappan), artefact-based descriptive classifications (Early Iron Age) and socio-economic processes (Developed Village Farming Communities) is not unique and others, such as Singh (2008), have presented similar categories which treat the Indus Valley and the Early Historic Traditions in very different ways and thus reinforce established divisions which prevent easy comparative discussion.

We will adopt Shaffer's framework in this volume in order to better understand and explore the processess which led to the two main urban-focused developments in South Asia and, in the following chapters, we first investigate the developmental sequence of the Indus Valley Tradition. This approach will also allow us to escape that paradox highlighted by B. D. Chattopadhyaya, whereby current divisions between the 'Protohistoric' cities of the Indus and 'Historic' cities of the Early Historic appear to pivot on interpretations of the nature of the Indus script and its use (2008: 8). Following this new scheme, we will characterise the Indus urban-focused tradition, from its food-producing origins to its post-urban fragmentation and transformation, and we also compare these stages with the developmental trajectories in neighbouring regions. We then compare the Indus developmental character with the characteristics of the succeeding Early Historic Tradition utilising Shaffer's approach. We also begin to replace the traditional terminologies of 'Chalcolithic', Iron Age, Proto-Historic, Early Historic and Mauryan with those of a 'Localisation Era' followed by an Era of 'Regionalisation' and an Era of 'Integration'. We argue that Kenoyer's (1998) suggestion that the Era of Integration was only reached with the Mauryan period (c. 317 BCE) was overcautious and that such a cultural and economic stage became evident in the archaeological record as early as 600 BCE, although the actual stage of political integration is much later according to 'historical' sources.

This task is likely to be controversial and we acknowledge that not all scholars will be receptive. Indeed, we note that some academics have advocated even the abandonment of more traditional terminology and advocated the phasing of the archaeology of the Sarasvati River within a sequence which leads from Period I: Rigvedic through Period II: Brahmana Period and Period III: *Mahabharata* Period to Period IV: nineteenth century CE (Gupta 2010: 17). There are also a number of issues still to be refined, and it remains questionable whether there is sufficient difference and distinction between Shaffer's definitions of Regionalisation and Localisation. Shaffer's own definition (quoted earlier) observes the similarities of the two eras, with some differentiation in the form of contact between groups. In turn, we have retained this separation and nomenclature, although we recognise the overlap, and part of our aim in this volume is to further differentiate between the regionalisation (emerging complexity) eras and localisation (declining or contracting complexity) eras for both the Indus and Early Historic periods. Indeed, such a cyclical process had been successfully piloted by Louis Dupree, who referred to phases of 'fusion' and 'fission' when discussing the history of Afghanistan (1973: 344). We can also question the relevance of the term Integration to refer to the period of Indus urban development as large swathes of northern and southern South Asia were unaffected by what was, on a subcontinental scale, a regional feature. This issue is easier to address as the Era of Integration is linked to the coverage of the Indus Valley Tradition and areas interacting with it, rather than being applicable to the entirety of the Subcontinent. Chase et al. have also questioned the extent to which the 'borderlands' were ever fully integrated and have suggested that in such areas "residents of various backgrounds and interests negotiated novel social identities in the context of ever-changing social, economic and political networks." (2014: 64). The application of such a question to the Mauryan Empire is similarly complex, particularly if one endorses the suggestion of Monica Smith that cities were effectively linked, but ideological linkage suffered severe distance decay beyond the main networks between nodes (2003). Certainly, Sengupta and Chakraborty have stressed that the majority of the populations of Early Historic South Asia were rural rather than city dwellers (2008: xxiii). However, as Manuel has noted, it should be remembered that the temporal and spatial boundaries of Shaffer's Phases should be considered flexible and possibly overlapping as "they are purely modern archaeological constructs derived from artefactual typologies and (admittedly few) scientifically obtained dates" (2010: 148). Manuel has also focused on the beneficial flexibility offered by Shaffer's concept, a flexibility which allows a focus on social processes and dynamics as well as the ability to integrate new discoveries, such as the ease with which the Ravi Phase was introduced (Manuel 2010: 151). These are all issues which we will investigate further throughout the volume, and we stress that there was a difference in scale, as the Indus Tradition was focused on the north-west of the subcontinent and the Early Historic on its entirety – in the words of Jaya Menon "Unlike the Harappan, the early historic does not offer us, either chronologically or geographically, a compact entity for analysis." (2008: 15). We feel strongly that we need to both utilise a single uniform yet flexible terminology to effectively bridge between both eras of development but, at the same time, are keen to avoid the creation of another new periodisation scheme.

After considering the available data, we will also briefly address the ongoing debate about whether there is an inherently 'South Asian' character to these urban-focused developments, or whether they owe their characteristics to developments on their flanks. We will also reassess the nature of the intervening timespan by tracing strands of cultural continuity between the two before considering why South Asia's first urban-focused development lost its integrated character. Once we have presented and analysed key material culture from a range of selected sites, we will carry out a critical comparison of the two traditions, which remains one of the fundamental themes of this volume. This focused approach will simplify the dated and overspecialized terminologies for the region while allowing us to link its sequence with those of neighbouring regions. Using Shaffer's terminology will also allow us to demonstrate that not only are the sequences in the two urban-focused developments internally similar, but also that they are fundamentally different in character from those in neighbouring regions, such as West Asia. Moreover, we will argue that these sequences, and their material culture, do not respect many of the current generic archaeological models for explaining cultural change or evaluating cultural complexity. For example, the notable lack of evidence of ranking within the Indus cities, where the absence of royal burials, palaces and temples have suggested that models based on normative values of wealth and rank clearly fail (Miller 1985; Possehl 1998; Rissman 1988).

DATING CONVENTIONS IN THE TEXT

What is the difference between the abbreviations BC and BCE or AD and CE when it comes to dating? BC and AD are the abbreviations most commonly used in archaeological, historical and general literature, and they are abbreviations for the terms 'Before Christ' and 'Anno Domini' respectively. 'Anno Domini' is a Latin phrase meaning 'in the year of our Lord' and has come to refer to a numbering system for years following after the birth of Jesus Christ. 'Before Christ' derives from the Ancient Greek word 'Christos' or 'Anointed One' and has come to refer to the years prior to the birth of Christ. Although a clear and widely accepted system for recording chronologies, the BC/AD system has some major drawbacks for many archaeologists – as it is western-derived, European-centric and bound up with Christianity. When working in areas outside Europe, we are of course working largely outside the Christian framework, and because of this, attempts have been made to find alternatives to the BC/AD notation.

The Islamic or Hijri calendar differs from the Western or Gregorian calendar in a number of ways. The Hijri calendar is a lunar calendar, meaning it is based on the moon, rather than on the solar Gregorian calendar. Because of this, the Hijri year is about ten or days days shorter than the solar year, which is why Islamic festivals are assigned different dates in each year. The Hijri calendar is also linked to the Prophet Muhammad, who established Islam. It begins with the Prophet's journey from Mecca to Medina and is abbreviated to H or AH, the latter meaning 'Anno Hegirae', which is Latin for 'In the year of the Hijri'. The Prophet's journey is generally agreed to have taken place in the western calendar year of 570 AD, although there is some debate about this. However, there are many other groups in South Asia who are not Muslim and therefore do not follow the Hijri calendar. In an attempt to find a more universally acceptable and religiously neutral alternative, the abbreviations BCE and CE have been suggested. BCE stands for 'Before Common Era' and replaces BC, with the years being equivalent. CE stands for 'Common Era' and replaces AD, and again the years are equivalent. Although we recognise that there are still links to the Christian calendar, we will be using BCE and CE as dating conventions in this volume as they are relatively neutral, while still being widely understood and accepted. Where we draw directly from published scientific work, for example, palaeoecology studies relevant to the environmental background of our study region, we use the abbreviation BP as given in the original text in order to minimise the possibility of cumulative error through translation. BP refers to years before the standard benchmark date of 1950.

CONCLUSIONS

This volume is subdivided into four main parts, the first of which lays the foundations for the analytical and interpretative study of the other three. In this introductory chapter, we have outlined our main themes and approaches and, in the remaining chapters of Part I, we will introduce the geographical and environmental context of South Asia as well as a review of the historical development of South Asian archaeology as a discipline. Part II is concerned with the Indus Valley Tradition in the north-west of the subcontinent between circa 6500 and 1900 BCE and will present the four eras of the Indus urban-focused tradition, from food producers and regional proto-urban communities, through the emergence of an integrated urban and rural system, before considering the evidence for the apparent end of this tradition. Each of the three chapters in Part II will also draw on selected evidence from neighbouring communities in order to investigate the comparative development of this region and to test the extent to which diffusion or autochthonous development occurred.

The third part of this volume will consider the Early Historic Tradition between circa 1900 and 200 BCE and begins with a re-examination of the period which separates the two urban-focused traditions and will stress the elements of continuity and transformation through the sequence. We then outline the developmental stages by which urban forms re-emerged during the Early Historic throughout the subcontinent and compare them with Indus Valley Tradition and those of the contemporary developments to the west. In the fourth and final part, we will return to some of the fundamental issues raised by the volume such as the similarities and differences between the two major urban-focused developments, the role of indigenous development and the diffusion of ideas and innovations in South Asia, and the nature of complexity. We will also consider Tainter's 1988 model of marginal returns, and other archaeological models and interpretations dealing with the collapse and transformation of civilisations, in order to consider why the first urban-focused tradition ended with such a loss of communal traits, whilst still passing on a number of fundamental continuities. We will also identify certain key areas and phases in South Asia which we believe should be investigated in more detail if we are to better understand the social and economic dynamics involved in these transformations.

CHAPTER 2

ENVIRONMENT AND CULTURE: SOUTH ASIA'S ENVIRONMENTAL, LINGUISTIC AND RELIGIOUS PATTERNS

INTRODUCTION

This Chapter will introduce South Asia's main geographical and environmental characteristics and the linguistic and religious patterns of its habitants, both of which provide context for our study of the two urban-focused traditions and beyond. We will begin with a geographical definition of South Asia and explain why parts of the archaeological sequence of neighbouring countries such as Afghanistan and Iran will, at times, be included within this study. We also consider some of the wider potential spheres of influence, such as the Indian Ocean, Arabian Sea, Persian Gulf, Central Asia, Western Asia, and South East Asia, and how they relate to South Asia. The major geographical boundaries, such as key mountain ranges and rivers, will be discussed in the light of the opportunities and barriers they may have presented to the movement of people, goods and ideas over time. In turn, this will lead to a discussion of the major changes in the environment of South Asia which are thought to have occurred over the last 10,000 years and the impact such changes may have had on the populations of the two urban-focused developments, both directly and indirectly. More detailed environmental change in individual regions and at specific times will be considered, where appropriate, within later chapters in relation to key archaeological events and developments. The drying of the Ghaggar-Hakra River, for example, is thought by many to have had a major effect on the stability of the Indus Civilisation, and will be discussed again in greater depth in Chapter 7.

We will also introduce the major linguistic families of the region in this chapter, Indo-European, Dravidian, Sino-Tibetan and Austro-Asiatic, and discuss the attempts to use and misuse their current and postulated ancient population patterns by archaeologists and historians in constructing historical frameworks and narratives. Another issue which will be introduced is that of caste, the common English term for the complex South Asian concept of *varna*. One of the most fundamental socio-economic forces within contemporary South Asia, caste is found throughout South Asian communities from Hindu and Roman Catholic to Muslim and Buddhist, and geographically from Nepal to Sri Lanka. Although affected by different phases of imperial and colonial rule and administration, it continues to govern access to occupation, diet, sex and housing for millions of people. Thought by many scholars to have been present in the Early Historic period on the basis of textual and epigraphic references, there is still debate as to whether it was also present during the occupation of the Indus cities. Finally, the extremely complex patterns and relationships between South Asia's religions will be introduced, highlighting the problems of attributing single, simplistic identities and heritages to the modern human populations of the region. This, in turn, indicates that exploring the ideological affiliations of communities in the past is both difficult and challenging.

DEFINITIONS OF SOUTH ASIA

South Asia is sometimes referred to as the Indian subcontinent or the Indo-Pak subcontinent, and comprises the modern nation states of Bangladesh, Bhutan, India, the Maldives, Nepal, Pakistan and Sri Lanka. Today, they are linked by membership of the South Asian Association for Regional Cooperation (SAARC), which extended membership to Afghanistan and observer status to China and Japan in 2005; Iran has also held discussions about joining. While SAARC is primarily aimed at the core South Asian countries, such broader links demonstrate clearly that South Asia is well aware of its wider regional position and connections. Indeed, many of the geographical, linguistic, historical and archaeological factors which unify many areas of South Asia also include parts of Afghanistan and Iran, as well as China and Tibet, parts of Central Asia and South East Asia. Physically, South Asia is recognisable as a roughly triangular landmass covering some 4.5 million square kilometres with self-defining boundaries. To the east lies the Bay of Bengal, where the Ganges or Ganga and the Brahmaputra Rivers link the mountains to the sea. To the west is the Arabian Sea, where the desert plateau of western Pakistan and eastern Iran meet in the provinces of Baluchistan. In the north, the mountain ranges of the Hindu Kush, Karakoram and Himalayas provide an almost continuous barrier separating South Asia from the Tibetan Plateau and Central Asia beyond (Figure 2.1). To the south lies the Indian Ocean, Sri Lanka and the island chains of the Andamans, the Laccadives and the Maldives (Robinson 1989). This definition is by no means uniform and other scholars have further subdivided South Asia into the 'Himalayan States' of India, Pakistan, Bangladesh, Bhutan and Nepal and the 'Indian Ocean Nations' of Sri Lanka and the Maldives (Hoffmann 1998: 44). As we will demonstrate in the following chapters, the lands and oceans around South Asia have played far more important roles than just as neighbours or boundaries. They have also provided opportunities for human contact, movement and expansion, and have done so

Figure 2.1. View of the Himalayas from Pokhara, Nepal.

for centuries as urban centres and their inhabitants' demand for resources and luxury goods have ebbed and flowed in different localities and polities.

Twenty-four percent of the world's human population live in South Asia (Bloom and Rosenberg 2011), and within this wider grouping, some 80 percent of South Asians live in India. These figures give an indication of the importance of this region in the modern world, and an understanding of the history and prehistory of South Asia is essential if we are to approach any of the issues relating to land and people which have arisen from this complex trajectory of interaction and contact. Today, as in the past, the density of population varies enormously across South Asia. Bangladesh, the most densely populated country, has an average of 1,142.29 people per square kilometre, whereas in India this drops to 393.83 people per square kilometre and is 332.64 in Sri Lanka, 208.99 in Nepal and 225.19 in Pakistan, according to 2010 World Bank figures (Trading Economics 2012). This high average density and the growing trend for the expansion of urban populations in megacities have huge implications for the lifestyles of South Asia's modern nation states. Indeed, Dhaka, the capital of Bangladesh has a population of 12 million and is subject to the highest population growth in the world. The city has a population density of 27,700 people per square kilometre and a massive 47 percent of the city's residents live in poverty. Notwithstanding their impact on social issues, such as health, literacy and education, these population issues also have a number of implications for archaeological investigation and preservation, as well as urban heritage management and preservation, and we will return to these issues in our final chapter. Beyond the cities of South Asia, it is possible to perceive

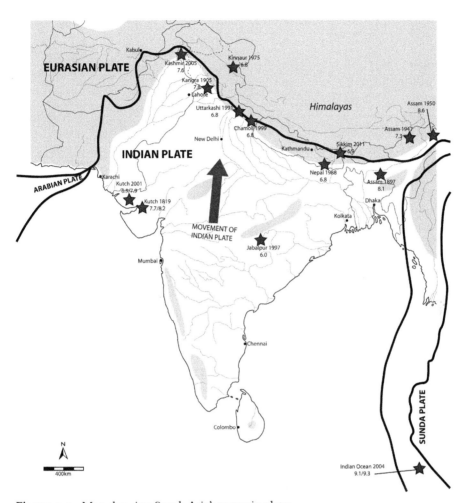

Figure 2.2. Map showing South Asia's tectonic plates.

some general correlations between rural population densities and land fertility (Farmer 1993: 4), although human intervention in the form of political settlement and irrigation, among many other factors, has done a great deal to obscure underlying and historical trends.

THE MAIN GEOGRAPHICAL FEATURES OF SOUTH ASIA

As noted in Chapter 1, describing South Asia as 'the subcontinent' has numerous colonial overtones, but this name is derived from the physical fact that the region rests on the Australian-Indian tectonic plate, which is separate from the rest of Asia. The boundaries of this plate are shown in Figure 2.2 and are marked above ground by the extensive Himalaya, Karakorum and Hindu Kush mountain ranges in the north, separating South Asia from the neighbouring states of China and Tajikistan. While the physiography of South Asia can be divided into three broad areas of plateau, plain and mountain, the reality is far

Figure 2.3. View of the Padma River, Bangladesh.

more complex than such a simple description suggests. There are numerous physical regions within the larger areas, all of which have their own distinctive geology, weather patterns, hydrography, soil types and vegetation cover (Farmer 1993: 5–10). Regional geographies will be explored in greater detail in relation to specific archaeological issues and sites throughout this volume but it is useful here to describe some of the physical features which have helped define South Asia, both in the past and the present.

As already noted, South Asia's northern boundary is provided by the Himalaya, Hindu Kush and Karakorum mountain ranges with peaks up to 8,848 metres (Sagarmatha/Everest), 7,708 metres (Tirich Mir) and 8,611 metres (K2) respectively, and many of the great rivers of South Asia have their source in these mountains, including the Indus, the Ganga, and the Brahmaputra (Spate and Learmouth 1967: 457). The Indus River, which is 3,180 kilometres long, rises in the Tibetan Plateau and flows for some distance in a north-westerly direction before reaching Kashmir and then continuing to the south-west, meeting the coast near modern-day Karachi. The Ganga rises in the Himalayas, where it flows from the north to the south-east before being swollen by a number of other rivers along the way (Figure 2.3), until it meets the coast after a course of 2,252 kilometres in the Bay of Bengal, in what is today Bangladesh (Spate and Learmouth 1967: 427). The region's third great river, the Brahmaputra, also originates in the Himalayas in western Tibet and flows 2,900 kilometres eastward before turning south and joining with the Ganga and Meghnarivers to form the largest river delta in the world at the mouths of the Ganga and Sundarbans National Park in the Bay of Bengal. The interaction of sea and

Figure 2.4. Ploughing in Rajbari District, Bangladesh.

river at this point creates one of the few tidal bores or tidal waves in the world, where the sea periodically forces its way up river against the current in the form of a large wave (Farmer 1993).

Many other great rivers flow across South Asia. Some, such as the Kabul and Sutlej, are connected with the Indus, while the Yamuna joins the Ganga and, in Peninsular India, important rivers such as the Narmada and the Krishna flow from east to west and west to east respectively. The rivers of South Asia have played an important role in prehistory and history, in economic and ideological capacities. The regular alluvial deposits of those rivers originating in the Himalayas and other northern mountains support millions of people; some 400 million alone in the case of the Ganga (Figure 2.4). The Ganga and Indus are estimated to each transport around 1 million tonnes of suspended alluvial particles each day, and the Brahmaputra even more than this (Spate and Learmouth 1967: 43). In contrast, the rivers of Peninsular India carry much less in the way of matter, and are far more reliant on rainfall, which means far greater human input is required in order to exploit them for irrigation (Spate and Learmouth 1967). The effect of river-borne sediment on archaeological visibility is also an important area for consideration. For example, when conducting a surface survey in the Vale of Peshawar in northern Pakistan, Ali (2003) found very few prehistoric sites and very few small Early Historic sites, which may well be the result of the deep alleviation noted in this area (Young and Ali 2007). Rivers are also intimately involved in issues of ritual and identity. The Ganga is perhaps the most readily recognised Holy River in the world, in a country where the water of certain rivers is

Figure 2.5. View of Brahmagiri, India (courtesy Peter Johansen).

considered sacred by Hindus, who constitute the majority religion in India (Singh and Khan 2002: 21).

The Indo-Gangetic plain stretches from the Indus River and the Aravalli Hills in the east across northern India to the Bay of Bengal in a great arc, taking in the Ganga River. The southern edge of the plain is marked by the Vindhyan escarpment, the Satpura range and the Chota Nagpur plateau, and in the east meets the Great Thar Desert. The Indo-Gangetic plain thus forms a natural divide between Peninsular India and the northern and western regions of South Asia, and this divide is further marked by the 1,312 kilometre long Narmada River. To the south of the Indo-Gangetic plain, Peninsular India is bounded by the Bay of Bengal, the Laccadive Sea and the Arabian Sea. The main geographical features include the Deccan Plateau, which is a large triangular-shaped upland area sitting between the Vindhya escarpment and the Satpura range to the north (Figure 2.5), and the Eastern and Western Ghats in the south-east and south-west. The Western Ghats (Sahyadri Mountains) and Eastern Ghats (Mahendra Pravata) run separately up each side of the Peninsular and have an important impact on regional climate and biodiversity as they rise to a maximum of 2,524 metres (Figure 2.6). Sri Lanka is an island lying off the south-east coast of Peninsular India but, in geological terms, is an extension of the peninsula itself, separated some 12 million years ago by rising sea levels (Cooray 1984). In the Palk Straits, which separates Sri Lanka and India, a series of limestone islands are visible above the sea, indicating the remnants of a natural land bridge linking the two areas, called either Rama's or Adam's Bridge. The Palk Straits are only about 64 kilometres wide at its narrowest

Figure 2.6. View of the Western Ghats from Madurai, India (courtesy Jo Shoebridge).

point and has caused a natural break of bulk for larger ships wishing to avoid the Basses Reefs off the south of the island (Carswell et al. 2013). Broadly, Sri Lanka may be divided into wet and dry zones, and lowland and upland zones, with the north and eastern areas of the island being relatively dry, while the west and southern areas receive far higher levels of rainfall (Deraniyagala 1992: 1–2). These lowland dry zones can be heavily populated with the assistance of artificial tank and bund technology (Figure 2.7). The highest land is found in the south central part of the island, including Sri Pada (Adam's Peak) at 2,243 metres and Pidurutalagala (Mount Pedro), which is the highest peak in Sri Lanka at 2,524 metres (Figure 2.8). The Maldives lie 700 kilometres to the south-west of Sri Lanka and comprise an archipelago of 1,192 islands, most of which are no more than 1.5 metres above sea level.

MOUNTAINS AND RIVERS: BARRIERS OR OPPORTUNITIES?

South Asia is an area of great physical contrast containing, as it does, the world's highest mountains, some of the wettest places on earth, deserts, lush tropical forests, sparse plains, extreme cold to extreme heat, and dryness to monsoon (Box 2.1) (Figure 2.9). During the course of this volume, we will demonstrate that such regional extremes act as unifiers for humans in some circumstances and in others have resulted in a history of separate, isolated development.

Figure 2.7. View of tank and bund complex from Yapahuwa, Sri Lanka.

Figure 2.8. View of the Horton Plains, Sri Lanka.

Box 2.1. The South Asian Monsoon

The monsoon refers to a seasonal reversing wind accompanied by changes in precipitation and was first scientifically observed by Colonel James Capper of the East India Company in his monograph *Observations on the Passage to India* in 1784. There are two monsoon systems which affect South Asia; the south-west monsoon (SWM), which is also called the summer monsoon because it brings rainfall from June to September; and the north-east monsoon (NEM), which is also called the winter monsoon, bringing rain from October to December (Aguado and Burt 2007). Figure 2.9 illustrates the main patterns of both monsoons. Variations in the SWM particularly can have far reaching and devastating consequences as these variations can cause flooding or drought that affects nearly two-thirds of the world's population (Morrill et al. 2003: 465). The SWM is both longer and stronger than the NEM, and it has been the subject of more research and focus. In terms of weather and climate, there is known to be some link between the two monsoon systems: "long instrumental records have shown that the wider the geographic area of India receiving above-normal SWM rainfall, the wider the area of southeast India receiving surplus rainfall during the consecutive NEM season" (Gunnell et al. 2007: 211).

Many researchers of environmental change and archaeology have noted that there was a monsoon 'event' occurring around 10,000–7,000 years BP (c.8000–6000 BCE) with an above-average increase in rainfall and temperature. The wetter and warmer conditions of this event are viewed by many as the trigger for domestication, sedentism and ultimately civilisation in South Asia (Gupta et al. 2006: 1085). Although it is noted that an increased SMW may well have led to localised flooding and probably even inhibited farming near rivers, some researchers suggest that this may in fact have stimulated water storage and management for crop production outside of the monsoon season (Gupta et al. 2006: 1085–1086). Whether or not the environmental and archaeological data support environmentallydetermined theories of critical cultural development, whereby key events are the result of environmental factors, there is little doubt that the monsoon is a critical cycle for human life in South Asia today, as it would have been in the past. In particular, predicting the reverse of the monsoon winds has been central for those communities who trade with other Indian Ocean maritime populations as winds shift direction every six months.

Within each modern nation state of South Asia, there are numerous regions with their own character, and these regions are often, at least partly, defined by physical parameters. However, contact, trade and movement of goods, ideas, plants, animals and people between these regions occurs today, and the archaeological record shows this to be true in the past as well.

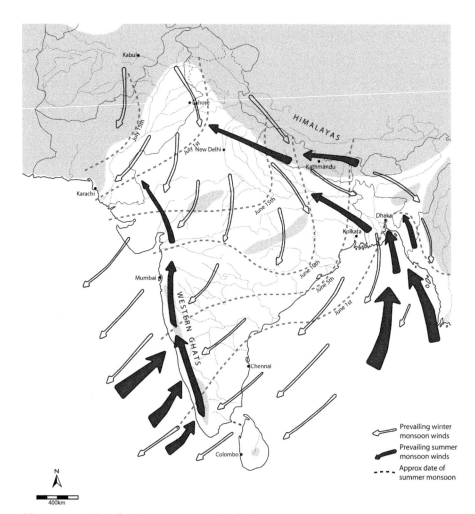

Figure 2.9. Map showing monsoon circulation.

Many archaeologists and historians have viewed mountains as physical
and social barriers and have argued for the isolation of peoples living in and
around them. For example, the explorer Aurel Stein (1862–1943) travelled
extensively in the north-western parts of South Asia and eastern Iran in the
early twentieth century and perceived mountains and passes as barriers and
boundaries, restricting communities to limited areas on either side of them
(1929). However, more recent archaeological research on the Gandharan Grave
Culture within the Vale of Peshawar and its feeder valleys offers a good example of how alternative interpretations may present very different explanations
of cultural change and adaptation. Tusa (1979) and Dani (1967), for example,
both argued that the character of the Gandharan Grave Culture was determined by the isolated position of the sites within mountain valleys and the lack
of contact with other groups and areas (Figure 2.10). However, archaeological and ethnographic work within Pakistan's Khyber Pakhtunkhwa Province

Figure 2.10. View of the Hindu Kush from Malam Jabba in the Swat Valley, Pakistan.

(formerly North-West Frontier Province) makes it possible to suggest that mountains integrate more than they isolate communities, and also that transhumance was an important vehicle for the movement of people, ideas and even goods (Young 2003). Moreover, Dichter (1967: 104), a geographer of South Asia, has made an important point about the symbolic division of space and barriers from a geographical standpoint – he suggested that the Indus, particularly where it joins the Kabul River as it reaches Attock, is the main barrier between Central and South Asia, rather than mountain ranges themselves. Dichter argued that the river acted as a barrier at least in part because the land to the east of the Indus at this point is arid and dry, while to the west, the Vale of Peshawar is lush and fertile.

Rather than just representing boundaries and divisions, mountain passes and rivers are also extremely important as trade routes and, in South Asia, there is a wealth of historical data indicating the significance of the Indus River and passes over the Karakorum Mountains at Kunjerab within the Silk Route (Figure 2.11). Chinese pilgrims from the early centuries CE onwards recorded the presence of numerous passes and routes across mountains and along major

Figure 2.11. View across Karimabad to the Hunza River and the Hindu Kush, Pakistan.

rivers from their travels around South Asia (Legge 1965; Xuanzang 1996). Archaeological data has also demonstrated that trade along rivers and across mountain ranges has been important for many millennia, with lapis lazuli from Afghanistan found at a number of 'Chalcolithic' sites in Pakistan as well as the presence of carnelian from Gujarat in India in many inland Early Historic sites (Lahiri 1992). Moreover, the movement of Buddhists and Buddhism across the northern ranges and into Central Asia is attested at numerous points along the Hindu Kush, Karakoram and Himalaya ranges as well as to South-east Asia (Dani 1991). It is also clear that many mountains or peaks may play important roles as pilgrimage points for disparate communities, such as Adam's Peak in Sri Lanka or Mount Kailash in Tibet.

Mountains also play an important role within the seasonal movement of people and animals, whether this is transhumance or pastoral nomadism. Pastoral mobility has been recognised as an extremely important subsistence strategy from many different areas of the world throughout antiquity. For example, Gilbert recorded archaeological evidence for pastoral nomads in south-west Iran from 6000 BCE (1983: 107), while Mughal's survey of the Cholistan Desert in central Pakistan has demonstrated that pastoral nomadic groups in this region were numerous, and had considerable contact with sedentary groups identified as part of the Indus urban-focused Tradition (1997; 1994: 53). Detecting transhumance and pastoral mobility in the archaeological record is a challenging issue, but important in order to understand population and settlement dynamics (Young 2010; Young et al.

2008). We will return to the role of transhumant and nomadic groups in future chapters when we consider the multiple lifeways pursued by the disparate communities of South Asia.

AREAS OF ATTRACTION AND AREAS
OF RELATIVE ISOLATION

These debates are not, of course, restricted to the mountainous barriers or conduits of South Asia as illustrated by the thesis of Subbarao, who analysed the nature of the environmental setting of Protohistoric and Early Historic settlement in his volume '*Personality of India*' (1958). Notwithstanding concerns raised about his overemphasis on the influence of geography and barriers on the shaping of the cultural development of South Asia (Chakrabarti 2001a: 21), he identified key areas of attraction, areas of refuge and, finally, areas of relative isolation. Subbarao defined areas of attraction as mapping well against the major river basins of the Indus, Ganga, Narmada, Tapi, Godavari, Krishna and Kaveri, where they could be exploited by large-scale agricultural communities (1958). In contrast, he identified isolated refuge zone areas in Peninsular India, where the river valleys and land masses were separated by ridges of hills and forests. Finally, he defined the areas between the "perennial nuclear regions and the area of isolation" as areas of relative isolation as they were away from the major routes of transcontinental communication (ibid.: 56). Based on this geographical analysis, Subbarao suggested that later cultural differentiation was partly influenced by the initial differences of the first large-scale agricultural communities but noted that the isolation of most areas had been broken by the Early Historic period due to the expansion of large-scale agricultural and their subsequent colonisation of adjacent areas (ibid.: 63). Whilst most scholars would reject the driving premise of environmental determinism, Subbarao's definition of zones has had a lasting effect (Chakrabarti 2001a; Parasher-Sen 2008). With this in mind, it is interesting to note that the History Database of the Global Environment (HYDE 3.1) has provided more recent parallels to these earlier mappings of the most fertile land by offering a long-term global change study through the combining of historical population, cropland and pasture statistics with satellite information and allocation algorithms over the period between 10,000 BCE and 2000 CE (Klein Goldewijk et al. 2011). However helpful, the resultant maps fail to acknowledge variable levels of technology or environmental changes and, for example, predict that the north central plains of Sri Lanka hosted fewer than 175 people per 10 square kilometres by 0 CE – a result significantly at odds with the data from the intensive settlement and survey and clearly a pattern resulting for intensive investment in artificial irrigation (Coningham and Gunawardhana 2013).

MAJOR CHANGES IN THE ENVIRONMENT OF SOUTH ASIA, THE LAST 10,000 YEARS, AND THEIR IMPACT

Understanding environmental conditions and environmental changes is an important aspect of learning about past interaction with the land. Humans have shown that there are few areas of the world that they cannot, and indeed will not, inhabit. However, environment does shape the way humans live, and changes in environment will almost certainly affect this too. 'Environmental Determinism' as an interpretative theory in archaeology has had periods of great popularity as an explanation for change, and key to this theoretical approach is the concept that environment determines all human responses. It is closely linked to ideas of cultural ecology, whereby it is argued that all societies are determined by their material surroundings, and thus adapt to them, and to any changes in them. Such modelling devices as site catchment analysis, optimal foraging theory and the least effort principle, risk and seasonality, have developed from the cultural ecology movement, and been used within archaeology (Johnson 2010: 144).

Critics of environmental determinism and cultural ecology argue that ideological issues are at least as important as are environmental factors, if not more so, and that concepts such as 'risk' and 'least effort' are modern, and originate largely in western capitalism. Given that humans have developed complex, state-level societies, in different parts of the world in very different environments (Trigger 2003), it is clear that environment alone is not a determining factor in social organisation. Indeed, this becomes clear in our study of South Asian settlement patterns where increasing and decreasing complexity is known from the archaeological record across a very diverse environmental trajectory. On the other hand, environmental resources clearly do play a role in shaping the way people live, and one of our aims in this volume is to explore these differential developments, but we will be examining them as a facet of material culture, rather than as a primary determining force of human activity. In order to begin this process, here we summarise some of the major environmental changes that are currently known, by looking at a range of sources of evidence. In future chapters, we will then be able to consider direct archaeological evidence within this environmental context, without placing undue emphasis on environment as a prime mover for change.

SUMMARY OF SOME OF THE MAJOR ENVIRONMENTAL CHANGES IN THE HOLOCENE

In this section, we look at some of the main changes in the Holocene, the period since the Last Glacial Maximum (LGM), which is approximately the last 10,000 to 11,000 years worldwide. We present the results from the analysis of a range of different proxy climate indicators, and these results will be considered against human activity in South Asia in the same timeframe (Box 2.2). A summary of various published studies gives us a broad outline of some of the better recorded and widely agreed upon climate changes (Morrill et al. 2003). Although many short-term and relatively localised changes are noted, the most important are at the start of the Holocene, when abrupt world-wide changes included a temperature increase, which in Europe is known to have been between 4 and7 °C within a few decades. This change to a moister and hotter climate around 11,500 BP is also clearly visible in the South Asian records. The next major climate change occurred in the mid-Holocene, and was a move towards much more arid conditions. This aridification has been noted in other parts of the world, such as Mesopotamia, although this is quali-fied by the information from marine varves off the coast of Pakistan which indicate that conditions became moister around this time. This reinforces the difficulties in analysingenvironmental data and attempting to apply it to large areas, and highlights the importance of local variations and changes.

Box 2.2. Proxy Environmental Indicators

There are many analytical techniques used by geographers, geologists, cli-matologists, archaeologists and others to reconstruct and explore changes in climate and environment in the past. Different types of data are used, including sea level fluctuations, tectonic activity, glacial activity, riverine activity, palaeolakes and associated wind activity; marine and terrestrial sedi-mentological analysis, including analysis of Aeolian deposits, palaeosols, cave sediments, lake and swamp sediments. There are a number of biological sources of information about past environments such as pollen analysis (or palynology), diatoms, plant macrofossils (e.g. wood charcoal), insects, small mammals and reptiles, and molluscs (both marine and land) (Lowe and Walker 1984). Many of the analytical techniques used to study these, and other related sources of evidence about past environment and climate, are the product of non-archaeological research, drawing on geological and geo-graphical methods and research questions. While geological and geographi-cal studies provide a wealth of information, they do not necessarily provide a framework of environmental and climate change that archaeologists can easily use in studying their own particular research questions. The rise of environmental archaeologists with specialisms directly aimed at exploring the ways in which environment have been affected by and affect human activity in the past have helped this understanding immensely. However, the work of such specialists within South Asia remains relatively limited, and this has given rise to concentrations of coverage, rather than a full understanding of environmental and climate change from an archaeological perspective. In the course of this volume, we will be discussing environment

(continued)

and climate in relation to each area and cultural complex we address, and considering the different interrelationships.

Proxy environmental indicators rely on two main principles: the use of modern analogues and uniformitarianism. Uniformitarianism is the concept that processes which can be observed happening today in the natural world can be reasonably assumed to have happened in a similar way in the past too. Originally developed to explain geological processes as a series of regular events, rather than as the result of singular catastrophes, uniformitarianism has been applied to many other natural sciences, as well as formation processes in archaeology. Within the field of environmental reconstruction, uniformitarianism is used to predict rates of flow, sedimentation, and so forth, which can then be analysed in order to understand different processes and events.

Modern analogues are used in many areas to aid identification and interpretation. Insects are a good example of this, where scientists have identified many modern and recent insect species, and developed a good understanding of the different habitat requirements each species has. They are able to determine whether a certain species requires moist, shady conditions or whether they require arid, sunny conditions. This understanding of modern species is then applied to species recovered from archaeological or geological contexts – they are assumed to have had the same habitat requirements in the past, and by looking at an assemblage of insects (or pollen, plants or reptiles) an understanding of a particular environment and the way it has changed is then possible.

There are of course many challenges associated with environmental reconstruction, not least of which are flaws in the principle of uniformitarianism and the use of modern analogues. Rates of change may well have been different at different times in the past, and different environmental factors may have had a greater or lesser impact on other factors. Species may change their habitat requirements over time, or be tolerant of a range of environmental factors. An understanding of events in one region of the world may not translate to another, albeit relatively close in distance, meaning that there is a great need for numerous, localised studies. Dating environmental processes and events is also very difficult – not only because of the error margins and intrinsic issues in almost all archaeological and geological dating methods, but also because of inconsistencies in application and interpretation by researchers in this area. For example, in South Asian environmental studies published since 2001, radiocarbon dates are presented as both calibrated and uncalibrated, as dates BC and BP, and this of course leads to great variation (see Box 2.3 for a further example of dating problems).

Different proxies use different time scales, and they are also applicable on different geographical scales – some give very localised information while some are regional in scope. The results of different proxies are at times also contradictory – see the discussion later where sea varve data is at odds with terrestrial data – which requires great knowledge about the physical processes at work and careful interpreting in order to understand what is actually happening where, in terms of environmental change. In summary, environmental reconstruction is invaluable for archaeologists, but all studies and techniques need to be considered critically, and linked carefully to the archaeological evidence.

The Nilgiri Highlands in South India have provided peat cores for analysis, and cores for the analysis of carbon isotopes (Caner et al. 2007). These peat cores show more humidity and higher temperatures between 18,000 and 10,000 BP, which coincides with other records for the south-west monsoon maximum circa 11,000 BP. From circa 10,000 BP to the present, there has been a long-term trend towards an increasingly dry climate, which was accompanied by an increase in grass cover in the region. Interestingly, the records from the Nilgiri Highlands show that grasslands were in fact more extensive at the LGM than at any time since, although with the move towards a moister and hotter climate came an increase in forest cover. The analysis of carbon isotopes agree with the peat data, showing that extensive grassland was replaced by forest, which in turn has been replaced by grassland again. Differences between the carbon isotope and peat analysis lie primarily in the dating of the main events.

Yadava and Ramesh (2005) carried out oxygen and carbon isotope analyses on speleothems from two limestone caves in Orissa and Chhattisgarh (formerly Madhya Pradesh). Although the caves were some 30 kilometres apart, there were nevertheless interesting differences in the results, with indications of an arid phase between circa 3700 and 3200 BP from Dandek in Orissa, and indications of a more humid phase between circa 3400 and 3000 BP from Gupteswar in Chhattisgarh. The authors compared these results with river varves on the Karachi coast, and again, they found that there were many differences for each time period. For example, the speleothem isotope analyses indicated a period of higher than average rainfall between 1000 and 500 BP, which compares to results from pollen cores in Rajasthan, while the varve data for circa 600 BP shows evidence for lower than average rainfall, and the analysis of nitrogen levels in sea cores from the Arabian Sea show similar results. The varve and speleothem data also show differences in rainfall levels in the period circa 1000–2000 BP, but between circa 2000 and 3400 BP, both show higher than average rainfall.

Work at Sanai Lake in the Indo-Gangetic plain (Sharma et al. 2004, 2006) draws on both pollen analysis and carbon and oxygen isotope analysis, and indicates a number of climate changes. At around 15,000 BP, the lake is believed to have formed during conditions that were less humid than the long-term average, and this coincided with a decrease in the south-west monsoon known from other sources. The vegetation around the lake points to open scrub and grassland in the region, and very importantly, the pollen record shows that *Cerealia* pollen, and other 'cultural' pollen or pollen associated with human disturbance and activity were present from the beginning of the Holocene, and from quite early in the core itself. From circa 13,000 to 5800 BP, the lake expanded as there was an increase in rainfall due to a strengthening of the monsoon, and more varied vegetation around the lake. This coincided with the known mid-early Holocene climatic optimum. From circa 5000 to 2000 BP, the pollen and isotope records indicate a much more arid phase, with reduced monsoon activity, agreeing with a recorded dry phase in Rajasthan at this time. There is a great lack of tree and shrub pollen throughout the whole period of the pollen core (Box 2.3). This suggests that over the last 15,000 years, the Gangetic plain was largely a savannah landscape with some forest thickets (Sharma et al. 2006: 976). This grassland was established before the appearance of the cereal and other cultural pollen, which contradicts the argument that this area was thickly forested prior to the arrival of humans and the spread of agriculture (Sharma et al. 2006). Interestingly, there was a decline in pollen indicators for cultural activity in the period circa 10,000–5000 BP, which was the climatic optimum, and the authors suggest that this may be due to the expansion of the lake and inundation of the lake margins (Sharma et al. 2004: 156).

Box 2.3. Pollen Evidence for Environmental Change

Pollen analysis, or palynology, is one of archaeology's most reliable and effective techniques for looking at long-term environmental change (Moore et al. 1991). Some regions of the world have been better served with intensive pollen research than have others, along with the production of pollen diagrams, and these regions have in general been linked to active programs of archaeological and geographical sciences. In South Asia, there has been an increasing awareness of the valuable information that can be obtained from pollen studies, especially when combined with site-specific analyses, although these have tended to be mainly in India, and then further west in Iran (Singh 1991: 283).

Pollen diagrams from northern India suggest an increase in both temperature and rainfall from circa 8000 to 2500 BCE (Singh 1991: 285). Human impact on vegetation can also be detected in pollen diagrams, most noticeably when tree cover decreases while cereal, or species such as plantain, associated with disturbed, agricultural ground, increase commensurately. The detailed work carried out at a series of salt lakes in the Thar Desert region, as summarised in Singh (1991: 286–288), has produced a clear record of environmental change which is closely linked to human activity. The pollen records for the salt lakes show that during the early to mid-Holocene period rainfall levels increased markedly, and at the same time, cereal pollen increased in the pollen diagrams. When pollen and charcoal results from sites such as Sambhar, Lunkaransar and Didwana were published in the 1970s (Singh et al 1974), the results were challenged, and even discounted by some other researchers as being far too early to support the traditional model of agriculture, which until then had placed the earliest agricultural activity at circa 4000 BCE in South Asia. However, the analysis of pollen cores showed not only the appearance of cereal pollen in the region around 7000 BCE, but charcoal associated with this pollen could be both radiocarbon dated and interpreted as an indication of increased forest clearance by fire to create areas for cereal cultivation. Excavations at the site of Mehrgarh in modern Baluchistan have revealed a great deal of archaeological evidence to indicate an indigenous domestication of animals and plants as early as circa 6500 BCE (see also Chapter 4). The research at Mehrgarh has overturned earlier models of agricultural adoption and sedentary settlements in South Asia, and the early dates from the site seem to support the indications of the Thar Desert pollen studies.

More Recent Pollen Studies

In their summary of pollen analyses from lakes in Kashmir and Rajasthan, and from coastal areas of Karnataka, Korisettar and Ramesh (2002: 36) note that results from recent studies using high precision dating techniques do not always agree with earlier results, in some cases even contradicting them. Similarly, recent research by Premathilake in the peats of the Horton Plains in central Sri Lanka has suggested the presence of oat and barley pollen grains at a date of 13,000 BP (2006: 468), although there is no known evidence in the island of a distinct Neolithic tradition. These contradictions have many implications for environmental models of change; not least, those developed to explain the emergence of urban periods in light of ameliorated environmental conditions, and will be considered further in sections dealing with the emergence and contraction of each urban period in turn.

Between 6000 and 4000 BP, the Thar Desert received year round increased rainfall and dunes stabilised (Korisettar and Ramesh 2002: 47), but it seems clear from other studies in this area that overall there have been many fluctuations and short-term increases and decreases in such aspects as precipitation and temperature. This is reinforced by faunal studies in the Holocene (Chattopadhyaya 2002: 368), which demonstrate that while changes in species profiles occurred, along with changes in human practices with regard animals, these were by no means unilateral or unidirectional changes. However, it has been suggested that, in northern India at least, it is possible to discern changes in fauna due to expansion of forest cover due to rise in rainfall in early Holocene (Chattopadhyaya 2002: 369), where the archaeological record indicates a rise in the number of deer as compared to larger fauna.

Despite this very uneven background, there are several broad climatic trends that most researchers agree on. Firstly, following the LGM, the climate in South Asia became more humid and warmer with increased south-west monsoon activity between circa 10,000 and 7000 BP (Gupta et al. 2006). This was followed by increasing aridity in the early-mid Holocene, peaking circa 5000–4000 BP, although there is considerable regional variation associated with the onset and duration of this dry phase, perhaps as much as 1,500 years between different places across South Asia. Many researchers have linked climate change to cultural developments, and this is particularly true of the cities of the Indus Tradition. The transformation of early agricultural communities into a flourishing urban-focused, state-level society has been attributed to climate change and, equally, to the demise or collapse and transformation of the Indus Tradition network of cities, and integrated materials has also been explained by climate change. While climate is undoubtedly of great importance to human activity, the impact of human agency should never be underestimated. We also need to remember that scientific advances allow us to continually critically reassess earlier work and results, and update our interpretations. For example, early work by Singh (1971) and colleagues (Singh et al. 1974) on pollen sequences with associated radiocarbon date estimates from Rajasthan were interpreted as showing a period of increasing rainfall during the third millennium BCE as the Indus developed, and then a period of increasing aridification during the second millennium BCE as the Indus collapsed. However, the radiocarbon dates used in this study were not calibrated and the effect of calibrating the dates provides a rather different interpretation, which places the rise of the Indus during a period of increasing dryness. Given the agreement of many studies (of which a few are noted previously) on the long-term increase in aridity, and decrease in south-west Monsoon strength from around 7000 BP (c. 5000 BCE) onwards, reaching the greatest intensity of dryness around 5000–4000 BP (c. 3000–2000 BCE), it seems clear that the Indus Tradition was indeed expanding and developing during an established change in climate towards drier conditions.

Many archaeologists, who have moved beyond the early climate change models for the demise of the Indus, are more convinced by the evidence supporting changes in river courses (e.g. Madella and Fuller 2006; Possehl 1997, 2002a; Kenoyer 1998; Ratnagar 2000) and this will be considered further in Chapter 7. Human and social adaptation remains a very powerful intervention within South Asia, and there are numerous examples of how technological development has enabled the populations of settlements to develop resilience to environmental challenges. For example, Anuradhapura, one of the great Early Historic cities of Sri Lanka, was founded within the island's dry zone in an area with an average annual rainfall of between 120 and 190 centimetres between October and January and a natural carrying capacity of only 0.4 people per square kilometre (Coningham 1995a). Anuradhapura's success as a permanent urban settlement of 100 hectares with a suburb of 25 square kilometres of Buddhist monasteries lay within the development of a simple gravity irrigation system storing and conserving rainfall during the wet season and then using it for irrigation agriculture, and for animal and human needs during the dry season. This simple system was later augmented with storage reservoirs, channels from other watersheds and diversions to cope with the city as its needs expanded. In this way, the population's resilience was developed and a system established which lasted for more than one and a half millennia (Coningham and Gunawardhana 2013).

MAJOR LINGUISTIC FAMILIES OF SOUTH ASIA

The theme of unity and diversity which can be seen in the physical geography of South Asia is evident again when we come to consider the region's languages. There are four main language families in South Asia: Indo-European, Dravidian, Austro-Asiatic and Sino-Tibetan (Chaubey et al. 2007: 96), but there is such great diversity of linguistic forms that in India alone there are 22 official languages and a further 179 'important languages' (Kaminsky and Long 2011: 422). Languages in South Asia are not simply a means of spoken communication, but they can represent changing ethnicity, and indeed have been drawn into debate about cultural origins, development and identity. For this reason, we feel that an introduction to the different language groups and some of the controversy that surrounds their presence in South Asia is important.

The Indo-European language family is the most widely spread throughout South Asia with 1.5 billion speakers, and is found mainly concentrated in the north, central and western areas, as well as the south and central regions of Sri Lanka (Chaubey et al. 2007: 96) (Figure 2.12). Indo-European languages are related to each other and are assumed to have branched out from a common root or ancestor in Eurasia. They are found in a wide arc from eastern South Asia, across Iran, Anatolia, and then both northwards through western Russia to the Baltic States and westward to the Atlantic Seaboard and the United Kingdom (Renfrew 1987). Within South Asia, the earliest known Indo-European language is Sanskrit, the language used in many historic and sacred texts, such as the *Vedas* (in a form known as Vedic Sanskrit or Vedic) and the *Puranas* (Thapar 2006a). Sanskrit is, of course, related to a number of extinct Indo-European languages, such as Latin, Ancient Greek and Persian, and is also recognised as the ancestor of many of the Indo-European languages

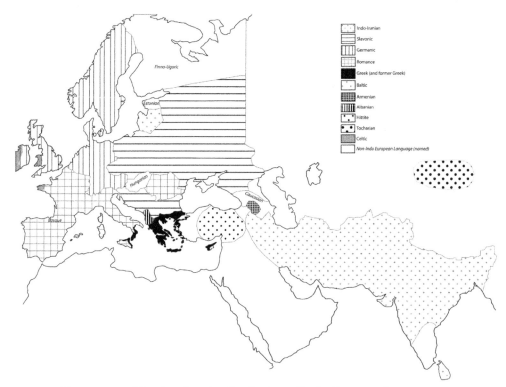

Figure 2.12. Map showing the distribution of Indo-European languages.

spoken in South Asia today, such as Hindi, Sindhi, Gujarati, Nepali, Bengali and Sinhalese (Mallory 1989: 15; Renfrew 1987: 10).

As introduced in Chapter 1, one ongoing controversy in South Asian archaeology involves conflating Indo-European languages with a separate Indo-Aryan (or even simply Aryan) ethnic and cultural grouping or identity. While there is little doubt in linguistic terms that the languages spoken in northern and central South Asia belong to the major linguistic Indo-European family, equating the language with the archaeological evidence of a single population group is far more problematic and in great part results from nineteenth-century antiquarian explorations into physical biology and language (Thapar 2006a). The implications of this controversy will be explored further in later chapters, but Trautmann has offered the following summary of the key problem with what he calls the 'racial theory' of South Asian civilisation, whereby: "India's civilization was produced by the clash and subsequent mixture of light-skinned civilizing invaders (the Aryans) and dark-skinned barbarian Aborigines (often identified as Dravidians)" (1997: 4). This explanation recurs frequently in South Asian archaeology and history, with Indo-Europeans or Aryans presented as an actual people, often an invading presence in South Asia, overrunning 'native' Dravidian peoples and bringing with them chariots and horses (Sharma 1999; Lal 2005).

The 'Indo-European Question' and the search for the homeland of Indo-European speaking peoples, has been debated for several hundred years since William Jones's 1786 report of a degree of similarity between Sanskrit, Latin and Greek so strong that he believed they must come from the same root. Over the next two and a half centuries, many other scholars have pursued the study of linguistic roots for languages. Once the idea of a proto- or ancestral language had been established, scholars then wanted to reconstruct the people they believed responsible for the language and its spread, and where they came from; a practice that Thapar refers to as 'monogenesis' (2006a: 4). Researchers broadly agree that there is a similarity between the major languages of Europe, Iran and India – not only in vocabulary, but also in pronunciation and grammar, and comparison of such a wide range of languages over a wide geographical area suggests that these Indo-European languages may have originated from one common but extinct language, now known as *Proto-Indo-European (*PIE). Many archaeologists and linguists have taken this idea further and believe that there was a cohesive group or culture speaking *PIE, living in a designated homeland, and various archaeologists have used elements of *PIE combined with their interpretation of archaeological data to propose *PIE homelands in Anatolia (Renfrew 1987) and Central Asia (Gimbutas 1971, 1989; Kohl 2007). In Chapter 3 we will explore the impact of models of change based on the movement of people and, in particular, consider the impact of Mortimer Wheeler's research on the transmission of ideas in archaeology and his understanding of the Indo-European debate (1950) which has been continued by others (Lal 2005; Sharma 1999). At many stages of the archaeological sequence, Indo-European movement has been proposed as an agent of change in South Asia, although even one colonial scholar commented that "At times one despairs about ever making contact with these very elusive people" (Gordon 1960: 93). We will consider both the models and the archaeological data that have been used to support it.

Of course, Sanskrit was only one of the many languages spoken in India, and a number of languages, particularly in the south, are not part of the Indo-European family. These non-Indo-European languages have been designated Dravidian and so from a very early point in the construction of the cultural history of South Asia, there was a major division. This language division 'naturally' divided people and cultures, and this has led to a number of major issues in South Asian archaeology. Most modern speakers of Dravidian languages, some 164 million people, live in Peninsular India but the presence of a Brahui-speaking pocket, a Dravidian language, in western Pakistan has suggested to some scholars a much wider distribution of the languages in the past (Coningham 2002) (Figure 2.13). This pattern, when overlain by the distribution of Indo-European languages, has led many archaeologists and historians to suggest that Dravidian speakers were displaced from the northwest by an invasion of Indo-European speakers (Parpola 1994). This pattern

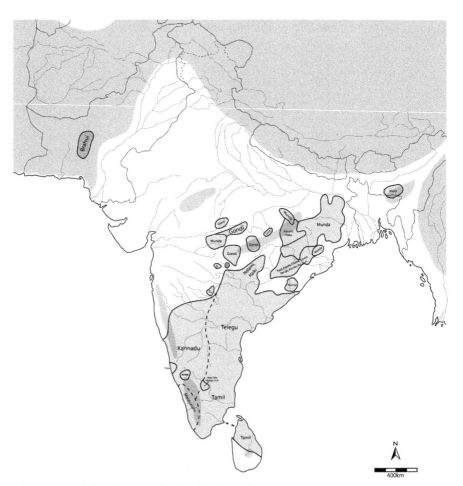

Figure 2.13. Map showing the distribution of non-Indo-European Languages.

is repeated in microcosm in Sri Lanka where the majority speak Sinhalese, an Indo-European language, but there is a distinct northern and eastern distribution of Tamil speakers, a Dravidian language (de Silva 1981). However, recent genetic studies involving the comparison of mtDNA have indicated that there is a closer affinity between the Brahui speakers of Pakistan and Indo-Iranian speaking populations to the west, than with Indian Dravidian speaking populations to the south, questioning these linguistic links (Chaubey et al. 2007: 96). Such advances in our understanding of languages and, through genetics, the relationships between populations, show that this is an ever-changing and developing field. Alongside the well-documented difficulties of using languages as an indicator of population movement, it is clear that archaeologists need to avoid simply equating languages with people or ethnic and cultural groups. It is also clear that archaeologists beyond South Asia are still motivated by the search for Indo-European homelands and the physical signature of such speakers as illustrated by David Anthony's recent book (2007).

Austro-Asiatic languages are widely spread across South and East Asia and are thought possibly to have been linked to agricultural population expansions from southern China (Chaubey et al. 2007: 96). Some tribes in the Central Indian states of Chotanagar and Orissa speak a Mundari branch of Austro-Asiatic, while there are speakers of the Mon-Khmer branch in Khasi in Meghalaya. Genetic studies indicate that the Mundari group have mainly Indian mtDNA, while the Mon-Khmer group have East Asian mtDNA (Chaubey et al. 2007). Sino-Tibetan speakers are found in the north-eastern part of South Asia, and it is thought that their language family originated in China. Genetic studies of populations in the north-east show a closer relationship to East Asian populations than to Indian populations, which is thought to be consistent with their recent spread to India from East Asia (Chaubey et al. 2007: 96). Whilst many scholars have been preoccupied by the dynamics of linguistic change within ancient South Asia, it is useful to reflect on a study of contemporary linguistic changes within Baluchistan by Fredrik Barth (1972). Barth worked on the premise that based on their more warlike and aggressive reputation, speakers of Pushto would increase in numbers in Baluchistan as Baluch lost ground and more individuals adopted Pushto. Barth was surprised to find the reverse was actually the case as disgraced Pathans could not be reassimilated within their own clans but were more freely inducted into Baluch communities – indicating that group organisation and self-perception dictate language assimilation rather than perceived cultural superiority and dominance.

CASTE IN SOUTH ASIA

While there is a great deal of debate about the definitions and origins of caste in South Asia, there is agreement that caste was, and remains, a major force shaping social, economic, political and ideological relationships in the whole region. Caste has been studied by anthropologists, sociologists, ethnographers and historians within South Asia, but less work has been carried out by archaeologists. Those archaeologists that have attempted to explore caste in prehistory or Early Historic periods have encountered the difficulties involved in using historical models and ideal patterns of behaviour to explore actual behaviour (e.g. Coningham and Young 2007; Kenoyer 1998). Yet caste is a critical part of modern South Asia, affecting almost all aspects of life and playing a major role in politics and economics (Khare 2007), and thus it has been argued that it also needs to be considered by archaeologists (Gupta 2013; Boivin 2005 and 2007) although some scholars have indicated that they are less willing to engage (Sinopoli 2003: 309).

Within academic circles there are currently two major views of the origins of caste (Rogers 2004a: 2–3). The first view of caste is that it is a set of practices that characterise Indian social organisation, that these are concrete and absolute and may be recognised and analysed from historical, late pre-colonial,

colonial and post-colonial periods. While there may be regional variants of the practice of caste, the fundamental ordering or rules remained and remains constant. The second view of caste maintains that caste is the primary construct of British officials, missionaries and orientalists transforming an existing sacred order based on *varna* (as discussed later) into an imposed rigid social system which allowed the British to consolidate their own positions of power at the apex. Whether or not we agree that caste has its roots in history if not prehistory, and has shaped modern South Asia, or that caste is an essentially colonial construct that drew on earlier forms of social organisation purely to subordinate indigenous populations and allow colonial rulers to extend their power, caste is a key part of South Asia and is present not only in Hindu societies, but in Muslim and Buddhist societies as well. What follows is a brief explanation of what caste is generally agreed to be, and how it operates within a range of different examples.

One of the most influential and wide ranging definitions of caste was compiled by Hutton (1946: 49) and may be summarised within seven key elements which ranged from endogamy to respect for Brahmins. Gough agreed with this broad definition of caste, arguing that it also offered a means of ranking a group according to birth status (1960: 11). Caste is usually endogamous, associated with occupation, and the formal ranking of castes is defined through concepts of ritual purity and pollution, and the distances and differences between castes stem from these beliefs. Gough also noted that the recording of caste and beliefs was carried out by the Brahmins, who were the educated caste of religious specialists at the top of the caste hierarchy.

The word 'caste' itself derives from the Portuguese word '*casta*', meaning race, breed or lineage (Quigley 1993) and was used by the Portuguese settlers in South Asia to describe the social system they encountered. Indian Hindus today use the term '*jati*' when describing their birth group, tribe or caste, and *jati*, although usually translated as caste, actually is closer to 'genus' in meaning (Boivin 2005: 228). The hierarchical system observed by the Portuguese and others, and now commonly known as caste or *jati*, is based on *varna*, a term known from historical texts such as the *Rig Veda* and Laws of Manu. *Varna* is believed to equate to a term similar to 'colour' or 'rank' and in the societies described in the *Rig Veda*, there were four ranked *varnas*, with *Brahmans* (priests) above, then *Kshatriyas* (rulers and warriors), followed by *Vaishyas* (merchants) and *Sudras* (cultivators and servants) below. Below the *Sudras* were the untouchables, not even accorded a ranking (Boivin 2005: 234). The *Rig Veda*, traditionally dated within the first millennium BCE, is the earliest known reference to *Varna*, whilst the Laws of Manu or *Manavadharmasastra* were compiled between the second century BCE and the second century CE (Buhler 1886).

There are, of course, many dangers involved in the use of a historical description of an ideal social network such as this. Many studies of religious and other practices show that there is frequently a large gap between orthodoxy (right thinking) and orthopraxy (right practice), in other words, what we should do, what we would like to do, and even what we say we do is not always the same as what we actually do. Classificatory systems also tend to ignore local variations and adaptations, as Kosambi (1944) pointed out in his critique of a mid-twentieth century description of caste in South Asia, and he gave numerous examples of social activities and practices that seemingly breached strict caste and class rules. Texts are usually written by dominant groups who write their own histories and, as Gough noted in her work in Tanjore Villages in Southern India, it was Brahmins who carried out the recording of caste and ideological issues (1960: 11). Caste is also known to vary considerably from region to region throughout South Asia, and to have changed over time (Rogers 2004b: 51), and it is also possible for lower castes to undertake a process of 'Sanskritisation' whereby they emulate certain behaviours and practices of upper classes in order to improve their own status in society (Jayaram 1996: 78). Yet this issue of Sanskritisation, and potential de-Sanskritisation, is in direct contrast to the sixth part of Hutton's definition of caste noted earlier, which clearly stated that caste is decided at birth and is almost always immutable. This contrast is reiterated by Yalman's observation that when a high caste family relocated to part of a Sri Lankan village traditionally inhabited by lower castes, they were treated socially in accordance to their geographical standing not their own social or ritual standing (Yalman 1960). Within anthropology there have been recent challenges to the use of collective cultural categories such as caste and religion in order to define and explore people, with an emphasis on the individual and their roles and relations with wider social groups (Mookherjee 2013: 3–5). In line with archaeology's growing awareness of the importance of agency and the individual, this poses a further challenge to archaeologists working in South Asia and who are concerned with exploring the ways in which hierarchies and inclusive/exclusive social groups were constructed.

Colonial accounts such as the writings of Robert Knox, a British sailor captured by the Kandyan King Rajasingha II (r. 1624–1687 CE), described the honours and ranks of the people of Sri Lanka as being based on descent and blood. This record provides an interesting insight into how caste shaped many aspects of life quite early in this period of contact with European colonising nations (Knox 1681: 105). Knox noted that marriage and sexual relations outside marriage, social ranking, occupation, and interaction between groups were all subject to this overall ranking or caste system. Such accounts inform us that there was in place a rigid system of social organisation that has some similarities to the modern and anthropological definitions of caste in South Asia, but we need to remember that such descriptions are place specific, lack detail, and are the subjective record of the individual author.

Caste is closely linked to Hinduism and some authors have argued that caste is a purely Hindu phenomenon, as elements of Hinduism have been utilised to underpin the framework to justify and maintain the Indian caste system (Dumont 1966). Yet others claim that caste is a more universal means of ordering social relations (Barth 1960; Leach 1960) and a way of ensuring that communities may reproduce themselves even with the absence of central state or polity control (Quigley 1993). Various studies have explored caste systems in non-Hindu South Asian countries, for example, Buddhism was introduced to Sri Lanka in the second century BCE and has remained closely associated with state identity ever since (Coningham 1995b). Rogers's (2004b: 53) discussion of caste in Sri Lanka draws on historical records to demonstrate that in the Kotte Kingdom, under the Portuguese and then the Dutch, hereditary groups were used for organising and activating labour, economic practices and taxation. The groups in the south-west recognised by the Portuguese and Dutch included the Goyigama or cultivators, who were the most numerous and highest status caste; Karava or fishers; Durava the toddy tappers; and Salagama, the cinnamon peelers. While these occupational groups were called 'natural occupations', the occupation of a caste could be officially changed – for example, the Salagama were formerly weavers, but as the importance of cinnamon grew, their occupation was changed (Rogers 2004b: 54). Although subject to great local variation and an absence of Brahmins, there was a clear caste-like system in place in Sri Lanka controlling not only occupation, but dress, housing, marriage, funeral customs and so forth which was continued and reinforced by the Portuguese and Dutch "not out of any ideological commitment, but in order to maintain social order" (Rogers 2004b: 55). In economic, administrative and labour terms, colonial rulers also extended this control to non-Sinhalese and non-Buddhist groups such as Tamil-speaking Muslims, thus demonstrating that this system was not simply restricted to the numerically dominant religion or group (Rogers 2004b: 53, 57). In the 1830s the British, who succeeded the Dutch as the colonial power in Sri Lanka, decided that the caste system was no longer desirable as a social or economic force and, through a series of legal moves, ostensibly removed the caste system from the island. In practice, however, caste has continued to shape Sri Lankan society up until the present day, albeit in an altered form and with less formally recognised powers (Rogers 2004b: 51). Although beyond the chronological coverage of this volume, it is notable that a number of scholars have identified a clear social stratification amongst some Muslim communities in India and Pakistan, which has many similarities to the caste system as outlined earlier, although is by no means identical to it (Ahmad 1978; Barth 1960: 117).

Caste then has many implications for everyday life, as it controls not only hierarchically ranked groups and their interaction, but also the access of individual people to dress, food, habitation, marriage, and occupation. Further codification of caste came in the *Arthashastra* of Kautilya, a textbook of the ideal for rulers, written in the third century BCE (Kangle 1965) and also the Laws of Manu (Buhler 1886), and a great deal of our understanding of the historic practice of caste comes from these two texts. Present within the Early Historic period, some scholars have also attempted to identify caste within the cities of the Indus Tradition (Lal 1998; Malik 1984) and the role that the presence of rigid manufacturing communities may have contributed to the production of very uniform artefact categories across time and space.

RELIGIOUS IDENTITIES IN SOUTH ASIA

One of the oldest living religious traditions in the world, Hinduism remains the majority religion for India and Nepal today – indeed, until recently Nepal was the only official Hindu state in the world. While there have been various attempts to identify the origins of Hinduism within the Indus Valley Tradition, this remains a matter for active debate, and we will explore various ideas and issues further in Parts II and III of this volume. This section offers a brief account of the main religions of South Asia and an indication of how they are linked together, thus reinforcing the complexity of social identity and organisation in our study region and this underlying issue of simultaneous diversity and unity. Hinduism is not only linked to the oldest religion in South Asia and possessing the most significant numbers of adherents, it also shares origins with numerous other religious communities, including those still practiced not only in South Asia but also worldwide, such as the Jains and Buddhists, and also at least in part, the Sikhs. However, like 'caste', the term 'Hinduism' is a relatively modern construct and one that was externally created and applied. Just as the name 'Hindu' was developed by Muslim rulers from the fourteenth century CE onwards and used to describe the inhabitants of India, in other words non-Muslims, so 'Hinduism' was developed by the British and other European powers to describe the religion and religious practices of the non-Muslim majority living in India (Narayanan 1996a: 14). Because Hinduism is thus a blanket term, used to refer to what would have been numerous local and regional practices, with probably certain shared elements, it is of course very hard to offer one single, simple definition or even description of 'Hinduism'.

Early Hinduism is correctly referred to as Brahmanism and is believed to represent the oldest and purest form of the religion, the traditions of which were largely complied by *Brahmans* or priests (Parrinder 1957: 31 and 34). Records of an early tradition of Hinduism come from the Vedic texts, which have been attributed to the end of the second millennium and the beginning of the first millennium BCE (Box 2.4). Both Jainism and Buddhism emerged contemporaneously from mainstream Brahmanical tradition in the northern half of South Asia with a number of other heterodoxical sects, and although the Jains have remained quite a small but influential religion, Buddhism developed into a major missionary and monastic-focused tradition. Founders of both religions were members of *Kshatriya* or the warrior-ruler caste, not *Brahmans* (Parrinder 1957: 41), which was at least in part due to the major social, political

Box 2.4. **Early Historic Texts and Traditions**

There are a number of Early Historic texts and traditions which have been
used by archaeologists and historians in order to shed light on the prehistoric
and protohistoric periods of South Asia. These texts are of course subject
to the same caveats as all texts used by archaeologists: they may well have
been written hundreds of years after the events they narrate having been
passed on orally and subjected to multiple changes and interpretations; they
may have been compiled by politically, socially or economically dominant
groups or their hired scribes; they may have been intended to be associated
with ritual practice or as poetic entertainment; they may have described an
ideal or state to aspire to, rather than offer a realistic description of practice;
and so forth. It is useful, however, to have an understanding of the main
texts to which are commonly referred as these have shaped a great deal of
scholarly work in South Asia, and indeed continue to contribute.

The Vedas

Veda translates as 'knowledge' and there are four main Vedic texts or books:
the *Rig Veda, Sama Veda, Yajur Veda* and the *Athura Veda*. All contain hymns,
prayers and formulas for incantation. The Vedas are generally believed to
have been composed between 1500 and 600 BCE (Narayanan 1996a: 20)
and the oldest and most important of these is generally considered to be the
Rig Veda, or 'Song of Veda', which contains 1,028 hymns to gods arranged in
subdivisions or circles (Parrinder 1957: 34–35). There are thirty-three gods or
devas in the *Vedas*, belonging variously to the sky, air and earth, and there is
no single, supreme god. Many Hindus uphold the belief that the *Vedas* were
divinely constructed and, as such, are transhuman – eternal and authorless –
and they are known as *sruti*, or 'that which was heard' (Narayanan 1996a: 23
and 35). The four *Vedas* came to have commentaries associated with each
which contain directions for performing sacrificial and other rituals, and
these commentaries are called *Brahmanas*.

The Upanishads

In addition to the *Vedas* themselves containing hymns and prayers, the
Brahmanas, and *Aranyakas*, or 'compositions of the forest', comprise the
Upanishads. Upanishad is a Sanskrit word meaning 'session' or 'communication', and the *Upanishads* are thus theological and philosophical treatises,
essentially presenting the philosophical development of Hindu thought
(Parrinder 1957: 38). Although there were some 300 *Upanishads*, only 13 are
known to have survived, and these teach the importance of such practice
as repetition and meditation, including an explanation of the syllable '*Om*'
within recitation of the *Vedas*. One doctrine of the *Upanishads* deals with

reincarnation of the soul and the idea of good action and *karma*, or 'deed' (Parrinder 1957: 38–40).

The Epics

The epics are known as *smrti* or 'that which is remembered' and are therefore of human origin, although still divinely inspired (Narayanan 1996a: 35). Two of the most widely known epics are the *Ramayana* and the *Mahabharata* and are generally believed to have been completed around the first or second century CE, although undoubtedly this was the formalising of older oral traditions with some scholars setting the former to the fifth century BCE and the latter to 400 BCE (Singh 2008: 18). The *Ramayana*, the story of Rama, is set in northern India where the young prince Rama is born in Ayodhya. He is exiled by his father on the eve of his coronation, and so sets out for the forest with his wife Sita and brother Laksmana. Sita is captured by Ravana, the demon king, and Rama, helped by Hanuman, the monkey god, searches for her. When they find Sita, Rama and the monkeys go to war with Ravana in Lanka, eventually killing him and winning Sita back. Rama then returns to Ayodhya and is crowned king. In later accounts, this becomes the story of Vishnu descending or appearing in the form of Rama to slay Ravana, and this incarnation of Vishnu is said to be the seventh descent or avatar of the god (Parrinder 1957: 46).

The *Mahabharata*, the 'Great Epic of India' (or 'the Great Sons of Bharata') is nearly three times as long as the *Ramayana* and narrates the relationship of Bharata, a major house of northern India, and one of the neighbouring houses. The story of two tribes and two chiefs, Arjuna and Karna, in this epic, Krishna is believed to be the ninth incarnation or *avatar* of Vishnu. One of the most important sections of the *Mahabharata* is the *Bhagahvad Ghita*, which is one of Hinduism's holiest books (Narayanan 1996a: 38), meaning song of the Lord, or Song of Blessed One. In the *Bhagavad Ghita*, Krishna describes three ways to achieve liberation from the cycle of birth and death: firstly, the way of action or *karma yoga* (where *yoga* simply means discipline); secondly, the way of knowledge or *jnana yoga*, through scriptural knowledge; and thirdly, the way of devotion or *bhakti yoga* (Narayanan 1996a: 41–42).

The Puranas

The *Puranas* or 'Old Tales' were composed between circa 300 BCE to circa 1000 CE, and they are devotional books, praising the deities and their actions. The deities covered in the *Puranas* are those that have become important in modern Hinduism, while many of the older Vedic gods such as Varuna were now less regarded (Naryanan 1996a: 43). They include references to a number of ancient dynasties, including the Nandas and Mauryas.

and economic transformations taking place in central India during the seventh and sixth centuries BCE (see Chapters 10 and 11). Jainism as a spiritual teaching was developed by twenty-four great ascetics, called *Jinas*, meaning conquerors or forders (Parrinder 1957: 41). The last of these *Jinas*, Mahavira or Great Hero, known as Vardhamana Mahavira was born circa 599 BCE and established the Jain community. Jainism teaches the idea that there are many individual souls, which exist for all eternity and that the Self is a stable and eternal principle (Parrinder 1957: 42). Key to Jainism is the concept that through a life of non-violence and non-hatred and practicing of right conduct, one's soul is cleansed and restored and one is liberated from the cycle of life and death – this is achieved through spiritual practice, not the intervention of some divine being (Narayanan 1996b: 136).

With Hinduism recognised as the earliest extant religious tradition within South Asia, generations of South Asian archaeologists have sought to identify the presence of related gods and practices within the archaeological record. For example, John Marshall interpreted the seated figure on an Indus seal as "a prototype of the historic Siva" (1931a: 52), and Wheeler suggested that phallic-like stone pillars indicated that "Siva and linga-worship have been inherited by the Hindus from the Harappans" (1968: 109). Such identifications were not just restricted to colonial archaeologists but to those active in the years after independence too. One of the best known examples are the 'fire altars' from the Indus city of Kalibangan as reported by B.B. Lal, who linked the presence of apparent firepits and washing facilities, suggesting that they represented "a tradition still in vogue in India amongst Hindus" (Lal 1979: 78). Other fire altars have been reported, such as the one at Nageswar, but alternative interpretations have suggested that it was a ceramic kiln (Hegde et al. 1991: 6). This particular example illustrates the complexities of trying to differentiate an individual's ritual practice from an imperfect archaeological record. A number of more recent researchers have tried to demonstrate that the Indus Tradition was Vedic in nature (Tiwari 2010). However, we should also remember the comments made by the archaeologist Dilip Chakrabarti whilst reviewing the archaeology of Hinduism: "There is no Vedic Age. Similarly, there is no Vedic Archaeology. ... In such a situation archaeology can do only one thing: try to trace different ritual behaviours which Hindus traditionally associate with Hinduism" (2001b: 35).

Buddhism is thought by many to have emerged in the same century as Jainism; certainly within the latter part of the first millennium BCE (Barnes 1995; Amore and Ching 1996: 221; Parrinder 1957: 43; Coningham 2001). Buddhist philosophy offers a belief in the impermanence of the human self, social egalitarianism and a desire to be free of suffering and want. Like Hinduism, it ascribes successive re-birth cycles, the spiritual ideal of ascetic, and also many gods, demons and spirits alongside central Buddhist doctrine (Amore and Ching 1996: 220). Siddhartha Gautama, a royal prince, was born at Lumbini in what is now Nepal but the date of his birth has been uncertain as there are different regional chronologies for his life, both long and shorter. In Sri Lanka and South-east Asia his life has been dated to between 624 and 544 BCE; Indian and some Western scholars date his life between 566 and 486 BCE using Greek sources, or alternatively between 563 and 483 BCE; Japanese scholars use Chinese and Tibetan texts and date his life to between 448 and 368 BCE (Amore and Ching 1996: 221). Recent archaeological evidence from the Maya Devi Temple at Lumbini in modern Nepal has demonstrated the presence of a structure sequence at the shrine from the sixth century BCE onwards, favouring the longer chronology (Coningham et al. 2013). As a young man Siddhartha Gautama was taken outside the protected atmosphere of his childhood palace at Kapilavastu and saw three sights: a sick man, an old and suffering man, and a dead man. He then saw a fourth sight – a renunciant whose calmness and peacefulness showed the way to overcome suffering. After many years as a wandering ascetic, Siddhartha Gautama finally achieved enlightenment or *nirvana* (thus he became a *Buddha* or enlightened one) under the Bodhi tree (*Ficus religiosa*) at Bodh Gaya in modern India. He continued to wander and preach for the rest of his life, and when he died at the age of eighty, he entered the state of *parinirvana*, in which the necessity for rebirth was gone, there is no more suffering, and perfect happiness is achieved (Amore and Ching 1996: 230). In Chapters 11 and 12, we will explore the impact of Buddhism on the Early Historic Tradition of South Asia and its patronage by the early rulers and merchants – including the Mauryans.

Difficulties in assigning a single religious or ideological identity in archaeological contexts can be illustrated by reference to some of the material culture of religion in South Asia. For example, the architectural entity of the *stupa*, now closely identified with Buddhism, was used by both Jains and Buddhists in the Early Historic periods. Likewise, tree shrines are both Hindu and Buddhist in nature and even Lumbini, the birthplace of the *Buddha,* is a place of pilgrimage for Buddhists as well as Hindus. There are many other local examples, and this sharing or blending is important to recognise when trying to assign religious identity, or even trace origins of particular religions through material culture.

Within the timeframe of this book, these are the main religious identities with which we are concerned. There are other smaller religious communities such as Parsis, who are modern followers of the ancient Zoroastrian religion founded in Persia and are believed to have arrived on the coast of western India in the first millennium CE (Mushrif-Tripathy and Walimbe 2012). Christianity was known from very early years CE in South Asia through trade contacts with the Persian world and beyond, and the advent of Islam of course has had a huge impact on South Asia, not least of which is the development of the Sikh religion from the fifteenth century CE onwards, which began as a blending of elements of Hinduism and Islam (Oxtoby 1996: 178). Christianity, Islam and Sikhism, however, are of importance at periods later than those covered at the end of this volume and, for this reason, we offer no discussion of the religions themselves or their development here. We also consider the evidence for the development of religion and ritual behaviour within the two great urban-focused traditions and examine the debate which surrounds a number of the aspects of the Indus tradition and its possible affiliations with modern Hinduism, as well as the use of the state sponsorship of Buddhism in the Early Historic period.

CONCLUSIONS

The main purpose of this chapter has been to familiarise readers with the main features of South Asia's environmental, linguistic and religious landscapes which act as a context for our study. Beginning with a definition of the region under focus, it explained why parts of the archaeological sequences of neighbouring regions, such as Afghanistan and Iran, are included within the study. It also introduced some of the major geographical boundaries such as mountain ranges and rivers, and considered them in terms of the opportunities and barriers they may present for the movement of people, goods and ideas. This was followed by a discussion of some of the major changes in the environment of South Asia that have occurred over the last 10,000 years and the impact they may have had on the two urban-focused developments and their inhabitants. We also introduced the major linguistic families of the region, Indo-European and Dravidian, and discussed their use and misuse by archaeologists and historians in constructing culture-historical frameworks and narratives. Whilst 'mosaic' is a rather over-used term in modern archaeology, there is little doubt that South Asia represents a mosaic of languages, ethnicities, religions, caste groups and environmental and geographical zones today and did so throughout the past. To fully explore all aspects of this diversity in all the regions and time periods we cover in this book would be impossible, but equally, we wish to avoid the overemphasis of homogeneity where it did not exist. As a result, we will acknowledge and characterise the major cultural developments under study whilst endeavouring equally to reflect the mosaic pattern in which that development occurred. Finally, we should note that as the history of the practice of archaeology in South Asia is crucial for understanding the nature of its discipline, and is particularly important in understanding the different approaches taken following Independence and Partition, the following chapter will review the development of archaeology within South Asia.

CHAPTER 3

HISTORIES OF SOUTH ASIAN ARCHAEOLOGY

INTRODUCTION

An understanding of the history of the practice and theory of archaeology in South Asia is crucial for understanding the development of the discipline, and this becomes increasingly important when we explore the different explanations made before and after Partition and Independence (Figure 3.1). Not only is this history closely tied to the history of foreign and colonial activity and domination within South Asia, but it is also possible to demonstrate that the very nature of empire and imperialism over the last 300 years has also had an impact on the way archaeological narratives are now practiced by many within South Asia, particularly with regard to postcolonial discourse. We will not provide a definitive history of the development of archaeology within South Asia as there are a number of general synthetic volumes already available, such as Dilip Chakrabarti's *History of Indian Archaeology* (1988a) and *A History of Indian Archaeology since 1947* (2003) and Upinder Singh's *The Discovery of Ancient India* (2004). There are also more detailed autobiographies and biographies of specific individuals such as Mortimer Wheeler's *My Archaeological Mission to India and Pakistan* (1976) and *Still Digging: Interleaves from an Antiquary's Notebook* (1955), Himanshu Ray's *Colonial Archaeology in South Asia: The Legacy of Sir Mortimer Wheeler* (2007), Jacquetta Hawkes's *Mortimer Wheeler: Adventurer in Archaeology* (1982), Abu Iman's *Sir Alexander Cunningham and the Beginnings of Indian Archaeology* (1966), Shanti Pappu's *Prehistoric Antiquities and Personal Lives: The Untold Story of Robert Bruce Foote* (2008) and B. B. Lal's autobiography (2011). There are also more detailed studies of specific themes such as Charles Allen's *The Buddha and Dr Fuhrer* (2008), Donald Lopez's *Curators of the Buddha: The Study of Buddhism under Colonialism* (1995), Nayanjot Lahiri's review of colonial Indology (2000), and Tapati Guha-Thakurta's (2004) volume *Monuments, Objects, Histories: Institutions of Art in Colonial and Post-Colonial India*, which all explore ways in which pasts have been created and some of the motivations behind the processes involved.

Figure 3.1. Map of sites mentioned in Chapter 3.

We begin by examining the colonial origins for modern archaeology within South Asia, primarily reviewing the work undertaken by William Jones and other pioneers of the Royal Asiatic Society. These individuals laid down a number of concepts and models that are still perceived by many as fundamental to a study of not only South Asian archaeology, but also linguistics, numismatics, inscriptions and related areas today. As already noted in Chapter 2, amongst these enduring concepts is that of an Indo-European language family and the related debate as to whether modern patterns of languages represent ancient movements of peoples (Tiwari 2010). We will also consider the pervasive impact of the diffusionistic models of Mortimer Wheeler, Gordon Childe, D. H. Gordon and Stuart Piggott, which suggested that people from outside the region played critical roles in the emergence of the Indus and Early Historic civilisations. Moreover, we will consider the evidence supporting Wheeler's and Piggott's suggestions that the Indus Civilisation was destroyed by a wave of Indo-European speakers, and the way this model has permeated explanation throughout South Asian archaeology. Closely linked were the preoccupations of colonial scholars with linking South Asia to Western chronologies, which has greatly contributed to the perception that South Asia was a largely 'passive' realm throughout its history and prehistory (Wheeler 1959).

Following this, we will briefly consider the nature of postcolonial archaeology in South Asia and the shift in focus by some of the nation states from diffusionistic explanations to indigenous explanations (Chakrabarti 2003). The influence of nationalism will also be traced, and different aspects of the relationship between archaeology and politics in modern South Asia will be explored, primarily by recent claims by a number of Indian scholars that the Indus civilisation was Vedic (Tiwari 2010; Lal 2005). We will return to this issue in Chapter 12, when we consider some of the ways in which the development of cities and states in the early years CE has shaped South Asian social organisation in more recent times, but it will also recur at many points throughout this book.

TRADING AND COLONIAL BEGINNINGS

Awareness of, and interest in, South Asia's past did not originate with European colonial contact, although it was under colonial expansion that such an interest became more concentrated and eventually systematic in approach. An example of this early interest in the past comes from Firuz Shah Tughlak (r. 1351–1388 CE), a Muslim ruler and Sultan of Delhi who was well known during his own lifetime as a respecter of other faiths and of scholarship. He was also aware of the importance of legitimation and the value of the past, and took care to transport two Asokan pillars, one from Meerut in Uttar Pradesh and the other from Ambala in Haryana, to his palace in Delhi where they were re-erected (Chakrabarti 1988a: 1) (Figure 3.2). Even during the Raj, South Asian leaders and scholars were concerned with their own heritage, and it was not left solely to the British to preserve and explore the past. The support given to John Marshall by the Begum of Bhopal during his field activities at the Buddhist site of Sanchi illustrates this relationship (Marshall, Foucher and Majumdar 1940), as does Ratan Tata's sponsorship of the Archaeological Survey of India's excavations at ancient Pataliputra (Spooner 1913). However, the early history of archaeology in South Asia is more closely linked to the activities of European travellers, military officials and those linked to trade, particularly in the form of the East India Company (1600–1834 CE). The English East India Company obtained permission from the Mughal Emperor Jahangir (r. 1605–1627 CE) to begin trading in India in 1619, but by 1764 had extended their role to one of territorial control and conquest when the army of the East India Company

Figure 3.2. Asokan pillar on the Firoz Shah Kotla, Delhi, India.

ensured the subjugation of Bengal. This process of territorial hegemony continued until the conquest of Punjab and the annexation of Awadh in the 1840s
and 1850s. Britain remained the primary colonial power in South Asia until
Independence in 1947, although Portuguese and French enclaves legally survived until 1961 and 1963 respectively.

With the expansion of British mercantile, military and administrative capabilities within South Asia, the number of officers and officials expanded dramatically, and many of these early expatriates took an interest in their new
surroundings. Whilst some immersed themselves in the contemporary literature and culture of the Mughal courts like James Achilles Kirkpatrick, Resident
at the court of the Nizam of Hyderabad in the 1790s, others developed interests in the ancient past of South Asia. One of the earliest influential antiquarians was William Jones (1746–1794 CE), who travelled to India as a Judge
of the Supreme Court at Fort William in Calcutta (Kolkatta). Jones was an
'Orientalist', who admired and studied the achievements and cultures of Asia
and was an accomplished linguist and scholar (Figure 3.3). In 1784 Jones and
other like-minded individuals founded the Asiatic Society of Bengal, which
invited select members of the East India Company and the British military
to share their knowledge and investigations of history, geography and natural

Figure 3.3. Engraving of William Jones (1746–1794).

history. This society was the first to collectively explore the history of different cultures in India and later produced papers on the importance of antiquity and archaeology in the subcontinent, and even hosted a museum.

Many of the antiquarians involved in the Asiatic Society had been educated in Britain prior to their arrival in India, and this had a great impact on their studies and findings, with many linking the monuments, coins and cultural remains of South Asia to perceived counterparts in the European and Classical world. For example, William Jones identified the Indo-European language family by drawing links between Sanskrit and Greek and Latin in 1786, while James Prinsep (1799–1840) dated the inscriptions of the Emperor Asoka through references made to them by Ptolemy II (Figure 3.4). Alexander Cunningham (1814–1893) identified sites in what is now Pakistan according to their association with Alexander the Great, and even managed to draw parallels between Stonehenge and the great *stupa* of Sanchi (1854) (Figure 3.5).

Like William Jones, Prinsep was also an important figure within the Asiatic Society and is best known for deciphering early Brahmi and Kharosthi scripts. He was something of a polymath, undertaking research into chemistry, meteorology, Indian scriptures, numismatics, archaeology and mineral resources, while fulfilling the role of Assay Master of the East India Company mint in East Bengal (Kolkatta). It was his interest in coins and inscriptions that made him such an important figure in the history of South Asian archaeology, utilising inscribed Indo-Greek coins to decipher Kharosthi and pursuing earlier

Figure 3.4. Early illustration of an Asokan edict by Postans in 1838.

Figure 3.5. Alexander Cunningham (1814–1893) as a young man.

scholarly work to decipher Brahmi. This work was key to understanding a large part of the Early Historic period in South Asia, as Brahmi was the script used on a series of known stone pillars and rock inscriptions in Delhi, Allahabad and central areas, while Kharosthi was the script used on rock inscriptions and coins in the north-west at Mansehra and Shahbazgarhi. Prinsep was able to demonstrate that these pillars and rock inscriptions had all been the work of a single ruler, the Mauryan Emperor Asoka (r. 273–232 BCE), and he determined the dates of the inscriptions through references to contemporary rulers in western Asia. This of course was a hugely significant development as it gave a clear chronological and political link between India and the West, one on which much has been built, often uncritically, to this day (Box 11.1).

Following the political upheavals associated with the military reversals of 1857 (Box: 3.1), direct power was transferred to the British Government in London, and all facets of the newly acquired crown territories were

---

Box 3.1. The East India Company

The East India Company was founded by royal charter on 31 December 1600, and was originally named the *Company of Merchants of London Trading into the East Indies*. The Company was formed by a group of London merchants to import spices and other exotic goods from Asia. Spices, of course, had been imported to Europe for many centuries along various land routes. However, during the sixteenth century, Portuguese navigators and explorers such as Vasco de Gama had identified a sea route down the west coast of Africa, around the Cape of Good Hope and up the east African coast to India and thence the East Indies, or directly across the Indian Ocean to the East Indies. This allowed the Portuguese, and then the Spanish, to trade directly with the spice-producing regions and cut out the numerous traders and markets that goods had previously passed through on their overland routes. The destruction of the Spanish Armada in 1588 allowed the Dutch and then the British to break the former Portuguese and Spanish monopoly in the east and create what would become the East India Company, which itself had the monopoly over British trade. However, British merchants still met with opposition from the Dutch in the Dutch East Indies (what is now Indonesia) and the Portuguese in India. In 1612 the British defeated the Portuguese in India, and were subsequently granted trading rights by the Mughal rulers of the time. It was because of these encounters, and numerous other threats to safety and security from other European traders as well as local leaders, that the company developed its own military and administrative capabilities, which allowed it to become an imperial power in its own right over time.

In 1615 negotiations with the Emperor Jahangir allowed the British to establish factories and trading posts at the port of Surat, in what is now the modern state of Gujarat and, over the next hundred years, British trade flourished. Numerous trading posts were founded and significant British communities emerged, particularly in the cities of Calcutta, Bombay and Madras (now known as Kolkatta, Mumbai and Chennai). The company had more than twenty factories around India by 1647, with major factories becoming the walled towns of Fort William in Bengal,

(continued)

Fort St George in Madras and Bombay Castle. The most important goods traded by the Company included spices, cotton, silk, indigo, saltpetre and tea, but one of the less attractive products traded by the East India Company was opium, which was grown in India and smuggled in great quantity from Bengal to China, despite being illegal in the latter. The proceeds of this drug were used by the Company trading post at Canton to purchase Chinese tea, and the drug trade reached such proportions by the 1830s that it resulted in the Opium Wars between the Chinese Government and the Company. The Company was awarded a royal dictat or *farman* in 1717 from the Nawab of Bengal, Siraj-ud-daulah, which exempted the Company from paying export taxes in Bengal. It then extended steadily, both geographically and in terms of political and economic control, until Robert Clive, one of the Company's military commanders defeated Siraj-ud-daulah and his French advisers at the Battle of Plassey in 1757. This was followed by a period of increasingly punitive rule by the Company, which contributed to the Company's short-term financial difficulties and eventual demise.

The East India Company did not restrict itself to the South Asian region – it established trading posts in China, including Guangzhou, Singapore, and Hong Kong in the east, and the Table Mountain region of South Africa, and the island of St Helena along the sea route. Towards the end of the eighteenth century, the British Government began to take steps to limit the powers of the Company and take some of its power into Crown hands. In 1773 the British Government passed Lord North's 'India Bill' which allowed much greater governmental control of the Company's activities in India, as well as assisting the Company financially and placing India under the rule of Governor-General. Under Warren Hastings, and subsequent Governors-General, the British expanded their rule in India, with notable 'victories' over competing independent rulers such as Tipu Sultan of Mysore and the Marathas in the Peninsula, and over the Sikhs in the Anglo-Sikh wars of the 1840s. The Government had put an end to the Company's trade monopoly in 1813, and from 1834 to 1857 the Company operated as a government agency. In 1857 the Indian Mutiny, or First War of Independence, led to London taking full control of the Company and its activities in India, although the Company itself remained in existence for another sixteen years, finally finishing in 1873.

investigated through the creation of a series of surveys. In addition to separate Geological and Ordinance Surveys, an Archaeological Survey was established in 1861, which went some way towards formalising the antiquarian activities across the region. The newly formed Archaeological Survey of India (ASI) played a major role in developing a more systematic approach

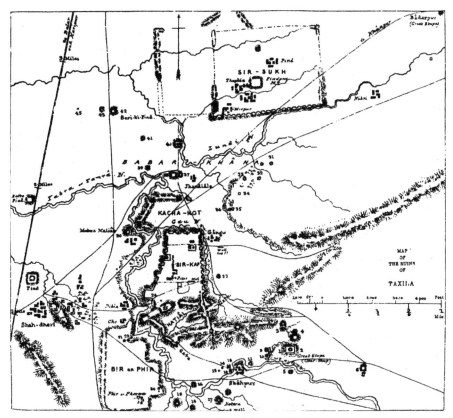

Figure 3.6. Alexander Cunningham's plan of the Taxila Valley.

to discovering and recording archaeology. Under the leadership of General Alexander Cunningham (1814–1893), first as Surveyor and then between 1871 and 1885 as Director-General, numerous historical sites, including many associated with the life of *Buddha* were identified. Cunningham undertook a series of tours or surveys of the Indus-Gangetic valleys and central India, and he was meticulous about publishing his findings in twenty-three volumes of *Archaeological Survey Reports*.

Cunningham is particularly remembered for his rediscovery and identification of the great cities of early South Asian literary tradition, such as the Early Historic cities of Charsadda and Taxila, and other sites of note that had been documented in early texts (Figure 3.6). Because of this activity, Cunningham is often described as a 'historical geographer', by which we mean that he tried to locate sites of antiquity within a landscape by identifying unique or outstanding geographical features by which to place them. Indeed, recording and identifying monuments are what gave Cunningham his place in South Asian archaeology, as he undertook little excavation (Menon 2008: 17). As testimony to his detailed and thorough identification and recording, his study of early coins, and his 1854 monograph on the Buddhist remains at Sanchi in India,

The Bhilsa Topes are still used by scholars today (Willis 2000). However, and this is an issue to which we will return in later chapters, many of the identifications by Cunningham and others of this period have been accepted with little attempt at archaeological verification, and this has brought a number of problems and issues to South Asian heritage and archaeology.

This legacy of Cunningham, and of course William Jones, shaped the course of the study of prehistory and early history in this region right up to the early twentieth century. Rather than focusing on archaeology and material culture as a means of understanding the development of different cultures, and the way they changed over time, linguistics, numismatics, epigraphy, architecture and the analysis of early texts were seen as the most important approaches to understanding the past. With reference to methodology, Cunningham's background as a military surveyor has provided a legacy of extremely accurate plans of archaeological sites set within their landscapes prior to the expansion of population and settlement. For example, Cunningham's topographical studies and interpretations of the Taxila Valley and other sites offer a unique perspective, particularly as those landscapes have since been encroached by modern farming and habitation. His other great contribution was to offer holistic studies of sites as demonstrated by the Bhilsa Topes volume, which attempted to study a complex of Buddhist monuments with reference to its landscape, individual architectural monuments, artefacts, sculpture, and inscriptions rather than studying only one aspect (1854). Some scholars have accused Cunningham of having ulterior motives in his study of ancient South Asia, suggesting that he focused on Buddhism as an alternative to Hinduism in the belief that Buddhists could be made to convert to Christianity more freely (Chakrabarti 1988b: 44). Although disputed, it is quite clear that Cunningham subdivided the ancient South Asian past into broadly religious periods with a period of Buddhism succeeded by one of Hinduism and then one of Islam followed finally by European Christianity (Cunningham 1871). However, it is also clear that Cunningham's political superiors were aware that others were observing their behaviour with the Governor-General stating that "It will not be to our credit, as an enlightened ruling power, if we continue to allow such fields of investigation ... to remain without more examination than they have hitherto received. Everything that has hitherto been done in this way has been done by private persons, imperfectly and without system. It is impossible not to feel that there are European Governments, which, if they had held our rule in India, would not have allowed this to be said" (Canning 1862).

By the end of the nineteenth century, much was known about the Historic, Early Historic and even Protohistoric periods of South Asia but what sort of enquiries into prehistory had taken place? Those involved in the Geological Survey of India were of course ideally placed to observe the landscape and artefacts within it of the regions being surveyed, and this is indeed what happened. Robert Bruce Foote was a geologist with the Geological Survey of India, and many modern archaeologists agree that he was a key figure in the prehistory of South Asia (Chakrabarti 1988a: 8–9; Kennedy 2000: 11–12; Pappu 2008). In 1863 Foote formally identified the first Palaeolithic tool in South Asia, which he recovered from a gravel bed in Pallavaram near Chennai. Foote discovered and recorded over 460 Palaeolithic sites across southern India, along with many more sites with microlithic finds that he believed to be later in date. Foote also linked early human activity sites with finds of Pleistocene fauna, thus opening up a whole new area of study. A contemporary of Foote's in the Geological Survey was William King who also devoted a great deal of time and effort to the discovery and recording of stone artefacts from southern India. They were supported by many colleagues, both South Asian and European, but their extensive survey and publications provided a solid foundation for early prehistory, in the south at least. Another remarkable achievement by Foote was his correct identification of the Neolithic ash-mounds of Peninsular India in 1872. Foote (1887) suggested on the basis of his observations that these mounds were in fact cattle pens that had been repeatedly burnt, this interpretation was largely passed over by archaeologists for many years, with the purpose of the mounds the subject of great debate until work at sites such as Utnur and Pikhlihal confirmed Foote's interpretation as correct (Allchin 1963). However, despite the enthusiasm of individuals such as Foote, the archaeology of Peninsular India was thereafter largely neglected on account of the strength of historic and other texts associated with northern areas of the Raj. This neglect did not always extend into field techniques as Meadows Taylor was already experimenting with stratigraphic recording whilst excavating megalithic burials in the Deccan in the 1850s (Figure 3.7).

FROM THE EARLY TWENTIETH CENTURY TO PARTITION

Field archaeology largely stopped at the ASI on the retirement of Cunningham in 1885 as he was replaced by James Burgess, an architect. In 1902, however, John Marshall (1876–1958) was appointed as the Director-General of Archaeology in India, and almost immediately began a systematic excavation at Charsadda, in what is today the Khyber Pakhtunkhwa Province in the north-west of Pakistan. This signalled a change of approach in the way archaeology was carried out in India, as Marshall was a Classical scholar and archaeologist, with solid experience of excavation and archaeological technique, particularly large area trenches in Crete with Arthur Evans. Marshall is credited with having 'discovered' the Indus Civilisation, with his recognition of the site of Mohenjo-daro and his later excavation and publication of '*Mohenjo-daro and the Indus Civilization: Being an Official Account of Archaeological Excavations at Mohenjo-daro Carried out by the Government of India Between the Years 1922 and 1927*' in 1931. The ASI's campaign along the Indus was extremely

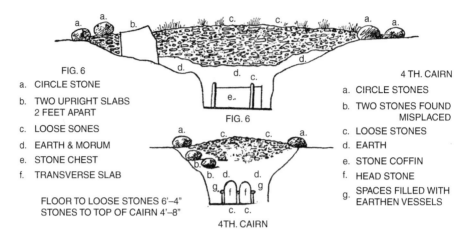

FIG. 6

a. CIRCLE STONE

b. TWO UPRIGHT SLABS
   2 FEET APART

c. LOOSE SONES

d. EARTH & MORUM

e. STONE CHEST

f. TRANSVERSE SLAB

FLOOR TO LOOSE STONES 6'–4"
STONES TO TOP OF CAIRN 4'–8"

FIG. 6

4 TH. CAIRN

a. CIRCLE STONES

b. TWO STONES FOUND
   MISPLACED

c. LOOSE STONES

d. EARTH

e. STONE COFFIN

f. HEAD STONE

g. SPACES FILLED WITH
   EARTHEN VESSELS

4TH. CAIRN

N.B.   THE POTTERY SPEAR HEADS A C IN THE OTHER PARTS OF THIS
       PLATE ARE ONEFOURTH OF THE SIZE OF THE ARTICLES THEY
       REPRESENT

Figure 3.7. Meadows Taylor's early recording of stratigraphy in the 1850s.

Figure 3.8. Harappa railway station, Pakistan.

timely as many of the structures on Mound AB at Harappa had already been stripped by contractors looking for ballast for the Multan railway (Figure 3.8).

Under Marshall's twenty-six years of leadership, archaeology and its related subjects advanced greatly in India and, in addition to regular 'scientific' excavation, he produced publications and journals such as '*Memoirs of the Archaeological Survey*' and began programmes of conservation and preservation with a mission to "dig and discover, to classify, reproduce and describe, to copy and

Figure 3.9. Taxila Museum, Pakistan.

decipher, and to cherish and conserve" (Marshall 1939: 13). He also promoted the founding of site museums, thus demonstrating a major shift in focus from the collection of individual objects to the preservation and conservation of monuments in situ. Following his excavations at Taxila (see Chapters 10 and 11), he established a museum at the site which is still running today, along with a Government Rest House for visiting officials and scholars, which still contains some of the furniture and the dinner service he had brought out from England (Figure 3.9). As with many of his contemporaries, not all of Marshall's contributions have been without their critics, and Indra Sengupta has shed light on an early and rather naive example of Marshall questioning the sanctity of space during his tour of temples in Orissa in 1904, quoting his retort that "[i]f the Government decides that the pavement is sacred and belongs indisputably to the temple, then it should be fenced and a notice warning people not to step on it should be posted up." (2010: 168). This espisode aside, most scholars would agree that a further service Marshall rendered to South Asian archaeology was his facilitation of the surveys by Aurel Stein, whose extensive travels throughout South and Central Asia and Iran provided a wealth of archaeological and historical detail (e.g. Stein 1928), although the methods by which Stein collected materials have been subject to considerable scrutiny and question. Marshall also introduced the concept of major horizontal excavations to South Asia and his archaeological campaigns were typified by the opening up of major portions of ancient South Asian cities, whether at

Mohenjo-daro and Harappa, or in Bhita and the Taxila Valley. These campaigns offered unique opportunities to study town planning and urban morphology as well as to recover large numbers of artefacts to publish and display in the new museums. His discoveries across the northern portions of South Asia provided a clear chronology for the region. In turn, this enabled him to link the antiquity of South Asia firmly to the Old World Civilisations of Egypt and the Near East and, when he retired, it was said of him that he left India 3,000 years older than he had found it.

When Marshall retired in 1928, he was succeeded by a series of elderly Directors-General – Hargreaves, Rai Bahadur Daya Ram Sahni, Blakiston and Rao Bahadur K. N. Dikshit – the last of whom coincided with a review of the ASI by Leonard Wooley. Wooley was deeply critical of the ASI, its plans, its excavations and its training (Woolley 1939) and his report resulted in the appointment of the next notable figure in South Asian archaeology – Mortimer Wheeler – perhaps one of the most charismatic and influential archaeologists in world archaeology in the twentieth century (Box 3.2). Wheeler (1890–1976) had an impressive background in British archaeology, excavating at both Verulamium (St Albans) and Maiden Castle (Dorset) before

---

Box 3.2. Mortimer Wheeler (1890–1976)

Sir Robert Eric Mortimer Wheeler was born in Glasgow, but brought up in Saltaire, Bradford, attending Bradford Grammar School before reading Classics at University College, London. He married Tessa Verney in 1914, joined the Royal Field Artillery, and was subsequently posted to Italy and Germany where he was awarded the Military Cross. After the war he was appointed Keeper of Archaeology in the National Museum of Wales, where he stayed until 1926. He then moved to London to take up the directorship of the London Museum. In 1937 he founded the Institute of Archaeology at University College London and became its first director. Wheeler excavated many sites in Britain between 1920 and 1939, including the Lydney Roman Temple, Gloucestershire, Roman Verulamium, and Maiden Castle, an Iron Age hill fort in Dorset. Tessa Wheeler, who had become a noted archaeologist herself, died in 1936 and he married his second wife Mavis de Cole in 1939. This marriage lasted until 1942, when the couple divorced, and then Wheeler married Margaret Norfolk (a former pupil), in Simla in 1945.

Wheeler served again in the Second World War in the 42nd Royal Artillery Regiment at El Alamein, Tunisia and Italy. He became Director-General of the Archaeological Survey of India in 1944, taking on the task of restructuring the organisation, as well as providing training at Harappa, Taxila, Charsadda and Arikamedu, and developing publications. He became adviser to the Government of Pakistan following Partition in 1947, and was then appointed Professor of Archaeology of the Roman Provinces at the Institute of Archaeology, London (1948–1955), continuing to direct excavations within Britain. At the same time he continued to spend part of the years 1949 and 1950 in Pakistan as an adviser to the Government, overseeing the establishment of the government's Department of Archaeology in Pakistan and the National Museum of Pakistan in Karachi. He was knighted in 1952, and was president of the Society of Antiquaries in Britain from 1954 to 1959 and secretary of the British Academy between 1949 and 1968.

He returned to Pakistan in 1958 to carry out excavations at Charsadda and then joined the UNESCO team concerned with the preservation and conservation of Mohenjo-daro during the 1960s. Mohenjo-daro was eventually inscribed as a UNESCO World Heritage site in 1980. In addition to his scholarly reports, he introduced the archaeology of South Asia to the wider public through his many popular books and radio and television appearances, which brought archaeology to the attention of the listening and viewing public. He hosted *Animal, Vegetable, Mineral?*, *Buried Treasure* and *Chronicle* and was named British TV Personality of the Year in 1954.

Wheeler made an immense contribution to archaeology and archaeological techniques, particularly in stratigraphic excavation and the principles of stratigraphy. The 'Wheeler box-grid' is still used frequently in South Asia today, whereby baulks of unexcavated earth are retained in a grid pattern between larger areas of excavation. This means that a record of stratigraphy is held in the sections of the baulk, thus allowing relationships across a site to be better understood and recorded.

being appointed Director-General of Archaeology in India (1944–1948) and then acting as Archaeological Adviser to the newly formed Government of Pakistan (1948–1950) (Figure 3.10). Wheeler was particularly committed to scientific principles of excavation, following on from those established by Pitt Rivers. Wheeler's box grid technique crucially allowed him to expose both open areas and stratigraphy on sites, and is the basis of techniques widely used today. The box grid is one of Wheeler's long-lasting methodological legacies and is still used across South Asia although it has been replaced in Europe by open area excavation (Figure 3.11). Wheeler also needs to be recognised for his use of trained volunteers and students in excavation in Europe, rather than workmen. When Wheeler was appointed Director-General of Archaeology in 1944, he realised that he had a short time to re-establish the Survey before Independence and quickly identified a list of priorities. The first of these was

Figure 3.10. Mortimer Wheeler (1890–1976) on fieldwork at the Bala Hisar of Charsadda, Pakistan.

Figure 3.11. Wheeler's box grid in action in Sri Lanka.

to undertake the training of key field excavators, and it is a tribute to this regime of field training schools that many of its graduates were to play major roles in the development of archaeology in Post-Partition archaeology, such as B. B. Lal and A. H. Dani (Box 3.3). He also ensured that the training camps were focused on key archaeological sites such as Mohenjo-daro, Harappa,

Box 3.3 B. B. Lal

Professor Braj Basi Lal was born in the village of Baidora, some 20 kilometres from Jhansi in Uttar Pradesh, India in 1921, and his passion for archaeology and ancient history has led to his status as one of the most influential teachers and researchers on India's past. He attended Allahabad University and achieved a first class MA in Sanskrit but also participated in the archaeological training camp set up at Taxila by Mortimer Wheeler in 1944–1945 along with Professor A. H. Dani, with whom he became good friends. B. B. Lal also worked at Arikamedu under Wheeler and then joined the staff of the Archaeological Survey of India at the age of twenty-three as an assistant superintendent. He excavated at Harappa, where he first came across Wheeler's idea of Vedic Aryans destroying the Indus Civilization and then Brahmagiri, also under the training and teaching of Wheeler. B. B. Lal went on to direct his own excavations at the sites of Sisupulgarh and Hastinapura, and then at many other sites in the course of his long career (Lal 2011).

Lal moved to Kolkata to take up a post as superintending archaeologist in charge of the Eastern Circle of the Archaeological Survey of India in 1953, taking care of the area from Orissa in the south to Assam in the north. In 1955 he was placed in charge of the Agra Circle, which included the world renowned Taj Mahal, the Fort at Agra, and the monuments at Fatehpur Sikri. Lal undertook some of the most important excavations of his career at Kalibangan in Rajasthan between 1961 and 1969. His career went from strength to strength and ultimately he served as director general of the Archaeological Survey of India from 1968 to 1972.

In 1959 he was the first director of the School of Archaeology founded under auspices of the Archaeological Survey. This school expanded Wheeler's original training vision by covering both the practical and theoretical sides of archaeology. The school was open to students not only from India but from the wider region, including countries such as Thailand, Nepal and Afghanistan. The school was renamed the Institute of Archaeology in 1985 and its campus is located in the Red Fort, Delhi. B. B. Lal also worked outside India, leading a team to Nubia and Egypt in 1962, which threw valuable light on issues such as Egyptian prehistory and the possible domestication of cotton in Sudan. In 1971 he was the Alexander White Visiting Professor at the University of Chicago.

In 1972 he left the Survey and joined the Jiwali University in Gwalior, School of Studies in Ancient Indian History, Culture and Archaeology and carried out research and training excavations at the Gupteshwar Valley among others. At this time the 'Archaeology of the Ramayana Sites Project' was initiated in order to systematically explore the key sites named in the *Ramayana*. B. B. Lal then left Gwalior and took up a National Fellowship with the

(continued)

Institute of Advanced Study, Shimla which enabled him to continue the
Ramayana Sites Project, specifically targeting Ayodhya, Bharadvaja Asrama,
Sringaverapura, Chitrakuta and Nandigrama. Professor B. B. Lal has received
many honours and awards, including presentation of the VS Wakankar Award
in 2010 and being honoured with Padma Bhusana by K. R. Narayanan,
President of India, in 2000.

Throughout his career, two research questions have played a major
role in shaping B. B. Lal's scholarship; these are determining the historical and archaeological basis for the two great epics, the *Mahabharata* and
the *Ramayana*, and exploring the Aryan Invasion. A controversial figure on
account of his interpretations at Ayodhya, his long and wide reaching career
means that his research has greatly influenced the development of both
academic and popular narratives of Indian prehistory and proto-history.

Figure 3.12. The old French Jesuit Mission at Arikamedu, India (courtesy Jo
Shoebridge).

Taxila and Arikamedu and were geared towards examining deep sequences,
chronology and links between the two great civilisations, as well as attempting
to bring a more certain chronology to the south in the form of contact with
the Near East, the Roman world and Indian Ocean trade (Figure 3.12). He
also focused on the need to publish swift and full excavation reports and to

provide artefactual and ceramic typologies to allow the cross, or relative, dating of sites throughout the region. Wheeler trained many students in archaeological practice, and his legacy is apparent throughout Pakistan and India, as we discuss further later.

FOUNDATIONS OF POSTCOLONIAL ARCHAEOLOGY

Having outlined some of the key events and key characters in the pre-Independence history of archaeology in South Asia, we now need to consider the legacy that such scholars as Marshall, Piggott, Childe and Wheeler left for the twenty-first century. In this section we will consider explicitly archaeological theories, although many of these are inextricably entwined with textual material and interpretations. John Marshall excavated extensively at Mohenjo-daro, and his three published volumes on the site remain the most extensive text to date (1931a). When it came to interpretation and explanation, he was convinced of the similarities between the artefacts and structures of the Indus Civilisation and those of Mesopotamia to the west (1931a: 102). He claimed that the similarities indicated not only that they were contemporary, but also that there was extensive contact between the two. Marshall suggested that there must have been a long period of development, perhaps as much as 1,000 years, before the urban form known through excavation was reached (ibid.). With regard to the origins of the Indus Civilisation, Marshall outlined two main speculative theories of the time – that the people of the Indus Civilisation were Vedic Aryans, thus dominant incomers; or that they were connected to the Sumerians – but stated emphatically that there was no evidence to support either theory (ibid.: 107). Although he ultimately suggested that the people of Sindh and the Punjab were likely to be of mixed origin, he did subscribe to the then highly fashionable practice of unearthing ethnic origins through cranial measurements and morphology. Now widely discredited in anthropology, such practices continued to be used into the 1960s and were used by Dani at the site of Timargarha in Dir (1967).

Although he discounted the Vedic Aryans as contenders for the architects of the Indus Civilisation, Marshall did consider that they existed as a group, and that accounts of fair skinned, fine featured Aryans in the Vedic literature were more or less statements of facts (1931a: 110). It was this uncritical acceptance of the oral and historical sources that has led to one of the most enduring and widely debated issues of South Asian archaeology throughout the twentieth century and unfortunately on into the start of the twenty-first century. The existence of a group of people called Indo-Europeans or Vedic Aryans has achieved the status of received wisdom – it has been repeated so often that it is now accepted fact, despite there being no satisfactory archaeological evidence whatsoever to support the presence of an incoming group of such numbers as historical and archaeological explanations require (Trautmann 1997).

Marshall's acceptance and promulgation of descriptive material found in epics and chronicles was not new but, given his role as a key South Asian archaeologist in the early twentieth century, he helped to solidify ideas which had no legitimacy outside these oral accounts and myths, yet which have shaped the direction of much archaeological enquiry for nearly a century. With regard to his work at the later Early Historic site of Taxila, Marshall himself was keenly aware of projecting his own knowledge of the Classical world into South Asia (1951: xv), although he did not consider that this in any way impacted unfavourably on his interpretation of the archaeology there. In his discussion of the origins of the earliest phases of the Bhir Mound, then considered the earliest settlement in the Taxila Valley, Marshall suggested that the urban form was the product of Persian influence or instruction, although he was aware that there was little evidence to support this surmise (1951: 12–13). He was, however, very little concerned in his interpretations with the form of settlement or culture prior to this historically recorded contact with the West.

Although highly critical of much of Marshall's field archaeology, Mortimer Wheeler developed many of Marshall's earlier ideas and suggested that the different industries and cultures to be found in Baluchistan were the result of stimuli from "the west: across Afghanistan … from the Persian Plateau" (1968: 23). He went on to suggest that the earliest known towns and villages on the Indus Plain itself, such as Amri and Kot Diji, were the successors of earlier Baluch towns (1968: 24). When considering the origins of the Indus Tradition, Wheeler was aware of the many differences between Mesopotamian and Indus culture, but was nevertheless convinced that the urban form of the Indus was the result of diffusion from the west. He claimed that "[a]s the evidence stands, civilization emerged in Mesopotamia some centuries before it emerged in Sind[h] or Punjab…. It is difficult to suppose that, in spite of a parallelism of opportunity, so complex a conception can have arisen independently in each of the great riverine regions, related as they are to a common stem on the Irano-Afghan plateau" (1968: 25). Wheeler reconciled the issues he raised by suggesting that it was primarily 'ideas' that had been transferred or diffused, which went some way in explaining similarities in urban development, domestication, as well as differences in pottery styles, script and types of metal artefacts. He was aware that although excavations had been limited, the earliest known levels at both Mohenjo-daro and Chanhu-daro showed continuity from pre-urban to urban stages. Despite this evidence for continuity, he remained convinced that the driving force of urban development had come to South Asia from the west, and then certain forms and features of an urban civilisation were given a local twist. Wheeler said, "[I]t can at least be averred that, however translated, the *idea* of civilization came to the Indus from the Euphrates and Tigris, and gave the Harappans their initial direction or at least informed their purpose" (1968: 135). Although he noted the presence in both Sumer and the Indus of artefacts from the other civilisation, he declined to call

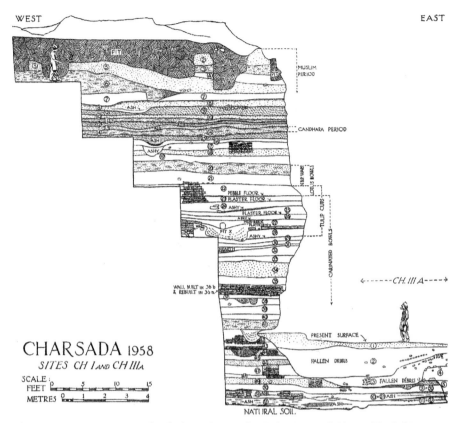

Figure 3.13. Mortimer Wheeler's section at the Bala Hisar of Charsadda, Pakistan.

this contact 'trade' as the evidence he had seen was so small in quantity. Rather, he viewed it as further evidence of contact between the two civilisations that would have allowed the movement of ideas from Sumer to the Indus without the more formalised links that trade implies. As we will see in Chapter 7, excavations carried out at Indus Tradition sites since the 1950s have provided archaeologists with a great deal more in the way of material culture which has been interpreted as part of an extensive trade network.

Wheeler also worked on the Early Historic site of Charsadda (see also Chapter 10). Charsadda had already been identified by Alexander Cunningham as Pushkalavati, one of the ancient capitals of the Persian province of Gandhara, through his analysis of historical texts; an identification which Wheeler later accepted without question (1962: 3) (Figure 3.13). This identification provided Wheeler, and all other early scholars working there, with a solid historical date to which they could link their archaeological investigations – that of the invasion of Alexander the Great and his troops in 327 BCE. Wheeler considered the period between the end of the Indus Civilisation during the early second millennium BCE and the arrival of the Achaemenid or Persian kings in the mid-sixth century BCE to be one of localised activity based around minor leaders, indeed a major cultural transformation (see Chapters 8 and 9). While he acknowledged that Charsadda (ancient Pushkalavati) and Taxila (which became another major city), were in existence prior to the sixth century BCE, he suggested that their development as urban centres was entirely due to the spread of Persian control (1962: 5). The presence of iron objects in early levels allowed Wheeler to suggest that the site was first occupied sometime around the sixth century BCE, and further, "it is here inferred that, at any rate as a city, Pushkalavati should be associated with the pacification of the region by Cyrus or Darius" (1962: 13). Iron, Wheeler asserted, was not found in South Asia prior to the sixth century BCE, and that the spread of iron after that time was due to Achaemenid rule in the north-west (1962: 33–34).

Although Stuart Piggott was primarily a prehistorian of Europe, he carried out various desktop surveys within South Asia during the Second World War, as well as studying museum collections and synthesising earlier published works, which allowed him to comment on both Pre and Protohistory (1950). Piggott's greater knowledge of the Near East and Mesopotamia greatly influenced his interpretations of South Asian material, just as the Classical world influenced Marshall's work. Piggott was similarly explicit in his work about this Western leaning: "So far as India is concerned, therefore, we must look westwards for the introduction of the arts of agriculture, and it will be seen throughout this book how the Indian material can be properly understood only in terms of its general Western Asiatic setting" (1950: 50). Piggott also repeatedly referred to the links between South Asia and the Old World Civilisations to the west, particularly in Mesopotamia, when exploring the origins and development of the Indus Civilisation (1950: 67). Indeed, Piggott went further than simply finding connections between the Indus and neighbouring Mesopotamia; he attempted to find connections that stretched from South Asia through to the Near East, building up an almost pan-continental network of links and influences (1950: 110–111). Piggott was also struck by the uniformity of much of the Indus material culture, not only over a large geographical area, but also over a chronological period that he estimated to be at least 700 years in duration (1950: 139). He contrasted this uniformity in technologies and forms with similar artefacts from the Mesopotamian civilisations, and concluded that the "stagnation and uniformity" of Indus material was the product of fixed ideas and lack of forward development, or progress (1950: 140). When discussing the end of the cities of the Indus Tradition, Piggott strongly supported the idea of a relatively sudden demise of extended urban living, which he claimed is shown through evidence for burning and violence and intrusive populations from the west (1950: 215ff). He stated that "the long-established cultural traditions of North-Western India were rudely and ruthlessly interrupted by the arrival of the new people from the west" (1950: 238–239), and went on to liken the end of the Harappan with similarly abrupt and violent occurrences in Mesopotamia.

Piggott drew heavily on the *Rig Veda* to demonstrate that Aryan peoples had invaded or moved into northern South Asia in great numbers in what he called a 'Dark Age' in the period between the end of the Harappan and the Early Historic urban-focused phase (see Chapter 8). Piggott did not commit himself to absolutely claiming that the Aryans were directly responsible for the end of the Harappan, but he did believe that, as a migrating people, they were entirely non-urban and more 'tribal' in their social organisation (1950: 263). Piggott presented a somewhat confusing picture of the developments of the Early Historic period, when he moved directly from the apparent cultural, linguistic and social transformation in northern India in the second half of the first millennium BCE to the Greek accounts of the court of Chandragupta Maurya, the Mauryan Emperor based at Pataliputra on the Ganges dated to circa 300 BCE. Piggott wrote effusively of Chandragupta Maurya's great state and organisation, and suggested that there must have been some Harappan legacy at work there (1950: 287–288). What Piggott failed to address here was the importance of the other Early Historic developments across the region and the impact of the Achaemenids and Greeks, whose activities in South Asia have been the subject of considerable historical records by eyewitnesses, unlike the Aryans.

Finally, reference should be made to Vere Gordon Childe who, like Stuart Piggott, was not a South Asian archaeologist but a Professor of Prehistoric Archaeology at Edinburgh University. Like Piggott, and very much in keeping with the approach of the mid-twentieth century, he attempted to synthesise knowledge about the early Old World Civilisations. In his discussion of the Indus Civilisation, Childe emphasised the homogeneity of the material culture, despite the distance between the main sites known at the time, being Mohenjo-daro, Chanhu-daro and Harappa (1954: 173). Childe noted similarities in the form of certain pottery types, metal objects and other artefacts between the Indus and Mesopotamia, but he was also clear that these civilisations were in fact very separate: "Enough has been said to show that India confronts Egypt and Babylonia by the third millennium with a thoroughly individual and independent civilization of her own, technically the peer of the rest. And it is plainly deeply rooted in Indian soil" (1954: 183). However, he then went on to point out that the three civilisations all had the same basic concepts, and suggested that it was unlikely that all three were the result of entirely separate, indigenous development. Trade was acknowledged as one means of sharing both goods and ideas, but in Childe's view, trade "may explain some rather superficial agreements between the two civilizations, but not the underlying technological and economic bases, common to both" (1954: 186). He expanded this concept further by explaining that in his view, both Mesopotamia and the Indus were based on the same fundamental inventions and discoveries, but during the third millennium BCE there was great divergence and separate development.

Like Piggott, Childe claimed that there was no internal development within the material culture of the Indus; that there were no cultural changes to distinguish different levels or stages over time in the civilisation itself (1954: 186). This is of course partly a product of limited data from a limited number of sites available at the time Childe was writing, and also the difficulties of closely dating stratigraphic events and changes. While Childe was cautious in his commentary on the origins of the Indus, he was very clear about its end and focused on a period of internal degradation in the civilisation, evident through the reuse of brick and the much smaller scale of building carried out. This was then followed by a barbarian invasion which destroyed the cities and most of the civilisation itself (1954: 187). While not fully committing himself to identifying these invaders as Aryans, he did suggest that they came from the region of north-western Iran, and attributed to them a gap in the cultural record, which lasted until the time of the Persian King Darius (1954: 188). Finally, reference should be made to Colonel D. H. Gordon, whose *'Pre-Historic Background of Indian Culture'* epitomised earlier diffusionistic narratives although it was published as late as 1960. With a clearly stated philosophy that "[a]s we trace the cultural progress of man in India we shall see how influences in the shape of immigrants or invaders made their way into India" (1960: 35), all of South Asia's major cultures were attributed to Western Asia. Collectively, this group of foreign scholars were to greatly influence the development of archaeological explanation and theory within South Asia, and their concepts have been repeated and delivered to generations of students and scholars through key textbooks. However, it is also important to recognise the contributions made by large numbers of South Asians during this period. This contribution included patrons, as foreign governments were not the only sponsors of excavations as demonstrated by the financial support of the Begum of Bhopal and Ratan Tata, but also included the pioneering fieldwork undertaken in the region of Sindh by Majumdar, who was killed by dacoits whilst surveying, or the mapping of Lumbini, the birthplace of the *Buddha*, by P. C. Mukherji in Nepal or, indeed, the discovery of Lumbini itself by General Khadga Shumsher J. B. Rana in 1899. Similarly, it is worth noting that some of the individuals may have sponsored archaeological activities for more personal reasons and Basak has suggested that Ratan Tata's focus at Pataliputra may have been partly driven by a wish to explore his own "Persian roots" (2008: 47).

POST-PARTITION ARCHAEOLOGY

As is clear from Wheeler's own memoirs, the devastating events and mass migrations associated with Partition were to make the latter half of the 1940s extremely unsettled for archaeological professionals, but archaeology within South Asia was soon to recast its role by contributing to the emerging identities of the new nation states. To an extent, such a contribution had already been made by scholars like Marshall. Indeed, he had clearly demonstrated a substantial depth to the cultural sequences of South Asia, identified the presence of a literate, urban civilisation much earlier than those of Europe, and his conservation programme has created what he termed a "national heirloom for posterity" (1939: 27). Wheeler also contributed as he assisted the archaeologists of the new state of Pakistan to recognise the distinct character of the cultural heritage of West and East Pakistan in a volume called *Five Thousand Years of Pakistan*, which he admitted was a wilful paradox (1950). Acknowledging the territorial allocation of the Indus Valley and its cities to the new state of Pakistan, he then advised the archaeologists of the new state of India that "recent Partition has robbed us of the Indus Valley.... We now have therefore no excuse for deferring longer the overdue exploration of the Ganges Valley. After all if the Indus gave India a name, it may almost be said that the Ganges gave India a faith" (Wheeler 1949: 10). The professionals of the new nation-states needed little encouragement and quickly developed a level of state sponsorship, scarcely seen before within the region, as Pakistan launched archaeological missions to Bahrain whilst India sponsored missions to Afghanistan, Indonesia, Cambodia and Nepal as well as European exhibitions (Lal 1964).

It is important to note, however, that this new Independence-inspired archaeological agenda was still largely fuelled by a continued reliance on diffusion and the movement of people as the main explanation for cultural change. Thus Banerjee initiated a search through Iron Age cultural assemblages in order to identify the presence of the diffusion of Aryan colonists (1965). Even later, Sankalia considered contemporary Western trends for processual models of indigenous cultural development before rejecting them in favour of diffusionism (1977). Not all research was driven by earlier diffusionistic antecedents, as illustrated by B. B. Lal's 'Epic Archaeology', a term utilised by Menon to describe attempts to link archaeological sequences within India with the textual content of the *Ramayana* and *Mahabharata* (2008: 25). Despite the collective influence of the colonial scholars discussed earlier, huge changes have occurred within South Asian archaeological method, theory and practice over the last forty years. For example, concepts of a diffused Neolithic have been replaced by not one but multiple Neolithic developments in different regions. This includes the chance discovery of Mehrgarh in Baluchistan, which is the sixth millennium BC archaeological site from which we can see clear developmental links to the later cities of the Indus Tradition. Similarly, the apparent appearance of the Indus cities is now known to have been presaged by the presence of a series of proto-urban planned forms from the middle of the fourth millennium BC. Similarly, sites like Inamgaon, Pirak and Charsadda suggest that the intervening period between the two major urban-focused developments was actually a period of innovation and growth in many aspects, and that a number of later Early Historic cities had their genesis in the preceding late 'Chalcolithic' and Iron Age periods. Menon has suggested that the acceleration in the study and excavation of Early Historic sites in India reflected this desire "to fill the gap" between Harappan and Early Historic (2008: 19). The vast majority of these developments and discoveries were initiated after Partition, and this event also caused the development of very different trajectories of archaeological practice within each separate South Asian state. Moreover, there was also a growing critical awareness of the impact of colonialism and postcolonialism on the discipline (Chakrabarti 2003, 1988a; Thapar 1995, Tiwari 2010) (Box 3.4).

Box 3.4. Romila Thapar

Professor Romila Thapar is one of the leading authorities on ancient South Asia, particularly Indian history, and her work spans both textual sources and material culture analysis. She obtained a BA from Punjab University and then went on to study for a PhD on the Mauryan Empire at the School of Oriental and African Studies (SOAS) in London in 1958. Born in India in 1931 in Punjab, Thapar's career has been both illustrious and influential. For example, she has defended the right of universities to teach broadly debated interpretations of the *Ramayana*, and has engaged with discussing the motivations behind different interpretations of South Asian history, particularly in relation to religious tradition. Thapar has taught ancient Indian history at Delhi University and Jawaharlal Nehru University (JNU), and has been an Emeritus Professor at JNU since 1993. She has also been awarded numerous honorary degrees and distinctions, including honorary degrees from Peradeniya University, Sri Lanka, University of Chicago, University of Calcutta, Oxford University, and Edinburgh University. Some of her recent distinctions include being appointed to the Visiting Kluge Chair at the Library of Congress, Washington DC, and being awarded the Kluge Prize, being voted a Corresponding Fellow of the Royal Society of Edinburgh, elected to the American Academy of Arts and Sciences, and being elected an Honorary Member of the American Historical Association. Such international recognition is in keeping with the scope and impact of Thapar's research.

What has made Thapar such an important figure in the study of South Asia's ancient history? One of the key elements of her research is her use of social context and her attempts to place analysis and interpretation within a specific cultural context, that of South Asia. Thapar's work has also challenged two major narratives of ancient India; the first of which cast South Asia in terms of past glory, a once-great culture that had degenerated; and the second which portrayed ancient South Asia as a non-violent and progressive region up to colonial contact. Thapar's work challenged both these views and this has led to a great deal of intellectual debate. Arising from her PhD research on the Mauryan Empire, Thapar has also carried out much analysis of the role of religion in the history of South Asia and, in particular, the development of both Hinduism and Buddhism in social terms. She has cautioned against the uncritical use of texts (1985: 16), stating: "the chronological stratification of literary texts, particularly those which arose out of religious needs or came to serve a religious function and which have been preserved as part of an oral tradition before being edited and recorded in writing, do present multiple problems in providing data on precise points of historical and social change".

Professor Romila Thapar continues to publish widely on ancient South Asia, and to promote debate and discussion about many different aspects of her work. She remains based in New Delhi, although she travels widely in order to lecture about her work and undertake visiting research and teaching fellowships.

Up to the mid-twentieth century, archaeology throughout most of South Asia came under the auspices of the ASI and of course the British, with a separate Archaeological Survey Department in Sri Lanka. Following independence from Britain, and in the case of Pakistan and Bangladesh, each country developed its own agenda for the study and practice of archaeology. In Post-Independence India, the major change was in the scale of support and approach. As we saw earlier, it was not until 1902 that archaeological excavation became accepted in South Asia within the ASI. After Independence, India retained the structure of the Survey, but greatly extended its scale and activity. As Dilip Chakrabarti has commented "The basic shape of the central Archaeological Survey remains the same, but in scale there can be no comparison between the official strength of the pre-1947 Survey and that of post-1947 India. In terms of approved human resources, budget and the number of its 'circles' and 'branches', the modern Indian 'Survey' is truly an archaeological juggernaut" (1999: 17). In addition to the national survey, states took control of research and conservation within their own territory, and the Indian University Grants Commission has provided funding for universities to conduct teaching and research in different parts of the country. This means that Indian archaeology is well-funded and multi-tiered, and this has resulted in a great deal of exploration since 1947, as well as a very strong commitment to archaeology and archaeological science in higher education. Bishnupriya Basak observed that there has also been parallel growth in the development of regional archaeologies and histories, reflecting individual states, some of which were newly formed such as Gujarat and Maharashtra (2008: 49). In some cases, this in turn has influenced how the archaeological sequences of larger areas or regions have been presented and researched with Aloka Parasher-Sen stating that some "corridors of cultural interaction ... were now blocked out only to highlight the archaeological personality of a newly constructed administrative entity" (2008: 316). Finally, it is necessary to note that the impact of increasing numbers of Buddhist pilgrims from Japan, South-east and East Asia has acted as a catalyst for an investment in ancient Buddhist sites across northern India.

The other countries of South Asia have also inherited a similar structure from the ASI – in all, archaeology is the affair of the government, either directly through both federal and state departments (or circles), or indirectly through state-funded universities. The major differences are in the amount of funding and the size of the departments. In Pakistan, for example, archaeology is taught at fewer institutions, and still owes a huge debt to Mortimer Wheeler for its interpretation and approach. More recent legislation has divided archaeological jurisdiction of sites between UNESCO World Heritage sites under the care of the Federal Department of Archaeology and Museums whilst other sites are now entrusted to provincial governments. Nepal has an active government Department of Archaeology as well as a Lumbini Development Trust archaeological unit, but little formal tertiary teaching in the subject, while Sri Lanka is fiercely proud of its own separate archaeological tradition, with high standards of training and excavation. Moreover, its departmental activities have been augmented by fieldwork and excavation sponsored by the Central Cultural Fund and the Universities of Kelaniya and Peradeniya. The Central Cultural Fund is also now responsible for management and research within the island's UNESCO World Heritage sites, which include a striking range of important Early Historic and Mediaeval capitals and their hinterlands. Finally, one should note that whilst Bangladesh has an established Department of Archaeology, the archaeology of the Maldives and Bhutan is as yet underdeveloped. A number of Myanmar's senior archaeologists were trained at the ASI's Institute of Archaeology and now its Department of Archaeology and National Museum runs its own programs under the auspices of the Department's Field School of Archaeology (Moore 2007).

From the late 1960s and 1970s, a growing interest in environmental and scientific archaeology may also be traced, particularly within India. Examples of this include the palynological work by Singh (1971) (see Chapter 2) and work within the field of archaeometallurgy by D. P. Agrawal (1971). This was in line with a broader concern with these sub-disciplines in archaeology worldwide, and contributed greatly to the environmental determinist approaches which dominated much archaeological explanation and interpretation in the 1970s and 1980s. Whilst some departments and universities have remained more traditional in approach, both Deccan College, Pune and the MS University of Baroda pursued routes of science-based archaeology in their publications in the 1970s and 1980s. The impact of radiocarbon dating was also quickly recognised as reflected in the initial publications of scholars such as Agrawal and Ghosh (1973), Agrawal and Kusumgar (1974) and Mandal (1972). This scientific and environmental approach allowed the development of alternative explanations for both the origins and the demise of the Indus Civilisation (see also Chapters 2, 6 and 8), as well as attempting to explain many earlier cultural developments, such as the advent of the Mesolithic or periods associated with the use of microlithic tools (see Chapter 4) or the general health of ancient populations (Lukacs and Walimbe 1996). Additional archaeological science units were developed across India, including at Banaras Hindu University, Garhwal University, the Birbal Sahni Research Institute of Palaeobotany, Tata Institute of Fundamental Research, and the Bombay and Physical Research Laboratory. While an understanding of prevailing and changing environmental conditions is obviously important to gain a full picture of landscape use and the exploitation of plants and animals, to rely on environmental determinism as a single or main driver of change ignores human agency and the importance of cultural adaptation. Other important foci, such as the postgraduate Centre for Historical Studies at Jawaharlal Nehru University, are committed to investigating reconstructions of the past through the interface between socio-economic history and archaeology. In the following chapters we will, of course, cover environmental issues, but we will consider them as just one part of a suite of factors that have contributed to, shaped, and been shaped by human activity.

Similarly, settlement and landscape archaeology has become of increasing interest to South Asian archaeologists, just as it has developed as an archaeological sub-discipline in other parts of the world. In South Asia, survey archaeology ranges from the compilation of gazetteers of sites by archaeologists such as Rafique Mughal (1997), George Erdosy (1988), and Ihsan Ali (2003) to consideration of religious landscapes (e.g. Shaw 2000; 2013), the place of rock art in landscapes (e.g. Dani 1995) and the links between landscape and identity (e.g. Young 2010, 2009). There have also been developments in the application of different methodologies and different interpretative approaches to understanding urban-rural landscapes and their development (e.g. Bandaranayake and Mogren 1994; Coningham and Gunawardhana 2013, Coningham et al. 2007a; Mohanty and Smith 2008). Moreover, there have also been limited but successful transborder collaborations, such as the participation of Indian specialists like B. K. Thapar, P. B. Karunaratne, P. P. Joglekar and M. D. Kajale in the excavations at Mantai in Sri Lanka (Carswell et al. 2013). These methodological and technological innovations have occurred in parallel with increasing recognition of the challenges and limitations presented by culture history (Johansen 2003), as well as consideration of the negative impact of colonialism and neo-colonialism on contemporary South Asian archaeology as a whole (Chakrabarti 2010). Alongside these focused developments, however, there is still strong diffusionist or anti-diffusionistic debate even today as illustrated

Figure 3.14. Looters excavating the Indo-Greek city of Shaikhan Dheri, Pakistan.

by the collection of papers presented by Tiwari in 2010 and the 12th World Association for Vedic Studies conference on 'Harappan Civilisation and Vedic Culture'. That these opposing views still exist, and result in such polarised debate, demonstrates the power of the legacy of early archaeologists.

CONCLUSIONS

Whilst it would be true to say that never has there been so much archaeology practised within South Asia, whether by the state or national government or by South Asian or international universities, it would also be true to say that the threats to South Asia's heritage have never been greater. Urbanisation, industrialisation and the development of more intrusive farming technologies in addition to the development of national and international markets for South Asian antiquities are taking their toll. With regard to the illegal trafficking of antiquities, a series of surveys in north-west Pakistan in the 1990s estimated that over half of all known Buddhist archaeological sites in Charsadda District had been targeted by illegal excavators (Ali and Coningham 2002), and similar evidence has been produced from Anuradhapura District in Sri Lanka, where two-thirds of all Buddhist sites had been targeted (Coningham and Gunawardhana 2012) (Figure 3.14). As the population grows, this human risk to the preservation of heritage keeps pace. To this may be added the destruction of sites and monuments from 'nationalistic' and 'ideological' motives. The oft-cited example of the destruction of the Mughal Emperor Barbur's mosque in Ayodhya in 1992

Figure 3.15. The standing Buddha of Bamiyan before its destruction, Afghanistan.

demonstrated that even the modern nation state of India was unable to protect certain monuments as political popularism and fundamentalism focus on individual sites. This disaster also saw archaeologists turn against each other with some even loosely associated with the destruction of the mosque on account of the postulated presence of a Hindu temple beneath (Ratnagar 2004). Sadly, at the same time that the Babri mosque in Ayodhya was destroyed, similar

Figure 3.16. The Bombing Temple of Tooth in Kandy, Sri Lanka.

damage was sparked in Multan when Hindu temples were targeted by furi-
ous crowds. The destruction of the Bamiyan Buddhas in Afghanistan in 2001
(Figure 3.15), the bombing of the Temple of the Tooth in Kandy, Sri Lanka, in
1998 (Figure 3.16), the attack on the Sacred Bodhi tree at Anuradhapura, Sri
Lanka, in 1986 and the bombing at the shrine of Bodh Gaya in India in 2013
all demonstrate that heritage in South Asia is highly vulnerable, and that dominant and separatist ideologies have few scruples over the targeting of heritage

Figure 3.17. Graffiti on Buddha carving in the Swat Valley, Pakistan.

as in the case of the recent destruction of Buddhist images in the National Museum at Male.

This current state of affairs shows that while archaeology is now integral to South Asia and highly professional, it also has a high profile, and attempts to control the use and misuse of the past will make its preservation increasingly difficult, although this is the context of archaeology globally (Chakrabarti 2010) (Figure 3.17). It is also important to note, however, that not all popularism is necessarily damaging to sites. For example, neither the Sri Lankan government's Department of Archaeology nor the Sri Lankan Royal Asiatic Society has been able to control the current popular interest in sites associated with the *Ramayana* as hundreds of thousands of pilgrims come to the island seeking authentic evidence of Lankapura, Ravana, Sita, Rama and Hanuman as sites without any archaeological evidence are transformed into cult pilgrimage stops (Dissanayake 2010). These developments are not without their positive aspects as there is also growing awareness of the social and economic benefits of cultural heritage across South Asia with a range of exemplars stretching from the Asian Development Bank's investment in infrastructure to support international Buddhist pilgrimage, to the original model of Sri Lanka's Cultural Triangle which has generated sufficient income to both preserve and conserve its monuments. This promotion shares a parallel in the surge of interest in the search for the submerged continent of Lemuria. Identified by some scholars as the lost ancestral homeland of Dravidian speakers, Sumathi Ramaswamy has charted how they have used this concept to explain why there is an apparent lack of early complexity in Peninsular India – its cities and temples lie beneath the Indian Ocean (2004). The SAARC member states have also had a number of major monumental sites inscribed on the UNESCO World Heritage Site list, although the pervasive and arguably intrinsic imbalances of the list are reflected in the types of sites inscribed and the number of sites from each of the different countries. This context suggests that the next phase of the development of archaeology as a discipline within South Asia will witness increasing pressure on the archaeological resource as professionalism and popularism clash, but will have a clear path forward, one which will offer the potential for archaeologists to blend research objectives with real societal impact and benefit. Finally, it must be recognised that these challenges do not face only South Asian archaeologists, but also confront their colleagues and contemporaries around the world. Once again, it is this sheer diversity which makes the study of archaeology in South Asia so challenging and so rewarding.

PART TWO

THE INDUS VALLEY
TRADITION (c.6500–1900 BCE)

CHAPTER 4

FOOD PRODUCERS: MULTIPLE NEOLITHICS (c. 6500–2000 BCE)

INTRODUCTION

The next three chapters of the volume will explore the development, formation and transformation of the Indus Valley Tradition between the seventh and second millennia BCE, with additional consideration of archaeological material from key sites in adjacent parts of South Asia and neighbouring regions where appropriate (Figure 4.1) (Timeline 4.1). We take this approach because the 'Neolithic' in South Asia was not one single event or development, but took place at different times, different speeds and scales, and in different places across the region as a whole. Diversity is again a key theme in the archaeology of the subcontinent and when we discuss settlement, people and society in Neolithic South Asia, we are not only referring to developments such as sedentism and domestication and particular pottery assemblages, we are also considering a whole range of lifeways that might adopt all, or some, or none of the typical Neolithic package (whatever that might be). The variability of early food producing, or agricultural populations in South Asia is important to grasp, and this variability or diversity makes the eventual emergence of the Indus with a marked degree of homogeneity (discussed further in Chapters 5–7), across such a large geographical area and over a relatively long span of chronological time, even more striking.

While the Mesolithic prelude to the Neolithic of Baluchistan remains uncertain, the sequences from the Ganga, Sindh, western India and northern valleys of Pakistan indicate that the Neolithic populations of South Asia did not emerge fully formed from a physical and cultural vacuum. Indeed, people had already occupied South Asia for millennia prior to the advent of domesticates and a sedentary lifestyle. Many Mesolithic sites have been excavated in South Asia, and the subsistence evidence points towards groups of mobile and egalitarian hunter-gatherers. Wild plants and animals were exploited and a microlithic stone tool set consistent with hunting and gathering has been recovered alongside the faunal and floral material. Certainly, this is true of the Ganga region where sites such as Chopani Mando demonstrate sequences

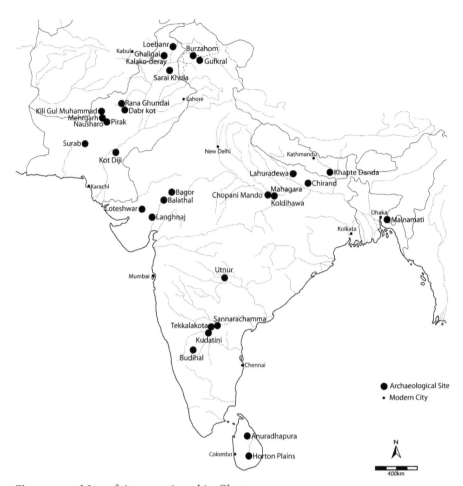

Figure 4.1. Map of sites mentioned in Chapter 4.

from the upper Palaeolithic right through to a Microlithic assemblage, and the styles and changes in the stone tools throughout this period led its excavators to suggest that there was strong evidence of continuity at this site.

With regard to the Indus Valley Tradition, we will focus on selected key sites such as Mehrgarh in Baluchistan and Kot Diji in Sindh, and demonstrate how the archaeological evidence supports their interpretation as precursors of sites belonging to the Indus Civilisation. In modelling the first evidence for domestication, permanent structures, long distance trade, the conservation and storage of agricultural surplus, and analysing ceramic and aceramic traditions, the village of Mehrgarh and its associated communities are the crucial backdrop for understanding the origins and foundations of the cities of the Indus Valley Tradition. Issues of continuity and transformation are important in many areas of archaeological interpretation in South Asia, not only when looking at the appearance and form of plant and animal domestication, but also in respect to questions relating to the movement of communities of people, animals and

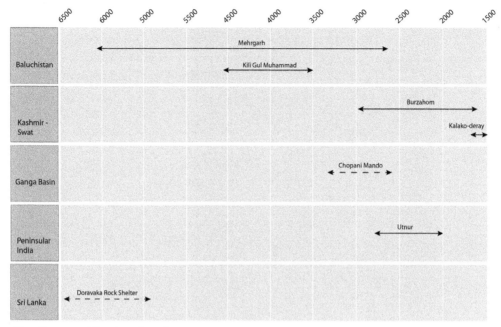

Timeline 4.1. Timeline for Chapter 4.

plants. We have already touched on the Indo-European debate in previous chapters, but there are many wider implications that affect modern South Asia, as shown in the brief discussion of the role of archaeology in politics in Chapter 3. The shaping of personal and political identity through the manipulation of archaeological findings is certainly not exclusive to South Asia, but tensions between Tamil and Sinhalese groups, for example, or the events at Ayodhya, indicate that this debate has a particular resonance.

In this chapter, we will also examine the archaeology of one of the most significant developments in human prehistory, the initial adoption of sedentary lifeways and the exploitation and domestication of a narrower range of plants and animals. In many parts of the world this development is often referred to as the Neolithic, which has almost become a shorthand way of referring to the settling of humans in permanent villages and the domestication of plants and animals. This use of the term 'Neolithic' has taken over from the chronological period called the 'New Stone Age' and was introduced by John Lubbock in 1865, exemplified culturally by the use of ground stone tools alongside plant cultivation and animal husbandry (Box 4.1). The widespread adoption and use of pottery by people is also strongly associated with the Neolithic, particularly in Europe. As noted earlier, we will highlight some of the many different 'Neolithics' across South Asia in this chapter, and we examine the different subsistence strategies in place across different areas, and where and when sedentism, cultivation and animal husbandry developed and spread.

Box 4.1 The Neolithic

The Neolithic or 'New Stone Age', is a widely used term for the period during which the domestication of plants and animals occurred, pottery production and use developed, and ground stone tools such as axes and arrowheads
were made and used. The term was first introduced by Sir John Lubbock
in 1865 and gained greater importance when Gordon Childe wrote about
a 'Neolithic Revolution' in 1935. Childe argued that the domestication of
plants and animals was one of the most important developments in human
history: "Food-production – the deliberate cultivation of food-plants, especially cereals, and the taming, breeding, and selection of animals – was an
economic revolution – the greatest in human history after the mastery of
fire. It opened up a richer and more reliable supply of food, brought now
within man's own control and capable of almost unlimited expansion by
his unaided efforts" (1954: 23). Childe carried out detailed research into
the spread of agriculture, considering both geographical and chronological parameters, and his work has had considerable impact on archaeologists
throughout the later twentieth century and into the twenty-first century.
'The Neolithic' has essentially become a shorthand term for a package of
domesticated plants and animals, sedentary settlements, pottery manufacture and use, and polished stone tools. The Neolithic had been preceded by
the Mesolithic or Middle Stone Age, where hunter-gatherers were mobile
and, in social evolutionary terms, existed in a state of less complexity. The
Neolithic or the period of 'Barbarism', then represented a great advance
over the Mesolithic and, in turn, paved the way for the development of
metallurgy in the succeeding Bronze Age and, eventually, 'Civilisation'.

Archaeological research has dramatically changed our understanding of
this key stage of development since Childe's first use of the term 'Neolithic
Revolution'. Early research focused on the Fertile Crescent, an arc of land
broadly stretching from Mesopotamia at the head of the Persian Gulf, up
to eastern Anatolia, through Syria, Jordan, Lebanon, Palestine, Israel and
down to Egypt, and stressed that this region was the source or origin of
domestications, pottery production and use. It was argued that a Neolithic
package of domesticates, pottery and a sedentary lifestyle spread out from
this core Fertile Crescent region to other parts of the world through the
movement of people. However, it is now clear that there were multiple areas
of domestication and that the mechanisms by which developments spread
are still not fully known. As a result, the concept of a 'Neolithic package'
has also broken down in the face of research with many sites having one
or more elements considered 'Neolithic' but not others. For example, some
sites such as Ain Mallaha in Jordan have evidence for year round settlement by occupants practicing hunting and gathering (Watkins 2004: 210).

Childe's concepts and definitions have not been entirely abandoned and Zeder has suggested they still offer "insight into the broader evolutionary context of the emergence of food production" (2009: 13).

Some of the earliest pottery in the world has been uncovered in Japan and dated to circa 10,000 BCE and is part of a pottery culture known as Jomon, which was also very long-lived – extending over some 10,000 years (Mizoguchi 2002). The manufacturers of early Jomon were not settled farmers but they were hunter-gatherers, exploiting plants, birds, animals and sea resources. As our knowledge of early domestication has expanded, it is also clear that on many sites there was a period when plants and animals were cultivated and husbanded and the occupants lived in sedentary communities, but pottery was not manufactured or used. This is commonly called the 'Pre-Pottery Neolithic' and is known from such key sites in southwest Asia as Abu Hureya in Syria, as well as sites such as Mehrgarh in South Asia. Pottery, or baked clay, was also used in the Upper Palaeolithic period in Europe to produce figurines, which are the earliest surviving ceramic artefacts known in the world. Dated to circa 30,000 BCE, these 'Venus figurines' from Dolni Vestonice in the Czech Republic have been the subject of extensive debate regarding their meaning and purpose.

It is also now recognised that there were different centres of domestication for different plants and animals – while wheat and barley were almost certainly domesticated in the Fertile Crescent, many pulses are thought to have been domesticated in their region of origin, including those in southern India (Fuller 2006). Goat and sheep are also thought to have been first domesticated in the Fertile Crescent, but current evidence strongly supports the domestication of humped cattle (zebu) in Pakistan (Wright 2010; Meadow 1989; 1991). What remains less well understood are the mechanisms by which domestication and sedentism as concepts and practice spread, and the reasons for their widespread adoption. Some scholars remain of the opinion that the focus on faunal and floral remains actually masks the real transformations which occurred during the process of Neolithicisation, that people were domesticated too and adapted and changed their lives fundamentally (Hodder 1990).

We will start with Baluchistan, the area with the earliest evidence for domesticated plants and animals, and arguably, structures associated with longer-term communal storage. The sites of greatest importance are Mehrgarh and Killi Gul Muhammad, and these will be the focus of this first section, although not exclusively. We will then examine the evidence for settled occupation and farming in the Khyber Pakhtunkhwa Province of Pakistan as well as in the Vale

Figure 4.2. View up the Bolan Pass, Pakistan.

of Kashmir; explore the evidence for subsistence change within the Ganga region; then move south to Peninsular India and finally Sri Lanka. As we will demonstrate, the populations of each of these regions had their own distinctive food procurement characteristics, and time and manner of domestication, as well as how different subsistence strategies coexisted.

BALUCHISTAN

Baluchistan links the Indus basin of modern Pakistan with south-east Iran and forms the eastern fringe of the Indo-Iranian Plateau. It comprises a series of narrow alluvial valleys running north to south, watered by summer and winter rains and a limited number of perennial rivers, although these resources are frequently conserved by the construction of *gabarband* or low stone dams across the valleys. These valleys have traditionally provided access for traders, herders and armies across the Indo-Iranian plateau from the Kojak pass, through the Quetta Valley and out through the Bolan pass into the Kachi plain and the Indus River beyond (Figure 4.2). Despite its historically pivotal position between upland and plain, a number of early archaeologists dismissed its early role in the origins of the Indus cities, as exemplified by Wheeler's comment that "the ill-sorted industries and cultures of the hills are of no immediate concern save as a back-curtain to the main scene.... None of them shows any clear primary and organic relationship with the Indus Valley culture" (Wheeler 1968: 9). However, even when Wheeler was writing these words, his perspective had been challenged by Walter Fairservis's expedition to the Quetta Valley between 1949 and 1951 as Fairservis had already identified the presence of early Neolithic horizons in a small exposure at the base of the Kili Gul Muhammad mound near Quetta (1956).

Indeed, by the 1960s there was a growing anticipation that the region of Baluchistan was likely to yield the earliest evidence of Neolithic populations within South Asia and shed light on their Neolithic origins (Gordon 1960: 33). These origins were, however, clearly expected to be those of a diffused Neolithic as evidenced by Sankalia's statement that "Baluchistan received the first fruits of civilisation because of its proximity to Iran, a gateway to India" (1977: 84) or the Allchins' observation that "there was a considerable time lag between the appearance of a food-producing way of life in the Middle East, and even Iran, and in any part of the Indian subcontinent" (Allchin and Allchin 1968: 100). Indeed, as the 'Fertile Crescent' of south-west Asia had long been regarded as the centre of domestication, it seemed only logical that these crucial developments had then diffused outward through the movement of people first exploiting the Indo-Iranian plateau before reaching the Indus valley. Certainly, this time lag appeared to be proven by the earliest evidence from Kili Gul Muhammad, where Fairservis provided a radiocarbon date of the fourth millennium BC for the established early Neolithic levels encountered, commenting that "The dates for Kili Ghul Mohammad I do not seem to be too conservative, if one accepts the general tendency among Near Eastern archaeologists to consider the Indo-Baluchistan Area as on the fringe of a 'Nuclear Near East'" (1956: 357).

Mehrgarh

This model of population movement and agricultural diffusion, built on the evidence from Kili Gul Muhammad, was completely revised with the discovery of Mehrgarh at the entrance of the Bolan Pass in Baluchistan in the early 1970s by Jean-Francois Jarrige and his team (Jarrige 1979). Noting an archaeological section exposed by flash flooding, they found a site covering two square kilometres which was occupied between circa 6500 and 2500 BCE (Figure 4.3). The site comprises a number of different settlement areas or mounds that were inhabited sequentially over time and then culturally linked with the later neighbouring sites of Nausharo and Pirak. While Jarrige and his team have produced a number of preliminary reports and specialist studies related to all three sites, there is still no overarching monograph which leads to a number of difficulties trying to understand the individual excavation sites and interpretations, particularly when interpretations have changed from season to season as we would expect in light of new material. With reference to Shaffer's chronological scheme (see Chapter 1), the cultural developments and period we are exploring in this chapter fall within the 'Early Food-Producing Era' of the Indus Valley Tradition (1992: 443). However, there are very few

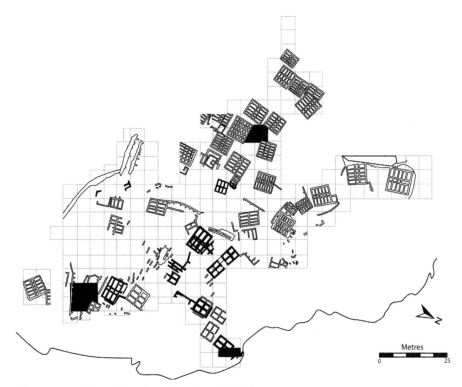

Figure 4.3. Plan of the site of Mehrgarh, Pakistan.

sites with evidence for the development of early food production within the
region and, of these, Mehrgarh is the best explored and analysed to date. As
Shaffer noted, chronologies for Mehrgarh itself were being constantly refined
through continuing work, but it is clear from the cultural material that it is the
earliest levels, however defined or labelled, that are of greatest importance in
the understanding of early food production. Interestingly, Shaffer also pointed
out that "Although subsequent phases defined at Mehrgarh are most strongly
affiliated with the Baluchistan Tradition, this initial phase reflects a cultural
pattern presently believed applicable to both the Baluchistan and Indus Valley
Traditions" (1992: 443). This makes an interesting point about the ways in
which different traditions may develop from what appears to have been a common core. As noted earlier, Mehrgarh was first excavated between 1975 and
1985, after which attention was turned to the nearby site of Nausharo which
was initially described by the excavators as a 'pre-Indus' and Indus site. Work at
Nausharo took place over eleven seasons, and work then resumed at Mehrgarh
between 1997 and 2000 (Jarrige et al. 2005: 129). This second phase of excavation was aimed specifically at clarifying the Neolithic sequence, particularly
the earlier, Aceramic Period. The excavators re-evaluated earlier sequences
and excavated new trenches, and now claim that there was a single Aceramic
Neolithic Period, Period I, which was followed by the appearance of ceramics

Figure 4.4. Mud-brick compartmentalised structure at Mehrgarh, Pakistan.

in Neolithic Period IIA but that there was no discernible transitional phase between these two periods (Jarrige et al. 2005: 130).

Remains from Period I, the Aceramic Neolithic, have been recorded across an area of at least 25 hectares, although the shifting nature of settlement suggests that not all of this area would have been fully occupied by people at any one time (Jarrige et al. 2005: 132). The earliest occupation of Mehrgarh in Period I was found in mound MR3 and has been dated to between 6500 and 5500 BCE. Nine different levels of architectural remains were identified during excavation, all within period I (Jarrige et al. 2005, 131). During Period 1, the small settlement consisted of a series of rectangular mud-brick structures internally subdivided into small compartments linked by corridors (Figure 4.4). More than seventy-five buildings of this nature were uncovered during the excavation, and most were built from hand-moulded mud bricks fairly uniformly measuring 62 × 12 × 8 centimetres in size and containing a wealth of plant impressions from the material used to temper the mud (Jarrige et al. 2005: 133). Many of the walls had internal mud plaster lining, and some of the external mud plaster had been painted. In level 1, the earliest architectural level identified, this external painting took the form of plain red ochre. In upper levels, the painting became more elaborate and included red, black and white patterns (Jarrige et al. 2005: 135).

From the earliest architectural levels, 1 and 2, the excavators recorded two roomed "dwelling houses" (Jarrige et al. 2005: 135), then in later levels (3 and 4) houses of four rooms occurred alongside two roomed houses. In levels 7, 8 and 9 a single six roomed structure occurred alongside the two and four

Figure 4.5. Deep section at Mehrgarh, Pakistan.

roomed structures and in level 9 a unique ten roomed structure was uncovered (Jarrige et al. 2005: 135–136). As some of the later compartments measure little over one square metre (1.19 square yards), it is unlikely that they were rooms used by families for habitation, but a more plausible interpretation is that they represented storage silos for grain and other materials. Buildings were grouped together in blocks, and these blocks were separated by alleys and larger open spaces (Jarrige et al. 2005: 136). Within each of the nine different architectural phases, similar patterns of occupation and abandonment were noted as the inhabitants of the village built structures and modified them before abandoning them and allowing them to fill with rubbish. Burials were then dug through this rubbish, although it is clear that graves were never dug through walls of abandoned buildings, only through the interior spaces. Human settlement would temporarily shift to other areas of the site, then levelling took place and settlement again resumed, and the whole cycle continued organically, seemingly without a coherent master plan (Jarrige et al. 2005: 132) (Figure 4.5).

The nine levels of burials within buildings interspersed with occupation phases resulted in the excavation of at least 315 individual burials, of which 244 have been analysed (Jarrige et al. 2005: 137; Jarrige and Jarrige 2006: 470) (Box 4.2). More than 70 percent of the graves studied were aligned on an east–west

---

Box 4.2 Mehrgarh Human Skeletal Material

Studying the human skeletons recovered from a site can be extremely informative in terms of understanding the impact of changing lifeways, population health and the relationships between populations. The excavations at Mehrgarh in Baluchistan have identified a number of cemeteries and burials from different periods allowing the comparison of skeletal material from the Neolithic, a period of increasing sedentism and adoption of agriculture and domesticates, with the 'Chalcolithic', a period of regionalisation, increasing complexity and incipient urbanism. The burials at Mehrgarh can be broadly summarised as:

- Period IA: the dead were buried in the spaces between houses in oval pits in a flexed position. The bones were often covered in red ochre and young goats were placed in several burials.
- Period IB: a formal graveyard with more than 150 burials was excavated and showed a clear transition to more elaborate burials, taking the form of a niche cut into the side of a pit in which the body and grave goods were placed. This niche was then walled up with cigar-shaped mud bricks. There were some double burials recorded and also secondary burials – where bodies were first exposed to the elements, then the bones collected and buried.
- Period II: flexed burials with substantial quantities of red ochre on bodies.
- Period III: another cemetery was excavated and attributed to this period with some ninety-nine individuals. The heads of some of the individuals had been placed on mud bricks, and there was one striking collective burial with wheel-thrown ceramic vessels included within the grave.

These mortuary excavations have the potential to provide archaeologists with important data about pre-farming populations and about the impact of the transition to farming on the general human health (Kennedy 2000: 279). However, because limited detail has been published to date, the majority of work has focused on dental analysis. The Neolithic sample of teeth from Mehrgarh comprised ninety-three individual specimens, giving rise to 1,273 permanent teeth, and ten juveniles with eighty-two deciduous teeth (Kennedy 2000: 279), and this sample has been studied and compared with the material from Chalcolithic Mehrgarh and from a range of other Neolithic populations from South Asia and beyond (Lukacs 1989, 1983).

Lukacs's studies have shown that tooth crown sizes from Neolithic Mehrgarh were the largest of any Neolithic population in South Asia.

(continued)

Indeed they are comparable to Mesolithic crown sizes, and this is significant as crown size is normally linked to diet, where larger crown sizes are thought to be an adaptation to a coarse diet (Kennedy 2000: 280). Dental health may also be inferred from the study of dentition and a notably low incidence of caries was recorded in the Mehrgarh Neolithic sample. The rate of caries was considered to be similar to that of hunter-gatherer groups or mixed subsistence groups, rather than to sedentary populations with more highly processed diets (Lukacs 1983: 390). However, the low caries rate may also be linked to the naturally fluoridated water in Baluchistan, and this receives support from the presence of yellow-brown stains on some Neolithic teeth which is a symptom of fluorosis (Kennedy 2000: 280).

Teeth have also been used to explore genetic relationships by studying the statistical occurrence of key genetically determined traits in particular teeth. Lukacs and Hemphill, for example, suggested that whilst the archaeological evidence of Mehrgarh suggests strong continuity from Neolithic to the 'Chalcolithic', the Neolithic populations do not appear to be ancestral to the 'Chalcolithic' populations. They concluded by stating that "Regardless of the type of multivariate analysis employed, once the dental morphology differences between Neolithic and Chalcolithic Mehrgarh are placed in a comparative framework with other prehistoric south Asians, the difference in dental morphology between them do not indicate biological continuity in a regionally isolated lineage but tentatively suggest moderate levels of gene flow coupled with some degree of random genetic drift. Neolithic and Chalcolithic Mehrgarh do not form a tight grouping when contrasted with all other samples, the result expected under conditions of in situ genetic change. Quite the contrary, specimens from Neolithic levels at Mehrgarh show much closer affinities to the late Chalcolithic series from Inamgaon than to the Chalcolithic sample from Mehrgarh" (Lukacs and Hemphill 1991: 114).

Lukacs and Hemphill also compared the chronological and physical differences of skeletal remains between Neolithic and 'Chalcolithic' Mehrgarh (about 1,500 years and half a kilometre apart) and those from Neolithic Mehrgarh and later 'Chalcolithic' Inamgaon (about 5,000 years and 1,440 kilometres apart) (1991: 114). They concluded their work by suggesting that "the direct lineal descendants of the Neolithic inhabitants of Mehrgarh are to be found to the south and to the east of Mehrgarh, in northwestern India and the western edge of the Deccan Plateau, rather than in post-Neolithic Baluchistan" (Lukacs and Hemphill 1991: 114). They also concluded that there were greater similarities between the skeletons of Timargarha in the north-west (Iron Age), populations of Central Asia, and the Neolithic

Mehrgarh population than between Neolithic and Chalcolithic Mehrgarh (Lukacs and Hemphill 1991: 113; Lukacs 1983: 392).

This study demonstrates that studying human skeletal remains is critical as it raises many interesting questions about our understanding of population continuity. It may be that increased aDNA analysis will help further understand links between different groups but this is a costly process and DNA does not always survive well. Teeth on the other hand are generally quite robust in archaeological contexts, and carry a number of genetically determined traits that can be incredibly useful in exploring genetic movement. In conclusion, although this dental analysis may suggest firm links between the north-west of South Asia and the Deccan, there is as yet no corresponding artefactual evidence – leaving this dental study as an intriguing data set.

axis, with the head generally placed to face south. Further analysis is required to examine whether there were gender or age-related patterns in grave goods which might lead to greater understanding of the ideology and social organisation at Mehrgarh (Jarrige and Jarrige 2006: 470). For example, it seems thus far that goats were buried only with women, and generally both the goats and women were young individuals. These goats, including one kid, were recovered from graves in level 3 through to level 9 (Jarrige et al. 2005: 137–138). Beads were mainly recovered from the graves of females but also within those of children, but what this actually means is yet to be fully considered. Many of the small and special finds from this early period were recovered from the settlement's burials and included beads of turquoise, marine shell, lapis lazuli and steatite which clearly indicate long distance contact and even trade. A single copper bead with what has been identified as mineralised cotton textile fibres attached was also recovered, and this presence of both cotton and copper in such an early context is very striking (Jarrige et al. 2005: 139; Jarrige and Jarrige 2006: 469). Polished stone axes and microliths, flint cores, and bone tools were also found in different graves arranged around the bodies, perhaps indicating a degree of craft specialisation amongst the village's inhabitants. Bone spindles from graves indicate textile production, and clay figurines hint at ideology. From a context in level 1, a mother-of-pearl object was recovered and the excavators suggested that it was carved in a human silhouette. Around eighty clay figurines have been recovered from different levels in period I, some having evidence for surface colouring of red ochre, some with appliqué patterns, and some with perforations suggesting that they were intended to be worn or hung (Jarrige et al. 2005: 139–140). In the absence of ceramics in the pre-pottery phase, woven baskets were lined with bitumen and used as liquid-proof containers. Bitumen was also used to fix short stone blades into wooden handles to form sickles for agricultural activities such as harvesting.

Recent analysis of the stone tool industry from the first period at Mehrgarh has also demonstrated some interesting trends. Within the flint tool assemblage, lunates, trapezes, borers and scrapers dominate from levels 1 to 4, then from levels 5 to 8, blades, drills, and trapezes dominate (Jarrige et al. 2005: 139). The craftspeople appear to have been more selective in the selection of raw flint used for tools in the later levels, and all of this is suggested as indicative of an increasing degree of specialisation. The tools from levels 1 to 4 are also considered quite similar to tools from other South Asian Mesolithic or microlithic sites found further east (Jarrige and Jarrige 2006: 468). This hint of societal specialism is also indicated by the presence of what appears to be a lithic tool kit of cores and blades within several tombs, marking the burials of specialist tool-makers (Jarrige and Jarrige 2006: 470).

Evidence for the exploitation of plants by humans comes from the impressions of a range of plants incorporated as temper in the mud bricks made at the site and used for construction. Impressions of both wheat and barley have been noted, although Lorenzo Costantini indicated that there was no evidence for the domestication process of wheat at Mehrgarh (1984: 31). However, barley was found in much greater quantities than was wheat, and more recent morphological analyses suggested that it had not been entirely domesticated, thus was likely to be part of a local domestication process. In the upper levels of period I and in periods IIA, IIB and III, both wild and cultivated barley grains were noted (Jarrige and Jarrige 2006: 466). In addition to evidence for cereals, remains of dates and jujube fruit have been recovered, along with one very special find of mineralised cotton fibres (*Gossypium arboreum*) on a copper bead recovered from Cemetery 9 (noted earlier), which is believed to be the earliest identification of cotton in the world (Jarrige et al. 2005: 139). Cotton seeds were also recovered from the later Period IIB, which suggests that cotton was important at the site from very early periods and challenges what had been broadly accepted as a Nubian source for its sole domestication (Chowdury and Buth 1970: 85–86; see also discussions by Moulherat et al. 2002; and Zohary and Hopf 2000) (Box 4.3).

The faunal remains from Mehrgarh have been equally illuminating, and Richard Meadow's analyses indicates that the population had an early focus on the hunting of wild species such as wild sheep (*Ovis orientalis*), wild goat (*Capra aegagrus*), gazelle (*Gazella dorcas*), water buffalo (*Bubalus bubalis*), wild pig (*Sus scrofa*), onager (*Equus hemionus*) and deer (*Cervus* spp.) (1984a: 35). Meadow notes that "by the end of the aceramic Neolithic period at Mehrgarh, almost all of the faunal remains that can be identified come from sheep, goat, or cattle, three of the domestic animals of principal importance in the Middle East and South Asia today" (1984a: 35). When we consider the relative quantity of bone from each different animal, it is notable that cattle (*Bos* sp.) represented only 4 percent of the bone weight in the earliest layers but by Period II they represented a massive 65 percent – an increase associated with a decrease

---

Box 4.3 How Do We Identify Domesticates?

How do we know whether something is wild or domesticated? How can we tell whether the bones or plant remains recovered from an archaeological site belong to a domesticated herd or crop, or to wild animals that have been hunted and wild plants that have been gathered? There is no simple answer to this, and many archaeobotanists and archaeozoologists have devoted whole careers to studying this issue. Like so many other archaeological debates or issues, domestication is best seen as a process rather than an event – some archaeologists suggest that it happened very slowly and some that it happened relatively quickly, but rather than trying to find a moment when we can see that something is 'domesticated' it is probably better to approach this as part of a continuum from wild to fully domesticated.

The work of Dr Richard Meadow, director of the Zooarchaeology Laboratory, Peabody Museum of Archaeology and Ethnology at Harvard University, on the animal bone assemblage from the site of Mehrgarh is an excellent example of the types of methodologies that can be applied to faunal assemblages to learn more about the whole domestication process at a particular site. Central to Meadow's study was the precept that the domestication process of animals resulted in individuals becoming smaller, which can be measured on surviving skeletal elements. Because there will always be individuals in a herd who are larger than average (perhaps due to sexual dimorphism or genetics) analyses of size changes need to be carried out on a large, closely dated assemblage in order to understand the whole picture, and not have results skewed by a few (physically very large or very small) outliers. The radiocarbon dates for Mehrgarh place period IA to circa 6300–5300 BCE, to circa 5300–4800 BCE; IIA to circa 4800–4300 BCE; IIB to 4300–4000 BCE (1984b: 301), and Meadow analysed faunal remains for a series of trenches and contexts from Mehrgarh Periods I-III. In addition to the change in average size of species within the assemblage over time, Meadow also found that the percentage of different animal types in assemblage changed over time. In general, the earlier contexts were dominated by wild types, while the proportion of what Meadow calls 'prodomestics' or taxa, which are relatively easily and commonly domesticated, increases over time, while the proportion of wild taxa decreases. Of the three prodomestics – cattle (in this case zebu or humped cattle), sheep and goat – two exhibit a decrease in size over time, and Meadow argues that "for both cattle and sheep, the trend of size diminution, coincident with increasing representation in the faunal record, can be used as an argument for the local domestication of these animals" (1984b: 310). In the case of goat, the presence of a significant amount of bones from large

(continued)

animals, combined with an abundance of goat from the earliest levels has led Meadow to suggest that domestic goats may have been present at the site from earliest settlement, and alongside this wild goats were hunted and exploited (1984b: 310).

Dr Dorian Fuller at University College London's Institute of Archaeology has carried out extensive archaeobotanical research across South Asia, including consideration of the origins and domestication of a range of common crops. He has published widely on this topic and his recent paper '*Agricultural Origins and Frontiers in South Asia: A Working Synthesis*' (2006) is an impressive and comprehensive consideration of the evidence for domestication across the region. Fuller explains that there are various morphological and genetic changes to plants that generally accompany selection and domestication, and these include the loss of natural seed dispersal mechanisms such as the brittle rachis found on wild cereals, or the dehiscent pod of wild pulses and legumes. Instead, humans select and encourage strains where the grain or seed remains in place until deliberately harvested (2006: 13). Further information about deliberate cultivation of plants may be gained from a study of all plant remains, as weed seeds can provide a great deal of information about land management and crop profiles. While there are many sites from which plant assemblages have been recovered, with species identified as both wild and domesticated, with regard to the domestication process itself Fuller suggests that "direct archaeobotanical documentation of domestication in South Asia is still largely lacking, and other approaches such as identifying weed assemblages suggestive of domestication are yet to be investigated" (2006: 14). Nevertheless, it is important that the evidence that has been recovered is considered alongside other available archaeological evidence for sites and regions in order to increase our understanding of this key period in prehistory.

in the size of animals – indicative of what Meadow has interpreted as a localised domestication of zebu or humped cattle (1984a: 37). Finally, these sources of evidence appear to be aligned with what is known of the palaeoenvironmental and palynological context of the site, and suggest that in both the Neolithic and 'Chalcolithic' the environment around Mehrgarh would have been appreciably wetter than it is today, with possibly even areas of lakes, and certainly forests of junipers, oaks, elm, willow and ash (Jarrige and Jarrige 2006: 465).

Whilst the early levels of Mehrgarh represent a unique archaeological discovery, it is clear that settlements of 'Neolithic' populations, that is sites with evidence for a degree of sedentism and increasing exploitation of certain plants and animals, had already spread throughout a number of the valleys of Baluchistan by the fifth millennium BCE. The sequence at Kili Gul Muhammad is indicative of this spread, and this site takes the form of a mound measuring 100 metres by 60 metres (Fairservis 1956). Radiocarbon dates on material from the lowest levels, Period KGM I, at Kili Gul Muhammad have provided dates of between 4400 and 4100 BCE; however, these dates have not been calibrated and Fairservis also reported a further estimated four metres of deposit below the layers from which these dating samples were recovered. Material from the earliest Kili Gul Muhammad I levels included bones of domestic sheep, goat and cattle amongst evidence for simple mud habitations but with a notable absence of metal artefacts and pottery (Fairservis 1956: 358). Chert, jasper and chalcedony blades and grinding stones, as well as bone tools, were also recovered. Only in the succeeding period, Kili Gul Muhammad II, did the excavators uncover what they have described as crude handmade pottery of red or yellow colour with basket impressions. Fairservis also suggested that the population of the basal level or Period I, of the site of Rana Ghundai in Loralai to the east of Quetta, shared a similar cultural affiliation as Period II of Kili Gul Muhammad (1956: 354) and Shaffer further attributed the sites of Surab, Sur Jangal and Dabr Kot to this extension and establishment of the Neolithic villages across Baluchistan.

KASHMIR-SWAT

From the fourth millennium BCE, a second and quite separate cluster of permanent or semi-permanent populations became established in the valleys to the south of the Karakoram and Himalayan mountain ranges (Figure 4.6). Called variously the Burzahom, Northern or the Kashmir-Swat Neolithic, there have been more than forty individual sites identified to date, and their communities were all characterised by use of an assemblage of ground-stone axes, rectangular stone sickles pierced for straps or handles, and structures in the form of bell-shaped pits (Figure 4.7). This tight and coherent association of artefacts and features was first recognised at the site of Burzahom in the Kashmir Valley during the 1930s, but the type-site itself was not subject to extensive excavations until the 1960s (de Terra and Paterson 1939; Singh 2002). Collaborative Pakistani and Italian excavations and survey within the Valley of Swat in the late 1970s and 1990s revealed an extension of associated sites with similar features and very similar artefact assemblages giving rise to the recognition that the archaeological adaptation was shared by populations across this band of high altitude regions. There is still some debate about the exact extent of this Neolithic cultural complex with some archaeologists suggesting that early phases at Sarai Khola, in the Taxila valley in the Punjab were also linked to Burzahom and other sites to the north (Halim 1972).

The type-site, Burzahom, or 'the Place of Birch', is located on one of the many elevated ancient terraces, or *karewas*, overlooking the old Pleistocene

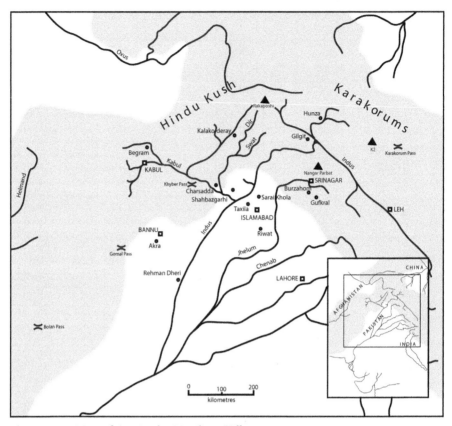

Figure 4.6. Map of sites in the Northern Valleys.

Figure 4.7. View across the Kashmir Valley, India.

Figure 4.8. The site of Burzahom, India (courtesy Bridget Allchin).

lakes in the south-east of the Kashmir Valley, a location shared by a number of other related settlements, such as Gufkral (Agrawal 1982:95) (Figure 4.8). The site, some 16 kilometres north-east of Srinagar at a height of 1,800 metres above sea level, had attracted the attention of de Terra and Paterson in 1935 on account of the numerous megalithic features and ceramics on the surface, but it was only during the 1960s that its Neolithic sequence was fully understood (de Terra and Paterson 1939; Singh 2002). It is now clear that Burzahom was first occupied by people between 3000 BCE and 1700 CE, and Neolithic layers have been identified as belonging to Phase IA (3000–2850 BCE), IB (2850–2250 BCE) and IC (2250–1700 BCE) (Sharif and Thapar 1992). The first phase, IA, appears to have been aceramic, then grey and black coarse, thick-walled vessels fired by potters in an over-reduced atmosphere appeared in the second phase, IB, with restricted shapes of bowls, vases and stems and a very characteristic mat-impressed base. Archaeological features from both of these early phases were similar, being bell-shaped pits, the largest of which measured 4.57 metres in diameter and 3.96 metres in depth. Some of these pits were lined with a clay plaster and some were provisioned with cut steps in their sides. The fill of these pits included horizons of ash and charcoal, a number of lithic and ceramic finds, and faunal remains of ibex, dog and deer (Sankalia 1977:165). Although the function of these pits is still debated, a number of scholars have suggested that they may have represented underground dwellings for the settlement's inhabitants, providing shelter for families from the cold winters of the foothills (Sharif and Thapar 1992). No further pits were cut during the third phase of occupation, phase IC, and during this period they were replaced by their inhabitants with larger rectangular mud and timber stake buildings erected on the surface – often directly above the earlier in-filled pits (Sankalia 1977: 164). Period II, to which we will return in Chapter 5, provided evidence of the use of a copper arrowhead, two engraved stone slabs including a hunting scene, a wheel-thrown red vessel containing 950 agate and carnelian beads, and a globular vase decorated with a distinctive horned figure with affinities in the Indus Valley Tradition (Singh 2008: 114).

These initial results were confirmed, and additional information obtained, during the later excavations at the site of Gufkral. Located in a similar position on a *karewa* some 41 kilometres from Srinagar, the archaeological mound is 35 metres high and measures roughly 400 metres north-south by 75 metres east-west (Kaw 2004: 28). Also crowned with megaliths as at Burzahom, the basal Neolithic sequence in Period IA confirmed the presence of a distinct aceramic phase associated with a variety of oval and circular pit features. Ranging in size between 3.8 metres and 1.5 metres in diameter and between 0.2 and 0.3 metres in depth, many pits were plastered and also associated with postholes and hearths (Singh 2008: 114). Confirmation of the artefact assemblage identified at Burzahom was made with the presence of distinct stone, bone and horn industries, including small bone arrowheads, bone needles with eyes, and bone harpoons in Period IA. It has been suggested that the edges of bone tools were heated to strengthen them. While the distinct absence of a stone blade industry has been noted (Allchin and Allchin 1982: 113), the population had access to ground stone tools, including axes and ringstones, and hammer stones were recovered in addition to a very characteristic rectangular or semi-lunar harvesting knife with pairs of drill-holes. Microwear analysis by Pant suggests that a number of the objects identified as axes had been resharpened and curated by their owners as well as having been used variously as adzes, chisels and axes (1979: 11).

Faunal remains from Period IA indicate that its inhabitants followed a broad spectrum subsistence strategy, which included wild sheep, goat, cattle, red deer, ibex, wolf and bear as well as domesticated sheep and goats, and these were augmented by the presence of barley, wheat and lentils (Singh 2008: 114). In the succeeding Period IB, the pits were replaced by mud and rubble structures as at Burzahom, and within the faunal remains there was a notable drop in the presence of wolf but a rise in reliance on sheep, goat and cattle, as well as the addition of the common pea (*Pisum arvense*). This direct evidence of subsistence data is augmented by information from pollen sequences taken from the lakes in the Kashmir Valley, which indicated frequent periods of decline followed by regrowth in the pine forests of the region from 7000 BCE onwards. Such a pattern of diminishing forest cover followed by forest regeneration has

Figure 4.9. The cave site of Ghaligai, Pakistan.

been interpreted as resulting from regular human forest clearance, for grazing or agriculture or both (Singh 1964).

In one of the earlier archaeological syntheses of the region in the 1970s, Walter Fairservis recorded his puzzlement by the absence of similar assemblages within Pakistan's former North-West Frontier Province and the Punjab stating "It may well be that future investigation of these regions will reveal a deeper penetration of the Burzahom cultural form" (1971: 317). Such a prediction has subsequently proved correct and the evidence from the Swat valley, in what is today the northern province of Khyber Pakhtunkhwa in Pakistan is extremely similar to Kashmir, although the majority of sites have been dated rather later, to between 1700 and 1400 BCE. The exception to this later occurrence is the deep sequence of the Ghaligai Cave, where the earliest occupation layers within the rock-shelter have been radiocarbon dated to between 2970 and 2920 BCE (Stacul 1987: 33) (Figure 4.9). The comprehensive nature of Giorgio Stacul's report has ensured that Ghaligai is also one of the best documented sequences for Pakistan's later prehistory (1967; 1969; 1987). This led Stacul to build what he calls the Swat Chronology, which comprises Periods I and II (at Ghaligai only), Period III (Ghaligai and Butkara I) and Period IV known at a number of sites in the region (Stacul 1987, 30). Stacul's Swat Chronology also extends up to Periods VI/VII which have been dated to 500 BCE and later, thus reaching into the Early Historic period (Young 2003: 24). We will meet the Swat Chronology again in Chapter 7 and beyond, when we explore the developments of the Northern Valleys alongside the localisation of the Indus Tradition, and the Regionalisation at the beginning of the urban phase of the Early Historic Tradition.

From the very earliest levels of the sequence at Ghaligai, designated Period I, coarse handmade pottery was recovered along with stone tools made from river pebbles. The lithics from this period were mainly unifacial and bifacial choppers, unifacial flat-based choppers, wedge-shaped flakes and discoid scrapers with a notable absence of ground stone tools. Some of the ceramics were burnished internally and belonged to a restricted repertoire of ovoidal jars, biconical bowls and bowls on stands (Stacul 1984a: 205). The plant and animal material recovered from these early layers consisted of wild plants, mainly hackberry, and wild barking deer (*Muntiacus muntjak*), wild hog deer (*Axis porcinus*) and cattle (*Bos indicus*) which may well be from domesticated specimens (Compagnoni 1987: 142). Period II at Ghaligai, which is dated to the third millennium BCE, witnessed an increase in the amount of pottery and a change in quality; not only was it much finer and with some black on red painting, but it was almost all wheel-made. There were far fewer lithic items, although those that have been reported are still made from local river pebbles. Both the plant and animal assemblages now show a mix of wild and domesticated types, including rice and wheat, as well as hackberry, and cattle, sheep and goat alongside deer and porcupine. Stacul attributed the development of this fine ceramic tradition to contact with the "southern plains" in the third millennium BC, although definitive evidence is as yet absent (1984a: 206).

The sequence at Ghaligai continued into Period III, which has been dated to the early second millennium BCE and showed a marked decline in the quality of the ceramics with a return to coarser fabrics, poor firing and a combination of hand and wheel-thrown pieces. More lithics were reported, again all from river pebbles and including geometric forms, but the plant and animal remains were similar to those noted in Period II, although joined by dog bones. However, it is at this point that the sequences of the two regions, Swat and Kashmir, were brought together by the new categories of material culture. The pottery assemblages from the Swat Valley included poorly fired handmade shapes, complete with basket and mat impressions, all of which have strong parallels with the ceramics of Burzahom (Stacul 1984a: 209). Strikingly, the sites of Kalako-deray and Loebanr III in Swat also possess archaeological features which are very similar to those found at Burzahom and other Kashmir sites. At both Kalako-deray and Loebanr III, large and small pits were recorded and excavated; the largest of these were bell-shaped and measure up to 4.7 metres in diameter and 3.6 metres in depth (Stacul 1977; 1994a) (Figure 4.10). Some of the pits were lined with stone paving and some contained evidence of burning or hearths, along with human and animal terracotta figurines, ceramics, polished stone objects, jade beads and rectangular stone sickles. Analysis of plant remains indicate that the subsistence of the inhabitants was based on

a   b

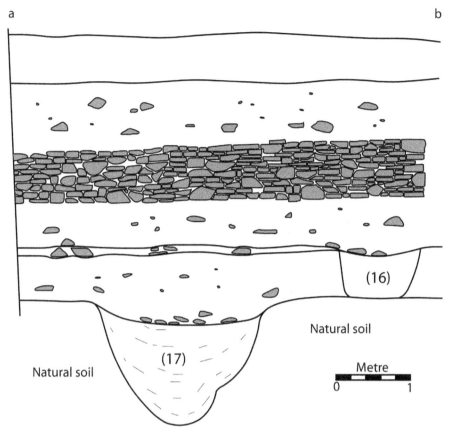

Figure 4.10. Section of pits at Kalako-deray, Pakistan.

the cultivation of barley, wheat, rice, lentils and the field pea, and the notable presence of a grape seed. In the later phases of Swat Chronology Period IV, the excavators noted that mud-brick structures, and structures with foundations of river cobbles were built on the surface. This paralleled the situation in Kashmir and, again, archaeologists have suggested that this demonstrated a move from underground or semi-subterranean dwellings, to fully above-ground habitation (Stacul 1987). Coningham and Sutherland have offered, however, an alternative interpretation of the pits, suggesting that they may have been used as subsurface grain storage pits over winter, while transhumant communities and their flocks and herds moved south, returning to the valleys in the spring for the sowing of crops (1998). Although this interpretation has been expanded, and supported by modern ethnographic studies of transhumant activity in this region (Young 2003), the presence of hearths and structures within the larger pits and signs of external super-structures over some of the pits still need to be fully explained. Nor do these alternatives explain why there are such a range of pit sizes and shapes, including a large, shallow oval pit, which has a maximum width of 7.70 metres (Stacul 1987: 56) (Figure 4.11).

Figure 4.11. 'Pit Dwelling' at Kalako-deray, Pakistan (courtesy Italian Archaeological Mission in Pakistan).

The recovery of jade beads and holed rectangular sickles from Loebanr III and Kalako-deray, along with the presence of pits interpreted as underground dwellings in the early occupation phases, succeeded by above-ground structures, has been interpreted by a number of archaeologists, including Giorgio Stacul as showing clear parallels between the Kashmir and the Swat sites. Furthermore, the earlier suggestion from Fairservis that this Neolithic assemblage represented "the southmost expression of a widespread North Asian complex" (1971: 318) is now broadly accepted by most archaeologists. Sharif and Thapar (1992:148) have commented that "we find unmistakable examples of two items of material equipment of the Yangshao culture of North China, namely the harvester and jade beads", and Asko Parpola has suggested that this may be linked with the prehistoric presence of peoples speaking languages related to those of Central Asia (1994). Whilst a simplistic model based on these similarities may just replace a Near Eastern diffusion of Neolithic population with a Central Asian one, the parallels are striking and Giorgio Stacul's concept of a broad Inner Asia cultural complex, whereby the primary links and influences of the Swat sites were from Kashmir, and then China as the source of jade, bitumen embedded blades and dog burials is quite attractive (1994a). However, this approach fails to explain the chronological gap between the earlier sequence of Burzahom and Gufkral as opposed to the dates of Loebanr III and Kalako-deray, as the Neolithic phases at Burzahom end about the same time as they begin at the two latter sites. Moreover, whilst there is chronological parity between Burzahom and the early phases of Ghaligai, there is little similarity between their material culture assemblages suggesting that whilst they present a broadly parallel chronological development, they are still distinct − a situation which the Allchins' interpreted as "a local adaptation to the special environment of the mountains, its people having rich sources of food from hunting and from agriculture" (1982: 116). Recent survey work in Kashmir shows that there are many Neolithic sites with great potential for learning more about contact and development here (Yatoo 2012). The issue of spheres of influence and connections in these northern valleys will be explored further in Chapter 8, when we explore the localised cultures from circa 1900 BCE onwards.

GANGA BASIN AND VINDHYAN ESCARPMENT

A third Neolithic complex was loosely centred on the Ganga basin, but the recovery of polished stone axes in eastern India, Bangladesh, Nepal and Myanmar, including shouldered examples, suggests a much broader distribution of associated populations. Some sites with Neolithic material were established close to the seasonal settlements of the preceding Mesolithic period in the Ganga Valley, and may have their origins within them. Indeed, some of these sites have been interpreted as continuations of sites with material and phases characterised as Mesolithic. This pattern is not surprising, as a number of sites associated with microlithic tools and a subsistence base, dominated by the exploitation of wild and domestic animals, also gathered plant resources for food, as suggested by the presence of stone querns for grinding cereals, as well as perforated and polished stone rings. In particular, a cluster of sites on the Belan River: Mahagara, Chopani Mando and Koldihawa, have provided much of the information we have to date about the emergence of settled human lifeways and domestication in this region (Sharma et al. 1980). The first of these, Chopani Mando is located on the middle terrace of the Belan river on a former meander of the river, some 77 kilometres south-east of Allahabad. It was excavated by G. R. Sharma between 1967 and 1978 and his 1.5 metre sequence is striking as it appears to have stretched from the beginning of the Holocene through to the early Neolithic (Sharma et al. 1980). The earliest occupation at the site, Phase I, was identified by the excavator as Epipalaeolithic and included a variety of large and broad tools, which were divided into both Upper Palaeolithic and Early Mesolithic assemblages. Phase I was succeeded by a phase of Early Mesolithic occupation, which was itself subdivided by the excavator into two on the basis of the later presence of geometric microliths. Two circular huts with diameters of between 3 and 8 metres were identified in Subphase A of Phase II, one of which was paved with stone. Similar structures were recovered from Subphase B of Phase II, together with microlithic tools, debitage, charcoal, animal bones and lumps of burnt clay with reed impressions from hut walls. The final phase of occupation, Phase III, has been dated to the fourth millennium BCE, where settlement covered an area of 1.5 hectares (3.7 acres) and consisted of at least thirteen structures more substantially constructed than those of earlier phases, thus suggesting more permanent population (Sharif and Thapar 1992: 149). A number of its artefacts and features, such as cord-impressed handmade ceramics, ground stone tools, querns and other food processing artefacts, are Neolithic in nature, but wild rice, and wild cattle, sheep and goat remains suggest that this may have been a transitional settlement, rather than one fully sedentary and exploiting domesticated plants and animals. However, until radiocarbon samples from the site are dated, it remains difficult to place Chopani Mando rightfully within the chronological sequence for this region.

G. R. Sharma strongly argued that there was an ill-defined cusp between the advanced Mesolithic and the Proto-Neolithic but that this cusp was physically realised at the site of Mahagara, located only 3 kilometres from Chopani Mando, and called it a later stage on the 'Neolithic evolutionary path' (Sharma et al. 1980). Mahagara had a single deposit of 2.6 metres of Neolithic occupation where the final structural phase, VI, covered an area of some 0.8 hectares (1.98 acres) and comprised a settlement of at least eighteen huts or structures centred around a stockade or supposed animal pen measuring 12.5 by 7.5 metres (Sharma et al. 1980) (Figure 4.12). Impressions of animal hoofs within the mud of the pen led Misra to suggest that "these animals were domesticated from their wild prototypes available in the area" (1999: 244), and Sharif and Thapar to calculate that it could have housed a herd of between forty and sixty individual animals (1992: 150). George Erdosy (1987) suggested that the village was grouped into eight individual households, and the site had a total population of around 250 people. Furthermore, he argued that the uneven distribution of querns and stone tools across the site in association with the structures showed that a degree of specialisation amongst the people had already been developed. The final phase at Mahagara was represented by an assemblage of wild cattle, deer and boar, alongside domesticated cattle, horse, sheep and goat, together with cord-impressed ceramics, polished stone axes and stone blades, strongly demonstrating its links to the preceding Mesolithic phases of the Vindhyan escarpment and the associated oxbows of the Ganga beyond. The third site of this complex, Koldihawa, shares a similar Neolithic assemblage with ground stone tools, handmade cord-impressed ceramic vessels as well as microlithic tools. Rice-husk within the temper of the vessels has been accepted by many as evidence of domestication and cultivation although the very early dates for the site, seventh to fifth millennium BC, are not widely accepted (Sharif and Thapar 1992: 150).

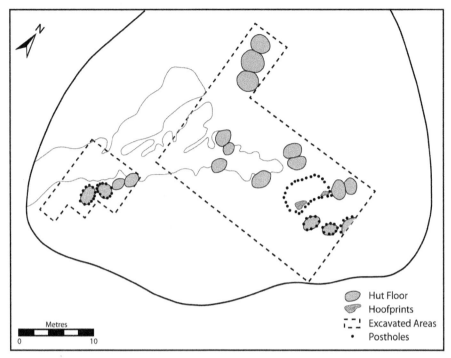

Figure 4.12. Plan of the site of Mahagara, India.

Although somewhat geographically isolated, a further site, Chirand, appears part of this broad adaptation. Chirand is located on the banks of the Ganga some eight kilometres east of Chhapra in Bihar and excavations at the 14.5 metre high mound identified an important historic and prehistoric sequence. The earliest occupation at Chirand, Period I, has been attributed by its excavators to the Neolithic and comprised 3.5 metres of in situ deposits (Roy 1989: 104). The ceramics from these levels were mainly handmade, some of which also had mat impressions and post-firing graffiti, and the excavators also recorded the presence of terracotta animal figurines, beads and balls. The forms of the vessels were restricted to vase, bowl, bowl on stand and footed cup. There were also bone and horn objects including arrowheads and needles, as well as polished quartzite, granite and basalt celts, hammers and pestles. Occupation took the form of a circular floor, four metres in diameter, in association with open hearths, and postholes and the recovery of lumps of fired clay with bamboo impressions, suggesting the presence of mud walls rather than open shelters (Sankalia 1977: 158).

In addition to faunal remains of rhinoceros, stag, deer, ox, elephant and buffalo, charred wheat, barley, gram and lentil were recovered, along with the presence of paddy-husk impressions within burnt clay fragments. The microlithic blades, scrapers, points and borers from Chirand demonstrate that the site's inhabitants shared a cultural continuity with the region's earlier lithic traditions, but the dates remain uncertain with a single radiocarbon date of circa 2000 BC from the upper part of the sequence (Allchin and Allchin 1982: 118). Now acknowledged as a distinct Neolithic development within South Asia, G. R. Sharma and his pioneering colleagues successfully demonstrated the presence of a deep archaeological sequence within the Ganga Basin (1980 et al.). Additional evidence has continued to be published, most recently with Rakesh Tiwari's report of domesticated rice and a sedentary village at the four metre high mound of Lahuradewa in Uttar Pradesh from the seventh millennium BCE onwards (Tewari et al. 2006). However, controversy continues over the specific dating and identification of domesticated rice at a number of the key sites as it is accepted by some scholars (Singh 2008: 110) and contested by others (Fuller 2006).

Equally uncertain is the distribution, chronology and character of associated Neolithic populations to the north and east of the Ganga Basin, as little systematic survey has been undertaken. However, surface finds of polished stone axes, adzes and ring-stones from the Mahabharat and Siwalik ranges of Nepal indicate their presence (Shreshtha 2008: 74). Bishnu Shrestha has also noted their presence in the lowland Terai region of Nepal and their similarity with similar artefacts from eastern India and Bangladesh (1982: 155). Similar examples have been recovered from the surface levels at the site of Khapte Danda near Lahan in eastern Nepal at the interface between the Himalayan foothills and the Terai. In parallel, archaeological surveys and excavations within Bangladesh have recorded the presence of 'Neolithic stone axes' and celts, although a number have been recovered from much later levels associated with the Ananda Vihara at Mainamati. Dilip Chakrabarti has cautioned against assuming that this evidence suggests the presence of a separate Neolithic development in this region and states that all it may indicate is "the persistence of a Neolithic-manufacturing tradition in this area up to the eighth-tenth century AD" (1992: 32). Indeed, the apparent presence of Northern Black Polished Ware (NBPW) and ground stone tools within the same erosion deposit at Khapte Danda may also suggest an Early Historic date for some examples.

WESTERN INDIA AND GUJARAT

There is substantial evidence in western India and Gujarat for activity associated with microlithic tool-using populations, as demonstrated by the rich sequences identified at Bagor and Langhnaj. Bagor is located on a six metre high sand dune above the Kothari River in Rajasthan and provided a sequence which appears to stretch from 5000 BCE to the Early Historic period (Misra 1973; Lukacs et al. 1983). Its earliest occupation comprised schist paving and semicircular stone alignments, presumably for shelters and its subsistence appears to have focused on hunting and gathering but with some early reports of domesticated sheep/goat. In Gujarat, Langhnaj was similarly located on the summit of a dune above a seasonal lake and appears to have first been occupied in the third millennium BCE. Comprising a midden deposit of charcoal, faunal remains and thirteen grave cuts, its inhabitants appear to have followed a broad spectrum subsistence strategy (Karve-Corvinus and Kennedy 1964; Sankalia 1965). More recently, the site of Loteshwar has also been excavated in Gujarat, and its inhabitants utilised pottery and appear to have had access to domesticated cattle (Ajithprasad 2004). Fuller has suggested that elements of the crop package within Saurashtra differed sufficiently from the native crop packages in other regions of South Asia "to raise the likelihood of local plant domestication processes in Western India, perhaps to be dated back to the fourth or early third millennium BC", but also stated that "[t]his region clearly received livestock from the Indus valley and Baluchistan" (2006: 38–39). Rather than advocating the movement of farmers and herders into this region, Fuller has further suggested "a local trajectory of plant cultivation beginning amongst local hunter-gatherers who presumably adopted livestock from their neighbours to the west" (Fuller 2006: 39). Fuller's hypothesis challenges the view of Meadow and Patel who suggested that the zebu present at Loteshwar may be evidence of a second, later domestication of cattle (2003: 74). In Rajasthan, the site of Balathal has also provided early evidence of a sedentary village with domesticated wheat and barley by 3000 BC (Misra et al. 1997; Misra and Mohanty 2000; 2001; Shinde 2000). Providing evidence of "the dispersal of winter-cropping systems east of the Indus Valley prior to the rise of the Harappan Civilisation", Madella and Fuller interpret this as evidence already of the successful spread of farming communities across the Indus alluvium at this early stage (2006: 1297).

PENINSULAR INDIA

The Neolithic of Peninsular India has been dated between the fourth and second millennia BCE and may be broadly divided into two categories of sites, ash mounds and larger open area settlements (Korisettar et al. 2002). The former category, ash mounds, are large accumulations of vitrified and non-vitrified cattle dung ash, and they are argued to have been created through the ritual clearing and cleaning of cattle penning sites through burning (Fuller et al. 2007: 755). Ash mounds were first reported by antiquarians and archaeologists in the early nineteenth century, but it was not until the 1860s that Robert Foote of the Geological Survey of India carried out survey and exploration (see also Chapter 3). Foote also correctly identified ash mounds as Neolithic sites and the product of cow dung that had been burnt at extremely high temperatures, thus resulting in ash and vitrification, and although numerous other interpretations were suggested over the next century and a half, scientific analysis confirms Foote's early identification (Korisettar et al. 2002: 155).

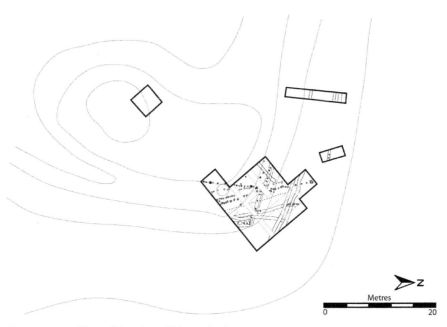

Figure 4.13. Plan of the site of Utnur, India.

There are more than 100 roughly circular ash mounds known to date between the Krishna and Pennar Rivers (Johansen 2004: 310). The largest example is Kudatini, which measured 130 metres in diameter by 10 metres high (Paddayya 1973). Excavations of the 3.5 metres high mound at Utnur uncovered the burnt and vitrified remains of four phases of double stockades (Figure 4.13). It was suggested that cattle were penned in the inner area, while the herders lived in the space between inner and outer stockades (Allchin 1963). Hoof impressions were also preserved at Utnur, and, along with the large quantities of cattle bone and the burnt dung, provided strong evidence for the pastoral function of these sites. The excavations at Utnur also revealed that there had been multiple layers of occupation in the form of stockade building, separated by episodes of burning (Figure 4.14). Early investigations of the ash mounds led to suggestions that these were seasonally occupied pastoral sites (Allchin 1963). Other cultural material from Utnur included ground stone axes, stone blades and pottery which was coarse, handmade, and similar to pottery found at settlement sites in the area such as Tekkalakota. Johansen has stressed that the ashmounds should not be considered in isolation from the many physically smaller habitation sites in their vicinity. Rather than representing separate communities, he has argued that the ashmounds served a cyclical function for stressing pastoral products and were binding artificial monuments within the Deccan landscape (2004: 328)

Less is known of the open air sites as they are frequently covered by overlying deposits with copper objects and even material with an Iron

Figure 4.14. Section through the ash mound at Utnur, India (courtesy Bridget Allchin).

Age date, but they appear to have consisted of villages of circular boulder and stake structures, covering areas less than 4,000 square metres. One of the best examples of an open air site to have been excavated is that of Tekkalakota, some 43 kilometres south of Bellary in Mysore (Nagaraja Rao and Malhotra 1965). The site was occupied for two main phases, Neolithic and 'Chalcolithic', and stretched over a series of undulating granite outcrops. Individual house structures appear to have been built where the ground could be easily levelled. Circular in plan and 5.53 metres in diameter, the walls of one Neolithic house were made of plastered bamboo screens secured on a framework of timber posts, and internal features appear to have been constructed of clay and flat-topped stone slabs (Nagaraja Rao and Malhotra 1965: 91) (Figures 4.15 and 4.16). In addition, a series of six burials were identified as dating to the Neolithic occupation of the site, with children buried in urns within the house floors but adults in separate pits (Nagaraja Rao and Malhotra 1965: 27). Recent work on the dating of the southern Neolithic has shed new light on the role of ash mounds and their relationship to the settlement sites or villages in the region (Fuller et al. 2007). Existing calibrated radiocarbon dates with error margins have suggested that the formation of ash mounds occurred over a longer time scale, with possibly

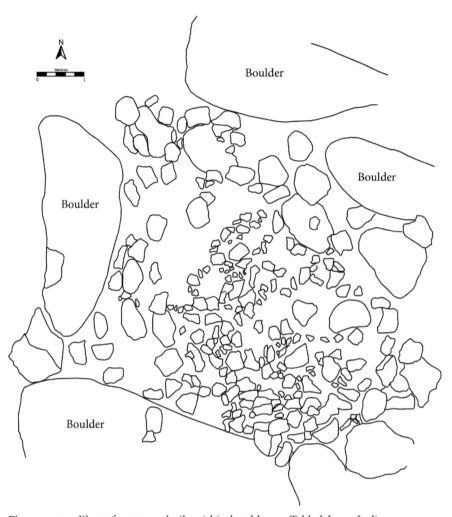

Figure 4.15. Plan of structure built within boulders at Tekkalakota, India.

two phases of creation, each lasting around 300 years. Budihal-south, one of three sites in the Budihal complex, is one of the most completely excavated ash mound sites, and much of its interest stems from being a site where both cattle penning and settlement structures were uncovered together. Traditional radiocarbon dates showed that there was an overlap between the two, with dates of circa 2450–2100 BCE for the ash mound and circa 2450–1600 BCE for the village. When these dates were reanalysed using Bayesian statistics, a rather different picture emerged – dung accumulation and the creation of the ash mounds took place over a relatively short period between circa 2300–2200 BCE, which is when the village was first occupied (Fuller et al. 2007: 765). The village at Budihal-south however, continued in use until circa 1700 BCE alongside the defunct ash mound. Of further interest is the butchery floor located near to the ash mound which has the same

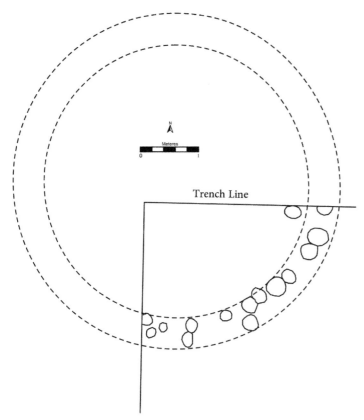

Figure 4.16. Plan of building at Tekkalakota, India.

dates – this has been interpreted as an area of feasting, and is linked to the ritual importance of ash mound sites (Fuller et al. 2007).

Fuller et al. (2007) have argued that the new dates indicate a change in pastoral practice, as ash mounds represented only a very small active phase in the longer span of the villages, and then became key monuments in the land-scape (2007: 765). Excavations at other sites such as Sannarachamma Hill have revealed occupation deposits overlying an ash mound and so it would seem that, over time, some villages replaced the ash mound rather than coexist-ing with them. Fuller et al. (2007: 767) argue that there was no single model of development for either ash mounds or villages in this region and some ash mounds were formed quickly, over perhaps 100 years. After this forma-tion stage, some sites such as Utnur were abandoned, while at others such as Budihal and Sannarachamma, sedentary occupation developed alongside or even over the ash mounds. At the very large sites, such as Kudatini and Pallavoy, there are layers in the sequence that may indicate natural soil for-mation during periods of abandonment, in between periods of activity and burning. Fuller et al. (2007: 767) suggest that dating evidence from these larger sites shows that the ash mounds here appear to have been formed over quite long time periods, in contrast to the dates from the smaller sites. Although there is extensive evidence for domesticated cattle at the ash mounds and other occupation sites, little is known about the origins of these domesticates – were they locally domesticated, or introduced from the north? Given the absence of evidence for local domestication, current thought favours introduction from the north (Fuller 2006). What is clear, however, is that cattle were augmented by a broad variety of other species, including deer, buffalo, sheep, goat, fowl and pig (Nagaraja Rao and Malhotra 1965). Recent archaeobotanical work on ash mound material gives a somewhat clearer picture of early plant exploitation, and shows that some of the earliest agriculture was based on native millets (*Bracharia ramose* and *Setaria verticillata*) and native pulses (*Vigna radiata* or mungbean, and *Macrotyloma uniflorum* or horsegram) (Fuller 2006: 50). These are thought to have been domesticated locally and they formed the core plant foods for the occupants of the site, while a range of other plants, including wheat, barley, hyacinth beans and pearl millet were introduced and appear in much smaller quantities.

SRI LANKA

For many years archaeological wisdom deemed that Sri Lanka did not host a Neolithic period, or more correctly, did not host a period of people either adopting domesticated plants and animals or increasing the manipulation and exploitation of native species over time. While in parts of southern India, sedentism and agriculture developed alongside continuing hunter-gatherer lifeways, there appeared to be little archaeological evidence to indicate that this had occurred in Sri Lanka (Deraniyagala 1992: 365). Siran Deraniyagala, former director-general of the Archaeological Survey Department of Sri Lanka, summarised the situation by claiming that "the present evidence indicates that Lanka was a cultural backwater, a refuge area, with respect to the advent of Neolithic/Chalcolithic subsistence practices of farming. None of the pre-Iron Age sites investigated so far has yielded any firm evidence of the prevalence of domesticates. The subsistence pattern appears to have transformed itself rapidly from a hunting and gathering basis to a full-fledged agricultural cum stock-raising economy with the advent of the Iron Age at c. >900 BC, with hunter-gatherer relict tribes such as the Yakka/Vaddas surviving in regions with low agricultural potential" (1992: 365–366). However, as Bandaranayake has pointed out, little is known about the transition from what appears to be a very long lived period of hunting-gathering and stone tool use (early Holocene until c. 1000 BCE) to the complex Early Historic society encountered in the early levels of the archaeological record at sites such as Anuradhapura, for example (Coningham and Allchin 1995). The widely accepted model of a swift transition from hunter-gatherer to sedentary farming lifestyles, without intermediate stages of domestication and technological development, is one which suggests human migration as the vehicle for metal and metal-working, domestic plants and animals, and ideas of incipient urbanism and social complexity (Bandaranayake 1992). This model, and the evidence supporting it, will be considered further in Chapters 9 and 10, when we explore the emergence of urbanism and the development of states in the Early Historic period across South Asia.

However, recent palynological work in the Horton Plains region in central Sri Lanka has provided some very different data on the chronology and appearance of agriculture on the island. Premathilake's (2006) analysis of the pollen diagrams suggests that wild cereals may have been domesticated as early as the beginning of the Holocene, and the types include wild progenitors of oat, barley and wheat (Premathilake 2006: 489). Of these, barley and oat species appear in the pollen record as the major cultivars of the early Holocene between circa 8000–7500 BP, but then there appears to be a decrease in cultivation which is linked to deteriorating climatic conditions (Premathilake 2006: 490). Whilst Premathilake links archaeological sites with microlithic tools and the appearance of Black and Red wares, at the Doravaka rock shelter for example, the absence of a major archaeobotanical and archaeozoological sampling programme weakens the associated certainty. While it is entirely possible that there were local domestications, and possibly introductions as well, until we have evidence from a number of excavations to support the claims of very early agricultural activity, we still have little idea of the processes and form of the development of agriculture. The analysis of the pollen cores suggests that cereals were present on the Horton Plains, and that their relative abundance fluctuated over time. However, this still needs to be situated within an archaeological context which allows us to understand the processes and mechanisms of the development and adoption of agriculture. Premathilake's pollen work points to the presence of non-wild cereal in the Horton Plains as early as 8000 BCE but this does not necessarily mean that people were actually practicing agriculture or even living in settled communities. It may simply mean that people were manipulating cereals as part of a seasonal regime, which brings us back to the difficulties of defining domestication and the Neolithic period itself.

CONCLUSIONS

In this chapter we have seen that there was no single chronological period or material culture package that can be termed 'Neolithic' in South Asia. Instead, we argue that there were multiple Neolithic populations across the region and note Meadow and Patel have already identified at least two domestications of zebu, one early in the north-west and a second in western India (2003: 74). This model is strongly supported by recent work on the domestication of plants and animals, which demonstrates that while wild progenitors may have become domesticates in some places, they were equally likely to have been supplemented with introduced species. Of course, different suites of plants and animals, both local domesticates and introductions, dominated in different regions, and the time frame for the adoption of domesticates and other Neolithic trappings by communities varied enormously from area to area. Recent research into the types of early faunal domesticates and environment demonstrates that there is no simple relationship between variables, and that agency is key (Fazeli and Young 2013). The earliest region to adopt agriculture, pastoralism and sedentism was the north-west, with the site of Mehrgarh providing key evidence, and, arguably, elements of this early development spread out to the north, east and south over time, but in each area there was a distinct local flavour and, as already noted, strong evidence for local centres of domestication of a varied range of plants and animals. Sri Lanka remains a largely unknown entity with regard to the Neolithic, although there are now two competing models for the emergence of agriculture.

Mehrgarh remains one of the key sites in South Asia because it has provided the earliest known undisputed evidence for farming and pastoral communities in the region, and its plant and animal material provide clear evidence for the ongoing manipulation, and domestication, of certain species. Perhaps most importantly in a South Asian context, the role played by zebu makes this a distinctive, localised development, with a character completely different to other parts of the world. Finally, the longevity of the site, and its articulation with the neighbouring site of Naushasro (c. 2800–2000 BCE), provides a very clear continuity from South Asia's first farming villages to the emergence of its first cities (Jarrige 1984). Prior to the work at Mehrgarh, many scholars had assumed that Neolithic communities in Western Asia gradually diffused eastwards bringing with them the Neolithic package of settled villages, ceramics, wheat, barley and sheep/goat (Fairservis 1971). The earlier dates for aceramic Neolithic levels at Jericho (8350–7350 BCE), and dates of between 8000 and 6500 BCE for Neolithic levels at Ali Kosh in south-west Iran, supported the model of population movement from West to South Asia at a speed of one kilometre per year (Renfrew 1987). However, the presence of a 'Neolithic' period at Mehrgarh with dates of at least 6500 BCE challenges this model of diffusion, as it would mean that colonists in Iran would have had to begin the process of diffusion in at least 8600 BCE in order to cover the intervening 2,100 kilometres. This has become increasingly unlikely in the light of new radiocarbon dates for the establishment of Neolithic communities in the Central Plateau of Iran being firmly placed in the seventh millennium BCE (Fazeli et al. 2013).

As with the Neolithic process elsewhere in Eurasia, a series of major transformations and distinct changes to South Asian human and animal lifeways occurred, accompanied by transformations in social and economic values. Indeed, Melinda Zeder has suggested that archaeologists should step back from obsessively focusing "on the exact demarcation between domestic and wild, and to turn, instead, to a consideration of the full span of the evolving nature of domestic relationships" (Zeder 2006: 105). For example, the first formalised burials of the dead, frequently within houses and structures, are interpreted as indicative of communal and individual senses of belonging, but equally importantly is the linkage between settled inhabitants with fields, and the associated cycles of seasonal activities which would have bonded people to their newly defined fields. Human labour was needed to prepare and clear fields and to tame and cull animals, leading to a greater "degree of incorporation of domesticates within the socio-economic organisation of the human groups investing in its production" (Zeder 2006: 108). This was, in turn, to lead to a situation where there was so strong a mutualism, that domesticates were dependent on humans for their own fertilisation. People were also needed to build and plaster the new structures within villages, and the absence of doorways at Mehrgarh suggests that such buildings were only accessible through their roofs. Additionally, the inhabitants of these growing settlements must have appeared distinct from the more mobile hunter-gatherers and pastoralists around them. Indeed, the very creation of such settlements further differentiated their populations through the process of degradation, erosion and rebuilding which led to the creation of an artificial landscape, the tell. Many of the structures demonstrate a continuity and may represent ownership, not necessarily individual but perhaps kin-related. Certainly the creation of compartmentalised storage units suggests that there was a need to differentiate the produce and material held in each individual silo. Such a transition has been marked as highly significant elsewhere by Kent Flannery, as he held it to reflect a major shift in risk ownership, from the collective to specific smaller groups (2002: 421). There was, however, little evidence of pre-planning and the development of these structures appears to have been organic or haphazard. Whilst we are uncertain as to their exact function, the growing production of terracotta figurines may indicate a growing exchange of physical ritual information between individuals, perhaps as a method of trying to control the undomesticated world by ritual and symbol as suggested by Watkins (1992).

As significantly, it is important to note that this development did not simply imitate the West Asian Neolithic package, as it relied heavily on the domestication of indigenous humped South Asian cattle (zebu), rather than sheep and goat. Furthermore, if the Neolithic in South Asia is considered to be a result of diffusion of a West Asian, ready-prepared package, then there are challenges explaining the earliest occupation at Mehrgarh, which was both aceramic and perhaps seasonal in form. When the current archaeological material for Mehrgarh is examined, it appears that there are clear local developments as well as some external influences. Intensive field survey within Baluchistan may provide additional evidence for such a development as demonstrated by the results of Biagi's recent research in upper and lower Sindh (2004). There, such an approach has identified the presence of numerous Early Holocene communities across the region, demonstrating that the lower Indus was already peopled before the advent of the first farming settlements. However, the chance discovery of Mehrgarh also highlights the challenges of archaeological visibility and Jarrige wisely notes that "It is still impossible to know if Mehrgarh documents the whole process of domestication in the greater Indus or, as is more likely, if it represents only an episode that was preceded by an earlier Epipalaeolithic phase" (Jarrige 1993a: 17). It is clear that the structures at Mehrgarh were strikingly communal, and Jarrige has pointed out, with regard to the storage units, that "such features were evidence of storage and [a] redistributive system on which depended an important part of the socio-economic organisation" (Jarrige 1993a: 28). These communal features, combined with the network of long-distance trading partnerships and mobile communities bringing ivory, shell, lapis lazuli and carnelian to Mehrgarh, allowed these new settlements to expand, grow and bud-off, which in turn resulted in the settlement of the alluvial valleys of Baluchistan all the way to the edges of the Indus River itself.

CHAPTER 5

REGIONALISATION AND DIFFERENTIATED COMMUNITIES (c. 5000–2600 BCE)

INTRODUCTION

This chapter introduces a broad range of regional developments and populations across South Asia and the concepts of 'diversity' and 'mosaic' are probably
more important in the period covered in this chapter than elsewhere in the
chronological range that we consider in this book. Yet from this diverse mosaic
of material culture, ideological practice, subsistence practices and connections,
a clear transition towards the integration of the later Indus period began to
coalesce. It is also important to remember that beyond the region covered by
the Regionalised Indus Era, numerous cultural developments remained that
were not absorbed (or in some cases even affected) by the spread and sharing of
Indus Valley Tradition cultural traits. While the urban-centric Indus Civilisation
has demanded a great deal of archaeological attention over many years, the
vast majority of South Asia's people would of course have continued to live
in villages and small farming settlements or have been involved in mobile
hunting-gathering-fishing or pastoral lifeways. We offer a similar focus on the
urban character of the Indus (and then the urban Early Historic Tradition) in
this volume; however, this focus should not prevent an awareness of the range
of different developments at this time across the whole of South Asia.

As noted in Chapter 3, the Indus Civilisation was viewed for many years as
an entity which emerged fully formed to take its place as one of the major Old
World Civilisations. This concept was reinforced by early models and theories
which presented it as a product of contact with Mesopotamia to the west, and
so the product of cultural diffusion (Dani 1968, 1978; Piggott 1950; Sankalia
1977; Wheeler 1968). However, extensive research over the last forty years has
provided archaeologists with a great deal of evidence which has allowed them
to refute such simple models. This research has demonstrated that the development of the Indus Civilisation was the result of many hundreds of years
of increasing complexity, rather than a sudden or self-contained phenomenon (Figure 5.1) (Timeline 5.1). This research has also uncovered indisput-
able evidence for the presence of a proto-urban transition. For example, the

Figure 5.1. Map of sites mentioned in Chapter 5.

Regionalisation and Differentiated Communities Timeline

Timeline 5.1. Timeline for Chapter 5.

occupation sequence stretches from the Aceramic Neolithic (c. 6500 BCE) to the 'Chalcolithic' (c. 2000 BCE) at the sites of Mehrgarh and Naushadro in Baluchistan. These sites are thus clear examples of both the increasing societal complexity evident at some sites in this region and of continuity over a very long period (Jarrige 1984), and we will consider them in some detail in the later parts of this chapter. The occurrence of a distinct proto-urban phase is also supported by evidence from sites such as Rehman Dheri, Harappa, Kot Diji and Kalibangan, whose populations were differentiated from a hinterland of smaller, undifferentiated farming villages by their larger size and greater range of function (Mughal 1990, 1997). Rehman Dheri's residents, for example, lived within a highly regular planned form, with grid-iron planned streets and high defining walls, which differentiated it from numerous smaller organic sites which lacked evidence of clear formal planning (Durrani 1988; 1995). Settlements such as Rehman Dheri, Harappa and Kalibangan stood out clearly and Mughal's (1997) survey in Cholistan in modern Pakistan illustrates this division well.

Whilst Rehman Dheri, Kot Diji, Harappa and Kalibangan also had evidence for the use of non-scriptural graffiti, complex trade and exchange networks, and increased evidence for administration as indicated by artefacts such as seals, it should be stressed that there was still an apparent gulf separating the primate settlements of this Era of Regionalisation from the later Integration Era of the Indus cities which will be discussed in Chapter 6 (Box 5.1). For example, there was a huge difference between the tremendous expansion in settlement size

---

Box 5.1. Seals and Sealings

Scripts and writing have long been perceived to be hallmarks of complex civilisations (Childe 1954), and seals engraved with animal motifs and an undeciphered script represent one of the most enigmatic artefact classes excavated from sites of the Indus Valley Tradition. There are more than 3,700 known Indus seals, of which some 87 percent have been recovered from the two major urban sites of Mohenjo-daro and Harappa (Possehl 2002a: 127). These artefacts have been largely interpreted as indicators of trade; part of a mechanism to stamp, record and trace the movement of perishable and non-perishable goods. Although their presence within the littoral of the Arabian Sea adds weight to the suggestion of their facilitation of a maritime mercantile network, it has been argued that the Indus seals do not simply reflect the seal-based administrative system encountered in Mesopotamia. Indeed, there are notable differences, such as the small number of clay seal impressions recovered within the Indus Valley Tradition. Secondly, most Indus seals have retained the sharp appearance of their initial carving and do not appear to have been affected by wear,

(continued)

which one might expect if they were used to make multiple impressions. This point is further reiterated by the fact that they were cut from a relatively soft steatite.

A number of these factors led Ernest Mackay to consider whether these square stone objects should have been classed perhaps as amulets rather than seals (1931b), and it is certainly a possibility that the seals were worn for visual identification or as markers of ownership (Possehl 2002a: 130–131). Some scholars have argued that the symbols carved onto these square stone seals identified rulers and their clans and that these motifs of animals were the most important symbols of power wielded by the rulers of the Indus Valley Tradition (Vidale 2005; Kenoyer 1998: 81). However, most would agree that the engraved seals represent a fragment of what may have been written on perishable materials and that records for more utilitarian purposes may have been fashioned from less durable materials (Coningham 2002: 98).

As noted previously, the presence of prehistoric seals and sealings is usually interpreted by archaeologists as evidence of administration and bureaucracy. Given the lack of textual information regarding the administration of craft specialisation for the prehistoric period in the Turan, Tosi argued that the organisation of labour could be reconstructed from the analysis of the distribution of devices for record keeping across a site (Tosi 1984: 45). Furthermore, Tosi hypothesised that increasing centralisation of administration would have accompanied the development of complex societies on the Turanian Basin and that such evidence would come in the form of seals and sealings becoming centralised and increasingly absent from individual households (Tosi 1984: 47). However promising the hypothesis and data set under scrutiny, analysis at the site of Shahr-i Sokhta found that such a centralisation was not apparent even though the site expanded in size and complexity and that there was no significant clustering of sealings across the site (Tosi 1984: 47). As a result, we suggest that whilst seals and sealings are indicative of increasing recording of ownership, they may not necessarily be directly mapped against increasing craft specialisation and centralised administration.

from the Regionalisation Era to the Integrated Era at the site of Kalibangan and there was also clearly a change in purpose and construction of the enclosure walls. In Period I, the population of Kalibangan occupied an area of no more than 4 hectares (9 acres) bounded by a mud-brick wall; by Period II, there was a walled 'citadel' mound and a walled lower mound, together covering an area of 11.5 hectares (28 acres) (Lal 1998: 21–25, 2003; Thapar 1975: 20–26). Similarly, whilst sherds with non-scriptural graffiti have been recovered from the pre-Integration town, they were very different in form from the later Indus script. In this chapter, we will explore both the continuities and the transformations within emerging urban forms evident in the archaeological record. We will examine the developmental sequences of a number of sites, including Kalibangan, Rehman Dheri and Harappa, where there is sufficient published material from excavations and explorations for us to be able to gain an overview of the general developments and innovation. We will also consider the nature and function of links between sites illustrating emerging social, political and economic differentiation within the Indus region with settlements which developed slightly earlier on the Indo-Iranian plateau. These sites, such as Shahr-i Sokhta, are important as they appear to represent nodes of population along clear trade routes between east and west (Tosi 1983). They demonstrated trading links within the proto-Elamite world and also functioned as a conduit for the exchange of peoples, materials and concepts. Regionally, the Era also witnessed the growth of key 'anchor' centres, a growth towards record keeping and occupational specialisation on a major scale as well as new systems and ideologies to justify and validate the changes and the potential of human migration into relatively unexploited areas with, of course, a reliance on the asymmetric geographical distribution of resources. This chapter will conclude by suggesting that the evidence demonstrates that there was a duality in the Era of Regionalisation within the Indus Valley Tradition; clear continuity at many sites and within their material culture but no evidence for a seamless, smooth transition from the Era of Regionalisation to the Era of Integration. We will argue that this may well be due to poor archaeological phasing and a reliance on relative ceramic dating, rather than indicating a diffusionistic model. At the same time, however, we also recognise that South Asia has never operated within a cultural vacuum and that contact, trade and the movement of ideas, goods and people have played a vital role in the development of this region, although not necessarily in the ways traditional archaeological models of explanation have suggested.

AN ERA OF REGIONALISATION? (C. 5000–3200 BCE)

What do we mean by 'regionalisation'? Regionalisation was the term used by Shaffer in his dating framework for the Indus Valley Tradition (1992) and broadly corresponds with the period often known in more traditional, simplified schemes as the Early Harappan. In this sense, regionalisation is a method of referring to this period of emergent urbanism or proto-urban forms in the north-western areas of South Asia. However, it also encompasses a great deal more when we begin to reflect about the sites and processes involved in the development and emergence of urban populations and urban forms. What we begin to recognise are 'regional' traditions, or certain aspects of material culture that were evident at many sites in particular regions. It is important here that we avoid charges of invoking culture history, or equating peoples with closely

defined cultural definitions, as explanation. Instead, we are referring to poly-
thetic rather than monothetic groupings, and trends and patterns rather than
absolutes (Clarke 1978: 247). It is also important to reflect on the differences
between each geographical region and note that different events and processes
were occurring in different regions within a wider arena, and that these different regional developments went on to take different forms again in the
Integrated Era or 'Mature' Harappan period, to use more traditional nomenclature. As noted earlier, there is no clear mapping of all proto-urban sites
from the Era of Regionalisation to fully urban sites in the Era of Integration;
and there is no clear mapping of urban sites from the Era of the Integrated
Indus Valley Tradition to the urban sites of the Early Historic period. It is also
important to note that the use of this term helps us escape the earlier use of
terms like 'pre-Indus' or even 'early Indus' by focusing on the core cultural
characteristics and processes at work.

As we discussed in Chapter 4, archaeological explorations in Baluchistan,
that is the eastern part of the Indo-Iranian plateau and the western edge of
the Indus plain, have revealed the presence of a number of early sedentary
populations, forming what have been described as 'villages'. With their origins in the seventh millennium BCE, the inhabitants of these settlements
exploited domesticated plants and animals, had evidence for the storage of
surplus and also evidence for involvement in the long-distance trade in exotic
materials and items (Jarrige 1984). A number of characteristics of the preceding
hunting-gathering-foraging lifestyles persisted alongside these new developments, illustrated by the continued use of microlithic tools, the presence of
wild plant and animal remains alongside domesticates, and probably continued
mobility in the form of transhumance for at least some of the communities or some elements of the communities. By the fourth millennium BCE,
some of these populations had successfully settled the Indus plain and, by
the third millennium BCE, had agglomerated sufficient population to create distinct walled, planned settlements (Mughal 1990), and it is this period
that forms the main focus of this chapter. The significance of this long period
of development of what is now believed to be the urban forms that became
the cities, towns and villages of the Indus Civilisation, was not fully recognised or understood by earlier scholars, and so this stage was generally referred
to as the 'pre-Harappan' or 'pre-Indus', which incorrectly suggested that it
formed a separate developmental stage from the 'Mature Indus' (Allchin and
Allchin 1968; Mohan 1998; Wheeler 1953). More recent work has challenged
and changed this interpretation, and we now know that this period was one
of dynamic experimentation, which culminated in a shared cultural complex
circa 2800 BCE, just prior to the emergence of the Integrated Era of the Indus
Civilisation (Shaffer and Thapar 1992). The sites associated with this shared
complex stretched from Rehman Dheri on the west bank of the Indus to the
Ghaggar River in the east, and from Balakot in the south-west to Surkotada

in the south-east. Current archaeological knowledge indicates that there are more 300 known sites attributed to this Era of Regionalisation. We will now explore the different regions with evidence for development during the period between 5000 and 2600 BCE, beginning with Baluchistan, moving on to the Indus plain itself, and then the areas to the south and east of the Indus plain. Within each section, we will examine selected sites, through Box Feature Case Studies, in greater depth.

VARIATION AND MATERIAL CULTURE

Aiming to find universal rules that define or explain human behaviour or cultural variation is of course impossible, as post-processual archaeological understandings and interpretations have clearly demonstrated (Hodder and Hutson 2003: 207–208). Indeed, the early ethnoarchaeological studies of Hodder remind us of the difficulties of even trying to map specific motifs and materials against living linguistic or tribal groupings (1982). This is not to deny that material culture has meaning but to state an awareness that the meaning of any artefact or assemblage is reliant on context and may be created and manipulated by people or by groups, and this can open up exciting ways of beginning to think about the ways in which people used objects: "Rather than assuming norms and systems, in the attempt to produce bounded entities, archaeologists can use their material to examine the continual process of interpretation and reinterpretation in relation to interest, itself an interpretation of events" (Hodder and Hutson 2003: 211). In order to find a framework within which to explain cultural similarity, Eerkens and Lipo (2007: 240) have made use of cultural transmission theory, which draws on exchanges of information. Whilst the legacy of culture history and culture evolutionary studies have given early work in cultural transmission a poor reception, the core issue at the heart of modern studies is that of the sharing of information by individuals or groups. These studies recognise historical context, human agency, and simultaneous independent development of knowledge, and Eerkens and Lipo cite examples where cultural transmission theory "has been used to explain the maintenance of group cohesion through common iconography or ritual behaviour" (2007: 259). Contact is essential for the transmission or sharing of ideas and artefacts, and this contact can take many forms. Trade and exchange are perhaps most commonly offered but the movement of individuals through marriage is also key (see Hodder 1982 for a discussion of this), along with movements of transhumant and nomadic groups, and movement of people seeking different or better places to settle. Adopting material culture might be driven by individual or group aims and, as well as fashion, taste is a powerful means of stating identity and allegiance as Eerkens and Lipo noted earlier. Moreover, the adoption of motifs and materials does not necessarily indicate that a community has been absorbed by wholesale acculturation but might reflect that a community has adopted and assimilated the material culture of others as part of a process of emulation and competition. With barriers to size of individual settlements resulting in the 'budding-off' of new settlements and chiefly authority limited by some scholars to no more than 30 kilometres by foot (Spencer 2010: 7119), such shared styles would have facilitated an awareness of broader community than just the people with whom one shared a valley or common water source. In the same way, we might perceive the breaking down of the mosaic of differentiated wares across Baluchistan and the growing adoption of single dominant assemblage as part of a process of growth, emulation and competition amongst individual populations rather than targeted colonisation. Indeed, Henry Wright has suggested that the widespread similarity or the spread of a specific ceramic type might represent the movement of one particular segment of a community, potters for example, rather than mass migrations or colonisation (2001: 124). Similarly, we should acknowledge that the very adoption and sharing of an integrating material culture might mask regional and even local cultural variation from archaeological analysis. Certainly, Chase et al.'s study of two small neighbouring sites in the 'borderlands' of Gujarat has identified distinct differences in economic production and object consumption despite the fact that both sites were occupied during the Indus Integration Era and were only 22 kilometres apart (2014).

THE BALUCHISTAN UPLANDS

In recent years, the "wide and growing assortment of ceramic industries of the central and southern Baluchistan", as termed by Wheeler (1968: 11), have been systematically ordered into a series of clearer chronological phases by Shaffer. Thus the individual 'Chalcolithic' Nal, Amri, Zhob, Togau and Quetta wares, which were geographically derived names, have been transformed into the Kili Gul Muhammad, Kechi Beg, Damb Sadaat and Nal phases, which stretched from 4300 BCE to circa 2500 BCE, contemporary with the urban complexes on the Indus to the east (Shaffer 1992: 452). We describe the major transformations at a number of key sites as their populations developed through this long time period from late Neolithic into 'Chalcolithic' centres and consider what these changes mean for the people and communities behind the material culture.

There are many other associated sites in Baluchistan that have been identified and dated to this Era of Regionalisation (c. 5000–2600 BCE) through the surveys and excavations of Piggott (1950), Beatrice de Cardi (1983) and Fairservis in the 1940s and 1950s (1956). This pioneering research has allowed the development of a relative chronology and the creation and comparison of pottery typologies. Perhaps most importantly, these archaeologists were able to construct links between the material from sites such as Amri in modern Sindh, to the south of Mohenjo-daro, and Kili Gul Muhammad in modern Baluchistan, near Quetta with certain aspects of Harappan material, particularly pottery. For example, the Amri Ware from the sites of Amri, Lohri, Ghazi Shah and Pandi Wahi (Sindh) demonstrated that Amri wares belonged to the Era of Regionalisation, but Piggott identified a mixture of Harappan and Amri styles at the site of Pai-jo-Kotiro in the Gaj Valley of the Kirthar Range (1950: 355).

There were also close links between Amri-Nal styles and Harappan styles, such as patterns on pottery, with Piggott commenting that "It appears therefore that the Amri-Nal style underlies the Harappan much as it does the Classic Nal style of southern Baluchistan and the Early Quetta style in northern Baluchistan" (1950: 355). Links between Harappan sites and sites in the Quetta valley itself were scarcer, although there is believed to be some Harappan-derived pottery at Quetta Miri and Damb Sadaat (Fairservis 1956: 355) and Mackay identified sherds of Quetta Ware at Mohenjo-daro in 'lower levels' of the site (Fairservis 1956: 356). The recognition of this shared developmental stage is key to our understanding more about the processes and drivers that led to the emergence of one of the Old World Civilisations, the Indus, although it has taken many decades of work before a full understanding of the time depth involved has been appreciated. Finally, it should be noted that the surveys and excavations in Baluchistan also demonstrated that different sites pursued different developmental trajectories. Sites such as Kechi Beg and Karez were single-period sites with little in the way of change in ceramics from earliest to latest levels, but others, such as Kili Gul Muhummad and Damb Sadaat, were shown to be multi-period sites with clear changes and development in ceramics and other types of material culture.

Kili Gul Muhammad Phase (c. 4300–3500 BCE)

Although represented at a number of sites such as Kili Gul Muhammad II-III in the Quetta Valley and Rana Ghundai I-III in the Loralai Valley (Shaffer 1992: 454), the best preserved and researched evidence for this phase comes from the early 'Chalcolithic' phases of Mehrgarh, close to the mouth of the Bolan Pass. Following its Neolithic origins, Mehrgarh continued to thrive with a steady growth in settlement size and, presumably, population (Jarrige et al. 1995). As the settlement expanded, it emerged as a regional centre of ceramic production, and these ceramics have played an important role in the characterisation of the 'Chalcolithic' in Baluchistan. More than 3,000 square metres of the circa 100-hectare site area (247 acres) was exposed through excavation (Samzun 1991: 66; Jarrige et al. 2005: 132). These excavations exposed two types of mud-brick structures; square or rectangular compartmental units, measuring an average of 20 by 15 metres, and residential units. Four ranges of the former were excavated and found to comprise individual compartments measuring a maximum of three by one metres each and set on either side of a central corridor. These types of structures represented a continuum from the compartmentalised structures of the Neolithic period at the site and have also been interpreted as granary silos and stores.

The residential units were often constructed with foundations of clay and gravel and the units were made up of four or five irregular shaped rooms with interconnecting doorways and internal fireplaces. These structures were interspaced with a large cemetery with a high density of two burials every square metre. The majority of the 100 excavated graves were individual crouched inhumations, oriented east-west, lying on their sides facing east. At the beginning of the fourth millennium BCE, there was also evidence to suggest that the site of Mehrgarh Period III was becoming transformed into a centre of craft production for the wider region. The evidence cited by its excavator, Jarrige, appears to strongly support such a hypothesis through the presence of workshops for the production of wheel-turned pottery as well as for working and drilling objects of lapis lazuli, steatite, turquoise, carnelian and marine shell (1993b: 83). A stand of ceramic kilns with circumferences of 2.5 metres occupied part of the site and were surrounded by a staggering six metre depth of ceramic wasters and terracotta beads and figurines indicating that pottery production "was carried out on a semi-industrial scale by specialised craftsmen" (Samzun 1991: 68). The find of crucibles for smelting indicated a further specialisation and was accompanied by a decline in stone and bone-working with the complete disappearance of microliths (Lechevallier 1987: 73).

As well as Mehrgarh and Naushero, sites in the Nal and Zhob watersheds have also been recorded and assigned to the 'Chalcolithic' (Shaffer 1992; Shaffer and Thapar 1992). Between the second half of the fourth millennium and the first half of the third millennium BCE, both Mehrgarh (3600–2700 BCE, periods IV-V-VI and VII A-B-C) and nearby Naushero (2900–2500 BCE, period I A-B-C-D) have evidence to demonstrate that ceramic production intensified to such an extent that it has been described as representing 'mass production' (Quivron 1997: 45). At both sites, buildings have been uncovered that have been identified as potteries with storage rooms containing hundreds of vessels, unfired vessels, potters' tools and many kilns and pottery wasters. Analysis of the unfired pottery has shown that many vessels had been incised with a mark or symbol, which has been thought to possibly be a forerunner of the Indus script or, at least, workshop identification or recording marks (Quivron 1997: 45). The social and economic organisation and investment in kiln infrastructure, labour and raw materials indicate both the growth of the potential markets as well as capacity for groups of specialists to emerge within the otherwise largely undifferentiated settlements.

The pottery assemblages from these sites were dominated by wheel-thrown wares with monochrome, bichrome and even polychrome decorations and, in addition to pottery, glass and other glazed objects were produced at Mehrgarh at approximately the same time they were being produced in Egypt and Mesopotamia, which is around 4500 BCE (Barthelemy de Saizieu and Bouquillon 1997: 63). This tradition continued in the Indus Valley Tradition right through to the Era of Integration Indus (see also Chapter 6). Steatite was also an important material for decorative objects and it has been calculated that during period III or the later Neolithic, some 93 percent of all beads were made from steatite. Although this figure dropped to around 80 percent during Periods IV and VII or the 'Chalcolithic' through to the 'Early Bronze Age', steatite was clearly one of the materials of choice for beads at Mehrgarh (Barthelemy de Saizieu and Bouquillon 1997: 63). These figures were echoed at Nausharo, where some 90 percent of beads were made of steatite during Period I, which these scholars equate to Mehrgarh VII or the 'Early Bronze Age'. Almost all of the steatite beads from the 'Chalcolithic' at Mehrgarh had been baked, and all of those that were studied had been glazed. In the next period, referred to by the excavators as the 'Early Bronze Age', there was another new technical development, the miniaturisation of beads, and these very tiny beads were not glazed. At the same time, those beads manufactured in 'normal' size and shape continued to be glazed (Barthelemy de Saizieu and Bouquillon 1997: 65).

Kechi Beg Phase (c. 3500–3000 BCE)

The succeeding Kechi Beg Phase is less well understood but is still represented across both north and south Baluchistan at the sites of Mehrgarh in Periods IV to V, at Damb Sadaat I, Kili Gul Muhammad IV and Surab III (Shaffer 1992: 455). Characterised by the appearance of the manufacture of distinct polychrome ceramics, the first stamp seals of terracotta, steatite and bone were recovered at Mehrgarh during this Phase (Jarrige 1993b: 84), and the presence of seals is commonly associated with the need to account, administer and indicate ownership. More specifically, the development of seals allowed the keeping of records beyond that of memory and indicates that already distinctions were being made between owners and their materials and perhaps exchange beyond face to face contacts. Jean-Francois Jarrige has also identified the presence of "a ditch, which was probably a canal" at Mehrgarh during this Phase and has suggested that canal irrigation might have had a substantial impact on settlement patterns and population agglomeration within the Kacchi-Bolan area (1993a: 31). It should be noted, however, that while this is currently the earliest known example of an artificial channel in South Asia, regions to the west have provided similar evidence of features on alluvial fans dating back to the sixth millennium BCE (Gillmore et al. 2009), indicating that earlier examples are to be expected within South Asia.

Damb Sadaat Phase (c. 3000–2600 BCE)

There are more than thirty-five sites associated with this phase (Possehl 2002a: 45), many of which were initially identified by Fairservis during his reconnaissance of the Quetta Valley in the 1950s (1956). Despite this large number of sites, the phase is best illustrated by reference to phases at two sites already established, Damb Sadaat II-III and Mehrgarh VI-VII. The 14 metre

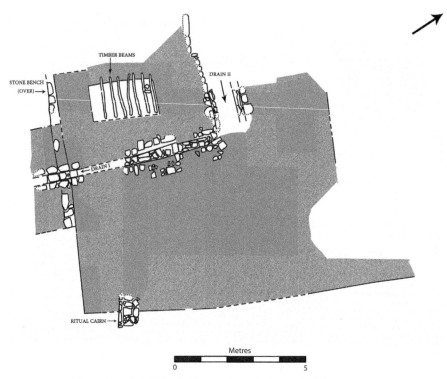

Figure 5.2. Plan of mud-brick platform at Damb Sadaat, Pakistan.

high mound of Damb Sadaat has an occupation which stretches from 3500 to 2395 BCE. Located some 13 kilometres west of Quetta, the mound covers an area of 140 by 105 metres and was divided into three main Periods I, II and III. Whilst the earliest occupation was established during the preceding Kechi Beg Phase, Periods II and III have been attributed to the Damb Sadaat Phase by Shaffer (1992: 456). Mud-brick walls on footings of stone continued to be built into Period II but Fairservis also uncovered evidence of a monumental square mud-brick platform or podium (1956: 358). Located at the highest part of the ancient mound, the platform stood 3 metres wide and measured at least 10 metres long, and although nothing remained of its superstructure, its surface was cut by a one metre deep drain delineated by rough limestone blocks (Figure 5.2). The presence of human skeletal remains in a foundation deposit below the platform, combined with the presence of eight terracotta female figurines led Fairservis to assume that it had served a ceremonial function for the settlement's population, a conclusion which was reinforced by his argument that the drain was far more substantial than needed to clear the platform from rainfall (Fairservis 1956: 216).

At Mehrgarh, the presence of large areas of open kilns and millions of wasters confirmed the continued economic and regional specialisation of some of its inhabitants during Period VI. Indeed, the excavators suggested that the settlement had functioned as a centre for "semi-industrial productions ... intended probably for a large market" (Jarrige and Lechevallier 1979: 502). Occupation then shifted to the southern part of the main mound along with the construction of a monumental mud-brick platform almost 40 metres in length during Period VII. More than 300 square metres of the monument was exposed during the excavations and it appeared to have been screened by a pilastered wall to its north side, although with a slightly different alignment. Unfortunately, its eroded nature makes it difficult to estimate its original height but the mass of collapsed bricks surrounding it led its excavator to suggest that "its original height must have been important" (Jarrige and Lechevallier 1979: 510). The associated cemetery continued to demonstrate the strength of Mehrgarh's long-distance trade through the presence of objects made of carnelian from western India and lapis lazuli from Afghanistan, and its continuing economic specialisation was demonstrated by the presence of large areas of kilns and wasters. It is interesting to note that the monumental structure and semi-industrial production were followed by the presence of compartmentalised stamp seals of terracotta and bitumen during Period VII (Jarrige and Lechevallier 1979: 527), again, indicative of the needs for administration, recording and ownership amongst some of the settlement's population. It is also apparent that whilst finished goods had been imported during the early occupation of the site, by the Era of Regionalisation, increasing amounts of raw materials were being sourced by the emergent centre for completion and redistribution to local and regional consumers.

THE LOWER INDUS PLAIN

Balakot Phase (c. 4000–3500 BCE)

In contrast with the uplands to the west, evidence for colonisation of the lower Indus basin is much more fragmentary, and this is partially due to the enormous degree of annual siltation which has buried earlier land surfaces. Current archaeological information indicates that the earliest evidence for sedentary populations was at the site of Balakot, which is located 88 kilometres to the north-west of Karachi on an old course of the Windar River. Excavated by George Dales and his team in the 1970s, and dating from the fourth millennium BCE, its shorter cultural sequence clearly contrasted with the long sequence of settlement within the Baluchistan uplands (Dales 1979). The site measured some 180 metres east to west and 150 metres north to south, and its 14 metre deep sequence contained two major Periods, I and II, of which the second had clear affinities with the period of Indus Integration. The wheel-made polychrome floral and zoomorphic designs of the earlier Period I ceramics were identified as having notable links to the assemblages of the Nal tradition in Baluchistan, perhaps indicating strong cultural and trading affiliations (Dales 1974). This lower 6 metre deep sequence contained occupation evidence in the form of mud-brick structures built on stone foundations, and brick pavements were exposed. Continuity was found in some materials, for example, the size of bricks was similar to those of the later Integration Era ratio of 1:2:4 (Agrawal 1982: 128). Parallel-sided chert blades were recovered as well as semi-precious stone and shell ornaments, including lapis lazuli beads. Finds of badly eroded objects of copper and bronze placed the site within the 'Chalcolithic' period (Shaffer 1992: 444). Terracotta figurines depicted only cattle, but archaeozoological evidence demonstrates that the inhabitants of this 2.7 hectare (6 acre) settlement relied on a broad spectrum of domesticated cattle, sheep and goat alongside hunted and gathered species such as gazelle, fish and shellfish, while also cultivating barley and jujube (Dales 1979). However, the fact that more than half of the bone weight was represented by fish bone, makes it is clear that the subsistence strategy of the inhabitants of this early settlement was notably adapted and focused towards the coast with evidence of seasonal inshore and near-shore exploitation (Belcher 2003: 144). Balakot remains the unique representative of this initial colonisation of the lower plain of the Indus River, but its later prehistoric ceramics have been strongly linked to a number of sites spread across the region, particularly the site of Amri.

Amri Phase (c. 3600–3000 BCE)

The early occupation at Amri has been dated between 3600 and 3300 BCE and thus represents a slightly later developmental phase than Balakot. Amri is the type-site of this early cultural assemblage and was first investigated by N. G. Majumdar in 1929 before being more fully excavated by Jean-Marie Casal between 1959 and 1962 (Casal 1964) (Figure 5.3). Amri is located close to the west bank of the Indus river but also only some 10 kilometres from the easternmost extension of the Baluchistan uplands and comprises two main archaeological mounds, A in the east and B in the west. Casal's research demonstrated that the earliest human occupation of the site commenced in the vicinity of 13 metre high Mound A but that its occupants had later spread westwards to include the four metre high Mound B (Casal 1964: 3) (Figure 5.4). The early occupation was termed Period I and was followed by an intermediate Period which was then followed by the Integration Era in Period II. Period I was further subdivided into four distinct phases, of which IA represented the earliest occupation of the site directly above natural soil. Restricted to Mound A, the only structural features identified in Phase IA were the remains of a ditch delineating an area of occupation marked by vessels sunk into old land surfaces, but corroded bronze and copper objects and handmade geometric-painted ceramics, chert blades and terracotta bangles and beads were recovered. This phase was succeeded by Phases IB and IC and, during the latter, occupation

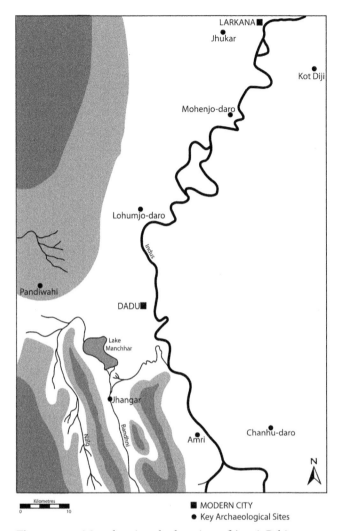

Figure 5.3. Map showing the location of Amri, Pakistan.

expanded to cover both mounds and an area of some 300 metres by 120 metres. The structures of Phases IC and ID were well preserved and comprised a series of cardinally oriented angular mud-brick walls, some on rubble stone footings, defining courtyards and larger rooms which were adjacent to rather distinctive "large compartmented buildings" with walls preserved up to a height of 1.6 metres (Casal 1964: 6). These distinctive buildings were formed by joined cells, which Casal interpreted as "storerooms or godowns" (1964: 6) and are highly reminiscent of the compartmented structures of Mehrgarh but now accompanied by residential ranges (Figure 5.5).

As noted previously, the pottery from the earliest phase was handmade and occurred alongside copper and bronze fragments, and chert tools. During the second phase, the pottery became more distinctive with reference to decoration

Figure 5.4. The site of Amri, Pakistan.

and style and, by the third phase, the pottery was mainly wheel-made with geometric and other decorations, both plain and polychrome. In parallel, the early occurrence of individual post-firing graffiti was succeeded by multiple individual marks in Phase IB, and painted humped bulls and gazelle were noted in Phase ID, presaging common ceramic decorative motifs associated with the Integration Era. The presence of triangular terracotta cakes within Phase ID are also interesting as they again anticipate later Integration Era assemblages, along with terracotta and shell bangles as well as terracotta figurines of humped bulls (Casal 1964: 157). Subsistence evidence from Amri indicates that the diet of its population was dominated by domesticated cattle from the very beginning, along with evidence of marine shellfish and the hunting of wild species.

As there are more than twenty other sites, newly founded during this period, associated with this distinct tradition across part of lower Sindh, including Tharo, Kohtras Buthi, Pandi Wahi and Ghazi Shah (Wright 2010: 99), we may conclude that it represented a second phase of the successful colonisation of the lower Indus plain, completing the earlier process evidenced at Balakot. This phase has long been identified as being developmentally linked to the later Integration Era, as appreciated by one of its perceptive early pioneers: "The earlier pot-fabrics of Amri ... should be looked upon as representing an earlier phase of the Chalcolithic civilisation than that represented by Harappan and Mohenjo-daro, the Indus Civilisation had undoubtedly a long history, and it is possible that the Amri Culture, while co-existent or identical with some of its phases, antedated others" (Majumdar 1934).

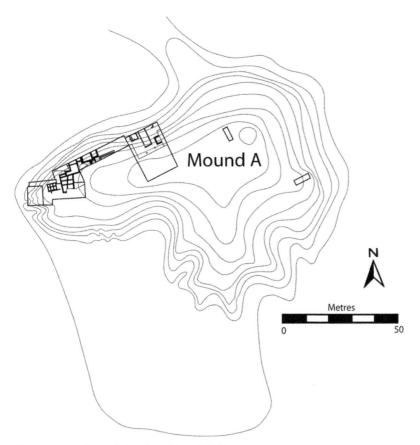

Figure 5.5. Plan of the site of Amri, Pakistan.

THE PUNJAB

Hakra/Ravi Phase (c. 3500–2700 BCE)

To the north of the Amri tradition, another regional ceramic grouping has been identified and termed the Hakra group after the plain where it was first recognised. The Hakra has a distinctive, wheel-made pottery tradition including painted and incised decoration, and covered a wide area from the Indus plain, the site of Sarai Khola in the Taxila Valley, up to sites such as Loebanr III and Bir-kot-ghwandai in the Swat Valley in the foothills of the Hindu Kush (Shaffer 1992: 446). Chronologically, the adoption of Hakra Ware emerged amongst the inhabitants of this region during the latter part of the Amri tradition circa 3500 BCE but continued in patches around the edge of the core of the Indus right up to the middle of the second millennium BCE. Our knowledge of the populations associated with Hakra assemblage is mainly due to the detailed settlement survey of Rafique Mughal within the Cholistan Desert where he identified a total of ninety-nine sites (1997: 40). These ranged from small, temporary camping sites occurring in considerable numbers, along

Figure 5.6. Ravi phase levels on Mound AB at Harappa, Pakistan.

with fewer, larger, permanent villages reaching sizes of around 26 hectares at Lathwala (64 acres). This type of site hierarchy, according to size, and often discriminated by function, continued throughout the succeeding Integration Era, and it is interesting to note that it emerged quite early in the trajectory of this area towards an urbanised state. In these early phases, the presence of two larger settlements of between 20 and 30 hectares (49.4 and 74 acres) dominated a hinterland with nearly forty known smaller sites, which suggests that increasing population agglomeration was achieved although there was a distinct lack of craft specialisation (Mughal 1997: 56). In addition to long blades and flakes, the presence of microliths was notable, occurring as they did alongside terracotta bangles and beads, copper objects and terracotta animal figurines (1997: 68). A closely associated and chronologically similar ceramic assemblage, termed the Ravi, has been recognised in some of the earliest levels at the site of Harappa in levels dating to between 3300 and 2800 BCE (Kenoyer 1997b). Whether the inhabitants would have asserted that they belonged to the same cultural grouping or whether they represented a slightly different localised characteristic is still open to debate (Wright 2010: 83). The evidence from Harappa suggests that the earliest inhabitants were dispersed across the edges of Mounds AB and E and that their structures comprised cardinally oriented huts of posts with plastered reed walls with an absence of mud-brick walls (Figure 5.6). Ceramics

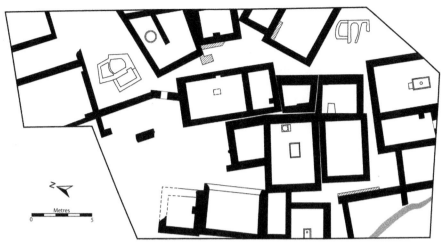

Figure 5.7. Plan of the residential structures at Area A at Mundigak during Period II-3, Afghanistan.

from these lowest levels were handmade but wheel-thrown ceramics were present at the end of the phase, and recent research has highlighted the presence of pre and post-fired graffito as at Amri.

THE HELMAND TRADITION (C. 3500–2800 BCE)

Whilst the populations of the Baluchistan valleys were developing their distinctive regional ceramic assemblages, an apparently separate but parallel transformation was occurring just north of the Indo-Iranian Plateau within the Helmand River basin. Whilst there is no evidence for an early Food Producing Era as at Mehrgarh in Baluchistan, the Helmand region has provided clear evidence of a similar process of Regionalisation (Shaffer 1992: 460). The first represented phase, the Mundigak Phase, has been found at the type-site in the Kuskh-i-Nakhud Rud Valley near Kandahar and has been dated to between 4000 and 3500 BCE. The limited exposures of Mundigak II-3 revealed an absence of residential structures, leading the excavator, J. M. Casal, to suggest seasonal occupation. He also noted a similarity between the handmade and wheel-thrown pottery of this phase and material from the early levels of Kili Gul Muhammad (Figure 5.7). The second phase, the Helmand Phase, has been dated by Shaffer to between 3500 and 2800 BCE (1992: 461) and comprised residential blocks of mud-brick structures separated by open areas with ovens and kilns. This phase also saw the establishment of the site of Shahr-i Sokhta in the fourth millennium BCE, adjacent to the Helmand Delta itself. The first phase of the settlement, Period I, saw its inhabitants occupy an area of between 15 and 17 hectares as they exploited its position on the banks of the Hamun Lake and formalised some of the ancient networks of trade across the borderland. Early evidence of the extent of their networks comes in the form of a Proto-Elamite tablet of Susa type and twenty impressions of proto-Elamite stamp seals (Asthana 1985: 166) as well as finds of marine shell, lapis lazuli and turquoise. The tablet has since been attributed to a late proto-Elamite writing phase, indicative of what Dahal et al. refer to as "a later trajectory that linked Susiana to the southern Zagros and eastern Iran" (2013: 375).

ANTICIPATING INTEGRATION

Kot Diji Phase (c. 3200–2600 BCE)

From the beginning of the fourth millennium BCE, we begin to have access to a more detailed archaeological understanding of settlement across the Indus plain and, in particular, we see one shared tradition clearly emerging from the mass of regional traditions, and coming to dominate a large area across and around the Indus plain. This tradition is known as Kot Dijian, after the type-site Kot Diji, which is located in the Rohri Hills, north-east of Amir and on the east side of the Indus River. Sites with similar material culture assemblages of the same period in what is now north-west India are frequently referred to as the Sothi-Siswal (Wright 2010: 95), although there are distinctions and Sothi wares are largely restricted to Cholistan, north-west Rajasthan, Haryana and the southern Punjab. The Kot Dijian Phase has been dated to between 3200 and 2600 BCE, and its pottery was almost all wheel-made, with a number of distinctive decorative types. These included vessels with plain rings of darkish brown, and this type of design seems to have developed into loops and wavy lines, and then the fish-scale patterns, which are a characteristic Integrated Era Indus motif. Other characteristics of the Kot Dijian style were wheel-thrown globular jars of red ware with everted or flanged rims, and further geometric decorations including fish-scales and intersecting circles, and also patterns of bulls heads, fish and pipal leaves. What is also important to note here is that, along with this distinct 'cultural complex', this phase also provided evidence for the presence of sizeable populations living within formally planned settlements of mud-brick behind fortification or defining walls. Alongside their pottery-shared tradition were stone and bone objects, at least one bronze bangle and terracotta bull figurines, carts and cakes – all of which become characteristic artefacts of the later Integration Era. As noted earlier, the type-site, Kot Diji, was excavated in the 1960s and was found to cover an area of 2.6 hectares during the Kot Dijian Phase (Khan 1965). As also encountered at the sites of Harappa, Rehman Dheri and Kalibangan, the inhabitants of this early 'anchor' centre defined it by constructing a major revetment wall. Unlike the other examples, however, Kot Diji's wall was constructed of mud brick on foundations of rough-limestone blocks, surviving in places to a height of 1.65 metres. The excavator, F. A. Khan, also exposed the presence of buttresses

Figure 5.8. Kot Dijian phase walls around Harappa, Pakistan.

further strengthening the wall, one of which measured 6.1 metres wide and between four and five metres high. Within the walls, mud-brick residential structures were also built on stone foundations, and the artefact assemblage included bone, shell, terracotta and semi-precious stone objects as well as terracotta cakes, figurines and carts (Khan 1965).

This pattern of pre-planned and fortified centres was present across the region at Harappa and Kalibangan as well as Rehman Dheri, close to the Baluchistan uplands. The well-known site of Harappa also contained a Kot Dijian assemblage succeeding the earlier Ravi Phase. This 1.5 metre thick phase, known as Period 2, saw human occupation expand to cover 26 hectares of Mounds AB and E and was notable for its inhabitants' creation of a series of massive parallel mud-brick walls which were exposed on the north-west of Mound E. These retaining walls appear to have run for more than 50 metres from north to south and were 2 metres wide and constructed from bricks measuring 10 × 20 × 40 centimetres in the well-known uniform ratio of 1:2:4 which dominated the later Integration Era (Kenoyer 1991a: 29–60). Kenoyer has interpreted these walls as the product of mobilisation of group labour far beyond an individual basis and has suggested that they "may represent some form of Early Harappan social organisation capable of mobilizing and controlling the production of large quantities of bricks as well as the labour involved in wall construction" (1991a: 47) (Figure 5.8). He has also suggested that the presence of Kot Dijian sherds under one of the massive walls exposed by Wheeler along the western edge of Mound AB may indicate that both mounds were walled at the same time. The creation of such walls also separated space, creating two distinct domains and surely accelerated differentiation between those people living within and those beyond the new barriers. The excavations have also identi- fied the presence of specialist kilns for stoneware bangles, again a mainstay of the Integration Era, and ceramic vessels as well as the presence of a cardi- nally oriented street marked with cart tracks to the southern edge of Mound E. Furthermore, the report of large mud-brick platforms also indicated what Wright refers to as "fairly large-scale community activities" (Wright 2010: 87). Networks of communication linking Harappa with the communities to the south were evidenced by the presence of dried or salted marine fish (Belcher 2003: 161) and marine shell bangles from the Arabian Sea and tan-brown chert from the Rohri Hills (Kenoyer 1991a: 47). Forerunners of the material culture of the Integration Era Indus cities included a single cubic stone weight and a single sealing bearing a 'unicorn' motif (Wright 2010: 89). Further standardi- sation has been identified in the broad use of mud bricks using a 1:2:4 ratio and also within spindle whorls (Kenoyer 2010) and may indicate that some inhabitants had taken up occupational specialisation beyond household mode of production.

The site of Kalibangan offers another example of an urban Integration Era Indus site with a proto-urban sequence established during the Kot Dijian Phase (Box 5.2). Situated close to a bend of the old Ghaggar channel, B. B. Lal exposed the presence of a cardinally oriented settlement measuring some 250 metres by 180 metres and defined by a 1.9 metre thick mud-brick wall (Lal 2003). With an entrance on the north, the wall was built of bricks measuring 30 × 20 × 10 centimetres and both inner and outer faces were plastered. The interior space of 4.5 hectares appeared to have contained cardinally oriented residential structures, built of mud brick of similar dimensions, and the remains of drains constructed of baked brick for water proofing were also exposed. The excavations indicated that its inhabitants had access to chalcedony and agate blades, objects of semi-precious stone, terracotta and bronze as well as terra- cotta bulls, carts and figurines.

Whilst the evidence of the construction of pre-planned sites is clear from the example of Kalibangan, the interior areas exposed through archaeological excavation were limited in size, and it is the site of Rehman Dheri in the Gomal Valley which offers the best understanding of the interior of sites in this period (Box 5.3). Rehman Dheri was first identified by A. H. Dani in 1971, who noted that erosion patterns on an aerial photograph of the site demonstrated "the ruins of a well-designed city making a rough parallelogram (Figure 5.9). The water channels that have been cut all follow a rigid pattern of parallel lines and it seems that these channels follow the old lines of street alignments" (Dani 1971: 28). Later surveyed and excavated by F. A. Durrani in the 1970s, 1980s and 1990s, the site was found to be a roughly cardinally oriented rectangle, measuring 500 metres by 325 metres, with a very pronounced division into

Box 5.2. Kalibangan

The site of Kalibangan is situated on the banks of the now dry Ghaggar River, some 200 kilometres south-east of Harappa, in north-western India (Lal 2003). Period I at Kalibangan has been dated to between circa 2920 and 2550 BCE, and during this early Regionalisation Era the extent of the site has been estimated as four hectares. Right from the early occupation, the site was surrounded by a massive mud-brick rampart, and although it has been speculated that this was built for protection, possibly from flood, wild animals or marauding tribes, the reasons behind this monumental building activity are not yet clear. Dried brick and stone were used for both domestic structures and the fortification wall, and there was a clear standardisation of the brick sizes used, in a ratio of 1:2:3. Although this ratio is slightly different to that found at sites from the Integrated Era of the Indus Valley Tradition, researchers have argued that the use of standard brick sizes is a good precursor of the homogeneity to come (Kenoyer 1991b: 347).

Hearths were uncovered within many house rooms, and one house had series of ovens. There were also lime-plastered storage pits, and saddle querns, indicating the importance of agriculture to the development of urbanism. This was greatly reinforced by the discovery of a field surface dated to Period I, with furrows indicative of the presence of ploughed fields to the south of the settlement area. Other artefacts recovered from Kalibangan included large numbers of stone tools, including many serrated blades, terracotta cakes and copper objects, including a copper bangle and flat axes. Shell bangles were numerous, as were beads made from steatite, faience, and also carnelian, gold and silver. Pottery from this early period was distinctively local, although analysis has also shown that there were some stylistic and decorative similarities with some Kot Dijian material (Lal 2003).

Kalibangan was occupied through into the Integrated Era without a clear hiatus or cultural transformation, but the site's layout was remodelled to include a higher walled 'citadel' zone and a lower town zone. This layout is shared by many sites of this period, including Mohenjo-daro, but Kalibangan's 'citadel' contained a unique range of seven structures identified by its excavator as fire altars (Lal 2003). An additional altar on a neighbouring platform associated with a clay-lined pit containing ash, charcoal and terracotta indicated to some researchers that "fire and water rituals as well as animal sacrifices were conducted" (Ratnagar 1991: 119). Kalibangan's 'Indus' layout will be discussed further in the next chapter.

Box 5.3. Rehman Dheri

Rehman Dheri shows clear evidence for an early planned settlement and, for this reason, is important in understanding incipient urbanism during the Era of Regionalisation. The site is located in the very south of Khyber-Pakhtunkhwa Province in Pakistan, on the west bank of the Indus River, and was excavated between 1976 and 1981 by a joint team from the Department of Archaeology, University of Peshawar and the Department of Archaeology and Museums, Government of Pakistan, under the direction of Professor Fazand Ali Durrani, with a further season in 1991 which included Dr George Erdosy from the University of Toronto. These excavations demonstrated that the site was first established circa 3300 BCE and aerial photographs illustrate the presence of a rigid grid pattern to the streets, which is indicative of very formal town planning. Rehman Dheri is not only the earliest example of planned urban form in South Asia but it is also one of the best preserved. Today, it is possible to see streets and individual buildings, and even concentrations of craft working debris on the surface of the site. Rehman Dheri takes the form of a large mound surrounded by a fortification wall, and the town is divided by a main street running from north-west to south-east. The settlement covers an area of some 550 × 400 metres (22 hectares), and a population of around 12,000 people has been estimated (Durrani 1988; Durrani et al. 1991; 1995).

Rehman Dheri is also important because it shows continuity from early occupation through to the Era of Regionalisation, alternatively referred to as the Kot Dijian or Early Harappan period, and excavations have shown that the town wall and layout of the streets were in place from the earliest occupation, around 3300 BCE. This continuity is apparent when we look not only at issues such as planned proto-urban and urban settlements, but also in material culture. Pottery is one of the most commonly found and analysed examples of material culture, and the development of designs from sites such as Kili Gul Muhammad and Kot Diji with specific motifs, such as the bull and certain types of geometric patterns, are found across a number of sites over time. Early levels at Rehman Dheri had a local style of pottery, and then by the later phases of the site Kot Dijian pottery dominated. Throughout the pottery sequence there were many sherds displaying graffiti and it has been suggested that they may have been a precursor to the Indus script.

The excavators of Rehman Dheri reported finds of wheat and barley, and the bones of cattle, sheep, goat, and fish. House structures from the earliest period were reported to contain packed mud and clay plaster 'silos' or storage containers for agricultural products. The excavators reached this interpretation on the basis of botanical materials recovered from the silos, and this of course points towards the importance of agriculture and agricultural surplus in the establishment of the town. In the second period of occupation, these silos were replaced by large storage jars, many buried upright to a quarter of their height in the house floors.

Artefacts from Rehman Dheri include beads made of lapis lazuli and turquoise and, as the nearest known source of lapis is in Afghanistan to the north-west of the site, this indicates both long-distance trade and contact and an awareness of the importance of 'exotic' materials. Sources of turquoise include Afghanistan, northern India and Turkestan, although Mashhad in north-eastern Iran remains one of the most important sources for good quality turquoise in significant quantities. In turn, this could indicate an emerging social hierarchy and differential access to certain goods for particular groups (Durrani 1988; Durrani et al. 1991; 1995).

A seal was recovered from the early period at Rehman Dheri, which has interesting implications for recording and trade. The seal was made from bone and engraved on one side with scorpions and what has been interpreted as a female figure, and two goats on the other. Early terracotta figurines are similar to those from Gumla and Mehrgarh Period IV; however, the form of these figurines changes in the latter two periods of occupation, and they become distinctively 'Rehman Dheri' in style (Durrani 1988).

One of the reasons Rehman Dheri is so well preserved is because there is no later city constructed over the Kot Dijian and earlier phases. The main occupation here ended circa 2500 BCE, but settlement continued in a much contracted form until 1900 BCE.

northern and southern halves (Durrani et al. 1991: 66). Durrani's excavations demonstrated that the 16 hectare settlement had been walled from the earliest occupation and that the wall sat on a five metre wide foundation which had been cut 0.3 metres into the natural soil; the wall itself was constructed of dressed blocks of clay slab. Durrani's excavations also demonstrated that the mud-brick and clay block walls of the earliest residential occupation of the site respected the parallel orientation of the town walls, further supporting the concept that the settlement followed a planned outline. Individual wheat and barley grain silos were noted within the structures of this initial phase and finds included the site's earliest seal. Whilst a number of the decorated sherds shared the repertoire of the Kot Dijian, such as terracotta cakes and carts as well as the 'horned deity', pipal leaves and fish-scale motifs, the presence of scorpions is notable, especially as they are also present on a unique ivory seal from Period IB, but as Durrani noted they did not survive into the Integration Era (Durrani 1981). This latter point is important as this emergent process of integration did

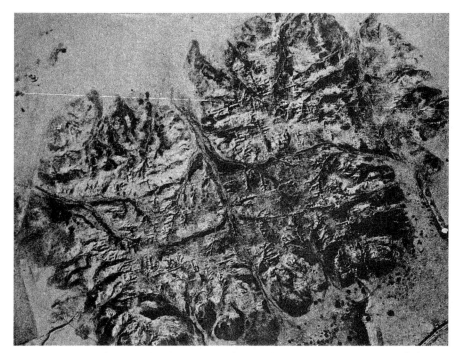

Figure 5.9. Air photograph of Rehman Dheri, Pakistan (courtesy Bridget Allchin).

not absorb and retain every aspect of the regional impulses. Later investigations at the site identified the presence of a heavily eroded mud-brick platform 50 metres inside the defensive wall on the western side of the town (Durrani et al. 1991: 75). It measured 22 by 6.4 metres and was associated with bone and lapis lazuli amulets and seals, suggesting to the excavators that it may have provided the foundations for a public structure (Durrani et al. 1991: 67). They also confirmed a concentration of kilns, marking an industrial zone in the western part of the mound, as well as four separate lapidary areas across the site (Durrani 1995: 5). The recovery of 314 inscribed sherds led the excavation team to suggest that "several signs may be treated as antecedents to the signs found in the Harappan script and this is reinforced by the impression … that the signs were written right to left" (Durrani 1995: 217). It is still possible to see lines of walls and streets if one visits the site early in the morning as dew clusters on the lines of ancient brickwork forming a visual impression of the old town layout (Figure 5.10).

Of course, not all Kot Dijian sites were fortified proto-urban sites, and there are numerous examples of individual village settlements. For example, the village site of Gumla, some eight kilometres to the south of Rehman Dheri, covered an area of 0.5 hectares and was investigated by A. H. Dani (1971). The total sequence at the site was six metres in depth and, of this, only 1.2 metres has been identified as contemporary with the Kot Dijian levels at

Figure 5.10. Building visible on surface at Rehman Dheri, Pakistan.

Rehman Dheri. Another important source of information about Kot Dijian settlement patterns is derived from the survey work conducted by Rafique Mughal in the Cholistan Desert (Figure 5.11). Mughal recorded ninety-nine sites belonging to the preceding Hakra Phase but this number then declined to forty in the Kot Dijian phase. However, within this decline the number of seasonal camping sites dipped sharply from fifty-two to three; they had accounted for half of all sites in the Hakra phase, but they now accounted for only 7.5 percent of all sites (Mughal 1997: 44–53). It was also notable that there was a shift in location of permanent sites between the Hakra and Kot Dijian phases, these permanent sites shifted in location from the preceding Phase and a far greater number, more than a third, were associated with specialised craft and industrial activities. This settlement specialisation was also accompanied by the emergence of a three-tiered settlement hierarchy in which 60 percent of sites covered areas of less than 5 hectares, 25 percent of sites covered between 5 and 10 hectares and four sites covered areas between 19 and 27 hectares (Mughal 1997: 45). The largest site, Gamanwala, covered just under 30 hectares, while the second largest site, Jalwali, was almost the same size as Rehman Dheri, demonstrating the presence of large agglomerated populations at the peak of the Cholistan settlement grouping. Although not as clearly differentiated, similar surveys around the Chenab, Ravi and Beas Rivers on the upper Indus have also revealed three-tiered settlement hierarchies as well as a further 165 sites around the Ghaggar-Hakra River in north-west India (Wright 2010: 90–91). A cluster of twenty sites was recorded in the Dubi complex to the south of Kot Diji itself as well as at Amri (Casal

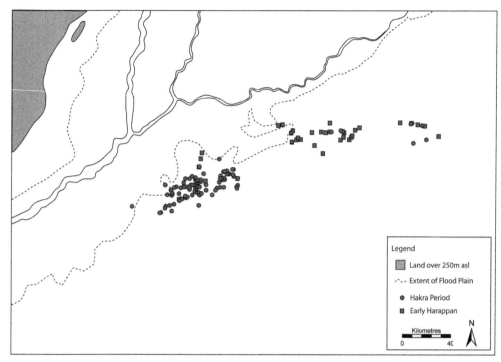

Figure 5.11. Map showing settlement patterns in Cholistan during the Regionalisation Era.

1964). Cultural links have also been made to clusters of slightly more peripheral sites, including Lewan, Tarakai Qila and Islam Chowki in the Bannu Basin (Thomas 2003: 406), Hathial in the Taxila Valley as well as further north in the Swat Valley and Kashmir (Morigi and Bianchetti 2005: 229). Finally, reference should be made to Gujarat, which later formed a distinct part of the Era of Integration of the Indus Valley Tradition. The Era of Regionalisation in this region also shows broad similarities with the presence of terracotta cakes and standardised mud brick (Shinde 1998) at Padri, Kuntasi, and even in the lower levels at Dholavira (Singh 2008: 145).

CONCLUSIONS

John Marshall is frequently credited with the 'discovery' of the Indus Civilisation, or at least being the first person in the recent past to recognise the significance of its remains. Indeed, as noted in Chapter 3, when he returned to England in the late 1920s, it was said of him that he left India 3,000 years older than he found it. He also left considerable debate as to the origins of the Indus Civilisation. Marshall himself was struck by the South Asian character of the great cities that he had excavated, believing that he could identify strong parallels between past and present structures and layout; indeed he even photographed their ancient streets filled with local inhabitants for scale

(1931a). This South Asian character appealed to other archaeologists, but they were also aware that there were no known antecedents for the civilisation in this region and so looked westwards. As a result, early researchers such as Stuart Piggott and Mortimer Wheeler were unable to find convincing evidence for increasing complexity or incipient urban-focused developments in the valleys and plains around the major cities of Mohenjo-daro and Harappa, so they turned their sights to the west and the great cities of Mesopotamia as the key source for the origins of urbanism and the state in South Asia (Piggott 1950). Wheeler noted the similarities between these two great civilisations, such as their 'urban way of life', their 'civic consciousness' and grid-iron urban plans, and as he was also aware of the greater age of Mesopotamia, he suggested that the communities of the Indus basin had benefited from the diffusion of the 'idea of civilisation' from the west (Wheeler 1953). Such conclusions were also shared by other archaeologists, with D. H. Gordon suggesting that immigrants from Western Asia had brought knowledge of "civilized living" and "were able by their drive and vision to establish within the matter of a hundred or so years the pattern of a culture which was to ensure for a thousand." (1960: 58). He also denied the possibilities of indigenous development stating that "No future search is going to bring to light either in India or some adjacent country a Harappan city site, where the constituents of this culture can be shown to have evolved for millennia, parallel to but separate from the development of Sumer, Elam and ancient Iran." (ibid.)

Despite Gordon's certainty, as we saw earlier, increased and varied archaeological exploration from the 1970s onward dramatically altered the way in which the origins and development of the Indus Civilisation are understood. Of primary importance was the identification of a distinctive proto-urban phase, which clearly demonstrated that the planned cities of the 'mature period' Indus Civilisation were not suddenly produced as a result of contact with city dwellers and builders to the west, but were constructed within an earlier context of experimental settlement and planning (Mughal 1990). For example, the site of Rehman Dheri, located in Kyber Pakhtunkhwa Province of north-western Pakistan is thought to be one of the earliest formally pre-planned urban agglomerations in South Asia (Durrani 1988). Its initial phases have been dated to between 3300 and 3200 BCE and it appears at a time very similar to that of the contemporary foundation of Shahr-i Sokhta on the Indo-Iranian plateau to the west (Tosi 1983) (Figure 5.12). The nature of this internal sequence is also paralleled by findings at Harappa and Kalibangan, all of which contributes towards the weakening of arguments of diffusion. The discovery of Mehrgarh in the 1970s was of equal, if not greater significance, as the material and sequence there pushed the cultural traditions for the development of the Indus Tradition back to the seventh millennium BCE and into the pre-pottery Neolithic, as well as presenting a stronger case for the indigenous development of many of the features which later became key to the Indus

Figure 5.12. The site of Shahr-i Sokhta, Iran.

urban-focused development, including the domestication of certain plants and animals, as discussed in Chapter 4 (Jarrige 1984; Meadow 1984a; 1989).

More than thirty years after Rafique Mughal renamed the 'Pre-Indus' cultures 'Early Indus' and more than twenty years after Jim Shaffer reclassified the period as an Era of Regionalisation, we are finally in a position to be able to begin to understand this process. It is now clear that the early Neolithic villagers of the Baluchistan uplands were able to thrive and expand as they exploited the alluvial fans of the narrow valleys and created *gabarbands* to curate excess silt and water. This, combined with their presence on a series of major continental trade routes for the movement of non-perishable goods, such as marine shell and semi-precious stone as well as perishables, permitted and promoted a steady expansion as well as the creation of a series of key population agglomerations. Their villages, such as Mehrgarh III, became major centres for craft activities, and their ceramic assemblages began to spread in popularity over substantial areas of Baluchistan. This period, the Kili Gul Muhammad Phase (4300–3500 BCE), also witnessed evidence for the continued colonisation of the Indus Plain itself as indicated by the evidence from Balakot. The succeeding periods in the uplands, the Kechi Beg and Damb Sadaat Phases (3500–2600 BCE) hosted the transformation of these agglomerated sites of craft specialisation into sites with semi-industrialised production, compartmentalised stamp seals and monumental communal structures, such as the platform and drain at Damb Sadaat II and the platform at Mehrgarh VII. Such structures represented the outcomes of communal activities and may be assumed to have been central to community meetings and perhaps ceremony. Moreover, despite the increasing size and complexity of the settlements, the lack of individuality within them suggests that strong preferences for common identities and values were already apparent. It is equally tempting to suggest that these community-level outcomes, the platforms, may have hosted community-focused activities which bound the populations of individual households together and counterbalanced the centrifugal effect of the privatisation of surplus. It may be further anticipated that these were shared but reinforced and maintained by authority, although whether this was through elders, priests or chiefs is unknown. The focus on monuments associated with drains and perhaps bathing and water, echoes a number of the later practices of the Integrated Era. Often distinct tell site features within the landscape, it is plausible to suggest that such settlements also began to act as what Akkermans and Schwartz have called "anchor sites" which "were invested with considerable social and ritual meaning" for their neighbours (2004: 150). With reference to authority, it is possible to equate the economies of such settlements as based on a model whereby surplus staples were collected and stored and then used to support communal activities. Of course, these developments did not take place in a vacuum, and a growth of population and societal complexity and in settlement size occurred in parallel in the Helmand Basin and also on the Indus Plain itself. The early occupation of Balakot was succeeded by the wider colonisation of the lower Indus during the succeeding Amri Phase (3600–3000 BCE), which itself had strong cultural links to the Baluchistan uplands, including a tradition of the use of compartmentalised structures well known at Mehrgarh. This distinct southern ceramic tradition then developed into the more broadly distributed Hakra tradition (3500–2700 BCE) in the vicinity of Cholistan and Harappa, and its users were further differentiated by the emergence of three-tiered settlement hierarchies.

All of this existed, however, as a prelude to the popularity, expansion and adoption of the Kot Dijian material culture, with associated ideas and emerging social and political developments, across the lower Indus, the western flanks of central Baluchistan and the Punjab between 3200 and 2600 BCE. The new evidence from Balathal in Rajasthan suggests that some farmers must have already successfully colonised the eastern alluvium by 3000 BCE (Madella and Fuller 2006: 1297). The movement to the plain area which was rich in fertile alluvium but poor in raw resources also necessitated the organisation of further networks of distribution and redistribution. Confronted by a similar imbalance in Mesopotamia, Guillermo Algaze has stressed that increasingly complex societies based on the alluvium had to access a significantly wider resource base, otherwise they "could neither develop further nor maintain themselves in the long term" (2005: xii). There is evidence to support such a hypothesis for the Era of Regionalisation, as Kenoyer has argued that trade between coastal and inland sites like Harappa began in the Kot Dijian period (2800–2600 BCE) on the basis of his analysis of shell-working (1997a: 275), and Biagi and

Starnini have suggested that the flint sources in the Rohri Hills in upper Sindh were already exploited at this time, a pattern which was to continue into the Integrated Era (2008: 81). A similar transference was of the basic weight system, in the words of Kenoyer, "the system developed by the Early Harappans became widely adopted during the Harappan Period" (2010: 116). For the first time, we find widespread evidence of formally tiered settlement hierarchies complete with specialised craft settlements, and while the larger agglomeration of population also appear to have possessed the communal mud-brick platforms known from earlier phases, they were now placed within what appear to be planned and walled settlements. In direct contrast with earlier practices, it appears that intramural burials ceased during this phase and the transition to distinct extramural cemeteries must have occurred and, with it, far greater visibility for the dead during funerary practices as well as far greater separation from the living.

Using analogies with functions associated with Early Historic examples, it is possible that the newly walled residents may have fashioned their barriers to protect against floods or marauders, or to compete with other centres or to recreate the universe; however, the organisation of the labour and the bricks must have needed a heightened social organisation as well as sufficient surplus labour and food. The shared ceramic designs across this vast area also seem to be shared with the presence of uniform brick ratios, suggesting a common concept of space and measurement – the presence of a single stone cube at Harappa also seems to hint that the precise weight system of the Integration Era cities was already anticipated. Similarly, the presence of compartmentalised seals across Baluchistan and the Indus Plains, accompanied as they were by non-scriptural graffiti, suggests that recording and ownership was becoming more important as was the recording of value and designation of individual ownership. As Spencer has suggested, if chiefdoms were increasingly centralised but not bureaucratic, their authority was limited geographically (2010: 7119). Once equipped with "internally specialised administrative organisation", that is, bureaucracy, they were able to undertake territorial expansion (ibid.). It is also notable that from the Ravi Phase onwards at Harappa, terracotta carts and wheels have been recovered, indicating the use of full-sized carts which would have provided a technical means for a greater scale of sharing "grain, wood, stone and other bulk commodities" (Kenoyer 2004: 94). Finally, the presence of shared norms for terracotta figurines, drains, terracotta carts and cakes, as well as the shared presence of the 'horned deity' motif across this huge area, suggests the presence of a converging ideology and, again at Harappa, the presence of a seal with the 'unicorn' suggests a pervasive continuity of cult, belief and tradition.

Precisely at this time of integration and transformation within the Indus Plains, similar transformative processes were at work within the Helmand Basin to the north-west, also beginning a somewhat earlier process of Integration

Figure 5.13. Seals from Rehman Dheri, Pakistan.

than that of the Indus between 2800 and 2300 BCE during the Shahr-i Sokhta Phase (Shaffer 1992: 462). At Mundigak IV, the site grew to 32 hectares and there was a period of general levelling on Mound A followed by the construction of surrounding walls with buttresses and bastions enclosing two monumental structures. The first was a 'palace' structure with a formal monumental exterior wall faced with pilasters, and the second, a 'temple' structure with a shrine. No such monumental structures were identified in this period at Shahr-i Sokhta, but that settlement reached a size of 45 hectares and the position of being a major industrial and exchange node. Shaffer has suggested that the key role in the development of these trade networks and interactions spheres was filled by mobile pastoralists undertaking their seasonal migrations (1978: 153).

As noted in the Introduction, despite this long developmental sequence for the Indus basin, it should be recognised that there are still many differences between the 20 hectare (49 acre) settlement of Rehman Dheri and the vast 200 hectare metropolis of Mohenjo-daro, for example. This suggests that the social and economic mechanisms for preventing fission at a particular maximum size of settlement had not yet been sufficiently developed but also may reflect the fact that readily available land and water resources were still available for pioneering sections of society. A similar difference exists between the stamp seals and non-scriptural graffiti of the proto-urban phase or Regionalisation Era and the Integrated Indus Era script and seals (Figure 5.13). There was also a notably different site distribution between the Kot Dijian and the cities of the Integration Era. While populations adopting Kot Dijian phase assemblages thrived in parts of Pakistan's Khyber Pakhtunkhwa Province to the west of the Indus River, there were very few settlements of the Integrated Era of the Indus Valley Tradition in that region. This physical shift in settlement is a theme which we will return to again in the third section of this book, when we examine the urban-focused developments of the Early Historic period, and recognise that these two major urban-focused developments do not mimic each other in terms of mapping their geographical locations.

Similarly, the early proto-urban sites were not uniform in character, and whilst both Kalibangan and Rehman Dheri's architects designed settlements which were rectangular and clearly oriented north to south, Harappa's appear to have constructed two separated walled mounds. The mechanisms driving the transformations and changes that led from proto-urban settlements to large, urban sites within a complex state-level society are not well understood and there is still debate as to whether this initial process was achieved through coercion. Interestingly, in sharp contrast to this early process of integration reaching the Kot Dijian, there appears to have been a notable transformation at a number of sites during the transition from the Kot Dijian to the Integrated Era in the centuries between 2800 and 2600 BCE. For example, brick proportions remained constant at Harappa whilst they changed at both Kalibangan and Banawali (Kenoyer 1991b: 347). More significantly perhaps, at Kot Diji, the type site, a distinct 'burnt level' between the Kot Dijian levels and those of the 'Mature' Harappan was recorded and the sequence at Amri offered a parallel transition with Period I and Period III, belonging to the integrated Indus Tradition, separated by an intermediate PII (Casal 1964: 6). Represented by a major levelling phase associated with both Amri and "Harappan types of pottery", Casal also noted the presence of blackish and ashy levels, although he also noted that "it is difficult to say whether this occurrence should be interpreted as evidence of some sort of violence or of a fire" (1964: 7). Similarly, at Gumla in the Gomal Valley, Dani recorded the presence of a thick layer of ash separating the Kot Dijian levels of Period III from the Period IV, the Integration Era, stating that "The end of this period appears to be violent" but that "[t]he reoccupation of the site must have been started soon after destruction. There is a continuity in the cultural tradition and at the same time new cultural elements were introduced from outside" (1971: 40–41). Similar discontinuities have been recorded at Balakot, Nausharo and Kalibangan (Possehl 2002a: 48–49). Possehl also noted that the Sindh settlement survey data demonstrated that thirty-three of the thirty-seven Kot Dijian sites were abandoned, and of the new Integrated Era sites, as many as 132 of the new 136 settlements were established on virgin land (Possehl 2002a: 48–49). However, at Harappa there was a picture of gradual continuum without "major hiatus or cultural break" (Kenoyer 1991a: 49), although Kenoyer suggested that the process was not peaceful everywhere stating that "the process of urbanisation and cultural integration in the Indus Valley probably did result in battles over control of resources and the destruction of some villages" (1998: 42). This conclusion echoes some of the earlier observations of Ratnagar, who suggested that the process of integration of the 'Sothi-Siswal' settlements was not through diffusion or "a gradual incorporation of the communities into a wide spread trade network. Instead, the threat or use of force must have compelled the temporary desertion of settlements and the overall change in the distribution and use of house plots" (1991: 84).

There are scholars who have attributed this general development to the movement of people from the now densely populated uplands of Baluchistan, suggesting that "the pressure of growing populations in comparatively restricted hilly tracts for agricultural pursuits pressed them in the last quarter of the fourth millennium BC to move into the plains. They came in the Indus Basin in different waves and several groups, often intermingling in different proportions, that is absolutely clear from the pottery assemblages" (Asthana 1985: 79). This postulated migration certainly coincided with a sharp decline in settlement within the Quetta Valley as recorded by Fairservis who stated that "[t]he reasons for this decline are unknown. No traces of violence have so far been identified. The existing sites, however, tend to be concentrated in the fertile plain where Quetta City is located. This may indicate a decrease of water sources ordinarily accessible to the population" (Fairservis 1956: 359). Shaffer and Liechtenstein have also suggested that a deteriorating climate led to independent ethnic groups defending their own resources and negotiating access to resources beyond their territories, thus rapidly fusing together (1989). Durrani et al. further developed this model by suggesting that the well-established "circulation of prestige goods was vital to the performance of rituals, and thus essential for the smooth functioning of society" and that over time this generated an emergent ruling class whose growing inequality led to greater need for intensive communications and the circulation of yet more prestige goods (1995: 91). However, the climatic information is by no means certain and is subject to review and, most recently, Madella and Fuller have suggested that agricultural surpluses were increased by periods of higher precipitation in the period leading up to urbanisation and may have encouraged the movement of communities down onto the alluvium (2006: 1297). They also observed that "[w]hile higher rainfall levels of the fourth millennium BC may have promoted the more widespread adoption of cultivation and sedentary settlement, subsequent decline in rainfall may have contributed to growing population density in certain regions" (Madella and Fuller 2006: 1297). Furthermore, they suggest that "[i]ncreasing aridity could have promoted further agricultural intensification efforts, requiring mobilisation of labour, and consequent landscape modification" (Madella and Fuller 2006: 1298).

Perhaps, these drivers towards societal coordination played a major role in the agglomeration of settlement and the process of urbanisation. It is also possible that the increasing agglomeration of a selected number of sites, or incipient urbanisation for want of a better term, had the connected effect of drawing population from across Baluchistan to join these steadily differentiating populations. Yoffee has called this process 'ruralisation' (1997: 260), and it is also possible that increasing demands for raw materials and perhaps even meat or wool increasingly set the two adjacent but asymmetric areas, the uplands and the alluvium, on increasingly divergent courses. Those settlements which differentiated themselves through agglomerated population were also equipped with the necessary staple and labour surplus to invest in surrounding walls and thus further differentiated themselves and their ways of life. Linked through an increasingly shared cultural and ideological perspective, or per-haps 'civilisation', such centres undoubtedly engaged in the process of peer polity interaction and further differentiated themselves (Renfrew and Cherry 1986). The resultant "competition (including warfare), and competitive emu-lation; symbolic entrainment, and the transition of innovations; and increased flow in the exchange of goods" (Renfrew 1986: 1) reflected the interaction between these walled centres but most probably also reflected the dynamics played out within each walled centre as intramural elites also engaged with one another. However, only further excavations of the quality and detail of the joint Pakistan-American team at Harappa, for example, and the wider use of chronometric and palaeoenvironmental dating will shed light on this, the most critical phase of the development of the Indus Civilisation. To conclude, we quote S. P. Gupta who wrote that "urban growth of the Indus kind is usu-ally so sudden and quick that within a generation or two, it may spread over a vast area, but the archaeological tool as applied to our protohistoric sites is too blunt to bring out the evidence of this kind" (1978: 144). Archaeological methods and interpretative theories have developed since the late 1970s, and great progress has been made in both obtaining data about this critical period of urban origins and in developing explanatory models. However, a great deal of refinement is needed before we can be entirely confident about the asym-metric trajectories of complexity in all the regions discussed earlier and how (and indeed if) they intersect.

CHAPTER 6

AN ERA OF INTEGRATION: THE INDUS CIVILISATION (c. 2600–1900 BCE)

INTRODUCTION

The Indus Civilisation has been frequently characterised as an example of great standardisation and uniformity, whether this refers to its settlement plans, artefact forms or ceramic motifs (Wheeler 1953). This type of characterisation has been repeated so often that it has now become received wisdom and is widely accepted by many scholars in this field, as well as by those comparing Old World Civilisations more broadly. However, as we will demonstrate in the course of this chapter, whilst there are many aspects of material culture from this Integrated Era that are remarkably similar over a very wide geographical and chronological range, recent research has demonstrated that this homogeneity is by no means as complete or absolute as has been presented in the past. The Integration Era, or Mature Indus period as it is more widely known, when urbanisation and other traits associated with state-level societies were at their peak, is generally agreed to have lasted some 700 years from circa 2600 to 1900 BCE. Whether this very long duration was as seamless and uniform as has been presented by a number of earlier researchers is another aspect of the Indus Valley Tradition that we will consider, asking just how much internal change and development occurred within this integrated period? When compared with the other early states such as Dynastic Egypt, Akkadian Mesopotamia and Shang China, it becomes clear that not only did the Indus Valley Civilisation integrate a huge area during this Era, but its settlements were located in a very diverse range of environmental settings. This indicates that a key element of this debate is whether we can distinguish differences within the artefact assemblages and settlements of these different settings.

We will consider some of the recent research on the Indus Civilisation in this chapter and also present evidence for the nature and form of the urban and rural sites, including evidence for the centralisation of surplus, writing, long-distance trade, planning, monumental buildings and public works, craft and settlement specialisation, and subsistence patterns. We will evaluate this evidence and its support for both similarity and difference across the wider Indus

region, throughout the duration of the Integrated Era. One of the ongoing
debates concerning the Indus region relates to the nature of social organisation as some archaeologists have questioned whether this phenomenon can be
understood as a cluster of city-states, or indeed whether it hosted states at all
(Possehl 1998). Can the Indus be described and explained according to traditional models of empire (Piggott 1950; Wheeler 1953) or should we be looking at models of competition among different groups to find the origins and
stimuli (Kenoyer 1998)? Some scholars rely on normative concepts of wealth
and hierarchy in their definitions of complex societies, and suggest that the
absence of palaces, royal burials, or clear evidence for an elite segment of society on the grounds of wealth and status marks a more fundamental difference
in social organisation (Coningham and Manuel 2009a; Fairservis 1986; Miller
1985; Rissman 1988). Once the evidence has been presented and explained, we
will then consider fit with explanatory models of social organisation, attempting to indicate which are the most satisfactory.

PHYSICAL SPREAD AND SETTING

At its peak, which is synonymous with its greatest extent and greatest
urban-based population, the Integration Era of the Indus Valley Tradition
covered an area of 3,133,886 square kilometres (Wright 2010) (Figure 6.1)
(Timeline 6.1). This is twenty times the size of Egypt and ten times the size of
Mesopotamia, two other contemporary Old World Civilisations. Integration
Era settlements stretched from the Makran Coast in the south-west, close to
the border of the modern states of Pakistan and Iran, to New Delhi in the
north-east and from Afghanistan in the north to Gujarat in the south-east.
Although the Indus Civilisation clearly extended far beyond the eponym-
ous river, one of the defining features of the north-west of the Indian subcontinent is the Indus River itself, which runs north to south from the
Hindu Kush mountain range to the Arabian Sea, effectively bisecting the
modern state of Pakistan. Running parallel to the Indus River in antiquity
was the Ghaggar-Hakra or Sarasvati River, which is now dry. Although now
divided between Pakistan and the Indian states of Gujarat and Rajasthan,
the settlements of the Integrated Era both surrounded the river itself, and
extended far beyond it. Its two main river systems were fed by snow melt
from the Himalayan and Hindu Kush ranges, leading to summer flooding
across the alluvial plain, which provided not only a reliable source of irrigation but also leaving pools and lakes which provided water for people and
animals alike.

The Indus River still brings immense quantities of silt with it down from
the mountains and hills which are deposited on lower lying ground. A number
of scholars have noted that these soft, deep very fertile soils could have been
cultivated by people without metal tools, and this has been considered an

Figure 6.1. Map of sites mentioned in Chapter 6.

important factor in explaining why this region was the site of South Asia's first 'civilisation' rather than the Gangetic region to the east (Allchin and Allchin 1982; Scarre and Fagan 1997: 120). Indeed, the Gangetic basin is one of the regions where urban-focused state-level societies appeared in the early first millennium BCE, coinciding with the large-scale appearance of iron and iron tools in the archaeological record of South Asia (see Chapter 10). The soils of the Gangetic area are described as black cotton soils, and many scholars have claimed that they were too hard and difficult to cultivate without the wide-spread availability of metal tools (Kosambi 1956) although this is increasingly questioned.

However, within the huge area incorporated by the Integrated Era of the Indus Valley Tradition there was a range of different environments where

The Indus Civilisation Timeline

Timeline 6.1. Timeline for Chapter 6.

smaller settlements as well as towns and cities were established, and the apparent uniformity of material culture was thus all the more surprising and striking. These environments ranged from the Kachi Plain of Baluchistan at the interface of upland passes and the Indus plain with the arid Makran coastal belt, the hot and arid Indus Delta, Gujarat and Kutch and the rich alluvium of the Punjab. Clearly there was great diversity within the environmental setting of the Indus; whether this shaped individual people, sites, settlement or regions is open to debate, and would require a detailed analysis of many variables from a whole range of sites. What we will do here is examine a representative selection of sites, both urban and rural from across the extent of the Indus and discuss the significance of any discernible patterns.

HISTORY OF DISCOVERY AND INTERPRETATION

The presence of a number of eroding mounds and ruined brick walls at the town of Harappa in what is now the Pakistani Province of Punjab had been noted by European travellers as early as the 1820s. Alexander Cunningham, director-general of the ASI, visited the mounds in the 1850s and recognised that they were of some, although uncertain, antiquity. In 1849 British hegemony spread to the Punjab, which is now separated into two provinces – Indian Punjab and Pakistani Punjab – and they extended their program of road, bridge, canal and railway building. This included constructing a railway line between the major cities of Lahore and Multan, which passed through an area of plain lacking suitable natural construction materials. Instead, use was made of the vast amounts of brick and rubble lying on the surface of these large mounds, situated very close to the proposed railway line. Meanwhile, Alexander Cunningham had carried out small scale excavations and surveys at one of these mounds – Harappa, with the express purpose of being able to identify this site as the city of Po-fa-to, a major Buddhist urban centre and described by the Chinese Buddhist pilgrim, Xuanzang who travelled in India between 625 and 645 CE. However, Cunningham was unable to make a positive identification, in part prevented by the extensive robbing of the site for bricks and other building materials, which essentially resulted in the stripping of the upper layers from the whole site. Cunningham did publish the finds of his work at Harappa – ancient coarse ware pottery, clearly not of the Buddhist period he was searching for, some stone tools such as chert stone blades, and worked shell, along with a worn stone seal. This seal was unlike any others known at this time; it was designed with a pierced knob or projection on its reverse side, and a peculiar animal with a single horn, resembling a bull or unicorn, on the obverse. Above the bull image was a short inscription in a completely unknown script, and this was the first modern recorded discovery of the Indus script.

Fortunately, Cunningham's lack of interest in Harappa did not prevent other archaeologists from wanting to know more about these unusual finds, but it was not until John Marshall took on the role of director-general in the 1920s that large-scale exploration at Harappa was initiated. While Marshall and his team worked in Punjab, the archaeologist R. D. Banerji began work at the site of Mohenjo-daro, located some 570 kilometres to the south of Harappa, in what is today the province of Sindh in Pakistan. Banerji's excavations uncovered what was clearly a very large city, with evidence for urban planning, a sophisticated drainage system, gold and bronze artefacts, monumental buildings, and some of the rare Indus sculptures and art objects that have been notably absent from other sites. Marshall recognised the similarities between the two sites and that they were part of what he believed was a civilisation, hitherto unknown in South Asia. Although unable to offer dates for this civilisation, he was confident that it was older than any other known. This was confirmed when he published illustrations of the seals which were recognised by archaeologists working within Iran and Mesopotamia as being very similar to seals recovered at Susa, located in what is now south-west Iran, and other Sumerian cities in what is now southern Iraq, from contexts dated to the third millennium BCE. As fieldwork at Indus sites increased and as dating techniques grew increasingly sophisticated, so our understanding of the chronology of the development of the Indus has increased and we can now assign a date range of between circa 2600 and 1900 BCE for the Integrated Era when this urban-focused tradition was at its height.

WHAT CHARACTERISES THE INTEGRATION ERA?

What do we mean by 'integration' and what do we understand by 'state'? These two terms are central to the discussions in this chapter, so it is worth ourconsidering how they are understood. In his exploration of Old World states, Yoffee (2005: 17) placed stress on the development of central political authority, with a range of key roles including "maintaining the central symbols of society, and undertaking the defence and expansion of the society". Ideology is key here and may, of course, take many forms; the dominant ideology may be coercive, inclusive, harsh or benign, and members of the state may have a very wide range of responses to the central ideology and leadership (Yoffee 2005: 39). We have also taken Shaffer's definition of integration as our starting point here: "pronounced homogeneity in material culture distributed over a large area reflecting an intense level of interaction between social groups" (Shaffer 1992: 442) (and see also discussion in Chapter 1). In this sense, integration draws heavily on definitions of state which include the sort of central political control noted earlier, which organises society very hierarchically and although (as Yoffee points out (2005: 17)) kin relationships would have been extremely important in the establishment of ruling dynasties, as well as in the majority of all settlements, non-kin relationships would have begun to emerge and become codified within the new forms of rule. Alongside this, craft specialisation and control of production would have emerged, and this may be seen archaeologically through homogeneity of design, shared skill sets and prevailing fashions over a notable physical area. The strength of ideology would play a critical role here too – without a strong ideology binding people under the centralised leadership, it would not have been possible to bind and maintain such an immensely complex economic and political entity as a state. It is also clear, however, that integration did not just infer a simple acculturation, as the structures and artefacts are almost identical and the underlying economies became firmly bound together. However, as previously noted, we do not assume that integration resulted in a single coherent state. Ideology would find expression through material culture, and some degree of uniformity or homogeneity would be expected. This uniformity, although not necessarily total or all-consuming, would be sufficient to demonstrate that people in different parts of the civilisation were acknowledging the common ideology in one form or another.

A number of structures and artefacts that are common to the Integration Era sites have been identified and these include the existence of large urban forms with all the accompanying implications for the need of agricultural surplus and organisation to support their agglomerated population. There was evidence for town planning within these cities, and large urban areas and walled angular subdivisions are frequently encountered, effecting differentiation. Although early theories suggested that the fortifications around the western mound of Mohenjo-daro were to repel invaders and therefore had a primary if not sole function of defence, later theories have suggested that the walls may have been symbolic and perhaps involved marking distinctions between public and private buildings or even to protect the site against floods and changes in river levels. In addition to this same broad plan of distinct walled and mounded communities, sites of the Integrated Era were characterised by the presence of public architecture, such as the Great Bath at Mohenjo-daro, and the so-called granaries at Harappa. The Indus script, still undeciphered, has been recovered from sites throughout the vast area covered; seals, weights, decorative styles in pottery and terracotta figurines are among the artefacts that make up this technological and cultural complex. There was evidence of long-distance trade and contact in the form of lapis lazuli from northern Afghanistan. These artefacts and structures typified the Integrated Era, and so are interpreted as representing the adoption or imposition of a homogeneous culture across such a vast area for a long time period. Furthermore, they have also been used to demonstrate that the inhabitants of the cities and towns of the Indus were indeed truly urban and formed an integral part of a major Old World Civilisation, fitting the classic but often misleading definitions of 'urban' and 'civilised' established first by Childe, and further developed by later writers (Yoffee 2005).

SETTLEMENTS OF THE INDUS VALLEY TRADITION

More than 1,000 settlements belonging to the Integrated Era have been identified (Singh 2008: 137), but there are only five significant urban sites at the peak of the settlement hierarchy (Smith 2006a: 110) (Figure 6.2). These are Mohenjo-daro in the lower Indus plain, Harappa in the western Punjab, Ganweriwala in Cholistan, Dholavira in western Gujarat and Rakhigarhi in Haryana. Mohenjo-daro covered an area of more than 250 hectares, Harappa exceeded 150 hectares, Dholavira 100 hectares and Ganweriwala and Rakhigarhi around 80 hectares each. The majority of these major settlements were on alluvium far from raw resources, resulting in what Algaze has called "disequalibrium" in parallel environments in Mesopotamia (2005: 2). Other settlement categories include smaller cities and towns ranging in size between ten and 50 hectares, and walled settlements between five and ten hectares, but by far the most numerous settlement category comprised small villages. These data suggest that the core part of the Integration Era possessed a four-tiered settlement pattern and that together they formed a network of settlements of different sizes and locations with different, often specialised or semi-specialised, functions. Analysis by the late Greg Possehl (1993) further suggested that the five major settlements were all located as central places or primary centres within the lower Indus, western Punjab, western India and on the Ghaggar-Hakra and acted as focal points for networks of exchange and integration.

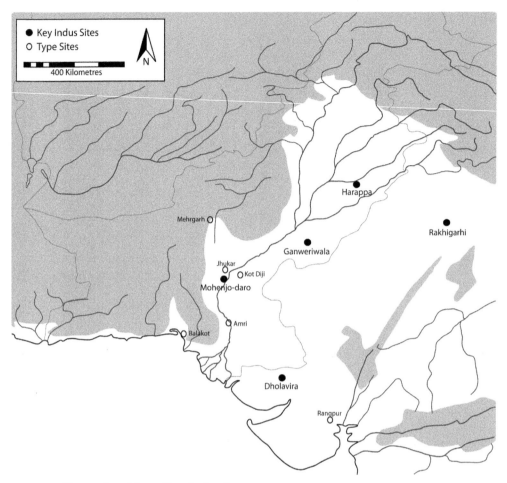

Figure 6.2. Map of key Indus sites.

Mohenjo-daro

The city of Mohenjo-daro is one of the most explored and publicised Integration Era cities and comprised two main areas; a raised occupation mound in the east, known as the Lower Town, and a second smaller raised mound in the west, known as the Citadel (Figure 6.3). The Citadel Mound is the highest at Mohenjo-daro, rising up to 9.15 metres above the present plain. It was formed by a mud-brick podium built on natural soil, but a Buddhist *stupa* dating to the third century CE was later erected on top of the much earlier structures on this mound. Covering an area of some 10 hectares, it was thought to have been surrounded by a retaining wall, and although its streets were cardinally oriented, the plan was not grid-iron. Several exceptional structures have been exposed on the Citadel mound, and these structures have been subject to extensive analysis, debate and interpretation. One of these is the Great Bath complex with its own outer wall, which is entirely

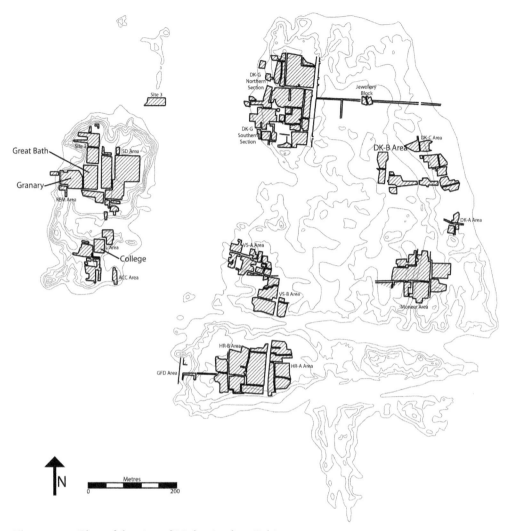

Figure 6.3. Plan of the city of Mohenjo-daro, Pakistan.

surrounded by streets and lanes and enclosed an area of 49 metres north to south by 33 metres east to west (Figure 6.4). Access to and from the complex was through two doorways on the southern side which led through an antechamber before opening into a central colonnade which measured 27 metres by 23 metres and was pierced by thirty openings. This colonnade led directly to a 7 metre deep, fired-brick faced basin measuring 12 metres by 7 metres (Mackay 1931a: 131). The brick facing was waterproofed by a three centimetre layer of bitumen, and the side walls were strengthened against the weight of the 1,600 cubic metres of water it would have contained, with buttresses below the floor level of the courtyard. The eastern side of the colonnade was flanked by eight brick-floored cells, some of which were equipped with drains, and on the north by a further colonnaded space with a chamber

Figure 6.4. The Great Bath at Mohenjo-daro, Pakistan.

beyond. The bath must have been filled by hand from a 15 metre deep well in one of the eastern chambers and was drained through a brick-corbelled vault 1.8 metres high. Across the lane from the eastern facade of the bath complex was a series of mud-brick podia covering an area of some 50 by 27 metres and although nothing above the mud-brick foundation survives it has been named the Granary (Wheeler 1968: 38) (Figure 6.5 and Figure 6.6). Other exceptional structures on the Citadel included a pillared hall in Area L, measuring 27 by 27 metres and formed from four rows of five brick podia and lined with benches (Marshall 1931b: 23). The presence of a shell-working area within Area L is also interesting, as this indicates that the Citadel was not only reserved for monumental, public structures but also manufacturing (Mackay 1931a: 170).

In contrast, the majority of the city's population lived in the 4.6 metre high lower town which comprised an area of low mounds, measuring 820 metres north to south and 330 east to west at its northern edge and 720 metres wide at its southern edge. It was covered in cardinally oriented mud-brick structures, subdivided by a rough grid-iron arrangement of streets and lanes (Figure 6.7). Only 20 percent of this area has been excavated, and Anna Sarcina believes that all structures in this part of the city generally conformed to one of a limited number of residential models (Sarcina 1979: 437). The most common, with fifty-eight examples, Sarcina's 'yellow model', was found across all areas and was formed by a northern courtyard with rooms on three sides and is thought to have represented private housing. The second most common was the 'red model', with forty-two examples recorded which were also found in all areas and comprised a corner courtyard and rooms on two sides and are thought

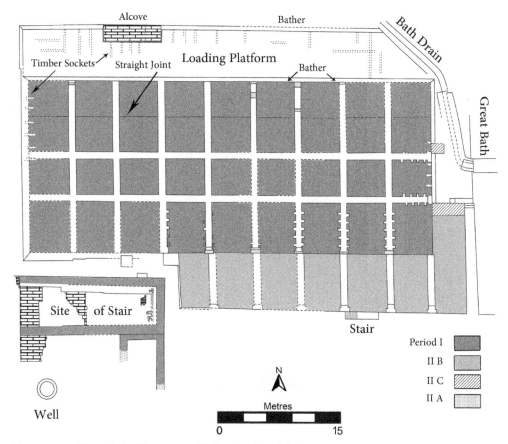

Figure 6.5. Plan of the Granary at Mohenjo-daro, Pakistan.

Figure 6.6. The 'Granary' at Mohenjo-daro, Pakistan.

Figure 6.7. Lane view in the Lower Town of Mohenjo-daro, Pakistan.

to have been residential structures hosting artisan activities. There were twelve other complexes, which generally comprised a central courtyard surrounded by rooms, or a courtyard occupying the rear half of the structure but separated from the street by rooms on one side only. In addition to these relatively uniform units, Marshall identified a number of "spacious and elaborate" structures (Marshall 1931b: 22), and more recently, a series of large mud-brick platforms have also been recorded (Possehl 2002a: 103) giving more diversity to the record of the settlement. When analysis of craft-working activities was undertaken across the Citadel and Lower Town, the resultant pattern was something of a surprise, as shell-working (Kenoyer 1985), ceramic production, metal working and even faience-working and steatite-working (Pracchia et al. 1985: 241) were carried out by hundreds of residents throughout the site rather than being located in specialist areas of the city. This state of affairs has led scholars to conclude that at Mohenjo-daro "the average size of production appears to be restricted, something between the size of a room and a courtyard" (Coningham and Manuel 2009a: 173). Whilst most scholars have been unwilling to advance population estimates due to a lack of information as to densities, figures in the region of between 30,000 and 40,000 have been advanced (Kenoyer 1997b: 54).

Harappa

When they were first excavated, Harappa and Mohenjo-daro were thought to be remarkably similar in plan, comprising a high western walled mound, or citadel, where public buildings were located, and a lower eastern unenclosed mound where occupation and craft working areas were located (Allchin and Allchin 1982: 171). However, more recent work at Harappa has demonstrated that this is a rather misleading pattern and that there were many differences between these two major cities. The major difference is that instead of the presence of just two mounds at Harappa, the excavators have now confirmed that the inhabitants of Harappa delineated themselves within at least four walled mounds surrounding a central depression which Mark Kenoyer has suggested may have acted as a large pond or reservoir for its inhabitants (1998: 55). The most prominent of these mounds was AB, which Wheeler demonstrated had been enclosed during the Integration Era by a 14 metre thick and 11 metre high wall faced with baked bricks. Sadly, most of the brick structures and their drains on the summit of this parallelogram-shaped mound were stripped for ballast by railway builders in the nineteenth century, but Wheeler was able to trace the course of a number of gates and towers on the western and northern edges (Wheeler 1968: 30). One of these gates led north towards Mound F, whose 274 square metre area is now also known to have been enclosed by a mud-brick wall (Kenoyer 1998: 55). Mound F appears to have been more public in nature and included a series of mud-brick structures that were initially interpreted as circular brick grain-threshing platforms (Figure 6.8), two granary blocks (Figure 6.9) and a well-planned residential quarter close to a series of sixteen furnaces (Wheeler 1968: 32). Mound E stands to the east of Mound AB and recent excavations have exposed a nine metre wide mud-brick wall facing its southern edge, thus demonstrating the presence of yet another independently walled mound at the site. These excavations have also exposed the presence of a 2.8 metre wide gateway in the centre of the southern wall which connected with a five metre wide street running directly north with evidence of structures on either side (Kenoyer 1991a: 50). This gate appears to have opened into a market or merchandise checking point with shell and agate workshops to its east and copper-working to its west. A further gate has been identified to the east, close to the junction between the walls surrounding Mounds E and ET (Kenoyer 1998: 55). It is clear that the different mounds or walled neighbourhoods at Harappa were established as the city's population grew but were inhabited by people who shared similar styles of ceramics, figurines, seals and ornaments. It is not clear, however, why they built the different walls or how the residents of different areas were articulated to form a single city or civic community. It has been estimated that the settlement was occupied by a population of over 30,000 inhabitants (Schug et al. 2012: 147).

Figure 6.8. Circular brick 'grain-threshing' platforms on Mound F at Harappa, Pakistan.

Figure 6.9. The 'granary' at Harappa, Pakistan.

Dholavira

Dholavira is located on Kadir Island in the Rann of Kutch, in what is now the state of Gujarat (Kenoyer 1998: 53). Its position not only allowed access to estuarine and coastal resources, but also put the population of this major site in an ideal position to control sea and river trade with other parts of

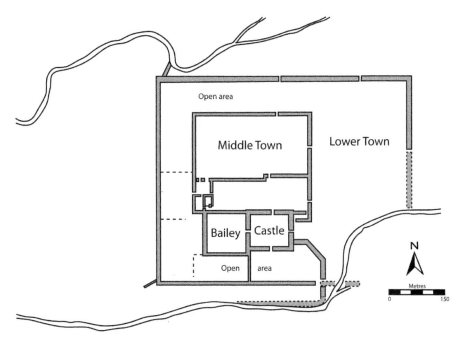

Figure 6.10. Plan of the city of Dholavira, India.

the integrated region. Archaeologists have identified an early phase of settlement here, contemporary with the Kot Dijian period of the Regionalisation Era, although with a somewhat different material culture. Dholavira appears to have adopted the characteristic material culture associated with the Indus Civilisation quite early in the Integrated Era, around 2600 BCE.

During the Regionalisation Era, the outer wall already in place was extended and reservoirs were constructed, which gave rise to the concept that the city form was in place by the beginning of the Integrated Era and was not changed throughout that phase of the city. However, Dholavira is interesting because its layout is completely unlike that of the other known Indus cities. Whilst it was oriented in the traditional cardinal directions and enclosed by a mud-brick wall faced with stone blocks, the similarities in layout end there (Figure 6.10). Its builders had subdivided its interior into three rectangular enclosures, built within each other, and further occupation and activity areas have been recorded outside the walled area. The outer wall enclosed an area of 768 metres by 614 metres (47 hectares) and was equipped with large bastions at each corner and gateways located in the middle of the northern and southern walls. The middle town enclosure measured 360 metres by 250 metres and had four gates, one in the middle of each wall. The citadel or acropolis area was further divided into two roughly equal sections and rose 13 metres above the lower town and again had one gateway in each of its four walls. In front of the north gateway in the citadel area, there was a large rectangular open space which might have been a meeting space or market area. Near the northern gateway of the citadel, the remains of a large board was discovered with ten large white gypsum paste symbols, each measuring 40 centimetres high and about 25 centimetres wide, suggesting that this could have been a large sign erected near this northern gateway or public space and highly visible across most of the town. A number of large buildings have been identified within the upper town or citadel area, and while their exact function is not yet known, it is thought that they were likely to have had some administrative or ritual function. In the lower town, areas of craft manufacture have been identified, such as agate bead-making, shell-working and ceramic production. Rock-cut cisterns and reservoirs have also been identified in the lower town areas, and would have been filled with seasonal rainwater; these water collection areas account for nearly 36 percent of the area of the walled city which is located in an extremely arid region.

Rakhigarhi and Ganweriwala

Rakhigarhi is located in Hissar District of Haryana is more than 100 hectares in size. Five mounds have been identified at Rakhigarhi, including what has been labelled a citadel mound complete with a mud-brick enclosing wall around it (Lal 2002). Evidence for planned settlement in the Early Harappan or Regionalisation period was recorded by the ASI during their extensive excavations, with types of pottery similar to those known at Kalibangan (Lal 2002; Singh 2008: 144). Ganweriwala is located in the Cholistan desert and covers an area of around 80 hectares (Mughal 1997: 47). It has not been excavated, but surface examination shows two mounds, thus similar in layout to other Indus cities. Wright has noted that all surface materials indicate occupation during the Integrated Era only and that its emergence occurred at a time when larger settlements of the preceding period had been abandoned (2010: 132).

URBAN AND RURAL SITES OF THE INDUS VALLEY TRADITION

Below the uppermost tier of cities or major urban sites of the Integration Era was the next rank of settlements, whose population covered areas of between 10 and 50 hectares, making them significantly smaller than the central places noted earlier. There are more than thirty known sites in this category and their forms vary considerably, but most of their residents lived behind formal walls within cardinally planned interiors. Kalibangan is a particularly interesting city to examine as it was occupied in the preceding Kot Dijian Phase, and the early walled enclosure of the Regionalisation Era was reoccupied as a citadel mound, whilst a new walled settlement was laid out to the east (Figure 6.11). It is the only site to share such a striking similarity with the layout of Mohenjo-daro, although there is no evidence to suggest that the latter's lower town was ever fortified, and the streets of the former do not run parallel with the alignment

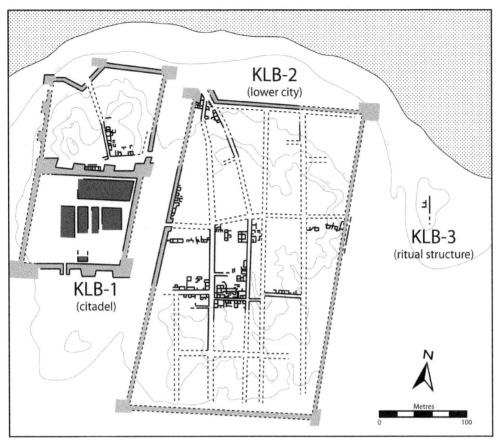

Figure 6.11. Plan of the site of Kalibangan, India.

of its enclosing walls. As noted in Chapter 5, Kalibangan was located close to the former course of the Ghaggar-Hakra River and its rectangular citadel measured some 250 metres north to south by 170 metres east to west and rose 12 metres above the plain (Lal 2003). Its builders subdivided it into two equal parts with a massive wall, and externally, the wall was strengthened by bastions. The northern portion was provided with a major entrance gate at its north-west corner, giving access to a street lined with what appear to be residential units, which ran to a central stairway giving access to the southern portion. The southern portion was distinctly different in character and contained at least five massive mud-brick platforms, one of which contained a roughly square brick-lined pit containing antlers and bovine bones and another which contained a row of oval firepits, which a number of scholars have identified as religious in nature (Sankalia 1974: 350), and a well and bathing platform (Dani and Thapar 1992: 307). Some 40 metres to the east of the citadel, the majority of inhabitants lived in the lower town which was surrounded by a wall measuring 360 metres north to south and 240 metres east to west, and subdivided by a grid of streets and lanes. Following a similar alignment to the street grid

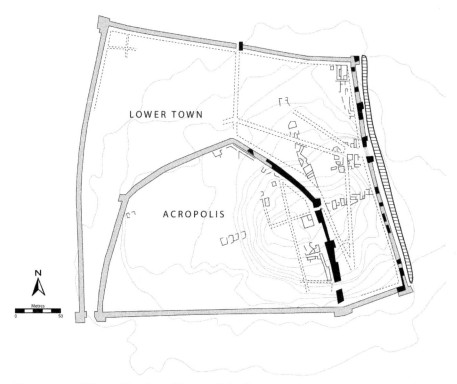

Figure 6.12. Plan of the site of Banawali, India.

within the citadel mound, two of the streets of the lower town converge on a main gate set in the north-west corner of the enclosure.

The presence of large walled and subdivided enclosures has also been encountered at other sites during the Integration Era, for example, at Banawali on the Ghaggar River, Sutkagen Dor on the Makran coast and at Lothal in Gujarat. Although on the same river as Kalibangan and also succeeding a Sothi-Kot Dijian settlement, an entirely new urban plan was laid out above at Banawali during the Integration Era. This contrasts with the development at Kalibangan which linked both phases of planning (Bisht and Asthana 1979). The new settlement measured some 275 metres north to south and 130 metres east to west and was clearly divided into two with the construction of a massive mud-brick wall measuring 105 metres long, 6 metres thick and surviving to a height of at least 4.5 metres (Figure 6.12). Sutkagen Dor is the most westerly of all known walled settlements and is located 48 kilometres inland, beside what George Dales believed to have once been an inlet close to the mouth of the Dasht Kaur (Dales 1962). The settlement appears to have comprised two distinct parts, a lower or outer town to the north and the east and a walled citadel mound containing at least one mud-brick platform. The latter was oblong measuring 173 metres north to south and 103 metres east to west and defined by a wall of semi-dressed stone set in mud mortar topped by mud

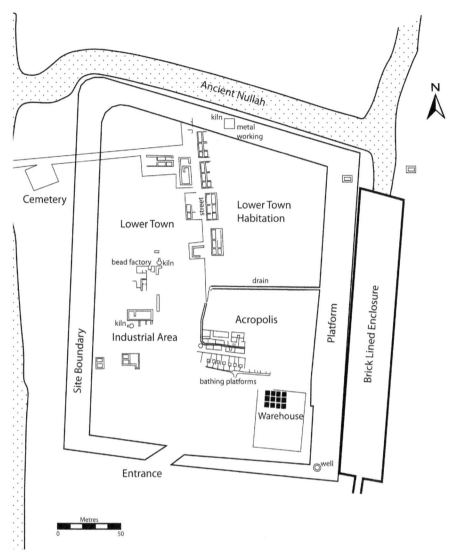

Figure 6.13. Plan of the site of Lothal, India.

brick. Constructed during the initial occupation of the site, the wall measured almost nine metres in width, was strengthened by towers or bastions, and most of the excavated ceramics were characteristic of the Integration Era. Dales did note, however, that the ceramics of the initial development phases of the site were all highly micaceous, were probably direct imports from the lower Indus Valley and had probably been brought to the site by its "original settlers" (Dales 1962: 89).

In contrast, Lothal is one of the easternmost sites and has a somewhat different plan again with a rectangular mud-brick wall measuring 300 metres north to south by 400 metres east to west (Rao 1973: 61) (Figure 6.13). Rao's excavations of the 4.2 hectare site have exposed the presence of a grid-iron street

Figure 6.14. Street view in Lothal, India.

plan lined with cardinally oriented mud-brick structures in the south-west, north-west and north-east quadrants whilst the south-east corner appears to comprise a series of major mud-brick platforms. Despite its small size, its residents lived in units complete with brick-paved bathrooms, drains and soakage pits, whilst their streets were also provided with main drains (Rao 1973: 73) (Figure 6.14). There was also good evidence for their manufacturing activities on the site with the presence of separate areas for bead production, copper and metal working, and shell-working, as well as one set of postulated dyeing-vats. The raised mud-brick platforms in the south-east quadrant, referred to as an 'acropolis' by its excavator, appear to have housed a series of larger complexes including a series of small cells on platform B, each of which were provided with a bath which fed into a major drain system and a flat compartmentalised structure on platform C interpreted as a warehouse foundation (Figure 6.15 and Figure 6.16). Whilst in some respects Lothal conforms to many architectural characteristics of the Integration Era, the large fired-brick lined rectangular basin on the eastern side of the town was a unique feature. Measuring 212 metres by 36 metres and 4.15 metres deep, it had a clear brick-lined 12 metre wide sluice at the south end (Rao 1973: 70) (Figure 6.17). The excavator interpreted this feature as a dock for shipping, as ships of less than 75 tons are able to clear a 2 metre depth of water, and noted the presence of large perforated stones which he suggested were anchors (Rao 1973: 72). Whilst other scholars have suggested that it played the role of a fresh-water reservoir (Leshnik

Figure 6.15. The 'Warehouse' at Lothal, India.

1979), the exact function of the structure is still unknown, although it has not been attributed a ritual role unlike the tank at Mohenjo-daro. Whatever the function of this particular structure, the role of Lothal in the manufacture and transportation of goods within the Integration Era and beyond is unquestionable and this is supported by the presence of a Dilmun (Bahrain) type circular seal amongst the city's Indus seals.

A third category of settlement was represented by the populations of small walled sites of between two and four hectares with industrial activities which have been identified in western India (Dhavalikar 1995). Their inhabitants lived within simple enclosures, although others were more complex with two separate walled zones, such as at Surkotada. Despite their relative simplicity of layout, the presence of weights, seals and assemblages of raw materials and partially processed objects at these sites indicates their social and economic integration. Surkotada in Kutch measured 130 metres east to west and 65 metres north to south and was divided into two equal sections with bastions at the four corners and also where the internal dividing wall joined the main exterior walls (Figure 6.18). The excavator termed the western enclosure the 'Citadel' and the eastern enclosure the 'Residential Area' (Joshi 1990) and both contain mud-brick and rubble structures, but it is notable that a grid-iron street pattern appears to have been absent.

Most of these smaller settlements were not subdivided even though they were walled, as illustrated by the diminutive two hectare site of Kuntasi (Figure 6.19).

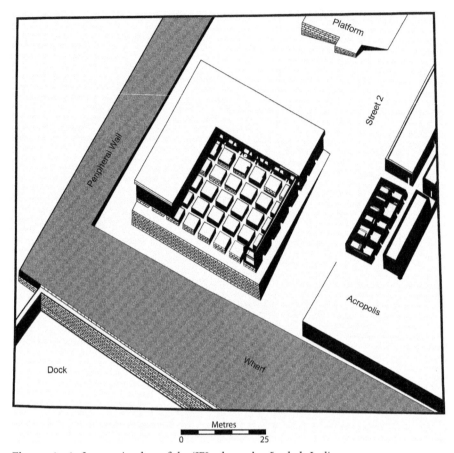

Figure 6.16. Isometric plan of the 'Warehouse' at Lothal, India.

This roughly cardinally oriented site measured some 125 metres square and was defined by a wall ranging between 1 and 1.5 metres wide with an entrance to the east (Dhavalikar 1995: 83). Although the majority of the structures at Kuntasi observed the orientation of their surrounding walls, the main street was less precise and the interior contained a number of working areas with unfinished beads of locally available chalcedony, agate and carnelian, ceramic kilns and copper working furnaces as well as weights and seals. Recent excavations at Gola Dhoro indicated another type of site in this settlement category, where a 5.2 metre thick stone wall enclosed a cardinally oriented area of some 50 by 50 metres, although additional structures were identified to the south of the enclosure (Bhan et al. 2005; Chase 2010). One of the buildings within the enclosure has been identified as a workshop, complete with distinct piles of shell bangles and uncut *Turbinella pyrum* shell as well as numbers of shell wasters and grinding stones. The excavators have suggested that the shell had been brought to the site from distances of more than 100 kilometres to be sorted, traded and manufactured into bangles. The recovery of drills and partly worked

Figure 6.17. Lothal 'dock' and sluice, India.

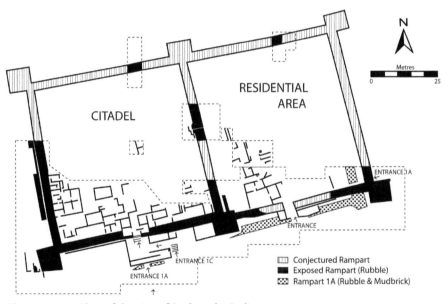

Figure 6.18. Plan of the site of Surkotada, India.

semi-precious stone beads as well as stockpiles of raw stone materials from 70 kilometres to the south-west have suggested that a similar process was being undertaken in the manufacture of beads. Clearly this category of site appears to have been a highly specialised settlement focused on the collection of raw

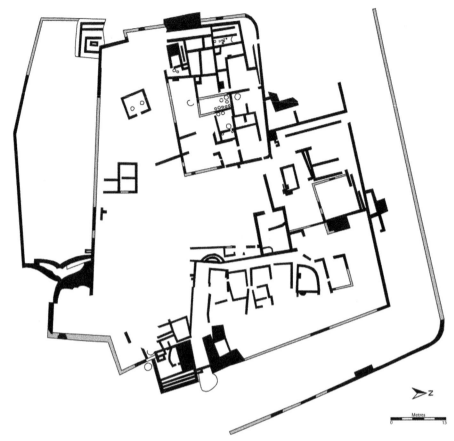

Figure 6.19. Plan of the site of Kuntasi, India.

materials, their processing and completion as objects for trade within the settlements to the north and west. This category of settlement was probably not only involved in localised collection, processing and export, as illustrated by the recent excavations at Shikarpur. This 3.4 hectare walled site near the Gulf of Kutch has yielded evidence of chert imported from the Rohri Hills and processed at the site, presumably for use by its inhabitants (Gadekar et al. 2014). Significantly, although only 22 kilometres apart and contemporarously occupied, these two small sites appear to have notable differences within their respective corporae of artefacts (Chase et al. 2014). Whether such heavily focused procurement sites were occupied full-time or seasonally, still remains to be debated.

   At the base of the settlement categories, the majority of the inhabitants of those within the integrated zone lived in more than 1,000 sites, measuring less than one hectare in area, which represent agricultural village populations or economically specialised settlements. A good example of the functional split has been demonstrated by the survey work conducted by Mughal in Cholistan, where almost half of the 174 settlements recorded have been identified as being solely industrial and a further 29 percent as solely agricultural (Mughal

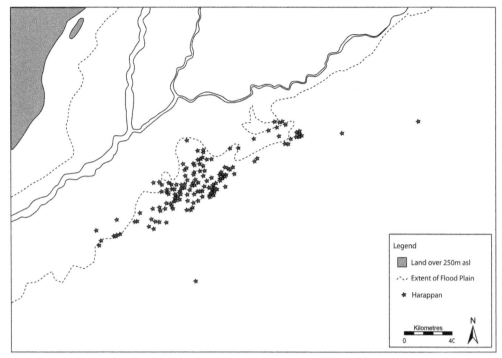

Figure 6.20. Map showing settlement patterns in Cholistan during the Integration Era.

1997: 49) (Figure 6.20). Similar settlements include the shell processing site of Nageshwar in western India (Hegde et al. 1991) and Balakot in Sindh (Dales 1979). It is also interesting to note that many of the smaller settlements still shared many cultural aspects of the larger sites as illustrated by Nausharo, successor settlement to Mehrgarh close to the mouth of the Bolan Pass. During Period III of its construction, Nausharo comprised cardinally oriented blocks of housing delineated by a five metre wide street and lanes 1.5 metres wide (Jarrige 1994: 283) (Figure 6.21). The 700 square metres of Block 2 exposed during excavations have provided evidence of eleven household units, each of which was oriented around a courtyard or open area and each provided with a "flat water-resistant platform" or bathroom complete with drains.

It would be incorrect, however, to suggest that all the Integrated Era population was settled and sedentary, and Possehl has argued that the large voids between known distributions of settlement sites would have been filled with nomadic pastoralists who have left few permanent archaeological indicators (Possehl 1979: 546). Possehl went on to stress the roles that such individuals may have played stating that "the presence of pastoral nomads makes very good sense if we see them as the mobile population which bridged the gap between settlements, as the carriers of information, as the transporters of goods, as the population through which the Harappan Civilisation achieved its remarkable degree of integration" (Possehl 1979: 548). This suggestion of interaction

Figure 6.21. Buildings at
Nausharo, Pakistan.

and coexistence has more recently been supported by clear evidence from
Mughal's Cholistan survey, where 6 percent of the 174 sites occupied during
the Integration Era were found to be camp sites (Mughal 1997: 49). Whilst this
is lower than in the preceding phases, it is still notable and indicates the presence and significance of "nomads in marginal areas within the fully urbanised
society of the Indus Civilisation" (Mughal 1997: 49). Such groups, many of
whom practiced hunting and gathering, were engaged with settlements of the
Integration Era as indicated by the presence of copper tools and objects at the
seasonal camping sites of Langhnaj and Bagor (Misra 2002: 122), and it may
be anticipated that their inhabitants may have played roles in the collection
and transportation of raw materials and thus functioned within the integrating
networks of more sedentary communities.

PUBLIC BUILDINGS, PALACES, GRANARIES,
GREAT HALLS OR WAREHOUSES?

The mud-brick platforms that provided the base for the citadel mounds of
many Integration Era urban sites alongside the massive settlement walls also
offer clear evidence of public or communal investment in monuments, but

there are many other individual examples of possible monumental or public architecture. For example, John Marshall also noted the presence of a 'curious' baked-brick construction immediately to the south-west of the Great Bath at Mohenjo-daro. The structure was later fully cleared and proved to be a six metre high fired-brick platform measuring 50 metres by 27 metres and covering an area of 1,350 square metres surmounted by twenty-seven individual plinths or podia. Each of the latter measured 1.4 metres high and they were organised into three rows east to west and nine north to south, each separated by a 0.8 metre gap (Jansen 1991: 147). Jansen has demonstrated that the platform represented an earlier phase of construction and that the podia were constructed at the same time as was the Great Bath. Recording that the gaps between the podia were filled with cinders and charcoal, Marshall suggested that the building was the foundation for a "hammam or hot-air bath", complete with air passages or "hypocaust flues" between the podia (Marshall 1931b: 26). Mortimer Wheeler reinterpreted the complex as a large granary with a timber superstructure resting on podia foundations to provide "the circulation of air beneath the main body of the Granary overhead" and identified an associated loading bay (Wheeler 1968: 43). The presence of granaries on the Citadel mound of Mohenjo-daro suggested to Wheeler that "the flow of grain, doubtless the principal source of civic wealth, was regulated and distributed by government officials with their clerks and labourers" and that they "fulfilled in the state economy the function of the modern state-bank or treasury" (Wheeler 1968: 35). Wheeler also noted the presence of a complex of other "municipal or state granaries" on Mound F to the north of the Mound AB at Harappa, further confirming this link between authority and the collection, storage and redistribution of agricultural surplus. These granaries, however, followed a rather different plan and comprised an eastern and western block, both measuring 45.72 metres by 17 metres, constructed 7 metres apart. The blocks were subdivided into six rectangular units measuring 15.77 metres by 5.33 metres separated by corridors, and it was assumed that the timber superstructures rested on a series of low walls for air circulation rather like Roman granaries in Britain (Vats 1940: 213).

As Marcia Fentress has noted, although Wheeler identified both these structures as granaries, they have quite different floor plans, morphology and locations and should not necessarily be treated the same (1984: 95). Moreover, excavations at neither provided evidence of charred grain, although both structures were associated with deposits of burning. There is possibly more of a case for the presence of a granary at Harappa on account of the presence of eighteen circular fired-brick platforms to the south, each of which measured 3.3 metres in diameter, which have been identified as locations for husking grain (Chakrabarti 1995: 85). Fentress also dismissed the suggestion that the Mohenjo-daro structure represented a hammam as there was no evidence of a furnace, water source or drain system and has suggested that this structure may have been a market place and was probably "social and multifunctional in use" (Fentress 1984: 95). Reconfirmed as storage facilities by Ratnagar (1991: 134), more recently Kenoyer has rejected both these interpretations and, instead, suggested that the granary at Mohenjo-daro was a "Great Hall" as it was "a large and spacious building with wooden columns" set in the podia (Kenoyer 1998: 64). However, Possehl reinterpreted the Mohenjo-daro granary as a warehouse and has suggested that the "people in charge of the Great Bath ... probably stored things for their use as well as for patronage or 'giveaways'" (Possehl 2002a: 192). This interpretation is more reasonable as there are distinct similarities between the 'Great Granary' of Mohenjo-daro and the 'Warehouse' of Block C within the south-east corner of the walled 'Acropolis' platform at Lothal. The latter comprised sixty-four individual 1.5 metre high mud-brick podia measuring 3.6 metres square each sitting on a four metre high mud-brick platform covering an area of almost 2,000 square metres (Rao 1973: 66). Separated from each other by one metre square, Rao suggested that this arrangement allowed for the movement of labour and customs officials between the podia as well as the safe storage of traded goods. Strongly confirming Rao's interpretation of the complex as a warehouse was his recovery of sixty-five clay sealings from the structure, bearing impressions of Indus seals on one side and the impression of mats and cloths which covered the bales of produce on the other (Rao 1973: 119).

As noted earlier, most studies of the cities of the Indus Valley Tradition have failed to identify evidence of major monuments or palatial structures within their lower towns (Sarcina 1979; Miller 1985). This is, of course, not entirely uncontested as "spacious and elaborate" structures were recorded by Marshall (1931b: 22) and later discussed by Ratnagar (1991: 44). To this list we may add Possehl's large mud-brick platforms (2002a: 103) as well as House A1 in HR District. Wheeler referred to it as a possible shrine (1968: 52), although Jansen suggested that it might also have been a palace (Jansen 1985). Similarly, Dhavalikar and Atre suggested that Structure No. XXIII of HR Area was a temple (1989), and Vidale re-identified Block 2 of HR-B District as a single palatial complex close to a smaller bath rather than seven individual compounds (2010). Finally, Kenoyer noted that whilst all lacked the distinctive colonnades of the structures on the Citadel, they may have been "elite or administrative/ritual centres which competed with those found on the Citadel Mound." (1997b: 60). This situation suggests that additional research and reanalysis may yet demonstrate the presence of major inequalities and differentiation within the lower town settlements of the Integrated Era.

BATHS, DRAINS AND WELLS

In addition to the Great Bath complex of Mohenjo-daro and bathing facilities on Platform B at Lothal, the Integration Era is extremely well known for the investment in both public drainage systems and private bathrooms; in Dales's

Figure 6.22. Bathroom and drain in the Lower Town of Mohenjo-daro, Pakistan.

words "The controlled use of water is an architectural characteristic of Indus settlements" (1991: 139). There were parallels within the preceding phases to the provision of such features as the stone-lined drain across the mud-brick platform at Damb Sadaat II or the presence of bathroom platforms at Kot Diji I; however, in the Integrated Era the controlled use of water was very wide-ranging, from major civic initiatives, such as the drains in streets and lanes, to individual domestic bathrooms (Figure 6.22). The complexity and ubiquity of the former was summarised by one of the early excavators at Mohenjo-daro thus: "A remarkable feature of the city of Mohenjo-daro is the very elaborate drainage system that exists even in the poorest quarters of the city" (Mackay 1931a: 278). Streets were provided with channels covered with brick or stone and they drained individual households, while larger channels were encased within corbelled culverts as at the Great Bath or under the gateway of Harappa (Kenoyer 1998: 61). The majority of the houses at Mohenjo-daro were provided with bathrooms with carefully laid fired-brick platforms, which sloped gently to drains which emptied into the street and lane drains, although some first discharged into silt traps (Mackay 1931a: 273, 280).

These drains and bathrooms appear to have been fed by rainwater and water drawn from cylindrical wells. Lined with waterproof fired brick, these wells also dated to the Integrated Era, and Jansen has estimated that there was one well-placed at every 15 metres within Mohenjo-daro, that is, within every third house (1991: 160). The investment in the management of the flow of water does not seem to have been part of a water conservation strategy as the main street drains did not lead to cisterns nor did they appear to be intended to reduce localised flooding as there was no attempt to lead the water beyond the city walls; the main street drains simply terminate in soakage pits (Marshall 1931b: 17). Indeed, the original excavators were struck by the nature of the over-engineering of drains and bathrooms and commented that "it is even possible that the water ... had some religious significance and that, therefore, all due care was taken that it should not escape elsewhere than to mother earth" (Mackay 1931a: 274). This provision has also struck later scholars, and the late Greg Possehl was to borrow the phase 'wasserluxus' to allude to the physical and symbolic role of water as a cleansing agent in the Indus Valley Tradition (2002a: 58). As we have seen with other categories of features across the Integration Era, although the provision of drains and bathrooms is known across almost all categories of settlement, there are also exceptions and differences. The frequency and density of wells at Mohenjo-daro is unmatched elsewhere, which perhaps reflects different regimes of water collection, availability and use across the Indus, as the populations of both Dholavira and Harappa appear to have had central reservoirs or catchment areas for seasonal water collection.

CEMETERIES

Whilst formal extramural cemeteries are known of from the Integration Era, it is clear that the number of individuals interred must only represent a very small sample of the population of the settlements to which they were attached. As also noted in relation to urban form and layout, there was an apparent uniformity within the cemeteries whereby extended burial was the norm, but there was vast diversity in practices as well as location of cemeteries. The largest sample of human remains comes from the urban site of Harappa, and the careful excavations at Cemetery R37 have provided a degree of information lacking from many other Indus sites. R37 is located some 300 metres to the south of Mound AB and produced 106 burials in the 1920s and 1930s and a further ninety in the 1980s (Hemphill et al. 1991: 139). The best preserved thirty-three human remains from the latter set were analysed and the sample found to represent a young to middle-aged adult population in which males and females were equally represented (Hemphill et al. 1991: 139–141). In all but one of the graves, the extended body was placed in a rectangular grave cut with head to the north, but it was notable that earlier burials appear to have been disturbed or entirely removed as later graves were cut in the cemetery (Dales and Kenoyer 1991: 195) (Figure 6.23 and Figure 6.24). Some mud-brick lined pits were identified, presumably graves, and distinct timber coffin shadows were confirmed in Burials 147a and 127a. Grave 127a was found to have been furnished with four shell bangles, carnelian and lapis lazuli beads and a steatite

Coffin

Figure 6.23. Plan of burial within Cemetery R37 at Harappa, Pakistan (i).

disc bead anklet, although the excavators argued that "the persons buried in this cemetery were not from greatly diverse socio-economic segments of the society" (Dales and Kenoyer 1991: 210). The presence of coffins had already been recorded at R37 by Wheeler, who noted a female burial in a coffin with sides of local rosewood but a lid of deodar imported from the foothills of the Himalayas (Wheeler 1968: 67). The palaeopathology of the sample from R37 suggests that there was a remarkable lack of differential dietary stress suggesting that they were "healthy and well fed, probably from among the upper classes" (Kenoyer 1998: 122) but that girls were subject to greater growth disruption than were boys (Hemphill et al. 1991: 171).

A formal cemetery at the urban site of Kalibangan was located 300 metres to the west-south-west of the Citadel Mound and contained some 102 inhumations attributed to one of three very different types of burial practice. The majority of burials, eighty-eight in total, conformed to the widespread tradition of extended inhumation with grave goods in oval or rectangular grave cuts. The other two types comprised vessels in circular pits and vessels in rectangular or oval pits. Sharma noted that whilst the first group contained human remains, the latter two groups had no evidence of inhumations leading him

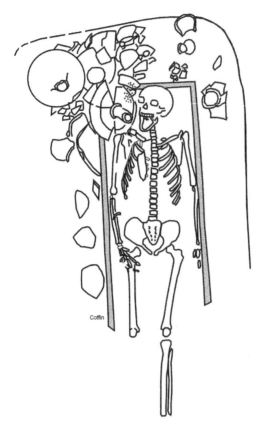

Coffin

Figure 6.24. Plan of burial within Cemetery R 37 at Harappa, Pakistan (ii).

to suggest that they were cenotaphs (1999). He also noted that whilst the first and third groups were mixed together, there was a distinct concentration of pit burials to the north of the cemetery and suggested that this indicated separate family or social groupings. Whilst the empty cuts may be interpreted as a different form of practice, it is also possible that the human remains have been differentially preserved across the cemetery or may even represent different phases as the city site itself was occupied for over 700 years. One extended burial in particular, Grave 29, was noted as pre-eminent on account of its having been lined in mud-brick with a plaster finish and furnished with seventy-two individual vessels (Agrawal 2007: 244). More recently, evidence has been produced at Dholavira for the presence of a cemetery of stone-lined pits to the west of the city (Agrawal 2007: 239). The absence of a formal cemetery at Mohenjo-daro is notable, but it may still remain masked under the very deep alluvium which has accumulated around the site, and indeed covered much of the known city itself.

Cemeteries are also known from the smaller categories of walled settlements and a cemetery measuring 40 by 36 metres was also identified at Lothal but to the north-west of the Lower Town, beyond the walls (Rao 1973: 146) (Figure 6.25 and Figure 6.26). Comprising "an overwhelming majority of

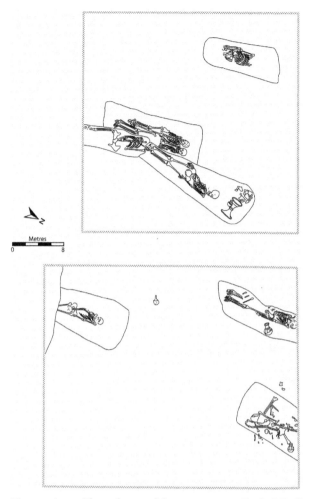

Figure 6.25. Plan of part of the cemetery at Lothal, India (i).

males most of whom belong to the age-group 20–30", Rao has suggested that they were not representative of "the true population of Lothal" due to the unusual age and gender composition (Rao 1973: 151). A total of eleven north to south oriented graves belonging to Period A (Integration Era) were excavated and found to conform to the practice of extended burials with the head in a northerly direction, although at this cemetery they were also recorded as being tilted to the east. Three of the graves included two skeletons and one grave had been lined with mud-brick as at Kalibangan. The excavator noted that the graves were "poorly furbished" but also recorded the presence of goat bones in one grave and a cattle jaw in another (Rao 1973: 147–149). The cemetery at Surkotada was located 300 metres north-west of the walled settlement and comprised charred and uncharred human remains in urn burials within oval pits, some of which were marked by stone slabs (Joshi 1990: 365). Finally, reference should be made to the presence of a formal cemetery 900

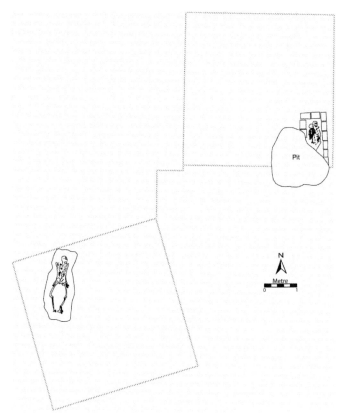

Figure 6.26. Plan of part of the cemetery at Lothal, India (ii).

metres to the north-west of the small town of Farmana on the course of the
Ghaggar–Hakra River (Shinde et al. 2009: 19). The town measured 18 hectares
with a grid-iron street and lane configuration oriented north to west to south
to east and its cemetery appeared to cover an area of 3 hectares. The seventy
burials were interred in three phases with distinct changes in burial orientation in each phase. This was marked with a move from north to west to south
to east between the first and second phases, and then, finally, to north to east
to south to west between the second and third phases. It is also notable that
a number of the later burials cut across earlier ones and there appears to have
been both primary and secondary burials. The excavators suggested that the
different orientations indicated "at least three distinct groups in a settlement at
Farmana and each had burial customs differing slightly from others" (Shinde
et al. 2009: 63), suggesting a significant degree of change within the sequence.
Significantly, Paul Rissman noted the presence of far greater "secular value"
placed in hoards than in cemeteries, suggesting an ideology of equality within
public cemeteries, than caches hidden or deposited within private residential
units (1988: 218). Finally, reference must be made to the recent reanalysis of
human skeletal material from Harappa, where a team of palaeopathologists

have identified differentiated patterns of 'interpersonal-trauma' and have suggested that "Indus statehood was … based on exclusion and this structure determined the risk for violence" (Schug et al. 2012: 148).

SEALS, SEALINGS AND SCRIPT

One of the major innovations of this Era was the development of what is called the Indus Script, a new method for facilitating the recording of both ownership and transactions. There are now over 3,700 known examples of the Indus script from a range of sites of different types and sizes, from Afghanistan and Turkmenistan in the north, and the Persian Gulf and Arabian Sea in the west, to Gujarat in the east (Parpola 1994) (Figure 6.27). Found on a wide range of materials including stone, metal, ceramic, terracotta, shell, bone and ivory, these examples of script are present on an equally diverse range of objects, including seals, tablets, tools, vessels, bangles and clay impressions. They comprise between 170 and 220 simple signs and between 170 and 200 composite ones and are thought to represent a logo-syllabic script, that is, one which has both word-signs and phonetic syllables (Coningham 2002: 81). In addition, most scholars would also agree that the script was written right to left and that numerical signs are represented by single strokes and semicircles. Despite this consensus, the script defies decipherment, and scholars also disagree on the identity of the language family underlying it with some advocating Dravidian and others Indo-European (Parpola 1994). In the absence of a bilingual text, a knowledge of the language depicted, and an inscription more than twenty-six characters long, it is unlikely to be deciphered. The most numerous category of inscribed object is the seal, of which over 200 have been found. Both square and rectangular in shape, many were manufactured from steatite or soapstone which was first carved and polished and then kiln-fired which would have whitened and hardened the surface so that it could stamp wet clay. The majority have an animal carved on them, often a bull or a unicorn, and a short inscription (Kenoyer 2013) (Figure 6.28). Ratnagar (1991) has interpreted these animals as representing different trading guilds and descent groups, a point more recently considered by Vidale with the suggestion that "the unicorn was the symbol of scribes … and small-scale urban bureaucracy" whilst the gaur or short-horned bull was the symbol of trading communities to the west (2005: 153). Whatever they may have actually represented, Kenoyer (1998) has suggested that they may have acted as badges and been worn by individuals (Figure 6.29). Script was widely used in Mesopotamia by a growing bureaucracy for recording the movement of grain and flocks, and although the Indus Script has not yet been successfully deciphered, we suggest that it played a key role in allocating resources amongst specialists as well as recording loans and allocations. However, the extent to which trade and manufacture, major segments of the economy of those living within the walled centres, was controlled

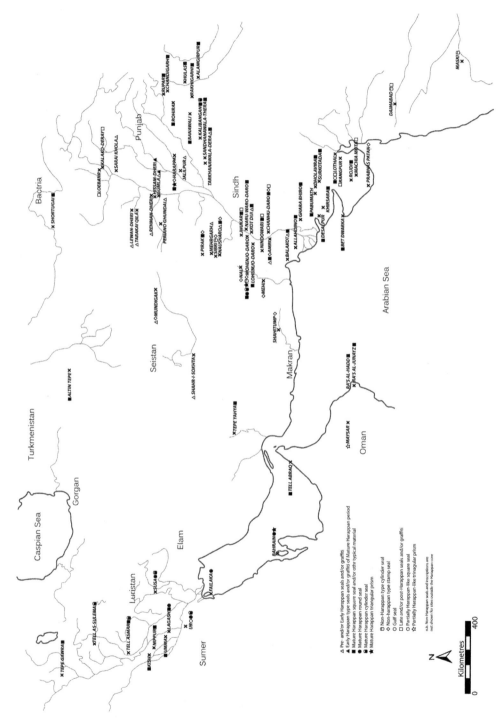

Figure 6.27. Distribution map of seals.

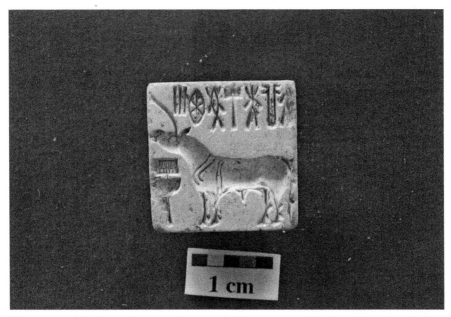

Figure 6.28. Indus unicorn seal (courtesy Department of Archaeology and Ancient History, The Maharaja Sayajirao University of Baroda, India).

by the 'state' or the 'private sector' is unclear. Similarly, whether the presence of seals at sites like Gonur-depe in Turkmenistan (Kohl 2007: 199) indicates the full extent of such networks and the reach of individual Indus merchants or whether it was a collected curio is also unclear.

WEIGHTS AND MEASURES

Many scholars have noted the presence of uniformity and standardisation throughout the region covered by the settlements of the Integrated Era (Miller 2013) and further suggested that this was underpinned by the widespread adoption of a shared unit system of weight and measures by its inhabitants. It is important to understand that this system was not the result of simple import or diffusion from the Near East, but had its origins in the Kot Dijian and Hakra phases as suggested by the early presence of a weight at Harappa and continuity in ratios of bricks from the sites of the Regionalisation to Integrated Eras. That there was a uniform system of weights during the Integration Era is demonstrated by the presence of small polished rectangular or cuboid blocks of banded chert across the region and beyond, although examples of limestone, gneiss, steatite, chalcedony and truncated spherical weights are also known (Figure 6.30). Hemmy conducted one of the early studies of 147 blocks from Mohenjo-daro and Harappa and found that there was "no local variation between the weights in the two places, although 500 miles apart" and concluded that the ratios ran 1, 2, 4, 8, 16, 32, 64, 160, 200,

Figure 6.29. Indus seals and sealings (after J. M. Kenoyer).

320, 640 and 1600 (1931: 591). He also found that the Indus weight system was binary in the smaller weights and then became decimal, and noted that the most frequently discovered weight, ratio 16, bore no relation to Babylonian weight systems (Hemmy 1931: 596). Mark Kenoyer has suggested that banded chert predominated amongst weights as it provided a highly recognisable and standard weight (1991b), and to this we may add Marshall's comment that it is also fine-grained and thus possible to be ground to reach the appropriate weight as well as being "hard enough to defy ordinary wear and tear" (Marshall 1931a: 37). Kenoyer noted a concentration of these weights close to the gateway at Harappa and has suggested that they may have been associated with the weighing and taxing of goods brought into the city (1998: 99). The excavations at Harappa have also provided evidence of scale pans, complete with cross beam (Kenoyer 2010: 116). Heather Miller's recent analysis has reconfirmed the

Figure 6.30. Indus weights from Shikarpur (courtesy Department of Archaeology and Ancient History, The Maharaja Sayajirao University of Baroda, India).

presence of a standardised Integration weight system but she has also drawn attention to the presence of what may be secondary systems at different sites, either indicating articulations with subregional variants or traders from outside the integrated zones (2013: 173).

The presence of a shared system of measurement amongst the inhabitants of the Indus Civilisation is less certain but anticipated by the common use of fired and unbaked mud bricks with a ratio of 1:2:4 (Kenoyer 2010), and Dales has noted that "stone seals, figurines, jewellery and other classes of artefacts appear to have been made according to accepted size and proportion standards" (Dales 1991: 133). In addition to this more indirect evidence, three extremely rare finds of rulers or measuring rods have also been discovered at Lothal, Mohenjo-daro and Harappa. The first is an ivory length, measuring 128 millimetres and is rectangular in section (Rao 1973: 105). Apparently damaged at one end, a 46 millimetre length of the broader face was marked with twenty-seven parallel cut marks. Each cut was 1.7 millimetres apart and the sixth and twenty-first were longer, perhaps indicating larger units. The second measuring rod is a graduated fragment of shell divided into nine surviving individual units of 6.62 centimetres with a group of five demarcated by dots, one of which is further marked by a circle. The third measure is a bronze rod from Harappa marked in lengths of 0.367 inches (the numbers and unit or measure are those given by the original excavators) (Wheeler 1968: 83–84). Wheeler has proposed that this evidence suggests a decimal system was in place but that there may have been two units of measurements in place; a Harappan foot measuring between 13.0 and 13.2 inches and a Harappan cubit of between 20.3 and 20.8 inches (1968: 84). Parpola has suggested that individual strokes on Indus seals represent single units and that semicircles represent units of ten (1994: 82–83). We can further hypothesise that the shared nature of weights and measure would have been accompanied by skills in town-planning and calendrics allowing the creation and integration of shared time and space across the Indus by specialists.

SOURCING, MANUFACTURING AND REDISTRIBUTION

Whilst a shared system of weights and measures explains a degree of the uniformity of artefacts and features, it is still striking considering the fact that the majority of agglomerated and walled populations were located within the floodplains of the Indus and Ghaggar-Hakra rivers at elevations below 1,200 metres (Schuldenrein 2002). Such locations allowed the supply of grain to larger settlements and cities by boat or raft, as otherwise the costs of overland transportation would have been immense. These settings also allowed the control of major rivers and the communities which relied on them for exchange and trade and enhanced the position of such 'Gateway' communities. This location, like those of the cities of Mesopotamia and Egypt, allowed a concentration of population near fertile land that benefited from seasonal inundation but far away from raw resources. In order to overcome this locational bias and articulate with settlement in other areas, urban-focused economies would have had to produce sufficient surplus to have allowed the movement of goods as well as the time of resident specialists. Mark Kenoyer has proposed the presence of a series of resource routes linking the urbanised centres and hinterlands with source materials such as lapis lazuli, carnelian, steatite, shell for objects and inlay and chert for blades as well as tin, copper, and gold (1998). For example, the Rohri Hills in upper Sindh and the Ongar, Daphro and Bekhain Hills in lower Sindh have provided evidence of hundreds of open-air flint quarries, many of which have been attributed to this Era (Biagi and Starnini 2008). Moreover, the exploitation of the lapis seams of the Afghan province of Badakshan all attest to this system of redistribution. The presence of copper tools and drilled beads within settlements of hunter-gatherers, at sites such as Bagor, suggest the exchange of nodules of semi-precious stone for finished goods. The strength of this link has led M. K. Dhavalikar (1995) to draw analogies between the small processing sites of western India and the early European 'factories' in Surat, suggesting that the focus on manufacturing and trade also required a protective or coercive element, hence the frequent presence of populations behind fortification walls, and that hunter-gatherers and pastoralists brought raw materials to these factories for processing (Box 6.1) (Figure 6.31). This not to suggest, however, that each of these sites matched against a single colonising model as recently illustrated by the analysis of two neighbouring sites in Gujarat (Chase et al. 2014). Brad Chase and colleagues have demonstrated that although these

Box 6.1. Reconstructing the Location of Craft Activities

Investigating craft waste is an important component of archaeological research as the finished products are often missing in archaeological contexts because of reuse and the continued circulation of more valuable goods. Many early archaeological pioneers utilised architectural form in an attempt to identify areas associated with craft activities, as their own methods of recording tended to lack contextual control and a detailed recording of artefact assemblages and by-products. For example, Stuart Piggott drew analogies between a series of fifteen small, single-storeyed regular structures on Mound F at Harappa and worker accommodation (Piggott 1950: 169) and suggested that they marked the location of subordinate communities in comparison to higher status groups in nearby structural complexes due to their relative smaller size (Coningham and Manuel 2009a: 172). However, such identifications were based on architectural evidence alone and are thus problematic, and Danny Miller argued that these structures were more likely to have contained powerful individuals who were conspicuous through asceticism, rather than slaves (Miller 1985: 61).

In response to these weaknesses and partly due to the influence of Processual Archaeology, an increasing number of researchers began to study artefactual variability across sites with a distinct focus on identifying craft waste and, through the archaeological signature of this activity, areas of craft production. For example, Mariani (1984) and Tosi (1984) worked on the Proto-urban sites of the Turanian Basin, whilst Pracchia et al. (1985) and Kenoyer (1985) studied Mohenjo-daro. Their studies analysed surface distribution of craft waste such as slag, stone debitage, crucibles, furnaces, blanks and moulds, on the basis that these materials were of low value but were well-preserved. Moreover, as waste products, there was also agreement that such items would not have been moved far from their original location with Mariani (1984: 118) stating that "[t]he presence or absence of these elements certainly indicates the kind of craft activity performed in that area. It is most unlikely in fact that such elements were moved away from their place of production, since they had at that time no intrinsic value which might have led to their removal".

A number of Early Historic texts, such as the *Arthashastra*, suggested that differing craft activities and communities should be located in different parts of urban forms (See Box 11.2). On the basis of Mariana's hypothesis, one might anticipate that such a city plan would provide a signature of different crafts (and craft waste) being located in different parts of Early Historic cities. Whilst surface surveys of tell sites clearly suffer from issues such as post-depositional taphonomic processes, craft

(continued)

waste excavated from secure sealed archaeological contexts across a site may provide more robust evidence. As a result, the craft waste from twelve excavated trenches across the Citadel of Anuradhapura was analysed to test the hypothesis that if the *Arthashastra's* ideals had been adhered to in the past, a segmentation of different craft activities would be visible, whereas co-location of craft would refute it (Coningham 1997: 356). The results indicated that there was no separation of crafts at the site, and very clear evidence for the co-location of craft activities was highlighted in the largest sample in Trench ASW2. Whilst such activities at Anuradhapura were on a limited household scale of production, this was not true for all Early Historic cities, as recent evidence from Tilaurakot indicates craft production on a massive scale.

There, in the southern portion of the Nepali Terai, an industrial area was identified on a low mound characterised by an extremely high surface density of iron slag to the south of the city rampart and beyond its moat. Excavations were conducted in 2012 to scientifically date the industrial activity, and thus connect it to the cultural sequence of the ancient city. The excavation exposed a 3.5 metre deep section of dumps of furnace lining and approximately eight tonnes of slag recovered from a four by three metre trench. Radiocarbon measurements indicated that the metal working activities at this site outside the city were first established in the fourth century BCE. These radiocarbon determinations indicate a concerted industrial-scale activity at this locality at Tilaurakot in the Early Historic period and suggest a degree of city planning in order to locate polluting activities beyond the city limits.

two small sites both shared elements of material culture associated with the Integration Era, they were differentiated from one another in terms of economic practice and consumption.

There was also, in general, considerable uniformity in a range of craft manufacturing activities throughout the Indus, but ceramics in particular also reveal important regional variations. For example, the populations of Harappa and Mohenjo-daro both favoured underlying regional styles, which contrast with local Baluchistan, Gangetic and Gujarati 'styles'. The larger urban population agglomerations and regional centres became centres for the manufacture of crafts, thereby creating and controlling access to items both everyday and prestige, and it is also apparent that some ceramic wares, such as Reserved Slip Ware, were so standardised that researchers have hypothesised that it was the "specialist product of a single or limited number of production centres" (Krishnan et al. 2005: 701). A great deal of research has been carried out on traded goods and long-distance networks in the integrated era (Kenoyer 1998). Lapis lazuli from Afghanistan and jade from China have been recovered, along with gold

Figure 6.31. Semi-precious stone debitage and working in Kutch, India.

(likely to have been imported along with more local sources), silver (from Afghanistan or even Iran) and coastal shells at inland sites. The inhabitants of the Indus settlements exported etched carnelian beads and lapis lazuli, particularly to the west. However, there is also substantial evidence of trade of both goods and raw materials within the Indus system itself: different types of stone, copper, gold, shell, turquoise and of course agricultural products from villages and the countryside into the urban areas. The rock and mineral assemblages excavated at the site of Harappa have been studied in detail and during the Integrated Era reached their greatest variety with thirty different types (Law 2006). These ranged from grinding stones, which were sourced from 200 kilometres away, and limestone and sandstone ringstones, each of which weighed more than 130 kilograms, down to small blocks of steatite. Law has suggested that these would have been transported through a variety of ways, including by boats and rafts, carts, perhaps sheep and goat, and human porterage (ibid. 308).

One of the easternmost sites of the Indus, Lothal was a trading outpost, situated on the border between the agricultural Indus and the contemporary hunter-gatherers of western India. Lothal was some 20 kilometres from the sea on a tributary of the Sabarmati River and thus a trading own ideally placed for access to the carnelian sources in Gujarat, and for sending out finished products (Rao 1973). The number of specialised bead workshops throughout this small town demonstrates the importance of manufacturing and trade to its inhabitants. There were also ivory carving workshops as the town was near a supply of elephants, possibly sourced in Gujarat. Manufacturing was on a large scale with the production of beads and objects from gold, copper, shell and ivory all shown in the archaeological record through the presence of both workshops and tools, and objects themselves in various stages of manufacture and waste material. The estimated output of all the workshops would have been far greater than production to meet the needs of the population of quite a small town, indicating that it fed far greater markets. Whether such settlements represented newly established entrepots of traders from established settlements elsewhere, or whether they represented local elites taking advantage of the demand for processed goods remains unclear.

Shortughai in eastern Bactria (modern Afghanistan) has yielded etched carnelian beads, steatite and agate beads, shell bangles, terracotta bull figurines and cart fragments. vessels with pipal motifs and even an Indus seal depicting a rhinoceros (Francfort 1984: 171). These 'typical' items of Indus material culture might well indicate strong trading links between Shortughai, beyond the frontiers of the Indus civilisation proper in Afghanistan, with access to the nearest significant supply of lapis lazuli, and the cities and towns of the Integrated Era. Indus seals and impressions of Indus seals, like the unicorn impression at Tell Umma, have also been found in Mesopotamia indicating the possible presence of traders (Possehl 2002a: 229). As noted earlier, specialised populations were also established within the Indus system and Belcher has suggested that Balakot may have been re-established as "a commercial station in order to supply fish for inland communities" (2003: 144). Its inhabitants undertook fishing alongside the procurement of shell and manufacturing of shell bangles, and they also followed Integration Era planning and administrative norms with the presence of cardinally oriented lanes, drains and wells on the High Mound as well as yielding five steatite stamp seals (Dales 1979: 269). The latter suggests that they may well have controlled access across the Las Bela Valley mouth and Sonmiani Bay and have been, as suggested by Dales, "a coastal way-station" and "Harappan frontier settlement" (Dales 1979: 271–272). As to the recipients of the fish, Belcher also identified fragments of marine fish such as jacks and mackerel in dumps and street deposits at Harappa, suggesting that dried or salted fish were traded and moved over 850 kilometres (2003: 160) (Box 6.2). Other recent analysis of the lead isotopes in copper ore from Integration sites has matched with samples from the Khetri/Singhana region of Rajasthan, demonstrating the export of both finished products and raw material (Hoffman and Miller 2009).

Of course, archaeological visibility has played a major role in the focus of scholars investigating the sourcing, manufacturing and redistribution of raw materials and finished products and, as a result, less attention has been focused on archaeological textile evidence from the Integration Era. Traces of such materials have only survived through metallic corrosion products or impressions in clay, but include cotton from Lothal preserved on the reverse of

---

Box 6.2. Indus Subsistence

Whilst discussing the archaeological evidence for plant and animal exploitation in the major cities of the Indus Valley Tradition, it is immediately apparent that the most systematic sampling strategies and systematic analysis of any assemblages come from Harappa itself. Stephen Weber's research at that site has been combined with the collection and analysis of extensive botanical samples, which has permitted the identification of the types of plant remains present. Furthermore, the combination of good stratigraphic excavation and sampling has allowed Weber to identify changes in both plant types and cropping strategies over time (2003: 175–198). He has recorded two major types of agricultural strategy within the Punjab: winter cropping and summer cropping. Winter cropping, known in South Asia as the *rabi* (or spring) crop, where sowing takes place in autumn, the crop is fed by winter rainfall and is then harvested in the spring, is known in the north-western area of South Asia, and the main plants include barley, wheat, oats, peas, lentils and so forth. Summer cropping, known in South Asia as the *kharif* (or autumn) crop, where sowing takes place in summer, the crop is fed by the summer monsoon rainfall, and is then harvested in the autumn, is known in Gujarat and western India, and the main plants include millet, sorghum, rice, cotton and dates (Weber 1999: 818). Weber believes that he has identified the winter strategy at Harappa and also suggests that it is likely to have been the agricultural strategy followed at the other major cities. Indeed, wheat, barley, peas, sesame and melon remains were all recovered and identified during Vats's 1920–1921 and 1933–1934 excavations at Mohenjo-daro, and Vats also noted the recovery of faience sealings in the shape of date seeds and other artefacts decorated with date twig patterns (1940: 466–467). Weber has further argued that the summer cropping strategy was developed later than the winter strategy and that it was "linked with pastoralism" (Weber 1999: 818). Whilst winter and summer crop plants have been recovered from both Harappa and Mohenjo-daro, Weber has argued that it is the quantity of each type of plant that indicates its importance. For example, he has stated that "while rice phytoliths and a few carbonized rice grains have been recovered from each occupational Harappa, rice appears to have played a minor role in their agricultural strategy. Rice cropping was probably not well suited to the environment surrounding Harappa, just as it is not the prominent plant cropped today" (1999: 819–820).

The extensive dating of contexts at Harappa has allowed Weber to present plant remains from the different phases of social development through the Eras of Regionalisation and Integration to Localisation, and

(continued)

this allowed him to develop sophisticated models of changing plant use in relation to changing political, social and economic conditions. Weber (1999) noted that during the Integration Era, Harappa yielded a limited range of cereal types with wheat dominating the assemblage, along with other winter crops. In addition to wheat, barley was also recovered, but it is clear that during this major urban-focused phase, wheat was the most significant cereal. Weber explains this dominance as the separation of functions between urban and rural, that is, that the place of production was also the place for preliminary processing, at least, as social complexity increases. Weber's model proposes that as the urban area and population increased, agricultural activity became divorced both physically and socially, and crops were moved over ever greater distances. This, he believes, accounts for the narrow range of plant types and also the presence of human food crops (wheat) in greater quantity than animal food crops (barley) (1999: 823).

In terms of animal husbandry and hunting, Mark Kenoyer has suggested that zebu (humped cattle), non-humped cattle and water buffalo were the most important animals of the Indus cities (1998: 164), and this is supported by the archaeozoological assemblages recovered from Harappa and Mohenjo-daro. Both zebu and buffalo are used for traction as well as milk, meat and other secondary products today, and finds of model carts and animals from archaeological contexts strongly support this pattern in the past. Although Vats work also recovered animal bones from Harappa, they were not quantified and often not identified. In relation to Mound F, for example, the excavation report noted "a number of hardened bovine bones including the forepart of a skull with two horns" (1940: 96), and on Mound AB, a large heap of loose animal bones is described, including bones from dog, sheep, ox, and horse. However, more recent research at Harappa has resulted in the systematic recovery, recording, and identification of animal bones, including the work by Meadow (1991). Meadow's work has focused particularly on understanding transitions to domestication and the impact of domestication on animal bone morphology, but within the reports published to date it is also possible to determine the type and range of animals recovered from the site (Kenoyer 1998; Meadow 1991). In addition to zebu, non-humped cattle, and buffalo, other domesticates identified at Harappa included dog, cat, camel, donkey, domesticated pig, sheep and goat. Considerable amounts of bone were recovered from the streets of Harappa and, as well as giving interesting insight into disposal of rubbish and the development of different areas of the city, this also demonstrates that animals were being kept within the urban space (Meadow 1991). Today animals are still kept within major cities in South

Asia and are used for regular access to milk and milk products, as well as for drawing carts.

Whilst we may comment on the advantages of science-based archaeological research within contemporary South Asian archaeological practice, it is interesting to note that one of the most comprehensive animal bone studies from Mohenjo-daro remains the report by Sewell and Guha (1931), which formed part of Marshall's excavation volume. In addition to various notes about bones recovered during excavation, Sewell and Guha were able to identify and describe bones from fish and tortoise in addition to the mammal remains, including zebu (but interestingly not non-humped cattle), sheep, camel and pig. Approximately equal numbers of wild and domesticated types were recognised at Mohenjo-daro, including four different types of deer and elephant, whereas at Harappa, domesticates outnumbered the wild species. It is clear, however, that wild resources remained important in Indus cities and, as well as representing pests, wild animals were likely to have been hunted, and may also have been an important source of supplementary protein.

sealings, and cotton from Mohenjo-daro preserved on silver vessels (Janaway and Coningham 1995). To this corpus, recent evidence of silk threads from Harappa and Chanhu-daro may be added, although it should be noted that they may have been sourced from wild indigenous silkmoth species within South Asia (Good et al. 2009). Timber for the deodar coffins at Harappa (Kenoyer 1998: 122) must also have been brought to the alluvium, probably down rivers on account of their bulk weight. Smith has stressed the importance of the production and trade of textiles between and within West and South Asia, suggesting that "textiles might well have been produced and consumed at a high enough rate to support dense networks of down-the-line exchange throughout the region" (Smith 2013: 152). Such a perspective on these archaeologically 'unseen' and perishable products may assist us in differentiating the relative importance of the trade in textiles to merchants as "bulk goods for regional consumption" rather than the "elite-destined special goods [which] served as a grace note of consumption" (ibid.: 153). An indicator of the fuller character of this trade has been presented by Good's research on the extremely well-preserved materials from Shahr-i Sokhta, which has demonstrated the presence of wool, hemp and linen (2006). Finally, Vidale also noted the complexities of post-depositional taphonomic processes when trying to reconstruct the location of craft production but has noted that heavy industries, such as brick, pottery and metal working, were excluded from the core urban areas of Mohenjo-daro and Chanhu-daro. He also found that sophisticated luxury items at the former were distributed across small workshops within households, and at the latter, the centre hosted warehouses-cum-workshops (1989: 180). This pattern appears to suggest a mixed pattern of craft production with much remaining at a household level of organisation but others at a more state, or rather, settlement level.

THE BALUCHISTAN UPLANDS AND
THE INDO-IRANIAN PLATEAU

Southern and south-west Baluchistan were an integral part of the emergence of the Regionalisation Era of the Indus Tradition and, although directly contemporary with the Indus cities and settlements of the Integration Era between 2500 and 2000 BCE, were never integrated into the network of centres associated to the east. Classified by archaeologists as the Kulli Culture, its populations used distinctive wheel-thrown red-buff ware with black on red decoration which showed characteristically Indus humped cattle, and their terracotta repertoire demonstrated continuity with earlier upland phases through the presence of cart frames, wheels and animal and human figurines. As might be anticipated, cultural boundaries were very loose and Kulli cultural material has also been identified within Harappan phases at Balakot in Sindh on the lower Indus, and Dales noted that whilst the walled sites of Sutkagen Dor and Sotka-Koh on the Makran Coast may have had strong affinities with Indus Integration Era materials and acted as coastal stations, the hinterland behind them was characterised as dominantly Kulli (Wheeler 1968: 61). However, this is not to suggest that Kulli populations were not also engaged in trade and exchange within the Arabian Sea as Kulli-type material has been reported from Umm-an-Nar, which indicates the complexity of drawing cultural boundaries (McIntosh 2002: 175). Whether integrated assemblage-bearing sites were established by force or other means remains uncertain, but perhaps the benefits of being drawn into the networks of the Integration Era are unclear from the archaeological evidence available. This complexity is further illustrated by the five-metre-thick Harappan deposit identified at Miri Qalat in the Makran. Periods I to II were associated with a distinctive 'Baluchi' cultural assemblage but in Period IV, this was superimposed by an steatite Indus seal and ivory comb and weights, in addition to Kulli Phase wares (Besenval 1994: 89). It is also important to note that not all sites within Baluchistan shared this sequence as the excavations at Sohr Damb in the Nal Valley have demonstrated with an apparent "absence of a classical Kulli horizon" (Franke-Vogt 2005: 75). It should be noted that the late Greg Possehl had suggested that the Kulli was the highland expression or variant of the Integration Era of the Indus Valley Tradition and, as such, belonged to one of the Indus domains (2002a). Smith is somewhat less convinced and refers to it as the "seat of a distinct culture" and suggests that it may have performed the role of "a merchant interface between the Indus, the Iranian Plateau, and the Persian Gulf" (2013: 155). Within such a role there is also the distinct possibility that sites apparently conforming to an Integrated assemblage may therefore represent local elites establishing themselves at key network nodes and emulating an integrated style to further their own differentiation from their peers (Algaze 2005: 143). Such a mechanism might have transformed social orders, improving storage and distribution structures, and have created the need for "the ritual displays needed to validate the changes taking place in the realm of social relationships" (ibid.: 4). Certainly, both these observations strengthen Ratnagar's earlier interpretation of the Kulli lying beyond the Integration zone and hosting linked yet independent chiefdoms (1991: 59).

Two Indus seals were excavated at Nindowari on the right bank of the Kud River, a site associated with distinctive monumental constructions (Casal 1966), the centre of one of these potential chiefdomships. Nindowari is 250 kilometres from Karachi and measured about 1,000 metres north to south and some 500 metres east to west. Its excavator, Casal, focused on the central mound where he identified a series of structures, including granaries which contained two Indus seals but was clear that the settlement did not represent a town nor an individual residence. In the KD area he identified the presence of a monumental tower constructed as three stepped terraces of boulders surrounded by a wall running for at least 460 metres. The Edith Shahr Complex in the Walpet area of Las Bela had a similar location and morphology and comprised a series of rectangular stepped boulder and cobble enclosures, the largest of which measured 10 metres high with at least three terraced steps with a connecting ramp (Fairservis 1971: 189). Never fully excavated, these centralised and agglomerated population centres represented the final response to the urbanisation to the east, but they were also to be transformed by the second millennium BC in parallel with the Indus cities. Further west on the land routes to Mesopotamia, this trade and exchange also incubated the development of an additional entrepot at Jiroft, paralleling that of Shahr-i Sokhta to the north (Kohl 2007: 225). Initial reports have indicated the presence of major mud-brick architecture complexes and extremely rich cemeteries from the vicinity of the tells of Konar Sandal located in the basin of the Halil Rud in south-east Iran. The presence of finished and semi-prepared objects of carnelian, chlorite and lapis lazuli at sites and within cemeteries attest to the broad network of contacts linking Jiroft to both east and west, and Potts has noted that "Seals and sealings indicate the presence of Mesopotamians, Harappans and Central Asians, whilst ceramic links suggest the presence of denizens from across eastern Iran, Baluchistan and the Persian Gulf / Oman Peninsular" (Potts 2012: 604). When reflecting on the character of such networks, Rita Wright has argued that there was no single controlling community and that much of the trade appears to have involved "small-scale exchanges that carried symbolic meaning" as well as the transmission of technologies (2013: 119).

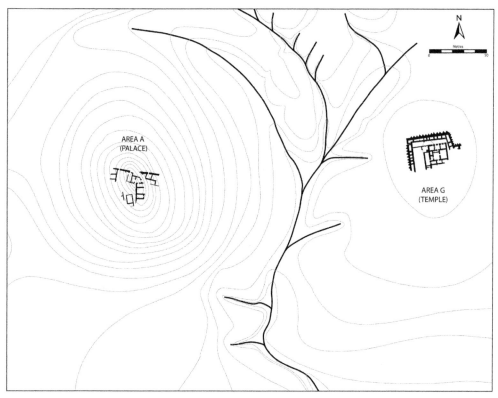

Figure 6.32. Plan of Mundigak, Afghanistan.

THE HELMAND BASIN

Across the Helmand Basin to the north, two of the region's smaller trading centres, Mundigak and Shahr-i Sokhta were also transformed as their inhabitants fed the raw and finished material needs of the Indus to the east and Mesopotamia to the west. At Mundigak, these changes were accompanied by a major increase in size from eight hectares of irregular building units in Period III to 60 hectares in Period IV (Tosi et al. 1992: 204). This expansion was termed the "Epoque du Palais" by the excavator (Casal 1961: 47) on account of the building of a remarkable pair of monumental structures on Mounds A and G as well as the creation of a series of enclosing walls covering an area of some 450 metres east to west by 200 metres north to south (Casal 1961: 65–66) (Figure 6.32). When Casal excavated the summit of the 11 metre high Mound MG A, he identified that the various structures of the preceding phase had been levelled and a 1.5 metre thick wall of fired-brick constructed along the 35 metre long north face of the MG A and presumably around the entire summit, although this is now eroded. This 2.3 metre high wall was plastered, painted and decorated externally with a colonnade of pilasters surmounted by a frieze of stepped bricks whilst most of internal face was occupied by individual cells forming a casement wall (Figure 6.33). In contrast to this monumental

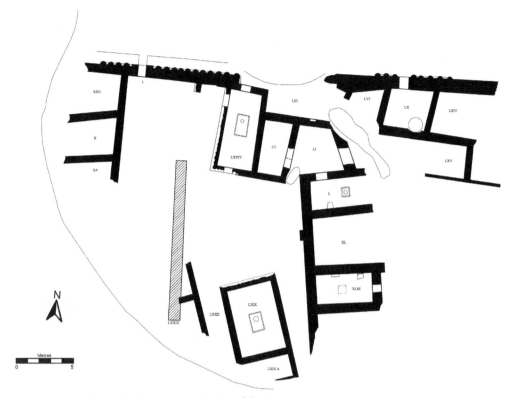

Figure 6.33. Plan of Palace at Mundigak, Afghanistan.

facade, the interior courtyard was partially occupied by a rather irregular set of large rooms although later phases were more cardinally planned and a drain of terracotta pipes installed in Room XXVII (Casal 1961: 53).

The second monument was located at MG G, on a direct alignment 200 metres east of the 'Palace' on the summit of mound MG A, and has been interpreted by Casal as a 'Temple' on account of the presence of structures identified as offering tables and a small sanctuary room complete with drain (Casal 1961: 65). Although only part of the structure was exposed, it is clear that the 'Temple' shared a similar orientation to the 'Palace' and comprised a compound defined by a 5.5 metre thick fired-brick outer wall faced with triangular buttresses on the exterior and individual cells on the interior. The interior of the courtyard was provided with a substantial basin and drain but was largely occupied by a brick structure consisting of a series of square and rectangular rooms, many of which opened from one another rather than opening directly into the courtyard. As noted earlier, they contained a variety of "installations si speciales", including benches and a large rectangular red-painted hearth (Casal 1961: 65). Casal also exposed sections of a least two surrounding curtain wall alignments, complete with bastions at Mounds B, C, D and E (Casal 1961: 56). Again forming casement walls with very regular exterior square buttresses every 2.5 metres, the interiors were lined with individual cells, and it

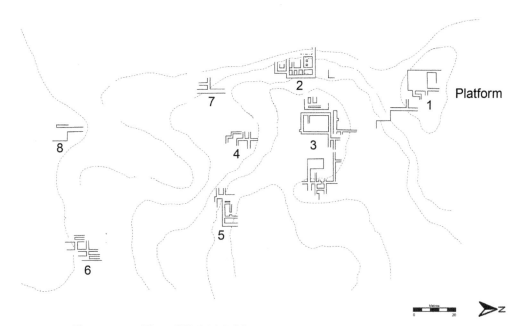

Figure 6.34. Plan of Shahi-i Sokhta, Iran.

is notable that as the settlement grew there was encroachment on these walls
(Casal 1961: Fig: 28). The presence of compartmentalised stamp seals indicated
enhanced administration as did the mobilisation and planning necessary for
the construction of the monumental public works, and whilst the find of a
stone head within MD D Period IV is intriguing, it is worth noting Shaffer's
statement that "to designate it as a 'palace' implies a degree and level of political
organisation which cannot be presently established" (Shaffer 1978: 102).

To the east of Mundigak on the trade routes across the Indo-Iranian Plateau,
the site of Shahr-i Sokhta also expanded dramatically from its Period II coverage of 17 hectares to 150 hectares by Period III (c. 2500 BCE) (Tosi et al.
1992: 204) (Figure 6.34). The majority of this area appeared to have been occupied by regular residential quarters, some of which housed craft activities, but it
is also notable that no palaces, public buildings or temples have been identified.
However, there was also the twenty-five-roomed 'Burnt Building' of Period
IV, which appears to have covered an area of 800 square metres as opposed to
the average housing unit area of 169 square metres, and Tosi has argued that it
has analogies with a monumental construction at Altyn-depe (Tosi 1983: 94).
No bathrooms have been identified, but an intriguing length of terracotta
drainage pipe has been excavated, suggesting that part of the site may have
been provided with "a system for conveying and discharging part of the water
used for consumption in the town" (Tosi 1983: 125). However, as Tosi noted
"The general impression of cultural unity of the entire Shahr-i Sokhta structural sequence is further confirmed by the minor structures required by the
household economy" (Tosi 1983: 131).

There was clear evidence to suggest that this overall expansion in size was accompanied by the agglomeration of those involved in craft activities from across the residential units and within the agricultural villages, into an area of between 30 and 40 hectares in the western and southern areas of the settlement after 2600 BC (Tosi et al. 1992: 205). It is notable that only ceramic manufacturing and metal working appeared to have become industrialised. These craftspeople were also recognisable within the separate 21 hectare cemetery of the settlement as they were interred with their tools and products (Tosi et al. 1992: 205). More than forty drill-bits have been recovered from Periods II and III at the site (c. 2800–2200 BCE) and have been identified as having been used for the on-site manufacture of beads of lapis lazuli, cornelian and turquoise as well as for cutting and drilling stamp seals (Piperno 1983). The importance of manufacturing here was further stressed by Tosi's observation of a ratio of 9:1 between finds of rejected semi-precious stone objects as opposed to completed ones (Tosi 1983: 169). The presence of painted potters' marks in Period II was replaced by more frequent incised ones in Period III, suggesting a greater need for recording, (Tosi 1983: 144) and these were accompanied by 200 compartmentalised steatite seals in Period II and a further fifty bronze ones in Period III (Tosi 1983: 156). The recovery of wooden combs for wool processing is also indicative of the full spectrum of production taking place at the site (Janaway and Coningham 1995). These industrial and long-distance trade networks still had to be supported by a framework of smaller settlements, and Shahr-i Sokhta presided over more than forty settlements covering between 0.5 and two hectares in this region, with a second tier of a single site of 4 hectares (Tosi et al. 1992: 204). Interestingly, some of these smaller sites appear to have been specialised ceramic productions centres like Tepe Rud-i Biyaban, but others were geared towards agricultural production and hunting on the edges of the Basin (Tosi 1983: 97).

THE ARABIAN SEA

Unlike the established trading settlements on the Indo-Iranian Plateau and in the Helmand Basin during the Regionalisation Era, there was little evidence for such complexity within the confines of the Arabian Sea and the Persian Gulf. This does not suggest that there was a lack of established seafaring communities in the region but that their inhabitants' involvement within trade and exchange networks during this early Regionalisation Era in South Asia is not yet clear. In contrast, by the time of the Indus Integration Era, there was clear evidence of contact between the cities of the Indus Basin and communities within and beyond the Arabian Sea (Tosi 1987) (Box 6.3). Evidence of such contact has been found at the coastal site of Tell Abraq in the United Arab Emirates during the excavation of a stone and mud-brick fortress-tower and surrounding complex of four hectares (Potts 1994a: 617). The contact came

Box 6.3. Searching for Dilmun

The name Dilmun appears on many Mesopotamian cuneiform clay tablets, and these records referred to mainly commercial records and Sumerian literary compositions. The oldest of these dates to the middle of the third millennium BCE and the name appears to have fallen out of use by the sixth century BCE. Written with letters that were reserved for place names, it is generally agreed that Dilmun must refer to a real geographical location (Crawford 1998). These commercial records suggest that Dilmun was a centre of international trade and it was frequently referred to in association with the entities of Magan and Meluhha and each are thought to denote separate geographical domains. Magan has often been identified as Oman, Meluhha as the Indus Valley, and many scholars have attempted to reconstruct the economic relations between Dilmun, Magan, Meluhha and Mesopotamia (Potts 1990; Possehl 2002a). However, although there is a general agreement that such a place existed in antiquity, a major point of contention remains: Where and what exactly was Dilmun?

In addition to being a trading centre, it is also clear that Dilmun was also conceived in Sumerian myths as a paradise island, inhabited by gods and demigods, and in the early nineteenth century, Arno Poebel published the "deluge" tablet in which it became clear that there was a Sumerian concept of an 'Abode of the Blessed' (Bibby 1972). In a section of this poem, the gods decide to destroy mankind through a flood, but the god of wisdom, Enki, forewarned the pious king Ziusudra of this catastrophe, advising him to construct a boat. Ziusudra duly did so and survived the ensuing destruction, showing thanks to the sun-god Utu after the deluge by prostrating and providing sacrifices. The gods An and Enlil then granted him eternal life and placed him in Dilmun (Kramer 1944: 18).

However, there also appeared to be an inherent contradiction between these portrayals of Dilmun. How could a place viewed as a pure land and a paradise be the same location mentioned in the economic texts as a hub of trade for copper, staple crops and luxury goods? In response, it has been postulated that the mythical concept of Dilmun emerged in the early third millennium whilst there was little direct contact between it and Mesopotamia, as the mythical aspects of the island built up over time through stories picked up on trading routes. However, it was not until after direct trade had developed and flourished that its commercial aspects became more well known, whilst its paradise image had already become entrenched (Crawford 1998).

Sir Henry Rawlinson was one of the first scholars to make a formal connection between Bahrain and the paradise island of Dilmun mentioned in early texts (Lamberg-Karlovsky 1982: 45). Indeed, it has been suggested that Bahrain's springs and rich vegetation may have aided the myths of Dilmun's paradise status in the early texts. In 1878 Captain E. L. Durrand undertook the first archaeological survey of Bahrain and, amongst his findings, the report contains a reproduction of the 'Durand stone', what has become one of the island's most treasured artefacts. This stone contains an Old Babylonian inscription recording an individual named Rimum, who described himself as the 'servant' of Dilmun's tutelary divinity. Although some have suggested a location in south-west Iran (Kramer 1944), the majority of scholars are in agreement that ancient Dilmun had Bahrain as its epicentre, but may also have extended to the island of Failaka and the eastern coast of Arabia (Crawford 1998).

One of the main features of Bahrain's archaeology are the thousands of ancient burial mounds, and it has been estimated, through aerial photography, that these total more than 170,000 (Hojlund 2007). The presence and density of these numerous monuments to the dead, in association with the presence of sweet water springs with reported magical properties, led early scholars to suggest that Bahrain was a sacred island for the dead, the paradise of Dilmun. Indeed, these scholars supported such assertions through contemporary observations of the wishes of Shia Muslims throughout the Near East to be buried in the sacred sites of Karbala and Najaf in Iraq (Crawford 1998). However, Geoffrey Bibby suggested that the tumuli exclusively belonged to the people of Dilmun due to the lack of material culture in the graves from elsewhere in the region (Bibby 1972), although this was countered by Lamberg-Karlovsky (1982). The latter argued that Bahrain was the burial ground for the entirety of the Persian Gulf and that individuals chose to be buried there to enter the underworld and stressed that "[o]nly the existence of a funerary cult, directed toward burial in a sacred region, can explain the 150,000 tumuli-tombs of Dilmun" (Lamberg-Karlovsky 1982:47). He backed this hypothesis on the status of Dilmun as a paradise land and abode of the blessed in Sumerian texts and that there was insufficient evidence of indigenous settlement to account for the sheer volume of tumuli, which was unprecedented in the ancient Near East (Lamberg-Karlovsky 1982: 46). Indeed, he also suggested that Dilmun's elites capitalised on their control of pilgrimage and the construction of tumuli to become an important node in international trade networks (Lamberg-Karlovsky 1982: 48).

However, intensive archaeological research has subsequently identified the presence of a number of substantial settlements on the island, such as Saar and Qal'at al-Bahrain (Potts 1990). Furthermore, it has also been shown that the tumuli were built over a long period of time, continuing into the first centuries CE, not just during the late third and early second

(continued)

millennium BCE, and it is now more mainstream opinion that the burial mounds represented the final resting places of the island's own inhabitants, rather than individuals from elsewhere (Crawford 1998). Despite this, the textual evidence of trade between Dilmun and the wider region is corroborated through excavated materials. Due to its geographical position in the Persian Gulf, Dilmun could tap into the potential of trade routes being somewhat equidistant between Mesopotamia and South Asia, as well as possessing many sheltered harbours. Evidence for trade interactions come from textual references, which record the trade in copper as well as of non-durable goods such as timber, foodstuffs and textiles. One of the most concrete indicators of trade is provided by seals and circular stamped seals made from steatite and chlorite, which have been found in great quantities at Saar and Qal'at al-Bahrain and have been identified as a key indicator of Dilmun material culture (Potts 1990). Dilmun seals have been found across Mesopotamia, including the find of a clay tablet recording an economic contract which was written in Susa but sealed with a Dilmun seal, raising questions as to the control of Arabian Sea trade (Potts 1999: 179). They have also been found within Indus Valley sites, such as Lothal (Rao 1973), and excavations at Saar have uncovered a chert Indus Valley Tradition weight, two haematite bullet-shaped weights, most likely Mesopotamian, as well as beads manufactured from bitumen, which analysis suggests have an Iranian origin (Crawford 1998). However, we should remember that the exact geographical location of Dilmun may well have shifted and changed over the millennia that it traded; only further research will aid the debate.

in the form of three polished Indus weights, one of jasper and two of banded chert in addition to a copper axe adze, micaceous red ware from Gujarat and two sherds of locally produced wares with incised Indus signs. The latter is interesting as it may suggest that individuals with knowledge of the Indus sign system were resident or visiting the site. On the eastern coast of Oman, further evidence of maritime connections with the cities of Mesopotamia and the Indus have been identified at the site of Ra's al-Junayz in buildings dating to between 2500 and 2200 BCE. These include slabs of bitumen with impressions of reed bundles and wooden planks, presumably parts of the caulking envelopes of boats, as well as a copper stamp seal with unicorn and script, a painted vessel and ivory comb which have all been identified as 'Harappan' by the excavators (Cleuziou and Tosi 1994: 748). Its presence in Oman should not be too confusing as we are reminded by Tosi that it is only 450 nautical miles (833 kilometres) to the Integration Era sites of Sotka Koh and Sutkagen-Dor on the Makran coast (Tosi 1987: 123). The presence of Mesopotamian vessels with cuneiform signs also indicates the broad nature of the networks engaging

Figure 6.35. Two of the tower tombs at Bat, Oman (courtesy of the Bat Archaeological Project).

these traders as does the presence of Dilmun seals inland at the site of Susa in modern Iran (Potts 1999: 179).

Potts has indicated with certainty that the polished weights which have also been recovered from Susa, Qalat al-Bahrain and Shimal in Ras al-Khaimah, are all direct imports from the Indus Civilisation and imply strong commercial ties (Potts 1993: 327). Whilst the exact nature of this trade is largely unknown, its impact on the communities within range of the Arabian Sea is demonstrated by the construction of tower tombs as at Bat (Thornton 2013; Cable and Thornton 2013), early Bronze Age cairns in Shajah (Jasim 2012) and the numerous burials mounds of Bahrain. Subject to increasing complexity from this contact, Hojlund has suggested that "The generally small-scale socio-political development in Dilmun (Bahrain) through the 3rd millennium may be a direct consequence of Mesopotamian intervention along the Gulf shores" (2007: 123) (Figure 6.35). Moreover, the presence of rich copper sources in the Oman Peninsula, combined with the presence of copper and bronze objects, hammer stones, slag, crucibles and moulds in contemporary Umm an-Nar period sites indicates that metallurgy was well developed within the area and that there is evidence for the "export of copper ingots and finished products ... to sites in southern Mesopotamia" (Potts 1990: 125). Vidale has further suggested that there were also "Indus communities in Mesopotamia" (2004: 276) and that Sumerians and Akkadians interacted with "Dilmun sailors and traders, Indian immigrants" (ibid.). Whether the evidence is sufficiently strong for such an assumption is questionable, but it is clear that rather than just being passive recipients of supply and demand from the Indus Integration Era sites or the sites of Mesopotamia, Thornton advises us to consider them as "a number of overlapping economic and cultural spheres of influence emanating from distinct and empowered polities of varying scales" (2013: 613) within what has been referred to as a broad 'Middle Asian Interaction Sphere'.

CONCLUSIONS

One of the most important challenges facing South Asian archaeologists is further understanding the nature and character of social and political organisation within this Era of Integration. The pioneering work conducted by archaeologists such as Marshall (1931a), Piggott (1950), Childe (1939, 1942, 1950) and Wheeler (1953) is known to have had a major impact on later interpretations of the Indus Valley Tradition (Chakrabarti 2010; Coningham and Manual 2009). In particular, key figures placed great emphasis on the homogeneity of material culture across the Indus, from the layout of the two main cities, to the system of weights and measures, and the pottery styles and decorations. This allowed the Indus to be understood as a culturally uniform entity, not only across the huge geographical area where sites have been recorded and explored, but also temporally, as the excavators reported little change during the Integration Era. Cultural uniformity allowed an interpretation of social uniformity, which in turn allowed Wheeler (1953, 1959), Piggott (1950) and Childe (1942, 1950) to explain much of what they saw as contradictions in the material evidence or difficulties in applying normative models of political and social rule developed in the Near East and the Mediterranean to the Indus. At the core of these explanations was the need to demonstrate that the Indus could be fitted within the imperial frameworks that had been developed and applied in the study of Dynastic Egypt, Ancient Greece and Rome as well as Akkadian Mesopotamia. Fairservis was one of the first scholars to critique these models and interpretations, and summarised the interpretations as largely comprising "kings, urban capitals, slaves, citadels, and alien invasions in the Indus Valley" (1986: 43), that is, a very simplistic transferral of models used in the west, or in historical contexts, to the third millennium BCE South Asia. A key part of the early interpretations of the Indus rested on subordination of a large part of the population by a smaller, ruling elite group. As Coningham and Manuel (2009a: 169) point out, however, more recent studies have entertained the idea that there may have been at least an element of willingness to be subordinated, but earlier scholars were all keen to promote interpretations of subordination by force or at the very least, coercion.

The earlier interpretations of the Indus Civilisation and explanations of its social organisation rested very strongly on this analysis of the material culture showing that there was almost total uniformity right across the Civilisation. This uniformity allowed Wheeler (1959) and Piggott (1950) to refer to the Indus as an empire with a centralised government whose power was rooted firmly in agricultural production and surplus, and subsequent redistribution, and the ability to mobilise a vast labour force. Piggott argued strongly that agricultural production would have been under state control, with the identification of public buildings as granaries facilitating this (1950: 138). The similarity in layout at Mohenjo-daro and Harappa, the twin capitals of the empire, further allowed Wheeler to promote this idea of a strong central governance that controlled urban planning to a high degree, and along with other evidence of uniformity in areas such as weights and measure, and craft production, supported the whole concept of uniformity through strong laws, commercial codes and control of technologies and manufacturing. For this to occur across such a vast geographical area, where sites were located in highly diverse environmental conditions, certainly provided testament to the extreme power of those ruling the civilisation. The identification of what Piggott believed were standardised workers' quarters (1950: 169) and Wheeler called barracks or priest's quarters (1953: 32–34) at Harappa further supported their development of a hierarchical society, with subordinated groups, possibly even slaves. D. H. Gordon tentatively identified imagery of slaves within the terracotta corpus of squatting figures clasping their knees (1960: 71). The power of ideology in establishing and maintaining this type of hierarchy was also recognised, and led to the identification of a rare human statue from Mohenjo-daro as that of a 'Priest-King'. It is interesting to note, however, that this imperial model was also adopted by a number of scholars after Independence (Rao 1973).

However, as discussed earlier in this chapter, a wealth of recent and ongoing research, including the reanalysis of earlier material and analyses, has demonstrated that the Integration Era was not as resolutely uniform as the early scholars believed and strenuously promoted. This recognition has increasingly led archaeologists to distance themselves from the concept of a single state with many favouring the concept of city-states (Possehl 2002a; Kenoyer 1998; 1997b). Greg Possehl, for example, identified the presence of at least six regional domains within the settlement distribution of the Integration Era based on the "point of cleavage between major geographic features, settlement clusters and the distribution of the largest of the Harappan centres" (1982: 22). These frequently conform to what Algaze has called "gateways", which marked nodes at which land and riverine routes intersected (Algaze 2005: 145). Some of the domains were based on the location of larger sites but others were founded on perceived differences within material culture, such as distinctions between the Sorath, Kulli and Sindhi. Possehl referred to both "Sindhi Harappans" and "Sorath Harappans", suggesting that the latter lent "diversity to the character of the Indus Civilization" (2002a: 59). This point has been reiterated by Wright who has suggested that the 'Sorath Harappa' of western India "appears to have lain outside the Harappan central core" as represented by the 'Sindhi Harappan' (2010: 319). A number of the geographical limits of Possehl's domains are similar to the 'economic pockets' identified in north-west India by Joshi et al. (1984). Reflecting on these earlier suggestions, Mark Kenoyer suggested that during the Integration Era, the Indus Valley Tradition was unlikely to have been subjected to the hegemony of a single ruler and instead suggested that "[e]ach of the largest city-states may have been organised as an independent city-state, with different communities competing for control. At times a single charismatic ruler may have ruled the city, but most of the time it was probably controlled by a small group of elites, comprised of merchants, landowners and ritual specialists" (1998: 100). Kenoyer has also stressed the evidence from Harappa which indicates that there were dynamic power relationships within the city-states themselves and competition within their populations of elites and merchants (Kenoyer 1997b: 56).

Dilip Chakrabarti has further developed this projection to suggest the presence of "multiple kingdoms centred around the major settlement of a region" but that "in each distribution zone there could have been more than one kingdom. It is also likely that some of them were nothing more than city states" (1999: 199). He reiterated this model to suggest that "many, if not all, of the fortified settlements of the period may have been the urban centre of a polity" and warns that cultural uniformity has never meant political uniformity in South Asia (2000: 375). These concepts are close to the model most recently adopted by Rita Wright who has suggested that "Indus cities were organised into several city states loosely integrated by a common material culture. Individual cities were centres of political and economic activities for rural networks of outlying settlements with which they interacted" (2010: 138). Other scholars have remained uncertain concluding that "It is not, however, certain whether we need to think in terms of a Harappan empire or a number of separate, perhaps inter-related states. Another possibility that cannot be ruled out is that there may have been several states with different kinds of political organisation" (Singh 2008: 179). The concept of heterarchy may also be invoked as it is quite possible that not all the settlements were ordered within a single power or rank hierarchy, thus Mohenjo-daro might have been a major ritual centre and Dholavira a trading town, with both independent in their own right. Moreover, influence and authority between settlements may also have been economic and ideological rather than political, a far more cost-effective form of organisation. Such an organisational link may have been in place to co-ordinate the activities of the 'factory-forts' in western India and Gujarat as, otherwise, the administrative costs of supporting such a hierarchy of small and duplicate enclaves would have been enormous and inefficient. Indeed, recent analysis of two of these smaller walled sites in Gujarat has demonstrated they are not simple copies of one another but supported distinct variability in material culture and economic activities (Chase et al. 2014). Whether their links were to individual cities or clusters of cities remains unclear, as does whether they were seasonally occupied or whether some may have been established by local elites responding to external resource demands. Therefore, on a macro-scale, it would be sensible to assume that the economic and ideological hegemony of the Integrated regions far outstretched the political control of any single individual centre.

This recognition of greater diversity alongside recognisable uniformity has also allowed archaeologists to offer different interpretations for the social and political organisation of the Indus Civilisation, and perhaps most importantly, argue that not only does the Indus evidence not fit into models developed in the Near East and eastern Mediterranean, but also that we should be actively developing models and explanations for the Indus alone. For example, arguments about whether the Indus can be defined as a 'state' or a 'non-state' have occupied archaeologists for some time now (Possehl 1998), but perhaps this argument itself is not particularly helpful, as it is primarily an exercise in determining whether the Indus fits a rigid set of criteria for identifying archaeological states. Instead, scholars such as Miller (1985) and Rissman (1988) have attempted to explore power relations within the Indus using material culture such as buildings and hoards, and from this develop a unique understanding of social and political control. Miller argued, for example, that the uniformity of the Indus material culture was a direct reflection and result of the particular controlling ideology where "extreme normative order was valued and combined control over the world. Such an order was antagonistic to anything which threatened it, which meant anything not generated by it" (1985: 63).

In other words, the geographical and temporal Indus uniformity was the result of a strong leadership, firmly rooted in ideological power which imposed and supported a standard view of the Indus world within the civilisation and strongly opposed any influences or impacts from outside. This is further supported by the argument that while raw materials may have been imported into the Indus, finished goods as imports were very rare with most materials being manufactured into artefacts within the Indus itself. Ideological manipulation was also important to Rissman's work and his analysis of hoards within the Indus Civilisation. Having confirmed that four out of seven hoards at Harappa were located in 'barracks', he argued that hoards in the Indus (i.e. the accumulation of great wealth, then hidden from view) did not support the idea of a subordinated community, but rather a community where there was differential access to wealth and status, but that these differentiations may well have been cleverly inverted and deliberately masked, perhaps in order to support an ideology based in apparent equality (1988: 219). The shared repertoires of artefacts suggest that across this vast area, individuals and families were performing similar practices daily. Vidale has suggested the presence of "inter-site economic and social patterning of the labour-force employed in craft production" allowed "well defined socio-economic bonds among the different groups of craftsmen working or living within the cities" (1989: 180). This concept has also been applied to smaller categories of walled settlements by Chase et al., who suggest that 'extended families' "provided the multigenerational structures necessary (to) organize space and labour to construct the walled enclosure and maintain order within the close residential quarters" (2014: 76).

Alongside the state or non-state debate, issues such as whether political rule would have been hereditary, or invested through individual power and achievement have also been considered. In looking beyond the state, the role and position of pastoralists have been studied, and the value of cattle and certain challenges in the archaeological record have led to alternative models being proposed. For example, in response to an apparent lack of Indus elites evidenced through the absence of royal burials and monumental art, Walter Fairservis suggested that archaeologists were wrong trying to infer the presence of a state and proposed instead the presence of a number of chiefdoms and a mode of political organisation based on pastoralism rather than on urbanism (1986; 1989). He was to further develop this idea by suggesting that it was wrong to apply normative values of wealth to the Integration Era as wealth and prestige may have been associated with cattle herds beyond the city walls.

To this list of alternative forms of social organisation, we also add the possibilities suggested by B. B. Lal, that the cities and settlements of the Integrated Era were organised on the caste system (1998). Based on his analysis of Kalibangan, he postulated the presence of three spatially distinct, occupation-based groups: a priestly class (or *Brahmans*) located in the northern part of the citadel; an 'agricultural-cum-mercantile' class (or *Vaishyas*) in the lower town; and craft and other workers (or *Sudras*) living and working outside the two fortified areas (Lal 1998: 101). Lal argued that similar divisions could also be distinguished at sites such as Banawali and Lothal, and he was thus able to make links between historical and contemporary Hindu caste groups, and Indus material culture. Malik had already reached this conclusion in 1984 when he suggested that the presence of "class-caste system, of class guilds and their internal structure which also follow kin-based ties" had allowed the passing of tradition through descent rather than superimposed sanctions of political leadership (1984: 208). In truth, we know very little about the rulers of the Indus, and by extension, we know very little about the politics or religion of the state system. Instead, we have absences where other state systems such as Egypt or Mesopotamia have a great deal of archaeological and historical material. There were few if any major palaces in any of the cities and very few large houses that could have been occupied by elite members of society. There were few public spaces that can be suggested as areas of worship or temples and even fewer (if any) where this can be conclusively proved. Instead, some researchers such as Fairservis (1986), and Shaffer and Lichtenstein (1989) have claimed that cattle, particularly humped zebu, were an object of veneration as shown by their presence on seals and on pottery, and as a subject of terracotta figurines.

Indus rulers appear to have controlled through trade and religion rather than the military – there were no monuments to glorify power, no pictorial displays of conquering and power. Instead, we have the inscribed seals and the ornaments made from rare materials and complex technologies – they are symbols of wealth and power and also reflect the many different social and economic levels controlled by rulers.

It is possible to make reference to Algaze's model of an "informal empire" comprising individual integrated polities associated with centralised cores in continual competition or of a "world system" (2005: 115–116). Indeed, this concept may also draw on Colin Renfrew and John Cherry's earlier model of Peer Polity Interaction in which roughly equal Early State Modules are drawn closer together by the transition of innovations, increased flow in the exchange of goods, competitive emulation, symbolic entrainment and warfare (Renfrew 1986: 1). Indeed, for 'Early State Modules', we might substitute 'city-state' with reference to the comparative work of Charlton and Nichols (1997: 1) – sometimes aligned and sometimes in competition with one another. One hesitation is created, however, by the apparent absence of evidence for warfare in the Indus Civilisation. Weapons are few, and most could as easily be used for hunting as warfare. The massive 'fortification' walls have been shown to be of little use in real warfare, and are more likely to be a show of unity and power, or perhaps to keep out floods and animals as much as people. This is why the Indus Civilisation is often referred to as both an egalitarian state and a peaceful one (e.g. Kenoyer 1998; McIntosh 2002). However, Ratnagar has noted the presence of both stone mace-heads and clay slingshots (1991: 155), and a re-evaluation of the artefacts usually classified as either tools or status symbols has suggested some similarities with artefacts identified as weapons in areas to the west (Cork 2004). As we do have extensive evidence for the importance of both trade and crafts, many archaeologists have thus suggested that real authority within this state system lay within the control of trade and craft production. Clearly, to manage the quantities and distances involved in trade, a good recording and administrative system was vital, and therefore a writing or notation system, weights and measures were all critical in maintaining this vast flow of goods and raw materials, and the people who were able to control this, are likely to have had great power. The difficulty, of course, remains how to recognise them as there seems to have been a pervasive tradition of 'levelling' which reaches back to early Food Producing and Regionalisation Eras of the Tradition. There were additional changes present such as a change in the role of the house from a single structure, difficult to differentiate from surrounding properties, to a multi-roomed complex arranged around an inner courtyard. Such a transformation might be understood as reflective of environmental adaptation but may also reflect increasing differentiation of individual houses and families, and, of course, privacy. That the Integrated urban-focused settlements of the Indus Valley Tradition represented a major socio-economic entity in the Old World is beyond doubt, no matter how we attempt to define or explain it. It was highly successful in so far that it extended and exerted power over a vast geographical area for some 700 years. There is still much that is unknown about the mechanics of this power, and when we come to look at this power in decline, or contraction, as we do in the next chapter, it is clear that our archaeological understanding still has many gaps. Perhaps equally important, traditional approaches to understanding the later transformation of the Tradition still lack an adequate theoretical framework in which to explore the currently available evidence.

CHAPTER 7

LOCALISATION: TRANSFORMATIONS OF A SYSTEM (c. 1900–1200 BCE)

INTRODUCTION

There is considerable academic debate focused on explaining why the urban-focused Era of the Indus Valley Tradition did not maintain its integrated form for more than 700 years, although this may be seen as part of a much wider debate about the transformation of contemporary early Old World Civilisations (Yoffee 2005: 131–140). Indeed, more recent estimates of the urbanised phases of other Old World Civilisations have suggested that they were also integrated for little more than this length of time, for example, the Old and Middle Kingdoms of Egypt are generally dated to between 2700 and 1780 BCE, and the span from the Early Dynastic II to the Old Babylonian periods in Mesopotamia (2500–1600 BCE) covered around 900 years. While the Integrated Era of the Indus Valley Tradition was (slightly) shorter in duration than these two, this was arguably not necessarily a significant factor in itself (Trigger 2003: 28), and it would be equally valid to state that it is surprising that such an integration lasted so long, bearing in mind the apparent absence of explicit mechanisms of authority and coercion. Whether we use the term collapse, contraction, deurbanisation or transformation, there is little doubt that after 1900 BCE the integrated character of the Tradition radically changed. Most scholars have agreed on the physical manifestations of this transformation, even if they cannot agree on what caused it. Generally, we encounter a loss of traits associated with the urban-focused settlements, such as the presence of pre-planned urban forms hosting major population agglomerations, monumental public architecture and the shared system of script and weights. At the same time that this transformation was occurring, we may also note that a number of regional traditions were reasserting themselves, thus providing a situation that in some respects paralleled the immediate proto-urban developments of the Regionalisation Era. It is equally important to stress that what took place was not just a simple uniform transformation across the whole of the region but different transformations were occurring in different regions. For example, what happened in Gujarat was rather different to what occurred in the lower Indus Valley, and the timescales for transformation were also different in different regions. However, wherever we investigate this period, it is clear that what we are observing was not an abrupt cessation. There is no evidence for an invasion or mass migration of new peoples from outside which destroyed the networks of the Integration Era, and there is no evidence of a sudden plague or natural disaster which wiped out cities and towns and their populations. Instead, there is evidence in the form of both artefacts and structures which demonstrates that there was a degree of continuity, although the form, scale and patterns of human communities and their settlements altered; or as many researchers describe it, there was a distinct transformation.

In this chapter, the final one of Part II, we examine the features and challenges associated with the transformation of the Integrated Era Indus urban-focused system. Firstly, working on a region by region basis we trace the loss of urban traits and other significant evidence that indicated the transformation from the Integrated to the Localised Era in Jim Shaffer's framework (1992). The abandonment of the major urban settlements of the Indus Valley Tradition and their hinterlands by their populations was a major transformation, but it was also accompanied by changes in key areas of material culture such as ceramics and food production, a general decline in sedentary settlements in most regions, and the appearance and adoption of new cultural traits, such as those found in the Gandharan Grave Culture of the north-west, and the Jhukar and Cemetery H cultures, will also be considered (Box 7.1). We will then discuss the various theories presented to explain these transformations, and evaluate the evidence that has been cited in support of the different theories. We begin our consideration of the various models developed to account for the transformation with mono-causal explanations such as invasion and migration; flooding, river shift and the drying of the Ghaggar-Hakra; trade collapse; deforestation, salination and climate change; new crops; and epidemics. This will be followed by explanations which are multi-causal and then by Tainter's concept of complexity and marginal returns (1988), considering that the latter approaches are more relevant than seeking single or primary factors. We also note Yoffee's argument that collapse and transformation was not a surprising or unexpected outcome, but rather it was the emergence and existence of states at all that was exceptional (2005: 132). This links with our own argument that many archaeologists have considered this period as a distinct transformation largely through a lack of evidence, which in itself is the product of an over-concentration on the conceptualisation of the preceding period as one of 'civilisation' and 'statehood'. This theme is pursued further in Chapter 8, where we explore this notion of a transformation between the cities of the Integration Era and the settlements of the Regionalisation Era, which also hosted the emergence of the first cities of the Early Historic Tradition.

Box 7.1. Settlement Survey Methods

Settlement and landscape survey has formed an important component of archaeological research within South Asia since the nineteenth century. For example, Alexander Cunningham's methodology of historical geography located Early Historic sites within large-scale regional landscapes whilst his investigations at structural complexes, such as at Sanchi (Cunningham 1854), placed monuments within their immediate topography (Coningham 2011: 932). Similarly, John Marshall's explorations and excavations at sites within the Taxila valley led to a detailed understanding of the development and settlement of the landscape (Marshall 1951: xvii). However, these long-term and resource-draining endeavours were not to be continued and later large-scale explorations usually coincided with rescue archaeology such as the responses to dam building and the associated flooding of landscapes at Nagarjunakonda and Devnimori (Sarkar and Misra 1966; Mehta and Chowdhary 1966). However, such surveys were framed as responses to mega-development rather than to research questions and, due to the unsystematic nature of most archaeological surveys in the early and mid-twentieth century, much work has focused on the identification of larger urban sites, whether belonging to the Indus or Early Historic traditions.

Influenced by processual archaeological survey methods successfully employed in the Middle East, more research-driven landscape archaeology was undertaken in South Asia from the 1980s onwards to gain evidence of long-term landscape development. For example, Makkhan Lal (1984a) in Kanpur District and George Erdosy (1988) in Allahabad District in India and Senake Bandaranayake in Sri Lanka (Bandaranayake et al. 1990) utilised village to village surveys to identify and map regional settlement dynamics. This method utilised large modern villages as bases for survey and information, and the location of these settlements largely determined the areas selected for field-walking. However, such a method has undoubtedly led to a bias of identifying sites near areas of current settlement as well as along modern communication routes. Similarly, the focus of field archaeologists towards highly visible mounds, such as those investigated by Verardi in his survey of the Nepali Terai (2007), also reinforced a bias towards more evident landscape features. Furthermore, these reports did not specify which areas were and were not surveyed, and the definition for criteria of a site was not made explicit. Mughal's (1997) survey of Cholistan and the dry riverbed of the Hakra suffered from a comparable site bias, and the predominance of large sites within this survey region may be a reflection of site visibility rather than site density, reflecting challenges within

(continued)

the methodology. Furthermore, all these surveys were focused towards a goal of creating settlement hierarchies, which were to be based upon site size as a marker of importance and complexity. Moreover, there was little attempt to integrate or differentiate religious sites within the landscape. However pioneering, the lack of robust systematic methodologies and theoretical assumptions have provided an imbalanced view of the archaeological record.

More recent survey programs have begun to deploy more complex strategies and a number of researchers have come to accept that although religious sites may be relatively small in size, they "may wield greater political and/or economic power than spatially larger villages or towns" (Coningham et al. 2007a: 714) and thus represent a separate settlement hierarchy with the landscape, a concept referred to as heterarchy (Crumley 1995). Indeed, an increasing number of landscape studies in South Asia have incorporated the identification and recording of religious complexes into their approaches and discussions. For example, recent surveys in the environs of Sanchi (Shaw 2000; 2013), Thotlakonda (Fogelin 2006) and Bharhut (Hawkes 2009) in India as well as in the vicinity of the sites of Sigiriya and Dambulla in Sri Lanka (Bandaranayake et al. 1990; Bandaranayake and Mogren 1994) have all stressed the central role that religious institutions, specifically Buddhist monasteries, played in the administration and development of their respective landscapes. Unfortunately, only preliminary results of the Sigiriya-Dambulla survey were ever published, and in India there is a lack of available detailed textual records to augment the archaeological evidence, which itself suffers from a lack of chronological resolution (Coningham 2011: 938–939).

Utilising systematic transect survey and integrating science-based archaeological, epigraphic and textual data, the Anuradhapura (Sri Lanka) Project has linked excavations conducted at the Citadel of Anuradhapura with its non-urban hinterland communities. More than 700 archaeological sites were identified in a 50 kilometre radius survey universe centred on the Citadel, a sample of which was then subjected to further investigation through non-intrusive survey methods and excavation (Coningham and Gunawardhana 2013). Rather than the five-tiered settlement hierarchy extolled within the *Arthashastra*, which suggested an entirely secular administration of landscape, the two main categories of sites identified were shallow ceramic scatters and deeply-stratified monastic sites, whilst urban forms were noticeably missing. The monastic sites were stratigraphically deep and associated with imported ceramics, glass, semi-precious stones and monumental structures, material culture and architectural characteristics lacking at the shallow and small ceramic scatters. The working hypothesis was advanced that the ceramic scatters represented small, short-lived, shifting village settlements, whereas the Buddhist monasteries performed the dual role of religious centres as well as administrative, economic and political centres. It was further postulated that the monasteries controlled localised autonomous territories, or temporalities, throughout the landscape, which were linked to the large monasteries in the near vicinity of the city, rather than the secular court (Coningham et al. 2007a: 717). The additional examination of epigraphic records and the Sri Lankan Chronicles, in conjunction with the archaeological evidence, is beginning to extend our understanding of the central roles of Buddhist monasteries in the management of irrigation and the colonisation of land for agriculture. Such systematic surveys provide evidence for the potential of what landscape archaeology can bring to the archaeology of South Asia, as well as highlighting the potential heterarchical interrelations of urban forms and hinterland, in addition to placing secular and religious sites in the landscape dynamics and sociopolitical developments of society in the past.

REGIONAL ANALYSIS

The purpose of this section is to review the evidence from within the area formerly covered by Integration Era settlement as well as neighbouring areas, in order to identify and evaluate changes in human behaviour and their choices of material culture (Figure 7.1) (Timeline 7.1). For the purposes of this study, we have used subdivisions which respect acknowledged archaeological assemblages, such as associating the Jhukar Phase with the Lower Indus, and Cemetery H Phase with the Punjab, but we are aware that there are other links and overlaps as well. Additional challenges involve the poor dating of these phases, partly because many archaeologists have been rather more interested in studying the earlier levels, and partly because this period is associated with occupation on the summits and uppermost surfaces of a number of the archaeological mounds and thus been most prone to erosion and post-depositional damage. This has resulted in a situation at Harappa, for example, where the site has been provided with one of the best dated sequences of the Integration Era in South Asia with more than thirty radiocarbon dates – but few belong to the period under study in this chapter (Kenoyer 1991a: 43). This challenge of poor chronological resolution means that we are not entirely sure how individual sequences at individual sites link and articulate with one another, even though some of the most cited sequences have been reanalysed and their results disseminated (Herman 1997; Mughal 1992). The numbers of reliable dates and sequences have increased, and now most scholars have abandoned the old terminology of Post-Harappan (Agrawal 1982: 192) to use Late Harappan or post-urban Harappan to reflect a more nuanced understanding of this era,

Figure 7.1. Map of sites mentioned in Chapter 7.

although we prefer to use the term 'Era of Localisation' to reflect the processes at work across the regions under study.

The Northern Valleys

Despite the presence of characteristic material including seals and weights at Shortughai in Afghanistan, there were no known Integration Era sites within the northern valleys of Pakistan. As a result, Possehl has argued against reviewing the sequence of this region whilst discussing the 'Late Harappan' cultures of South Asia (2002a: 241). However, reports of ceramics with Cemetery H affinities within the Swat Valley (Stacul 1984b: 271) lead us to do so in this chapter. Despite this fragmentary link, it is clear that new Late 'Chalcolithic' burial traditions were adopted by populations in the region of the northern

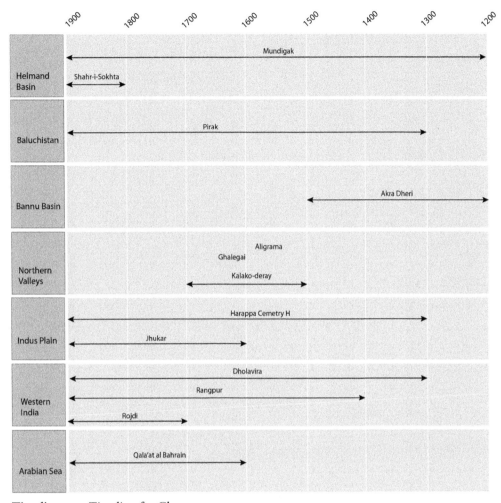

Timeline 7.1. Timeline for Chapter 7.

valleys during Swat Valley Period IV, between 1800 and 1400 BCE (see also Chapter 5), contemporary with the Localisation Era of the Indus Basin (Stacul 1987). This period is represented within the Swat Valley at a number of sites, including the Ghalegai rock shelter and at the open-air sites of Loebanr 3, Bir-kot-ghwandai, Aligrama, Damkot, Barama, and Kalako-deray (Stacul 1987: 53). Located on low slopes and saddles within the valley, the earlier pits of the Kashmir-Swat Neolithic were replaced by surface structures of rectangular stone walls and the valley's inhabitants instigated the first formal cemeteries (Stacul 1994a; 1987: 71) (Figure 7.2). As black-on-red painted vessels became phased out of fashion, new black and grey burnished wares were introduced alongside the establishment of trade networks bringing shell and carnelian from the Arabian Sea and western India and lapis lazuli and jade from

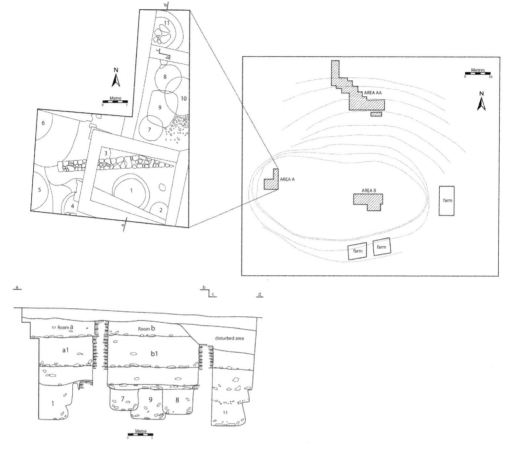

Figure 7.2. Plan and section of structures at Kalako-deray, Pakistan.

the north (Stacul 1987: 81–85, 101, 121). Identifying an Iranian and Central Asian connection for the black and grey wares (1979: 672; 1989a: 250), Stacul has also attributed links with the Kachi Plain for similarities between terracotta figurines and other materials suggesting the presence of "a dynamic system of multidirectional contacts in the framework of a process of integration and fusion" (1989b: 269). More details of the sequences in this critical area will be discussed in Chapter 8, but is clear that a number of key settlements continued to be occupied during this Era of Localisation, and that revitalised trading networks remained in place articulating the populations of these valleys with those close to sources to the north and south, forming a key attribute of the Localisation Era according to Shaffer (1992: 442).

Western India

The Localisation Era is also known as the Rangpur Phase within western India and has been dated to between 2100 and 1380 BCE (Shaffer 1992: 451).

As elsewhere within the Indus basin and its extremities, towns were largely abandoned by their inhabitants and this was the case with Lothal during Period B, although the excavator has cited a major flood as the main cause (Rao 1973: 60). The public and private structures of the settlement were razed and the brick-lined basin to the east silted up but during Phase V, Rao noted that the inhabitants constructed "jerry-built houses … with their mud-floors, reed-walls and thatched roof stand[ing] in marked contrast with the spacious brick-paved dwellings of the earlier years" (1973: 60). Recognising elements of continuity in the form of ceramics and stone tools, and even the continued creation of bathing 'basins' albeit constructed from robbed brick, a number of transformations occurred within the material culture of the site as its craft specialists manufactured tools from local chalcedony rather than from distantly sourced chert, and locally available spheroid sandstone weights appear to have replaced imported chert cubes (Rao 1973: 61).

A similar loss of urban traits was also encountered by the inhabitants of the city of Dholavira during Stage V, which the excavator has characterised as a period of "general decline'" (Bisht 1996: 29. This decline was illustrated by the poor maintenance of the Citadel, although Bisht has noted continuity in that "classical pottery, seals script, weights and others continued as before" (Bisht 1996: 29). During Stage VI, the population at Dholavira was reduced to an area surrounding the Citadel, and the cardinally oriented structures of the Integration Era were replaced with poorly constructed buildings of robbed out materials (Bisht 1996: 29–30). Continuity was observed in the use of some ceramic forms and decoration although Bisht noted the presence of Jhukar-style ceramics and seals and described this period as one where "the overall picture that emerges is that of progressive impoverishment and crumbling urbanism" (Bisht 1996: 30). Dholavira was not entirely abandoned by its inhabitants, however, and by Stage VI, rectangular and square structures were replaced by round buildings. A similar pattern was recorded at Kuntasi, where the industrial activities of the site were abandoned circa 1900 BCE and new rubble structures were erected above the old settlement (Dhavalikar 1992: 81).

This regional pattern had exceptions, of course, and one of these was at Rojdi in Saurashtra during its Period C, which has been dated to between 2000 and 1700 BCE (Possehl and Raval 1989: 171). At the beginning of the Localisation Era, it appears that the inhabitants of the 7.5 hectare settlement invested in the major construction of a two metre wide retaining wall of boulders, rammed earth and stones around the main mound. They also constructed the 10 metre square 'Large Square Building' within the new circumvallation (Possehl and Raval 1989: 29). With choices of ceramics reflecting both Integration and more local styles, it is notable that the excavators recovered no evidence of manufacturing, suggesting that the inhabitants of this large settlement mainly pursued a sedentary agricultural economy relying on millet, cattle, sheep, goat, buffalo and some hunted species (Possehl and Raval 1989: 84). Weber pointed out that an agricultural strategy based on summer crops (crops sown in early summer, fed by the summer monsoon, and harvested in autumn) was implemented at Rojdi, where millets were the dominant cereals (Weber 1999: 818, 820). Evidence for multi-cropping was recovered from the earliest occupation and this practice intensified over time. Weber has argued that regardless of the types of crops being grown "There seems to be an overall pattern throughout the Indus Civilization towards gradually broadening and intensifying the agricultural system by cropping plants more intensively throughout the year and by using a greater variety of plants during any given season" (Weber 1999: 820). Weber also found that in the Localisation Era, a wider range of crops were being grown by farmers than in any of the preceding periods, alongside a measurable decline in the density of seeds being recovered. While the range of millets and other cereals at Rojdi either remained similar or increased in the Localisation Era, there was a shift from finger millet (*Eleusine coracana*) and little millet (*Panicum sumatrense*) dominating assemblages in earlier periods, to foxtail millet (*Setaria italica*) being dominant in the later period (Weber 1999: 822). Reddy has argued that an increase in millet production at the site of Oriyo Timbo in Gujarat during the Localisation Era was linked to its use as animal fodder (1997; 2003) and, as such, may indicate that overall subsistence approaches transformed in this period with a greater emphasis on pastoralism.

The site of Rangpur was also illustrative of the human and residential trans-formations which were repeated across western India as the mud-brick plat-forms and cardinally oriented structures with bathrooms and public drains of Period IIA (the Integration Era) were replaced by structures built of mud in Period IIB, associated with the adoption of a new ware, Lustrous Red Ware as well as the loss of a number of 'Harappan' traits (Ghosh 1989: 371; Herman 1997: 194). However, IIC witnessed a return to the use of mud brick and the continuation of a number of established styles from earlier periods. Covering an area of more than 50 hectares, Rangpur remained one of the largest popu-lation agglomerations in the region with a sequence which lasted until circa 1400 BCE (Herman 1997: 190). Finally, note should be made of the dramatic changes in settlement numbers within Gujarat as twenty known sites of the Integration Era were succeeded by 152 sites of the Localisation Era (Possehl 1980). These figures are in direct contrast with other areas during the Era, although each site appears to have been much smaller in area than sites of the previous period (Mughal 1992: 217).

The Punjab/Cemetery H

Referred to as the Punjab Phase by Shaffer (1992: 451), this phase has also been called Cemetery H by others, or Late Harappan by Mughal (1997: 34) (Box 7.2). Most scholars agree that the phase commenced circa 1900 BCE,

---

Box 7.2. Cemetery R37 and Cemetery H

The early excavations at Mohenjo-daro and Harappa uncovered little evidence of Indus Valley Tradition burial rites leading to suggestions that the main cemeteries of Mohenjo-daro would have been located outside the urban area and were now buried deep beneath the rising level of the plain (Allchin and Allchin 1982: 217). Whilst no formal cemetery has yet been discovered at Mohenjo-daro, most skeletal remains have been found within domestic contexts within the uppermost levels of the site, leading to sensationalist theories about the 'Massacre of Mohenjo-daro' (Dales 1964). In contrast, two of the best known and most studied cemeteries of the Indus Valley Tradition are found at Harappa: R37 and Cemetery H. These provide some of the greatest number of human remains from any Integration Era site and both were located in low-lying areas to the southwest of Harappa's main habitation zones (Wright 2010: 263).

Cemetery R37 is the earlier of the two burial grounds at Harappa and dates to between 2450 and 2150 BCE. It measures roughly 50 × 50 metres (Possehl 2002a: 169), and the burials were all aligned north to south, with the skull toward the north and the majority of skeletons supine and extended. Many individuals were buried in rectangular pits of varying size, but some were associated with wooden coffins whilst some individuals in the cemetery were placed in brick-lined cuts (Wright 2010: 264). Palaeopathological and genetic analysis of skeletal remains from R37, in conjunction with study of associated artefacts (Hemphill et al. 1991), has potentially provided new evidence for the social relationships, burial practices and health conditions of this segment of Harappa's population (Kennedy 2000). This study suggested that the individuals buried in R37 were from a restricted section of society, with strong genetic links between the cemetery's female population. Furthermore, it has been argued the females had a strong genetic affinity to those found in Stratum II of Cemetery H, leading to suggestions that matrilocality, a system by which families move to where the bride's kin group resides, was practiced, highlighting a strong continuity of population over time (Wright 2010: 264, 267). This hypothesis has been further supported as males in the R37 cemetery had biological affinities to populations outside Harappa, indicative that the male population moved into the site from elsewhere (Kennedy 2000: 306).

Although research indicates that the general health of the individuals making up the cemetery population was good, differences in the dental remains of males and females is suggestive of preferential treatment for males, as females suffered higher incidents of lines on their canine teeth, indicative of periodic disruptions of growth (Wright 2010: 264). Unfortunately, the arrangement of grave goods is ambiguous at best but

(continued)

principal grave goods were ceramic vessels and, although types varied, there was a distinct uniformity in their shape and standardised motifs. Wright has suggested that plates with deep cut marks, found in some of these burials, was evidence of feasting during a funerary ritual, which were then placed with the dead as an offering. Furthermore, she has linked finds of pointed-base goblet forms of pottery scattered over the ground surface of R37 with such ritual feasting related to funerary activity (Wright 2010: 265). Although other grave goods were sparse, evidence of shell bangles, copper objects and beads of lapis lazuli, carnelian and Jasper were found within some burials, but seals and figurines were absent (Wright 2010: 265).

Cemetery H was established adjacent to Cemetery R37 and dated to between 1900 and 1500 BCE. The cemetery may be divided into three distinct areas; Stratum II: Eastern Section, Stratum II: Western Section; and Stratum I. Stratum II: East was comparable to Cemetery R37, containing extended supine inhumations interred in lined pits but contrastingly aligned east to west or on a north-east to south-west orientation (Possehl 2002a: 179). Stratum II: West did not include complete burials but comprised skeletal remains interred within ceramic vessels. Whilst evidence of trauma is not clear, it is thought that these remains may have been exposed before burial, but whether this was deliberate excarnation or natural is unknown (Possehl 2002a: 170). The most recent burials within Cemetery H were found within Stratum I, which contained evidence of a differing funerary practice. Ceramic vessels, measuring between 25 and 60 centimetres in height and painted with geometric and figurative designs, were found to contain human remains alongside the bones of various different species of animals, especially those of birds and rodents (Vats 1940: 242–245).

It was common for multiple individuals to be deposited within these burials, and also many contained a mixture of adult and infant bones. However, it is unclear whether the animal bones were the result of cultural or natural processes, and Possehl has suggested that the remains belonged to individuals left to decay in a specific place and later collected by the living who had more concern with gathering bones than identifying specific individuals (2002a: 171). Whatever the cultural reasons behind such funerary contexts, the burials at Cemetery H and R37 show a dramatic shift in practice from north-south to east-west orientations to the adoption of vessel burial, and these changes parallel the many elements of continuity and change across the region during the Era of Localisation. A number of these skeletal remains have subsequently been reanalysed by Schug et al., who have identified evidence of 'interpersonal-trauma' and a differentiated pattern of violence (2012: 148).

but there is a greater range for its terminal date with Mughal, for example, advocating 1500 BCE (Mughal 1997: 34) and Shaffer 1300 BCE (1992: 451). As with the other main Integrated Era urban sites, the population of Harappa largely abandoned their city, with some traces of occupation noted in the area of Mounds H and F during Period 5 (Kenoyer 1991a: 40). Archaeobotanical work by Weber at Harappa has demonstrated that agricultural strategies broadened over time, with a similar move to multi-cropping practices as seen at smaller sites in Gujarat (discussed earlier) alongside a greater variety of plant types. An increase in weed seeds in the plant assemblage may have been indicative of more localised crop processing, or as a supplement to cereals, while a move away from wheat to barley as the dominant cereal may have been indicative of environmental change (barley is a tougher plant than wheat), or barley may have been grown as animal fodder (Weber 2003: 183, 185).

Whilst this occupational evidence was mainly derived from surface scatters of sherds, the clearest evidence for this period comes from Cemetery H which was excavated by Vats (1940) and is located between Cemetery R37 and Mound AB. Cemetery H has been divided into two phases, the first of which consisted of both extended and fractional burials, including animal remains and artefacts. The second phase, of which there were twenty-six excavated examples, comprised individual vessels filled with fractional human bones, often of more than one individual, but without grave goods. Both phases were characterised by red wares painted with stylised black birds, bulls, fish and plant motifs which marked their difference from the plain ceramics of Integration Era burials, but the changes in burial practice from Period I to II have been interpreted by Kenoyer as indicative of a relatively limited transition (1998: 175) (Figure 7.3). Although early work by Wheeler led him to claim that the cemetery was "alien" and the result of new, incoming peoples to the region (1968: 69), more recent scholars have suggested that the material culture showed "strong links with earlier Harappan styles" (Kenoyer 1998: 175). The abandonment of individual burials and the adoption of new practices indicates, however, a major change in relationship with the dead. As in earlier periods, Rafique Mughal's data on the settlement patterns of Cholistan is invaluable for understanding the nature of population and settlement change, and it has demonstrated a distinct drop in the overall number of settlements from 174 during the Integration Era to only 50 associated with Cemetery H material, whilst their location indicated a population shift away from the Bahawalnagar District of Cholistan (Mughal 1997: 51). Significantly, Mughal also noted that only one site of the preceding period remained occupied during this phase and that the number of sites with evidence for only specialist industrial functions had also decreased to below one-fifth of the preceding period, while at the same time the number of multi-functional sites had increased (1997: 52) (Figure 7.4). Mughal also reported an apparent increase in the proportion of camp sites to make

Figure 7.3. Urn burial from Cemetery H in the Harappa Museum, Pakistan.

up 26 percent of the total number of sites, and suggested that this reflected a population "shift in the mode of living and a renewed focus on exploitation of the desert environment" (1997: 52). The presence of one site covering 38.1 hectares and another six between 10 and 20 hectares suggests that a degree of settlement specialisation and hierarchy may have survived into this Era of Localisation. Although less cited, the evidence from surveys on the Indian side of the border has indicated the presence of a further 563 sites belonging to this Era (Joshi et al. 1984), including occupation at Banawali, where inhabitants continued to live within the remains of the Integration Era walled settlement (Chakrabarti 1999: 133).

The Lower Indus

Across the Lower Indus, the major sites such as the city of Mohenjo-daro ceased to operate as urbanised centres of population, resource procurement and object production, and many of the smaller settlements such as Balakot and Allahdino were entirely abandoned by their inhabitants. However, some sites demonstrated reoccupation or continuation during the Jhukar Phase, which succeeded the Integrated Era (Allchin and Allchin 1982: 243). Many scholars

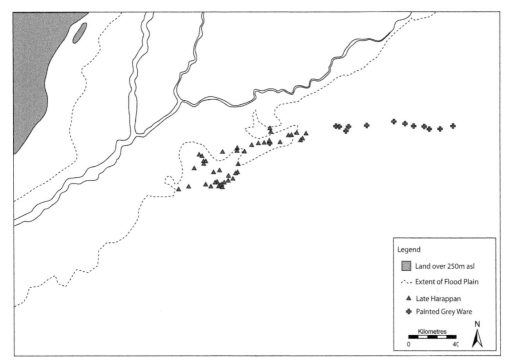

Figure 7.4. Map showing settlement patterns in Cholistan during the Localisation Era.

have characterised the Jhukar as a distinct and post-urban stage of occupation and are undoubtedly influenced by Majumdar's early label of it as 'degener-ate' (1934). For example, Marshall suggested that the Jhukar represented "a mere shadow of its former self" (1931a: 112), and Wheeler, that it represented "squatter-cultures of low grade" (1966: 92). Wheeler also interpreted any sty-listic links with the central Asian and Iranian worlds as evidence of contact with the incoming Aryans and concluded that "there is a notable absence of any real continuity in the Indus valley between the great Civilisation and its beggarly successors" (1966: 93).

Much of what we know about this phase comes from limited exposures on, or close to, the surfaces of the sites of Amri, Chanhu-daro, Mohenjo-daro, Jhukar and Lohumjo-daro. From these sites, it has been possible to identify characteristic red or pink wares with red or cream slips and painted bands of red to reddish yellow or black bands (Dales and Kenoyer 1986: 58). At Mohenjo-daro itself, Mackay noted the erosion of civic authority with the construction of ceramic kilns within the DK Area, including one in the middle of Central Street (Mackay 1938a: 6), and he also encountered a similar break-down of civic control at the bead-working town of Chanhu-daro (Mackay 1938b). Casal assumed a general abandonment after Amri IIIC before its reoc-cupation in the Jhukar on the basis of stratigraphy and occupation evidence at the site (1964: 9). Aspects of this breakdown were reinforced by Dales and

Figure 7.5. The site of Jhukar, Pakistan (courtesy Bridget Allchin).

Kenoyer's conclusion that the well-known human remains at Mohenjo-daro were also associated with late ceramics "following the major abandonment of the city" (Dales and Kenoyer 1986: 485). This late occupation was associated with finds of circular steatite stamp seals with geometric designs, quite different from those of the Integration Era as represented by the find at Amri (Casal 1964: 50) as well as a number of personalised copper objects with Iranian or Central Asian affinities such as the shaft-holes axes and axe-adzes from Chanhu-daro and Mohenjo-daro (Allchin and Allchin 1982: 232).

Evidence from Jhukar, the type-site for the Localisation Era in the Lower Indus region has, however, begun to suggest more continuity than transformation. The site was first formally identified by N. G. Majumdar in 1928. Measuring an area of 396 by 259 metres, it comprised two main mounds some 91 metres apart (Figure 7.5). Rafique Mughal, who re-excavated the site between 1973 and 1974, recorded that Mound A was five metres high and measured 259 metres east to west by 91 metres and that B was 18 metres high and formed a rough circle of 228 by 213 metres (Mughal 1992: 213). Mughal's sequence on Mound A indicated three phases of Jhukar occupation and he suggested that "the so-called Jhukar Culture refers to certain pottery designs and shapes which are different from those of the characteristic Mature Harappan ceramics but are found with them in the later period" (1992: 215). This point has been reinforced by Dales and Kenoyer who argued that "Jhukar pottery is a stylistic development out of Harappan that is partly contemporaneous with it" (Dales and Kenoyer 1986: 57), while Allchin and Allchin firmly dated this pottery to between 1900 and 1600 BCE (1997: 210). The Jhukar was succeeded by the Jhangar Phase which was represented by a scatter of sherds of burnished grey ware, often with an incised decoration, found at Amri during Period IV and at Chanhu-daro during Period III (Casal 1964: 10–16).

The Baluchistan Uplands

The Baluchistan uplands have long been linked by archaeologists with the abrupt transformation of the Integration Era on account of parallel destruction and abandonment of a number of settlements. Indeed, D. H. Gordon reflected that evidence of "such widespread destruction arguing for an invasion on a large scale." (1960: 79). These included sites belonging to the Indus Valley Tradition, such as Nausharo Period IV which was abandoned, and other associated sites which had clear evidence of destruction such as Rana Ghundai and Dabarkot (Allchin and Allchin 1982: 231). Alongside this destruction of sites in the west of the region, the settlement of Gumla in the Gomal Valley during Period V was also destroyed and abandoned by its inhabitants. The excavator of Gumla recorded the presence of "ash and charcoal and the destruction of walls together with the smashing of huge amounts of the material objects" (Dani 1971: 49). Subsequently, the site was utilised as a cemetery with circular grave pits containing cremated remains, terracotta figurines of horses and bulls, and horse bones. Similar material culture was recovered from the site of Hathala, which led Dani to make analogies with the cemetery of Sarai Khola in the Taxila Valley to the north and he suggested that it formed a separate 'Gomal Grave Culture' (Dani 1992: 399). Graves with Central Asian and Iranian affinities have also been found in the Kachi Plain to the south of the region at Sibri and Mehrgarh VIII cemeteries, established after the abandonment of Nausharo (Jarrige 1991: 94). The excavators noted the presence of a copper shaft-hole axe at Sibri similar to that from Mohenjo-daro (Santoni 1984). The cylinder seals from these two cemeteries were very different from those of the preceding period, but Jarrige also noted continuity through some of the vessels suggesting that despite the exotic materials "many elements of the material deposits from Mehrgarh Period VIII and Sibri have links with both local traditions and the Harappan Culture" and even that it was contemporary with the late phases of the Integrated Era (1991: 97). The joint German-Pakistani Archaeological Mission to Kalat has more recently added a chronometric aspect to this general abandonment with the suggestion that "At 2000 BC, settlements were abandoned in the Nal Basin and elsewhere" (Franke-Vogt 2005: 75).

Whilst the sites noted earlier were all represented by cemeteries with very little published evidence of habitation settlements, the site of Pirak, which is also in the Kachi Plain, has provided a distinctive continuous occupation sequence from 2000 to 1300 BCE (Shaffer 1992: 458) (Figure 7.6). Indeed, it is somewhat surprising to find such continuity so close to the mouth of the Bolan Pass, one of the historic gateways to South Asia, as the towns and

Figure 7.6. The site of Pirak, Pakistan.

cities of the Integrated Era were abandoned by their inhabitants (Jarrige and Santoni 1979: 9), although sadly there was no in situ stratigraphic link all the way through to the Integration Era. During this period, the nine hectare site progressed through two main phases I and II, and the material culture demonstrated clear continuity throughout. Although the trench only exposed 326 square metres of Period I's occupation, it was clear that this period represented the initial occupation of the site, which took the form of rectangular courtyards and cells, a number of which had silos and fireplaces. There was a possible civic or public construction to the west of these structures, a mud-brick platform with basins and drains which led off to a major brick-lined channel measuring one metre wide and over two metres deep (Jarrige and Santoni 1979: 21). The excavators noted the importance of structures associated with water during the Integration Era but suggested that they may have just performed drainage for higher areas of the settlement (Jarrige and Santoni 1979: 358). During Period II, the settlement continued to expand, and Phase IIB contained a particularly well-preserved block of cardinally oriented lanes, and courtyards around blocks of buildings provided with internal niches in Trench PKA (Figure 7.7). The site appeared to have hosted a manufacturing centre, and evidence in the form of ceramic wasters was recovered in Period I in addition to more than twenty terracotta seals, plus partially worked blades, bone-working, uncut ivory, and shell making as well as sixteen terracotta seals in Period II. Artefacts recovered from the site also included terracotta riders from Period IA and camels with two humps and horses from Period IB onwards (Jarrige and Santoni 1979: 171, 174–177) (Figure 7.8 and Figure 7.9). These finds were paralleled

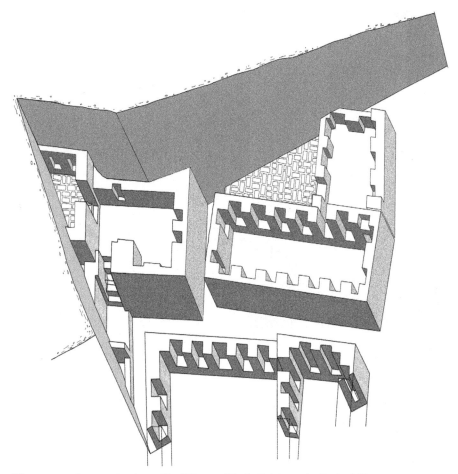

Figure 7.7. Isometric plan of building at Pirak, Pakistan, in Period IIb.

by the recovery of camel and horse bones within the animal bone assemblage (Meadow 1979: 334) and may represent key changes within transport networks. Certainly, the place of Pirak's population in long-distance trade was indicated by the presence of agate beads from Gujarat in Period I (Jarrige and Santoni 1979: 363) and uncut ivory and *Xancus pyrum* shell from the Arabian Sea in Period II (Jarrige and Santoni 1979: 372). Period III was to witness the appearance of iron working circa 1300 BCE but, significantly, without notable change to either the material culture of the settlement's inhabitants or the organisation of their other craft-working activities (Figure 7.10).

The Helmund Basin

In direct contrast with the end of investment in monumental communal constructions in the Indus watershed to the east during the Localisation Era, the 'Palace structure' of Period IV on Mound A at Mundigak was replaced by

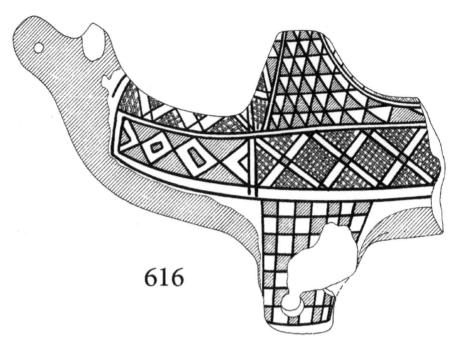

Figure 7.8. Terracotta camel from Pirak, Pakistan, Period II.

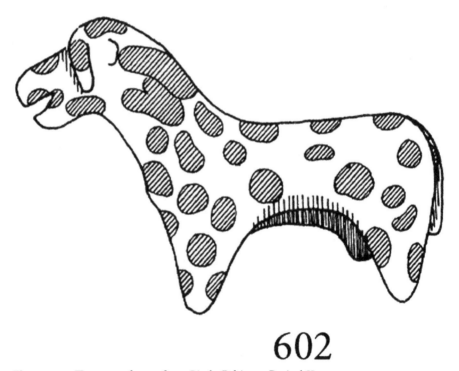

Figure 7.9. Terracotta horse from Pirak, Pakistan, Period II.

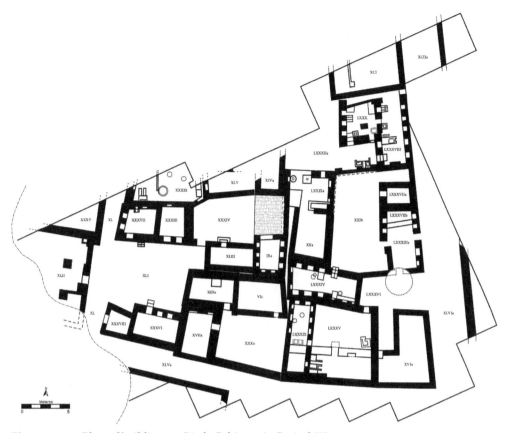

Figure 7.10. Plan of buildings at Pirak, Pakistan, in Period IIIa.

another major communal structure which Casal called the 'monument massif' (Casal 1961: 83). In the period dated to between 2000 and 1500 BCE by Shaffer (1978: 115), this new structure with foundations of stone supporting walls of mud brick was constructed directly above the Palace, although the period of time elapsing between the two was uncertain. The east to west casement wall of the palace complex with the colonnade on the exterior was entirely enclosed within a new platform, which was crowned with two rooms, XXI and XXIV, forming a further platform on its summit (Casal 1961: 87). South of the platform were a series of rectangular and square chambers and Casal suggested that the monument may have been painted red and white and accessed by a ramp (1961: 87) (Figure 7.11). The presence of this massive painted stepped structure on the summit of Mound A led Casal to suggest that it had been used for religious purposes, and the presence of human remains and a terracotta figurine were believed to confirm this interpretation (Casal 1961: 88). Casal also claimed a major transformation between the ceramics of Period IV and V, noting that while all preceding periods had demonstrated development set against continuity, the assemblage of Period V was "une complete revolution"

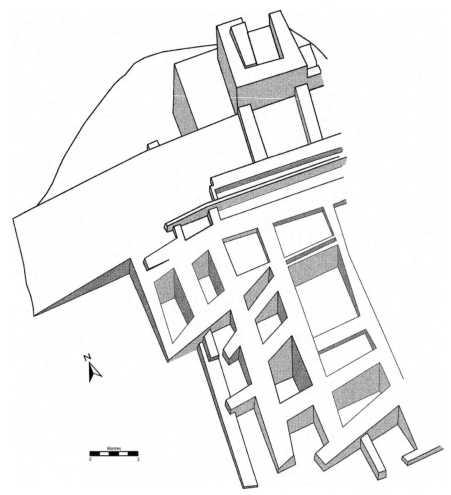

Figure 7.11. Isometric plan of the stepped structure on Mound A at Mundigak, Afghanistan.

(Casal 1961: 154). Furthermore, Shaffer noted that "The interactions with Baluchistan and the Indus Valley recorded earlier appear to cease with Period V" (1978: 139), although Dupree suggested that this transformation in ceramics and cultural linkages was due to the invasion or migration of new peoples from Ferghana in Central Asia (1973: 268).

The evidence of structural development at Mundigak V was paralleled to a degree by the sequence at Shahr-i Sokhta IV where although the settlement shrank in size to no more than five hectares, or what Shaffer called "a small agricultural village" (1992: 464), the largest single building of all its periods of occupation was constructed during Period IV. This complex, known as the 'Burnt Building', was entirely destroyed by fire, and the discovery of the remains of a boy within the charred remains has been interpreted by the excavator as evidence that "he died a violent death" and that the fire led to the "abandonment of Shahr-i Sokhta" (Tosi 1983: 88). Tosi also claimed that the ruins were used for "dwellings of a squatter settlement" and that the destruction may be dated to between 2000 and 1800 BCE (1983: 89). Shaffer has noted the complete cessation of lapidary production by its inhabitants as well as the absence of stamp seals from this period (1992: 464). At the site of Shortughai on the Oxus, evidence of links with Indus traditions disappeared by the end of the second millennium BCE, and the material culture clearly indicated that the occupants of the site replaced these with trading and exchange networks into Central Asia during Period IV (Francfort 1981: 191).

The Arabian Sea

As discussed in Chapter 6, a number of the Arabian Sea communities who had engaged in trading with the Mesopotamian and Indus Integration Era settlements had already began to undergo substantial social transformations. In Bahrain, in particular, as late as the beginning of the second millennium BCE, growing complexity was accompanied by the construction of "large-scale specialised storerooms" at Qala'at al-Bahrain, which itself now expanded to cover an area of 15 hectares and was differentiated and enclosed within a stone wall (Hojlund 2007: 124). These major communal investments were accompanied by the construction of religious monuments at Barbar and the establishment of cemeteries with a number of large burial mounds as at Aali, all of which have been identified by Hojlund as being indicative of the "material expression of the formation of a Dilmun state" (ibid.: 124). This development and its trading-orientation did not cease in the early second millennium BCE, and Potts has noted that cuneiform tablets continued to record the activities of a number of Mesopotamian traders in the region as late as 1800 BCE (1990: 221). This position was not to last, however, and the palace and warehouses of Qala'at al Bahrain and Temple of Barbar were abandoned by their inhabitants between 1740 and 1600 BCE as the southernmost Babylonian cities emptied of their populations and their trading networks ceased (Hojlund 2007: 127). Certainly in Bahrain, the creation of individual monuments and 'royal mounds' appears to have ceased and were replaced with communal and collective burials which may have been "related to a strategy of reuniting sub-groups of the clan/tribe that had previously been segregated and specialised into different economic activities during the expansion of Dilmun society" (Hojlund 2007: 135).

THEORIES OF COLLAPSE

Almost as soon as the Indus Civilisation was discovered, scholars were trying to identify when and why it ended. Whilst John Marshall focused on explanations based on floods and river shifts, some of his contemporaries were developing

Figure 7.12. Skeletons in the lane between Houses CVIII and XXXIII, VS Area, Mohenjo-daro (Courtesy Marshall Archive, Oriental Museum, Durham University DUROM.1957.1.771).

narratives which were more violent in nature, utilising some enigmatic human remains in the upper part of the ruins at Mohenjo-daro. When Mortimer Wheeler arrived in India, he reopened this debate and combined evidence from skeletal remains, 'exotic' metal objects and weapons, destroyed sites in Baluchistan and the *Rig Veda* to bind the advent of Indo-European peoples and languages with the destruction of the cities of Indus (Figure 7.12). By the time of Wheeler's own death, however, other scholars had begun to return to older models of natural catastrophes, such as floods and river course changes, in place of human agency. This has, in turn, moved to a focus on additional human factors, and now most scholars would argue that a combination of factors around 1900 BCE led to the general loss of many of the key characteristics of the Integrated Era Indus system, including its urban forms, centralised storage facilities, script, artefact standardisation and scale of its long-distance trade (Allchin 1995a; Ratnagar 2000). This longstanding perceived cultural uniformity was transformed into a combination of different cultural traditions, such as the Jhukar in Sindh and Cemetery H in the Punjab, as discussed earlier. The following section will briefly consider some of the major theories behind the demise of the Indus promulgated over the last eighty years before identifying those which have attained contemporary consensus.

Invasions

The putative movement and migrations of peoples towards the end of the Integration Era had long been advanced by archaeologists. Marshall, for example, suggested that the increase in fractional human burials present at Harappa in the post-urban period may have resulted "from extended immigration from the same quarter [Baluchistan and western Iran] which coincided with the decline in power of the Indus people" (1931a: 90). However, it was Wheeler who was to associate the movement of people with the ending of the Indus cities through violence. Wheeler found evidence for this invasion in the burnt settlements of Baluchistan, the presence of skeletons in the streets of Mohenjo-daro, the rapidly blocked gates at the Citadel of Harappa and the presence of material culture with new cultural affinities with Central Asia and the Iranian plateau (1968: 133). Wheeler also locked "traditional Indian history with the archaeological picture of the Harappan civilisation" (Fairservis 1971: 311) through his linkage of this invasion with the arrival of the Aryans in South Asia. In this way, he famously cited the *Rig Veda* as evidence and accused the god Indra of the destruction of the Mohenjo-daro and Harappa and of being the 'destroyer of forts' and interpreted the place name of Harappa as *Hari-Yupiya* or battleground of an Aryan victory (Wheeler 1966: 78). The *Vedas* describe the movement of a group of powerful people, the *Arya*, who were fair-skinned and war-like with horses and chariots and are recorded as destroying the cities of a people called the *Dasas*. Moreover, the *Arya* were thought to have brought with them an Indo-European language, which later developed into Sanskrit (Parpola 1994). Wheeler was so highly respected, and other scholars were so convincingly persuaded of the Aryan invasion, that synthetic archaeological volumes still included references to invasions and the movements of Aryans as late as the 1960s and 1970s (Gordon 1960: 87; Allchin and Allchin 1968: 144; Fairservis 1971: 311). It should also be noted that Wheeler was by no means the only scholar to have advocated invasions of Aryans and to have melded the *Rig Veda* with the archaeological record, as D. D. Kosambi followed such an explanation and even cited the Aryan destruction of dams as a contribution to the end of the Indus cities (1965: 80). More recently, other scholars have continued to try to trace the archaeological evidence of the Aryans within the sequence of South Asia, although back to the Integration Era itself (Lal 2005; Sharma 1999).

However, we also have to remember that most archaeologists at this time strongly advocated the concept of invasion and migration as a major form of explanation of cultural change as already encountered at Amri (Casal 1964: 7), Shahr-i Sokhta (Tosi 1983: 88) and Gumla (Dani 1971: 40). Confidence in interpretations based on invasion and violence were first actively questioned by George Dales in the mid-1960s as he re-examined the nature of the evidence for 'massacres' at Mohenjo-daro and suggested that there was no contextual evidence to show that the human remains were from the same period or that they represented a single event (1964: 38). Moreover, he questioned the absence of associated indicators of sustained violence such as burnt buildings, weapons and armour, and then suggested that the few individuals identified as victims were residents of a virtually abandoned city "and became easy prey for bandits from the Baluchistan hills" (Dales 1964: 43). There are also many problems trying to allocate a specific date to the *Rig Veda* or suggest that the events it described are of a historical rather than a ritual, symbolic or even poetic nature. Although advocating the presence of Indo-Aryan speakers within what he termed a "Period of Invasions", D. H. Gordon also sounded a note of caution that some of the *Rig Veda*'s descriptions may have been influenced by "a characteristic outburst of bardic spite" (1960: 97). As Edmund Leach later commented, the *Vedic* texts contain stories "about the past pegged to an identifiable relic and a place on the map. It serves as a chart for beliefs or actions in the present" and that they "are not primary in either a chronological sense or theological sense" (1990: 245). Furthermore, whilst a number of scholars have more recently tried to place the arrival of Indo-European languages (and people) within South Asia much earlier in the sequence (Renfrew 1987: 189) by arguing that the cities of the Integration Era were already populated by practices and traditions which are associated with Brahmanism, such as fire altars (Lal 1979, 2005; Agrawal 2007: 310; Tiwari 2010) (Box 2.4).

Wheeler was keen to stress the defensive nature of the cities of the Integrated Era (1968: 72), but it is equally possible to attribute symbolic functions to the walls and fortifications, or to suggest a more practical role such as flood defence or of course multiple functions. Hunting may have been responsible for the presence of many of the objects identified as 'military' by Wheeler and burnt layers at sites may have had a number of causes, such as earthquakes, accidents and ritual or hygienic cleansing, as in the case of the interpretations of the ash mounds of the Deccan. Finally, there is no evidence for invasions or mass movements of new peoples into the Indus region in the form of discontinuities in the skeletal record (Kennedy 2000: 304). Indeed, Sankalia's statement of 1962 still remains valid, that despite almost a century of investigations, "we have not found anything "Aryan" on the ruins of the Indus Valley Civilisation" (1962: 62). Whilst some readers may question why such a prime mover should still be included within a volume written in the twenty-first century, it is necessary to note that a number of scholars still consider the migration or large movement of peoples valid. For example, Philip Kohl has recently reiterated that "this urban phase ... developed into a less integrated, less centralised era of localisation ... an 'eclipse in the East' in terms of overall collapse in urbanism and social complexity that some scholars have associated with the arrival of the Indo-Iranians onto the Iranian plateau and Indo-Aryans into the Indian Subcontinent beginning sometime during the second millennium BC" (2007: 215).

Floods and Sea Level Change

Whilst interested in possible movements of new peoples into the Indus Valley, Marshall was also aware of a number of natural threats to the ancient cities which he had exposed on the Indus River. He noted that Mohenjo-daro's inhabitants "must have lived in ever-present dread of the river" and thus raised their buildings on mud-brick platforms to protect them (Marshall 1931a: 7). These early ideas were further developed by M. R. Sahni who suggested that tectonic activity had thrown up a barrier across the Indus channels and had led to the flooding of the lower Indus plain as far as Mohenjo-daro (1956). This explanation was based on the presence of freshwater shells on raised hillocks at Budh Takkar in Sindh and the levels of alluvium within Mohenjo-daro and Chanhu-daro, as well as reference to the flooding following the Allah Bund event in Kutch in the nineteenth century. The Allah Bund or 'Dam of God' was thrown up during the Kutch earthquake of 1819 CE and measured six metres high, 600 metres wide and over 80 kilometres in length. The Allah Bund blocked the course of the Pauram River and an area of more than 1,000 square kilometres was flooded. The hydrologist Robert Raikes further developed these ideas with reference to field-coring where he identified the presence of silts deposited during still-water events and suggested that this was further support for an ancient flood (1967). Working with Dales, Raikes developed a model in which a similar dam at Sehwan created a flood which led to recurrent raising of mud-brick structures at Mohenjo-daro until the inhabitants abandoned their city for good (Dales 1966). George Dales also combined the floods with an additional natural disaster in the form of a rise in the level of the Arabian Sea. He argued that this led to more serious flooding inland, which contributed to soil salination and contaminated valuable agricultural land (Dales 1964: 43). Claiming that the "enemy of the Harappans was Nature", he suggested that the populations of the Indus cities then largely abandoned the region for the Kathiawar peninsula and central India, leaving the remaining scattered occupants of the former capitals to the mercy of bandits or dacoits from the surrounding region (Dales 1964: 43). Thus the examples of violent deaths from the upper levels of Mohenjo-daro were integrated into his new explanation which placed them as post-urban. To these examples, we may add the presence of silting and associated damage within the sequence at Lothal where Rao recorded floods which destroyed the early settlement of Period AI in circa 2350 BCE. Rao recorded a further four floods circa 2000 BCE which damaged the settlement of Period AII, forcing its inhabitants to raise their floors and drains, and even damaged the structures on the 13 metre high mud-brick platforms of the acropolis (Rao 1973: 56). This sequence was then followed by another major flood in circa 1900 BCE, which "engulfed the town and destroyed all the buildings" (Rao 1973: 59), leading the majority of the population to finally abandon the site in favour of settlement on higher ground elsewhere.

Whilst recognising the severe danger to the populations of individual cities from flooding, this explanation is weakened by the fact that a large number of cities of the Integration Era would have been unaffected by damage
to one city or one region. The evidence from Lothal certainly showed that
the high economic importance of the settlement led to its recurrent reoc-
cupation by inhabitants after floods, demonstrating a high degree of societal
resilience within both its location and occupation. However, whilst individual
flood events might have occurred at sites such as Lothal, there is no reason to
suggest that this would have affected the other great sites such as Harappa or
Ganweriwala. Lambrick also questioned some of the environmental evidence,
suggesting that the Sehwan dam marked a late event and that the alluvium
and shells at Budh Takkar were the result of eroded mud brick made from
alluvial deposits (1967). He also noted that the Allah Bund was itself breached
by the first flood of the Parum River in 1826 CE, just seven years after its
appearance. It is also very difficult to correlate particular flood events with
specific levels of 'alluvium' within the Indus cities, as differentiating alluvium
deposited by flooding from alluvium eroded out of bricks made of alluvium
is complex. Finally, while many scholars cited flood defence as a main driver
for the construction of mud-brick platforms and retaining walls, there were a
number of walled sites which were not threatened by flooding, which reopens
the debate about the possible multiple purposes of these constructions, including symbolism and segregation, environmental protection or defensive. With
reference to sea level change, Dales was quite correct that a number of investigated sites, such as Amri, Balakot and Surkotada were once all coastal sites
(Flam 1981: 84) but that the sea had receded since occupation. The sequence
and chronology for such a movement remains largely under-researched, but
again, we argue that the impact of such changes on one or two sites would
not have been sufficient to affect the complexity of the Integration Era which
facilitated networks across an area of almost a million square kilometres (Singh
2008: 179).

River Shift

As early as the 1930s, archaeologists were also aware of the vagaries of the
courses of the river channels feeding the Punjab and noted the changes that
had taken place since the making of the first maps after the Arab conquests of
Sindh in the eighth century CE. Furthermore, they assumed that river capture,
and the accompanying human catastrophe, was the norm within this region
(Marshall 1931a: 6). This idea was further developed in the 1960s by Lambrick
who suggested that the Indus River had shifted away from the Indus cities leaving them without the benefit of communication by river and their
fields untouched by the annual inundation (1967). This model was followed by
Raikes' suggestion that the River Yamuna had oscillated between the Ganga

and Indus system but that its eventual movement to the former had resulted in the drying of the Ghaggar-Hakra and the abandonment of Kalibangan (Raikes 1968). Flam's study of prehistoric settlement patterns in Sindh went further to demonstrate that sites of the Integration Era were frequently located on riparian locations as opposed those of earlier settlement patterns (1981: 185). Undoubtedly, part of this shift in settlement was to exploit easily irrigated land, but also, it provided river access over short and long distances, allowing settlements to articulate with one another and transport bulk goods more cheaply (Law 2006: 308). Flam's study also demonstrated that the Indus River followed three different former courses between 8000 BCE and 1300 CE; namely the Jacobabad, the Sindhu Nadi and the Kandkot courses. The Sindhu Nadi course was identified as contemporary with the fourth and third millennium BCE and was joined by the Nara Nadi which formed a major tributary and fed a delta near the Rann of Kutch (Flam 1981: 83).

It can therefore be argued that shifts in these major rivers and river systems would have had a major impact on human settlement, which relied on water courses for both subsistence and communications. The impact of such a shift on habitation is exemplified by the findings of Mughal's settlement survey of the Cholistan Desert in modern Pakistan. Mughal was able to demonstrate that when the Hakra River was fed by the Sutlej, it supported a dense population in the middle of the third millennium BCE, but that once the Sutlej was captured by the Beas River in the second millennium BCE, the entire course of the Sutlej and Hakkra dried, leading to depopulation and a decrease in site number from fifty to fourteen (Mughal 1997: 26). Furthermore, the presence of two major Indus sites, Kalibangan and Harappa, both located next to dry channels, is an indication of the transformations which may have taken place. Of course, major difficulties with such explanations of change exist, including trying to date these changes and then conclusively link them to cultural change. One of the challenges with attributing the collapse and transformation of this major urban-focused civilisation to environmental causes such as river change is that the Integrated Era itself covered such a vast area that, while the change in a river course in one part may have had a major effect on the lives and livelihood of those immediately affected, it is unlikely to have had much effect on the rest of the network of populated settlements. Another challenge is of course timing, as river changes, unless precipitated by a dramatic and sudden event such as an earthquake, are likely to have taken place slowly, allowing alternative and ameliorating plans to be set in place by urban residents. Finally, recent studies of ancient soils in the Ghaggar-Hakra region have demonstrated that conditions became noticeably drier between circa 2000 and 500 BCE, but whether this contributed to the localisation of the Indus Valley Tradition is not yet well understood. It has been suggested this may have been part of a much longer-term cycle of regular seasonal river flooding interspersed with dry periods (Wright 2010: 313). However, as Ratnagar has pointed out

(2002: 17), we do not know how rapid the onset of these dry periods was nor do we know enough about their local impact, meaning that the current information available remains relatively broad-brush in approach.

Wearing Out the Landscape, Salinity and New Crops

Before he retired, Wheeler had already begun to broaden the factors he believed to have been involved in the transformation of the Indus cities and had started to cite the effect of urbanisation on the landscape during the Integration Era by 1966. In particular, he drew attention to the deforestation which he felt must have resulted from the widespread procurement of timber fuel for the brick kilns meeting the needs of the populations of the new settlements. Considered alongside an associated reduction of moisture within the soil as well as overgrazing and salination from poor irrigation practices, he concluded that "Mohenjo-daro was steadily wearing out its landscape" (Wheeler 1966: 77). Whilst he noted that this was simply conjecture on his part (1968: 127), it was a perceptive view, as similar problems continue to plague South Asian farmers and producers today. Whilst individually such factors may not in themselves have caused the beginning of the Localisation Era, it is highly likely that they contributed to decline in some areas and possibly even hastened it. Fairservis added to this environmental debate in 1971 by noting that the distribution of sites of the Integration Era appeared to be limited to "conventional regions for cereal growing" and that "the Harappans flourished essentially in the wheat-growing regions of Sind, Punjab and Gujarat" (1971: 311), although now we know that millets had already become established as the dominant cereal in sites such as Rojdi and Oriyo Timbo in Gujarat (Reddy 2003; Weber 1999). Suggesting that this distribution was caused by limits of effective cultivation of wheat, Fairservis postulated that farmers from Rangpur and Lothal augmented their own crops with locally available rice and that "it was experimented with until at last a successful development permitted the change from wheat to rice and the door was opened to the lower Ganges Valley and to south India. This would have been indeed a factor that caused the final disappearance of the Harappan style" (1971: 311).

Recent palaeoethnobotanical studies have demonstrated, however, that rice was already cultivated in Gujarat during the Integration Era as well as being present in a number of other major urban forms, including Harappa, as early as circa 2200 BCE (Madella 2003: 225). This then raises the questions of why such a population shift did not take place earlier and why it did not lead to a greater integration of the region to the east of the Indus Basin. Weber compared the assemblages from Rojdi in western India and Harappa in Punjab to ascertain whether major changes had taken place in the period that he defined as the 'Late Harappan' and found that both shared a broad range of crops but that barley had begun to predominate at Harappa (1999). He also found that both sites exhibited "a continuous, though gradual, effect to broaden and intensify the cropping strategy through an increased dependence on more species grown more regularly throughout the year" (Weber 1999: 824). Similarly, the increase in barley may suggest that an attempt had been made to shift from wheat to a more salt and drought-resistant crop. Additionally, as Weber has noted, barley also has softer straw and is better suited for animal fodder. This evidence suggests that towards the end of the urban-focused period of the Integration Era, cattle may have been husbanded closer to the cities, and that the shift in crops reflected the need for fodder as well as the reorientation of agricultural strategies away from feeding the needs of the population of a greater integrated regional system and towards local consumption for local communities (Weber 1999: 823). Finally, with respect to the deforestation of the Indus Plain, Possehl has calculated that in order to rebuild Mohenjo-daro, it would only have taken an estimated 161 hectares (400 acres) of forest to provide the necessary timber to feed the brick kilns (2002a: 238), thus lessening the impact on the timber stands available.

Climate Change

Climate change has steadily been identified as a major contributing factor to a number of major global challenges, and this is true for South Asia where it has become incorporated within national state level legislation. For example, one of India's recent Prime Ministers, Dr Manmohan Singh, recognised in 2008 that "Climate change may alter the distribution and quality of India's natural resources and adversely affect the livelihood of its people. With an economy closely tied to its natural resource base and climate-sensitive sectors such as agriculture, water and forestry, India may face a major threat because of the projected changes in climate" (National Action Plan on Climate Change 2008: 1). Long identified as a possible factor connected with the decline of the urban-focused settlement of the Integrated Era, some scholars raised concerns that much of the physical evidence for climate change had been obtained from regions outside the Indus Valley Tradition and little within. With this concern in mind, the research team of Dixit et al. focused on the sediments of Kotla Dahar, a former lake in Haryana, to reconstruct Indian summer monsoon variability (Dixit et al. 2014: 1). Their research indicated that the Indian summer monsoon in north-west India weakened about 4,100 years ago, which likely "led to severe decline in summer overbank flooding that adversely affected monsoon-supported agriculture in this region" (ibid.: 5). Although the researchers note that "dating uncertainty exists in both climate and archaeological records", they stressed that "the drought event 4.1 ka on the northwestern Indian plains is within the radiocarbon age range for the beginning of Indus de-urbanization, suggesting that climate may have played a role in the Indus cultural transformation" (ibid.: 1). However, as noted earlier, the Indus Valley Tradition spanned a number of differing environmental zones, making it unlikely that one event alone would cause this transformation.

Epidemics

Jane McIntosh has recently suggested that cholera, or a similar disease, may have been a major contributing factor to the general urban population decline encountered particularly at Mohenjo-daro (2002: 186). Given the reliance on public wells at the city for drinking water, contamination spreading from the extensive network of drains could have sparked an outbreak of cholera or similar disease linked to public health and sanitation. McIntosh argued that this, in turn, would have led to the type of general downturn in civic health and capacity that can be evidenced in the increasing absence of maintenance and planning in buildings across the city in the later periods. Whilst it is clear that cholera does not leave a skeletal signature (ibid.) and thus palaeopathologists would be unable to identify its presence, there are questions as to why such a disease only emerged after 700 years of successful drainage, and also whether such an outbreak within the population of a single city would account for the transformations across the whole network. Moreover, while the 'Black Death' plagues of medieval Europe spread across vast areas and decimated whole sections of society, they did not cause the kingdoms themselves to collapse. They also left a very distinct pattern of abandoned settlements in Europe, a pattern which is noticeably absent from the area occupied during the Integration Era. Unfortunately little palaeopathology has been carried out on human remains from the Integration Era, but recent analysis at Harappa found evidence of "increasing rates of interpersonal violence and infection" towards the end of its occupation (Schug et al. 2014), although how representative of the entire population remains unclear. As a result, this phenomenon remains uncertain.

Trade Collapse

The role of trade collapse and transformation at the end of the Indus Integrated Era has also been cited by a number of scholars, and Mortimer Wheeler was one of the first to note that Mesopotamian trade in the second millennium became "more indirect and complicated, and, no doubt, proportionately less profitable than in earlier days of more direct shipment" (1966: 77). This concept was later developed by Allchin and Allchin, who noted that such a decline would have left the Indus cities without alternative 'international' trading partners and only an internal market (Allchin and Allchin 1997: 211). Indeed, Vidale has suggested that Sargon's conquest may have led to a "sudden, unexpected fall of the Sumerian demand", which itself might have caused "a ruinous collapse of bead production, followed by a general crisis of the local craft organisation" in the Indus Valley (2004: 273). The paucity of dates from sites occupied during the Localisation Era means that it is difficult to compare phases across sites; however, we do know that the decline of the major trading centre of Shahr-i Sokhta, with its significant lapidary industry and role in long-distance trade, appears to have occurred at a similar time between 2000 and 1800 BCE (Tosi 1983: 89). This population and specialist activity decline was paralleled by the transformation of networks between the Indus settlements and the lapis lazuli producing site of Shortughai in Afghanistan (Francfort 1981: 191). These changes at Shortughai and Shahr-i Sokhta occurred when the major trading networks of Mesopotamia shifted from the Persian Gulf region in the east to focus on Anatolia and north-west Mesopotamia, which was in part corroborated by a reduction in the mentioning of Meluhha in the Mesopotamian texts (Potts 1994b: 290). As noted earlier, Hojlund has attributed the economic and social downturn in Bahrain to the aftermath of the collapse of the Babylonian state, stating that "the disappearance of the lucrative South Mesopotamian markets is probably responsible for the depression in the Gulf" (2007: 127).

There were also a number of notable transformations within the Indus Basin during the Localisation Era, such as the apparent failure of networks supplying banded chert to the residents of Lothal in Gujarat from its source in the Rohri Hills in the lower Indus region (Rao 1973: 61) and the increasingly local focus of agricultural produce and fodder strategies (Weber 1999). This feature was identified by Madella and Fuller as "a shift from more centralised labour in prior-to-storage crop-processing to something of smaller scale and more household based" and that "the shifts in the nature of settlement that are seen in the Late Harappan transition might be seen in part due to agricultural readjustment to slightly altered climatic circumstances" (2006: 1298). Lahiri also suggested that "an archaeological gloom settled over Sind – central Indus routes, and the Gomal – central Indus lines of movement" and that "the Cholistan tract, also … ceased to buzz with the movement of trade and other cultural items" (1992: 143). This is echoed by Franke-Vogt who noted that the abandonment of settlements within the Nal Basin was not due to river or climatic shift but that "the gradual cessation of the Indus civilization as a strong integrative and economic power can be considered an important factor" (2005: 75). The diversity of stone sources exploited by the inhabitants of Harappa during the Integration Era also shrank, but analysis suggests that sources to the east were increasingly accessed, reflecting what Law has called "the general eastward shift of the Harappan peoples" (Law 2005: 188). However, it is notable that a number of long-distance networks were still operational as demonstrated by the presence of 'exotic' objects within the Indus watershed, for example, at Pirak. It is equally possible to attribute the growing number of shaft-hole axes and axe-adzes in Baluchistan and across former urban centres during the Jhukar phase to the functioning of either continued or fresh exchange networks across the region.

A further weakness with a reliance on this particular prime mover is the fact that a number of southern Mesopotamian and Arabian Sea entrepots did not cease to act as major regional traders until circa 1750–1600 BCE (Hojlund 2007: 136), somewhat after the abandonment of the cities of the Integrated Era by their residents. However, Ratnagar's point that as the political economy of the Integrated Era appeared to have focused predominantly on articulating the numerous disparate regional groupings which constituted the urban-focused settlements of the Indus Valley Tradition, any disruption to long-distance or international trade would have caused major damage to the longevity and resilience of those integrated systems and networks and the elites which relied upon them (2000: 25). A further, but yet unexplored factor may be the apparent weakening of the Monsoon from 2100 BC onwards (Dixit et al. 2014), as not only would this have affected agricultural and pastoral economies delivering the surpluses to under-pin the trading, but it might have weakened the reliability of the trade winds which fed Arabian Sea trade networks. In any case, as Algaze has noted, asymmetric exchange patterns between urban-based alluvial communities and more dispersed resource-rich peripheral populations would have led to a focus of labour-intensive processing networks within cities, networks which relied on a reliable flow of raw resources (2005: 5). If disrupted, this would have led to the serious social and economic dislocations within urban populations as well as challenges to the highly, if not over-specialised, entrepots and enclaves with whom they engaged.

Multicausal Explanations

The previous discussion demonstrates that there are weaknesses within each of the prime movers advanced as explanations for the transformations from the urban-focused Integration Era to the new Era of Localisation. However, a number of scholars had already started bundling these prime movers together in the 1960s arguing, as Wheeler did, that a civilisation covering such a wide area need not succumb finally to a single or abrupt ending: "For a Civilisation so widely distributed, no uniform ending need be postulated. Circumstances which affected it in the sub-montane lands of the central Indus may well have differed widely from those which it encountered south or east of the Indian Desert and in the watery coastlands of the Rann of Kutch" (1966: 72). Wheeler further reflected that "[t]he fall, like the rise, of a civilisation is a highly complex operation which can only be distorted and falsified by easy simplification" (Wheeler 1966: 73), and finally suggested that the combined effect of raiders floods, coastline change, deforestation, overgrazing, salination and a decline in trade would have played a part in the end of the Indus. H. D. Sankalia, too, favoured a combination of factors, suggesting that invasions in the north-west, salinity and invaders in the Punjab, submersion in Sindh, desiccation, coastal uplift and invasions in Baluchistan and the Makran, and flooding in western

India all contributed (1977). The Allchins added trade collapse to this mix (Allchin and Allchin 1997: 211), and most contemporary scholars agree with such multicausal explanations, usually offering differing combinations of these variants. For example, Mark Kenoyer has suggested that the key components of the Integration Era had been the extended networks of trade and political alliances and that these had been vulnerable to changes in the environment and agricultural base, and that floods and changes in the river course had forced people to both move to new areas and develop new subsistence strategies like rice cultivation in the Ganga-Yamuna Doab and Gujarat (1998: 173). Dilip Chakrabarti similarly noted the impact of hydrographic change but suggested that "the political fabric of the Indus civilisation" was weakened by its expansion into areas where it "did not have a long period of antecedence" (1999: 140), whilst Greg Possehl stressed that the ideology of the Integration Era had already begun to fail but that it still continued to offer no alternatives but collapse (2002a: 245). Tainter's evaluation of overshoot as an explanation for collapse, however, argues that there is little convincing evidence for this to have played a role in the decline or contraction of the Indus (2006: 68).

Coningham and Manuel (2009a) have argued that willing subordination was one of the communal attributes which cemented disparate communities within the Integration Era and perhaps we are actually witnessing a rather different process in the Era of Localisation. Perhaps the inhabitants of the Integrated cities and villages were consciously and deliberately moving away from integrated complexity and centralised control, and rejecting subordination, whether it was willingly embraced or otherwise. Despite Cork's (2004) reanalysis of possible weapons from a wide range of sites and contexts, there seems to be little convincing evidence of conflict and violence from the Indus, and certainly none on a scale commensurate with the decline of a whole state or cluster of city-states. Therefore scholars do need to look beyond the more usually accepted archaeological explanations and interrogate those that allow the ordinary people of the Indus Civilisation a conscious will and agency.

CONCLUSIONS

It is clear that between circa 2000 and 1700 BCE, the cultural, social and economic uniformity which had integrated settlements across the Indus river basin and its neighbouring areas contracted and transformed. The urban-focused settlement system was abandoned by its inhabitants, and with it, the integration offered by shared commonalities amongst the seals and script, weights and measures system, and general standardisation of artefacts. The procurement and manufacture of objects from raw materials was also transformed as long-distance and international trade across both the Indo-Iranian Plateau and the Arabian Sea diminished in scale and realigned. In place of this uniformity, a series of localised cultural groupings emerged which still demonstrated links with the material culture of the Integrated Era but evidenced the adoption of much stronger regional and local trends and styles. A notable exception to this occurred in Baluchistan, where "local and regional traditions ... reinforced by a play of influences and new contacts ... eliminate the visible marks of Harappan techniques and styles" (Jarrige and Santoni 1979: 409). Not all societal complexity was lost, however, as demonstrated by Mughal's data from Bahawalpur, which indicated that a three-tiered hierarchy continued to exist amongst the populations of the 'late Harappan' settlement sites of the region (Mughal 1997). We may also observe distinct increases in population in Gujarat and also within the eastern Punjab and Ganges during this period (Shaffer 1993: 54), increases which many have attributed to the movement of peoples from zones previously intensely populated during the Integrated Era (Wheeler 1966: 89, Thapar 1985: 21). Furthermore, there is a growing awareness of continuity rather than the earlier models of collapse and change, and Kenoyer has suggested that rather than finishing abruptly, or being the result of any single cause, the decline of the integrated urban-focused Indus settlements may instead be presented as a scenario whereby the cities faded into the background whilst new cultural traditions emerged in the north and east (1998: 173). Kenoyer has argued that this change was a slow one and based his assumption on dates which demonstrate a long period of decline for the Indus settlements after circa 1900 against the development of the second, Early Historic urban centres between circa 800 and 300 BCE. This possible version of events favours multiple factors leading to a situation where transformation was not only possible but was the only way forward. As Kennedy noted (2000: 295), given the various developments in areas outside the traditional core Indus area of Punjab and Sindh, what we see is a replacement of cultural traditions rather than a decline or eclipse of the civilisation itself.

We can also consider the seminal research of Joseph Tainter, who highlighted the role of diminishing marginal returns in the collapse of complex societies (1988). Reviewing a number of historic examples, Tainter reached a similar conclusion to that of Gordon Childe before him, that most ancient states had had to invest substantial energy or resource subsidies from their surpluses into supporting classes of non-primary producers. Tainter believed that these individuals were critical for the maintenance and development of those states, as they were engaged with information-processing and analysis and were also responsible for identifying and mitigating societal challenges. Most significantly, he also recognised that these individuals and the problem-solving institutions to which they belonged were not cost neutral and would frequently incur additional subsidy or investment, and whilst natural or human challenges to states might be an apparent cause of collapse, it was the relationship between resource subsidy for these institutions and the returns from their activities which was critical. For example, he suggested that when the Roman Empire was faced with resource depletion in the form of a decline in agricultural surplus and an increase in population (1988: 49), it resolved this challenge through the annexation of neighbouring supplies of labour, raw materials and agricultural output. However, the recurrent cost of investing in roads and communication networks, garrisons and punitive campaigns and construction of civil authority soon began to outweigh the economic benefits as the point of diminishing marginal returns was met. In such a light, we should also acknowledge the extreme cost of imposing (whether through choice or coercion) cultural and economic integration across the area occupied by the Indus Valley Tradition and consider whether the resources invested in creating what Danny Miller has called "the establishment of an order ... that opposes both the natural environment and the human" (1985: 59) eventually outweighed the benefits integration brought.

In summary, we would suggest that whilst natural events, such as changes in rainfall or changes in the course of major rivers, are likely to have occurred and would undoubtedly have had an effect on various economic, social and political aspects of most categories of settlement during the Integration Era, all these factors need to be placed in a much broader context. The environmental information that has been obtained remains patchy in places and is often quite localised. There are also many dating concerns, with a total absence of dates for some critical sites and other dates presented with such broad error margins as to make them unhelpful for understanding such a brief and specific episode in recent South Asian prehistory. Some of the environmental material also appears to be contradictory and whilst this might be resolved by examining very local events, such an approach is not particularly helpful in trying to grasp the broader perspectives when considering which factors might have contributed to the transformation of the Integrated Era of the Indus Valley Tradition to the Era of Localisation. When additional proxy climate indicators, such as pollen and charcoal are analysed, they may show a movement towards wetter or dryer conditions, but the time lapse between the actual environmental change and this being reflected in a pollen or plant profile is not always well understood.

However attractive in comparison with more traditional prime movers, mono-causal models still fail to address the ways in which change in a single region of the Indus Valley Tradition might have caused the transformation of the urban-focused settlement networks as a whole. Furthermore, such catastrophes do not account for the areas of continuity and growth within the archaeological record of the Punjab and western India (Coningham 1995a). Just as there was a clear move towards multicausal models when explaining the origins of complexity, such as the 'Power in Three Domains' model (Fagan 2001: 380), those studying collapse and transformation have moved towards multicausal models to explain the disintegration of complexity. Instead of advocating one disaster as opposed to another, there is growing consensus amongst South Asian archaeologists that a combination of some or all of these factors may have destabilised the networks of trade and redistribution which bound the Indus communities so closely, resulting in established elites losing their authority and control and the emergence of new regional elites with fresh symbols of currency and power. Norman Yoffee has noted that once centres are no longer able to 'disembed' resources from the peripheries, the "process of collapse entails the dissolution of those centralized institutions that had facilitated the transmission of resources and information" (2005: 139). He also carefully noted that "successful methods of gaining political ascendancy do not necessarily ensure success in maintaining the political system" (ibid.). In such a way, we may anticipate the drastic restructuring of both centralising institutions and their elites, and this may explain the increased emphasis on pastoralism thought to be visible not only in the faunal record of many sites, but also in the shift to producing crops of animal fodder. Certainly, the burial record appears to stress the exposure of personal individuality rather than the collective and anonymous uniformity and concealed hoards of the Integrated Era. Perhaps, after being driven by the enormous economic cost of investing in the order and regularity of the Integration Era, we should read the 'exotic' central and western Asian materials, so visible within the post-urban period, as newly imported symbols of new orders, institutions and relationships. However, until the Indus script is deciphered and its social organisation understood better, the end of the civilisation is likely to remain unconfirmed. We conclude this section with the statement by Jarrige and Quivron (2008: 62) that "[a] great difficulty for a scientific approach to deal with questions concerning the last period of the Indus civilization is the fact that notions such as a climax or a decline of a civilization, for which we have no written records and for which the majority of data come from excavations without a well-controlled stratigraphy, have a good chance of being highly subjective".

PART THREE

THE EARLY HISTORIC
TRADITION (c.1900–200 BCE)

CHAPTER 8

SOUTH ASIA: TRANSFORMATIONS
AND CONTINUITIES (c. 1900–1200 BCE)

INTRODUCTION

As discussed in Chapter 7, many of the archaeological pioneers were convinced that there were major social, cultural and economic discontinuities and
transformations associated with the disappearance of the cities of the Indus
Valley Tradition and their inhabitants at the end of the Integrated Era. Indeed,
Mortimer Wheeler was certain that there was "a notable absence of any real
continuity in the Indus Valley between the great Civilisation and its beggarly
successors" (Wheeler 1966: 94) and that this was a period characterised by
"insecurity and economic instability", invasions and mass human migrations
(Wheeler 1966: 96). It is important to note that this belief in the lack of continuity between the Indus and later developments was not limited to European
or North American scholars, as illustrated by Sankalia's later observation that
"India was once more turned into a country of villages and small towns, where
writing and reading seem to have been unknown" (1977: 98). D. P. Agrawal also
commented that, in comparison to the Indus cities, "[t]he Chalcolithic cultures
present a definite set-back in every sphere" (1971: 231) and B. B. Lal famously
referred to this period as a "Dark Age" (Lal 1955: 6). This apparent decline,
however, had to be explained against a backdrop in which it became increasingly clear that most regions of South Asia were home to numerous progressively complex communities during the first half of the second millennium
BCE following the disappearance of the Indus cities (Figure 8.1) (Timeline
8.1). This population and settlement growth was referred to as "colonisation"
by Sankalia (1977: 99), who also attempted to link the various 'Chalcolithic'
cultures of India with the mass movement of Aryans into South Asia (Sankalia
1974: 558). Far from being isolated in pursuing this explanation, the model
was also followed by Agrawal who linked the Ahar-Banas culture of Rajasthan
with Aryan migrants (Agrawal 1971: 240). Others, too, continued to follow
Wheeler's approach of trying to map the postulated movement of Aryans
against the archaeological record, including Fairservis (1971) and Stacul (1969).
More surprising were the subsequent attempts by Allchin in 1995, Parpola in

Figure 8.1. Map of sites mentioned in Chapter 8.

1994 and Kulke and Rothermund in 1990 to attribute change to incoming Aryans, particularly as a number of scholars were already stressing the presence of a distinct continuity between the two urban-focused developments. This apparent contradiction is now resolving itself with increasing consensus that the period between the two traditions was not a discontinuity but a period of steady development (Sengupta and Chakraborty 2008; Agrawal 2007; Shaffer 1993; Coningham 1995a; Kenoyer 1991b).

Despite the added value of the new archaeological evidence from the northern valleys of Pakistan, Baluchistan and the regions that we cover in this chapter, the abandonment of the urban centres by their populations and their abandonment of script is still undeniable. Indeed, whilst attempts have been made by scholars to trace individual Indus signs through the 'Chalcolithic' into

South Asia: Discontinuity or Continuity?

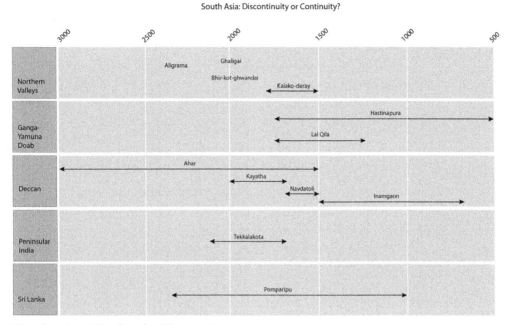

Timeline 8.1. Timeline for Chapter 8.

the Iron Age (Lal 1960), the results remain questionable. In place of the loss of a uniform script, there was instead the adoption of non-scriptural graffito inscribed on ceramics and some metal objects within the Ganga basin and in Maharashtra to the south, as well as the presence of terracotta seals and sealings at Pirak. These examples did not represent a shared script but they did represent an incipient demand for a system of individual ownership, perhaps paralleling the long use of such mechanisms during the earlier Regionalisation Era in Baluchistan (Coningham 2002). Spencer suggested that advanced tools of bureaucracy enabled early emergent polities to undertake periods of relatively rapid territorial expansion (2010: 7119). Whilst not entirely applicable, it may still be assumed that the technical developments of seals and graffiti expanded the geographical reach and influence of the leaders of these emergent communities.

Similarly, the major cities and highly specialised settlements, such as Kuntasi, were also lost from the archaeological record and the population estimates for Indus cities dwarf those for the 'Chalcolithic' settlements. For example, the lower town of Mohenjo-daro on its own may have housed as many as 40,000 people (Fairservis 1967), but the population of Daimabad would have been no more than 6,000 (Dhavalikar et al. 1988: 1001). While the construction of enclosing ramparts and ditches may have engaged substantial elements of the population of 'Chalcolithic' settlements in communal activity, they by no means compared with the scale of investment of surplus, technical knowledge and organisation needed to design and manufacture the walls surrounding the populations of Kalibangan or Harappa, despite Sharma's suggestions that the early defences at Kausambi closely resemble those of Harappa (Sharma 1960: 6). The patterns of uniformity and lack of prestigious burials as recorded by both Miller (1985) and Rissman (1988) during the Integration Era were also transformed, and intramural hoarding was replaced with richly furnished individual graves as in north-west Pakistan (Box 8.1). Perhaps also linked with the rich deposits of copper objects within the Ganga-Yamuna Doab

---

Box 8.1. The Gandharan Grave Culture

The Gandharan Grave Culture (GGC) of the northern valleys of Swat and Dir has attracted considerable interest within South Asian archaeology, largely because it seemed to offer an insight into what was happening between the two major urban-focused periods, the Integrated Eras of the Indus and the Early Historic Traditions, and also because it was a rural phenomenon rather than an urban one. The GGC offers a good case study of how different archaeologists, or in this case, different archaeological projects from different countries with different research paradigms, can reach rather different interpretations; and also how ongoing research utilising new methodologies can produce new data which can also change interpretations.

What theories have been developed to explain what was happening in these Northern Valleys? Not only within the graves but within the occupation sites too and across what is potentially a very long time span? Here we will consider some of the better known and influential theories that have been put forward to help us understand this region and cultural complex. There have been three main 'groups' of archaeological investigation into the GGC in north-western Pakistan: the Italian Archaeological Mission to Pakistan of the Istituto Italiano per il Medio ed Estremo Oriente (IsMEO), where some of the key scholars were Professors Tucci, Tusa, Silvi Antonini and Stacul and work focused in Swat; the early team from the Department of Archaeology, University of Peshawar under the direction of Professor Ahmad Hassan Dani, based in Dir and the later team under the direction of Professor Ihsan Ali, firstly at the University of Peshawar and then at Hazara and Abdul Wali Khan University, with projects based primarily in Chitral, but also carrying out work in Dir and neighbouring Bajaur.

IsMEO Interpretations

Tusa (1979) directed a number of the Italian excavations, particularly at Aligrama, and developed a theory to explain the GGC which was based on the inaccessible nature of the geography of the region. Tusa believed this whole area was marginal in terms of contact and cultural change, although up until Period IV, he claimed that there were clear links with the Kashmir Neolithic to the north – these links were based on the shared evidence of 'dwelling pits', dog burials, rectangular holed sickles in bitumen, and jade objects. However from Period IV onwards (1700–1400 BCE), Tusa claimed that the material remains showed a clear contraction in terms of outside contact and influence, while indicating internal cultural development which led to what could be understood as a discrete entity, namely the Gandharan Grave Culture.

Originally working with Tusa, and then leading many of his own expeditions in Swat, Stacul (1967; 1977; 1987; 1994a) proposed that this area was part of what he called an 'Inner Asian Neolithic'. Based on similarities between artefacts and structures (e.g. dwelling pits and jade objects) that Tusa had identified, Stacul stated that there were strong parallels between Swat and Burzahom, and there were links between these two areas and China to the north. However, Stacul also recognised that there were many differences between the Swat sites themselves, including subsistence base and function, with Kalako-deray in particular recognised as a possible stone tool factory, or as a dedicated agricultural processing site. Stacul has also emphasised issues of continuity from Period IV onwards within these Northern Valleys – like Tusa he believed that after Period IV there was more internal development within the valleys with far less reference to outside influences, and that the development and changes there could be traced through the material culture such as the pottery and burials.

Professor Dani's Interpretations

In contrast to these views, the work of Dani, professor of rchaeology first at the University of Peshawar and then at the Quaid-i-Azam University in Islamabad, focused on a model of population movement as the main source of development and change. Dani suggested that 'tribes' or 'tribal groups' had abandoned pastoralism and adopted sedentary agriculture by the end of the Indus Integrated Era (1967; 1992). He believed that these groups settled down within the northern valleys and became the 'Gandharan Grave people'. Following their settlement there, they had little or no contact with groups to either the north or south and contributed little in succeeding periods to the development of the second urban-focused period. Specifically, Dani argued that the GGC represented the successive invading waves of Indo-Aryans that had been identified through analysis of the Vedic literature (1968). Dani even argued that the location of the GGC in the northern valleys was a clear link to the inward movement of the Indo-Aryans to South Asia through mountain passes such as the Khyber Pass (1991).

(continued)

Dating the GGC – Swat and Dir

Both the Italians and Professor Dani developed dating schemes based on burial and grave typologies and radiocarbon date estimates primarily from settlement sites.

Dani's dating scheme was based largely on work at the site of Timargarha in Dir where he obtained two radiocarbon dates, and then carried out considerable work on pottery typologies, grave typologies and cross dating. Dani suggested that there were four periods; Period-I from the sixteenth to thirteenth centuries BCE; Period II from the twelfth to tenth centuries BCE, Period III from the ninth to sixth centuries BCE, and Period IV from the sixth to the fourth centuries BCE (Dani 1967: 48).

In contrast, the Swat chronology was developed largely by Stacul drawing on a series of radiocarbon dates mainly from settlement sites, but also based on the previous work by IsMEO in terms of pottery classification, burial typologies and so forth. This has allowed Stacul to propose the following chronology:

Period	Site	Calibrated dates
I	Ghalegai	2970–2920 BC
II	Ghalegai	2180 BC
III	Ghalegai	1950–1920 BC
IV	Loebanr 3 / Aligrama	1730–1300 BC

Source: (Stacul 1987: 167).

The graves were linked to this Swat chronology largely through pottery classification, but some radiocarbon date estimates were calculated, and these indicated that the GGC continued up into the second century BCE. However, a rather confusing situation has arisen whereby a further periodisation of the graveyards through an artefact seriation has been presented, which is additional to Stacul's Swat chronology:

Period	Site	Calibrated dates
??	Butkara II /Katelai I	1295+/– 155 – 550+/– 40 BC
IIB – III	Katelai I	370+/– 50 – 235+/– 45 BC
IIA	Loebanr I	585+/– 50 – 500+/– 500 BC
IB	Loebanr I	985+/– 155 BC
IA	Loebanr I	1120+/– 155 – 510+/– 100 BC

Source: (Vinogradova 2001: 35).

From the late 1990s and into the first decade of the twenty-first century, further work on the GGC has taken place by different groups of scholars from both Pakistan and the UK, linked by their connections to Professor Ihsan Ali. This work includes survey in Chitral, Dir and Bajaur, which identified a number of pre-Islamic cemeteries, though little further analysis was carried out (Ali et al. 2002; Ali et al. 2009; Ali and Lutf-ur-Rahman 2005). The main focus of this more recent work on the GGC has been Chitral, a valley to the north of both Dir and Swat where Stacul (1969) had carried out a limited excavation of some graves in the late 1960s. In the late 1990s a survey team recorded graves of a very similar construction to the graves of Swat and Dir in several places in Chitral, and in the years that followed, Professor Ali led a number of excavations of graves and cemeteries in different parts of the valley, observing that there were many large 'pre-Islamic' cemeteries throughout the whole area (Ali et al. 2002; Ali et al. 2005: Ali and Zahir 2005).

In 2007 a joint Pakistani-British team carried out excavations at a series of graves in Chitral specifically to obtain material for radiocarbon date estimates (Ali et al. 2008). The results from this are shown here:

Site and sample	Material	Calibrated date (95% confidence)
Gankoreneotek, Chitral		
Grave 1	Cremated human bone	790–420 cal BC
Sangoor, Chitral		
Grave 1	Human bone	50 cal BC – cal AD 90
Grave 21	Human bone	cal AD 440–460
Grave 22	Human bone	360–110 cal BC
Parwak, Chitral		
Grave 31, burial 1	Human bone	cal AD 770–980
Grave 31, burial 32	Human bone	cal AD 770–980
Grave 51	Human bone	cal AD 780–990

Source: (Ali et al 2008).

These radiocarbon date estimates provide an enormous range of dates, from potentially the eighth century BCE right through to the tenth century CE – what does this mean in terms of GGC? New work and re-evaluation of the GGC suggest that we are actually looking at a burial tradition spread across a wide geographical area rather than a specific culture that has endured from the early third century BCE, at Ghalegai in Swat, through to the tenth century CE, at Parwak in Chitral. Whilst there are certain similarities in terms of the graves themselves, this is no longer enough to argue for an encompassing 'culture' (Zahir 2012). Instead, it might be better to take into account the many differences between the valleys and the sites themselves, and focus attention on occupation sites in order to learn more about the different 'cultures' of Swat, Dir and other rural areas.

Figure 8.2. Anthropomorph from the 'Copper Hoard Culture' in the National Museum, New Delhi, India.

and beyond (Figure 8.2 and Figure 8.3), this transformation was focused far more on differentiation amongst the dead, on the individual person than on the collective – a divergence far from the establishment of an Integration Era order which opposed "both the natural environment and the human" (Miller 1985: 59).

Despite these major changes, most archaeologists now agree that there was a degree of cultural continuity or cultural survival and as D. P. Agrawal has suggested "Rulers come and go and the elite changes with new regimes; but the people continue. And so do the local cultural traditions. Despite the break, the Harappan legacy continues" (Agrawal 2007: 314). Other scholars have reached a similar conclusion with the late Greg Possehl suggesting that, although there were differences between the two urban-focused periods, they were not great enough to suggest that they were not part of a common cultural tradition (2002a). It is also worth noting that some pioneering scholars had also already acknowledged these traditions. For example, Malik (1968) pointed out similarities between the two urban-focused developments and included continuity in artefacts, such as similar ivory dice and combs, a similar weight system, etched carnelian beads, some pottery forms and some terracotta objects. However, Malik's theory was dismissed at the time because so

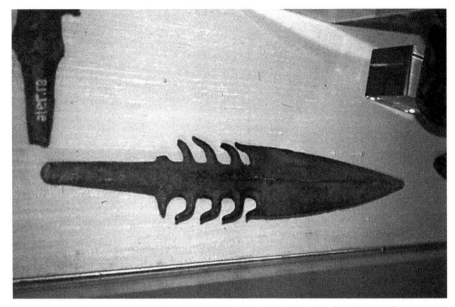

Figure 8.3. Harpoon from the 'Copper Hoard Culture' in the National Museum, New Delhi, India.

many scholars were convinced that there was a cultural hiatus between the two urban-focused civilisations (Shaffer 1993: 58).

Whilst the previous chapter examined the elements of transformation present at the end of the urban-focused phase of the Indus Valley Tradition, this chapter will consider those elements of continuity between the Indus and the later Early Historic urban-focused Traditions. Here we will evaluate the regional evidence and cite situations of continued occupation in areas previously united or linked by the tradition. One example of this is the evidence from Mundigak in Afghanistan, which showed the construction of a monumental structure in period V (Casal 1961), and we also consider the crucial evidence of cultural continuity displayed at Pirak through this period from circa 1700 to 700 BCE. As the Indus Civilisation itself was the focus of Chapter 7, this chapter begins with a focus on the regions surrounding the Indus Valley Tradition and then expands to consider a range of adjacent areas that have evidence for the development of differentiated settlements during the period 1900–1200 BCE. These include the established agricultural populations of the western Deccan at Inamgaon and Daimabad (Dhavalikar et al. 1988); the food-producers of the Ganga Valley (Sharif and Thapar 1992) and the Deccan (Korisettar et al. 2002), before considering the hunter-gatherers of Sri Lanka (Deraniyagala 1992) and the cemetery and associated settlement complex known as the Gandharan Grave Culture of the north-west region of South Asia. We will thus discuss the mosaic of regions, environmental settings and cultural developments which later became host to the second tradition of urban-focused settlement networks, stressing the clear elements of continuity but acknowledging the new regions and environments which were to become integrated in successive eras. We should also recognise that a number of these regions were immediately adjacent to the Integration zone of the Indus Valley Tradition and thus were directly affected by the processes of deurbanisation, disintegration and restructuring which occurred there. During the Era of Integration, trade, gifts and exchanges had "simulated the local growth of chiefdoms" (Ratnagar 1991: 61), and without the asymmetric draw of the cities, their inhabitants transformed and adapted to their new social and economic environments.

REGIONAL ANALYSIS

The Northern Valleys

GANDHARAN GRAVE CULTURE (C. 1700–1400 BCE)

As noted in Chapter 7, the Gandharan Grave Culture is the name that was given to what was believed to have been a distinct cultural complex that occurred in the north-west of the subcontinent (Dani 1967) (Figure 8.4). The name 'Gandhara' is derived from the name given to the province of the Achaemenid or Persian Empire which is believed by many to have included much of what is now the north-west of Pakistan. The early discovery and recording of what were distinctive grave sites within an area roughly corresponding to the boundaries of this ancient province adequately explains the use of this title, although these graves and associated 'culture' have also been referred to as 'Pre-Buddhist Cemeteries' (Stacul 1966) (Box 8.2). The name Gandhara, as well as being used for a geographical area and an archaeological grave culture, is also the name of a school of Buddhist art within the same region, although the material culture and period are quite separate (Young 2009). Originally, the defining material culture was known only through the graves of its communities, particularly cist graves, where a pit was lined with large stone slabs then covered and sealed by another large capstone. Further exploration, however, uncovered related settlement sites, and this has allowed archaeologists to build up a more balanced reconstruction of both life and death on the fringes of the Integrated Era and right through to the Iron Age and Early Historic periods (Stacul 1987). The Gandharan Grave Culture was thought in the pioneering years of research to have been focused primarily within the valleys of Swat and Dir, part of the area now known as Khyber Pakhtunkhwa. Although there was certainly a 'core' of known sites in these two valleys, recent explorations have demonstrated that similar graves were constructed in the Chitral Valley to the north, east across the Indus and south into the Vale of Peshawar (Ali et al. 2002). It is likely that they also extended west across the Afghan border, but it is rather hard to confirm this hypothesis through survey and excavation at present, and there are suggestions that it extended as far east as the southern Himalayas of Uttar

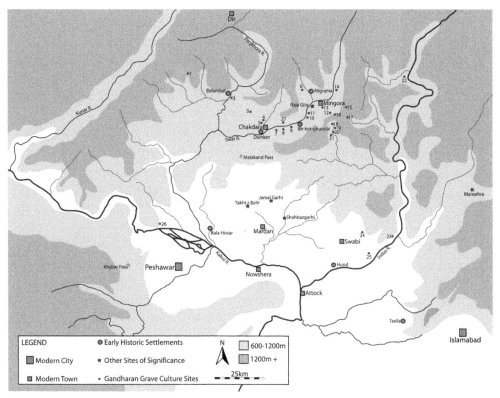

Figure 8.4. Map of sites associated with the Gandharan Grave Culture.

Box 8.2. The Copper Hoard Culture

The first copper hoard was discovered in 1822 in Kanpur District and, since that time, archaeologists have been trying to date and interpret more than 5,000 copper objects from 197 individual hoards (Sharma 2002). Some hoards have been more modestly equipped than others, as illustrated by the recovery of only five objects from Kiratpur (Sankalia 1977: 169), as opposed to the 424 objects weighing 376 kilograms in association with 102 sheets of silver discs at Gungeria (Agrawal 1971: 195; Ghosh 1989: 92). Originally encountered within the Ganga-Yamuna Doab, their core distribution range has been expanded to include Rajasthan and Bengal with stray finds as far south as the Deccan and as far north as the Nepali Terai.

The object categories associated with the hoards are well established and comprise flat anthropomorphic figures, antennae swords, harpoons, hooked spearheads, celts, shouldered celts, hatchets, double-edged axes, socketed axes and axe-adzes, bar-celts and rings. D. P. Agrawal has attributed functions to the majority of the tool types and suggested that

(continued)

bar-celts were used as crowbars for mining, rings as units of metal-weight, antennae swords for hunting big game, harpoons for catching large fish and anthropomorphs for hunting birds (Agrawal 1971: 198–201). These attributions are by no means certain and other scholars have suggested that the anthropomorphic figures may represent deities (Singh 2008: 220).

As the early hoards were recovered in isolation from other objects of material culture, it was very difficult to ascribe their contents to a distinct chronological range. However, this did not prevent a number of early archaeologists from associating them with the movement of Indo-Aryan speakers into the Indian subcontinent (Heine-Geldern 1936). Others, however, associated them with "the colonisation of the Ganges Basin by refugees and displaced persons from the Punjab and the Indus Valley during the time of the break-up of the Harappa empire and the coming of the raiders from the west" (Piggott 1950: 238). This degree of uncertainty has been steadily reduced with the 'in situ' recording and recovery of individual finds or groups of finds of characteristic copper objects from within residential and settlement deposits. For example, a copper anthropomorphic figure, two celts and rings were found in association with Ochre Coloured Pottery at Kiratpur, three kilometres from Lal Quila (Sankalia 1977: 169). More recently, the recovery of more than 5,000 copper objects, including sixty celts, in association with OCP Wares and round structures at the site of Ganeshwar in north-east Rajasthan has provided further verification as to a date of between 1750 and 1250 BCE (Hooja and Kumar 1997: 327).

It should be noted that although a number of early archaeologists assumed that the hoards were "unlikely to be a separate and independent evolution from that of Harappa metallurgy" (Piggott 1950: 237), metallurgical analysis has suggested that the technology and alloying were quite different (Ghosh 1989: 352). Although the source of raw materials remains unknown, the recovery of such a large single hoard from Ganeshwar has led Hooja and Kumar to suggest that the site must be close to the areas where they were manufactured (1997: 327). Finally, it should be noted that whilst early interpretations of the hoards supported concepts of this period as one of uncertainty and insecurity, the presence and frequency of such committed wealth might alternatively suggest displays of wealth enabling an individual or group to compete directly with other individuals or groups for power and hegemony. As such, it is increasingly possible to percieve such finds as evidence of a shared practice rather than evidence of a distinct 'culture'.

Pradesh (Agrawal et al. 1995). The Gandharan Grave Culture is in many ways a good example of how archaeological cultures are constructed, not necessarily always with reference to the material culture alone, and how interpretations can vary according to context (Young 2009; Young 2010; Zahir 2012).

More than thirty cemeteries have been assigned to the Gandharan Grave Culture by their various excavators. Many are in Swat but also in the surrounding valleys of Dir, Buner, Malakand, Chitral and down into the Vale of Peshawar to the south. Recent research on the definitions and dating of graves of a similar style across such a large geographical area has called into question many entrenched ideas about what constitutes a 'culture' and whether in fact many of these grave similarities result from a widespread burial 'tradition' which spans millennia (Ali et.al. 2009, 2008; Zahir 2012). The styles and types of burials that dominated at the cemeteries differed from period to period, but the main excavators, Stacul in Swat and Dani in Dir, have proposed a tentative three-fold grave typology (Stacul 1987; Dani 1992). The first phase has been dated to between circa 1700 and 1400 BCE and was characterised by the deposition of extended, single burials with grave goods of bronze and ceramics. The burial pits comprised a large upper pit, circular, oval or even rectangular, filled with earth or stones and marked on the surface by a circle of stone boulders, with a smaller pit below containing a rectangular grave chamber, often lined with dry stones and sealed with flat stone slabs (Figure 8.5 and Figure 8.6). The second phase has been dated to between circa 1400 and 1000 BCE and was distinguished by the use of cremations alongside grave goods of bronze, gold and ceramics. They were placed in large jars, often a visage vessel, and were in turn placed within a pit, frequently circular (Figure 8.7). The final phase has been dated between 1000 and 500 BCE and included fractional and multiple burials associated with iron grave goods, and are thought to have been contemporary with the emergence of the regional urban centres of Taxila and Charsadda, which will be explored in greater depth in Chapters 10 and 11 (Figure 8.8).

Whilst the cemetery sites are highly recognisable, settlement sites are also known from this period and have provided useful information with regard to such issues as population and cultural continuity and change within these valleys. For example, at the rock shelter of Ghaligai, Stacul (1969) noted that ceramics from the later levels of Periods III and IV demonstrated clear continuity with reference to choices of decoration and form, including mat impressions on the bases of many pieces; however, it was only in Period IV that copper objects were recovered for the first time in this region. It is uncertain still, however, whether this rock shelter was permanently occupied or whether it offered seasonal shelter for pastoralists. A further element of continuity within the later ceramic types of Period IV has also been found in the very earliest layers of the Bala Hisar of Charsadda, later the site of one of the large city sites of the second urban-focused period which we will examine at in some detail in

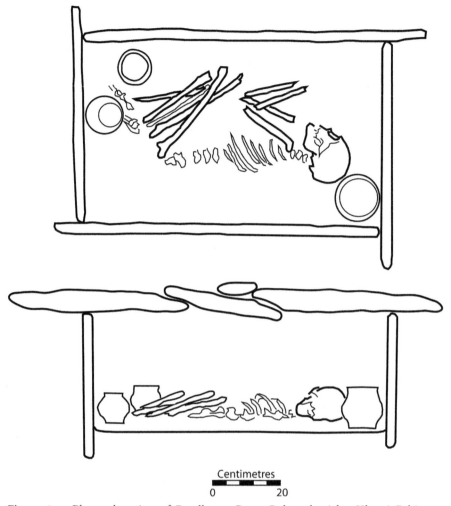

Figure 8.5. Plan and section of Gandharan Grave Culture burial at Kherai, Pakistan.

Chapters 10 and 11. A similar continuity has been found at Bir-kot-ghwandai, where what have been interpreted as pit dwellings by the excavators were succeeded by a phase of rectangular stone structures on the surface in Period IV alongside painted Black on Red Ware which showed great similarities with those from the sites of the Integration Era (Figure 8.9). The Period IV settlement of Aligrama also provided clear evidence that its inhabitants lived in rectangular structures of stone and earth floors with inset schist fireplaces and had access to limited numbers of copper objects (Stacul and Tusa 1975). This pattern of rectangular stone structures superimposed on earlier pit features was also present at Kalako-deray and Loebanr III, where they have also been associated with limited finds of copper objects.

Evidence of domesticated plants and animals has been recovered from most of the Gandharan Grave Culture sites in Swat and Dir, with cattle, sheep and

Figure 8.6. Gandharan Grave Culture burial at Timargarha, Pakistan.

Figure 8.7. Anthropomorphic vessel from the Gandharan Grave Cemetery at Timargarha, Pakistan.

goat, and barley, wheat, rice and lentils forming the most significant types. Interestingly, these plant remains have suggested that their inhabitants pursued both summer and winter cropping strategies (Young 2003). In contrast with the Integrated Era crop strategies at the sites of Harappa and Rojdi with

Figure 8.8. The Bala Hisar of Charsadda, Pakistan.

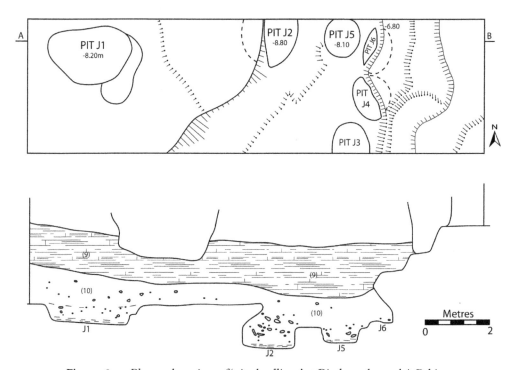

Figure 8.9. Plan and section of 'pit-dwellings' at Bir-kot-ghwandai, Pakistan.

a dominance of either summer or winter cropping, as suggested by Weber (1999), in the Localisation Era, a predominance of multi-cropping may be discerned within the northern valleys during the Localisation Era. Wild plants and animals such as deer and hackberry were also recovered, although not in as great quantities as the remains of domesticates. Trying to determine a single subsistence approach for the human populations of these northern valleys has not been possible, as there is as much variation as similarity between the sites (Young 2003). This may be due to multiple and diverse human lifeways being represented, including sedentary agriculture, summer transhumance, winter transhumance and even fully mobile pastoralism (Young 2003; Young et al. 2008).

The Ganga-Yamuna Doab

OCHRE COLOURED POTTERY PHASE (C. 1750–1250 BCE)
In northern India, in particular the Ganga-Yamuna Doab, there is a relatively strong concentration of archaeological evidence resulting from concerted excavation and survey work. This area is also particularly interesting as it later became one of the key foci for the second urban-focused development during the Early Historic period. As a result, the sequence with its evidence for the emergence of incipient urban forms is of importance, just as the incipient urban forms in Baluchistan and the Indus Valley were to the emergence of an urbanised-focused system during the Integration Era. Ochre Coloured Pottery, or OCP as it is frequently referred to in the archaeological literature, was first identified during B. B. Lal's excavations at Hastinapura (Lal 1955: 10) and has now been found at more than ninety sites throughout the alluvium of the Doab but also into Rajasthan and the eastern Punjab through to Uttar Pradesh (Hooja and Kumar 1997: 327). This red ware ceramic was wheel-thrown with a fine to medium fabric and was covered with a thick red slip, with some sherds decorated with black bands. When rubbed between the fingers, the slip leaves an ochre colour, thus giving the ware its name. Most scholars would agree that OCP vessel forms and decorations are closely associated with the regional assemblages of the Siswal tradition in the Punjab, and assemblages from sites such as Bara or Alamgirpur during the Localisation Era (Allchin and Allchin 1982: 254). This similarity led others to contend that "The upper Doab in particular receives the stragglers of the Late Harappan culture" (Thapar 1985: 21). However, Shaffer has suggested that OCP is predominantly an archaeological construct and only became differentiated because of its powdery surface which he believed is due to poor preservation within high water tables post deposition rather than representing "any distinct ceramic tradition" (Shaffer 1986: 228). As noted earlier, OCP is present in the lowest levels of occupation at a number of later important Iron Age and Early Historic cities such as Hastinapura, Atranjikhera and Kausambi. The small size of trenches in these very early levels means that little is known about the structural and cultural assemblages associated with the occupants of this Phase, although it has been broadly dated to between 1750 and 1250 BCE. Kausambi is located on the banks of the Yamuna River, and excavations there have yielded limited

evidence of the OCP occupation within Period I, but it may be suggested that Kausambi covered a little more than 6 hectares with the population living within an area measuring no more than 66 metres east to west (Lal 1955: 12). Whilst we do not know the extent of the OCP settlement at Atranjikhera, Period I was 1 metre thick and provided evidence that its inhabitants lived in wattle and daub buildings and the remains of rice, wheat and cattle indicate the focus of their subsistence (Gaur 1984).

Reference should also be made to Lal Qila, where R. C. Gaur exposed an area of 630 square metres, making it one of the largest OCP sites to have been explored, as most OCP sites ranged in size between 200 and 300 square metres (Gaur 1995: 7). Situated on the banks of a tributary of the Ganga, four structural phases with OCP Wares were identified within a deposit of 2.45 metres thickness. The excavators have suggested that their inhabitants lived within circular structures constructed of timber posts and wattle and daub, with either clay or mud-plastered floors (Ghosh 1989: 252) (Figure 8.10). A further structure enclosing a circular fireplace was exposed in Trench A6 at Lal Qila and interpreted as "a sacrificial-pit" (Gaur 1995: 12). Mud brick and fired brick were both recovered from Phase III contexts (Gaur 1995: 17). Five copper objects including one celt, bone tools and two extremely early female terracotta figurines were recovered from the site. Plant and animal remains included wheat, barley and rice, perhaps again indicating that its farmers grew two crops per year, one winter and one summer, as well as rearing domesticated cattle, sheep, goat, and pig, supplemented by deer (Gaur 1995: 20). The surprisingly large size of Lal Qila is reinforced by Gaur's excavations at Daulatpur, some 15 kilometres away, where a small mound with an area of less than 240 by 190 metres yielded evidence of OCP Wares and circular structures measuring less than three metres in diameter. Gaur has suggested that Daulatpur was a regional camping location, suggesting the presence of at least a two- or three-tiered-settlement hierarchy (Gaur 1995: 217). One particularly interesting aspect of OCP is the presence of the painted designs on a small percentage of the overall ceramic assemblages (Gaur 1995: 24), and analysis suggests that the populations of different sites appear to have favoured distinctive motifs as well as different non-scriptural graffito (ibid.).

Western India and the Deccan

Research by Deccan College and MS University of Baroda in Rajasthan, Madhya Pradesh and Maharashtra have demonstrated the emergence of a distinct settlement hierarchy and the presence of a number of long-distance trade links beyond the confines of the Indus Valley Tradition of western India. Emerging at the same time, or slightly later than the abandonment of the Indus cities, these 'Chalcolithic' sites have been mainly ordered through the presence of a series of distinctive wares restricted to the region. Whilst some

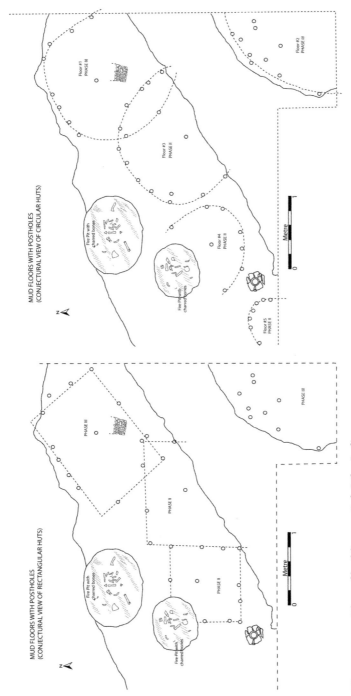

MUD FLOORS WITH POSTHOLES
(CONJECTURAL VIEW OF CIRCULAR HUTS)

Floor #1
PHASE III

Floor #2
PHASE III

Floor #3
PHASE II

Floor #4
PHASE II

Fire Pit with
charred bones

Fire Pit with
charred bones

Floor #5
PHASE II

Metre

MUD FLOORS WITH POSTHOLES
(CONJECTURAL VIEW OF RECTANGULAR HUTS)

PHASE III

PHASE III

PHASE II

PHASE II

Fire Pit with
charred bones

Fire Pit with
charred bones

Metre

Figure 8.10. Plan of buildings at Lal Qila, India.

299

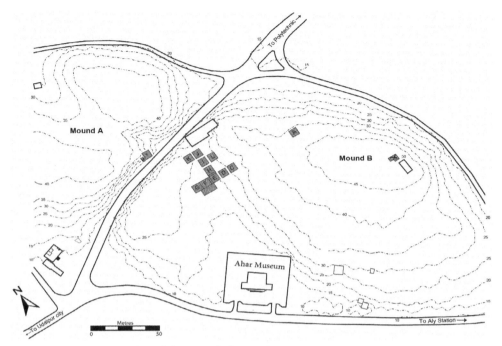

Figure 8.11. Plan of the site of Ahar, India.

scholars have sought to place a number of these developments within the Indus Valley Tradition's sphere of Integration, as at Daimabad (Sali 1984; Singh 2008: 229), others have acknowledged that they were parallel yet connected developments (Ratnagar 1991: 57). In any case, their populations formed what Dilip Chakrabarti has called an interaction zone "between the Harappan plough-agriculture and the incipient agriculture regime", an interaction which resulted in "the formulation of the neolithic-chalcolithic" (1999: 209).

AHAR-BANAS PHASE (C. 3000–1500 BCE)

One of the earliest and best documented sites known within Rajasthan is Ahar, which is located close to the city of Udaipur within the upper watershed of the Banas River. Close to significant copper deposits, Ahar is the type-site for the Ahar Culture and has a distinct sequence which began close to the beginning of the second millennium BCE (Sankalia et al. 1969). The excavation of the 14 hectare type-site has allowed the identification of more than ninety other sites within the Banas River area on account of the shared adoption of painted, black and red or cream coloured ceramics as well as vessels with distinctive incised, appliqué and cut-and-appliqué ornamental design (Hooja 1988). These sites also commonly have evidence of lustrous wares from western India and Jorwe Wares from the northern Deccan (Chakrabarti 1995: 146). Ahar itself covered an area of 500 by 275 metres and stands 12.8 metres above the adjacent drainage channels to the north and south-east (Figure 8.11). Established on silts deposited by the river, the occupants of the site's earliest period

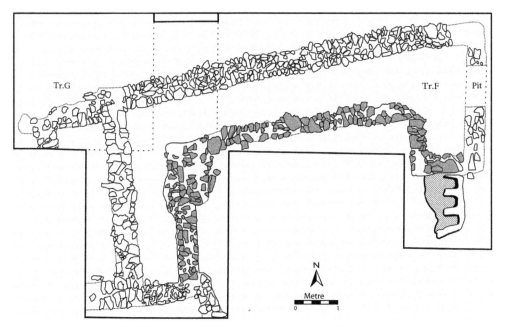

Figure 8.12. Plan of buildings in Trenches F and G at Ahar, India.

constructed buildings defined by mud walls on schist plinths. These buildings were rectangular and cardinally oriented, and one particularly well-preserved example measured six metres by 3.3 metres and another over 10 metres long; it is assumed that they would have had subdivisions internally (Sankalia et al. 1969: 11) (Figure 8.12). Querns were found inside these buildings, as well as ceramic vessels sunk in the floors, and rectangular clay fireplaces. One building contained an array of six fireplaces, prompting the excavator to suggest that the building may have hosted "community cooking" for the settlement (Sankalia et al. 1969: 12). Numerous beads were recovered, and in the earliest phase, Ia, these were mainly terracotta and schist but by Phase Ib beads were being manufactured from agate, carnelian, faience, shell and steatite, suggesting that its inhabitants had access to longer-distance trade networks, which was further reinforced by lapis lazuli examples in Phase Ic contexts. Although there were some possible affinities with Harappan vessel forms, such as dish on stand, there was a notable presence of copper tools and an absence of stone blades.

Further evidence of shared complexity during this phase has been recovered from joint excavations between Deccan College, Pune and the University of Pennsylvania (Shinde et al. 2014). Earlier excavations at the 25 hectare site of Gilund provided evidence for the use of mud brick as a building material as well as a complex of intersecting and parallel walls covering an area of 30 by 24 metres. Surviving to a height of two metres, the original excavators identified the building as a "very important structural complex of public utility" (Ghosh 1989: 150). Further explored between 1999 and 2005, the discovery of a clay silo containing more than 100 seal impressions within a storage magazine indicates the centralising role of the population of this important settlement as well as potential trans-regional linkages as far as Baluchistan and eastern Iran, including ones with Integrated Era settlements to the west (Shinde 2008). Topographic maps of the site indicate that there are currently two mounds, both of which have surviving elements of 'circumvallation'. Its excavators have reflected that should subsequent fieldwork find both these mounds independent, like Mohenjo-daro, it would "suggest fairly close inter-action between the peoples of Sindh and Mewar in the second half of the 3rd millennium (2500–1900 BC)" (Shinde et al. 2005: 162). Parallel research at the site of Balathal has provided evidence for the presence of a large central com-plex covering 600 square metres alongside a defined street and lane within a residential quarter, as well as evidence for copper working and ceramic kilns, all of which indicated the presence of incipient planning (Misra 2001: 513). Dating evidence from Balathal suggests that it was already established before the Integration Era but that it offered a continuity of occupation through into the Era of Localisation.

KAYATHA PHASE (C. 2000–1700 BCE)

Later in date than the initial phases of the Ahar-Banas to the north, the chron-ology of the Kayatha Phase of the Malwa plateau also suggests that the com-munities which adopted its distinct ceramics were contemporaries of the Integration Era of the Indus Valley Tradition but that they survived the demise of the latter's city populations. Although more than forty associated sites have been identified, the publication report of the excavation at the type-site in the 1960s continues to be one of the most useful sources for this archaeological phase (Ansari and Dhavalikar 1975). Located 25 kilometres east of Ujjain, Kayatha shared a common location with many of the settlements of Central India on black cotton soil and close to a water source; in the case of Kayatha, a tributary of the Chambal River. The sequence at the site was 12 metres deep, and Period I has been termed the Kayatha Culture, although it may be more useful to consider this as a phase rather than a culture. Unfortunately, no plans were published for this early phase, although structures appear to have comprised wattle and daub walls built around timber posts with floors of silt (Ansari and Dhavalikar 1975: 4). Although no evidence for the involvement of its inhabitants with manufacturing was found, this phase produced copper axes and bangles alongside a stone blade industry and beads of shell, carnelian, and agate, and over 40,000 steatite micro-beads. Three ceramic wares predomi-nated at the site: vessels with dark-brown slip with purple-painted designs; red painted buff ware; and comb-incised patterns. Although the site was aban-doned at the end of the phase, the excavators have identified the presence of Ahar-Banas material in Period II and then Malwa Phase material in Period III (Ansari and Dhavalikar 1975: 7).

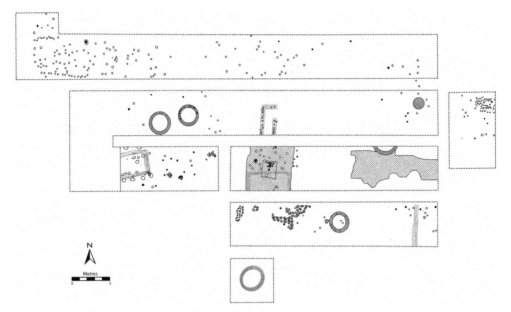

Figure 8.13. Plan of buildings at Navdatoli, India.

MALWA PHASE (C. 1700—1500 BCE)

The Malwa phase has been recognised at more than 100 sites within the watersheds of the Chambal, Narmada and Betwa rivers and into Maharashtra. Its communities were characterised by their use of distinctive Malwa Ware ceramics, which comprised a thick fabric strengthened with chopped husk, slipped in orange or buff, and painted with more than 600 motifs in black or red, plus cream-slipped ware. Although the sites of Eran, Nagda, Kayatha, Maheshwar and Navdatoli have all been excavated, the evidence from the latter has been most fully published. Navdatoli is located on the southern bank of the Narmada River, opposite the contemporary site of Maheshwar, and covered an area of roughly 400 by 400 metres. The occupation of the site has been divided into four phases which included Malwa Ware and painted Black and Red Ware in Phase I, the earliest phase; the disappearance of painted Black and Red Ware in Phase II; the appearance of Jorwe Ware and lustrous red ware in Phase III, accompanied by a fire; and in Phase IV, storage jars with appliqué decoration (Sankalia et al. 1971: 38) (Figure 8.13). A total of more than 7,000 fragments of broken chalcedony blades and rejects were recovered from most structures, allowing an interpretation that its inhabitants were self-sufficient or apparently lacked centralisation or differentiation. Little copper was recovered, although three of the more complete celts had deliberate individually distinguishing marks or symbols formed by circles. The presence of a fragment of a copper sword or dagger with a midrib on both sides has raised interesting analogies with Western Asia, and postulates the presence of far-reaching trading networks as well as a demand for individualising exotic items (Sankalia et al. 1971: 393).

The horizontal excavations on Mound IV at Navdatoli exposed a number of the structures from Phase I and these included five one-roomed square or rectangular buildings defined by wooden posts, the largest of which measured six by 4.5 metres. A further eleven circular posted buildings measuring between 2.4 and 3.6 metres in diameter were excavated and identified as stores. Additionally, the excavators recorded a series of pits, lime floors and a number of cardinally oriented burnt floors, one of which measured 6.7 square metres and appeared to have contained a rectangular firepit (Sankalia et al. 1971: 54). The second phase comprised a further eight circular and eight rectangular structures, with the largest rectangular structure measuring 12 by 6 metres, with a double thickness post interior wall dividing it. Some of these structures also had rectangular fireplaces inside them. There also seemed to have been a large, unoccupied space within the settlement, offering a community focus for its inhabitants.

Although Navdatoli does not appear to have been walled by its inhabitants, there is evidence for wall construction at the sites of Eran and Nagda. The former is located on the bend of a tributary of the River Betwa, which enclosed its north, east and west sides, and the site has a sequence of almost nine metres depth. The 'Chalcolithic' phases appear to have included Kayatha Ware in the earliest levels and Malwa Ware in its later occupation. During the Malwa Phase, the exposed southern side of the settlement was enclosed by a mud rampart, measuring 30 metres wide and surviving to a height of 6.41 metres, and a moat, measuring 36.6 metres long and 5.5 metres wide (Ghosh 1989: 135). Unfortunately, no information about possible internal layout and structural size is known. Whilst there is debate as to whether this wall represented a defence against humans or floods, the presence of what may be a mud and mud-brick rampart bastion at the site of Nagda has also been recorded (Ghosh 1989: 303). These monuments mark major communal investment and would have differentiated their walled populations from the surrounding villages.

As noted earlier, Malwa Phase sites are also known within Maharashtra and have been excavated at Daimabad, Chandoli, Inamgaon and Malvan, providing a broad range of more than 150 contemporary site types and locations. The largest of these sites is Daimabad with five metres of archaeological material, located on black cotton soil on the left bank of a tributary of the Godaveri River. Although occupied during the Malwa Phase, there is also clear evidence for three preceding phases at the site, including I, which has been attributed to the Savalda Culture (c. 2300 BC); II, which is thought to have had Late Harappan affinities (c. 2300–1800 BCE) and III, which was associated with buff and cream ware (Sali 1986). The settlement of Phase IV, the Malwa, formed a major population agglomeration and covered an area of 20 hectares. Its inhabitants lived in rectangular structures and the site also provided evidence for a copper workshop and sixteen urn and pit burials. The presence of a central "religious complex", comprising a residential block with a large mud platform with drain and soakpit, a variety of different shaped altars and an apsidal structure further contributes to the identification of this site as a primate regional 'anchor' (Ghosh 1989: 114).

In contrast with the very large settlement at Daimabad, Inamgaon only covered an area of five hectares, but open area excavations at the site have exposed the layout and structures of this small site rather more clearly. A total of thirty-two individual houses belonging to the Malwa Phase, the earliest at Inamgaon, were uncovered (Figure 8.14). Of these, twenty-eight were rect-angular, one circular and three had been constructed with pit foundations. Dhavalikar has identified evidence for planning at the site, as the individual structures appear to have been laid out in rows with roads or lanes between them, but there was a notable absence of the significant structures found in the following (Jorwe) phase discussed later (Dhavalikar et al. 1988: 1002). As in other contemporary sites, intramural double urn burials for children were identified within the houses (Figure 8.15 and Figure 8.16). Evidence for the site occupants' access to copper and stone tools as well as beads of terracotta, jasper, ivory and carnelian, shell, steatite, faience and gold are interesting as Inamgaon is an inland site. Similar cultural assemblages have also been iden-tified at the sites of Chandoli and Nevasa, both of which are also located on black cotton soils close to river courses (Deo and Ansari 1965; Sankalia et al. 1960).

JORWE PHASE (C. 1500–900 BCE)

The succeeding Jorwe Phase has been found throughout Maharashtra and its communities were characterised by their use of Jorwe Ware, a ceramic ware with a well-fired fine body with an orange or red matt surface painted with black geometric designs. There was an overall rise in site numbers to more than 200, which represents an expansion of farming populations across the black cotton soils, but it also witnessed the emergence of a three-tiered settle-ment hierarchy (Coningham 1995a: 61). The apex of the hierarchy appears to have been the 'anchor' settlement at Daimabad, which expanded in Phase V to 30 hectares and has provided evidence of rectangular and circular structures, complete with forty-eight urn burials within houses, as well as a distinct road and lane layout (Figure 8.17). The earliest levels of this phase also included ceramic kilns, an apsidal shrine, and altars and firepits along with the pres-ence of a notable ochre covered terracotta of four figures (Ghosh 1989: 114). Reference has also been made to the presence of a wall and bastions around the site, clearly indicative of the organising abilities of its population. The sites forming a second tier of settlement between five and 10 hectares included Prakash and Inamgaon. During the Jorwe phase, Inamgaon, which was sur-rounded on three sides by a meander of the River Ghod, was also enclosed on the fourth side by a wall and ditch measuring 195 metres long and 20 metres

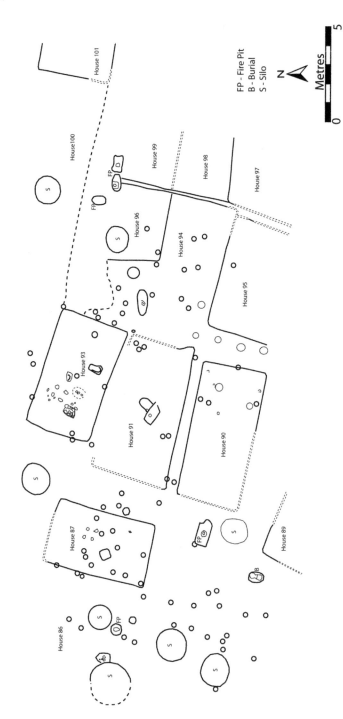

House 101

House 100

House 99

House 98

House 97

FP

FFP

House 96

House 94

House 95

House 93

House 91

House 90

House 87

House 89

FP

B

House 86

FP

S

FP - Fire Pit
B - Burial
S - Silo

N

Metres

0   5

Figure 8.14. Plan of buildings at Inamgaon, India, during the Malwa Phase.

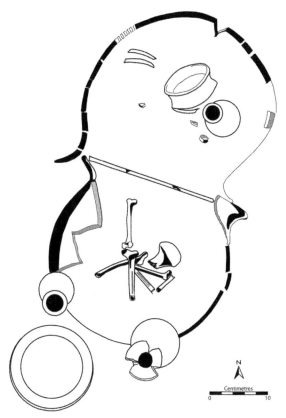

Figure 8.15. Intramural urn burial at Inamgaon, India (i).

wide (Dhavalikar et al. 1988: 237). Internally, the settlement appears to have been planned with rows of rectangular structures separated by cardinally oriented roads, and the excavators have suggested that the chief lived in the centre surrounded by wealthy farmers, with artisans to the west (Dhavalikar et al. 1988: 1002). The excavators also identified a public temple and central granary beside the chief's residence, complete with storage bins, pit silos and a firepit within a 100 square metre complex, dwarfing the average residences, which were 15 square metres in size (Dhavalikar et al. 1988: 193).

The settlement's inhabitants were clearly engaged in manufacturing and probably supplied completed objects to the third tier of small agricultural settlements (between one and three hectares). This suggestion has been based on evidence of workshops present within nine of the sixty-nine excavated structures at Inamgaon, including ceramic kilns and material consistent with smithing, and bone and stone blade working. There was evidence for trade over long distances in the form of gold and ivory, probably obtained from Karnataka, as well as shell from the Saurashtra coast. Ceramics manufactured at both Daimabad and Inamgaon appear to have been traded to the inhabitants of smaller Jorwe sites, and one Jorwe vessel has been recovered from Navdatoli

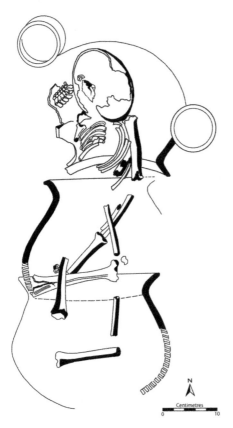

Figure 8.16. Intramural urn burial at Inamgaon, India (ii).

in Central India and others from late Neolithic and 'Chalcolithic' levels within Peninsular India (Paddayya 1973: 84). The period from 1200 to 900 BCE is considered a Late Jorwe Phase, and at Inamgaon there was a reduction in agriculture and an increase in hunting and, whilst the site continued to be occupied until circa 700 BCE, many other Jorwe sites in the northern Deccan were abandoned.

Peninsular India (c. 2100–1700 BCE)

As noted in Chapter 4, many of the earlier Neolithic settlements of Peninsular India were also occupied during the succeeding period, but many sequences were incomplete. Settlements of this phase were generally located on the top of granite hills or on plateaus situated between hills rather than on valley bottoms or plains. There was continuity in settlement form with occupants living in round wattle and daub huts, but the stone celts and blades of the earlier Neolithic phase were now joined by copper and bronze items. Evidence of this continuity is clear at Tekkalakota, where the granite outcrops which had hosted the Neolithic settlement were also occupied during Phase II, and the assemblage of microlithic tools and ground axes were augmented with copper objects and a dull red ware, and Black and Red Ware sherds (Nagaraja Rao and

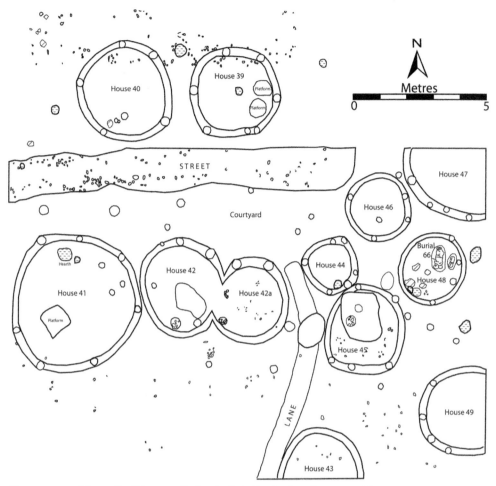

Figure 8.17. Plan of buildings at Daimabad, India, during the Jorwe Phase.

Malhotra 1965: 9). Continuity has also been indicated in the use of boulders to define circular structures, as exposed in Trench 5, and within burial practices. The latter included extended adult burials and intramural child burials within urns, although some burials were now furnished with Black and Red Ware vessels. As noted earlier, the presence of copper objects has been generally used to differentiate a distinct 'Chalcolithic' phase at the site. However, there were only five examples of copper artefacts, and a copper axe-adze from Period I may have been intrusive. As a result, whilst the excavator noted strong similarities with the site of Jorwe (Nagaraja Rao and Malhotra 1965: 76), the term 'Chalcolithic' may mask a fundamental continuity altered only by the addition of a few copper objects. Analogies between the Black and Red Ware burial vessels and the burial practices at Tekkalakota, including multiple vessel burial, and those of the northern Deccan were also noted (ibid.: 96). Paddayya has further recorded the presence of Jorwe Ware in a number of late Neolithic and 'Chalcolithic' sites in the Shorapur Doab (1973: 84). Whilst

Figure 8.18. View of the Prehistoric settlement at Brahmagiri, India (courtesy Peter Johansen).

two phases were clearly distinguished at Tekkalakota, such a definition is less easy at Brahmagiri, where Period IB was only distinguishable from the preceding Neolithic layer on account of the addition of a bronze ring, chisel and rod (Ghosh 1989: 82), again reinforcing the difficulties of attributing a title of 'Chalcolithic' (Figure 8.18). References have been made to clearer relevant sequences at the sites of Ramapuram and Singanapalli in Andhra Pradesh (Chakrabarti 1999: 156) but their full publication is still awaited.

Sri Lanka (c. 2300–1000 BCE)

As noted in Chapter 1, the long standing model of Sri Lanka's later prehistory is one where there was no evidence for the presence of a Neolithic or 'Chalcolithic' population, as the cultural technologies apparently transitioned directly from microlithic tool-using communities to iron tool-using ones (Deraniyagala 1992: 353). The appearance of iron objects and evidence for iron working seem to have occurred very suddenly at circa 1000 BCE and heralded a number of significant social, political, ideological, subsistence and economic changes. Indeed, Siran Deraniyagala has listed a number of sites across the island where there is clear stratigraphic evidence for an abrupt transition from what he calls the 'Stone Age', or Mesolithic, to the Iron Age. Furthermore, there is little evidence existing which indicates the mixing of characteristic materials between contexts from the two periods; that is, few stone tools have been found in Iron Age contexts at these sites (Deraniyagala 1992: 353).

Two sites appear to challenge this trend, Pomparipu and the Varana rock shelter. Pomparipu is an Iron Age cemetery located on the north-west coast of the island close to the mouth of the Malwattu Oya, where stone tools were recovered from individual burials, although they may have been redeposited (Begley 1981). However, ceramics dating to the Iron Age have recently been reported in association with stone tools within the sequence of the rock shelter at Varana (Gamini Adikari pers. comm.).

It is clear from the analysis by Deraniyagala (1992) that most of the island's distinct environmental zones were occupied by populations of microlithic tool users, whose subsistence strategies varied according to the zone or zones they inhabited. For example, communities at sites such as Mantai on the western coast and those around the coast of the Jaffna Peninsula exploited marine resources such as *Dugong dugon* or sea cow, oysters and other shells (Carswell et al. 2013). In contrast to these coastal and marine-based strategies, the site of Bellan-bandi Palassa in the inland hill country has provided evidence of an open air Mesolithic site with a broad spectrum subsistence based on snails, terrapins, land monitor lizards, fowl, water buffalo, elephant, wild board, deer, hare, pangolin, porcupine, monkey, jackal or possibly domestic dog and cat among other animals (Deraniyagala and Kennedy 1972: 37; Deraniyagala 1992: 306). At least twelve human skeletons were recovered at Bellan-bandi Palassa, and whilst the excavators did not report burial pits, they did note the presence of large, heavy stone slabs over the head and chest of some skeletons, suggesting a purposeful practice. A TL date generated from burnt quartz closely associated with one of the human skeletons at Bellan-bandi Palassa provided a range of 6500 BP+/−700 in the early 1970s (Deraniyagala and Kennedy 1972: 45), although more recent dating series have pushed the site's chronology into the terminal Pleistocene (Simpson et al. 2008). Excavations at one of the earliest Iron Age settlements in the island, Anuradhapura, have provided evidence of substantial occupation by microlithic tool users in the basal gravels at the site, although it is assumed that this occupation was seasonal as the site is within the Dry Zone. Like many other sites in Sri Lanka, there was no apparent transitional zone between these hunter-gatherers and the Iron Age populations which settled there (Coningham 1999; 2006a). We will explore the expansion of iron-using communities and the rise of urban forms in Sri Lanka further in Chapter 10.

CONCLUSIONS

The previous discussion clearly demonstrates that the timespan between the two urban-focused developments was a period where transformation is evident in the archaeological record; however, there is also convincing evidence for considerable continuity. The investment in excavations within the Ganga Basin and further south by the ASI and Deccan College, Pune and the MS

University of Baroda, has made a major impact on our knowledge of this period, as well as work in other parts of South Asia. Collectively, it has filled the gap observed by Amalananda Ghosh, who commented in Volume 10 of *Ancient India* in 1955 that "[t]he gulf of the Dark Age has been narrowed down but not filled" (Ghosh 1955: 3), a point reiterated by Jaya Menon who has stated that "[t]he 'Dark Age' has been largely filled." (2008: 33). By moving away from traditional explanations of change driven by the diffusion of ideas, or of human migrations and invasions, it is now possible to reframe the second development of urbanised populations within South Asia as part of a continuum, or longer term process. As Shaffer states "the cultural similarities of Harappan and NBPW [Northern Black Polished Ware] groups can be understood as a unique cultural tradition traceable for millennia" (1993: 54). In the place of early theories of human migrations, diffusions and associated chaos, we may instead suggest that this was a period of steady development, although clearly not on the scale of either the preceding Indus or succeeding Early Historic urban-focused eras (Coningham 1995a). This Era was also one which Sankalia and colleagues typified as being characterised by steady agricultural settlement by "Chalcolithic farming colonies" (1971: 429), and, as we shall see in the following chapter, new agglomerated and urbanised communities were to emerge across the entire subcontinent from these foundations, in association with the spread of iron-working during a new Era of Regionalisation by the beginning of the first millennium BCE.

It is also useful at this stage to look at the work of Guillermo Algaze, who applied the concept of Wallerstein's World Systems Theory to the role of long-distance exchange and the expansion of the Uruk in Mesopotamia (1993). Algaze traced the demand for timber, stone and metal of the southern Mesopotamian cities to the development of trade routes to eastern Anatolia and the raw resource-rich peripheries, and there are comparisons here with the major urban settlements of the Indus located in alluvial areas and their development of strong, long-distance trade routes. Driven by their need for exotic materials to confirm legitimacy and authority, rulers within the cities sought to control the flow of materials from their peripheries. In a later version of his model, Algaze refocused attention to those peripheries and stressed that the communities which engaged in this trade on the peripheries, or along such trade routes, were themselves transformed. He stated that "native elites controlling either the actual resources being exploited or access to those resources take advantage of their natural role as organisers of the means of production and (at times) mediators of the exchange to consolidate and extend their power, both in the context of their own societies and via-a-vis their rivals" (2005: 3). Perhaps directly applicable to the emergence of settlements in western India, Baluchistan and the north-west, he also observed that the outcomes of such asymmetric engagements were bound to be limited for the peripheral communities as the networks were geared towards the extraction of raw resources rather than greater socio-economic integration and that many became focused on specific or limited numbers of items (ibid.: 4). This asymmetric relationship has also been observed by Norman Yoffee who noted that "Tension between the center and periphery also exists, since the center is concerned with detaching the means for political action from the periphery, and groups on the periphery are reluctant to surrender their local political autonomies" (2005: 138).

Rojdi may offer an example of the result of this contact with evidence of both cultural connections and major communal activities, although a number of scholars have argued that "this settlement was not incorporated in the Harappan state(s)" (Ratnagar 1991: 57). It is also interesting to reflect that a similarly liminal position has been attributed to Nindowari with some scholars identifying it as part of the Integrated zone (Possehl 1986: 61) and others as beyond (Ratnagar 1991: 59). Although not urbanised or integrated on similar lines to the settlements within the core alluvium, it is also possible to suggest that not all these communities necessarily suffered adversely when the Integration Era fragmented. Indeed, it is possible that it was no longer advantageous for such populations to subscribe to integration and restructured their emphasis. Instead, it is highly possible that peripheral elites continued to benefit from their position on communication and exchange networks but engaged in different materials and perhaps with different trading partners. Wattenmaker also observed that the disintegration of centralisation, and its associated extraction of surplus which originally drove the circulation of 'display goods', need not end the value of such goods. In some cases, 'display goods' continued to be valued and exchanged and the specialists associated with them continued to be supported despite a degree of lower socio-economic integration (1994: 204).

A growth in individuality was also apparent in such sites, with examples of relatively disproportionately wealthy graves and the appearance of distinct weaponry and objects of authority and rank as recovered from hoards and cemeteries across Baluchistan and the north-west (Jarrige 1991) and perhaps exemplified by the personalisation of the chariot from Daimabad (Sali 1986). This would match with what Mizoguchi has termed a "vicious reflexive cycle", in which non-utilitarian imports become viewed an essential to the reproduction of daily life (2002: 163). Finally, it is noteworthy that Algaze also observed that "population dislocation as a consequence of environmental or political crises" might represent a major causal factor for expansion, more so than population growth (2005: 123). As a result, we have to at least consider the possibility of some shifts in population from the heavily occupied settlement of Indus and Ghaggar to the east and south (Thapar 1985: 21). It is also important to note, however, that such a model imposes a number of limitations on the human communities within the periphery and suppresses their ability to demonstrate societal resilience and resistance. Indeed, it is highly questionable whether their inhabitants would have ever considered themselves as peripheral. Such communities responded in different ways and over different timespans and, as this chapter has demonstrated, they were not dulled imitations of the Integration Era.

Whilst demonstrating transformation and restructuring within a context of continuity and sustainable growth, it is also relevant to return to the question of linguistic transformation as this time period is the one that many scholars would associate with the spread of Indo-European languages (Ratnagar 2006). Despite the challenges already raised in this volume concerning the complexities of mapping languages onto material culture and the dating of the *Rig Veda*, a number of leading scholars have hypothesised the movement of Indo-Aryan speakers from regions north and west of the Indus Valley Tradition through into the subcontinent (Kenoyer 2006). Indeed, much focus has been placed on the Bactria Margiana Archaeological Complex (BMAC) as representing the emergence of a series of chiefdoms in Central Asia between 1900 and 1500 BCE, chiefdoms which appear to have been associated with the Integrated Era of the Indus Valley Tradition through trade (Wright 2010: 229). Whilst clearly involved in exchange across the worlds of the Integrated Era, perhaps even as far south as Gilund, there is little evidence for demographic disruption identified amongst the skeletal collections from this period (Kennedy 2000: 304). To explain this apparent absence of evidence, Kohl has suggested that such movements were "largely peaceful and protracted, continuing throughout most of the second millennium BC" (2007: 235). While Mark Kenoyer has advocated the search for "ephemeral sites" associated with such possible movements, he also cautioned that "we must ask ourselves if archaeological evidence can ever be correlated with linguistic models about the origins of the Indo-Aryan speaking communities of South Asia" (Kenoyer 2006: 90). We would agree with this position and add that whether one looks at a broader perspective of the movement of Indo-European speakers into South Asia as a whole or just speakers of Sinhalese into Sri Lanka, for example, general archaeological evidence is unsuitable for this task. Whilst examining the latter, we concluded that issues of alternative language transition through trade or loans as well as issues of bilingualism or trilingualism were pertinent and suggested that linguistic change might also reflect issues of acculturation, legitimation and belonging rather than biological origin (Coningham et al. 1996). It may well have been the case that new 'exotic' individualistic objects were as attractive as new 'exotic' languages for new and old elites to differentiate and restructure themselves. Indeed, the English language was adopted by an emergent low country elite in colonial Sri Lanka and English is colloquially known as *Kaduwa* or the 'Sword' on account of its social divisiveness (Salgado 2007: 22). On the other hand, John Robb's modelling of random language change has demonstrated that "random, directionless processes can add up into directed results" (1991: 287), and thus random changes might account for the resultant linguistic patterns we find today across South Asia. At this point on the nexus between language, tradition and material culture, the volume will continue to review the archaeology of the Early Historic Tradition in the remainder of Part III.

CHAPTER 9

THE RE-EMERGENCE OF REGIONAL
DIFFERENTIATION (c. 1200–600 BCE)

INTRODUCTION

The aim of this chapter is twofold; firstly, to consider the emergence of regional differentiation within the area formerly hosting the Indus Valley Tradition and, secondly, to explore the impact of iron within a number of regions of South Asia (Figure 9.1) (Timeline 9.1). In so doing, we will examine in some depth the transformations which took place within the Indus Integration sphere. Changes which may be understood through the model of Regionalisation, whereby traits associated with strong centralised control diminished or disappeared, replaced by resurgence or restructuring of more regionally focused artefact complexes, suggesting that power had become decentralised. Naturally, this has similarities with the Regionalisation Era that preceded the Integrated Indus, although the following Early Historic urban-focused developments gave Regionalisation a rather different momentum. As noted in Chapter 5, these similarities included the growth of key 'anchor' centres, growth towards record keeping, occupational specialisation on a major scale, new systems and ideologies to justify and validate the changes taking place and the potential of migration into relatively unexploited areas based on an asymmetric distribution of resources. We are also interested in the many transformations which took place amongst populations beyond the Indus sphere as its integrated form only ever assimilated a relatively small proportion of South Asia, although its impact and influence was likely to have extended far beyond its physical boundaries. The appearance and adoption of iron in the archaeological record is also a significant development, and one that has been argued to have been a key to the development of significant differentiation in many parts of South Asia and, ultimately, the integration of much of the subcontinent during the Early Historic period (Box 9.1).

For many years, one of the most prevalent models explaining the appearance of iron in the archaeological record of South Asia, and the accompanying and significant socio-economic changes, was that both iron-working technologies and early artefacts were indicative of the mass movement of people. An

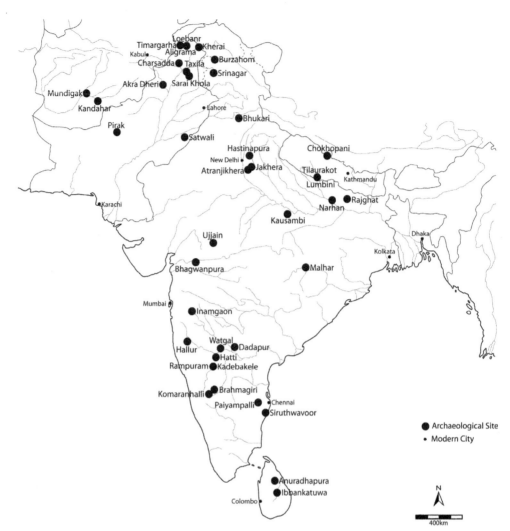

Figure 9.1. Map of sites mentioned in Chapter 9.

early example of this comes from Wheeler's work, who having found iron in the basal levels of trench CH.I at the Bala Hisar of Charsadda, attributed its presence to the introduction of iron technology by the Achaemenids during their annexation of the region in the sixth century BCE (1962: 34). As already discussed in Chapter 3, Wheeler was not alone in trying to co-ordinate and align archaeological sequences with the movement of peoples. As early as 1955, for example, B. B. Lal had attempted to equate the presence of Painted Grey Ware and iron objects in the Ganga-Yamuna Doab with the presence of Aryan peoples (Lal 1955). A. H. Dani had also attempted to explain the development of the Gandharan Grave Culture of the northern valleys of Pakistan as the product of an invasion of Aryans with bronze and grey ware ceramics following "the end of the Indus Civilisation" (1967: 54–55). The latter also claimed

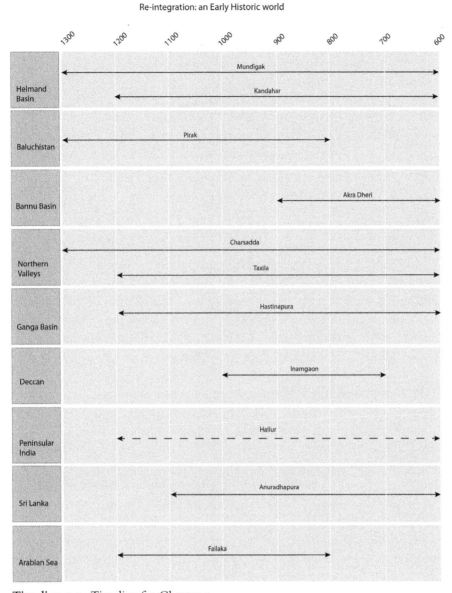

Timeline 9.1. Timeline for Chapter 9.

that a slightly later invasion, again from the west, had resulted in the introduction of iron and grey wares into the Ganga Basin (ibid.).

These discussions, often within excavation reports, were picked up and soon incorporated within the first synthetic volumes of South Asian archaeology with scholars such as Sankalia suggesting that the iron tool and Painted Grey Ware using communities "are likely to be a group of Aryans and possibly some of them the Mahabharata heroes" (1962: 76). Banerjee suggested in his review of the Iron Age in India that "the prime responsibility for introducing iron in India and spreading it far and wide within the subcontinent can be fixed

Box 9.1. Iron Technology

Iron ores are often more readily available in many parts of the world than are copper ores (Hodges 1989: 81), and South Asia certainly has abundant iron ore resources, particularly in the south and east. Dilip Chakrabarti (1976; 1974) has argued that ores suitable for smelting of iron may be found in all parts of South Asia and would have been used in prehistory. The term 'ore' refers to a naturally occurring mineral from which a metal can be extracted, and iron ores are found either on the surface or obtained through shallow mining. Ghosh (1989) has noted a number of iron artefacts at Atranjikhera during Period III (1200–600 BCE) associated with PGW, along with evidence for iron working in the form of iron slag and furnaces, and suggested that local iron ore was being mined and used for iron production. Radiocarbon date estimates from sites in Uttar Pradesh indicate iron-working activity in the early second millennium BCE, and the excavator has also suggested that "the sites at Malhar and the Baba Wali Pahari Valley are archaeologically linked to the area of Geruwatwa Pahar which appears to have been a major source of iron ore" (Tewari 2003: 542). Iron ores take two common forms: haematite (red oxide: Fe_2O_3) and magnetite (magnetic oxide: Fe_3O_4), and both are relatively easily worked.

Pure iron in its natural state is rare and is virtually unknown in archaeological contexts (Hodges 1989: 80). Instead, iron mixed with a small amount of carbon, in other words, less than 0.5 percent carbon (known today as wrought iron or low carbon steel), is commonly found, while what we would call 'steel' is a mix or alloy of iron and carbon in quantities of between 0.5 to 5 percent. When iron is mixed with carbon it produces a metal which is very hard – far harder than copper. The melting point of iron is about 1500 °C, which is around 400 °C higher than the melting point of copper, and thus requires specific technologies to achieve and maintain such temperatures. However, effective iron working may also take place when the metal is heated to about 1100 °C, although it will remain a solid. In order to heat or smelt iron, a furnace of some type would usually have been utilised. Understanding the technology of smelting – the type of furnace constructed, the use of bellows or tuyeres (the fired-clay air pipes inserted into the side of a furnace) to control air-flow, the addition of reducing or fluxing agents, the type of fuel used and so forth – can tell us much about the scientific knowledge of people in the past, and how this knowledge was applied.

As iron is such a hard metal and has such a high melting point, forging or shaping iron can only take place when it has been heated to a point of being 'red hot' (Hodges 1989: 84). This process would have required a means of heating the metal, plus specialist iron-working tools, such as an anvil (possibly a stone), tongs and iron-headed hammers. All of this means that in terms of archaeological recognition of iron working, such material evidence of furnaces, tuyeres, charcoal or other fuels in large quantities, iron slag, tools for iron working and the artefacts themselves are all important. Iron tools have often been invoked as the reason for the development of the second phase of urbanisation in South Asia in the Ganga Valley. Indeed, D. D. Kosambi (1965: 108) argued that the use of iron ploughs in agriculture permitted intensive farming on a greater scale than previously, which in turn permitted the creation and manipulation of an agricultural surplus, which permitted large sedentary settlements, which became towns and cities. This model was further supported by scholars, such as Agrawal (1971: 228), who pointed out that the black cotton soils of Doab region were not suitable for cultivation using copper tools and that only tools made from iron could be used here. Sharma (1983) also argued that iron tools permitted the large-scale clearance of forest necessary to provide large tracts of land for agricultural exploitation. This model has been subject to much criticism, with Chakrabarti (2003) pointing out that farming in this region had begun during the Chalcolithic, prior to the advent of iron working and iron artefacts. Forest clearance may well have been the result of fires, and iron technologies were adopted slowly in this region, and it is clear that there was no sudden appearance of iron on any significant scale (Singh 2008: 253). Whilst it is likely that both the production of an agricultural surplus and the development of metal-working technologies played roles in the development of complex urbanism in the Ganga Valley, they would both have been part of other social, political and economic changes at this time, just as we saw during the Regionalisation Era of the Indus Valley Tradition.

on the Aryan endeavour" (1965: 239), and even Wheeler was likewise later persuaded by the excavation of early iron in the Ganga region and suggested that "there is a possibility that a part of India may have marched closely with Persia in the introduction of iron-working" (1966: 113). Allchin and Allchin also followed Sankalia's identification of incoming iron-using Aryans within the communities using Painted Grey Ware, but acknowledged the much earlier dates from the associated sites and advocated the very early date of 1050 BCE for the commencement of the Iron Age in South Asia (1968: 211).

Clearly, the advent of radiocarbon dating and availability of more fully published archaeological sequences has vastly altered our general and specific understanding of the dating and spread of iron working across South Asia. Indeed, by 1996 Allchin and Allchin had advocated a three-phase development, which saw the earliest emergence of iron-working evidence at Pirak in Baluchistan and Hallur in Karnataka between 1300 and 1000 BCE; followed by a second phase dated between 1000 and 800 BCE during which iron working was more widely and commonly reported in the Doab, middle Ganga and Bengal; and finally, a phase between 800 and 500 BCE during which iron became more commonly used by people throughout the Indian subcontinent (Allchin and Allchin 1997: 227). It is clear from the previous discussion that even these adjusted phases need reviewing if one is to consider the evidence from two extreme ends of South Asia, Sri Lanka and the Vale of Peshawar, where excavations in the basal levels of the Early Historic cities of Anuradhapura and Charsadda have provided evidence that their inhabitants were engaged in iron working at dates of circa 900 BCE (McDonnell et al. 2006: 85) and the first quarter of the first millennium BCE respectively (McDonnell and Coningham 2007: 155). Moreover, Tewari has identified dates of between 1320 and 1140 BCE at Komaranhalli in Karnataka; between 1490 and 1185 BCE in the Vidarha region of Maharashtra; and from the first half of the second millennium BCE with dates of between 1880 and 2000 BCE at Malhar, and 1680 and 1880 BCE at Dadapur in the Ganga Basin (Tewari 2003: 537). Although none of these sites have been fully published yet and are still in preliminary reports, Tewari has advocated a three-phase introduction of iron working between 400 and 1200 BCE, 1200 and 900 BCE and the earliest between 1500 and 1800 BCE. He also noted that the type and shape of ceramics associated with the earliest phase generally agreed with those characteristic of the 'Chalcolithic' of the regions (Tewari 2003: 537). Whatever the earliest date of an iron object or iron-working debris may prove to be within South Asia, the presence of early examples has clearly swept away diffusionistic links to neighbouring regions. Indeed, since the 1970s Dilip Chakrabarti has been advocating the possibility of an indigenous development of iron working within the region, stating that "there is no logical basis to connect the beginning of iron in India with any diffusion from the west, from Iran and beyond" (Chakrabarti 1974: 354; 1976). The recent evidence from South Asia indicates that his perspective was both sound and correct.

With the release of the advent of iron working and iron artefacts from diffusionistic debates, discussion has continued to focus on the technical advantages which iron offered farmers over copper tools. Iron was undoubtedly important as a technological innovation because it was harder and more durable than copper or bronze, but it also required higher temperatures within furnaces and kilns to enable the smelting of iron. This meant that a major change in the technology of metal working was required for the introduction and spread of iron, and it should be remembered that iron on its own is still relatively soft, and only when a proportion of carbon was mixed with the iron that a metal that was hard and durable was produced (Hodges 1989: 80; Hurcombe 2007: 202). Many scholars have argued that iron tools were necessary for the colonisation of the Ganga Basin on account of its heavy clay soils and many trees (Kosambi

1965: 29). This was also illustrated by Agrawal's claim that "To colonise the Doab only iron technology and abundance of iron were the answer" and that "The Doab was as inhospitable to the Copper-age man for settled agriculture, as the wooded plateaux were" (1971: 205–208).

In this way, explanations of change based on the spread and migration of farming communities have continued within the contemporary archaeological narrative and this is illustrated by Dhavalikar's comments on the end of the farming villages of the Deccan. He suggested that the inhabitants of Inamgaon left the site for a more semi-nomadic existence but that "[i]n a short period of time they too were displaced by Iron Age invaders from the Southern Deccan" (Dhavalikar et al. 1988: 1008). A similar colonisation has been posited for the appearance of iron objects at sites located on the Reddish Brown Earths of northern Sri Lanka. Deraniyagala noted that the appearance of iron tools introduced from Peninsular India meant that these soils could be worked for agricultural and other purposes (1992: 710). These arguments still prevail with some scholars, for example V. N. Misra's recent summary of the Indian material stated that "[w]ith the help of iron tools enterprising farmers cleared the dense forests of the subhumid plains of the middle and lower Ganga valley and brought about effective human colonization of this vast fertile region. In the hilly and rocky peninsular India iron tools helped in quarrying stone for erecting megalithic sepulchral and memorial monuments and subsequently in digging wells and irrigation tanks in hard rock. The agricultural surplus generated by the combination of iron technology, fertile soil, perennial availability of water from rivers, lakes and wells, and human enterprise led to the emergence of [a] second urbanization in the country" (2001). Finally, note should be made of Erdosy's attempt to clearly link the advent of iron with an increase in warfare and control of economic resources (1988: 142–143), as well as noting that many of the earliest iron objects found within the Ganga Basin were weapons (Erdosy 1995a: 84) (Figure 9.2 and Figure 9.3). Such a model has also been advocated by Moorti for south India based on his review of objects recovered from a large sample of megalithic tombs (1990: 13).

This argument, that technological advantage accelerated an associated colonisation and spread of iron-using agricultural populations across South Asia is interesting but, as discussed in Chapter 8, ignores the origins of the trajectories of the preceding Era. Indeed, it is notable that the first categories of iron objects were not particularly different from those of the preceding 'Chalcolithic' period, but many archaeologists appear to have attributed items associated with copper hoards, such as spears and arrows, to hunting and fishing, but when such items were found in an Iron Age context they appear to have been given a role in warfare. Indeed, it should be noted that the advent of iron in the cultural sequence of Pirak resulted in very little change, and one might also comment on the apparent continuum within the Ganga basin with

Figure 9.2. Iron swords in the Indian Museum, Kolkata, India (courtesy Bridget Allchin).

the transition from the OCP to the PGW through settlements like Hastinapura or in the northern valleys at Aligrama. Where we do have regional survey data, it has also demonstrated that there was a steady growth in settlement as illustrated by Lal's survey where the combined coverage of human settlement during the 'Chalcolithic' phase was 17.25 hectares, and this increased to 53.58 hectares during the early Iron Age with an expansion of 32 percent (Lal 1984a, 1984b, 1989). The presence of communal monuments was also a very striking aspect of this period, although already identified within the 'Chalcolithic'. The walls and ditches at Kandahar and Charsadda were notable, as was their pre-eminent size within their regions, an aspect which was also shared by the Hathial Mound at Taxila. However, the multiple character of the early Iron Age was also very clear with regions characterised by unifying traits with Red Burnished Ware in the north-west, Painted Grey Ware in the Ganga Basin and Black and Red Ware and megalithic burial traditions to the south. This is not to suggest that the latter were in any way inferior. Indeed, as noted by Fuller, the adoption and spread of this distinct trait amongst the populations of the Deccan was accompanied by new systems of craft production, long-distance trade and exchange, and that the "megalithic of South India is

Figure 9.3. Antennae Swords in the Vellore Government Museum, India (courtesy Jo Shoebridge).

really a mosaic of local cultural traditions that shared traditions of constructing burial monuments from large stones and the use and production of iron tools and weapons" (Fuller 2008: 702). As with the Gandharan Grave Culture, those buried within the tombs cannot have represented the entirety of the population, and it may be suggested that such monuments involved the differentiation of elites through their preferential internment and thus the reconfirmation and legitimation of increasing social complexity. In conclusion, the appearance and spread of iron within South Asia took different forms in different regions. In the Gangetic region, iron was associated with the adoption of specific ceramic wares, although this was not exclusively so. The populations of several sites known from the early iron-using phases, such as Kausambi, were soon to gain importance in succeeding phases. In Peninsular India, we may trace the adoption and spread of iron largely through the region's striking megalithic burials, and can now begin to observe how they changed over time. In the far north-west, we have evidence for those communities associated with the Gandharan Grave Culture, which whilst outside the urban-focused developments of the Indus Valley and Early Historic Traditions, clearly had contact with other regions in South Asia. All these examples demonstrate how regions developed differently during the second and first millennia BCE but also demonstrate there were also both common elements, such as iron, as well as many unique aspects.

TAXILA, CHARSADDA AND THE NORTHERN VALLEYS (c. 1200–600 BCE)

The settlements and cemeteries of this period have been characterised by the presence of Red Burnished Ware, or Soapy Red Ware as it was earlier called, although it also shared a number of forms with burnished black/grey wares of similar paste (Coningham et al. 2007b: 104). Red Burnished Ware was first identified in the sequence at the base of the Bala Hisar of Charsadda by Mortimer Wheeler. Referred to as a "richly red or reddish ware, sometimes handmade and usually polished, with a pleasant soapy feel", its repertory included bowls, cups and pedestal vessels (Wheeler 1962: 39). Present within the Vale of Peshawar at the sites of Charsadda (Coningham and Ali 2007a), Sari Dheri (Wheeler 1962: 48), Sikander Abad and Nisatta (Ali 1994: 67–77) and Zarif Karuna (Khan 1973: 29), and very well attested at both burial and habitation sites within the Swat and Dir valleys, it has also been identified as far south-east as the Hathial mound of Taxila (Dani 1986: 37; Dani 1967; Stacul 1987). There is also a possibility that it may have extended as far south-west as Akra Dheri in Bannu, although this is based on published vessel profiles and has not been formally confirmed (Coningham et al. 2007c: 262). The ware was strongly associated with Swat Period V, which has been dated to between circa 1450 and 660 BCE (Vinogradova 2001: 35), and accompanied by an exponential expansion of population both within the northern valleys and into the plains below, but also in a number of cemeteries associated with the Gandharan Grave Culture. The latter appears to have developed from a single example in Swat Period IV at Kherai, throughout the Swat Valley and its tributaries with cemeteries established at Katelai, Loebanr I, Butkara II, Thana, Tilgram and Gumbatuna (Vinogradova 2011: Table 7), as well as down into the Vale of Peshawar at Zarif Karuna.

The individual burials remained very similar in morphology, generally comprising a deeper pit containing grave goods and flexed human inhumations, often fractional, sealed by slabs found at the bottom of a wider pit above, marked at its edges with stones. Of particular note were the horse burials within Katelai and fragment of iron horse furniture from Timargarha (Allchin and Allchin 1982: 238; Dani 1967). On the basis of burial practices, pottery and other artefacts, various attempts have been made to divide the Swat burials chronologically (Stacul 1966: 66; Vinogradova 2001), and this chronology has copper artefacts only in the earlier two periods (I and II of the graveyard sequence) and copper and iron artefacts in the later period (period III of the graveyard sequence). Stacul placed the earliest of the graveyard periods, in other words, Period I to Period V in the Swat chronology, which he dated to "the last centuries of the second millennium B.C." (1973: 197). Within the general interpretative umbrella of the 'Gandharan Grave Culture', a wide variety in tomb form has been recorded, including a number delineated by the presence of boulders marking their extremities. Recent surveys in the Chitral Valley and the Bajaur and Mohmand Agencies of north-west Pakistan have identified similar graves (Ali and Lutf-ur-Rahman 2005; Ali et al. 2005), although radio-carbon dates from the graves in Chitral cast doubt on these belonging to the 'Gandharan Grave Culture' (Ali et al. 2008). It is more likely that they formed part of an extremely long-lived regional burial tradition (Zahir 2012).

Such megalithic characteristics have led some scholars to suggest that there may have been links between those people who shared the Gandharan Grave Culture and those associated with the stone-lined burial traditions in the Himalayan Kumaon foothills of Uttar Pradesh, some of which have also been associated with horse burials (Agrawal et al. 1995). Whilst the megalithic circle at Burzahom has also been attributed to the second half of the second millennium BCE (Mohanty and Selvakumar 2002: 320), it is unclear whether iron was associated with such monuments. Further east, circular, square and rectangular sandstone cists have been reported in eastern Nepal in Udapur, Bhojpur, Khotang and Sankhuwa Sabha Districts. Although not published, reports suggest that their grave goods included chalcedony and etched carnelian beads, sun-dried terracotta vessels and iron objects (K. P. Acharya, pers. comm. 2012).

As previously noted, excavations at the long-lived rock shelter site of Ghaligai have provided the foundation for Stacul's Swat chronology, and iron artefacts are also present within the sequence from this site (Stacul 1987; 1969: 81). Stacul noted (1987: 53) that in Swat Period IV (c. 1700–1300 BCE) a number of open air settlement sites were now present in addition to the Ghaligai rockshelter, and these included Aligrama, Bir-kot-ghwandai, Damkot, Kalako-deray and Loebanr III in Swat, and the site of Balambat in Dir (Dani 1967). See Young (2003 24–25) for an overview of the dating and periodisation of the sites from both Swat and Dir. Aligrama has been extensively excavated, and research here has shown that it was first occupied in Swat Period IV and thus possessed a continuity of occupation (Tusa 1979: 681). During Swat Period V, the settlement's population covered an area of some 10 hectares and settled the alluvial deposits which sloped down to the Swat River with the cemetery at the base of a ridge to the west (Tusa 1979: 677). Excavations at Aligrama exposed rectangular structures dating to the eighth century BCE, made from river cobbles or sharp-edged blocks and even unbaked clay bricks (Figure 9.4). Its inhabitants built internal walls of clay brick or pise and some were fitted with stone benches and clay silos interpreted as grain stores. Tusa also noted that the buildings were oriented perpendicular to the hillside above and that there was evidence to suggest "the existence of strict property boundary lines" amongst the settlement's population (Tusa 1979: 685). A similar inventory of structures has been recovered from Balambat in the Dir Valley, although the dating is less certain (Dani 1966) (Figure 9.5). Stacul suggested that the newly established settlements in Period IV were located on hillsides and hilltops, whereas the site of Butkara I, which was first occupied in Period III, was found on a flood

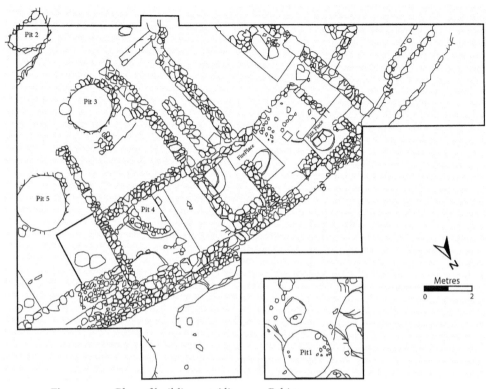

Figure 9.4. Plan of buildings at Aligrama, Pakistan.

bank (1987: 67). He argued that the difference in location was an important element of these new settlements in this later period, perhaps related to the need to provide a defensive position, protection from flooding or perhaps the need to maximise agricultural returns for resident populations (ibid.). Further evidence for agricultural developments also came in the form of a range of stone tools possibly associated with agricultural practices (ibid.: 69). Of particular interest here is the range of sickles, mortars and grinding slabs recovered from the site of Kalako-deray in Period IV (Stacul 1994b: 238), where the number of such tools led Stacul to suggest that the inhabitants of the site might well have been engaged in manufacturing stone tools beyond their own needs (1994b: 239). Engagement in long-distance trade was indicated by the recovery of a range of exotic items, including artefacts made from shell and coral (likely to have come from the coasts of the Arabian Sea), jade (showing trade links over the Hindu Kush range to the north and into China), lapis lazuli (originating in Afghanistan) and gold (possibly from the Hindu Kush mountains themselves) (Stacul 1987: 75–76). In addition to our knowledge of populations of the northern valleys associated with Swat Period V, we also have a great deal of information from the basal sequences of two of the greatest Early Historic cities in the north-west region, Taxila and Charsadda.

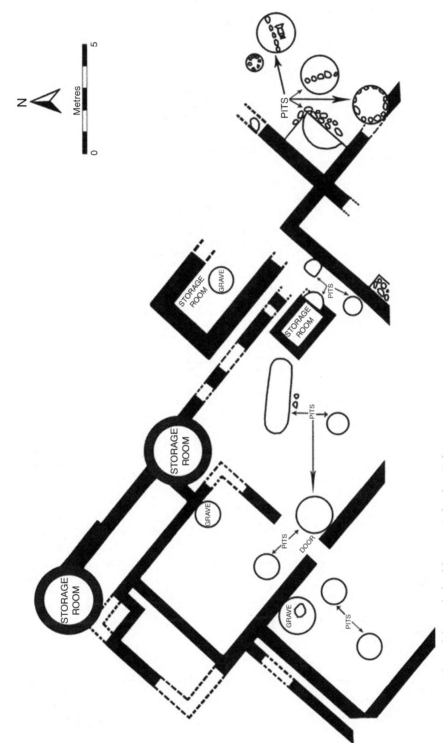

Figure 9.5. Plan of the early buildings at Balambat, Pakistan.

The first of these sites, Taxila, is located in a fertile valley fed by springs and water from the Haro River and was close to one of the major Early Historical routes, the *Uttarapatha* or Great Northern road, which linked the Ganga basin and Peninsular India with Afghanistan and Central Asia (Allchin 1993: 70). Already referenced in Chapter 5 on account of the presence of material linked to the Kot Dijian Phase at Sarai Khola, in many respects we know far more about the archaeological sequence at Taxila than of any other Early Historic site due to John Marshall's decades of excavations and the detail contained within his published reports (1951). Although not recognised by Marshall at the time, early Iron Age material has also been recovered from the Taxila Valley in the locality of the terminus of the Hathial ridge, surrounded as it is on three sides by the Tamra Nala (Allchin 1982). There, on eroding ridges, Raymond and Bridget Allchin identified scatters of Red Burnished Ware over an area of some 13 hectares in association with exposed cobble walls and structures. Allchin was keen to note both the possibilities of continuity from Later Kot Dijian occupation at the site, as well as the significance of such a large population already established in what was to become one of the core Early Historic urban-focused developments within the region (Allchin 1993: 73). Dani's illustrations of ceramics from the site have confirmed the identification of Red Burnished Ware, associated Grey/Black wares and pinched-nose terracotta figurines in association with rectangular rough stone walls (Dani 1986: 36). Both Allchin and Dani noted the very clear parallels between the Red Burnished Ware assemblage adopted by the inhabitants of the Valley of Taxila and those in the Vale of Peshawar to the north and west. There have been some issues and concerns with the radiocarbon dates that Allchin used as the basis of this chronological sequence (Thomas and Allchin 1986; Allchin 1993), but the key point here is that the Red Burnished Ware, or Soapy Red Ware, has been identified not only at Hathial but also from sites such as Aligrama in the Swat valley and at Charsadda within the Vale of Peshawar suggesting a wide distribution of a distinct regional character (Dani 1986: 37). It is also interesting to note that a number of the terracotta figurines recovered from some of the early levels of the Bhir Mound are similar to those from Charsadda and some of the Swat sites (ibid.: 36). Allchin has argued that this evidence demonstrated that the inhabitants of Taxila shared what he called a 'Gandharan culture', that is, one which was centred in the ancient geographical area of Gandhara. However, whilst he claimed that there was "little or no evidence of influences from outside" (Allchin 1993: 73), subsequent research in the Swat and Chitral valleys and at Charsadda have indicated that this region was part of a much wider network, although the character and intensity of contact is still only tentatively understood and much remains to be explored. Despite this detail, the presence of Red Burnished Ware has allowed us to link the presence of this type of ceramic with the initial establishment of urban communities at both Taxila and Charsadda, and it also means that with the more recent and reliable radiocarbon dates from Charsadda discussed later, we may augment and expand our chronological understanding of Hathial.

Antiquarian interest in the Bala Hisar of Charsadda has also been ongoing for nearly two centuries, and has been conducted by many of the same individuals who worked at Taxila, including Alexander Cunningham, John Marshall and Mortimer Wheeler. Whilst Marshall successfully identified the ancient site as the Early Historic city of Pushkalavati, known as Peukelaotis to the Greeks, Wheeler was driven by the opportunity to mesh the site's historic and prehistoric sequences with a Western absolute chronology based on historically attested events, including Darius the Great's annexation of the region in the sixth century BCE and the slightly later invasion of Alexander the Great in the fourth century BCE. In his single season of six weeks in 1958, he was able to demonstrate both links to his satisfaction. The first was proved through the identification of a slighted defensive ditch in trench Ch. III, which he linked to the events of 327 BCE, and the second through the presence of iron in the lowest levels of the site at the bottom of trench Ch. I. The latter confirmed to Wheeler that the site was no older than the sixth century BCE as he assumed the Achaemenids had brought both iron and cities to Gandhara during their hegemony (Wheeler 1962). Whilst his ceramic typology has remained critical for all subsequent studies of the region, a number of scholars were concerned that a foundation date of the middle of the first millennium BCE was too recent for material which had striking parallels with examples being excavated in the northern valleys of Pakistan, and they proposed a longer chronology extending into the beginning of the first millennium BCE (Dittmann 1984; Stacul 1979; Vogelsang 1988).

As a result of these concerns, excavations in the 1990s reopened a number of Wheeler's old trenches and confirmed the presence of an early Iron Age population at Charsadda, one which paralleled the site of Hathial in the Taxila Valley (Figure 9.6). There was evidence for a small settlement which had been established circa 1350 BCE on the edges of a natural clay mound standing some four to five metres above the surrounding alluvial plain and braided river channels. Whilst no evidence of individual house plans were recovered due to the small size of the trenches, we recorded clear evidence of the cutting of a linear ditch-like feature, measuring 2.75 metres wide and almost one metre deep marking the edge of the mound (Coningham et al. 2007d: 50). Within this postulated circumvallation, exposed features included postholes and clay ovens within trampled surfaces which yielded Red Burnished Ware vessels (Coningham and Batt 2007: 97). Other artefacts recovered from the trenches also demonstrated clear linkages with the northern valleys in the form of schist beehive-shaped beads and a single-holed sickle as well as fiddle-shaped human figurines and an anthropomorphic figure cut from a sherd of Black/Grey Burnished Ware (Coningham and Swati 2007: 171; Coningham 2007a: 188; Coningham et al. 2007b: 104). Wheat, lentil, rice, and fat hen, along with cattle, sheep, goat, pig and deer were recovered from contexts dated to this period

Figure 9.6. Excavation trench at the Bala Hisar of Charsadda, Pakistan.

(Young 2007a: 241, 244; Young 2007b: 257), indicating that while wild species were still being exploited, domesticates dominated both assemblages. From a study of recent settlement surveys in the vicinity of Charsadda, it is also clear that the site was substantially larger than a number of smaller sites such as Sari Dheri, Jhara Sikander Abad and Nisatta, all of which were located within 15 kilometres of Charsadda (Ali 2003; Coningham et al. 2007c: 262). This evidence suggested that the differentiated inhabitants of the Bala Hisar of Charsadda may have performed a centralising or 'anchor' role similar to the proto-urban forms in the Indus Era of Regionalisation. In addition, the presence of iron slag in the earliest levels of its sequence may suggest that its craftspeople may also have performed production for their neighbours.

THE BANNU BASIN (c. 900–600 BCE)

The Bannu Basin is located 190 kilometres to the south of Peshawar in Pakistan and is a distinctive landform created by the catchments of the tributaries of the Kurram River. Although the fertile basin has a rich prehistoric occupation and evidence of ancient trading networks expanding westwards, eastwards and northwards, until recently there has been little evidence of Iron Age population in comparison with the wealth of information available in the Vale of Peshawar and the Valley of Swat to the north. However, recent fieldwork has demonstrated the presence of a number of small iron-using settlements, such as Ter Kala Dheri around, what may have been a denser occupation at the Lohra Mound at Akra Dheri. Only two sites so far have been identified as using the distinctive regional late 'Chalcolithic' and early Iron Age Bannu Black-on-Red Ware: Ter Kala Dheri and the Area B mounds at Akra, where it has been dated to the first half of the first millennium BCE (Khan et al. 2000: 113; Petrie et al. 2008: 4). Distinct from the Red Burnished Wares to the north, its excavators have drawn analogies between this ware and Central Asian ceramic traditions in south Turkmenistan and Afghanistan. Whatever its cultural antecedents, this evidence provided a distinct and separate character for the inhabitants of the region and, in the words of the excavators: "It may be taken, therefore, as a definitive marker ceramic, probably representing a period anterior to the occupation of this region by later, better-known groups, the Achaemenids in particular. There is no doubt, however, that this ceramic type is a new variety and that it is not found in any of the great sites in the Gandhara region to the north" (Khan et al. 2000: 86). Excavation and survey work in this region demonstrate that in the late second and early first millennium BCE there was a clear regionalism in the material culture studied (Petrie et al. 2008: 1–2). Work has also focused on the mounds that make up the site of Akra (Area A mounds; Area B comprising Lohra and Hussani Boi Ziarat mounds), and it is clear that this was a significant site in the Iron Age or early first millennium BCE (Magee et al. 2005), of at least 20 hectares. The excavators of the site have also argued that the size of Akra pointed out that "the emergence of urbanism in this region was in no way linked to imperial episodes" (ibid.: 718) and that the presence of the smaller site of Ter Kala Dheri with dates of the same period and the shared Bannu Black-on-Red Ware "suggests that there was also an important hinterland for which Akra was the central place" (ibid.: 735).

THE HELMAND BASIN

Mundigak (c. 1500–1000 BCE)

Occupation continued to focus on the tell of Mundigak, as the "monument massif" of Period V on Mound A was replaced by another major complex of structures in Period VII, which have been interpreted as granaries by the excavators. Dating to the first half of the first millennium BCE (Casal 1961: 95), these comprised sets of solid platform foundations, measuring 0.5 metres wide and four metres long, running east to west as well as individual silos (Casal 1961: fig. 46). Although badly eroded, iron objects were recovered from these levels and McNicoll and Ball (1996: 366) have noted that the ceramics of Period VI and VII were very similar to those in the basal foundations of old Kandahar.

This regional continuity was important, as it provided a link between the occupation of the 'Chalcolithic' centre of Mundigak with the establishment of one of the Helmand's most significant Early Historic cities, Kandahar, less than 30 kilometres to the south-east.

Kandahar (c. 1200–600 BCE)

The site of old Kandahar, or Shahr-i Kuhna as it is also known, is located to the east of the Arghandab River and sheltered by the Qaitul ridge and has long been identified as the capital of the Achaemenid Satrapy of Arachosia (Helms 1982: 1). Although the main focus of the excavations at the site was to expose the Achaemenid and Hellenistic phases of the site, additional information on the very earliest occupation of the site was recovered. The bulk of the data were recovered during the cutting of a major trench through the 10 metre high eastern fortification wall, which stands 20 metres behind the 90 metre wide moat (Whitehouse 1978: 10). The four metre wide and 15 metre deep section was cut by mechanical diggers and exposed a sequence of fortification walls sitting above a primary clay rampart attributed to Period I. As the clay within the primary rampart was clean, it has been suggested that it had been freshly excavated from the new ditch around the site. The rampart was a major communal endeavour as it measured 14.6 metres wide and survived to a height of four metres. As noted earlier, the excavator also recognised very clear ceramic parallels between the ceramic assemblage of Period I, including Grit Ware, with Period VI of Mundigak and commented that "whereas Period VI is a phase of non-urban ... occupation at Mundigak, Kandahar I has a large earthwork and permanent, perhaps dense habitation. Accordingly, we suggest that at the beginning of Period I Kandahar replaced Mundigak as the principle settlement of the region, occupying a key position at the crossing of the Arghandab" (Whitehouse 1978: 32). Significantly, the presence of a 14 metre wide clay rampart dating to the first half of the first millennium BCE indicated the ability of the settlement's population to coordinate and mobilise sufficient numbers of people to construct it (Coningham 2007b: 22), as well as confirming and differentiating its presence at the summit of a regional settlement hierarchy.

BALUCHISTAN

Pirak (c. 1300–800 BCE)

As noted in Chapter 7, the site of Pirak in the Kachi Plain contained a continuity of sequence from circa 2000 to 800 BCE (Shaffer 1992: 458). In Trench PKA, a large new block of cardinally oriented rooms and courtyards measuring more than 40 metres square was laid out in Period III, defined clearly on the east and south by roads four metres wide. The presence of wall niches within individual buildings demonstrated a clear architectural continuity with the structures of preceding Period IIB as did the co-location of bone, ivory, antler and stone working with ceramic manufacture (Jarrige and Santoni 1979: 374). The inhabitants of this distinct craft quarter now also hosted furnaces for iron smithing alongside the other activities, questioning whether earlier models of the social and economic impact of the advent of iron are still tenable (Coningham 1995a: 65). The earliest identifiable iron objects at Pirak appeared to be weapons whilst stone blades continued to be used for harvesting (Jarrige and Santoni 1979: 54). Although the arrival of iron working appeared to have made little change to the organisation of pre-existing craft activities of the site's inhabitants, Shaffer noted a clear parallel between the grey ware, which was found in late Period II and through Period III, and the "early Iron age Painted Gray Ware culture in northern India" (Shaffer 1992: 459). It is also possible to draw parallels between elements of the ceramic assemblage of Period IIIB and that of Charsadda (Jarrige and Santoni 1979: Fig. 84.487), reiterating some of the common links and affinities shared by these distinct regional groupings.

THE ARABIAN SEA (c. 1300–600 BCE)

In Chapter 7, we noted the economic decline of a number of those proto-urban communities engaged in trading networks within the Arabian Sea. This is not, of course, to suggest that this region was abandoned or depopulated, as evidence has been presented from the excavations at the Qal'at al-Bahrain for large jars and storage vessels, with analogies to similar material from Susa and the island of Failaka between circa 1200 and 800 BCE (Potts 1990: 315). Similarly, scattered finds of iron and bronze objects with dates of the first half of the first millennium BCE have been reported from burials at al-Hajjar in Bahrain (ibid.: 326) and, more broadly, within the Oman peninsula. However, the degree to which such populations were actively engaged in trade and exchange networks with settlements within South Asia is less clear from the archaeological data. Indeed, textual records appeared to link Dilmun with Assyria. Finally, it should be noted that although the Omani burials were frequently associated with steatite and chlorite vessels, Potts has commented that "It has often been noted that the term 'Iron Age' is, in the Omani case, a complete misnomer. Practically no iron is attested, whereas the bronze industry appears to have flourished" (ibid.: 383).

THE GANGA BASIN

Painted Grey Ware Phase (c. 1200–600 BCE)

The Ganga Basin has long been the focus of discussions as to the character of the emergent Early Historic world, primarily due to the wealth of early post-Independence archaeological projects in this region. Indeed, in 1984 it was possible for Romila Thapar to state that "there is maximum data on these areas for an analysis of the process of state formation" (1985: 15). However, as this chapter demonstrates, increasingly strong archaeological data from the other regions of the subcontinent now allow us to review the Ganga within a broader context of increasing complexity. Painted Grey Ware, or PGW as it is often referred to, is the key fossil artefact for designating early Iron Age settlements within the Ganga Basin. The ceramic has a distinctive fine and well-levigated paste and its signature grey colour was produced through reduced firing conditions, and it was decorated with a variety of motifs painted in black on the surface. Most forms were straight-sided bowls, dishes and *lotas*, suggesting that the ensemble was designed to be deluxe tableware. As such, it is likely that it accompanied some major transformations in dining traditions which were adopted by people across a vast geographical spread. It was first formally recognised at Hastinapura by Lal (1955: 23) and has been generally dated to between 1200 and 600 BCE. Erdosy has noted that two of the main assemblages, from Hastinapura and Atranjikhera, share a number of simple geometric motifs, such as straight or wavy and solid or broken parallel lines, chequerboard and swastikas, whilst more elaborate designs have limited distribution (1995a: 95–96). For example, tridents, three-armed swastikas and trefoil designs, and three sets of parallel lines converging on the interior of the base were more common at Atranjikhera, whilst concentric rings, floral designs and concentric rings on the interior base were found at Hastinapura. Originally found only within the Ganga Basin, it has now been recovered from more than 700 sites across the Punjab, Haryana, northern Rajasthan, western Uttar Pradesh, the Nepal Terai and along the Ghaggar-Hakkra channel into Cholistan, and into central India at Ujjain (Singh 2008). It is likely that this distribution will continue to increase, as indicated by reports of painted grey wares from the Alaknanda Valley near Srinagar in Kashmir (Nautiyal and Khanduri 1986: 86). It should be noted that PGW was often only a minority within individual site ceramic assemblages and Mughal recorded that it accounted for only 5 percent of the ceramics from Iron Age Cholistan, whilst the remaining 95 percent were incised, cord-impressed and stamped red wares – a clear regional emphasis (Mughal 1997: 89). It is also interesting to record that some scholars have suggested that a late variant of PGW survived within the northern tributaries of the Ganga until the first half of the first millennium BCE (Mitra 1972), but this remains unproven with Lal categorically stating that "[t]he overwhelming evidence from all other sites is that this ware ceased to exist by about the middle of the first millennium BC" (Lal: 1978: 79).

With respect to Mughal's recognition of a regional Cholistan emphasis, it is important to note that PGW was not the only broadly distributed ceramic ware associated with this Era of Regionalisation, as a number of archaeologists have also identified distinct assemblages of Black and Red Ware, or BRW, in the middle and eastern Ganga, especially along the Ghaghara River and its tributaries. The lowest one metre of occupation at the site of Narhan, Period I, contained such an assemblage of bowls, basins and vases, of which 20 percent were decorated with white linear strokes (Singh 1994: 15). The vessels had a black exterior but a red interior. The site of Narhan also produced evidence that its inhabitants built structures defined by postholes with clay floors and clay-coated reed walls. Two iron objects were recovered from the uppermost levels of Period I (Singh 1994: 19) as well as a polished stone axe and two sherds of cord-impressed pottery which linked the site back to the traditions of the first food-producing communities of the Ganga Basin. Makkhan Lal's settlement survey of Kanpur District also identified nine sites with this distinct ware but noted that there was very little differentiation between the sites which were all below five hectares in size (1984a, 1984b). Interestingly, Lal identified this phase as a distinct period preceding the advent of Painted Grey Ware within the sequence of Kanpur, and Singh has suggested that it represented an interface between the 'Chalcolithic' and Iron Ages (Singh 1994: 49). As Allchin and Allchin argue, however, this sequence was by no means uniform as some sites have provided evidence of a sequence which ran from OCP through BRW to PGW as at Atranjikhera, whilst at other sites the sequence shifted directly from BRW to NBPW as at Narhan and Rajghat (Allchin and Allchin 1982: 259).

A number of preliminary settlement surveys have been conducted in this region, making it possible to begin to distinguish differing settlement categories. For example, Mughal's survey on the old Ghaggar channel in Cholistan provided evidence of fourteen sites associated with PGW despite what has been interpreted as evidence to indicate headwater shifts and the river becoming seasonal during this period (Mughal 1997: 53). There was an apparent division of settlement size into thirteen sites less than 4 hectares and a single site, Satwali, at almost 14 hectares. Whilst this represented a major decline in numbers and tiers in the hierarchy from the preceding Localisation Era within the area, Mughal recorded that there was a clear cultural, occupational and environmental hiatus between that Era and the Era represented by the assemblages of PGW (Mughal 1997: 53). A similar pattern has been identified by Joshi in Haryana and the Punjab, where 429 sites were associated with Localisation Era wares but only 50 with PGW (Joshi et al. 1984). Certainly, this pattern of decline in complexity, as indicated by decreasing hierarchical tiers and numbers, was not one encountered elsewhere across the Ganga Basin as illustrated by the results from the settlement surveys by Erdosy and Makkhan Lal. The latter surveyed Kanpur District and identified nine sites associated with Black and Red Ware and although all were less than 5 hectares, three were between 3 and 5 hectares. In the succeeding phase, the number of sites associated with PGW rose four-fold to forty-six, with forty less than 2 hectares and none more than 5 hectares (Lal 1984b: 79). In parallel, Erodsy focused on Allahabad District and identified sixteen sites associated with PGW, all near river courses.

Although fifteen sites were less than 5 hectares in area, the population of the future city of Kausambi had already occupied an area of 10 hectares during this period (Erdosy 1988: 46). Erdosy has suggested that the settlements were located close to water courses due to a combination of factors ranging from transport, fertile alluvial soils and defence, to the difficulties of colonising and clearing the forests of the upland areas. A similar two-tiered settlement hierarchy has also been identified in northern Haryana, where forty-two sites associated with PGW were identified, of which forty-one were less than 4.3 hectares and only one, Bhukari, covered almost ten hectares (Bhan and Shaffer 1978).

Despite this broad understanding of settlement distribution and size, rather less is known of the morphology and character of the larger sites in this period, mainly due to their presence in the basal levels of a number of very deep urban sequences. Excavations at Hastinapura have identified the habitation layers associated with PGW in Period II above the earlier settlement with its OCP assemblage. Although the archaeological deposit was damaged by later river erosion, the settlement appeared to have measured at least 66 metres east to west (Lal 1955: 12–13). Structures were of a similar nature to those of the preceding phase, with use of posts and plastered reed walls and an apparent absence of baked-brick. The presence of rice and the bones of cattle, buffalo, pig, sheep and wild deer have been interpreted by the excavator to indicate that its population was "an essentially agricultural society" (Lal 1955: 14). The excavations at Atranjikhera presented a similar sequence, where the late 'Chalcolithic' occupation was succeeded by the presence of deposits associated with PGW (Gaur 1984). This period at Atranjikhera, Period III, also provided evidence of manufacturing in the form of a kiln, an iron furnace, and slag. At Hastinapura, Period II provided evidence of a bone-working industry, and this combined evidence may have been an indication of a number of the manufactured goods or services that the inhabitants of this category of larger site provided for the smaller settlements. The populations of these larger 'anchor' settlements also appear to have been involved in longer-distance trade as indicated from the finds of agate and carnelian at Hastinapura. The presence of terracotta horses and horse bones in the same levels (Lal 1955: 13) indicated that mobility and transport routes were not necessarily restricted to the use of water courses (Lal 1955: 13).

Whilst excavations at various sites have exposed the remains of timber structures with reed walls, such as the oval and rectangular structures at Jahhkera (Ghosh 1989: 180), the small semi-circular huts of Period IB's earlier phase at Bhagwanpura were replaced by a large and distinctive complex of thirteen rectangular and square rooms set around a courtyard (Bisht and Asthana 1979: 236). Some of these rooms measured as large as 3.35 by 4.2 metres, and were found to have contained artefacts of copper, faience and glass, bone styli and horse bone. Early claims that Kausambi had been enclosed by walls by circa 1000 BCE have been revised down substantially to the middle of the first millennium BCE, and whether the site itself was "an early town", as claimed by the excavator (Sharma 1969: 13), is still open to debate. However, this is not to suggest that the populations of such large settlements lacked the ability to engage in communal activity, as illustrated by the construction of a low mud embankment, measuring 4.8 metres wide and surviving to a height of 1.2 metres around the site of Jakhera, enclosing and differentiating its community and their settlement of oval and rectangular structures (Sahi 1978: 102). Similarly, a 1.45 metre high and 35 metre long bund at Atranjikhera was also indicative of the ability to mobilise large workforces for the construction of major communal or public works (Gaur 1984: 100). Such activities also have the effect of defining social affiliation and linked people to a specific site as well as contributing to their self-identification as its community (Mizoguchi 2002: 200).

Finally, it should be acknowledged that a small number of archaeological sites in the Terai of southern Nepal have also been recorded with evidence of sherds of PGW, including Lumbini and Tilaurakot (Bidari 2004, 2007; Mishra 1978; Rijal 1979), Ramagrama (Shrestha 2005), Banjarahi (Deo 1968) and Panditpur as well as corresponding sites on the Indian side of the border (Srivastava 1986; 1996). A somewhat different cultural package was adopted by communities further north into the Trans-Himalayan belt of Nepal. For example, human burials have been excavated and been found to have been accompanied by finds of bone arrowheads, shell ornaments and copper objects, including anthropomorphic figures in Thakakhola on the Kali Gandaki River of Central Nepal (Tiwari 1985). Further north, at Chokhopani on the right bank of the river in Mustang District, two further burials were recovered in a cave in 1984 and found to be associated with handmade grey vessels, copper objects including anthropomorphic sheets, shell ornaments and chert arrowheads. The excavator has suggested analogies between the channel spouted bowls and similar vessels from Tepe Sialk B and Tepe Giyan and ascribed a date of the first half of the first millennium BCE (ibid.). These finds and dates demonstrate a distinct stylistic and cultural boundary between these two regions of the modern nation state of Nepal.

THE DECCAN

Late Jorwe Phase (c. 1000–700 BCE)

During Period III of Inamgaon, which has been dated to between circa 1000 and 700 BCE, the character of the settlement transformed dramatically with a large reduction in the number of rectangular structures and their general replacement by circular structures (Dhavalikar et al. 1988: 204) (Figure 9.7.). In addition, the earlier nature of internal planning where the town had been divided by clear paths and lanes also changed to a more haphazard placement

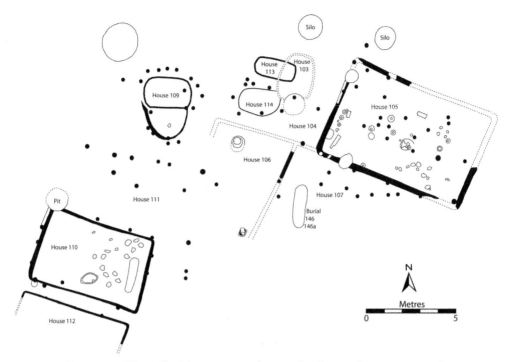

Figure 9.7. Plan of buildings at Inamgaon, India, during the Late Jorwe Phase.

of structures in relation to one another. The excavators noted that an "overall economic degeneration was visible in every field of human activity during this period" (ibid.: 204). Dhavalikar also noted similarities between the ceramic assemblages of the southern Deccan and those of the Late Jorwe Phase, and suggested that cultural contact must have occurred for this sharing to take place, possibly through the movement of farmers north in the first half of the second millennium BCE (ibid.: 417). There are still some contradictions associated with the nature of this phase as there was also a clear rise in the number of copper objects recovered from Period III, indicating that its inhabitants had access to rare objects. Alongside these changes, the physical anthropologists Gogte and Kshirsagar have suggested that trace element analysis of the human remains from this period demonstrated that the population shifted to a semi-nomadic phase from a settled agricultural lifeway (1988: 998), and that this coincided with the abandonment of the diversionary water channel from Period II. This is an interesting observation as nomadic and semi-nomadic lifeways are often (incorrectly) associated with the absence of material wealth. There were limited numbers of sites associated with this phase in Maharashtra and Inamgaon itself was abandoned by 700 BCE. The absence of iron at Inamgaon is all the more striking considering its wider distribution amongst contemporary communities to the south and north. Whilst considering reasons for this transformation and adaptation to pastoralism, P. K. Thomas has suggested that prolonged human interference in the surrounding habitat by Inamgaon's farmers had resulted in environmental degradation (2000: 148).

PENINSULAR INDIA

Black and Red Ware (c. 1200–600 BCE)

MEGALITHIC SITES

Megalithic sites have been a subject of interest since the nineteenth century, and Udayaravi Moorti has estimated that more than 1,700 of them have been identified within Peninsular India (1990), while Brubaker's recent work estimates "well over 2000 megalithic cemeteries have been documented in South Asia, the vast majority being located in south India and Sri Lanka" (2008: 1). The populations responsible for building the megaliths have also been associated with the adoption of Black and Red Ware and iron objects, and these assemblages have been found broadly spread across the modern states of Maharashtra, Andhra Pradesh, Karnataka, Tamil Nadu and Kerala (Moorti 1994: 4; Haricharan et al. 2013; Ramachandran, 1980; Narasimhaiah 1980) (Figure 9.8). Most early synthetic studies focused on the morphological variations of their funerary architecture (Allchin and Allchin 1982; Agrawal 1982). For example, classification by Agrawal included the categories of pit circle graves, cists, laterite chambers, alignments, sarcophagi and urns (1982: 261). However, Leshnik and McIntosh were amongst the first scholars to attempt to divide them into clear chronological bands based on artefactual seriation, that is, links to dated artefact sequences from other known sites (Leshnik 1974; McIntosh 1985) (Figure 9.9). In particular, McIntosh subdivided the funerary architecture into four main periods with Period I dating to between 1100 and 800 BCE; Period II dating to between 800 and 550 BCE; Period III dating to between 550 and 300 BCE; and Period IV dating to between 300 and 100 BCE (1985: 469). Of relevance to this chapter are Periods I and II, which McIntosh termed early Iron Age and Early Megalithic respectively. The first of these, Period I, was associated with individual human burials within simple pit graves, some of which were lined with stone slabs and some of which were covered with stone capstones, but all of which "differ little from those of the preceding Neolithic/Chalcolithic period" (McIntosh 1985: 471).

Recent evidence has been advanced for the use of stone within a burial at the site of Watgal with dates of between 2700 and 2300 BCE, which links well with McIntosh's suggestion of some form of continuity in burial practice (Korisettar et al. 2002). However, even with this suggestion of continuity, it is important to note that the megalithic tradition of Peninsular India was accompanied by a distinct ritual shift from intramural burial practice to the use of separate and defined extramural cemeteries. Literally, this redefined people's

Figure 9.8. Cists with portholes at Hire Benekal, India (courtesy Peter Johansen).

lives from living beside the dead to the creation of artificial monuments to differentiate the dead from the living. The ceramic assemblage adopted also had some affinity with those of the preceding period, but the graves were distinguished by the presence of simple daggers and arrowheads of iron. Concentrated in areas with evidence of preceding 'Chalcolithic' and Neolithic population, megalithic cemeteries have been mainly found in the uplands of Andhra Pradesh, Tamil Nadu and Karnataka whilst the first megalithic burials in Maharashtra only date to Period II. Indeed, Period II witnessed both an expansion in the distribution of this burial tradition and a far greater investment in the use of stone to monumentalise and perpetualise. This is illustrated in Maharashtra with the advent of stone circles around shallow burial mounds, as well as the development of stone cists within stone circles elsewhere. Period II was also characterised by the presence of fractional inhumation in addition to complete inhumation, and by an increase in the presence of iron objects and an extension of forms from iron daggers and arrowheads to include iron spears, sickles, axes and hoes. Horse burials, and the presence of horse furniture, have also been recorded (McIntosh 1985: 475).

The interpretation of such monuments has been contested and, as early as the nineteenth century, a number of scholars have tried to explain the emergence of a megalithic culture in the Deccan through population migrations and human diffusion. For example, Meadows Taylor suggested that they were the burial mounds of wandering Celto-Scythian tribes in 1852, whilst W. J. Perry suggested that they had been constructed by Egyptians (McIntosh 1981: 463).

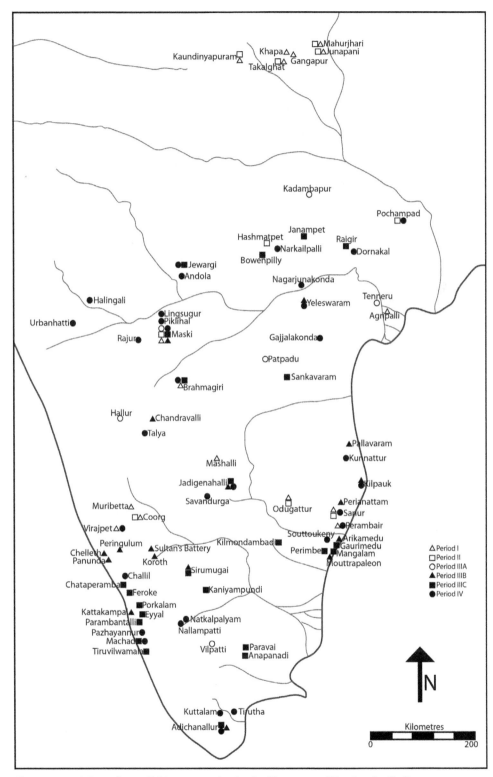

Figure 9.9. Map of megalithic cemeteries in the Deccan and Peninsular India.

Figure 9.10. Terracotta sarcophagus in the Kanchipuram Government Museum, India (courtesy Jo Shoebridge).

Although Sankalia concluded that "the authors of these megaliths remain unknown" (1977: 157), a number of scholars continued to attempt to link the movement of Aryans with the distribution of horse furniture and iron in south India (McIntosh 1981). Of much greater significance are the later attempts to analyse the contents of the various excavated megalithic tombs in an attempt to find trends of ascribed or acquired wealth, including the study by Moorti. Moorti analysed the artefacts and human remains from a sample of 186 well documented excavated burials from a total of twenty-nine sites, and identified a distinctive positive correlation between age and the number of items of status and weapons, with the highest numbers being associated with middle-aged or older adults (1990: 11) (Figure 9.10). It is also interesting to note that, in contrast to the preceding 'Chalcolithic' period, few child burials were represented (Mohanty and Selvakumar 2002: 322), suggesting that not all children were buried and that older adults possibly acquired wealth and status over their lifetimes. Brubaker's work in the provinces of Andhra Pradesh and Karnataka has been based on intensive landscape recording and analysis, and he has suggested that although there are large numbers of megalithic cemeteries, they would have accounted for only a very small percentage of the Iron Age population in this area. Brubaker has therefore argued that these monuments and associated burials are those of an elite section of society, thus representing the increasing social differentiation of this period (2008: 1). Brubaker's survey points to differentiation within the

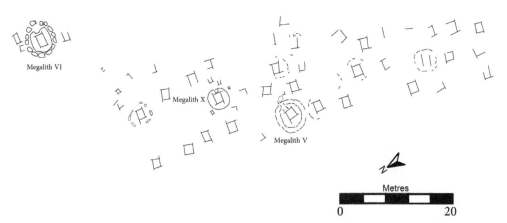

Figure 9.11. Plan of the megalithic cemetery at Brahmagiri, India.

cemeteries themselves, with few that are very large in size, and many more much smaller cemeteries. He has interpreted this feature as a possible marker of settlement hierarchies and emergent central places (2008:2).

Whilst the construction of individual monuments would have necessitated a coordination of labour, perhaps in linked groups such as extended family members, Allchin and Allchin pointed out that such activities would have needed a degree of technical and specialist knowledge, such as of fire-setting (1982: 339). Moorti has suggested that for larger monuments and alignments or menhirs "intercommunity cooperation" would have been needed, necessitating further organisation and support of surplus labour (Moorti 1990: 13). Indeed, Mohanty and Selvakumar have calculated that it would have taken a workforce of between seventy and eighty young adults three and four days to construct a simple cairn circle of 13.5 metres diameter (2002: 320). As noted earlier, Moorti's analysis of individual burials also recorded high numbers of iron weapons in the burials of adults; 285 examples from ninety-two burials (Moorti 1990: 13). When one considers the size of some of the cemeteries in the Deccan, such as Brahmagiri, it is clear that they represent a vast cumulative communal investment (Figure 9.11). It was assumed that mining had already been developed to exploit gold and iron sources, as indicated by dates of the eighth and ninth centuries BCE for artefacts of these materials at the site of Hatti in Karnataka (Moorti 1994: 42) and the recovery of iron slag and a goldsmith's die within the residential site of Paiyampalli in contexts dated to the first half of the first millennium BCE (Ramachandran 1980: 72).

Allchin and Allchin noted that whilst there was clear diversity within burial practices within the megalithic tradition of Peninsular India, there was also a striking uniformity across the forms of the iron artefacts recovered from them, including flat axes with crossed hafting bands. They also suggested that this uniformity may have been the result of a small group of iron workers with certain skills and styles either moving themselves around the region or diffusing their knowledge and products (Allchin and Allchin 1982: 335). Certainly iron working was a relatively fresh innovation at this time, and it is likely that with its increased use and presence, specialist groups of iron workers developed. Perhaps they guarded their craft closely passing on their skills to selected family or group members who then moved out to new areas where their skills would have been in high demand, or perhaps a prestigious group of iron workers moved around whole regions working and selling their products. Whatever the scenario, this uniformity of iron artefacts is striking. Whilst some of the objects recovered may have been agricultural in function, Moorti has concluded that the presence of large numbers of weapons suggests that this period was associated with a rise in warfare connected with attempts to consolidate resource-rich zones (1990: 13).

SETTLEMENT SITES

In contrast with the large amount of data recovered from the very visible megalithic cemeteries and individual or grouped megalithic monuments, there is relatively little information from habitation sites. The situation in the mid-1990s was summarised by Moorti, who pointed out that out of 399 known habitation sites in south India, only 19 had actually yielded occupational data (1994: 6) and, as Johansen observed more than ten years later, "The character of settlement and residential dynamics during the South Indian Iron Age (1200–300 BC) has been a perplexing and somewhat elusive issue in South Asian archaeological research for several decades" (2008: 20). A number of sites appear to have demonstrated a continuity of settlement, as illustrated by Brahmagiri, where the three metre 'Chalcolithic' deposit of Period I was overlain by a metre of Iron Age or Period II deposits (Box 9.2). Wheeler described Period II as "an Iron Age culture identical with that of the local megalithic tombs and pit-circles" (1948: 199), and his own excavations in Trench Br21 exposed fragmentary plans of posts holes and low walls of boulders in all periods, and what appeared to be an intramural urn burial, complete with bronze rod in Period IB (1948: 203). Recent work in Karnataka has extended knowledge of settlement sites, particularly the 'Early Historic landscapes of the Tungabhadra Corridor' project, which has identified and explored the Iron Age site of Kadebakele. This site has coverage of more than 60 hectares, and a number of distinct areas have been identified, including residential, waste dump, and megaliths (Srinivasan et al. 2009: 119). Preliminary analyses on some of the metal objects suggest that use of early crucible technology allowed the production of very early high carbon iron alloys. Both crucible technologies and resulting high carbon steel artefacts have also been noted at the site of Mel-siruvalur in Tamil Nadu (Srinivasan et al. 2009: 117). The site of Bukkasagara in Karnataka was constructed on a series of terraces on the side of a hill, and different terraces were used as the location of different activities,

Box 9.2. Brahmagiri

A major component of Mortimer Wheeler's archaeological enquiry in India between the years of 1944 and 1948 was to build up a chronological framework for South Asia through the excavation of key sites. In order to address the 'Indian Megalithic problem' – what he defined as the chronological lacunae for Peninsular India, he chose to excavate at Brahmagiri in Chitradurga District, Karnataka, where there was the "[p]resence of almost unnumbered megaliths" (Wheeler 1976: 62). In order to understand the chronological sequence of the megaliths at Brahmagiri, Wheeler chose not only to investigate several Megaliths but to also excavate the 'town' site as well, as he had reached the conclusion that "1000 megalithic cists might be scrupulously excavated without any significant addition to our knowledge of their chronology". Wheeler held that by contextualising them within a related culture-sequence, such as an adjacent town site, it would be "possible to ensure a substantive advance of knowledge" (Wheeler 1976: 62). He also anticipated that the related culture-sequence would be provided through association with artefact types for which he had developed typologies from his excavations at Arikamedu. There, he had linked South Asian ceramic industries with imported Italian Arretine Wares and amphorae as well as a ware adapted for the local market, Rouletted Ware. As prior investigations had uncovered Roman coins as well as Rouletted Ware at sites within the interior, and Asokan edicts were found in the vicinity of Brahmagiri, it was hoped that a long excavated sequence could be obtained and linked to Roman and Mauryan material culture providing "a fixed chronological point for a representative series of South Indian megalithic tombs" (Wheeler 1948: 183).

Excavations were conducted in 1947, and ten megalithic structures were investigated at Brahmagiri whilst additional cuttings were made through the town. Three major chronological phases were identified; the 'Brahmagiri Stone Axe Culture', which was dated to the early first millennium BCE to the beginning of the second century BCE on the basis of polished pointed-butt axes as well as handmade pottery of a coarse grey fabric; the 'Megalithic culture' dating to after circa 200 BCE to the middle of the first century CE which was thought to provide the first evidence of iron working and Black and Red Ware; and finally, 'Andhra culture' which includes evidence of Rouletted Ware (Wheeler 1948: 202–203). Wheeler's research had seemingly solved the puzzle of the 'Indian Megalithic problem' in terms of chronology, and he later reflected that "[t]owards the end of our work at Brahmagiri I found myself wondering from time to time whether it was not just a trifle too easy. Where was the catch?" (Wheeler

(continued)

1955: 208). The resultant chronological sequence has, for the most part, been accepted by archaeologists, and most narratives of South Indian prehistory and ceramic typologies remain largely indebted to Wheeler's sequence (Morrison 2005: 257).

However, a number of Wheeler's chronologies and sequences at various sites across South Asia have begun to be challenged, such as at Charsadda (Coningham and Ali 2007a) but also in relation to Peninsular India at Arikamedu (Begley 1996) and Brahmagiri (Morrison 2005). At Arikamedu, Begley (1996) demonstrated that Rouletted Ware was also present within pre-Arretine levels and this corroborates evidence from Anuradhapura, where excavations have revealed the presence of extensive pre-Roman trade networks across the Indian Ocean (Coningham 2002). Furthermore, Kathleen Morrison (2005) has reappraised Wheeler's excavations at Brahmagiri and Chandravalli utilising radiocarbon determinations from wood collected from the original excavations. Charred wood from Megalith 6, a deposit defined by Wheeler to be of a 'Megalithic' phase, provided a radiocarbon determination of between 2140 and 1940 BCE, firmly dating to the southern Neolithic (Morrison 2005: 258). In addition, a radiocarbon sample was recovered from cutting Br 21 at the town site, a key sequence upon which Wheeler based his chronology. This provided a date range of CE 1190 to 1280, clearly a medieval feature, again refuting the chronological sequence that had been developed (Morrison 2005: 261). As with many avenues of archaeological research in South Asia, further stratigraphic excavations linked to scientific dating programmes, as recently undertaken by Haricharan et al. (2013), are required to finally bring some chronological resolution to the 'Indian Megalithic problem'.

including residential areas, iron working, brick making, reservoirs, agriculture and mortuary rituals. The site included a large animal enclosure with ashy and vitrified dung, and Johansen has suggested that the terraces themselves allowed the occupants of Bukkasagara to "physically and symbolically demarcate(d)" these different areas (2008: 317). At Rampuram, also in Karnataka, terraces were used in a similar way, and the site included a stone circle, and what Johansen described as a "spatially segregated ritual place for mortuary preparations situated deep within the settlement's central occupational zone" (2008: 317), which offers interesting insight into the ways in which the dead were treated and their place within Iron Age society. Additional settlement information has come from the excavations at the settlement at Paiyampalli in Tamil Nadu, where the excavators recorded an apparent overlap between Neolithic and early Iron Age levels in the seventh century BCE without an intervening 'Chalcolithic' (Ramachandran 1980: 45). The earliest dates for the presence of iron in association with Black and Red Ware come from the site of Hallur in Mysore, where Period II has been identified as an overlap between the Neolithic and Iron Age occupation and has produced radiocarbon dates of circa 1100 BCE (McIntosh 1985: 473).

Complete examples of excavated structures from the Iron Age are few but those from Paiyampallu's 1.5 metre thick sequence indicated that its inhabitants built circular or oblong buildings defined by postholes and of walls and roofs contrasted of timber frames and perishable materials (Ramachandran 1980: 43). The site's circular structures measured between 1.5 and three metres in diameter and the oblong ones as long as four metres, and their floors were constructed of a layer of stone chips coated with a thin lime plaster (ibid.). Wheeler's dating of the sequence within Brahmagiri's settlement, and thus its links with the adjacent megalithic cemetery, was based entirely on stratigraphy and typological similarities, and thus has been open to question (Morrison 2005). However, more recent surveys indicate that most cemeteries appear to be linked with settlements, but often at a distance of between 10 to 20 kilometres. Moorti's analysis has also demonstrated that habitation sites were situated close to major river courses or their tributaries and on fertile black cotton soils (Moorti 1994: 11–12). In contrast, Rajan's survey in Arcot District of Tamil Nadu has suggested that cemeteries were located on less productive land, often granitic uplands, but that they were usually associated with a settlement site (Rajan 1994: 28). Most of these surveys and excavations have also failed to identify evidence of fortification or defining walls around settlement sites, but this is not to deny the presence of increasing complexity and site differentiation. Indeed, based on an analysis of settlement size across eighteen different physiographic zones of south India, Moorti has suggested that whilst the majority of settlements were smaller than 5 hectares, there were at least twenty-six with "a population of more than 1000" and that "some of them might have served in all probability, as regional centres" (Moorti 1994: 17). This recent research has assisted a shift of focus from interpretations of the early Iron Age in Peninsular India as a period dominated by pastoral transhumance, to interpretations that suggest that the Iron Age or Megalithic period was one of greatly increased population in comparison to the preceding Neolithic-Chalcolithic, with evidence for emerging craft and settlement specialisation but practicing what is believed to have been a mixed economy with "a predominance of pastoralism" (Mohanty and Selvakumar 2002: 331). Furthermore, a minority of scholars have suggested the initial construction of simple gravity irrigation tanks also occurred at this time and was accompanied by ploughing with the use of iron tipped hoes (Ramachandran 1980: 69). The heart of this complexity has been usefully summarised by Aloka Parasher-Sen, who has stated that "we cannot suggest a unilinear state of development from pastoralism to agriculture and then to urbanism for the whole region taken together. In fact, as a result of this complexity details of not only the economic structures but also the political and social systems that controlled and manoeuvred these differed conspicuously in each of the regions and sub-regions of Peninsular India." (2008: 333). Finally, reference to the difficulties of attributing date ranges to megaliths may be illustrated by the recent study of the megalithic burials at Siruthwavoor in Tamil Nadu which demonstrated that the cemetery of over 500 individual monuments had been utilised for almost a millennium between 300 BCE and 600 CE (Haricharan et al. 2013).

SRI LANKA

Anuradhapura (c. 1000–600 BCE)

As discussed in Chapter 7, Sri Lanka's cultural sequence appears to have transformed abruptly at the beginning of the first millennium BCE. The evidence suggests a swift transition from populations of microlithic tool-using hunter-gatherers to the earliest iron tool-using communities; although recent evidence from sites such as Varana suggests that there may have been an overlap in the areas occupied by these very different groups. The earliest evidence for the presence of early Iron Age populations within the island comes from the basal levels of the city of Anuradhapura in the island's North Central Province. There, in the dry zone, the low natural mound beside the Malwattu Oya river which had been previously occupied by hunter-gatherers was now occupied by a settlement of small, lightly constructed round houses with diameters of less than 2.5 metres (Coningham 1999: 127). Covering an area of some 18 hectares, the inhabitants of Period K appear to have relied on a subsistence based on herding cattle and hunting deer with iron objects, and iron smithing slag was present from the beginning of the sequence (Coningham and Harrison 2006: 59; Young et. al. 2006: 524–525) (Figure 9.12). Unfortunately, there are no other known settlement sites within the island for comparison, but the Black and Red Ware assemblage from Anuradhapura and the early dates allow us to make reference to some of the megalithic cemeteries within the dry zone, such as the site of Ibbankatuva which has been dated to the middle of the first millennium BCE (Coningham 1999: 137) (Figure 9.13). One of the more fully excavated of the island's thirty megalithic cemeteries, it covered more than 13 acres and comprised hundreds of individual cist burials with finds of carnelian beads imported from western India (Deraniyagala 1992: 734) (Figure 9.14). The absence of a 'Chalcolithic' phase, combined with the presence of iron and Black and Red Ware, some of which were inscribed with non-scriptural graffiti, has led some Sri Lankan scholars to suggest that these early Early Iron communities were initially part of the Iron Age population of Peninsular India and migrated across to the island (Seneviratne 1984: 283).

Figure 9.12. Circular buildings within the Citadel of Anuradhapura, Sri Lanka.

Figure 9.13. Megalithic cemetery at Ibbankatuva, Sri Lanka.

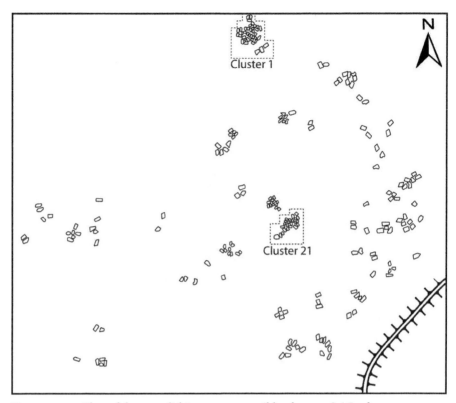

Figure 9.14. Plan of the megalithic cemetery at Ibbankatuva, Sri Lanka.

CONCLUSIONS

Having discussed the transformational processes and sequences of the Era of Localisation in Chapter 8, this chapter considered the development and growth of the new era of regional differentiation apparent within South Asia. In particular, we discussed the introduction of iron into the archaeological sequence of South Asia and examined the accompanying elements of continuity and transformation. We also illustrated the evidence of what is now considered to be a period of increasing complexity with pockets of incipient urban and differentiated populations in different parts of South Asia, and considered some of the apparent parallels between the Era of Regionalisation of the Indus Valley Tradition and this new Era of Regionalisation within the Early Historic Tradition. These emergent Early Historic urban-focused developments have been interpreted in many ways, and one of the earliest interpretations, which has had a widespread, long-term impact on scholarship in South Asia and beyond, was that urbanism at this time first appeared in the north-west of the subcontinent as the result of diffusion from developed cities and states to the west. In particular, the expansion of the Persian or Achaemenid Empire in the sixth BCE into the region known as Gandhara has been very influential as an explanation (Ghosh 2008: 69), and this was largely based on Mortimer Wheeler's excavations at Charsadda in the 1950s.

As will be discussed in more detail in Chapter 10, Wheeler suggested that the ancient city of Charsadda was founded as a direct result of Persian occupation and was specifically created along Persian and western urban forms, and he also argued that iron had been introduced at the same time (Wheeler 1962). This explanation has since been challenged and refuted by radiocarbon dates from this key site, placing the earliest settlement circa 1200 BCE. Supported by parallel evidence from the sites of Taxila, Kandahar and Akra Dheri, it is now suggested that the emergence of a number of differentiated regional centres or 'anchor' sites occurred prior to contact with the Persian world (Ali et al. 1998). This pattern of the establishment of large differentiated regional population agglomerations involved in long-distance trade has also been found in the Ganga Basin to the east as well as further to the south in Sri Lanka. In the former, the inhabitants of settlements like Hastinapura, which have been linked loosely with the Era of Localisation of the Indus Valley Tradition, expanded and became host to a regional grouping characterised by its adoption and spread of Ochre Coloured Ware and then Painted Grey Ware (Erdosy 1987). In the same period, the Iron Age settlement at Anuradhapura in the northern plains of Sri Lanka emerged as the dominant and differentiated regional population concentration with long-distance maritime links (Coningham 1999), whilst the populations of the Deccan appear to have followed an alternative trajectory with investment in vast mortuary complexes rather than the development of agglomerated proto-urban or incipient urban centres (Moorti 1990). Although these regional developments were relatively tightly geographically constrained, again, in parallel with the earlier Era of Indus Regionalisation, many were linked by active networks of trade and exchange with one another and began to share an increasing number of common cultural and technological features.

Whilst a number of earlier scholars attempted to link the presence of megalithic burial practices in different parts of the subcontinent with one another through chronological or ethnic linkages (McIntosh 1981), others proposed more functional explanations for their growth and spread. Borrowing heavily from processual explanation, McIntosh argued that they reflected a societal response to an environmental context of increasing aridity, and functioned as territorial links or anchors to ancestral lands for subsequent generations of more pastoral-focused communities (1985). Her assumptions have since been refuted by the results of a number of regional settlement surveys and by the increasing antiquity for the megalithic phenomenon, but many scholars would still attribute a territorial function to the megalith. The function of such monumental investments has also been queried by anthropologists who question the expenditure (or waste) of energy on such cultural elaborations as they do not necessarily improve societal fitness, or rather, improve surplus levels or the general carrying capacity of the environment (Madsen et al.

1999). In response to this apparent contradiction, R. C. Dunnell suggested that such waste purposely invested surplus and labour in elaboration in order to prevent the reinvestment of that 'energy' in reproduction (1999: 246). In unpredictable environments, this process had the effect of artificially depressing the population below the local carrying capacity and thus ensured societal survival. Further developing this concept, Nolan and Howard have suggested that ceremonial behaviour and elaboration involving the seasonal disturbance of forested environments would have resulted in the maintenance of more open landscapes, perhaps encouraging the growth of both edible plants for low energy investment and deer populations (2010: 130). Whilst not necessarily directly applicable to the Deccan, such a model may be helpful when considering the impact of megalithic cemeteries in the dry zone of Sri Lanka as "small ceremonial sites could serve as a substantial subsistence buffer and supplement to the local carrying capacity" (ibid.: 137).

As noted in the Introduction to this chapter, the causal link between the introduction of iron tools and the clearances and settlement of the heavy clays of the Ganga Basin has also been generally discarded. So too have the causal links between the introduction of domesticated rice and the exploitation of the Ganga Basin, particularly in the light of the cultivation of rice within the Integrated Era of the Indus Valley Tradition. However, it does need to be noted that an increasing reliance on irrigated rice would still have had a major social and economic impact on the human communities actually farming the land. This is illustrated best, perhaps, by reference to the ploughed field found underneath the Integration Indus Era settlement of Kalibangan in Rajasthan. This field was covered with a grid of plough furrows with one set 30 centimetres apart running east to west and another set 1.9 metres apart running north to south, presumably for two different crops (Thapar 1973). On a roughly levelled field, we can imagine that with the use of a pair of cattle and a timber plough, similar to the terracotta models recovered from a number of sites (Kenoyer 1998: 163), such fields would not be particularly labour intensive to prepare, maintain and cultivate. Rice cultivation based on water management, in comparison, represented a vast initial human investment and then substantial contributions throughout the year (Scarborough 2003: 93). The fields need to be carefully levelled, all trees and stumps removed and the necessary infrastructure of canals, bunds and reservoirs designed, constructed and linked. Moreover, this initial investment necessitated maintenance and paddy transplantation, additional coordination of labour and water sources, and associated administrative and technical support. Once such an infrastructure was constructed, and this was on a communal rather than a family scale of investment, the farmers and their families were bound to its collective regulation and maintenance, even more so for transplanted paddy. As Vern Scarborough has also noted, once such water systems are instigated, they also bring with them significant risks and may actually accelerate conflict (Scarborough 2003: 93).

So final was this alteration or adaptation to the landscape that much of the region exploited during this Era still adheres to the basic infrastructure laid down. This newly created economic and social landscape was, in many ways, an irreversible step.

This was also an Era which a number of scholars have considered to have been 'Protohistoric' on account of the survival of a number of oral traditions which were later codified and preserved by writing (Avari 2007: 73). As noted in Box 2.4, these include the *Rig Veda*, or 'Song of Veda', and have been analysed by Thapar, who has suggested that they stress the concept of wealth through the ownership of cattle which appear to have functioned as "the unit of value" (1985: 25). Whilst the horse is another indicator of rank, the defence and ownership of cattle was synonymous with the role of raja or ruler. Concepts of territory were also increasingly conceptualised within these traditions with Thapar commenting that "A group of clans constituted the *jana* and the territory where they settled was referred to as the *janapada*, literally where the tribe places its feet. Since the economy of the *jana* included hunting and pastoralism, large forested areas adjoined the settlements and could even carry the name of the *jana*" (Thapar 1985: 35). In the next chapter, Chapter 10, we will discuss the steady assimilation and integration of this mosaic of regional communities into a co-joined and increasingly historic world of *janas* and *mahajanadapas*.

REINTEGRATION: TOWARDS AN EARLY HISTORIC WORLD (c. 600–250 BCE)

INTRODUCTION

It is very clear that urban forms re-established themselves and were adopted by communities across much of South Asia during the period between 600 and 350 BCE, with the growth of a number of agglomerated populations enclosed within high walls and ramparts, as well as the appearance of coinage and the first written recording systems of the Early Historic Tradition. These new towns and cities demonstrated vast communal investment in their construction and layout, and although they differentiated communities into urban and non-urban, there is archaeological evidence to show that they drew on sizeable areas of hinterland in order to support their increasingly complex social and economic structures (Coningham and Gunawardhana 2013; Erdosy 1987) (Figure 10.1) (Timeline 10.1). This process is one which Norman Yoffee has referred to as 'ruralisation', stating that "the urban demographic implosion was accompanied by an equally important creation of the countryside" with the re-networking of existing villages to emergent urban forms and the creation of new specialist centres (2005: 60). There was also a degree of shared standardisation and uniformity in the construction and layout of these new cities, and there were transformations in material culture as regional characters were overlaid by increasingly shared developments in style, practice and technology. Examples of regional styles being subsumed into an overarching style or practice included the adoption of Northern Black Polished Ware from the Ganga Basin outwards and Tulip Bowls across the west and north-west and the spread of megalithic burial practices across the Deccan and Sri Lanka (Allchin 1995a). The Early Historic Tradition is of course distinguished from the Indus Valley Tradition by the presence of a distinct historical character in the form of textual accounts and sacred texts, allowing the identification of a number of these cities as the centres of named independent states, states which were recorded as being in competition with one another. The innovation and introduction of coinage also provided a unique transportable and storable commodity which rulers and elites could receive as tax, and thus utilise as wealth

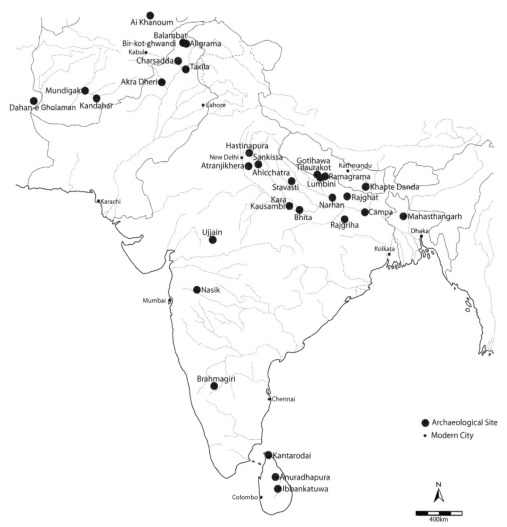

Figure 10.1. Map of sites mentioned in Chapter 10.

to wage war on one another or compete with each other for exotic imports, monumental building programmes and even to attract ascetic wanderers and religious teachers. Merchants could also use coins to transform perishables into imperishables, and they also began to erode elite patronage of ritual. We will consider the nature and dating of the 'historical' element in this chapter and the extent to which it does not always articulate with the archaeological data available to us. Some of the examples on which we touch include the peopling of Sri Lanka, the invasion of Alexander the Great and the annexation of the north-east of the subcontinent by the Achaemenid rulers. We begin this chapter by outlining some of the key challenges and debates facing scholars researching this period and follow this with an overview of sites and evidence from regions across South Asia as this Era of reintegration was to involve the entire subcontinent.

Re-integration: an Early Historic world

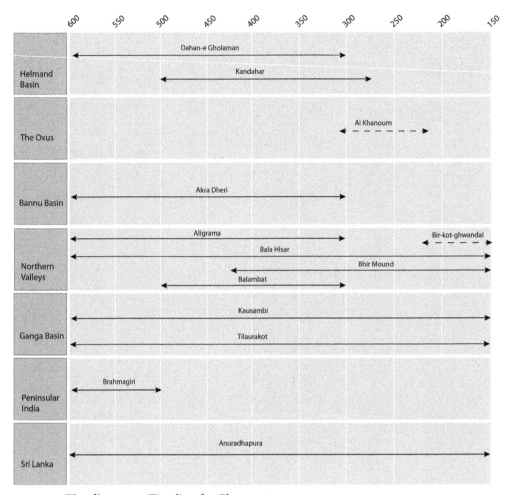

Timeline 10.1. Timeline for Chapter 10.

KEY CHALLENGES AND CONSTRAINTS

This Era of increasing integration is also referred to by some scholars as the 'Early Historic Period' due to the presence of interconnecting texts and oral traditions (Allchin 1995a) as well as/or the 'Indo-Gangetic' by others to reflect an initial developmental focus on the north of the subcontinent (Thapar 1985; Kenoyer 1998). However, we prefer to use 'Reintegration' to reflect the extension of Shaffer's model and its focus on the processes under discussion as there are a number of issues concerning both the interface between the relevant historical material and the archaeology and, as noted earlier, the fact that this Era was to integrate the entire subcontinent, not just the Indo-Gangetic plain. Indeed, this Era witnessed a steady integration across South Asia through the establishment and expansion of key networks of trade routes (Figure 10.2), but

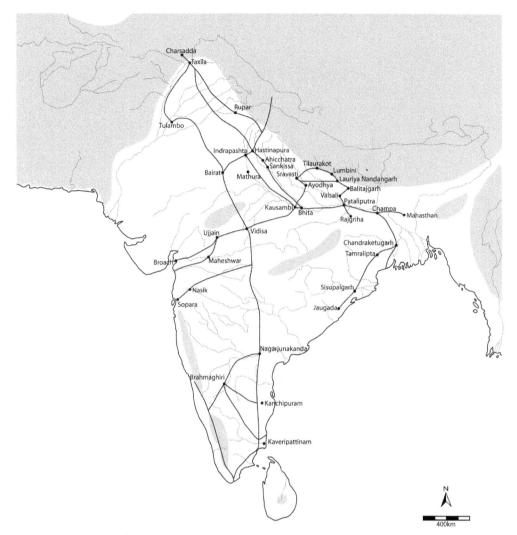

Figure 10.2. Map of major Early Historic trade routes.

it is also as important to note that this process was also closely associated with increasingly shared texts, ritual and belief practices and oral traditions. In the case of the latter, however, it is also clear that these sources are often at odds with the archaeological evidence. For example, although there is strong textual evidence to attest to the presence of Achaemenid Satraps in Hindush, Gandhara and Thatagush, the archaeological evidence for such hegemony remains poor. There are also dangers, however, of relying too heavily upon such texts and this is true of almost all Achaemenid, Hellenistic and South Asian texts and traditions as they may represent contrived 'kingly' narratives rather than independent records (Duncan 1990). We may illustrate this by examining Darius's DPh text, which cited his hegemony over Hind and was enshrined in the foundations of his new palace at Persepolis. However, Hind was named alongside the other three corners of the known world, suggesting a very strong degree of symbolic and cosmological quality to the inscription. This use of geography as microcosm has suggested to some scholars that Hind was a critical element of "the creation of the world and empire" (Nimchuk 2010: 227) but not necessarily a temporal ingredient. Similarly, there are frequent unexplained differences in detail between individual sources and the naming of those satrapies, such as the differences between those on the inscription at Behistun and those recorded by Herodotus (Dandamaev and Lukonin 1989: 98).

A further relevant category of textual and oral traditions are those of South Asian tradition, which described the emergence of the sixteen states or *Shodasa Mahajanapadas,* and the associated historical religious and secular leaders such as Mahavira and *Buddha,* and Bimbisara, Ajatasatru and Udayana (Erdosy 1995b) (Figure 10.3). The *Mahajanapadas* or 'great territories' were frequently referenced in early Jain and Buddhist traditions and were recorded as Gandhara and Kamboja in the north-west; Kuru, Matsya and Surasena in the Indo-Gangetic divide; Magadha, Anga, Kasi, Vrijji, Pancala, Asvaka, Kosala, Malla and Vatsa in the Ganga Basin; Avanti and Cedi in Central India; and Asmaka in the Deccan (Allchin 1995a: 115). Each of these territories was equipped with a capital and, according to tradition, was ruled by a Raja with the support of a hierarchy of ministers, chaplain and officers supported by a comprehensive taxation system. Indeed, Thapar has drawn attention to the fact that the *Arthashastra* later codified the seven elements, or *prakrti,* necessary for the definition and function of a state (1985: 121–122). These included the *svami,* the king or ruler; the *amatya* or ministers and the administration; the *janapada* or territory; the *durga* or fort; the *kosa* or treasury; *danda* or coercive power, law and authority; and, finally, the *mitra* or ally. It should be noted, however, that not all the *janapadas* were absolute monarchies as some are recorded as having been classified as *ganas* or *sanghas,* to which some scholars have attributed modern characteristics ranging from republics and democracies to oligarchies, although not without some translational reservations (Singh 2008: 266).

The physical remains of a number of the capitals of these sixteen states have been clearly identified, including the capital of the *Mahajanapada* of Gandhara at Taxila, that of Magadha at Rajagriha (modern Rajgir), Kasi at Rajghat (modern Varanasi), Vatsa at Kausambi, Kosala at Maheth (ancient Sravasti), Campa at Campanagar and Avanti at Ujjain. The traditions encapsulated within the *Dharmasutras* of Apastamba, Baudhayana and Gautama, and the *Astadhyayi* of Panini also recorded the rise of competition between these territories and the pursuit of 'the maxim of the fish', *matsya nyaya;* that is when larger fish prey upon smaller fish but are then themselves consumed by larger fish. This law of the fish resulted in the emergence of four victorious states – Avanti, Vatsa, Kosala and Magadha (Erdosy 1995b; Thapar 1985). With reference to the peopling of Sri Lanka, the early texts and traditions such as the *Mahavamsa* and *Dipavamsa* recorded that the island was only populated by spirits, demons, *nagas*

Figure 10.3. Map of the *Mahajanapadas.*

and *yaksas* at the time of the *Buddha*'s 'Great Passing Away' or *Mahaparinivana* in the first half of the first millennium BCE (Coningham and Lewer 2000). The island was then recorded as having been colonised by Vijaya and 700 companions from western India, who settled the north of the island and founded a number of settlements including Tambapanni on the north-west coast and Anuradhapura further inland (Coningham 1999).

We should note, however, that whilst a number of the capitals of the *Mahajanapadas* have been successfully identified, many are still undiscovered. For example, the capitals of Cedi and Asmaka in Central India remain unconfirmed, although various scholars have cited numerous possible sites (Allchin 1995a: 134–139). These early records did not include the presence of the kingdom of Kalinga amongst the sixteen great states, and this is particularly puzzling as Kalinga was the only state to be able to withstand the might of the Mauryan Empire until the middle of the third century BCE. Finally, neither the *Mahavamsa* nor the *Dipavamsa* make reference to the very long sequence of occupation within the island of Sri Lanka and the early occupation of Anuradhapura. Far from being just the home of spirits, demons, *nagas* and *yaksas*, its early inhabitants had already exploited many of the areas which were to become core parts of the Early Historic kingdom of the island. Certainly, the words that Ghosh placed in his forward to the Hastinapura report in the journal *Ancient India* still ring true with relevance for the historic character of the Early Historic Tradition: "a word of caution is necessary, lest the impression is left on the unwary reader that the Hastinapura excavation has yielded archaeological evidence about the truth of the story of the Mahabharata and that here at last is the recognition by 'official archaeology' of the truth embodied in Indian traditional literature. Such a conclusion would be unwarranted. ... It is indeed tempting to utilize archaeological evidence for substantiating tradition, but the pitfalls in the way should be guarded against, and caution necessary that fancy does not fly ahead of facts" (Ghosh 1955: 2–3). There are also challenges associated with the histories of Alexander the Great, particular as the majority of them date to the Roman period, such as the second century CE writer Arrian and the first century CE writer Curtius Rufus (Dandamaev and Lukonin 1989: 398). It is also interesting to observe, as Aurel Stein did, that "Alexander's triumphant invasion passed by, indeed, without leaving a trace in Indian literature or tradition" (1929: viii). This statement was later echoed by D. D. Kosambi, who commented that "[t]he invasion, or rather raid, for it was too ephemeral to be called anything else, passed completely unnoticed in Indian traditions, though a school of foreign historians still presents it as the single greatest event in ancient Indian history" (1965: 138).

With such a focus on historical sources, there has been less active pursuit of chronometric dating and phasing and, although there are a number of radiocarbon dates from this period, there remains a heavy reliance on the presence or absence of key ceramic vessel shapes or wares. As we shall see later, two of these critical categories are Tulip Bowls and Northern Black Polished Ware. The former has been described as a small round-bottomed wheel-turned vessel of a buff or brownish coarse ware with a distinct kick or carination half way down the side (Coningham et al. 2007b: 106). It has been strongly associated as a vector indicating the spread of Achaemenid influence and dominance in Afghanistan and Pakistan and has been dated to between the fourth and third centuries BCE (Dittmann 1984: 172). However, this date is controversial as Vogelsang has attributed a post-Achaemenid date to Tulip Bowls on account of their recovery from the Indo-Greek city of Shaikhan Dheri in Pakistan (1988: 104), while Magee and Petrie have attempted to push its dating back to between 600 and 300 BCE and link it firmly as a fossil indicator of Achaemenid influence (2010: 508). To add to this controversy, it is possible to note that a similar form had also been recorded in Period II of Hastinapura, alongside PGW vessels (Lal 1955: 49. No. XXVIa), suggesting a date of the first half of the first millennium BCE within the Ganga, thus weakening a blanket Achaemenid provenance.

The second category of ceramic from this period is known as Northern Black Polished Ware or NBPW. The ware and its forms have been broadly identifiable with the traditions associated with the production of PGW, and it is broadly agreed that NBPW is a development and refinement of Painted Grey Ware (Krishnan 2002a: 382). Like PGW before it, its clay was well-levigated and well-fired and its surfaces were black, lustrous and burnished. Fired at a temperature of 950 °C, the notable exterior appearance was reached by enriching the slip with potassium and iron, the former probably in the form of plant ash (Verardi 2007: 249). Ghosh has noted that, in addition to predominant finds of monochrome, there are also examples of bi-chrome vessels of NBPW with contrasting inner and outer colouring, haphazard colouring or distinct strokes (1989: 253). The dominant forms were all tableware, including thalis and deeper, smaller bowls, and the assemblage has been frequently described as 'deluxe' tableware (Lal 1955: 15). First identified by John Marshall during the Bhita excavations in the Ganga basin in 1910, its adoption is now known to have been extremely broad, stretching from communities in Sri Lanka in the south to Nepal in the north and from Afghanistan in the west to Bangladesh in the east.

During his excavations at Gotihawa in the Nepal Terai, Giovanni Verardi identified the presence of vessels of similar shape and technology as NBPW but noted that they appeared to have been fired in a slightly cooler kiln and had red or orange spots on their surface. As they occurred in the middle of the first millennium BCE, which is generally earlier within the sequence than "NBPW proper" and occurred in comparatively small amounts, he termed this material "Proto-NBPW" and believed that it represented "an experimental stage in the production" (Verardi 2007: 248). Such a sequence has also recently been encountered at Lumbini in Nepal (Coningham et al. 2013) and it is interesting to note the presence of a bowl of NBPW with "patches of brown" in the early levels of Period III at Hastinapura (Lal 1955: 52), perhaps indicating a broader distribution of this formative stage of development. However, it is generally accepted that NBPW had an early phase of between 550 and 400 BCE, a middle phase between 400 and 250 BCE and a late phase which terminated circa 100 BCE (Erdosy 1995b: 105). This wide chronological spread of 450 years makes it particularly complex when trying to date sites solely on the presence or absence of NBPW, although later forms are thought to demonstrate less control of colour and surface.

There was also the suggestion of communal investment in infrastructure as illustrated by the presence of exposed road surfaces at Rajghat (Tripathi 2008: 147) and outside the ramparts at the site of Kausambi and outside the casement wall at Kandahar, dating to the latter half of the first millennium BCE. The earliest of these was just over three metres wide and 15 centimetres thick and comprised rammed brickbat fragments, clay, ceramic sherds and grit (Sharma 1960: 40). Similarly, a reservoir appears to have been constructed at Ujjain, where archaeologists identified the presence of a tank of fired mud brick measuring 10.36 by 7.92 metres in Period II (Ghosh 1989: 448). Tripathi included the provision of distinctive refuse pits as part of the indication of "a greater complexity in the settlement system" at Rajghat, Sravasti, Rajgir and Taxila (2008: 147). Ringwells have also been recorded at many sites throughout this period, a further indication of the recognition of the need for investment in physical urban infrastructure and well as the necessity for the development of specialist kiln facilities and technicans to fire them. Whilst defining walls were associated with the monumentalisation of each capital's inhabitants within the *Mahajanapadas*, it was clear that there was a great variety of urban forms and materials being adopted in the fifth century BCE, ranging from an irregular pattern at Rajgir as dictated by the hills, to the crescent profile of Sravasti, the circular form of Sankissa and the triangular form of Ahicchatra (Allchin 1995a: 206). Equal diversity has been found within the materials and technology with which those urbanised populations defined themselves. For example, some of the new urban forms surrounded themselves with mud brick as at the Bala Hisar of Charsadda, others, clay ramparts as at Ujjain or stone blocks as at Rajgir.

There is also some debate as to whether these defining walls were all associated with warfare and defence, or whether these walls were linked to some other protective purpose such as flood protection or even symbolic or ritual protection. However, whilst flood protection might arguably be one function of the walls at some sites close to rivers, such as at Rajghat, it does not hold for other sites, such as Rajgir, where there was no danger to its population from flooding. Furthermore, it has been suggested that only part of the enclosed area of such cities was fully settled by human occupation. For example, less than 60 percent of the area enclosed within the new wall around the Citadel of Anuradhapura was actually occupied, and it is highly likely that the rampart and ditch complex may have been constructed to protect the kitchen gardens and fields within against the depredations of deer, wild pig and elephant (Coningham 1999). Whatever their function, all were associated with a vast increase in labour investment in their construction, and the largest, such as at Kausambi, had bases as wide as 75 metres, heights as great as 14 metres and covered circuits as long as 6 kilometres (Erdosy 1995b: 111). As such, they must have represented the mobilisation of thousands of individuals, far more than could have been found amongst the urban dwellers themselves, and thus they demonstrated the authority and ability of the emerging *Mahajanapadas* and their rulers to differentiate their urban inhabitants yet mobilise and integrate populations far beyond their walls and out into their hinterlands (Coningham

1995a: 70). It is important to recognise that some of these populations may have been recent migrants to the cities and their immediate hinterlands, as suggested by Tripathi (2008: 160) and Basant (2008: 197). In the light of such a suggestion, it is interesting to consider whether children, women and men were coerced in order to contribute their labour to such vast undertakings, but it is equally likely that, as identified by Mizoguchi (2002: 200), such communal activities were also methods by which individuals contributed to self-identification and affirming a particular social affiliation with a particular centre. Having thus set out some of the main limitations and challenges connected with the sources of evidence associated with this Era, we will now investigate the regional patterns and the process at work during this Era of increasing integration.

THE HELMAND BASIN

The city of Dahan-e Gholaman was established at the foot of a Plio-Pleistocene terrace, close to the old northern edge of the Sana Rud delta and 30 kilometres south-east of Zabul, the modern capital of the Iranian province of Sistan-Baluchistan (Figure 10.4). Unlike many long-lived tell sites in this region, Dahan-e Gholaman was founded as a new site on virgin land and "was designed fundamentally as a single project, at least in broad outlines" (Scerrato 1979:711). The excavator continued to suggest that this distinct planned urban character "presupposes a precise political plan and a well-established State" (Scerrato 1979: 711). The city was laid out over an area of 1.5 kilometres by 800 metres, parallel with a natural east-west terrace, and equipped with canals. Three monumental mud-brick and pise buildings were erected towards the eastern end of the settlement within a large open space which the excavator suggested formed the political, religious and economic core of the city: "the centre of the city's political administration, as well as the religious and perhaps also economic centre" (Scerrato 1979: 711). The first of these buildings, QN3, measured 53.2 by 54.3 metres and was centred on a square courtyard defined by a portico of pairs of pillars with four corner chambers or towers (Figure 10.5 and Figure 10.6). Entered from the south, the excavator identified pairs of 'ritual installations' within the walls of the cardinal porticos. These ritual installations were described as "a sort of fireplace or rather fire container or oven" (Scerrato 1979: 716) and were identified as facilities to prepare sacrificial offerings of food (Figure 10.7). A second phase of the structure, Phase B, saw the construction of three large stepped altars in the middle of the courtyard on an east-west axis and the creation of new ovens in the east and north porticos (Scerrato 1979: 719) (Figure 10.8). The presence of these features, and ash and fragments of crushed bone within the ovens of the western portico, led the excavator to conclude that QN3 was "the holy building of Dahan-e Ghulaman" (Scerrato 1979: 725).

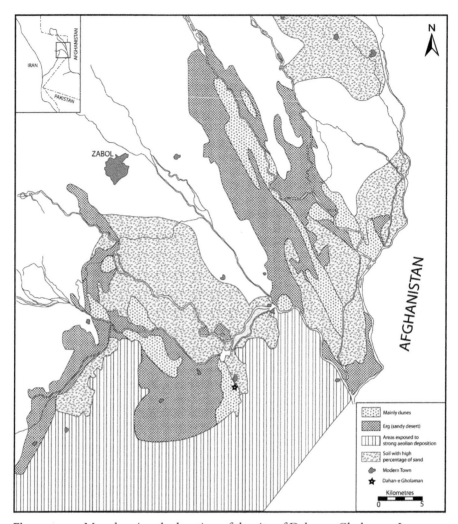

Figure 10.4. Map showing the location of the site of Dahan-e Gholaman, Iran.

Across the open space to the west of QN3 were a further two monumental buildings, labelled QN1 and QN2 respectively. QN1 was the largest of these public buildings and measured 70 by 53 metres. It comprised a large central courtyard surrounded by a portico on all four sides and has been identified as a building for civil ceremony. QN2 was located to the south of QN1 and was slightly smaller, measuring 51 by 41 metres, and has been identified as an administrative office and treasury. Again, it possessed a central courtyard with a portico, but it also had a double portico on the north side. This northern area yielded two seals, a large number of tin ingots weighing 4 Persian *minas* (a sixtieth of a talent) each, and ceramic vessels with Neo-Babylonian sealings.

The majority of the city's population lived in the residential area, which covered an area of more than 100 hectares. Whilst most exposed structures were small rectangular buildings set around internal courtyards and have been

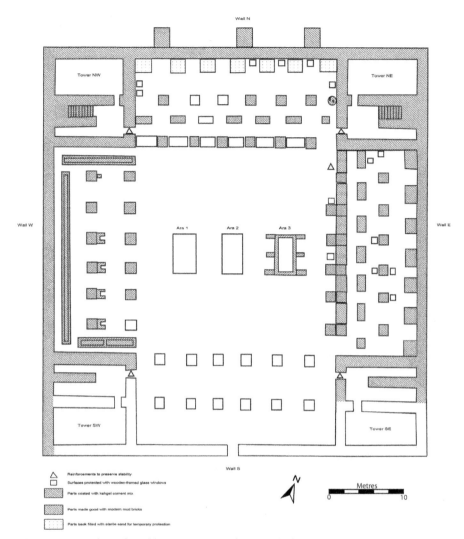

Figure 10.5. Plan of Building QN3 at Dahan-e Gholaman, Iran.

interpreted as residential in nature, there were a number of larger structures as well. Some of these residential buildings were also provided with stepped fire altars, as in the main central chamber of House QN6. The excavator identi-fied this distinct three-stepped altar format as dedications to the three most powerful Achaemenid deities, Ahura Mazda, Anahita and Mithras (Scerrato 1979: 732). This combination of imposed city plan, monumental architecture and major religious installations led the excavator to assume that the settle-ment represented the capital of the newly established Achaemenid province of *Zranka* (Sistan). Moreover, the construction of the temple and city was inter-preted as "an out-and-out occupation of the territory by means of a 'tolerant' taking over of the local religious traditions of oriental Mazdaism" (Scerrato 1979: 732). This is not to suggest that the settlement was entirely an 'imperial'

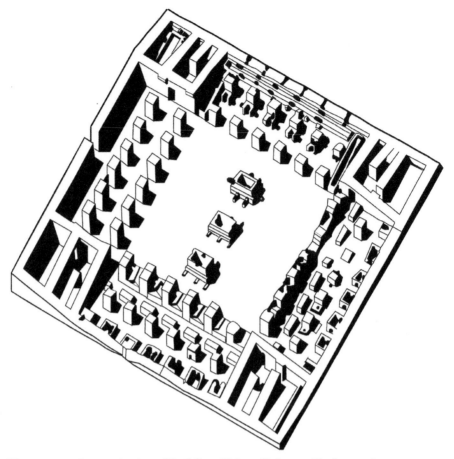

Figure 10.6. Isometric plan of Building QN3 at Dahan-e Gholaman, Iran.

Figure 10.7. Altar oven in Building QN3 at Dahan-e Gholaman, Iran (courtesy Armineh Marghussian).

Figure 10.8. Portico of QN3 at Dahan-e Gholaman, Iran (courtesy Armineh Marghussian).

imposition in nature, and it was clear that there were many local traditions which continued. For example, most of the main entrances, including those of NQ3 and NQ1, were situated on the southern faces of the buildings, and it has been suggested that this represented a local adaptation to the region's climate and its famous *bad-i sad-o-bist rooze* or wind of 120 days. The site was notably unfortified and there was no evidence of a citadel, such as that at the nearby Achaemenid centre at Kandahar (discussed later). Scerrato has interpreted the foundation of the settlement at Dahan-e Gholaman as material evidence of Darius the Great's expansion eastward, and it has been further suggested that the city was established in the late sixth and into the fourth century BCE in two main phases with a period of inactivity between (Genito 2010: 83).

As discussed in Chapter 9, the first settlement at old Kandahar, the Shahr-i Kuhna, was established in the first millennium BCE and was fortified by a moat and clay rampart (Figure 10.9). However, these early defences were levelled during Period II and acted as the foundation for the construction of a major casement wall made of a mixture of gravel and clay with a mud plaster finish on the outer face (Figure 10.10). With a thickness of 9.3 metres at its base, the wall comprised a series of rectangular inner chambers defined by the 2.3 metre thick front wall and 1.6 metre thick back wall (Whitehouse 1978: 12). The outer walls were battered and the walls stood at least 5.6 metres above the level of the floors of the chambers within. Immediately beside the wall's interior face, the excavators identified the presence of an intervallum road which allowed access to the walls. Whilst Whitehouse recorded the

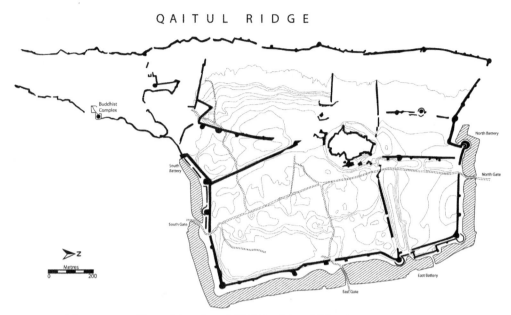

Figure 10.9. Plan of the city of Old Kandahar, Afghanistan.

presence of a degree of continuity with the ceramics from Period I, and thus
with Period VI of Mundigak, he also noted the appearance of carinated bowls
(Tulip Bowls) and ring-feet and suggested that they "may imply that Period II
was built under Achaemenian influence towards the end of the sixth century
BCE" (Whitehouse 1978: 33).

McNicoll's excavations within the walls of the settlement at old Kandahar
identified clearer evidence of Achaemenid occupation, as indicated by the
presence of characteristic ceramics, as well as the presence of a major structure
of small chambers with characteristic false arched doors at Site H (McNicoll
1978: 43). Later excavations at the Citadel mound in the centre of the city
provided evidence that filled pise casements covering an area of 200 metres
square had provided the foundation for a 30 metre high artificial platform
which formed "the administrative core of the ancient city" (Helms 1982: 11).
Attributed to the Achaemenid period, this hypothesis was confirmed by the
recovery of a clay tablet with an Elamite text from within the Citadel. This led
the excavator to state that the city of Kandahar "was undoubtedly one of the
greatest in the satrapy of Harahuvati and, until contrary evidence is discovered,
the best known candidate for a capital city" (Helms 1982: 18).

Whitehouse's excavations across the southern fortification revealed that the
Achaemenid casement wall of Period II was then partially levelled in Period
III and its chambers filled with gravel to provide a solid 8.5 metre high foundation. This foundation was modelled to provide a 10 metre wide external
glacis and was again provided with an access road on the interior and a new
casement wall constructed above. The excavator was struck that the new wall

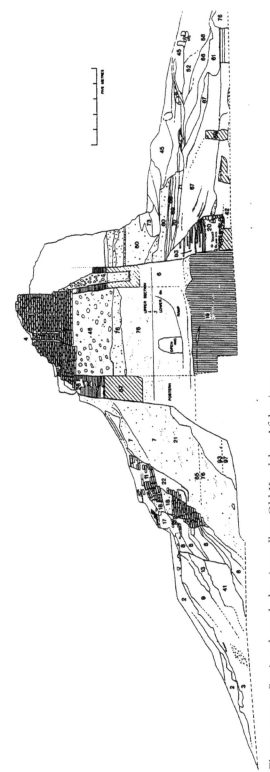

Figure 10.10. Section through the city walls at Old Kandahar, Afghanistan.

"reproduced the earlier scheme in every major respect", although it was constructed in mud brick rather than the earlier gravel and *pakhsa* (clay and finely
chopped straw) mix (Whitehouse 1978: 14). The height of the wall itself was
difficult to estimate as subsequent remodelling of the fortifications had levelled
it to a height of only 2.3 metres. On the basis of residual sherds of black gloss
wares in the layer directly above, Whitehouse concluded that "the casement of
Period III may be 'Greek'" (1978: 33). McNicoll's 1974 excavations within the
settlement found "[n]o evidence of the Alexander period" (1978: 44) but did
recover evidence of what he termed Mauryan/Greek material, which will be
discussed further in Chapter 11. Later seasons of excavations provided more
evidence of this phase and a Seleucid occupation, including the discovery of
a Late Hellenistic alabaster statue-base with a metrical dedication from 'the
son of Aristonax'. Dating to circa 275 BCE, the latter's discovery suggested the
presence of a sanctuary with Olympian cults serving a population of Greeks
in the first half of the third century BCE (Fraser 1979: 12). Indeed, Helms
suggested that the city underwent an abrupt cultural change at the end of the
fourth century BCE, accompanied by the influx of a distinct Greek population
(1982: 18). However, Helms was equally keen to note that "Old Kandahar was
still essentially an oriental city and not a new foundation ordered by Alexander
the Great in 330/329 BC or shortly after, as Ai Khanoum on the Oxus may
well have been" (1982: 18). The rebuilding of the city's fortifications along earlier established lines, using the same military architecture of the Achaemenid
period reinforced this character of mixed influences and styles.

THE OXUS

The founders of the city of Ai Khanoum selected a strongly defensive position in the north of modern Afghanistan at the confluence of the Oxus and
the Kockcha Rivers, one of the Oxus's tributaries. Established on virgin soil,
the plan of the new city was triangular, measured 1.8 by 1.5 kilometres, and
was watered by a canal (Bernard 1994: 109). It was divided roughly into two
sections by an axial road running north-east to south-west through the site,
and was surrounded by a seven metre thick wall of unbaked mud bricks. The
eastern side of the road was largely dominated by a 60 metre high hillside,
with buildings and a series of fortified enclosures constructed on this natural
acropolis. On flatter ground beside the road, structures within the western
half of the city included a theatre and an arsenal. This theatre was one of the
largest known in Hellenistic Asia and, with a radius of 42 metres, was thought
to have had capacity for an audience of at least 5,000 people. The arsenal
measured 140 by 110 metres and comprised a courtyard or parade-ground
lined with storerooms. The most important sanctuary of the settlement was
located in the middle of the settlement on the eastern side of the road. This
sanctuary measured 20 by 20 metres and stood above a three-stepped base,

although its resident deity or deities remain unidentified. Set back behind this building were a series of large enclosures, identified respectively as a palace and gymnasium (complete with sundial), as well as some smaller structures. These structures included a mausoleum for the founder, Kineas, which was designed in the shape of a small Greek temple. A formal cemetery was established in the north-east beyond the walls of the city for the rest of the population.

The excavator, Paul Bernard, noted that the settlement had a royal character as illustrated by the fact that the palace complex took up an area of 350 by 250 metres of prime land in the centre of the city. The palace was approached from the north through a large courtyard measuring 137 by 108 metres, whose four porticos were formed by stone columns capped with Corinthian capitals (Bernard 1994: 110). Some of the stone used for the columns was sourced up to 50 kilometres away, indicating the nature of the influence of the city's inhabitants over their hinterland. South of this courtyard were further courtyards, reception halls, kitchens, and private rooms, some of which were decorated with mosaics, but to the west of the main courtyard was a further complex measuring 60 by 40 metres and identified as the Treasury. Comprising a courtyard surrounding storage chambers, its function was ascribed through the discovery of worked and unworked semi-precious stone, coins and inscribed vessels.

Although it is unclear whether Ai Khanoum was founded by Alexander himself, 40 percent of all the coins recovered from the site were rather later having been struck within the reigns of Seleucus I (r. 311–281 BCE), Antiochus I (r. 281–261 BCE) and Antiochus II (r. 261–246 BCE), suggesting an importance under Seleucid rule (Dani and Bernard 1994: 95). Whilst the presence of Greek colonists is confirmed by graffito and inscriptions at the site, it is also interesting to note the distinct presence of Bactrians with Iranian names, some of whom were treasury officials, indicating that despite the Hellenistic appearance of the city, there was "a certain symbiosis with the local population" (Bernard 1994: 105). Indeed, this symbiosis was stressed further by the presence of a stele replicating the maxims set up at the oracle of Delphi in Greece as well as the discovery of a potsherd, or ostracon, written in Aramaic, the old imperial Achaemenid language. Further diversity was illustrated by the use of flat earth roofs throughout the city as well as the plan of the palace which drew its "inspiration largely from the Neo-Babylonian and Achaemenid models" (Bernard 1994: 110), whilst the form of individual residential houses was modelled on traditional Greek plans with a courtyard at the front of the property and rooms arranged around a living room set behind. Despite the presence of maxims direct from Delphi, and Doric, Ionic and Corinthian capitals within the palace courtyards, the excavator noted that "the architecture of the temples discovered at Ay Khanum owed nothing to Greek tradition" (Bernard 1994: 115). This included the main city sanctuary, the "Temple a redans", which measured 20 metres square but comprised an oblong vestibule which led into a central cella flanked by two sacristies. It has been generally agreed that this plan had been derived from Mesopotamian prototypes, although it probably housed a Hellenic cult image (MacDowall and Taddei 1978: 225). Similarly, a vaulted mud-brick mausoleum has been identified as sharing similar regional prototypes and Bernard has suggested that one of the stepped altars on the Hellenistic city's acropolis "recalls directly Iranian religious sites" rather than Greek or Hellenistic ones (Bernard 1994: 115).

THE BANNU BASIN

In Chapter 9, we noted the establishment of a number of small iron-using settlements in the Bannu Basin, distinguished by their use of Bannu Black and Red Ware and dating to the first half of the first millennium BCE (Khan et al. 2000: 113). One of these sites, Akra Dheri, also had evidence of substantial later occupation and comprised two mounds (divided by a *nullah* or seasonal stream) covering an area of 30 hectares and reaching a maximum height of 35 metres. Excavations on the northern, or Lohra Mound indicated that its inhabitants had access to a ceramic assemblage, including Tulip Bowls, which caused the excavators to suggest firm Persian linkages and a date of between 600 and 300 BCE. On the basis of this evidence, they also suggested that this "provides some archaeological confirmation for the argument, hitherto based on epigraphy and historical data, that Akra might be the capital of the Achaemenid satrapy of Thatagush" (Magee and Petrie 2010: 508). It should be noted, however, that there was no evidence of an associated Achaemenid building programme of the kind observed at Kandahar and Dahan-e Gholaman, and no evidence of Achaemenid coinage or cuneiform tablets. Acknowledging this problematic lack of evidence, and faced with strong continuities in settlement organisation and subsistence practices from the preceding prehistoric period, the excavators have suggested that "the Achaemenid policy in Bannu appears to have been of acquiescence to local systems rather than alteration" (ibid.: 518). If this was the case, certainly the absence of later Hellenistic occupation at the site would suggest that Alexander and his successors pursued a very similar policy of acquiescence.

THE NORTHERN VALLEYS

The inhabitants of the northern valleys continued to utilise a mortuary practice of burial in stone cists until the middle of the first millennium BCE, albeit with a number of small changes in the relevant period IIB (Vinogradova 2001: 19). Accompanied by the continued adoption of 'Gandharan Grave Culture' cemeteries within the Vale of Peshawar, it is highly likely that the burials at Zarif Karuna belonged to this period as did the settlements of Aligrama and Bir-kot-ghwandai (both in the Swat Valley). As early as the 1920s, Aurel

Figure 10.11. The town wall at Bir-kot-ghwandai, Pakistan.

Stein had identified the imposing site of Birkot in the middle Swat Valley as Bazira, one of the Persian cities besieged by Alexander the Great (Stein 1929). Although there remains considerable debate about the accuracy of Stein's claims, the site location is certainly impressive, with a crescent-shaped outcrop rising to a height of 943 metres over the settlement, which covered 10 hectares of the south-facing lower slopes (Callieri 2007: 140). The recent Italian and Pakistani archaeological mission at Bir-kot-ghwandai was focused on understanding the development of the occupation sequence at the site as well as generating evidence for its Achaemenid and subsequent Greek occupation. In addition to providing a deep settlement sequence, the excavations also exposed the presence of a major city wall enclosing the lower slopes of the town. This wall measured 2.7 metres thick and was strengthened by the presence of rectangular or pentagonal bastions placed every 29 metres, with a moat beyond. The morphology of this defensive complex was recognised as having clear analogies to those of the "Hellenized East" by the excavation director (Callieri 2007: 141) (Figure 10.11). According to Callieri, the presence of this wall alongside sherds with Graeco-Macedonian names indicated the "Hellenistic' origin of this town at the beginning of the historical period" and, more specifically, a date of the second century BCE and a link to the dynasties of Indo-Greeks who spread their hegemony south over the Hindu Kush from Afghanistan (ibid.: 142). Regardless of its relatively late date, as Callieri noted, "a fortification wall is a major building in the history of a town, implying a large economic effort or a strong political will" (Callieri 1992: 343). However, distinctive Achaemenid and Alexandrian levels continue to prove elusive at

Figure 10.12. The settlement of Aligrama, Pakistan.

the site, and one scholar has commented that the archaeological evidence for Bir-kot-ghwandai's historic identity "is not yet sufficient to prove categorically that the archaeological site … actually corresponds to the Bazira mentioned by Alexander's historians" (Olivieri 1996: 50).

During Swat Period VI (660 to c. 300 BCE), the inhabitants of Aligrama continued to expand their settlement and it reached a maximum size of 10 hectares along the base of the north-facing ridge (Tusa 1979: 684) (Figure 10.12). Despite this expansion, the excavators noted a clear continuity in material culture and architecture and a clear lack of differentiation between rooms and houses across the site. This occupation came to an abrupt end between the fourth and third centuries BCE. As described by Tusa, the excavator of the site, "the township of Aligrama came upon a comparatively tragic time during the expedition of Alexander the Great", and he also recorded that he had noted the "traces of violent destruction by fire and violent death of several individuals buried hastily near the ruined dwellings" (Tusa 1979: 688).

Finally, reference should be made to the east-west group of buildings excavated by A. H. Dani at Balambat in the Dir Valley above the confluence of the Panjkora and Swat rivers. Cardinally oriented, Dani noted that the end of the previous phase was abrupt and that the new diaper stone building ignored the alignment of the older structures and cut their foundations down through them. Dated to between the sixth and fourth centuries BCE, the group was at least 40 metres long and comprised at least seven small rectangular and square chambers, measuring up to 7.3 metres square, and forming the northern edge of an opening into a set of larger rooms to the south (Figure 10.13).

Figure 10.13. The 'Achaemenid' buildings at Balambat, Pakistan.

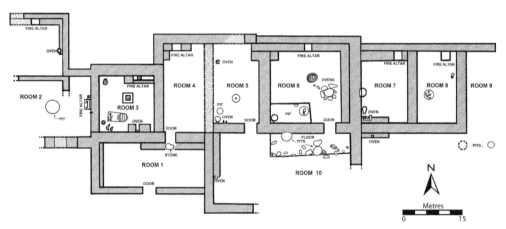

Figure 10.14. Plan of the 'Achaemenid' buildings at Balambat, Pakistan.

Each chamber had an oven on bench installation on its northern wall and Room 2 had a very distinct mud plastered altarpiece (Figure 10.14). Dani noted that their "obvious comparison is with the 'altar-ovens' found at Dahan-i Ghulaman" and that "when we remember that the whole complex belongs to the Achaemenid period, the presence of such fire altars is all the more justified" (Dani 1967: 245). In the absence of radiocarbon dates from the site, the dating has remained uncertain, but there were clear links with the lower levels of Charsadda through the presence of Rippled Rim and Red Burnished Ware and it is possible to recognise an Indic ceramic influence in layer 2 (Dani 1967: Figure 53). The settlement was apparently destroyed by fire, based on the discovery of charred roof timbers and ash on the floors, after which the site was abandoned. Dani commented that "the firing was deliberate, caused by the destructive hand of some invaders", although he also noted that "[e]ven if we recall the march of Alexander the Great through this part and his fight against the Gourais, generally located in this neighbourhood, the archaeological material has not produced any evidence to identify the invader" (Dani 1967: 244).

THE VALE OF PESHAWAR

As discussed in Chapter 9, Mortimer Wheeler had assumed that the Bala Hisar of Charsadda had been established as a city by the Achaemenids in the sixth century BCE. Indeed, he suggested that iron, currency and script "were the symbols of that new security which advancing imperial rule imposed along the highways, and of a new burgeoning of inter-regional trade. Local capitals which were also caravan-cities sprang up beside the main routes" (Wheeler 1963: 172). Despite these assumptions and statements, it is interesting that Wheeler only recovered iron from the basal levels of Charsadda with no alternative evidence of Persian hegemony, save the presence of a clay sealing whose "style is that of the Achaemenid tradition" in a much later structure dating to the third or second century BCE (Wheeler 1962: 121). Wheeler's second major chronological foundation was based on the fact that he had deemed that Charsadda was the Persian city of Peukelaotis, which had been besieged by Hephaestion and a large portion of Alexander the Great's army for thirty days in 327 BCE (Wheeler 1962: 34; Badian 1987: 118). Discovering a defensive ditch and rampart enclosing the site, he linked the fortification complex to that historical event, also citing the fact that the ditch fill suggested a single episode, which fitted neatly with historical reports of the slighting of the defences. Again, little actual evidence of Macedonian or Greek material has been recovered from the site apart from the stray find of a small terracotta head of Alexander the Great and an alabaster statuette of Heracles, both of which were referred to as being from the "Greek world" but it is quite possible that both belonged to the later Indo-Greek occupation at the site. Despite the paucity of evidence, many scholars have followed Wheeler's original identification with statements such as: "Charsada was probably the capital of the satrapy of Gandhara, added to the empire either by Cyrus himself or in the first years of Darius I" (MacDowall and Taddei 1978: 217), or that there "seems little doubt that the ancient city of Pushkalavati was one of the primary satrapal capitals of Gandhara" (Magee and Petrie 2010: 514). The extension of the identification of Charsadda as Peukelaotis, the satrapal capital, and also the site of a later Macedonian garrison was made by Fraser, further intensifying this historical link (Fraser 1996: 173).

As also noted in Chapter 9, the more recent excavations at Charsadda have provided very clear evidence of the adoption of a strongly regional ceramic assemblage from the earliest occupation of the site. Dating the earliest occupation and ditch to the end of the second millennium BCE has provided a very clear linkage between the site and the settlement of the Taxila Valley and the northern valleys, particularly through their shared adoption of Red Burnished Ware and Rippled Rim Ware. This regional pattern was joined by what Vogelsang has called a distinctly 'Indic' assemblage in the first millennium BCE and then by a third influence, a Western or 'Agaeic' assemblage (Vogelsang 1992: 250). One of the most characteristic forms of the latter was the Tulip Bowl, which was held by Vogelsang to have distinctive Achaemenid links (1988: 104).

In the recent excavations at the Bala Hisar of Charsadda, only eight of these forms were recovered, most redeposited, but one was from levels dating to the middle of the first millennium BCE (Coningham et al. 2007b: 106). Providing somewhat limited evidence for the presence of an Achaemenid satrapal capital or a Greek garrison, the archaeological sequence at the site recorded the cutting of a 4.25 metre wide and two metre deep v-shaped ditch along the eastern side of the settlement in the middle of the first millennium BCE. Set four metres back into the settlement from the early Iron Age circumvallation, this new ditch was backed by the presence of a mud-brick wall which was at least 1.6 metres wide. Whilst the identification of Charsadda as the ancient city of Peukelaotis, or the City of Lotuses, is not questioned on account of the presence of so many sherds with lotus impressions and Marshall's discovery of a nearby inscription (Marshall 1904: 176), whether Achaemenid or Macedonian influence over this differentiated and agglomerated community was ever as strong as claimed by Wheeler remains highly questionable.

THE TAXILA VALLEY

As we have already discussed, the early Iron Age occupation of the Taxila Valley was in parallel with that of Charsadda to the north-west and comprised a large spread of occupation on the Hathial Mound associated with Red Burnished Ware (Figure 10.15). These parallels also continued as the site has been the subject of frequent historic identifications as the satrapal capital of Gandhara as well as the capital of King Taxiles, who surrendered to Alexander the Great. Although initially proposed by Marshall in 1951, others have continued to reinforce this identification with Wheeler stating that Alexander visited the Bhir Mound (1968: 104) and MacDowall and Taddei recording that "[t]he Achaemenian town of Taxila may be identified with the earliest levels of the Bhir Mound excavations" (MacDowall and Taddei 1978: 218). It should be noted that not all scholars accept this linkage, for example, Magee and Petrie have suggested that "One possibility is that … the area east of the

Figure 10.15. The Hathial Mound in the Taxila Valley, Pakistan.

Indus developed into a separate entity that was free of Achaemenid control"
(2010: 515). Whilst commenting that there was not much evidence at Taxila
to show the extent to which "Persian domination made a durable impression
upon the conquered Indian peoples" (1951: 13), John Marshall did note the
presence of Aramaic, an official Achaemenid language as well as early silver
coinage based on a Persian standard and a number of scaraboid and eye beads
(1960: 57). Unlike Charsadda, which had a continuous development on the
same settlement site, the urban population of the Taxila Valley appears to have
shifted from the Hathial ridge down to the Bhir Mound by the side of the
rivulet known as Tamra Nala. The new site was represented by a six metre
high mound measuring 1.1 kilometres north to south by 670 metres east
to west and was excavated by Marshall between 1913 and 1934 and then by
Wheeler and Sharif. Marshall opened up an area of 1.2 hectares within the
habitation mound but only small areas of the lowest levels, Strata IV and III,
were exposed. The lowest of these, IV, he identified as being Achaemenid, and
the upper level he identified as Greek (1960: 57). As noted earlier, Marshall
recovered scaraboid and eye beads from the former and "Hellenistic black and
imbossed wares" and a hoard of coins of Alexander the Great and his brother
Philip Aridaeus (r. 323–317 BCE), as well as worn Achaemenid silver *sigloi*
(ibid.: 57–58).

Wheeler also opened further trenches in the Bhir Mound between 1944 and
1945, but these were restricted to levels close to the surface. Then Mohammad
Sharif opened a deep trench in 1967 in order to "acquire more knowledge
about the early phases of the history of the region" (1969: 11). Sharif's 5.6
metre deep sequence was divided into four periods, and he noted the presence

of iron in the lowest, Period I, and Northern Black Polished Ware and angular structures formed by cobble and rubble limestone walls, and circular-shaped pillar bases of the same material. It is possible that the pillar bases, rather than standing above the ground were, in fact, the fill of pillar pits as recently identified at Charsadda (Coningham and Ali 2007b: 68). Similar structures were found in the succeeding level, and it is interesting to note the presence of Vogelsang's category of 'Indic' ceramics forms, including carinated bowls and flat tray or thali forms from the very lowest levels (Sharif 1969: Figure 11). It is also important that Vogelsang's 'Agaeic' or western assemblage was not present within the sequence until Period III (Sharif 1969: Figure 19.1). This indicates that there was very little evidence of Achaemenid or Macedonian influence at the Bhir Mound, but between Hathial and the Bhir Mound there was a clear parallel with the sequence of Charsadda; a regional assemblage with links to the northern valleys, followed by an 'Indic' assemblage and, finally, a western or 'Agaeic' assemblage. Radiocarbon dates from the basal levels of the Bhir Mound would appear to support such a chronology with a cluster of four radiocarbon dates between 402 and 394 BCE (Allchin 1995a: 131). Again, evidence for an imperial presence at Taxila is not as compelling as at Kandahar and Dahan-e Gholaman, and the reported hoards of Achaemenid-style coinage or jewellery may have represented stocks or caches of traded goods, and we might even question the Achaemenid provenance of such seals. Although these seals belonged to a 'Graeco-Persian' style, they often featured South Asian iconography and motifs and may have been local products made by local craftspeople for local markets (Callieri 1996).

THE ARABIAN SEA

In parallel with the lack of clear evidence for an Achaemenid presence in the north-west of modern Pakistan, Daniel Potts has noted that "[n]either the archaeological nor the historical sources on Bahrain, eastern Arabia, or Dilmun in the Kassite to Achaemenid periods are abundant" (1990: 352). In contrast, there have been numerous finds of Persian-style metalwork and other material within the settlements and cemeteries of the Oman Peninsula in the latter half of the first millennium BCE (ibid.: 390). A number of scholars have also suggested that *aflaj* (underground irrigation channels) technology was introduced from the Persian heartland during this time (Wilkinson 1977), but this is by no means certain. Direct rule from the Persian Empire has been postulated by Potts on the basis of a number of references to the country of Qade in both royal archives as well as on Darius I's inscription at Naqs-i Rustam, and he has suggested that it was ruled during this period by Persian Satraps (Potts 1990: 395). This presence is, however, qualified, and he also noted that "the picture of an isolated Persian garrison stationed at Sohar may not be far from the truth, for as with the Sasanians and even the Portuguese, Achaemenid 'rule'

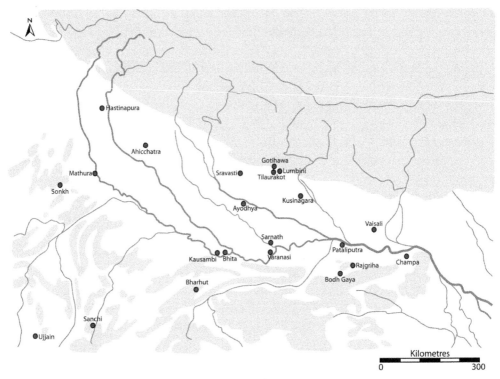

Figure 10.16. Map of key sites within the Ganga Basin.

in Maka may not have exceeded a coastal military presence with little or no claim to the nearly always independent and hostile interior" (ibid.: 400).

THE GANGA BASIN AND CENTRAL INDIA

As noted in the introduction, the urban-focused settlement development associated with the Early Historic Tradition also offers a series of opportunities to compare textual traditions with archaeological evidence, and this is certainly the case for the Ganga Basin and Central India as this region hosted a large number of the sixteen *Mahajanapadas* (Figure 10.16). At a macro level, the settlement survey analysis by Erdosy has provided evidence for increasing complexity within this period and clearer site differentiation by size and function. For example, although still located close to river courses, Erdosy identified a growing size differentiation between Kausambi and its surrounding sites during the preceding period which was associated with PGW. This differentiation increased, and he recorded the presence of four distinct tiers of settlement in the Era of Integration between 600 and 350 BCE (Erdosy 1988: 55). These included Kausambi, which increased in size to 50 hectares, two sites between 10 and 49.9 hectares, two between 6 and 9.99 hectares and seventeen less than 5.99 hectares. The smallest category of sites was represented by simple ceramic scatters and has been interpreted as agricultural sites, as they had no evidence of craft activities. Craft activities were represented in the next category, sites between 6 and 9.99 hectares, as slag was recovered from a number of those settlements surveyed. Erdosy has termed the next category, between 10 and 49.9 hectares, towns, and the site of Kara has provided evidence of metal, semi-precious stone and shell working and coins.

However, dominating the landscape was the pre-eminent population resident at Kausambi, who were differentiated within a total area of 200 hectares by a rampart some 6.44 kilometres long. According to Erdosy, these ramparts were erected in the fifth century BCE and were associated with uninscribed cast copper coins (Erdosy 1988: 61). Erdosy has also argued that these ramparts presented a strong illustration of the ability of the ancient *Mahajanapada* of Vatsa to mobilise the necessary workforce for such a massive undertaking. Its earliest phase was represented by a seven metre high clay rampart, Rampart 1, but there has been much debate as to its dating and phasing (Erdosy 1987: 5). It was later topped by mud blocks and then faced with a skin of fired brick (Revetment 1 1.3) (Sharma 1960: Figure 3). Although little is known about the internal layout of the city, G. R. Sharma exposed a large walled complex covering an area of 315 by 150 metres in the south-west corner of the ancient capital on the banks of the Yamuna (IAR 1960–1961: 33). Constructed in three phases, the earliest comprised rough blocks of stone, joined with lime mortar and coated with mud mortar set on a 2.5 metre high platform of mud and mud brick. The plan remains unique, although few other structures of this period have survived, and the excavator has described how its six metre wide northern wall ran for 130 metres and terminated in circular towers at either end, from where the eastern and western walls joined. A second phase saw the introduction of dressed stone blocks and has been associated with the recovery of NBPW from within its levels. The excavator identified the structure as a palace, although the associated artefacts have never been published.

Similar evidence for the construction of major fortified urban forms has also been identified at a number of sites interpreted as capitals of the *Mahajanapadas*, such as Rajghat, Rajgir and Ujjain. Rajghat, the capital of Kasi, was located on the Ganga close to the holy city of Varanasi and is represented by a 15 metre high mound covering an area of one kilometre square at the confluence of the Ganga and Varuna rivers (Narain and Roy 1977: 2). It shared, like many sites in the middle Ganga, a sequence which started with Black and Red Ware in Period IA and was then represented by NBPW in Period IB, which has been dated to the fifth century BCE. This transition was accompanied by the construction of a major clay embankment on the northern side of the settlement measuring almost 20 metres wide and surviving to a height of 5 metres. The excavators were at pains to stress that the embankment was to prevent erosion and flooding rather than for defence (Narain and Roy 1977: 7), but little evidence for any internal structures were recovered. To the east, the site of Rajgir, which was the old capital of Magadha until the fourth century

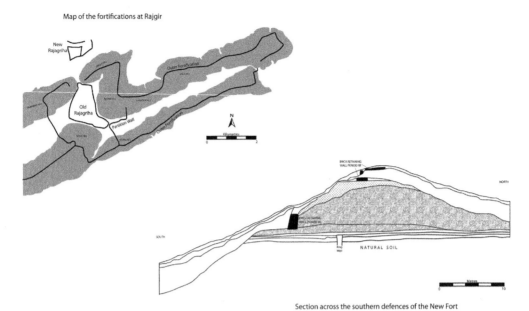

Figure 10.17. Plan of the city of Rajgir and section through the rampart of New Rajgir, India.

BCE, presented evidence of huge communal investment in the creation of a curtain wall of roughly shaped stone blocks which followed a circuit of 40 kilometres (Figure 10.17). It fortified an area of some 200 hectares of valley, slopes and caves within its surrounding rocky ridges (Figure 10.18). Measuring just more than 5 metres wide, and surviving to heights of 3.7 metres, the wall was strengthened in places with rectangular bastions (Ghosh 1989: 363) (Figure 10.19). An inner stone wall, 8 kilometres in circuit, further differentiated the settlement area in the interior, which had access to water from springs located within this inner wall (Marshall 1960: 84). Believed to have been fortified in the middle of the first millennium BC, the site was also famous for its associations with the Gautama *Buddha* and Mahavira, one of the *Tirthankara* of the Jains (Mitra 1971: 72). Whilst Rajgir's irregular profile was directly dictated by its circuit of rocky ridges, it is notable that the vast majority of the Early Historic cities on alluvial plains were also irregular in layout.

The settlement at Narhan on the banks of the Ghaghara in the modern state of Uttar Pradesh continued to be occupied, and during Period III, the structures of mud brick were accompanied by greater numbers of cord impressed vessels (Singh: 1994: 22). Whilst recognising their visual link to the Ganga Neolithic ceramic tradition, Singh observed that this genre "belongs to an altogether different tradition and ... it may be pointed out that some sherds of this type were present at other sites also in the early historic strata but they did not receive due attention" (ibid.: 107). Singh attributed a date of between 600 and 200 BCE for Period III (ibid.: 34). Largely associated with the central

Figure 10.18. The fortified valley of Rajgir, India.

Figure 10.19. Gateway through Rajgir's walls, India.

Ganga region, this late version of Cord Impressed Ware has also been recovered from Kausambi (Sharma 1960: pl. 53) as well as from a cluster of sites associated with the tradition of the Gautama *Buddha* within the Nepal Terai. These sites include Kodan, the settlement site of Tilaurakot (Mitra 1972: Pl. XXIV), the *stupa* complexes of Ramagrama (Shrestha 2005: Pl. 100) and Gotihawa (Verardi 2007: 246) and the birthplace of the *Buddha* himself, Lumbini, from within both the ancient Maya Devi shrine and the Village Mound (Coningham et al. 2013). The regional distribution of this distinctive ware demonstrates that whilst reintegration may have been drawing a number of the major urban sites together, a number of important regional traditions had successfully survived. Moreover, in some areas, these traditions continued to link important cult sites together as within the Nepal Terai, perhaps indicating the presence of heterarchy at this stage. The later sequences of these sites included the adoption of NBPW, indicative that the inhabitants of this region were steadily being integrated more closely into the trading and pilgrimage hegemonies of the major *Mahajanapadas*. It is also clear that even after sharing such a broader trait, there were still distinct differences in settlement types within the Terai with tell-like habitation sites at Tilaurakot, the Lumbini Village Mound and Panditpur, shrines at Lumbini and more dispersed settlement layouts close to the Himalayan foothills like at Khapte Danda in eastern Nepal.

Further eastwards, Mahasthangarh represents one of the most important archaeological sites in Bangladesh, being the prime urbanised population centre for much of the region from the third century BC until at least the thirteenth century AD (Alam and Salles 2001). The citadel itself is surrounded by one of the best preserved Early Historic fortification complexes in South Asia as its ramparts, capped by later additions, still rise some 8 metres above a 100 metre wide moat. Enclosing some 130 hectares, it is generally agreed to have functioned as a Mauryan provincial capital in the third century BC. Although there is no evidence of an Asokan pillar inscription in the site's vicinity, the discovery of a third century BC Brahmi inscription on a small slab from the site has suggested to some a variant of the Asokan series (Allchin 1995a: 212). Excavations at the site have provided evidence of NBPW. Found in the lowest levels of the site and dated to between the late fourth and beginning of the third century BC (Alam and Salles 2001: 159), this evidence suggests a slightly later establishment of urban communities in this region. We should, however, also cite the cautions of Sharmi Chakraborty who has noted both the cloaking nature of the delta's silts as well as the possibility that its settlement categories may have been different from those within the middle Ganga region (2008: 133).

Many of the recognised urban-focused traits associated with this wider Era of Integration have also been found to the south at Ujjain, capital of the *Mahajanapada* of Avanti in Central India, whose ramparts are thought to have been erected by the middle of the first millennium BC (Banerjee 1960). With

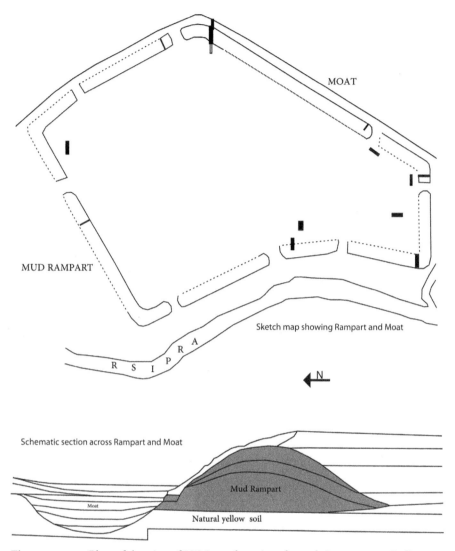

MOAT

MUD RAMPART

Sketch map showing Rampart and Moat

R A
R S I P

N

Schematic section across Rampart and Moat

Mud Rampart

Moat

Natural yellow soil

Figure 10.20. Plan of the city of Ujjain and section through its ramparts, India.

a circumference of five kilometres, the ramparts were 75 metres wide at the base and, as they were built of clay stabilised with a timber framework, they were able to reach an intimidating height of 14 metres. Forming an irregular pentagon of 95 hectares, the western side of the city faced the Sipra River whilst the southern and eastern sides were protected by a ditch, 27 metres wide and 7 metres deep, fed by the Sipra (IAR 1957: 20) (Figure 10.20). Breaches within the ramparts appear to indicate the presence of ancient gateways, with three opening onto the river frontage allowing its inhabitants to directly access a major communication network. Apart from the published account of the presence of a variety of structures built of mud, mud brick, stone rubble and brickbats, there has been little discussion as to the city's plan, although streets were reported as having been laid with rubble and clay and the presence of a reservoir noted (ibid.: 24). Finally, reference should also be made to the settlement of Hastinapura, which although having been described as a capital in the *Mahabharata* was not the capital of a *mahajanapada*. Apparently abandoned due to a flood in Period II, the settlement was reoccupied and expanded dramatically, almost doubling in size during Period III (Lal 1955: 12). Dated to between the sixth century and third century BCE and associated with NBPW, the inhabitants of this new settlement had access to buildings of unbaked and baked bricks, terracotta tube wells and drains of baked brick. In addition to the presence of NBPW and imported beads of agate and carnelian, the excavators recorded copper and silver punch-marked coins and cast copper coins, of which it was noted that "[t]he introduction of coinage must have gone a long way in augmenting the trade and commerce of the Period" (Lal 1955: 16).

PENINSULAR INDIA

This phase of the Iron Age in Peninsular India has been largely associated with Period III of McIntosh's subdivisions of the south Indian megaliths (McIntosh 1985: 469). Dividing this period into two, McIntosh identified continuity between Periods II and IIIA, with the construction of cist burials surrounded by a stone circle but differentiated by the presence of three-legged urns and sarcophagi and a far greater abundance of bronze and gold objects as well as the first evidence of cremation within Maharashtra. However, McIntosh also identified a distinct change in the succeeding Period IIIB, with the steady decline of megalithic burial practices in Maharashtra and northern Andhra Pradesh as the influence of the emergent northern states spread, although megalithic tomb complexity intensified to the south. This complexity involved the creation of slabs, ramps and a greater use of portholes which supported an interpretation of the multiple reuse and accessing of these funerary complexes. The presence of iron weapons with burials appears to have increased alongside the presence of tridents and lamps. With reference to accompanying settlement patterns, McIntosh noted that little evidence for settlements in Period IIIA had been recorded. Although McIntosh attributed this to a growth in pastoralism as a response to increasing aridity (McIntosh 1985: 479), this lack of settlement data was partly a reflection of gaps in archaeological survey methodologies. In contrast, she recorded an "explosive expansion of settlement over hitherto unoccupied areas of Tamilnadu and Kerala" and suggested that this may have been accelerated by the introduction of irrigation agriculture (McIntosh 1985: 478).

Most of the 300 megalithic burials surrounding the site of Brahmagiri identified by Wheeler have been attributed to Period IIIB, and the cemetery has been estimated to have covered an area of some 96 hectares, with six separate areas of megaliths. In 1947 Wheeler excavated ten megaliths: six of

Figure 10.21. Cist burial at Brahmagiri, India (courtesy Peter Johansen).

Figure 10.22. Pit burial at Brahmagiri, India (courtesy Peter Johansen).

the cist circle style, and four of the pit circle style (1948) (Figure 10.21 and Figure 10.22.). Much of Wheeler's chronology for the Brahmagiri megaliths and associated settlement at Isila was based on his ceramic typologies from the sites of Arikamedu and Chandravalli and subsequent analysis by Morrison (2005) has cast doubt on the accuracy of Wheeler's initial claims. Morrison's work, based on radiocarbon estimates of wood gathered by Wheeler from

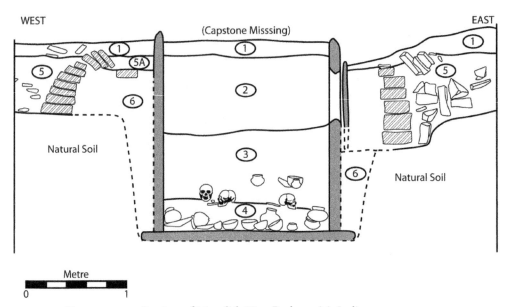

Figure 10.23. Section of Megalith X at Brahmagiri, India.

Megalith 6 and reanalysis of the ceramics in combination with Wheeler's stratigraphic sequence, strongly suggests that the settlement was occupied far later
than Wheeler had claimed, and the earlier activity was far less easily delineated
in chronological terms (Morrison 2005: 257, 261). Despite these concerns as to
the dating of Brahmagiri, it is illustrative to describe the construction details
and grave goods of one of the best preserved megaliths at the site, as it empha-
sises the focus on the ancestors and the dead in direct contrast to the developments in the Ganga Basin where the dead were generally cremated. Megalith
X was a cist-circle within Megalithic Area A of Brahmagiri to the west of the
Isila town site. The monument had been begun with the excavation of a pit
with a diameter of some 2.4 metres cut 1.2 metres into natural soil (Wheeler
1948: 196) (Figure 10.23). A square gneissic granite slab was then laid at the
bottom of the pit and four overlapping granite orthostats, measuring between
2.1 and 1.5 metres long and 1.8 metres high, were erected on edge to form a
square cist. Roughly cardinally oriented in a clockwise swastika plan, the cist
was accessed through a porthole carved through the western orthostat, and it
is assumed that the cist was topped by a capstone, although missing (ibid.: 194)
(Figure 10.24). Beyond the edges of the foundation pit, a circular dry stone
granite wall with a diameter of 3.7 metres was built around the cist to a height
of at least 11 courses and infilled behind. The porthole was accessed on the
western side of the wall through a passageway lined with orthostats and access
itself sealed by a door slab and later by walling up the entrance. The stratigraphy of the cist indicated that a primary deposit of fifty-six individual ceramic
vessels had been made and with at least two further deposits, of which the
second included three skulls and a number of disarticulated bones. As noted by

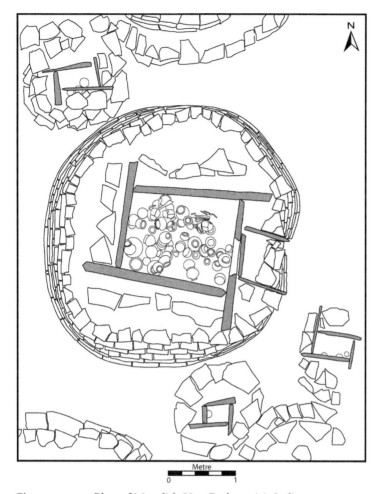

Figure 10.24. Plan of Megalith X at Brahmagiri, India.

Mohanty and Walimbe, it has been calculated that a single cairn circle of 13.5 metres in diameter would have taken a group of between seventy and eighty adults between three and four days to build, and this would only have been possible from a wider population of between 400 and 500 individuals (1993). Although the cist circles at Brahmagiri were smaller than those experimented with by Mohanty and Walimbe, it must be recognised that the concentration of more than 300 examples at Brahmagiri must have represented as many as 1,200 labour days, notwithstanding the preparation of the stone blocks and slabs. This indicates the presence of highly organised communities, perhaps competing with one another through a shared focus on funerary architecture. This of course raises questions about the role of tombs and burials in the living communities and of the continued role of such monuments into the Early Historic Tradition as a method of integration through "some sort of communal spirit … for people who are producing iron, growing crops and herding animals" (Haricharan et al. 2013: 500).

A rather more informative habitation sequence may be taken from the excavations on the Matichi Gadhi mound at Nasik on the upper stretches of the Godavari River, where the excavators identified an incomplete sequence extending from the 'Chalcolithic' to the Maratha Period (Sankalia and Deo 1955: 20). Period IIA at the site has been termed Early Historic by the excavation directors and dated to between the third and fifth centuries BCE, and the presence of Rouletted Ware in Period IIB suggests that the earlier phase concluded by the second century BCE (Coningham and Batt 2007). The inhabitants of the early settlement constructed huts with rammed clay floors and had access to Black and Red Ware identified by the excavators as being "closely analogous to the Megalithic ware" as well as NBPW and ceramic vessels with non-scriptural graffito (Sankalia and Deo 1955: 61). A great deal of organisation and labour resources would have been required to create the many complex megalithic monuments, which reflects distinctive choices and practices in this region. While there were no sites here with major wall and ditch constructions, in contrast to those in the north at this time, there is no doubt that there was a very clear political and ideological organisation at work. In this light, Peninsular India appears to have remained outwith the ongoing process of population agglomeration and urban-focused integration, and there is little evidence further to the south along the coasts of Tamil Nadu or Kerala to suggest otherwise – indeed, some scholars have suggested that megalithic monument construction continued until as late as the fourth century CE despite the close juxtaposition of and interaction with alternative lifeways (Ramachandran 1980: 76).

SRI LANKA

To the south, and in contrast to the investment in megalithic complexity across the Palk Straits, the newly established population at Anuradhapura witnessed substantial growth of the settlement during this period from an area of 18 hectares to 26 hectares in the middle of the first millennium BCE and a further increase to 60 hectares by the beginning of the fourth century BCE and Phase I (Coningham 2006a: 648). This increase in area was accompanied by the introduction and adoption of rectangular buildings with clay tiles replacing circular mud and thatch structures, as well as the construction of a ditch and rampart enclosing an area of 100 hectares (Figure 10.25 and Figure 10.26). Although only partially exposed, the rampart measured more than 2 metres wide, survived to a height of 2.1 metres and was composed of redeposited bedrock, presumably from an accompanying rock-cut ditch (Coningham 1999: 52) (Figure 10.27). The construction of this rampart and ditch has been interpreted as a communal activity and it has been estimated that it represented a volume of just over 50,000 cubic metres and would have taken a population of 575 people a total of 150 days to build. This simple

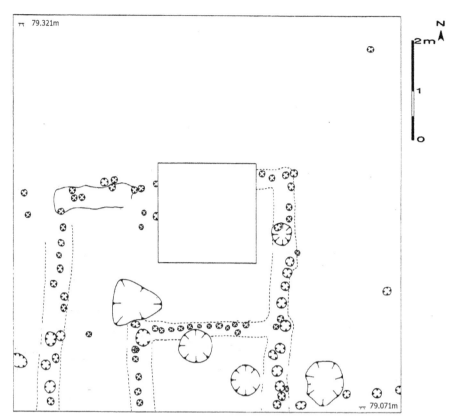

Figure 10.25. Plan of square building within the Citadel of Anuradhapura, Sri Lanka.

Figure 10.26. Square building within the Citadel of Anuradhapura, Sri Lanka.

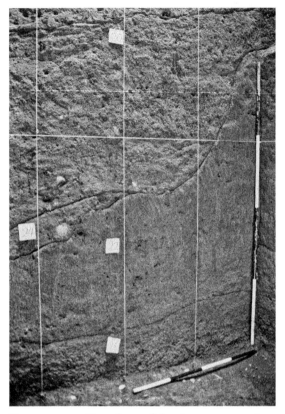

Figure 10.27. First phase of the city rampart at Anuradhapura, Sri Lanka.

rampart and ditch technology was also probably utilised to create irrigation reservoirs as there was an accompanying and notable increase in the depth of wells within the settlement, and this was associated with the presence of fresh water terrapins and rice within the subsistence record of the site's inhabitants (Coningham 2006a: 649; Young et al 2006; Young 2006) (Box 10.1). Despite these co-ordinated communal activities, it is clear from Siran Deraniyagala's sondages at various loci across the settlement, that the settlement's population were engaged in the manufacture of metal, bone and stone objects all across the site rather than concentrating craft production in a particular zone (Deraniyagala 1972, 1986). This distributed pattern is surprising considering the standardised forms of artefacts and the fact that some raw materials, such as carnelian, were imported from hundreds of kilometres away. Other exotic raw materials included lapis lazuli as well as crystalline limestone from the central hills of the island and mangrove timber from the island's coastal lagoons. Further proof of the growing mercantile links of the city's inhabitants come from the early presence of horse within the sequence and Early Brahmi characters inscribed on ceramic vessels, perhaps designating ownership of shipments as they are names in the dative or genitive cases (Coningham et al.

Box 10.1. Ideology and Food

Can we explore such abstract concepts as religion and ideology through analysing material culture, and in particular, something as fundamental to everyday life as food? Some archaeologists argue that we may use material culture to compare orthodoxy (right beliefs) with orthopraxy (right practice) (Edwards 2005; Schopen 1997). After all, we all know there is often a big gap between what we are told to do, what we say we do, and what we actually do when it comes to consumption of any kind, and how this is translated by archaeologists is an area of great interest (O'Sullivan and Young 2012). Food and diet is known to be an important aspect of the creation of religious identity – think about dietary taboos in relation to religious teaching (orthodoxy) for many major religions today such as Judaism, Islam, and Hinduism (Insoll 2004: 71). The introduction of Buddhism to Sri Lanka during the third century BCE and the conversion of the Royal family from Hinduism to Buddhism was certainly portrayed as a major event. Indeed, the *Mahavamsa* records that Buddhism became the official religion with the Royal family sponsoring Buddhist monks and monasteries, alongside the mass conversion of many ordinary people living in the royal capital city, Anuradhapura. This historical event allows us to look at the orthodoxy of diet for each religion at the time, and then consider the animal bone assemblage in terms of the dietary laws associated with both Hinduism and Buddhism.

A total of 3,544 animal bones were recovered during recent excavations in the Citadel of Anuradhapura and identified to species and element (Young et al. 2006, 592). Indian wild pig (*Sus scrofa cristatus*), Ceylon spotted deer (*Axis axis ceylonesis*), cattle (*Bos indicus*) and corrugated clam (*Parreysia corrugata*) stand out as the most numerous of the species recovered and identified, although there was a range of other animals. We can begin to explore the expression of orthopraxy, or the physical manifestation of orthodoxy in archaeological assemblages by considering meat consumption in relation to Hindu dietary rules, and the animal remains from Periods J and K (the two periods prior to the advent of Buddhism). The '*Laws of Manu*' (Buhler 1886) is a key text thought to have been formulated in the middle of the first millennium BCE, which codified the practices of Hindu caste, and covered dietary rules, setting out which animals were permitted and which were forbidden. The '*Laws of Manu*' stated that the following were forbidden (Buhler 1886, 171–172):

- All carnivorous and one-hoofed animals
- All solitary and unknown beast should be avoided

(*continued*)

- All five-toed animals
- Animals which eat fish
- Any man who kills a horse, deer, elephant, fish or snake will be degraded to a mixed caste.

If we compare this list to the animal bones that were excavated, we find that the following forbidden animals have been recovered from Periods J and K: deer, cattle, pig, dog and fowl. Buffalo, porcupine, hare and terrapin were all permitted animals recovered from Periods J and K. Shellfish are not mentioned within the *'Laws of Manu'*, and may have been considered an acceptable source of food. However, given the status of fish, and the fact that shellfish feed on waste materials and organic matter, they are likely to have been considered unfit for human consumption. While Hindu orthopraxy might have dictated clear rules about the types of animals that could be consumed, the animal remains from Anuradhapura indicate that a range of both permitted and forbidden animals were in fact consumed.

The greatest number of animal bones came from Period I in the archaeological sequence at Anuradhapura, which was the period of both urban expansion and the introduction of Buddhism. While Buddhism ostensibly advocates vegetarianism as part of the Five Moral Precepts which forbid killing, in practice meat is consumed. Monks, particularly mendicants, were expected to consume any food placed within their alms bowls and this included meat. While we might thus expect the vegetarian doctrine of Buddhism to result in a marked decrease in animal remains, the expansion of the city and increasing social complexity require a food supply which certainly appears to have involved the extensive exploitation of a range of other animals. Thus the impact of major ideological change may be masked within the changes linked to social, economic and political change in the same period. With regard to ideology and consumption, we would expect that major events such the introduction of Buddhism to the island in the second half of the third BCE would have had a discernible impact on the animal assemblage; or that a clearly articulated and disseminated guide to orthopraxy would have had an impact on behaviour, and thus orthodox beliefs reflected in material culture assemblages. Yet neither of these seems evident in the ASW2 animal remains. The advent of Buddhism had little impact on the animal bones recovered from Period I, and the animal assemblage for Hindu Periods J and K, contained bones from animals expressly forbidden for consumption, as well as from those permitted.

We may suggest that the increase in numbers of animal remains in Period I was linked to expansion of the city, but rather than the expected decrease in range of animals exploited which accompanied increasing social complexity in other parts of South Asia, we see continuation of exploitation of a broad range of animals. It is equally clear that there was no simple link between changes in ideology and changes in the faunal assemblage – in order to learn more about ideology and religion through food and consumption, we would need to be able to look for more subtle markers than simply expecting a change of eating habits in accordance with the religious ideal or the laws set down by those in authority (Young and Coningham 2010).

Figure 10.28. Grey Ware vessel from Anuradhapura engraved with a ship, Sri Lanka.

1996). Note should also be made of the use of vessels of Grey Ware, which appeared to have presaged the technologies later utilised in manufacturing Rouletted Ware (Figure 10.28).

A recent settlement survey within the hinterland of Anuradhapura has identified a total of fifty-six smaller settlements from this period within a radius of 50 kilometres from the walled population (Coningham and Gunawardhana 2013). Dated with reference to a combination of radiocarbon dates and the presence of Black and Red Ware, all of these sites were smaller than Anuradhapura with a maximum size of 25 square metres. It is interesting to note that all the sites, including Anuradhapura, were closely associated with river channels, suggesting that they were located on the fertile and easily irrigated alluvial deposits rather than on the areas which necessitated the construction of large-scale artificial irrigation works to cultivate (Gilliland et al. 2013). Anuradhapura was not the only agglomerated population established in the island during this period, as illustrated by the presence of Kandarodai in the centre of the Jaffna Peninsula, although its populations does not appear to have differentiated itself with a rampart or ditch. Covering some 16 hectares, its first phase was defined by the presence of Black and Red Ware as well as a Grey Ware similar to that from Anuradhapura and dated to between 480 and 130 BCE (Coningham and Allchin 1995: 171). A number of megalithic tombs have also been attributed to this period, considerably more than the single early example at Ibbankatuva. Assigned to a period of between 750 and 400 BCE (Deraniyagala 1992: 278), more than thirty megalithic cemeteries within Sri Lanka have been identified in the northern half of the island with particular clusters in the Yan Oya and Kala Oya watersheds. Many were cist burials with capstones and ranged in coverage from only fifteen individual cists at Vadigawewa to cists covering an area of 10 hectares as at Ibbankatuva (Bandaranayake 1992: 19). Whilst it is possible that some of these cemeteries were associated with settlements which have not yet been identified, it is interesting to note that some known settlement sites of this period are yet to provide hard evidence of associated cemeteries, thus weakening a direct link between the two. Additional evidence of specialist settlement and activity has been identified within the island's central highlands where sites associated with metal working in the vicinity of the modern Samanalawewa dam have been dated to the fourth century BCE (Juleff 1990).

CONCLUSIONS

As discussed in Chapter 1, in 1992 Jim Shaffer recast the concept of the Mature Harappan period as an Era of Integration in order to focus on the key processes at play. Stating that such an Era hosted "pronounced homogeneity in material culture distributed over a large area reflecting an intense level of interaction between social groups", we have applied it to the current period under consideration (Shaffer 1992: 442). Certainly, the re-emergence of major differentiated urban populations, artefactual homogeneity, long-distance trade and settlement hierarchies in this period all point to a second Era of Integration. This integration builds on the regional characteristics and developments of Chapter 8 and demonstrates how these regional characters intensified and expanded in many cases, just as they did in the Regionalisation Era prior to the Integrated Era of the Indus Valley Tradition. The appearance of massive defining walls at many sites, roads and urban water management in the form of ringwells are all examples of large-scale communal activities, requiring strong central coordination and staple surplus. That there remained great variation in the different size and shape of fortified settlements, does raise questions about the extent of sociopolitical hegemony of such centres during this time span, but the textual traditions indicate the influence of imperial models towards the west of the

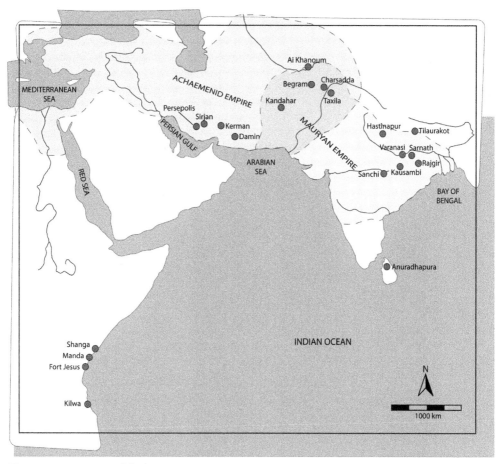

Figure 10.29. Map of the Persian Empire.

region as well as the presence of a mosaic of competing city-states. The associated presence of coins and an increasing abundance of historical material for analysis has also clearly brought with it new challenges. The annexation of the western and north-western regions by the Achaemenid or Persian Empire is a good example of textual and art historical data being analysed in support of archaeological understandings and may be considered in two main phases. The first phase included the campaigns of Cyrus (r. 558–530 BCE) in the provinces or satrapies of Bactria, Sogdiana, Arachosia and Gandhara between 545 and 539 BCE, and the second, under Darius the Great (r. 521–486 BCE), recorded the annexation of north-west up to the Indus River between 519 and 512 BCE and Skylax's expedition to the Indus estuary in 518 BCE (Dandamaev and Lukonin 1989: 90–95). These geopolitical details were drawn from primary sources, such as the Behistun inscription which identified Darius's sovereignty over the eastern satrapies of Bactria, Gandhara, Scythia, Sattagydia, Arachosia and Maka (Dandamaev and Lukonin 1989: 98) (Figure 10.29). This primary textual evidence also included the DPh inscription on the gold and

Figure 10.30. Gold Achaemenid foundation slab in the National Museum, Tehran, Iran

silver tablets in Darius the Great's foundation deposits in his newly constructed Apadana palace at Persepolis. Written in the three official imperial languages of Old Persian, Elamite and Late Babylonian, it recorded that the eastern extent of Darius's rule stretched from "beyond Sugdu (Sodiana), and from there as far as Kush, from Hind (Sind)" (Nimchuk 2010: 222) (Figure 10.30). The carvings on the great staircase at Persepolis also depicted representatives from these satrapies bringing tribute to the great king at his ceremonial capital (Figure 10.31). Gandharans have been recognised in its base reliefs as individuals carrying spears and bringing a zebu cow and the Arachosians by bowls and a camel. The satrapy of India was represented by men leading a donkey and carrying baskets. Scholars have also combined such pictorial evidence with Herodotus's description of imperial taxes, which recorded that the satrapies of Sattagydia, Gandhara and Arachosia had to pay an annual tribute of 170 talents (5,140 kilograms) of silver and the satrapy of India a tribute of 360 talents (10,886 kilograms) of gold dust (Dandamaev and Lukonin 1989: 185–187).

The state archive at Persepolis also recorded the missions of state officials between the capitals and the satrapies and noted that the Indian Abbatema travelled from India to Susa with twenty others in 499 BCE and returned after a month's stay whilst the Indian Karabba was sent with 180 others to India in 498 BCE (Dandamaev and Lukonin 1989: 293) (Figure 10.32). However, not all people travelled of their own free will as illustrated by contemporary Babylonian texts which recorded the transport and sale of female slaves from Bactria and Gandhara in 512 BCE (Dandamaev and Lukonin 1989: 156).

Figure 10.31. The Great Staircase at Persepolis, Iran.

The price of empire was also illustrated by the DSf text from the reign of Darius I which recorded the flow of raw resources from the satrapies, and that wood from Gandhara, gold from Bactria, ivory from India and lapis lazuli from Sogdiana were all used in the construction and decoration of Darius's new palace at Susa (ibid.: 256). Further evidence of the diverse character of the Persian Empire has been recently derived from an isotopic analysis of the extremely well-preserved male bodies recovered from within a series of collapsed deep shafts in the salt mines of Chehr Abad in Iran's modern Zanjan Province (Ramaroli et al. 2010). Dating to between 430 and 350 BCE, three 'salt mummies' demonstrated diverse geographical origins and, dressed in a 'Median' style, carried with them acorns from the Zagros Mountains and medlars from the Caspian Sea. This evidence has augmented our knowledge of exchange and trade networks operating within the empire and further illustrate the records of the Achaemenid archives which noted the major urban trade in "salt, beer, wine and ceramic vessels" (Dandamaev and Lukonin 1989: 215).

The Persian Empire, with its administrative and economic activities, was connected by a vast network of roads and caravan routes, but Alexander the Great was able to use these routes to bring war to the satrapal capitals and to gain control over the empire itself. Again, textual reports from some five different ancient historians have noted, in varying detail, the names and places of the cities and settlements along the campaign trail and these have provided generations of scholars with ancient itineraries to compare with modern topographies. For example, Aurel Stein undertook a survey of the Swat Valley in 1925 and used "a careful comparison of the topographical and archaeological

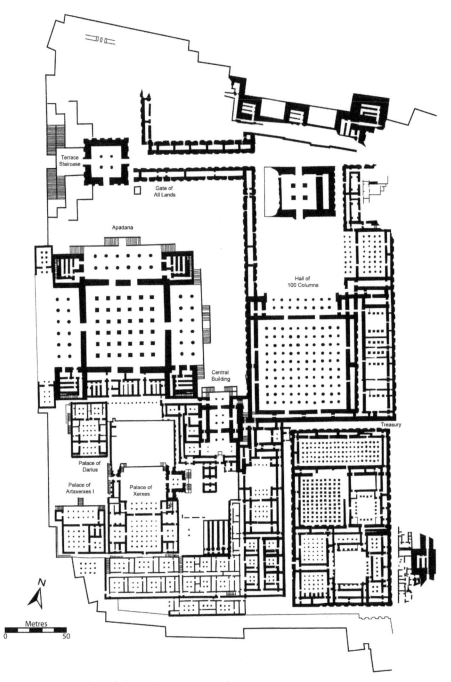

Figure 10.32. Plan of the palace at Persepolis, Iran.

facts with the notices of Alexander's historians" to identify the modern site of
Birkot as ancient Bazira or Beira and modern Pir-Sar as ancient Aornos (Stein
1929: 40; 113). This has resulted in a situation where Classical scholars and
archaeologists alike have blended modern geographical names with ancient

Figure 10.33. The Citadel of Kandahar (courtesy Warwick Ball).

ones and modern city names with ancient ones. This is exemplified by Fraser's study of the cities of Alexander where he recorded the campaign and the foundation or refoundation of urban forms in its wake (1996). Thus Alexander is described as having crossed over the Hindu Kush in the summer of 327 BCE and followed the valley of the Kophen or Kabul where he then divided his forces with Hephaestion who then moved on to besiege Peukelaotis or Charsadda, while Alexander followed the Kunar River and entered and pacified the Swat Valley. Climbing the Malakand Pass and travelling onto Taxila, he defeated King Poros on the Hydaspes or Jhelum in the summer of 326 BCE but halted his march at the banks of the Sutlej and then followed the Indus River down to the Makran coast (Fraser 1996: 68–71). There are, of course, many other variants of Alexander's route – almost as many as there are scholars who have studied his campaigns in this region. Although compiled later, and despite limited confidence in references to the exact size of the armies fielded by Porus and his fellow rulers, it is also clear that the field armies of the *Mahajanapadas* in the Punjab were substantial, even by Eastern Mediterranean standards (Coningham and Manuel 2008).

Kandahar may have had its massive casement wall and Elamite sealings in its Citadel (Figure 10.33), and Dahan-e Gholaman its monumental buildings and fire altars, but no such evidence has been recovered from within the eastern extremes of South Asia. As Raymond Allchin noted in 1993, there were hints of Achaemenid contact as represented by the silver bars and coins from the north-west or in the presence of later Aramaic inscriptions, but there was little else in the way of hard evidence (1993: 75) (Box 10.2). The presence of

Box 10.2. Punch-Marked Coins

Alongside inscriptions, which can often provide historical information at fixed points in time, coins are one of the most chronologically indicative artefacts that can be recovered from stratigraphic archaeological excavations. However, due to issues of residuality and reuse – factors often associated with coins due to the propensity for valuable commodities to be kept in circulation, such evidence can only provide a *terminus post quem* for the archaeological context in which the coin was found. The advent of coinage within South Asia is generally attributed after the middle of the first millennium BCE, and many cite the silver 'bent bars' of Gandhara as the earliest examples (Singh 2008). These oblong coins were struck on a Persian standard and were impressed by wheel or sun-like stamps at either end. As examples have been found in hoards alongside Persian *sigloi* at Taxila, it has been suggested that they were a localised reaction to the introduction of Persian currency.

Less restricted in distribution, the classic coin type of the Early Historic period was the punch-marked coin (Bhandare and Garg 2011). Made from copper and silver, punch-marked coins were manufactured through the hammering out of thin metal sheets or bars, which were then cut into squares, oblongs or discs with the weight of the coin adjusted through the clipping of corners. Although they were not inscribed with dates, they are held to provide a good artefactual marker of Early Historic occupation, activities and even territorial identities. Punch-marked coins were, as the name suggests, punched with numerous designs and symbols, such as the sun, a crescent on an arch and peacock on a hill. Whilst it has been noted that on the reverse, the punch-marks are smaller and often few in number, there is evidence of numerous punch-marks on the obverse, sometimes overlapping, indicating that these were stamped at different times. They were augmented by cast copper coinage in the fourth century BCE and fresh issues appear to have stopped by the second century BCE.

Kosambi (1965) suggested that the different stamps on the punch-marked coins could be associated with different rulers, dynasties and states, and he further asserted that coin hoards at Taxila provided evidence of a sequence of three successive types: silver bar coins and silver punch-marked coins of an earlier and later series with those of the later series being smaller and thicker than were the earlier coins. Indeed, the presence of the peacock above a hill has generally been identified as a symbol of the Mauryan dynasty – the Sanskrit term for peacock being Maurya (Falk 2006). Cribb (1985) has suggested that the later punch-marked coins were distributed throughout South Asia and represented a 'national' coinage, whilst the earlier series had localised concentrations and were evidence of 'local' coinages. However, more research is needed into punch-marked coins, including studies of distribution and metallurgical analysis. In addition, more secure scientific dating from stratigraphic excavations at Early Historic sites is required to gain more insights into the development of the earliest coinage in South Asia. The spread of coinage across South Asia is generally attributed to the influence of Mauryan expansion, including the advent of punch-marked coins in Sri Lanka (Bopearachchi 2006).

In addition to being one of the most dateable artefact categories, coins may also provide information on social and political conditions. The Early Historic period saw the development of urban centres and, out of the geopolitical transformations occurring in the Ganga plain, trade networks flourished, leading to the emergence of guilds of merchants and craftsmen as also noted by textual sources. Archaeological evidence attests to such a situation with the identification of innovations such as coinage and stamp seals – signs of the exchange of consumables for non-consumables, a growing economy and the movement and transfer of surplus and wealth (Coningham 2011: 933). Although the inherent limitations of textual sources must always be taken into account, the political treatise *Arthashastra* represents a major resource for understanding the role of coinage in the Early Historic world. Its text presents the ways in which society was conceptualised around monetary values and reflects the state's ideology regarding the use of money and wealth production and tax, even if this is an idealised view. Furthermore, finds of coins not indigenously produced in South Asia have also been recovered from excavations at Early Historic sites. For example, Roman coins have been recovered from Arikamedu (Begley 1996) and Anuradhapura (Bopearachchi 2006) providing further evidence of the extent of Indian Ocean trade networks, although there is a debate as to whether they represented an exchangeable currency or bullion.

Whilst punch-marked coins continued in circulation, they were augmented by localised copper currencies associated with the newly emergent independent post-Mauryan states which arose between circa 200 BCE and 300 CE (Bhandare and Garg 2011). Many of these provide insights into the political ideologies of Asoka's successors as exemplified by coins from the Kushan Empire, which developed across what are now the modern nation states of Afghanistan and Pakistan. Indeed, a plurality of belief systems is apparent, whereby the Emperor Kanishka was portrayed on coinage alongside the Hellenistic deity Helios, the Iranian divinity Adsho, Siva and the *Buddha*. As noted in Chapter 12, this numismatic evidence supports archaeological evidence of the diverse array of monuments constructed for

(*continued*)

the variety of faiths patronised in the Kushan Empire (Coningham and Manuel 2009b: 239). Finally, it should be noted that whilst many scholars have postulated the presence of formal state mints in the Early Historic period, the evidence is to the contrary. Indeed, only two examples of coin moulds have been identified, one at Anuradhapura and another at Taxila, and both consisted of simple tablets of baked clay bearing the impression of punch-marked coins. These moulds were then joined and coins cast; in the words of Thapar "punch-marked coins were therefore a transitional form between traders' tokens as units of value and legal tender issued by royalty" (1985 102–103). This reinforces the concept that whilst Mauryan ideology portrayed the presence of a strong centralist state, the absence of mechanisms for imposing authority indicates that this was more of an ideal than a reality.

stray finds of 'Graeco-Persian' style seals and the use of Tulip Bowls at various sites have often been cited as evidence of the north-western regions having "being drawn within the limits of the Achaemenid empire" (Magee and Petrie 2010: 518–520), but these objects may also represent the 'exotic' fruits of long-distance trade or exchange. Perhaps such increasingly agglomerated and specialised communities functioned as trade or mercantile interfaces on the periphery of the empire as well as central hubs within their own regions. Indeed, it is worth remembering Algaze's comments that "native elites controlling either the actual resources being exploited or access to those resources take advantage of their natural role as organizers of the means of production and (at times) mediators of the exchange to consolidate and extend their power, both in the context of their own societies and vis-a-vis their local rivals" (2005: 3), as applicable to these 'borderlands' as to the borderlands of the Indus Valley Tradition. It is also highly likely that the imperial Achaemenid model was very different in different parts of the empire as already suggested by Vogelsang (1992) and reiterated by Magee and Petrie with regard to the sequence in the Bannu Basin (2010: 518–520). Similarly, there is little to assist us with the identification of archaeological evidence for the campaign of Alexander the Great, although the later impact of the successors of the colonies that he founded north of the Hindu Kush was unmistakable (Narain 1957). Within such a context, one must again mark the parallel developments between the Regionalisation Era of the Indus Valley Tradition and the Regionalisation Era of the Early Historic Tradition. From a mosaic of distinct cultural lifeways, it is clear that numbers of population began to agglomerate at key regional centres, centres which began to be bound loosely together through networks of exchange and trade. Whilst dismissing earlier models which relied on the colonising influences of the Persian and Greek worlds, it is still possible to recognise that they had impacted on the extreme edge of the subcontinent.

The Achaemenid desire for raw materials, from timber to slaves, undoubtedly accelerated the process of integration and specialisation within South Asia but, again, whether such regional communities perceived themselves as peripheral is highly unlikely. Whilst we fail to find evidence of Persian or Greek cities or artefacts within the South Asian sequences, the presence of shared ceramic assemblages and motifs on seals indicate the exchanges which were taking place; exchanges which helped transform the emergent regional centres of the Iron Age into subcontinental superpowers and began a final process of integration completed by the Mauryan dynasty. These emergent regional centres or 'Early State Modules' became increasingly bound together through exchange, competition and emulation and the very process of urbanisation created a series of foci which could perhaps be described as city-states. The growth of such foci was only possible through the agglomeration of people spread out across the landscape and, as Yoffee has noted, urbanisation was linked with the "equally important and coeval phenomenon of ruralization", and that "in the process of city-state formation, the countryside was created as a hinterland of city states and as a fertile no-man's land to be contested by rival city-states" (1995: 284). This process is amply illustrated by *matsya nyaya* or the 'law of the fish' as well as the *Mahabharata*.

CHAPTER 11

THE MAURYANS AND THE ASOKAN
IDEAL (c. 321–185 BCE)

INTRODUCTION

Full integration only occurred with the emergence of the Mauryan Empire, which developed from being one of the many competing *Mahajanapadas* in the middle of the first millennium BCE to become the pre-eminent state of South Asia. Indeed, this final stage of the second urbanisation and urban-focused integration appears to have been largely the result of an internal process, a process that culminated in the middle of the third century BCE with the ascension of Asoka to the Mauryan throne. Asoka's reign between 272 and 235 BCE is crucial for understanding the development and integration of urban forms and planning within Asia, as he is recorded as having expanded Mauryan cultural and political hegemony over much of modern India, Pakistan, Bangladesh, Nepal and Afghanistan, as well as establishing strong trading links with Sri Lanka and western Asia (Thapar 1961) (Figure 11.1). Establishing a network of provincial capitals throughout his empire, much of South Asia and many of its neighbours were thus exposed to Asoka's style of 'righteous rule' or *dhamma*, and Mauryan concepts of the state have survived as recorded in both his own inscriptions and within the *Arthashastra* of Kautilya, the Mauryan Chief Minister (Allchin 1995a). The fact that his edicts were inscribed in Brahmi, Greek, Kharosthi and Aramaic indicate the heterogeneous character of the new expanded empire and have been found as far south as the Deccan and as far north as Nepal and as far west as Afghanistan. The *Arthashastra* is the second major historical source for this period, purportedly written by the Chief Minister to Asoka's grandfather, and contains detailed instructions for the creation of city-centric landscapes, the importance of the sacred nature of urban space and the art of governing and expanding the state. Additional sources for this period have been derived from Roman copies of extracts from the writings of Megasthenes, an ambassador from the court of Seleucus Nikator to the Mauryans and Pali Buddhist literature from Sri Lanka, as well as the later testimonies and traditions recorded by Chinese monks whilst on pilgrimage to South Asia in the first millennium CE. The legacy of the Mauryan Empire

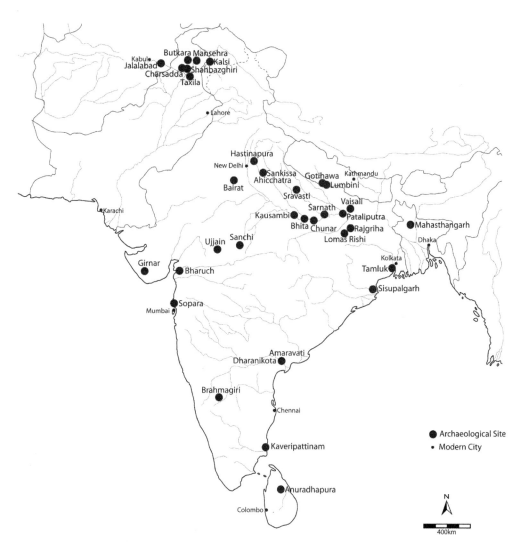

Figure 11.1. Map of sites mentioned in Chapter 11.

will be discussed in the next chapter as its model of integration and use of key urban and religious centres was to be utilised by successive Early Historic dynasties until Gupta hegemony in the fourth century CE.

We will also consider the archaeological evidence supporting the largely historical character of this period and suggest that there is a distinct lacuna between these two sources. As noted previously, many of the Western Classical sources were compiled centuries after actual events from fragments of earlier records. Similarly, the *Arthashastra* has been microscopically studied and elements found to have been compiled in the early centuries of the first millennium CE (Trautmann 1971). We will later evaluate the suggestion that the cohesiveness of the Asokan ideal owes more to early colonial scholars looking for a golden Indian age to legitimate their own imperial impositions as well as the pluralistic hopes and fears of early South Asian nationalists, as indicated by the choice of Asoka's lion capital for the Republic's crest, than actuality (Box 11.1). This early narrative was reiterated by Mortimer

---

Box 11.1. Prinsep and the Rediscovery of Asoka

James Prinsep (1799–1840) was employed as the assay-master of the East India Company mint at Calcutta but became a pioneer of antiquarian and historical scholarship in South Asia. Prinsep was keen to apply more scientific methods to the study of India's past and, as secretary of the Royal Asiatic Society of Bengal and founding editor of its journal, he became a focal point for the Society, guiding its activities along more systematic approaches. Understandably from his profession, one of Prinsep's major interests was numismatics, and he focused on the coins recovered from antiquarian investigations throughout South Asia which had been sent to the Society. Prinsep's attention was drawn to the many scripts stamped on the surface of these objects and, through a detailed study and classification, he became a key figure in the decipherment of ancient South Asian scripts, the development of which had gathered pace during the late-eighteenth and early nineteenth centuries (Chakrabarti 1988a: 330). It was such skills that led to his role in the rediscovery of one of the most revered and celebrated figures of the Early Historic world – the Emperor Asoka.

A series of enigmatic inscriptions, now known to have been composed in Early Brahmi characters, carved onto stone pillars and large boulders had been recorded by travellers and officials throughout South Asia in the 1830s. Whilst the content of the inscriptions remained unknown, Prinsep noticed that the inscriptions recovered from the Delhi and Allahabad pillars were identical, leading to the identification of the same script elsewhere. He then began working on other undeciphered inscriptions from Sanchi, which utilised a similar script, and noticed that many terminated with the same two characters. Working on the assumption that these inscriptions probably recorded donations and linking the symbols to previously translated scripts, he hypothesised the structure and potential letters which formed them. From this base, Prinsep made rapid progress and soon had a full understanding of the alphabet used in this script (Allen 2002: 178–180). Previously undeciphered coins began to be translated and the South Asian monarch lists updated, but Prinsep and his colleagues Ratna Paula and William Mill, recognised that the same sentence was repeated at many of the major boulder and pillar inscriptions: *Devanamapiya piyadasi laja hevam aha*, represented in English as: '*Thus spake King Piyadasi. Beloved of the Gods'.* This raised questions about the identity of King Piyadasi and why he had erected so many inscriptions across South Asia. It also became apparent that these inscriptions had the formula of royal edicts and that their contents provided evidence for "the workings of a most unusual mind, one that had been stifled for more than two thousand years and whose thoughts, carved into polished rock columns and boulders, had stood unread for almost as long. These three had broken that long, dark silence" (Allen 2002: 185).

In these edicts, King Piyadasi decreed that no living animals were to be slaughtered or used in rituals, religious tolerance to be observed and government was to be based on moral precepts (Thapar 1996). Such precepts of kingship differed from those found in Hindu and Vedic scriptures, and a monarch known as Piyadasi was absent from genealogical tables of royalty within the *Puranas* and was now thought more likely to have belonged to some long forgotten Buddhist dynasty (Allen 2002: 186). The answer to his identity was to come from the Sri Lankan Pali Chronicles, which had recently been translated by George Turnour. Initially attributed to the Sri Lankan monarch King Devanampiya Tissa, on the basis of the similarity in their names, this hypothesis was later rejected (Prinsep 1837). Indeed, although this king was recorded as a pious Buddhist, it was thought that if a Sri Lankan monarch had influence over northern parts of India, as the inscriptions attested to, this would have been recorded in the Chronicles. Furthermore, it became clear that the Sri Lankan Chronicles contained historical, rather than mythical individuals and, on reading a previously unstudied commentary, it was found that the Emperor Asoka had also utilised the title Piyadassi. In tandem with the Chronicles reporting that Asoka had sent missionaries to neighbouring lands to promote Buddhism, they also recorded that he had constructed monuments to this religion throughout South Asia. It was thus discovered that this major corpus of inscriptions belonged to the Mauryan Emperor Asoka rather than to King Devanampiya Tissa of Anuradhapura. However, it was not until 1915 that the Emperor's full name, *Devanam piyasa asokasa*, was found on an inscription with the discovery and decipherment of the Hyderabad rock edict (Allen 2002: 186–188).

This discovery, in tandem with evidence from the *Arthashastra* which was translated by S. Shamasastry in 1909 and published in English in 1915, led to a greater understanding and reconstruction of the social and religious character of the Early Historic world and the Mauryan Empire. Not only do the Asokan inscriptions bear testament to the influence of Mauryan hegemony across South Asia, but they also allow for the cautious reconstruction of the administration of this Empire. Indeed, the inscriptions

(continued)

identify the Mauryan capital and provincial centres but also demonstrate the attempts of the Empire to articulate diverse populations through the transcription of edicts into different languages and scripts, in addition to the promotion of proclamations of non-violence and the establishment of religious monuments (Falk 2006). Although there has been a heavy bias towards textual evidence, partially due to Prinsep's pioneering discoveries, recent archaeological re-evaluations of the nature of the Mauryan Empire are providing a greater understanding of the time and region that Asoka ruled (Smith 2005). However, interest in Asoka as a historical character still continues as illustrated by the coverage of the recent discovery of a later likeness of him on the stupa at Kanaganahalli in Karnataka (Poonacha 2007).

Wheeler, when he reflected that "[s]piritually and materially his [Asoka's] reign marks the first coherent expression of the Indian mind, and, for centuries after the political fabric of his empire had crumbled, his work was implicit in the thought and art of the subcontinent" (Wheeler 1959: 171). This continued debate is nowhere more clearly illustrated than by the differing interpretations concerning the distribution of rock and pillar edicts and discussions as to whether they marked the geographical and military extent of the Mauryan Empire or whether they marked routes of Mauryan pilgrimage and influence. The latter interpretation links more closely with Tambiah's (1976) concept of the galactic polity, whilst the former links to Kautilya's explanations of power being concentrated in the capital and its network of towns and forts rather than within places of worship and ritual. The Emperor Asoka has also been recognised as a powerful agent in the promotion of religious change from Pakistan to Sri Lanka, and his monumental investments and religious patronage started a trend still apparent today, but it has been argued that the traces of regionalism present within even the mainstream religions, such as Buddhism, again refutes the concept of a fully centralised state (Coningham 2001).

PHYSICAL SPREAD AND SETTING

Whilst the Mauryan Empire is generally agreed to have reached its greatest extent during the lifetime of the Emperor Asoka, the dynasty itself was recorded as having been established by Asoka's grandfather, Chandragupta Maurya (r. 321–297 BCE). Although his personal origins have remained uncertain, Chandragupta has been identified as the warrior Sandracottas within later western Classical texts, which recorded that he met Alexander the Great during the latter's expedition in the Punjab and along the Indus River. Although it remains unclear whether he actually served with Alexander himself, the historian D. D. Kosambi noted that whilst the latter's expedition "passed completely unnoticed in Indian tradition ... [t]here was an immediate, unexpected by-product of the utmost importance: it hastened the Mauryan conquest of the whole country" (1965: 138). Indeed, after Alexander's death at Babylon in 323 BCE, a vacuum occurred within South Asia, as powerful governors and warlords focused on the mastery of the Greek and Achaemenid satrapies further west. The Seleucid Ambassador Megasthenes later recorded that this vacuum allowed Chandragupta to organise a confederation of disaffected leaders to oust the remaining Macedonian-appointed governors occupying the Punjab and rule in their place. Then pursing an eastward campaign, Chandragupta steadily assimilated the city-states on the peripheries of the Kingdom of Magadha and, having had Dhana Nanda assassinated, expelled the Nanda dynasty from the throne of Magadha in 321 BCE. Now firmly established within the Gangetic heartland of Magadha, western Classical sources recorded that by 303 BCE he had campaigned against the eastern provinces of Seleucus Nikator (r. 305–281 BCE) as the latter was engaged in his own struggle for supremacy amongst Alexander's surviving generals. When Seleucus attempted to re-establish his hegemony over the eastern satrapies in 305 BCE, later western Classical historians recorded that he was defeated and exchanged sovereignty of those satrapies for 500 war elephants which he used against his Macedonian rivals in the west. Jain tradition recorded that Chandragupta renounced his worldly authority and wealth and retired to Sravana Belgola in the Deccan as an ascetic (Thapar 1961:17). Chandragupta was succeeded by his son, Bindusara, who reigned between 297 and 273 BCE and was recorded in Western Classical sources as Amitochates. Expanding his authority southwards and westwards, Pliny recorded that Amitochates sent a diplomatic request to Antiochus I Soter (r. 281–261 BCE), son of Seleucus Nikator, for sweet wine, dried figs and a Greek sophist for his court. Further expansion of the Mauryan Empire was recorded within Chandragupta grandson's own inscriptions as Asoka noted on his Thirteenth Major Rock Edict details of the final campaign against the independent eastern Kingdom of Kalinga in the eighth year of his reign.

In previous decades scholars suggested that "the geographical extent of the empire during the reign of Asoka can fortunately be indicated fairly precisely" and that the "distribution of his rock and pillar edicts is unchallenged evidence of his authority" (Thapar 1961: 123). This view has now been debated and challenged by many, including Thapar herself who no longer believes in this simple equation between the pillars, edicts and the extent of the Mauryan Empire under Asoka (Thapar 2006b). While the exact extent of the authority of the Mauryan ruler has remained uncertain, Asoka's inscriptions alluded to the presence of powerful neighbours at his borders, including Yonas, Kambojas and Gandharas to the north and west, and Colas, Pandyas, Satiyaputras and Keralaputras to the south, as well as references to the island of Lanka. Asoka's inscriptions also referred to the establishment of diplomatic communications with neighbouring rulers in Lanka as well as further west to Antiochus II Theos of Syria (r. 261–246 BCE), Ptolemy II Philadelphus of Egypt (r. 285–247 BCE), Antigonus Gonatas of Macedonia (r. 276–239 BCE), Magas of Cyrene (r. 258–250 BCE) and Alexander of Epirus (r. 272–255 BCE) (Thapar 1961: 41). This apparently involved the exchange of envoys, and a record of Asoka sending Buddhist missionaries to the court of King Devanampiya Tissa at Anuradhapura has also been noted within a number of the Sri Lanka's early Pali chronicles. In particular, the *Mahavamsa* and *Dipavamsa* record that Asoka sent his son, the monk Mahinda, and five companions to convert the island to Buddhism as well as a deputation carrying royal insignia for Devanampiya Tissa's coronation as King of Lanka (Coningham 1995b: 226). The chronicles also recorded that Asoka later collected and sent Buddhist relics to Mahinda as well as sending his daughter, the nun Sanghamitta, with a cutting of the Bodhi tree (*Ficus religiosa*), under which the *Buddha* had achieved enlightenment, for planting and veneration in Anuradhapura (Coningham 1995b: 226–228). Asoka's successors struggled to stabilise the territorial acquisitions of the Empire and the western extremities of the Mauryan Empire appeared to have reverted back to the Seleucids by 206 BCE. The Mauryan dynasty is generally accepted as having failed in 185 BCE with the death of Asoka's grandson, Brihadratha, following a coupe led by his commander-in-chief, Pushyamitra Sunga, founder of the Sunga dynasty (Kulke and Rothermund 1990: 71).

WHAT CHARACTERISES THE ERA OF MAURYAN INTEGRATION?

For many years, one of the key features of the Mauryan Empire was thought to have been use of the distinctive ceramic known as Northern Black Polished Ware or NBPW, which had a limited range of shallow black-slipped thalis and deeper bowls (Erdosy 1995b). As noted in Chapter 10, it was uniform in appearance and surface treatment and had clearly inherited features and forms from Painted Grey Ware, but far outstripped the latter's distribution and popularity. In its standardised forms, deposits of NBPW appear to have been largely limited in distribution to urban and religious sites. However, as we have already noted in Chapter 10, it is clear that NBPW was already well established as deluxe tableware before the reign of Asoka and before the final extension of Mauryan hegemony. This has led some archaeologists to assume that such sherds only penetrated "peripheral" areas in the north-west region in the fourth to third centuries BCE (Sharif 1969: 13) although more recent evidence has suggested that it reached this region at about the same times as the Gangetic core, further weakening a one-to-one link between the ware and imperial expansion (Erdosy 1995b: 105). As it has also been clearly identified in the sequence of Anuradhapura in Sri Lanka and other sites within the city's hinterland, there is the further issue that it was clearly distributed beyond the confines of the Empire and that the taste or style for this sought-after luxury item had become fashionable across South Asia as a whole and not restricted to Gangetic metropolitan or imperial markets (Coningham et al. 2007a; Coningham 2006b). A similar surface treatment has been found on a number of terracotta figurines, including elephants (Allchin 1995a: 272), and there is a class of female figurines associated with the Mauryan period, although their chronological resolution is based on art historical inference. They too may have been traded beyond the boundaries of Mauryan authority, refuting any attempt to relate them directly to Mauryan authority. A similar issue surrounds the distribution of Mauryan punch-marked coins as again they may have been transported beyond the political frontiers on account of their bullion value, or even as valued relics. Furthermore, the recovery of terracotta coin molds from a variety of 'unofficial' and small-scale production loci (Bopearachchi 2006: 16) suggests that central mint authority over coinage has been overstated and even their presence cannot be taken to directly represent a Mauryan territorial presence. Allchin has identified carved stone ringstones with the Mauryan period but whilst they have been found throughout the region covered by Asokan pillars, their chronological resolution is poor and their function unknown (1995a: 263).

As a result, rather than the highly mobile items such as NBPW vessels, terracottas and coins, the Mauryan period and empire has often been characterised by the find sites of Asokan edicts. However, there are even issues associated with this class of evidence as some have surfaced outside the known borders of the Mauryan Empire, such as from the bazaar at Kandahar, and others have apparently been moved out of their original context at a later date, such as the Niglihawa, Fatehabad, Hisar, Topra and Allahabad pillars (Falk 2006). Moreover, the only known Asokan inscription from the city of Taxila was actually recovered from within a building in the city of Sirkap, whose archaeological context was much later than the Mauryan dynasty and dated to the first century CE. There are also a number of fragments of uninscribed pillars and capitals which have been defined as "non-Asokan" and attributed to a post-Asokan period by Falk (ibid. 225). Evidence of a specific school of Mauryan urban planning has also been less clear to define, possibly because most of the provincial cities of the empire had long independent sequences as city-states before the arrival of Mauryan hegemony. Indeed, even within the Taxila Valley there appears to have been no desire to construct a new plan at the Bhir Mound, although the succeeding Indo-Greek and Kushan dynasties were to undertake such ventures. Having stated this, Erdosy has claimed to have identified a new tier of settlement associated with centralised control and there does appear to have been a distinct shared plan to the sites of Sisupalgarh and Bhita, both of which will be discussed later. At an individual monumental level, Romila Thapar noted that, while empires frequently manifested their elite and metropolitan culture through the construction of monumental palaces, temples and tombs, the pattern of Mauryan investment "suggests that much less was spent on secular monumental architecture than was the case under imperial systems in other parts of the ancient world" offering an interesting parallel with the urban-focused Era of the Indus Valley Tradition (Thapar 2006b: 296). Indeed, there has only been a single identification of a palace at Pataliputra and its character will be discussed later, but we should note that previous scholars have focused on the apparent 'Achaemenid' or 'Persianised' style of its pillared plan (Wheeler 1968: 133).

Whilst the presence of a pillar may not therefore represent direct imperial Mauryan rule, it is evident that the consistent use of bell-shaped lotus capitals has led many Western scholars to assume that the imperial monumental vocabulary of Achaemenid Persia had been adopted. Wheeler pursued such a theme and interpreted the Mauryan rise to power as an opportunity for the craftspeople of the old Achaemenid Empire stating that here "was the patronage of a dynasty with, as yet, no confirmed artistic tradition of its own in any way comparable with its wealth and ambition. Here was a new home for the accomplished artists and craftsmen of Persia" (Wheeler 1959: 173). The fact that the pillars appear to have been manufactured in a single quarry at Chunar on the Ganga and then distributed throughout northern India and Nepal certainly suggests the advent of a centralised monumental manufacturing and redistribution hub. This new style has also been found in the heart of the capital, Pataliputra, where a "Persianizing capital", complete with stepped impost, side-volutes and central palmettes was recovered and of which Wheeler remarked that "the formative influence of the mature craftsmen of Persia upon the immature experimentalism of India is plain to see" (Wheeler 1968: 134). This concept of cultural diffusion has continued to thrive and Harry Falk has clearly stated that "[s]ince there are no local predecessors, it was entirely logical that Asoka was inspired by learning about pillars erected outside India" and that "[t]he downfall of Achaemenid Iran had an immense impact on India. ... There was an intense exchange of goods and people" (2006: 139). It is, however, very possible that such prototypes may have been manufactured from timber and thus not have survived into the archaeological record.

Although unornamented, there was a further class of uniform monument throughout the Mauryan world, the *stupa* mound. A solid mound of clay, brick or stone built over a sacred Buddhist relic or at a sacred Buddhist location, the *stupa* is one of most resilient and widespread of early Buddhist monuments (Coningham 2001) (Figure 11.2). When the Chinese pilgrims Xuanzang and Faxian visited the holy Buddhist sites of South Asia in the first millennium CE, they reported that the emperor Asoka had opened a number of the earlier nirvana *stupas* of the *Buddha* and had redistributed the relics within 84,000 new *stupas* (Coningham and Gunawardhana 2012). Whilst nowhere near that number, partial corroboration for a campaign of monumental construction has been demonstrated archaeologically at a number of sites across South Asia, and

Figure 11.2. The Great *Stupa* of Sanchi, India.

it is possible to refer to a distinct 'Asokan horizon' at many of the key sites associated with the *Buddha*, including a number of sites associated with the lifetime of the *Buddha*, Lumbini and Sarnath, as well as sites beyond as at Taxila, Sanchi and Bairat (Coningham 2011; Coningham et al. 2013; Shaw 2000) (Figure 11.3).

SETTLEMENTS OF THE MAURYAN EMPIRE

In addition to advocating the ideal location, number and function of settlements within the landscape of the kingdom, Kautilya's *Arthashastra* also described the key social and economic elements of a city and their ideal subdivision (Box 11.2) (Figure 11.4). Detailing the correct ritual procedures for embarking on such a programme, the text advised the division of the site into a grid by constructing three roads running east to west and a further three roads running south to north (*Artha.* II.4.1). This initial process was then to be followed by the allocation of gods, castes and occupations throughout the site. The palace was to be established to the north of city's centre, the *Brahmins* or priests in the northern sector, the *Kshatriyas* or warriors in the east, the *Vaishyas* or merchants in the south and the *Sudras* or labourers in the west (*Artha* II.4.7–13). Representing the peak of the Mauryan settlement hierarchy, and hosting the Empire's key officials and administrators, generations of scholars have been tempted to compare the excavated plans of the Empire's major cities with the *Arthashastra*'s advocated plans (Dutt 1925; Allchin 1995a; Young and Coningham 2010). Reviewing the evidence for the presence of such features,

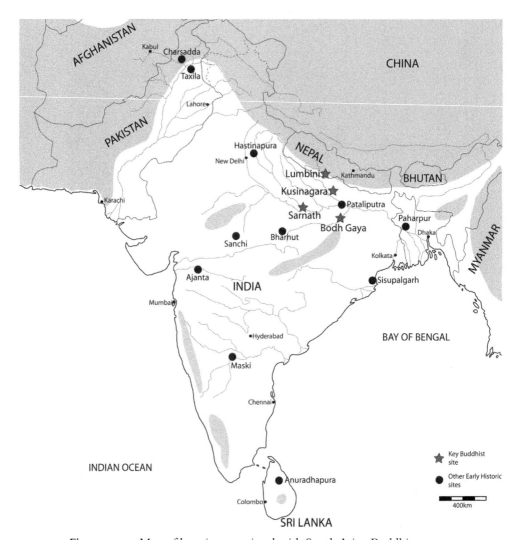

Figure 11.3. Map of key sites associated with South Asian Buddhism.

the following section will present the capital of Pataliputra and the cities of
Charsadda and Taxila in the north-west, Kausambi, Rajgir and Hastinapura in
the Gangetic heartland, Ujjain in Central India and Brahmagiri in the Deccan
before concluding by considering the cases of the sites of Sisupalgarh in Orissa
and Bhita in Uttar Pradesh.

The capital city of the Mauryan Empire, Pataliputra, was located along the
southern bank of the Ganga with branches of the Punpun and Son to the
west and south adding further riverine connectivity and protection. This ideal
location for a capital had already been identified a number of centuries earlier
when Udayin, King of Magadha, shifted his court there from the isolated rock
fortress of Rajgir. Whilst the city is now largely inaccessible beneath the modern city of Patna, capital of the State of Bihar, it is still possible to reconstruct
elements of its topography from contemporary and later records and the results

---

Box 11.2. Urban Microcosms

Ethnographic studies within South Asia have demonstrated that many contemporary communities have been spatially segregated on account of ritual hierarchies. For example, caste concerns are believed to have led to the settling of *Brahmans*, Non-*Brahmans* and Adi-Dravida in separate areas of the villages of Sripuram and Kumbapettai in Tanjore, South India, as were their own respective cremation grounds (Beteille 1965, Gough 1960). As noted in Chapter 2, the division of social groups and social hierarchies within settlements has a long history in South Asia, and a number of scholars have suggested that such divisions were also key to the structuring of settlement layouts in the past (Dutt 1925). Such concepts are also found within the work of Paul Wheatley, in particular in his seminal text '*The Pivot of the Four Quarters*', where he argued that pre-industrial cities were ritual and ceremonial centres (1971: 225) and exhibited cosmo-magical symbolism through their layouts (*ibid.*: 481). He thus conceived city layout as an image of social stability and harmony, in which imagery was linked to cosmology. Cities were therefore built as microcosms of the universe bringing the human realm into a relationship with the cosmos through the symbolic intersection point of the *axis mundi*, projecting cosmic order onto the human realm (Wheatley 1971: 418). Although Wheatley's analysis primarily focused on Chinese urban examples, South Asia's principle treatise – the *Arthashastra,* was cited to provide evidence for the influence of symbolism and microcosms in the planning of Early Historic urban forms.

Textual evidence from the Early Historic Tradition in South Asia certainly supports such a hypothesis as many treatises provide prescriptive details of how a city should be planned and organised (Eltsov 2008). Moreover, cosmological motifs were frequently used in South Asian settlements, as advised by Early Historic town planning treatises, and city moats and ramparts were built to represent the cosmic ocean and mountain range surrounding the universe. The central element of the city represented Mount Meru, the dwelling of the Gods, and implied that the monarch was the equivalent of a universal ruler or *chakravartin* (Wheatley 1971: 437, Coningham 2000: 350). The *Arthashastra* also stated that the city should be quadrangular, surrounded by three moats and a rampart (*Artha.* II.3.4–6) and be internally demarcated by six roads, three running north to south and three east to west with gates on either end of their lengths (*Artha.* II.4.1–20). It also advocated the spatial separation of people within a city and divided the four *varnas* spatially with *Brahmans* located in the north, *Kshatriyas* to the east, *Vaishyas* to the south and *Sudras* to the west of the city, with heretics and *Candalas* banished outside the city walls (*Artha.* II.4.7–23). However, although these

(continued)

texts advocated the construction of such a form, does the archaeological record support such physical representations within the Early Historic South Asian world?

In Myanmar, the Pyu period urban sites of Sri Ksetra, Beikthano and Halin appear to conform to such a plan and have been interpreted as cosmograms with their respective central citadel and palace areas thought to represent Mount Meru, their outer walls the mountains bounding the universe and their moats recalling the cosmic ocean. It has been further suggested that the smaller tanks and canals within the urban areas symbolised sacred lakes and rivers (Stargardt 1990: 108). Within one of the heartlands of South Asia's second urbanisation, the plains of the Ganga contain many Early Historic Integration Era urban sites with moats and ramparts although they are not quadrangular in form, such as Kausambi (Sharma 1960) and Hastinapura (Lal 1955). However, Sisupalgarh (Mohanty and Smith 2008), Bhita (Marshall 1912) and Tilaurakot (Coningham et al. 2010) do appear to mirror the *Arthashastra*'s description, being quadrangular shaped and internally divided by regularly laid out cardinally orientated streets and gateways.

Similarly, in Sri Lanka, the Early Historic Citadel of Anuradhapura was also roughly quadrangular in form and its architectural remnants have clear parallels with the *Arthashastra*. Excavations at Trench ASW2 have confirmed that by the fourth century BCE the Citadel of Anuradhapura exhibited a layout of rectangular cardinally orientated structures (Coningham 1999). Investigation of the city's fortifications also established that at this time there was a contemporaneous development of a moat and rampart, incorporating gateways at each cardinal direction (Coningham 1993: 121). Not only do the architectural remains from the Citadel appear to have aligned with precepts contained within Early Historic town planning treatises, but so too did the evidence outside the fortifications. For example, the *Arthashastra* advised that at a distance of 182 metres from the moats, sanctuaries, holy places, groves and waterworks should surround the city (*Artha*. II.4.20–21). Anuradhapura provided strong evidence for this precept (Allchin 1995a: 225), with shrines, sanctuaries and ecclesiastical structures located immediately around the Citadel (Bandaranayake 1974: 27–28). Anuradhapura was also provided with many artificial tanks, which were documented in the *Mahavamsa* and visible around the city today (Coningham 1999: 23). The architectural evidence from Anuradhapura thus would suggest that Anuradhapura was planned according to Early Historic texts and may be conceptualised as a celestial city and an *axis mundi* (Wickremeratne 1987: 45).

Although architecturally many Early Historic cities may match the *Arthashastra's* planning precepts, artefactual analysis of the spatial distribution of artefacts within Anuradhapura did not match the *Arthashastra's* ideals (Coningham and Young 2007). Rather than specific locales for specific crafts, potentially indicating the presence of differing social groups in separate areas of the city, the co-location of various craft activities throughout the Citadel, such as metal, semi-precious stone, glass, antler and ivory working indicated that the *Arthashastra's* precepts on the governance of space may not always have been practiced (*ibid.*: 90). Furthermore, as stated previously, many Early Historic cities did not match the quadrangular plan advocated by Early Historic planning treatises with Mortimer Wheeler referring to the urban plan of the Bhir Mound at Taxila as a "shambles" (1966: 109). The orientation of these streets bore no relationship to the surviving outlines of the mound (Allchin 1995a: 234), exhibiting irregularly aligned winding streets and lacking a fortification wall and moat (Chakrabarti 1995: 176). Therefore, whilst many urban forms did conform to the precepts of symbolic planning, this was not universally implemented across the Early Historic world, and whilst architectural aspirations for such layouts may be identified, much more analysis is needed for the artefactual variability across such sites to understand whether such precepts were fully implemented.

of a series of explorations between the 1890s and 1930s. The former was most vividly captured in the writings of Megasthenes, the Seleucid ambassador to Chandragupta Mauryan, who recorded that the city of Palibothra (Pataliputra) took the form of a parallelogram, had a population of some 400,000 and that its wooden fortification wall with fifty-four gates and 570 towers enclosed an area measuring 80 stadia long and 20 deep (McCrindle 1896: 66). Whilst some scholars have suggested a rather smaller area for the city, for example 2,200 hectares (Allchin 1995a: 202), all are of the opinion that the presence of the wooden walls was proven as early as the 1890s when various trenches encountered double lines of timbers 5 metres apart in particularly waterlogged areas. Particularly well-preserved in the modern suburbs of Bulandibagh and Gosainkhanda, they appear to have comprised a double row of heavy vertical beams joined together at the base and on top by a line of horizontal sleepers (Gupta 1980: 230–235) (Figure 11.5). Traces of the original clay rampart that this timber framework would have been used to anchor and stabilise have been lost over time, and it was not identified by the excavators. Apart from the presence of a monumental hall beyond the walls at Kumrahar, which will be discussed later, isolated finds of pillars (Falk 2006: 193) and sculpture within the walls in the suburbs of Sadargali and Lohanipur, little more is known about the internal layout of the city and its plan, although the Chinese pilgrims did

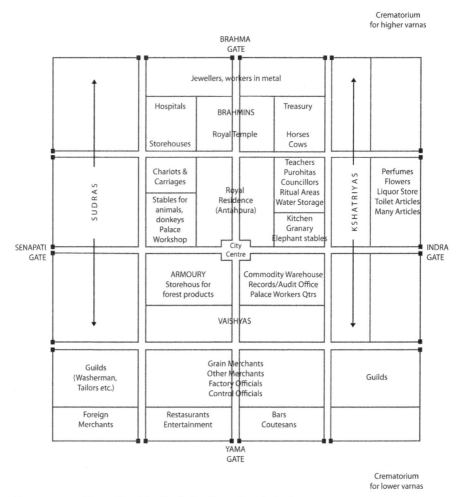

Figure 11.4. Plan of an idealised city from the *Arthashastra*.

record the presence of a *stupa* to its south, now indistinguishable, and a series
of stone pillars (Mitra 1971: 9).

A number of similarly monumental communal investments were also
undertaken in the other *Mahajanapada* capitals, later annexed and incorporated into the kingdom of Magadha. As noted in Chapter 10, Rajgir – the old
capital of Magadha, presented evidence of huge communal investment in the
creation of its curtain wall of rough blocks which fortified some 200 hectares
of valley within its surrounding rocky ridges. Whilst Rajgir's irregular profile
was dictated by its rocky ridges, the new fortification established just outside
its northern gate was remarkably regular in plan. Known as New Rajgir, the
city comprised two sets of enclosing walls, the inner of which was rectangular
and enclosed an area of about 30 hectares. The core rampart of the wall was 40
metres wide and 7.31 metres high and capped by a 5.48 metre thick and 3.35
metre high stone block wall. The archaeological sequence associated with the

Figure 11.5. The wooden palisade of Pataliputra, Patna, India (courtesy Marshall Archive, Oriental Museum, Durham University DUROM.1957.1.3443).

construction of this circumvallation lay above levels dating to circa 260 BCE, providing evidence of a clear Asokan horizon (Ghosh 1989: 364). Also associated with the life of the *Buddha* and provided with at least one Asokan pillar, Kausambi – the capital of the old *Mahajanapada* of Vatsa – was an irregular rectangle of some 200 hectares. Constructed in the fifth century BCE, the city layout was distinctly irregular as were the contemporary crescent profile of Sravasti, the circular form of Sankissa, and the triangular form of Ahicchatra (Allchin 1995a: 206), but all were associated with the vast investment in defining ramparts. As recorded by Erdosy, they had bases as wide as 75 metres, heights up to 14 metres and covered circuits as long as 6 kilometres (Erdosy 1995b: 111). These structures must have represented the mobilisation of thousands of individuals, far more than the urban population, and thus clearly demonstrated the authority and ability to mobilise the hinterland (Coningham 1995a: 70). The rampart of Mahasthangarh in Bangladesh has been similarly attributed to a Mauryan foundation and its 5 kilometre long rampart and 100 metre wide moats provide a very clear understanding of the vast human investment needed to construct and maintain them (Alam and Salles 2001) (Figure 11.6).

Many of these traits have also been found at Ujjain, capital of the old *Mahajanapada* of Avanti, to the south in Central India, whose ramparts are

Figure 11.6. City rampart and moat at Mahasthangarh, Bangladesh.

thought to have been erected by the middle of the first millennium BC (Banerjee 1960). With a circumference of 5 kilometres, the latter were 75 metres wide at the base and, as they were built of clay stabilised with a timber framework, were able to reach a height of 14 metres. Forming an irregular pentagon, the western side of the city faced the Sipra River and the southern and eastern sides were protected by the digging of a ditch, 27 metres wide and 7 metres deep, fed by the river (IAR 1957: 20). Breaches within the ramparts appear to indicate the presence of ancient gateways, although these were irregular in number with the largest number, three, directly facing the river front. Apart from the published account of the presence of a variety of internal structures built of mud, mud brick, stone rubble and brickbats, there has been little discussion as to the nature of the city plan, although streets were reported as having been laid with rubble and clay and the presence of a reservoir noted (ibid. 24).

Further south in the Deccan, the site of Brahmagiri has been identified as the most southerly outpost of the Mauryan Empire on account of its proximity to the rock edicts of Siddapur (Thapar 1961: 230). Often referred to as Isila, the headquarters of the officials referred to in the adjacent Asokan edict as the *Mahamatras* of Suvarnagiri, the site is located on the north flank of a 180 metres high granite outcrop which measures some 100 metres north to south and 500 metres east to west. The surrounding megalithic cemetery was excavated by Wheeler in the 1940s, but he also took the opportunity to excavate a sondage in the town, exposing a sequence which he believed to have stretched from the late Neolithic through the Early Historic into the period

Figure 11.7. Asokan rock edict at Mansehra, Pakistan.

of Satavahana rule in the first half of the first millennium AD (Krishna 1943; Wheeler 1948), although more recent work is potentially challenging these dates, as noted in Chapter 10 (Morrison 2005). In stark contrast to the contemporary fortified urban centres established in the Ganga basin, Central India and Sri Lanka, Brahmagiri appeared to have been entirely unfortified, although the presence of a well-laid street suggests some degree of centralised investment and planning. Whilst there may have been an absence of early urban enclaves of population within the Deccan, there is some evidence for the construction of infrastructure in the form of a timber wharf on the banks of the River Krishna at the site of Dharanikota, one kilometre away from the Buddhist complex at Amaravati, during the Mauryan period (IAR 1962–1963: 1–2). Excavations at the shrine and *stupa* at Amaravati have also indicated that occupation intensified at this period and relevant levels yielded Black and Red Ware alongside NBPW and a polished granite railing, and the excavator has attributed these activities to the advent of the Mauryans (IAR 1973: 4–5).

None of the monumentality identified within the cities at the core of the Mauryan Empire has been identified within the north-west of the subcontinent at either Charsadda or Taxila – twin capitals of the old *Mahajanapada* of Gandhara. This is despite the presence of three Asokan inscriptions within the region at Shahbazgarhi on a rock outcrop within the Vale of Peshawar, on an outcrop at Mansehra and on a stone slab within the Taxila Valley at Sirkap (Figure 11.7). As noted previously, the site of the Bala Hisar of Charsadda is represented by a 23 metre high tell, which was established close to the confluence of the Swat and Kabul rivers in the Vale of Peshawar (Coningham and Ali 2007c: 1). Later covering an area of some 25 hectares, the first settlement

Figure 11.8. The winding streets of the Bhir Mound, Pakistan.

at the site was established on a low natural mound of clay at the end of the second millennium BCE before having a series of defensive ditches cut around its circumference in the middle of the first millennium BCE. When Mortimer Wheeler investigated the site in 1958, he noted that the mud on cobble foundation structures belonging to the Mauryan period displayed little evidence of formal planning as they were crowded together and appeared to have been sporadically constructed (Wheeler 1963: 30). Wheeler also noted that the crowded nature of Mauryan Charsadda was shared by the structures and layout of the Bhir Mound at Taxila (ibid.). As noted in Chapter 10, a number of scholars have identified the lower levels of the Bhir Mound as the capital visited by Alexander the Great and that the uppermost levels were contemporary with Asoka.

Unlike the open location of the Bala Hisar of Charsadda, the Bhir Mound was sheltered in the bottom of the rocky valley of Taxila beside the Margala Hills. The Bhir Mound measured 1.1 kilometres north to south and 670 metres east to west, and the lower levels of the site were excavated to a limited degree by both Marshall and Sharif. Marshall had successfully exposed an area of 1.2 hectares of stone-built structures between 1913 and 1914, subdivided by a series of streets, squares and lanes ranging in width from between 6.7 and 0.91 metres (Marshall 1951, 1960). Built of rubble, Marshall identified small single cell structures facing out on to the thoroughfares which he interpreted as shops, behind which were individual dwelling blocks (Marshall 1951: 52). Throughout the settlement, however, Marshall noted that there was little evidence of civic planning as evidenced by the bending streets and lanes, lack of street drainage and the encroachment and blocking of passages (Figure 11.8). Confused by

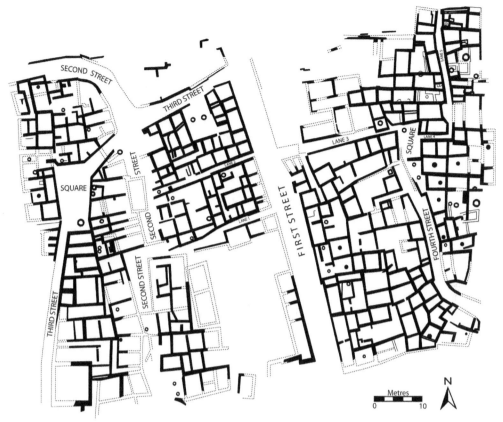

Figure 11.9. Plan of the street layout of the Bhir Mound, Pakistan.

trying to identify where one individual building ended and another started, he noted the presence of a single example of communal action; refuse bins within the streets (Marshall 1951: 91) (Figure 11.9).Whilst scholars continue to debate whether the layout was formally ordered or not, most have shared Dani's perspective that the layout had evolved organically according to the needs of the growing population rather than following a rigid imperially imposed plan (Dani 1986: 83). Although the Bhir Mound possessed none of the rigid planning which characterised its successor, Sirkap, its structures do appear to have comprised housing blocks of roughly cardinal courtyards surrounded by similarly oriented ranges of rooms and rows of individual chambers or units facing onto the streets and lanes, presumably shops. It is notable that scholars have been unable to identify a defensive circuit around the Bhir Mound, and some scholars have suggested that it was unfortified, in contrast with the cities of Central India and the Ganga Basin.

In stark contrast to the irregular patterns and plans of the cities of north India and Pakistan, as described earlier, two distinctive regularly planned Mauryan settlements were established at Sisupalgarh and Bhita. Sisupalgarh is located close to the mediaeval shrine of Bhubaneswar, adjacent to the course of one

Figure 11.10. Aerial photograph of the city of Sisupalgarh, India (courtesy Bridget Allchin).

of the braided channels of the Mahanadi River with two distinct hillocks to the south and west, Dhauli and Udayagiri respectively (Lal 1949; Smith 2001). Sisupalgarh's layout was particularly striking as it comprised a regular square of 1.1 kilometres, with indications of two gateways on each side, presumably subdividing the interior into nine main blocks (Figure 11.10). Roughly oriented to the cardinal points, B. B. Lal's excavations in 1948 exposed a heavily fortified 7.6 metre wide entrance gate, built of laterite blocks, set into a clay and brick rampart. Most significantly, when Lal cut a section through the city's rampart sequence, he identified that the plan had been in place since the beginnings of the settlement's fortification. Located in the heartland of the old eastern kingdom of Kalinga, Asoka recorded in his Thirteenth Major Rock Edict that "the beloved of the gods, the king Piyadassi, conquered Kalinga. A hundred and fifty thousand people were deported, a hundred thousand were killed and many times that number perished" (Thapar 1961: 255). Thapar suggested that those deported were then engaged in agricultural colonisation elsewhere

(Thapar 1985: 162). Such depopulation would have both weakened the capacity of Kalinga as well as creating a surplus population who could then be relocated for agricultural labour in direct support of the Mauryan state. It is highly tempting to associate this rigidly planned urban imposition with the process of Mauryan consolidation, pacification and integration following the annexation (Erdosy 1995b: 111), and it may be no mere coincidence that this fortress-cum-provincial centre was situated slightly more than 3.2 kilometres from Asoka's own rock edict on the hill at Dhauli. Recent fieldwork at the site has suggested that the site was occupied from at least the fifth century BCE (Mohanty and Smith 2008), but the exact dating of the fortifications is still awaited. Geophysical survey within the site has also demonstrated the existence of cardinal roads subdividing the site into nine main quarters as well as an apparently empty area around a monumental central complex. Monica Smith has suggested that these roads created and maintained "a clear line of sight between gateways and the economic effects of easy access to the exterior" and that the central area "provided a space for performance and communal activities" (2008: 227). It is likely that the Mauryan city was imposed on the pre-existing settlement and equally likely that other centres were established for this purpose elsewhere within the old kingdom.

URBAN AND RURAL SITES OF THE MAURYAN EMPIRE

Many scholars have been influenced by the *Arthashastra*'s section on the ideal organisation and location of settlements within all the provinces of a kingdom, contained within Book II Section 2, interpreting it as an indicator of how the landscape of the Mauryan Empire was physically ordered (Allchin 1995a: 196). Each province was to be furnished with a provincial capital or *sthaniya*, which serviced, administered and taxed the 800 agricultural villages or *grama*, which populated the province (Figure 11.11). However, Kautilya's model also advocated laying out a further hierarchical series of lower order service settlements within the province, including one *sangrahana* or local centre for every ten villages, one *karvatika* or sub-divisional headquarters for every group of twenty *sangrahanas*, one *dronamukha* or divisional headquarters for every two *karvatikas* and, finally, two divisional headquarters for every provincial capital (*Artha.* II.21.1–3). Whilst archaeologists and historians may have been influenced by the *Arthashastra*, it was not until the 1980s that archaeologists set out to test this pattern against the archaeological record in the heart of the Mauryan Empire in Allahabad and Kanpur Districts. The former settlement survey was undertaken by George Erdosy within the territory of the old *Mahajanapada* of Vatsa and he postulated the presence of a population of 50 million present within a five-tiered settlement hierarchy between 400 and 100 BCE (Erdosy 1995b: 107–109). Crowned by the provincial capital at Kausambi at 200 hectares, there was a second site of 22 hectares, two sites between 6 and 10 hectares,

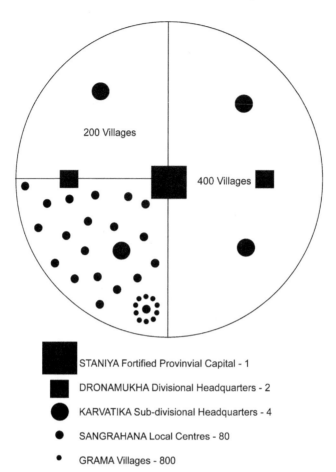

200 Villages

400 Villages

■ STANIYA Fortified Provinvial Capital - 1

■ DRONAMUKHA Divisional Headquarters - 2

● KARVATIKA Sub-divisional Headquarters - 4

● SANGRAHANA Local Centres - 80

• GRAMA Villages - 800

Figure 11.11. Plan of an idealised kingdom from the *Arthashastra*.

four between 3 and 6 and no fewer than thirty-seven under 6 hectares (Erdosy 1988: 66). Noting that the villages at the bottom of the size hierarchy were primarily occupied with farming and herding activities, Erdosy identified that the next tier, between 3 and 5 hectares in size, performed primary administrative functions but that the third tier were involved in the manufacture of ceramics, stone blades and iron objects. At the fourth tier, fortified towns between 10 and 50 hectares augmented these activities with production of luxury goods, such as semi-precious stone, copper and shell objects, but all were dwarfed by the primate capital, Kausambi. Erdosy has suggested that the four sites between 3 and 6 hectares may have represented a new tier of settlement established "by a central authority for the exercise of an administrative role in addition to economic ones", as over time, the "former political units – including the kingdom of Vatsa – were incorporated into the emerging empire without any major administrative reorganisation" (Erdosy 1988: 69).

This clear correlation between size and activities led Erdosy to note that his findings confirmed "the basic premise of Central Place Theory, that sites

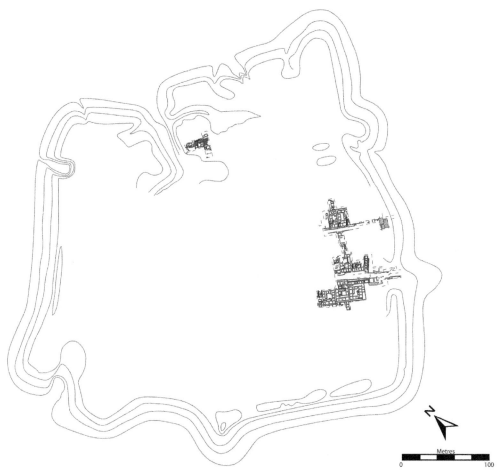

Figure 11.12. Plan of the site of Bhita, India.

of a higher order will contain larger populations and perform all the functions of smaller settlements in addition to some unique to themselves" (Erdosy 1995b: 107). In total, the old kingdom (which covered an area larger than Erdosy's survey) hosted at least seven settlements between 19 and 50 hectares, including Kara and Jhusi, which Erdosy referred to as towns. However, the most extensively sampled site of this category was the town of Bhita, 22 kilometres downstream the Yamuna from Kosambi, which was excavated by John Marshall between 1911 and 1912. Covering an area of 14 hectares, Bhita was laid out on a square plan and enclosed by a 3.4 metre thick wall on the top of an earth rampart which was pierced by three sets of gates, one on each side (Marshall 1912: 40) (Figure 11.12). Marshall excavated an area of 26,000 square metres on the south-east side of the settlement and exposed the presence of two parallel east-west roads, 43.5 metres apart with a grid of lanes and smaller streets at intervals of 16.7 metres at right angles, creating a network of blocks. Main roads were between 6.7 and 5.18 metres wide and

Figure 11.13. Plan of street layout in Bhita, India.

lanes between 1.5 and 0.9 metres, and individual blocks comprised houses flanked by shops facing onto the roads. These individual residential blocks covered 673 square metres and consisted of open courtyards surrounded by chambers (Figure 11.13). Excavation of the roads demonstrated that they were made up of rammed material and had been laid out at the same time as the site was walled. Furthermore, there was no evidence of encroachment on the roads, suggesting a strong degree of municipal control within the settlement. Marshall noted that many of the blocks and their residential compounds were serviced by drains which led into larger drains at the sides of lanes and passages. From Marshall's 7.8 metre section through the occupation sequence, it is possible to suggest that the defensive circuit and street blocks were laid out contemporaneously and that it is highly likely that this programme had been initiated during the Mauryan period (Allchin 1995a: 231). Whilst not associated with a garrison, Bhita may have nevertheless represented an imperial Mauryan imposition, as it appeared to have hosted a number of critical administrative and mercantile functions. Perhaps representing the creation of a new tier of settlement within the hinterland of the old *Mahajanapada*, the presence of NBPW at the site demonstrates a further degree of integration through its material culture.

Whilst some scholars have argued that Erdosy's five-tiered settlement hierarchy supported the idealised mapping contained within the *Arthashastra* (Allchin 1995a: 198), there are concerns that the hierarchy of Allahabad District was something of an isolated phenomenon, as illustrated by the contemporary survey by Makkhan Lal in neighbouring Kanpur District (1984b). Utilising a similar combination of village to village investigation and a desktop study of reports, Makkhan Lal reported the presence of only three tiers of settlement, namely small villages, larger villages and regional centres, although his survey area was not in the heart of one of the old *Mahajanapadas* (Lal 1984a: 189). It is also interesting to note that no subsidiary sites were found during Ihsan Ali's survey of Charsadda District in the Vale of Peshawar around the Bala Hisar (Ali 2003), again raising the potential for further questioning of the application of the *Arthashastra's* ideals across the entirety of the area incorporated within Mauryan hegemony.

It is also useful at this point to compare the evidence from Anuradhapura in Sri Lanka, which although beyond the established borders of Mauryan rule has provided one of the most comprehensive studies of Early Historic settlement within an urban hinterland. The city at this period certainly appears to have conformed to the monumentality of the *Mahajanapadas* to the north of the subcontinent, and its urban population was housed and differentiated within a settlement of some 71 hectares enclosed within a rampart and ditch complex measuring roughly half a kilometre square. As also noted in Chapter 10, the earliest round structures associated with the Iron Age phases of the site had been replaced with rectangular buildings, and whilst roof tile had already been used, limestone blocks were then introduced to pave courtyard floors, although the roofs appeared to have been supported by timber pillars bound by iron rings rather than stone pillars (Coningham 1999). Settlement survey within the hinterland of Anuradhapura identified 186 sites associated with this period, largely conforming to three categories: small towns, monasteries and small rural settle-ments (Coningham and Gunawardhana 2013). There were only two sites which appear to have conformed to the category of small town and these were associ-ated with the modern villages of Siyambalaweva and Rajaligama. Rajaligama was located 27 kilometres to the south of Anuradhapura and comprised a wide scatter of ceramics. Covering an area of some 200 metres by 300 metres, geo-physical survey identified a series of rectilinear anomalies which may mark the location of individual house floors. Although Rajaligama was one of the largest sites recorded within the hinterland, excavation demonstrated that the deposit was only 20 centimetres deep, suggesting that its occupation was only short lived. However, the trenches did produce evidence of metal-working slag, glass and imported fine wares. The second site, Siyambalaweva, was a low mound 100 metres from a natural ford of the Malwattu Oya at a distance of 7 kilome-tres to the north of Anuradhapura. It was also represented by shallow ceramic scatter of 200 metres by 150 metres but was distinguished by a monument formed by four clusters of rough stone pillars at the centre of the settlement. Both sites have been identified as small towns on account of their size, and it is notable that they possessed evidence of luxury goods and imports (including fine black slipped wares, perhaps NBPW), but it is equally clear that both were short-lived and have been interpreted as a failed attempt to install a medium tier of settlement within the city of Anuradhapura's hinterland (Coningham et al. 2007a).

The second major category of site identified within Anuradhapura's hin-terland was represented by sixty-nine Buddhist monastic sites, which were largely confined to granite outcrops. The most recognisable features of this site category were *lenas*, or natural caves, augmented with rock-cut drip ledges as well as the presence of Early Brahmi inscriptions (Figure 11.14). Associated with the spread of Buddhism in the third century BCE, *lenas* were commonly used as the wet season residences for monks and nuns although many became permanently inhabited (Coningham 1995b). The hinterland's monastic sites have proved to possess deep occupation sequences and to have been occupied for many centuries, clearly differentiating them from the category of small short-lived Early Historic towns. It is also interesting to note that the mon-asteries were often associated with literacy, manufacturing and communally constructed monumental architectural elements, suggesting that monasteries actually performed the same social and economic functions as towns but were closely articulated with the major monasteries around the city of Anuradhapura itself (Coningham 2011). A number of these sites, such as Veheragala and Sembukulama, also yielded evidence of access to long-distance trade items like NBPW but it is notable that the quantities of these types of material cul-ture were far lower than within the urbanised core itself (Coningham and Gunawardhana 2013). There was also evidence from Veheragala, a monastic site 27 kilometres to the south of Anuradhapura, that the Early Historic occupation

Figure 11.14. Early Brahmi inscription at Anuradhapura, Sri Lanka.

on the granite outcrop was accompanied by the contemporaneous construction of a small gravity-fed irrigation reservoir some 200 metres to the west. The final but most numerous category or tier of site were small ceramic scatters covering areas of less than 15 by 15 metres and which have been proved to be very shallow and short-lived. These sites were less than 0.2 metres in depth and have only produced coarse ware ceramics with a notable absence of fine wares or exotic or luxury goods, and have been interpreted as peripatetic village sites (Coningham et al. 2007a). It is therefore clear that the Early Historic attempt to impose a category of town within the countryside quickly failed within Anuradhapura's hinterland and that the established monasteries were to assume greater social and economic roles by binding the city with its hinterland of small rural settlements but at the same time forming distinctive temporalities. This landscape of heterarchies suggests that not all attempts to apply the guidance of planning treatises, such as the *Arthashastra*, were unopposed or successful.

PUBLIC BUILDINGS

As noted previously, while some scholars have observed that "much less was spent on secular monumental architecture than was the case under imperial systems in other parts of the ancient world" (Thapar 2006b: 296), others have observed that there is evidence of a recognisable Mauryan core within a

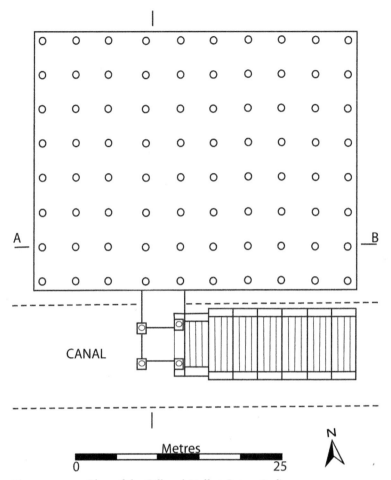

Figure 11.15. Plan of the Pillared Hall at Patna, India.

number of monumental structures, although they were religious rather than secular in nature (Allchin 1995a: 240). When considering metropolitan structures, the 'palace' at Kumrahar is the sole example of an imperial structure belonging to this period, and it is clear that the construction techniques and materials used in this structure were very different from the simpler brick-built merchant houses with their ranges of rooms set around a courtyard as encountered at Bhita or in the Bhir Mound. Located just beyond the southern wall of the city of Pataliputra, the palace was originally excavated between 1912 and 1914 and then again in 1959 (Spooner 1913; Altekar and Mishra 1959). These excavations suggested that the original building was rectangular in shape and that its roof was supported by eighty massive pillars arranged in ten rows running east to west and eight lines north to south (Figure 11.15 and Figure 11.16). Each pillar was highly polished and placed a distance of 4.3 metres apart. The palace was entered by a timber ramp to the south, which offered access to a 12.6 metre wide and three metre deep east to west canal and was presumed

ELEVATION FROM SOUTH

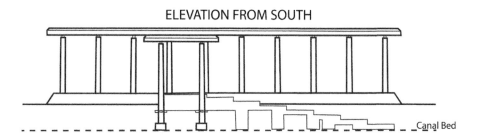

SECTION ON A-B

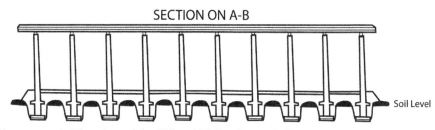

Figure 11.16. Elevation of the Pillared Hall at Patna, India.

to have joined the city moat. Although the stone pillars were all smashed and fragmented after the abandonment of the building, the complete pillars would have measured some 9.6 metres in length. They were set in individual foundation pits within substructures of timber and stone so that only 6.9 metres of the dressed pillar would have showed above the floor. It has been assumed that the roof was timber as the entire site was covered in charcoal from its burning and subsequent collapse in the second century BCE (Allchin 1995a: 238). When first exposed in 1913, its excavator declared that the entire Mauryan complex of Pataliputra was a "replica of Persepolis" (Spooner 1915: 69), although this interpretation was not generally adopted. This concept was, however, reanimated when Wheeler commented on Kumrahar's similarity to Achaemenid examples stating that "it is clear that we have in the main building a Persian *diwan* or *apadana* or audience-hall, and that we are dealing once more with a deliberate 'Persianization' that bespeaks the presence of imported ideas and doubtless of imported master-masons" (1968: 133). However, it is also clear that its construction was adapted to a localised environment with a high water table as the individual pillars were set on timber cradles and the entrance ramp on timber rafts (Allchin 1995a: 238). These deliberations aside, the identification and function of the structure remain uncertain and only further research will help us to identify whether it was an administrative centre, a waterside pleasure pavilion or a secular adjunct to the monastic complex to the south (Ghosh 1989: 335).

The second and more numerous category of Mauryan monuments comprises religious constructions and most of these have been attributed to the reign of the Emperor Asoka, although whether such an attribution is correct is questionable as we have little reference to the need to construct Buddhist monuments within the *Arthashastra*. Indeed, evidence for Asoka's patronage of these monuments comes largely from the travel itineraries compiled by the Chinese pilgrims Faxian and Xuanzang over half a millennium later or from the Pali texts of Sri Lanka in combination with the proximity of many of these constructions to Asokan pillars. There are distinct points at which these sources correspond with archaeological evidence but others where it is difficult to be so accepting, such as the pilgrims' assertion that Asoka personally constructed 84,000 *stupas* across his empire. Of these Mauryan monuments, most are *stupas* with a limited number of examples of associated *grihas* or shrines and *viharas* or monasteries. As noted previously, there was a distinctive Mauryan construction horizon across the northern half of the subcontinent with monumental *stupas* established at sites associated with the life of the Gautama *Buddha*, such as Vaisali or Sarnath (Allchin 1995a), as well as ones such as Sanchi in Central India (Marshall et al. 1940), at Gotihawa in the Nepali Terai (Verardi 2007), Taxila in the Taxila Valley (Marshall 1951) and Butkara in the Swat Valley in the north-west (Faccenna 1980). It is interesting to note that many of these structures were also associated with Asokan edicts (Falk 2006). These monuments were also distinctly extra-urban, as illustrated by the Dharmarajika *stupa* at Taxila which was established some three kilometres away from the Mauryan period settlement at the Bhir Mound. Possessing one of the better preserved *stupa* sequences in South Asia, John Marshall believed its core to be Mauryan and suggested that its original shape was a solid hemispherical dome of limestone blocks with a diameter of 14 metres with a height of some 10 metres, which was later encased within subsequent phases of enlargement (Marshall 1951). Only the brick-built Gotihawa *stupa* has been firmly chrono-metrically dated, and it has demonstrated a construction sequence that commenced in the middle of the third century BCE (Verardi 2007) (Figure 11.17). The construction details of Gotihawa's 19.5 metre diameter *stupa* provide an insight into Mauryan building technology, and its triangular and trapezoidal bricks appear to have been specially moulded (ibid.: 116). Moreover, the presence of multiple marks inscribed on bricks before firing have suggested to its excavator that "the marks on bricks denoted different workshops, which thus identified their production at the end of the firing in local, huge communal kilns, probably under imperial – although territorially compartmentalised – control." (ibid.: 117). Again, it is worth considering whether all the people involved in the construction of such monuments were coerced or whether, as with the construction of the city walls, their contributions also contributed to their self-identity and affiliations as well as allowing them to receive merit. It is also notable that not all the Mauryan Buddhist monuments commemorated the Gautama *Buddha* as illustrated by the Asokan pillar at Niglihawa in the Nepali Terai. This pillar recorded that fourteen years after Asoka's consecration,

Figure 11.17. *Stupa* of Gotihawa with Asokan pillar in foreground, Nepal.

he had the *stupa* of the Konagamana *Buddha* enlarged and that he personally worshipped at the site six years later (Deeg 2003: 45) (Box 11.3) (Figure 11.18). The Konagamana *Buddha* was the twenty-sixth *Buddha*, the Gautama *Buddha* the twenty-eighth, and Buddhist traditions hold that they will be superseded by the arrival of the final and future *Buddha*, Matitreya.

Providing roughly parallel evidence, a number of Buddhist *grihas* or shrines have been attributed to the Mauryan period, although most were dated through association with ceramics or inscriptions before the advent of scientific dating methods or even of contextual excavations. Two of these are at sites associated with the life of the *Buddha*; at Sarnath where the Gautama Siddhartha preached his first sermon following his enlightenment and at Lumbini in the Nepali Terai, where he was born. Not much is known of the stratigraphy of the former as it was excavated in the nineteenth century, but it appears to conform to an eastern facing apsidal shrine directly south of the central shrine and Asokan pillar. Allchin has suggested that it measured roughly 25 metres east to west and 15 metres north to south but little remains above its brick foundations (Allchin 1995a: 241). Falk has further suggested that there were at least two Asokan pillars within the monastic complex as well as a stone railing with a 'Mauryan' polish which he states "seems likewise to owe its existence to Asoka" (2006: 214). However, there is still debate as to whether the railing enclosed a pillar, a small *stupa*, a Bodhi tree or was a *harmika* erected above the drum of a large *stupa* (ibid.). In contrast, rather more is known of the Asokan shrine complex built around the birthplace of the *Buddha* at Lumbini, where

Box 11.3. Searching for Kapilavastu

The *Buddha*'s quest for enlightenment began with his *Mahabhinishkramana* or 'Great Departure', when he left through the eastern gate of the city of Kapilavastu and renounced his parents, wife, son and life as a prince of the Shakya lineage at the age of twenty-nine (Coningham 2001: 63). Whilst it was not one of the four major pilgrimage sites identified by the *Buddha* as he approached his *Mahaparinivana* or 'Great Passing Away', Kapilavastu was still greatly revered by Buddhists as the childhood home of the *Buddha* and was visited by the Chinese monks Faxian in circa 400 CE and Xuangzang in circa 630 CE, whose pilgrimages to the site were recorded in their travel itineraries. Although the archaeological pioneers like Alexander Cunningham rediscovered many of the sites associated with the *Buddha*'s life, such as Lumbini, Sarnath, Bodhgaya and Kusinagar, by retracing the steps of the Chinese pilgrims – the identity of the childhood home of the *Buddha* remains contested with two main contenders, Tilaurakot in Nepal and Piprahawa in India.

The potential locations of Kapilavastu were identified during the 1890s when, after a hiatus from Alexander Cunningham's unsuccessful endeavours in the Nepali Terai to identify sites associated with the natal landscape of the *Buddha*, new discoveries re-energised the search (Coningham et al. 2010). The first of these discoveries was the Niglihawa pillar, rediscovered by Anton Alois Fuhrer in 1895 and translated by Buhler in 1896. The Niglihawa pillar had a reference to the enlargement of the *stupa* of the Konagamana *Buddha*, and according to Xuanzang's record, Kapilavastu was situated close to the natal town of the Konagamana *Buddha* (Allen 2008: 127). Secondly, a further expedition to the Nepali Terai, undertaken by Dr Fuhrer and General Khadga Shumsher J. B. Rana, had uncovered another Asokan pillar next to the small shrine of Rummindei in 1897. Carved with an Asokan inscription identifying the site as Lumbini, the birthplace of the *Buddha*, the Chinese pilgrim itineraries suggested that Lumbini was to the east of Kapilavastu (Fuhrer 1897: 23). In addition to the evidence from the Niglihawa pillar, Fuhrer stated that "[t]he discovery of the Asokan Edict Pillar in the Lumbini Grove at Rummindei enabled me to fix also, with absolute certainty, the site of Kapilavastu and of the sanctuaries in its neighbourhood. Thanks to the exact notes left by the two Chinese travellers I discovered its extensive ruins about eight miles north-west of the Lumbini pillar, and six miles north-west of the Nigali Saga [the location of the Nigliva pillar]" (ibid.).

With the relative position of the ancient city seemingly secure, archaeological surveyor P. C. Mukherji of the Archaeological Survey of India was tasked with the continued investigation of Kapilavastu and identified it in 1899 at Tilaurakot, some 28 kilometres west of Lumbini (Mukherji 1901: 3–4). There, he mapped a fortified site within a hinterland of Buddhist monuments and undertook limited clearance of architectural features. Mukherji was convinced that Tilaurakot represented Kapilavastu asserting that "no other ancient site has so much claim ... as being situated in the right position and fulfilling all other conditions" (ibid.: 50). Such conditions were realised through similarities between textual descriptions of Kapilavastu, the Asokan inscriptions and his topographical and archaeological records at the site (Coningham et al. 2010). However, there were early doubts and criticisms to the claims that Tilaurakot was Kapilavastu. Not only were there discrepancies in terms of both the distances and directions of routes taken by Faxian and Xuanzang for their journeys from Sravasti to Kapilavastu (Coningham et al. 2010), but the discovery of an inscribed relic casket by William Peppe at Piprahawa added to the debate. This inscription read, "This shrine for the relics of the Buddha ... is that of the Sakyas, the brethren of the Distinguished One", suggesting that the site was also close to the location of Kapilavastu although being south-west of Lumbini across the Indian border (Allen 2002: 275). Attempts to harmonise these contradictions were attempted by a number of scholars, including Vincent Smith, who suggested that the two Chinese pilgrims had referred to different sites as there had been an interval of more than 200 years between their visits (Smith 1901: 10–12). Similarly, Rhys Davids suggested that "The old Kapilavastu was probably at Tilaura Kot. But Mr Peppe's important discoveries at the Sakiya Tope may be on the site of a new Kapilavastu, built after the old city was destroyed by Vijudabha" (1903: 18).

Since that time, Tilaurakot and Piprahawa have been subject to a series of archaeological investigations to confirm the cultural sequences of both sites. Debala Mitra, for example, excavated at the former across the northern rampart and, on the basis of the ceramic sequence, asserted that this area of the site was not occupied earlier than the third or second centuries BCE, well after the lifetime of the *Buddha* (Mitra 1972: 16). Further work was then undertaken by T. N. Mishra (1978) and B. K. Rijal (1979), and both these scholars pushed the earlier sequence of Tilaurakot back to the first half of the first millennium BCE on the basis of the recovery of Painted Grey Ware, therefore providing the evidence that the site was occupied during the lifetime of Gautama *Buddha*. However, these later excavations did not gain much attention in India whilst work at Piprahawa recommenced, directed by K. M. Srivastava of the Archaeological Survey of India (1996). He confirmed that the *stupa*

(continued)

of Piprahawa was built in multiple phases but also recovered a clay sealing dating to the first or second centuries CE with the legend "*Om Devaputra Viahre Kapilavastu Bhikkhu Sanghas*", which again pointed towards a link between Kapilavastu and Piprahawa (Srivastava 1986: 59). Furthermore, Srivastava's excavations at the adjacent mound of Ganwaria exposed a series of brick-built structures and a sequence that in its earliest phases was associated with Painted Grey Ware, convincing him of its identity as Kapilavastu (ibid.: 70).

None of these early excavations used scientific-dating measurements but in 1999 excavations were conducted at Tilaurakot in order to develop an absolute chronology for the site (Coningham et al. 2010). In addition to finds of Painted Grey Ware and Cord Impressed Ware, radiocarbon determinations from *in situ* occupation horizons in the sequence dated to the early fifth century BCE, whilst recalibrated radiocarbon determinations from redeposited material provided a date-range between circa 550 BCE and the beginning of the first millennium BCE (Coningham et al. 2010). These dates demonstrated Tilaurakot's antiquity and, in combination with a number of other factors, suggest that Tilaurakot is the more likely candidate for ancient Kapilavastu. For example, there are no other major Early Historic urban sites in the vicinity of Lumbini (Allchin 1995a), and the published evidence from Ganwaria does not suggest a city of the size and complexity of Tilaurakot. Indeed, excavations at Tilaurakot in 2013 demonstrated that the fortification sequence investigated by Mitra was far deeper than hitherto anticipated, as evidence of a timber palisade was exposed at the very base of the 3.5 metre sequence. Furthermore, the presence of seals and inscriptions at Piprahawa does not refute this identification as it is likely that the Kingdom of Kapilavastu would have had many monasteries within its territory and that they would have used seals marked with such an affinity, and of course the two sites are only divided by a modern geopolitical boundary not an ancient one (Coningham et al. 2010). However, although an important concern, the identification of Kapilavastu alone does not further archaeological enquiry into the Early Historic Period. Evidence from recent excavations at Tilaurakot and Lumbini as well as freshly initiated work at Piprahawa by the Archaeological Survey of India, in combination with published reports from the region such as Gotihawa (Verardi 2007), are only now beginning to provide the basis for furthering understandings of the shared material culture of the natal landscape of Buddhism and the sociocultural environments which resulted in its adoption and spread.

Figure 11.18. The Asokan edict at Niglihawa, Nepal.

existing structures of brick and timber dating back to the sixth century BCE were encased within a network of walls defining an area of 26 metres north to south by 21 metres east to west (Figure 11.19). Entered from the east, a central chamber was constructed in which was placed a white conglomerate that has been recognised as a key sacred marker. Although little survives above the wall foundations, recent excavations have provided evidence of ceramic tiles and plaster. These new findings suggest that, with the exception of its geographical centre, the shrine was roofed and its walls plastered and painted white. It must have offered a significant contrast to the thatch-roofed buildings in the village and the adjacent monasteries (Coningham et al. 2013). Recent chronometric dating indicates that these later activities occurred between 400 and 200 BCE. Immediately outside the shrine to the west, an Asokan pillar was erected, and although part of the bell has been preserved, there is no sign of its capital figure (Figure 11.20).

To the south, a further two Mauryan shrines have been identified at Sanchi in Central India and Bairat in Jaipur. Whilst the stone-built *griha* at Sanchi was apsidal and opened to the north on an alignment with the great *stupa* and Asokan pillar (Allchin 1995a: 242), the example at Bairat was circular (Sahni 1937). Also associated with an Asokan rock edict and fragments of at least one polished pillar, Bairat appears to have consisted of a small circular brick *stupa* enclosed within a circular brick shrine with a diameter of 10.6 metres. Roofed with ceramic tiles, a circumambulatory path was created by an inner colonnade formed by timber octagonal pillars (Piggott 1943)

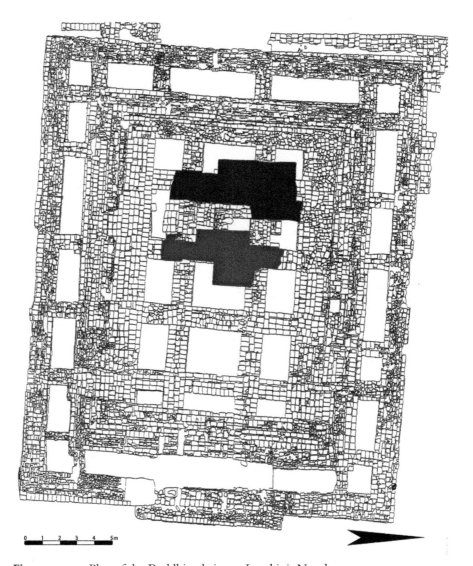

Figure 11.19. Plan of the Buddhist shrine at Lumbini, Nepal.

(Figure 11.21). Whilst some writers have suggested that Asoka was a convert to Buddhism (Falk 2006: 55), a number of his edicts indicate that he was accepting of many sects and traditions and that Buddhism was far from being a state religion sponsored by the Mauryans, as indicated by the rock-cut *grihas* in the Barabar and Nagarjuni hills. With walls smoothed to a Mauryan polish, they were dedicated to the Ajivika sect (Allchin 1995a: 247), indicating support for another heterodoxical sect. It is also clear that rulers were not the only patrons with resources to donate as indicated by the Jivakarama *vihara* at Rajgir, as well as by the fact that of the 1,345 contemporary caves with Early Brahmi inscriptions in Sri Lanka, less than 7 percent of patrons were royal (Coningham 1995b: 230). This is not to suggest, however, that Asoka did

Figure 11.20. The Asokan pillar at Lumbini, Nepal.

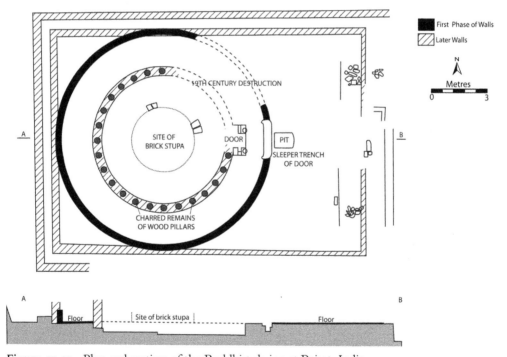

Figure 11.21. Plan and section of the Buddhist shrine at Bairat, India.

not intervene with the ritual practices of contemporary communities and attempt to realign their practices, as demonstrated by his First Major Rock Edict which forbade animal sacrifice and the holding of festivals at particular localities (Thapar 1961: 250).

SCRIPT, BOULDERS AND PILLARS

As noted in Chapter 10, there was already clear evidence for the development of Early Brahmi script at Anuradhapura in the fourth century BCE, although it seemed to have been associated with trade, exchange and individual ownership rather than with imperial records and proclamations which only later appeared in association with the Mauryan Empire (Coningham et al. 1996). As also noted earlier, the pillar and rock edicts of Devanampiya have all been attributed to the Emperor Asoka and comprise "some three dozen unique Asokan texts … at approximately fifty sites" across India, Pakistan, Nepal and Afghanistan, although "most or all of the fourteen rock edicts are found together in several locales" (Sinopoli 2001: 157). Since that time, additional examples have been identified and Falk has prepared an inventory of all fifty-four sites, subdivided them into seventeen examples of the Minor Rock Edicts, with separate edicts adjacent to two of those sites, nine Rock Edict sites, nineteen pillar sites, pillar quarry sites at Chunar and Pabhosa, seven Greek and Aramaic edict sites and three cave sites (2006). Most scholars agree that the pillars were quarried and distributed from the single site of Chunar on the Ganga (Jayaswal 1998) and have only been found within the modern states of Nepal and India. Falk, however, has suggested that Pabhosa, five kilometres west of Kausambi may be a better candidate (2006: 157). Whichever quarry was the source, the pillars were finished with a 'Mauryan polish' and they all appear to have been crowned with animal capitals.

Single lion capitals survive at Vaisali, Rampura and Lauriya Nandangarh with only the lower portion of the animal surviving at Bansi. Some 300 metres away from the pillar with the lion capital at Rampura was a further pillar with a bull capital, and the pillar at Sankissa was crowned with an elephant capital. The famous four lion capital at Sarnath was surmounted by a wheel and stood above a carved abacus depicting the four noble, or cardinal, beasts – the lion, the elephant, the horse and the bull (Allchin 1995a: 252) (Figure 11.22). We are uncertain whether such animals were depicted to create an *axis mundi* or microcosm but it does suggest the adoption of a shared concept of cosmography across South Asia. A similar capital with four lions was recorded at Sanchi but its abacus was decorated with birds. Certainly, other animals are attested such as Faxian's description of a horse capital, since lost, on the Lumbini pillar, and we can add the fine elephant carved on the rock face near the Dhauli edict and the elephant engraved on the rock at Kalsi. The bases of the pillars vary and when Verardi exposed the base of the Gotihawa pillar, he encountered a 0.26 metre thick sandstone saddle stone measuring 2.12 by 1.76 metres marked with a central circle indicating the location for the pillar and a hill-and-crescent graffito on the south-east corner (Verardi 2007: 112). It is notable that a similar sign has been found on the base of the Asokan pillar at Kumrahar, on the 62.2 centimetre long copper

Figure 11.22. Asoka capital at Sarnath, India.

dowel connecting the Rampura pillar with its capital, as well as on Mauryan punch-marked coins (Verardi 2007: 113), reinforcing the concept of the presence of a centralised production system. In contrast, the rock edicts were far more natural, comprising inscriptions on the polished faces of outcrops or large boulders beside major route ways, as at Shahbazgarhi and Mansehra, or at Kalsi where routes run up into the Himalayas from the Yamuna.

The inscriptions of Asoka are the earliest primary written sources relating to the history of the Mauryan Empire. Engraved between the eighth and twenty-seventh years of his reign, they documented both his personal path after the Mauryan annexation of Kalinga as well as his attempts to spread his *dhamma* or 'righteous rule' through his kingdom and beyond. It is also clear that the individual locations and edicts appear to have played varying roles, rather than just representing propaganda near subdued cities or marker stones at the edges of the empire. For example, his pillar at Lumbini is of polished Chunar sandstone, weighing 37 tons and was 9.45 metres long, of which 4.11 metres was unpolished and acted as a foundation (Bidari 2004: 63). Its early Brahmi inscription recorded the personal visit of the Emperor to the site: *"By King Piyadasi, the beloved of the gods (who) having been consecrated*

Figure 11.23. The Asokan edict at Taxila, Pakistan.

twenty years (having) come himself personally (here) to offer homage, or celebrate, because Shakyamuni Buddha was born here, was caused both a Silavigadabhica to be built and a stone pillar to be set up. (And), because the Lord was born here, the Lumbini village was made free from taxes and liable to pay (only) one-eighth part (of the produce)" (JBF 2001: 75). It is interesting to note that Asoka had already been active within the Terai six years earlier and had the *stupa* of the Konagamana *Buddha* enlarged in the fourteenth year of his reign, but this may have been enacted by decree rather than in person as recorded at Lumbini.

Other edicts were located within Buddhist monastic complexes, as at Sanchi and Sarnath, and both included the so-called Schism Edict which advocated the expulsion of dissenters from Buddhist communities so that unity and order could prevail (Tieken 2000). This indicates that such monastic complexes may have earlier formed their own heterarchies but now they were beginning to be linked into the authority structures and hierarchies of the Empire itself. Others were located close to cities and towns, such as the ones at Sisupalgarh, Kandahar, Brahmagiri and Taxila (Figure 11.23), whilst others were placed close to trade routes, such as those inscribed on boulders at Shahbazgarhi, Mansehra and Girnar or ports like Sopara. As noted earlier, any attempts to analyse the expansion of imperial authority as reflected by regnal year has been unsuccessful, as illustrated by those edicts known from Afghanistan where one in the Laghman valley near Jalalabad was dated to the tenth year of Asoka's rule, and another close to the confluence with Kabul River to his sixteenth. It is also interesting to note that different scribes appear to have been used for the carving of the inscriptions as Falk has recognised at least three different styles within the close grouping of the rock edicts at Brahmagiri, Siddapur and Jatinga-Ramesvaram (Falk 2006: 66). Other edicts recorded the digging of wells and the planting of trees along thoroughfares as in the Second Major Rock Edict, and the prevention of the killing of animals as in the First Major Rock Edict. These unique records provide all the information that we have of the character of the emperor, as his image has not survived and the earliest known portrait dates from between the first and third centuries CE, centuries after his death (Poonacha 2007).

SOURCING, MANUFACTURING AND REDISTRIBUTION

As noted previously in the description of more fully excavated towns and cities within South Asia, the first formal evidence for the presence of shops was uncovered during this Era of the Early Historic Tradition. For example, whilst the sites of Bhita and the Bhir Mound had very different town plans and were located in very different parts of the Mauryan Empire, both were provided with small, individual cells or units facing the streets, with evidence of manufacturing and redistribution. Certainly the analysis of patterns of craft-working residues at the Bhir Mound have suggested that craft activities were associated with such units, but also that there was no overall segmented distribution of such manufacturing, as metal working has been identified in Loci A, O and G, shell working in D, and textile processing in N, with clay sealings scattered throughout (Coningham 1995b: 234). Such a mercantile function also corroborates Erdosy's assumption that higher order settlements with craft activities were present within the Mauryan period in core regions (Erdosy 1988: 69). Certainly the newly established city of Ujjain appears to have conformed to such a model with the report of the presence of a house close to the gate containing evidence of unfinished agate beads as well as partially completed bone objects (IAR 1957: 27). Similar evidence of the economic role of such major settlements is suggested by the evidence from Anuradhapura, where most of the city's inhabitants appear to have engaged in the procurement of semi-precious stone rough blanks, often from overseas, as with the rough blanks of carnelian from western India, and then engaged in a process of manufacturing finished objects (Coningham et al. 2006: 413). This is of significance as it appears that the inhabitants of each area of the city were involved in similar craft activities rather than following a more centralised pattern of manufacturing, and that even the royal quarters appear to provide a similar pattern. This suggests that

Figure 11.24. Detail of Rouletted Ware from Anuradhapura, Sri Lanka.

whilst there might have been specialists attached to palaces or monasteries, the private sector was also highly active.

Indeed, the presence of long-distance trade networks has been well attested through the analyses of Lahiri (1992), Chakrabarti (2005) and others, and it has long been recognised that a number of the Asokan pillars and boulder edicts lay on key routes within South Asia. However, whilst Asoka referred to his provision of trees and wells along roads in the text of his Second Major Rock Edict (Thapar 1961: 251), little archaeological evidence of major infrastructure has been found beyond the religious buildings and cities, with the exception of the timber wharf on the banks of the River Krishna at Dharanikota (IAR 1962–1963: 1–2), the record of the construction of an irrigation tank in the vicinity of Asoka's rock edict at Girnar in Gujarat (Mehta 1969) and potentially a timber jetty at Kaveripattinam in Tamil Nadu (Smith 2006a: 121). However, these regional routes must have been sufficiently passable for the movement of the pillars weighing as much as 40 tons from Chunar. Most of the major cities are located near river systems, indicating that their location allowed them to benefit from the movement of heavier materials more cheaply, as well as offering them connectivity and control over key trade routes. It is also important to recognise that these networks extended far beyond South Asia itself as illustrated by the broad distribution of a slightly later ceramic type known as Rouletted Ware, which has been described as "a dish ... with an incurved and beaked rim. The ware has a remarkabl[y] smooth surface, is thin, brittle and well burnt, and has a metallic ring. The flat interior is normally decorated

Figure 11.25. View across Khor Rori towards the natural harbour, Oman.

with two, occasionally three, concentric bands of rouletted pattern" (Wheeler et al. 1946: 46) (Figure 11.24). Dated from the beginning of the third century BCE and emerging from the southern regions and islands beyond Mauryan authority, sherds have been recovered from Bangladesh, the southern half of Peninsular India, Sri Lanka and the Maldives, as well as far east as Bali and as far west as Berenike on the Red Sea (Coningham et al 2006: 133). They have also been recently reported from excavations at the site of Khor Rori in Oman, a fortified port developed close to the source of frankincense (Avanzini 2008: 14) (Figure 11.25). Finally, much of the literature related to the Early Historic period acknowledged the increasing influence of traders and merchants, and this was reflected in the epigraphic records that indicate that guilds and individual goldsmiths, potters and weavers were able to patronise Buddhist monks and even provide them with residences in Sri Lanka (Paranavitana 1970). The presence of an Asokan edict close to the port sites of Sopara near the mouth of the Vaitarna River in Maharashtra and NBPW deposits at key sites like Bharuch in Gujarat and Tamluk in Bengal further indicate the importance of trade within the Bay of Bengal and Arabian Sea, although few complete excavation reports have been published.

As might be expected, it is clear that both the *Arthashastra* of Kautilya and the *Astadhyayi* of Panini made reference to the presence of a system of standardised weights and measures during the Early Historic period, although both texts were finally compiled rather later than the Mauryan period (Allchin

1995a: 217). For example, the *Astadhyayi* referred to a *pramana*, or a measure
of length, and equated the *anguli* as the length of eight grains of barley and
the *sama* as representing a length of 14 *angulas* (Agrawala 1953: 255), whilst
longer measurements in the *Arthashastra* appear to have made reference to
the numbers of rod and bow lengths. Similarly based on available reference
material, weights were calculated in relationship to the seed of the ratti or
Abrus precatorius and the sources referred to a weight of one *masha* equating
to five ratti seeds and one *sana* to 100 seeds, and both terms referred to the
names of coins (Agrawala 1953: 252). The presence of such standards, the wide
availability of coinage and the ability of elements of literate society to record,
allowed the newly emergent state to ensure that taxes were recovered, and
Kautilya's *Arthashastra* dedicated an entire section to the Treasury, sources of
revenue, budget, accounts and audit with the very clear mission statement that
"Just as one plucks fruits from a garden as they ripen, so shall a King have the
revenue collected as it becomes due" and that "from wealth comes the power
of the government" (Rangarajan 1992: 253–254). Tax must have been both
widely accepted and understood, and the Asokan pillar at Lumbini specifically
records that the shrine's adjacent village was freed from part of this burden in
recognition of its proximity to the birthplace of the *Buddha* himself. Although
beyond the Mauryan Empire, the unique set of early Brahmi inscriptions from
Sri Lanka have assisted our understanding the nature of economic tenure and
mobility at a period contemporary with Asoka and his successors. Thus private donations to the Buddhist order were found from a Tamil ship captain,
mariners, a *Parakaradeka*, or superintendent of roads, as well as donations of
shares of privately owned irrigation reservoirs and channels, pasturage, income
from villages and even the revenues from a ferry (Paranavitana 1970: xcix-ci).
However, whether this evidence allows us to accept Thapar's early hypothesis
that "[i]ncreased centralisation under the Mauryas, more particular during the
reign of Asoka, meant an increased control of the state over the economy"
(1961: 68) remains uncertain with only the spread of uniform artefacts categories and Gotihawa's incised bricks as partial evidence.

CONCLUSIONS

As noted earlier, ever since the decipherment of South Asia's early Brahmi
pillar and rock edicts and the discovery of the linkage between the ruler
named Devanampiya Tissa and Asoka, the Mauryan Emperor, there has been
an anticipation that "the geographical extent of the empire during the reign of
Asoka can fortunately be indicated fairly precisely" and that the "distribution
of his rock and pillar edicts is unchallenged evidence of his authority" (Thapar
1961: 123). Although this was not a universally held conclusion with Gordon
stating that "[t]he Rock Edicts were frontier notice boards pushed far beyond
the bounds of normal effective government control" (1960: 185), Thapar's

concept has been reiterated by archaeologists and historians from South Asia and beyond. Even recent textbooks have chosen to restate that "[t]he distribution of Asoka's inscriptions suggests the extent of the Mauryan Empire, it extended up to Kandahar in Afghanistan, with the kingdom of Antiochus II of Syria lying to the west. Its eastern frontier extended to Orissa. It included almost the entire subcontinent, except the southernmost parts" (Singh 2008: 333). However, there are issues with a number of the key sources recording the Mauryan world as exemplified by the work of Thomas Trautmann, who undertook a statistical analysis of the *Arthashastra* and concluded that it had not been written by a single author but that it comprised sections from a number of sources and authors. Stating that parts included those of "previous teachers whose works, in condensed form perhaps were bound into a single work by a compiler who divided the work into chapters, added the terminal verses, composed the first and last chapters", Trautmann concluded that "[w]e can say with confidence that Kautilya cannot have been the author of the Arthashastra as a whole" (1971: 174–175). Attributed by Trautmann to a date of the second century CE (1971: 177), Basham commented in Trautmann's preface that "[t]o a historian the results may appear at first destructive. But the edifice which successive generations of Indian historians have built rests on very shaky foundations" (Basham 1971: xi). The records and descriptions of Megasthenes may be subject to similar questioning and may be dismissed as primary sources. Indeed, they are partial records which have survived in a fragmentary form through the Roman compilations many centuries later, such as that of Arrian in the third century CE (Kalota 1978). Similarly, whilst there are clear correspondences between the *Mahavamsa* and *Dipavamsa* and some parts of the archaeological and architectural records of Sri Lanka, there are also a number of distinct divergences (Coningham 1995b; Coningham and Lewer 2000).

With the textual sources for the presence of a strong uniform imperial authority weakened, it is necessary to revisit some of the evidence discussed earlier to reconsider the nature and consistency of the integration and hegemony of the Mauryan Empire on the basis of the archaeological data. Indeed, such a review demonstrates that there was huge variability in many aspects of life and activity within the urban-focused Era of the Early Historic Tradition of South Asia. Whether one considers the very different urban forms across South Asia or the haphazard nature of the streets of the Bhir Mound, only a handful of sites like Sisupalgarh and Bhita have indicated a clear pre-planned nature. Moreover, the attribution of individual designs on punch-marked coins with specific Mauryan rulers is by no means certain, and the distribution of the number of specific artefacts thought to have Mauryan affinities are by no means indicative of ancient boundaries or borders due to the very active trade networks of the time. Similarly, if one considers the orientation and material utilised to construct the various Buddhist monuments associated with the Emperor Asoka, there is similar disparity. At Lumbini, the brick shrine or *griha* was rectangular and opened to the east whilst the stone shrine at Sanchi opened to the north and was apsidal; the brick temple at Sarnath was apsidal and opened to the east and whilst the brick and timber built shrine at Bairat opened to the east, it was circular. In parallel, the Dharmarajika *Stupa* at Taxila was built of stone blocks but that of Gotihawa of bricks, further emphasising the very distinct individual nature of this long-established category of imperial monuments. Whilst it is tempting to compare the nature of the archaeological evidence against well-worn definitions of the material character of empires, it is clear that the cohesiveness of the very category empire has already been more broadly questioned (Alcock et al. 2001). Indeed, there is an increasing corpus of scholarship which has questioned the solidity of the Mauryan Empire, and a growing number of researchers would now agree with Smith's caution that the Asokan edicts may have "represented an area of maximum contact rather than streamlined bureaucratic control" (2001: 17).

Smith's additional provocative suggestion that "it is also possible that local leaders borrowed the concept of inscriptions as a means of emulation and sponsored the emplacement of such texts" (ibid.) remains a source of stimulus and debate; it still indicates the wider willingness to reinvestigate the nature of Mauryan power and authority. This reinvestigation had already been started by Thapar herself, who noted that Mauryan "[h]egemony was extended over a range of differentiated systems – hunter-gatherers, chiefships, a variety of peasant tenures and exchange relationships extending from barter to nascent market systems. ... Despite its size and administrative control, the Mauryan state does not appear to have attempted a restricting of all the areas under its control" (1985: 159–160). Fussman followed this by observing that the Mauryan Empire was far too large to have been fully centralised but was instead organised as a series of linked semi-independent units, a number of which reflected the pre-Mauryan *Mahajanapadas* (1988). Such an approach, Fussman argued, explained the regional character of the empire and the presence of different scripts and languages within different portions of the empire. Romila Thapar again returned to the study of Asokan edicts and noted the presence of three distinct "areas of isolation" within the empire – in the lower Indus plain, the eastern part of Central India, and the far south, but commented that, elsewhere, the Mauryans established routes between emerging centres of exchange (Thapar 1996: 287). Thapar also drew attention to the notable absence of "northern artefacts" in central Karnataka despite the "heavy cluster of inscriptions in the area", further commenting that such phenomena "requires us to view the possible divergences in the relations between the Mauryan administration and the local people of a region" (ibid.: 288). Revising her earlier models, Thapar has now suggested that the empire comprised relationships of control between three very different spheres, the metropolitan state, the core areas of previously established *Janapadas* and *Mahajanapadas* and, finally, the peripheral regions of

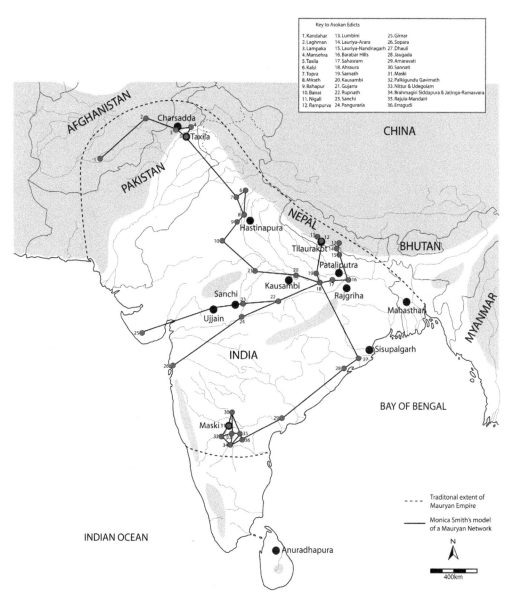

Figure 11.26. Alternative map of the Mauryan Empire (after Smith 2008).

"lineage-based societies" which "would be relatively liberated from the control of the metropolitan state" (ibid.: 318).

This refreshed and differentiated model, first developed by Thapar (1987), has been further developed by Monica Smith who has argued that, in addition to being located along trade routes as at Shahbazgarhi, at sites of religious significance as at Lumbini or close to settlements beyond traditional influence as at Brahmagiri and Kandahar, the edicts also broadcasted a set of imperial values in an attempt to "Mauryanise" local populations (Smith 2005) (Figure 11.26). Rather than utilising a standardised imperial language as in the

Figure 11.27. Pillars at Persepolis, Iran.

Persian or Hellenistic Empires, they were written in Greek, Aramaic and local Prakrits and reflected and respected the empire's distinct regional traditions. However, they equally projected an overarching *dhamma*, or philosophy, and exerted a 'Mauryanisation' effect by drawing or integrating local communities into networks of shared social, cultural and ritual relationships. Such an observation also has parallels with Falk's hypothesis that Asoka's Minor Rock Edicts were placed at locations of local cults and gatherings in an attempt to "oppose folk-religion" (2006: 57). Such models are close to the model advocated by Stanley Tambiah with his concept of the 'galactic polity' (1976). Although based on later Mediaeval Thai polities, Tambiah recognised the presence of a concentric ring or centre-periphery model in which the capital and arena of direct control was surrounded by a circle of provinces ruled by centrally appointed governors and princes with an outermost ring of "more or less independent 'tributary' polities" (1976: 112). Moreover, Tambiah predicted a highly fluid relationship between these units suggesting that "we have before us a galactic picture of a central planet surrounded by differentiated satellites, which are more or less 'autonomous' entities held in orbit and within the sphere of influence of the centre. Now if we introduce at the margin other similar competing central principalities and their satellites, we shall be able to appreciate the logic of a system that is a hierarchy of central points continually subject to the dynamics of pulsation and changing spheres of influence" (ibid.: 113). Such a constellation is directly linkable to the concept of Peer Polity Interaction (Renfrew and Cherry 1986) as we shall discuss in the final chapter.

Figure 11.28. The Asokan pillar at Lauriya-Nandangarh (courtesy Marshall Archive, Oriental Museum, Durham University DUROM.1957.1.3268).

In the light of this refreshed model of differentiated authority, it is also timely to revisit some of the models which have relied heavily on the concept of direct cultural loans from the Achaemenid Empire (Figure 11.27 and Figure 11.28). Such models have focused on the plan of the pillared hall at Pataliputra and the decorative character of the Asokan pillars. Features which caused the art historian Benjamin Rowland to observe that "the idea of such memorial columns is, of course, not Indian, but is yet another derivation from the civilisations of ancient Mesopotamia" (1953: 43) and that the pillared hall "corresponded very closely to the...Achaemenid palace ruins at Persepolis" (ibid.: 41). Whilst the Rowland and Wheeler models of the Achaemenid empire as the model for the pillared halls of Kumrahar were persuasive, not all scholars accepted it and Kosambi commented that it could not be taken literally as "it was built over 2000 miles way before 500 BC and had been burned down in 330 BC" (1956: 160). Falk has also noted that Asokan pillars were monolithic whilst Persian ones were composite (2006: 139); moreover, reference should be made to the fact that the foundation construction at Kumrahar was quite unlike any Persian *Apadana* and was clearly designed to cope with the extremely uneven and soft ground in the vicinity of the Ganga at Pataliputra. An additional point is that all of the inscribed Asokan pillars are single monoliths not grouped together in structural complexes as in the Persian world. South Asia also has had a long association with pillars representing the *axis mundi*, with some scholars suggesting that a number of the Asokan pillars were in fact pre-Asokan (Irwin 1973), although not all agree. Indeed, we cannot doubt that the timber pillar was an integral part of the architectural technology available to the Early Historic builders at the Bala Hisar of Charsadda, the Bhir Mound at Taxila and as far south as the city of Anuradhapura in Sri Lanka (Coningham 1999). The translation of established tradition of timber prototypes into stone experiments has also long been recognised within a number of Mauryan examples, such as the rock-carved Lomas Rishi cave (Brown 1956: 11; Kosambi 1956: 160). As such, it is perfectly plausible that the lone pillar as a concept originated in South Asia.

Reference to Tambiah's galactic polity projects the presence of a central core within the Ganga heartlands and secured with the development of a hinterland of towns, enhancing mercantile and tax collecting activities as at Bhita. Within the surrounding ring or band of more distant provinces, authority was established in different ways and acknowledged different languages and traditions but, as the example of Sisupalgarh and Kalinga demonstrated, some impositions of this authority were contested and brutal. Finally, the outermost ring was always likely to have been in flux but these two outermost rings or bands could be assimilated or influenced through the spread of a non-chauvinistic imperial *dhamma*, which was not restricted to a particular tradition or caste. This was accompanied by the sending out of Buddhist missionaries as recorded in the *Mahavamsa,* with the journeys of Mahinda and Sanghamitta to King Tissa of Anuradhapura as well as the travels of the missionaries Majjhima and Kassapagotta, teachers of the Himalayan region (Willis 2000: 75). This dissemination was following a policy noted by Asoka himself, when he stated "this inscription ... has been engraved so that any sons or great grandsons that I may have should not think of gaining new conquests. ... [T]hey should only consider conquest by *dharma*". The impact of such a conquest is clear from the epigraphic records of Sri Lanka where King Tissa referred to himself as Devanampiya Tissa in his own inscriptions (Paranavitana 1970: li) and where coinage with a tree and railing, perhaps to commemorate the arrival of the Bodhi tree, was issued. A number of anthropological studies have recognised the role played by Buddhist monks in steadily 'domesticating' or integrating peripheral regions within modern states (Taylor 1993), and one might anticipate a similar process occurring across South Asia as a whole and at the peripheries of imperial control in particular. Similarly, archaeological studies have also documented the processes by which Buddhism became embedded in regions beyond those visited by the *Buddha* himself, such as central India and Sri Lanka, frequently facilitated by the introduction of Buddhist missionaries and Buddhist relics (Coningham 1995b; Hawkes 2009). One might even consider parallels with promotion of Buddhism to Dalit communities during the campaigns of Dr B. R. Ambedkar in India in the 1950s. Finally, we should note the Mauryan building campaign in the Nepali Terai, where we have clear evidence of sacred sites associated with the historical and other *Buddhas* being personally visited by Asoka, and existing structures enshrined within larger imperial monuments as the local cults became transformed into imperial vehicles, offering the empire both legitimacy and a highly transferable mission (Coningham et al. 2013).

PART FOUR

CONCLUSIONS

CHAPTER 12

CONCLUSIONS AND CHALLENGES

INTRODUCTION

In this final chapter, we return to some of the challenges that we raised in the introduction. Perhaps the most important of these is that of the balance between models of indigenous development and those that rely on the diffusion of ideas and innovations from outside the region. Closely linked to this theme is the long-standing narrative of the presence of a major transformation and discontinuity between the two major archaeological urban-focused traditions of South Asia. Our review and analysis have clearly demonstrated the presence of continuity within the long-term developmental sequences of both the Indus Valley and Early Historic Traditions. Moreover, we have demonstrated that both were fundamentally and clearly differentiated from those of their close contemporaries to the west. In relation to the Indus Valley Tradition, these differences ranged from motifs used on ceramics, such as the Kot Dijian horned bull, to the very basis of its subsistence – cattle – a trait dating back to the initial aceramic levels at Mehrgarh. In the case of the Early Historic Tradition, we have witnessed the influence and adoption of monumental sculpture in the form of the Mauryan pillars of Asoka, but the messages carried were quite different from those of earlier and contemporary Achaemenid rulers. Moreover, we also have instances of continuity through both Traditions, as with the weight system or the focus on cattle, forming both an iconic image in the former tradition and representing a unit of value through the beginnings of the latter.

Alongside these distinctive elements of the two South Asian urban-focused eras, we have also acknowledged the importance and pervasive nature of the networks of long-distance trade and exchange across the Indo-Iranian plateau and Hindu Kush mountain range, and the presence and characterisation of 'exotic' elements, which linked the Indus Valley Tradition and the early phases of the Early Historic Tradition with those contemporary urban-focused and state-level developments to the west. Similarly, we cannot ignore the impulses and impacts of such networks on the connected communities within the

Arabian Sea littoral. Such elements may be assumed to have played important roles in assisting the internal integration and restructuring of many differentiated regional communities within South Asia as understood through concepts of emulation, competition and entrainment associated with Peer Polity Interaction (Renfrew and Cherry 1986) as well as core and periphery or World Systems (Algaze 2005). In the former, Colin Renfrew specifically identified that prior to the achievement of full social and economic integration, a number of regions which later became integrated had frequently hosted a series of "autonomous political centres" (1986: 1). This cluster of centres, called 'Early State Modules' (ESMs), usually shared "similar political institutions, a common system of weights and measures, the same system of writing (if any), essentially the same structure of religious beliefs ... the same spoken language, and ... the same 'culture'" (ibid.: 2). Moreover, as also indicated in Chapter 1, these centres were integrated and drawn closer to each other through a process of Peer Polity Interaction which operated through "competition (including warfare), and competitive emulation; symbolic entrainment, and the transmission of innovation; increased flow in the exchange of goods" (ibid.: 8). Aware of the value of innovations, imports and exports, this model states that "strong interactions between the autonomous socio-political units within the region are of greater significance than external links with other areas" (ibid.: 7). More than just a model, Bruce Trigger has noted a number of these characteristics through a comparative study, stating that "[b]ecause of their proximity and economic interdependence, city-states also tended to be culturally interdependent and to share religious beliefs, artistic conventions, and symbolism, especially as these related to upper-class culture" (2003: 101). Norman Yoffee has also commented on the importance of the internal dynamics and restructuring at play within each of these emergent city-states, alluding to the "new arenas of competition that are "invented" in city-states" (1997: 261). When faced with these lists and the scenario modelling, it is striking how effectively it is possible to project that model of competing and emulating ESMs across both Eras of Regionalisation within South Asia, and map the shared nature of these developments with reference to the presence of pre-planned settlements, ceremonial mud-brick platforms, Early Historic *Mahajanapadas* and the emergence of a shared repertoire of ceramic wares, motifs and forms. A good example of this shared taste in deluxe tableware is demonstrated by the spread of Northern Black Polished Ware in the Early Historic Tradition. Its adoption not only traces the movement of the vessels themselves but also the accompanying changes and transformations in eating habits and traditions.

While South Asia was largely situated beyond the direct political hegemony of its powerful and actively colonising neighbours to the west, we have also charted within this volume the processess by which core loan elements were introduced and, having been adopted, provided these ESMs with the fundamental mechanisms for integration and innovation. Intensifying the development of shared traits, or 'structural homologies', we may further draw on Renfrew's prediction that this process of integration drew individual developments together through processes of competition, symbolic entrainment, the transition of innovation and the increased exchange of goods – including warfare (Renfrew 1986: 8). Again, this process may be mapped across both Eras of Regionalisation and our detailed understanding is only limited by the quality of the archaeological data available. However, hints are there within the archaeological record in the burnt levels at Kot Diji, Amri and Gumla, and within Asoka's famous Kalinga edicts, and within the advice to rulers within the pages of Kautilya's *Arthashastra*. These fragments of evidence suggest that occasionally one or two of the increasingly integrated city-states were able to propel themselves into the role of what Bruce Trigger has called a "hegemonic city-state" (Trigger 2003: 113). Guillermo Algaze's model of the dynamic peripheries may also be cited, particularly with reference to the processes which occurred in the peripheries both before and after the failing of the largely asymmetric exchanges between population rich alluvium and resource rich periphery (2005: 143). It is probably better to exchange Algaze's own term of 'periphery' for that of 'littoral' or 'borderland' as being less theoretically charged and thus articulate with Renfrew and Cherry's own concept of dynamic endogenous transformations (1986). We may suggest that these processes were undoubtedly replicated in microcosm across the regions adjoining each of the steadily agglomerating and differentiating centres of population during each Era of Regionalisation and Integration.

Equally importantly, we have stressed that the apparent uniformity of the urban character of each of the Eras of Integration has been powerfully overstated by generations of academics and archaeologists, and that the continued survival of regional identities and narratives were very important characteristics of the populations of both the Indus Valley and Early Historic Traditions, although this may too reflect contemporary Provincial State agendas (Parasher-Sen 2008). Indeed, the inhabitants of individual regions later reasserted their cultural heritage following the broader dissolution of the integrated urban-focused communities and their urbanised cores, in the case of the Indus Valley Tradition, and reasserted themselves following the failure of the Mauryan dynasty in the Early Historic Tradition. We have also demonstrated that the apparent hiatus between the Indus Valley and Early Historic Traditions was largely the creation of archaeologists and scholars unable or unwilling to confront established models and accept evidence that did not fit neatly into the category of 'Civilisation'. This hiatus is demonstrably the legacy of colonial and post-colonial archaeologists and historians, such as Mortimer Wheeler (1959), D. H. Gordon (1960), N. R. Banerjee (1960), A. H. Dani (1971) and D. D. Kosambi (1956), who embraced the concept of a discontinuity to explain the period between the two urban-focused Eras rather than attempting to explore change and possible continuity. By examining the developmental stages of the

Indus Valley Tradition and comparing them with those of the Early Historic Tradition, we have been able to demonstrate the presence of remarkably similar structural sequences or cycles, so often masked by the use of separate specialist terminology, scholarly communities and publications. However, before concluding this volume, we wish to discuss the legacies of the Mauryan Empire and introduce the communities who immediately succeeded it.

LEGACIES OF THE MAURYAN EMPIRE

Many scholars view the Gupta Period as representing the watershed between the end of the Early Historic Tradition and the beginning of the Mediaeval Period, which brought its own distinct traditions. Indeed, our own volume has largely followed the precedents set by Dilip Chakrabarti (1999), D.P. Agrawal (1982) and Bridget and Raymond Allchin (1982; 1995a) with a similar terminal date. However, we are also aware that it should be possible to demonstrate the application of Shaffer's nomenclature to the succeeding archaeological and historical periods within South Asia, and we wish to stress that such terminology has been extremely useful whilst considering the legacy of the Mauryan Era of Integration. This is by no means a simple task as the period has been largely approached as a historical rather than an archaeological entity and synthetic studies have remained overwhelmingly textual in approach. Indeed, as Jaya Menon has pointed out, bricks, ceramics and other artefacts have been frequently ascribed to particular post-Mauryan dynasties despite the concern that "Whilst it is not inconceivable that ruling powers may be instrumental in bringing about technological innovation, they cannot be responsible for entire changes in styles of artefacts used." (2008: 29).

As noted in Chapter 11, most scholars place the termination of the Mauryan Empire with the death of Asoka's grandson Brihadratha in 185 BCE following a coup led by the latter's commander-in-chief, Pushyamitra Sunga but it is important to stress that this single event was part of a broader context of decline (Chakrabarti 1995: 277; Kulke and Rothermund 1990: 71; Smith 2005: 844). The archaeological evidence for this decline has remained largely unexplored but has attracted attention through the presence of rather differing perspectives of the Mauryan Empire and Asoka. A number of pioneering colonial scholars identified a pervasive legacy resulting from the Mauryan emperor's imperial experiment, including Mortimer Wheeler who stated that "Spiritually and materially his reign marks the first coherent expression of the Indian mind, and, for centuries after the political fabric of his empire had crumbled, his work was implicit in the thought and art of the subcontinent" (Wheeler 1959: 171). Whilst some of these concepts had been driven by research interest and scholarship, Dilip Chakrabarti has also suggested more political factors were at work in respect to Alexander Cunningham's statement of 1843 that "India had been generally divided into petty chiefships, which had invariably been the case upon every successful invasion; while whenever she had been under one ruler, she had always repelled foreign conquest with determined resolution" (1988b: 44). The argument is explicit, by lionising Asoka, these imperial agents were also using the past to legitimise their own presence and foothold within South Asia.

Whatever the underlying political ideology, Asoka and the Mauryan Empire also became a major reflection point for South Asians anticipating self-rule and Independence as it depicted "an indigenous precolonial South Asian state that had united the entire subcontinent under a single legitimate authority, governed by law and reason rather than coercion and despotism" (Sinopoli 2001: 162). Indeed, India's first prime minister after Independence, Jawaharlal Nehru, recognised the attraction of the Mauryan ideal and commented on it in the *Discovery of India*, written whilst imprisoned by the British in Ahmednagar Fort in 1944. When he later presented the Constituent Assembly with its new flag on the eve of Independence in July 1947, he further stated that "we have associated with this Flag of ours ... the name of Asoka, one of the most magnificent names not only in India's history but in world history. It is well that at this moment of strife, conflict and intolerance, our minds should go back towards what India stood for in the ancient days" and that "the Asokan period in Indian history was essentially an international period.... It was not a narrowly national period ... when India's ambassadors went abroad to far countries and went abroad not in the way of an empire and imperialism but as ambassadors of peace and culture and goodwill" (2010: 71).

Many of the pioneering scholars of independent South Asia echoed such sentiments in their own studies of the Mauryan period with D. D. Kosambi stating that the Asokan edicts provided "the first Bill of Rights for the citizen" (1965: 163). He further commented that the state had developed a new function under Asoka: "the reconciliation of classes ... [t]he special tool for this conciliatory action was precisely the universal *dhamma* in a new sense. King and citizen found common meeting-ground in freshly developed religion.... It can even be said that the Indian national character received the stamp of dhamma from the time of Asoka.... It is altogether fitting that the present Indian national symbol is derived from what remains of the Asokan lion-capital at Sarnath" (ibid: 165). Paralleled in part by Romila Thapar's pioneering *Asoka and the Decline of the Mauryas* (1961), more recently such models have been critiqued by scholars who have questioned the concept of legacy and the concept of the Mauryan Empire as a model nation state. For example, Upinder Singh has suggested many of the features attributed to the Mauryan Empire are features which "we should not generally expect to find in ancient states" (2008: 366) and Tambiah noted earlier that "ideas of a unitary state and of political loyalty ... are clearly inappropriate for the time" (1976: 71). With regard to the nature of the Empire and its decline, Singh also commented that the sheer extent and size of the Empire strained the Mauryan dynasty's ability to integrate and control its provinces through military force, administrative infrastructure and ideology (2008: 367). This echoes Gerald Fussman's observation that whilst the centre of the Empire depended on the individual force of the ruler, provincial officers had far greater freedom and were frequently drawn from the provinces themselves, creating centrifugal pressures (1988). Romila Thapar has subsequently reviewed her earlier perspectives on this decline and, remaining struck by the apparent speed of the break up, has suggested that "[t]he empire was short-lived and this may have been because it was primarily concerned with extracting revenue from existing resources and possibly not sufficiently with creating new resource bases" (1996: 320).

Monica Smith concurred with this general position and suggested that these concerns, and those of Sugandhi (2003) and Sinopoli (2001), as to the over-stated centralisation of the Mauryan polity, help us understand "[t]he apparent easy fragmentation of the Mauryans after Asoka and the lack of any large unifying polities in the subcontinent until nearly 500 years later with the rise of the Guptas" (2005: 843). Observing that the "Mauryan polity's construction of control was relatively ephemeral", she cited this as the reason that "[l]ocal inheritors of power did not seem to have reconstituted the territorial hold presumed to have been exercised by the Mauryans, and the tradition of inscriptions devolved from the continental scale associated with Asoka to instead commemorate local rulers' donations to regional Buddhist shrines and monastic communities" (ibid.). These considerations appear to agree with those of Stanley Tambiah, who dismissed traditionally cited factors such as the failure of Asoka's pacifist policy against the Indo-Greeks, excessive taxation, and Brahmanical reaction against the patronage of Buddhism. Instead, he concluded that the Mauryan Empire was based on a "galaxy-type structure with lesser political replicas revolving around the central entity and in perpetual motion of fission or incorporation" and that the Empire contained sufficient linguistic and cultural diversity to resist political unity following the Emperor's death (1976: 70–71).

Finally, it is worth recording that Asoka's own monuments were, in the words of Harry Falk, "regarded as signs of unusual ingenuity and technical ability, so that later kings felt induced to demonstrate their own abilities by producing similar pieces of art" (2006: 225). Indeed, pillars at Prahladpur and Sikligarh are both thought to date later to the Kushan period, and those from Latiya and ancient Vidisha from the Gupta period (ibid.). Moreover, the capital with four lions at Gwalior is so similar in style to Asokan prototypes that scholars cannot agree whether it represents a close Gupta copy or whether it was remodeled from a Mauryan original (ibid.: 233).

ASOKA'S SUCCESSORS

As noted in Chapter 11, it is generally agreed that the north-western territories of the Mauryan Empire had already reverted back to Hellenistic hegemony by the end of the third century BCE (Dani and Bernard 1994: 95). However, this was not a reversion or return to Seleucid imperial authority, as an autonomous Graeco-Bactrian kingdom had already been established there by Diodotus I Soter (c. 285–c. 239 BCE), formerly Satrap of Bactria-Sogdiana under Antiochus II. Paul Bernard has attributed a subsequent southern expansion of this polity over the Hindu Kush into South Asia to the Graeco-Bactrian ruler Demetrius I (c. 200–180 BCE), and his successors are commonly referred to as the Indo-Greeks (Narain 1957). Whilst rough timelines have been constructed for the various Indo-Greek kings and their dynasties by numismatists and ancient historians, it has proved almost impossible to allocate them to distinct geographical domains and we are left with the apparent emergence of numerous overlapping feuding principalities and city-states in Gandhara, the Punjab and adjacent regions, as Graeco-Bactrian authority was progressively challenged and weakened in the Bactria-Sogdiana heartland.

Notwithstanding issues of geographical jurisdiction, their dynasties established a number of new major urban sites south of the Hindu Kush, such as Sirkap and Shaikhan Dheri, and embellished a number of previously existing sites, such as Begram, Kandahar, Ai Khanoum (Bernard 1994: 108) and Akra (Khan et al. 2000). Sirkap and Shaikhan Dheri are particularly striking as both were re-established on virgin sites at a short distance from their urban predecessors, the Bhir Mound and the Bala Hisar of Charsadda respectively. The city of Sirkap was constructed less than 300 metres from the Bhir Mound in circa 175 BCE but, incorporating the terminal of the rocky Hathial Ridge as an acropolis, was planned as a walled rectangular form with regular bastions measuring 1,300 by 850 metres with a distinctive division between acropolis and lower town (Marshall 1951; Wheeler 1968: 113) (Figure 12.1 and Figure 12.2). Shaikhan Dheri was established at a distance of 600 metres from the old settlement of the Bala Hisar of Charsadda and, measuring at least 949 metres by 657 metres, was pre-planned and subdivided into blocks of 36.5 metres square (Coningham and Ali 2007a; Dani 1966).

Not all the urban sites were located within the plains, and excavations at Bir-kot-ghwandai have demonstrated the presence of a 2.7 metre thick fortification wall with regular bastions enclosing an area of 10 hectares below the isolated Birkot hill in the middle of the Swat Valley (Callieri 2007: 140). Dated to the second century BCE, its excavator has noted similarities between its defensive architecture and that of Sirkap. The site has also yielded potsherds inscribed with Greek letters in addition to Indo-Greek coins (ibid.: 142), confirming to the excavator that "Gandhara itself is a province of eastern Hellenism" (ibid.: 161). This is not to suggest that these populations did not

Figure 12.1. View across the Main Street of Sirkap in the Taxila Valley, Pakistan.

Figure 12.2. The city wall of Sirkap in the Taxila Valley, Pakistan.

adapt, as there is evidence to show that they did. For example, they used bilingual inscriptions on their coinage, firstly written in Greek and then translated into vernacular Prakrits and written in Kharosthi script (Bernard 1994: 126). Although vessels and coinage associated with the Indo-Greek period are present at numerous sites across the north-west of the region, few other definitive examples of the Hellenistic recolonisation of the region have been recovered. This new eastern Hellenistic province survived longer than the satrapy of Bactrian-Sogdiana, which was conquered by nomadic communities from Central Asia. Thus whilst Ai Khanoum was abandoned by circa 145 BCE, the last known Indo-Greek ruler Strato III, still issued coins in the western Punjab as late as the first decade of the first century CE.

As Demetrius I expanded his hegemony south of the Hindu Kush, the core of the old Mauryan Empire within the middle Ganga basin and Central India had crystallised around Pushyamitra Sunga, the commander-in-chief of the last Mauryan emperor. Establishing a dynasty which lasted between 185 and 73 BCE, reference to the *Puranas* and other textual sources indicates that the new domain was engaged at its north-western boundaries by the Indo-Greeks, at its eastern by a resurgent Kalinga in modern Orissa and in the south by a polity known as Vidarbha (Chakrabarti 1995: 278). Ironically echoing the Sunga dynasty's origins, it is further recorded that its final ruler, Devabhuti, was usurped by his own Minister Vasudeva, who then established a short period of Kanva rule. Despite what appears to be a full geopolitical history, most of its character has been reconstructed from later textual sources and traditions, and there are only a handful of reliable inscriptions associating monuments with the dynasty (Asher 2006: 58). Whilst the latter included the pillar at ancient Vidisha erected by the Greek ambassador Heliodorus from Taxila to the Sunga court (Chakrabarti 1995: 221), inscriptions at Bharhut and Sanchi may suggest that the two monumental gateways around the Mauryan *stupa* cores were erected during the period of Sunga hegemony, but whether this was under royal patronage remains uncertain. This largely textual narrative has also been challenged by Shailendra Bhandare who has suggested that the numismatic evidence indicated that following the break-up of the Mauryan polity, the Sunga period was associated with "a spurt in urban centres, supporting localised money economies and a gradual demise of the "uniform" silver coinage into several regiospecific coinages that are a quaint mixture of civic and nominative (monarchical) series" (2006: 97).

Dilip Chakrabarti has offered a clear summary of the current state of knowledge regarding the position of the Sungas and their successors, the Kanva: "One, in fact, does not really know the extent to which the Sunga-Kanva hegemony was pervasive throughout the Gangetic valley" (1995: 277). As Sunga-Kanva authority ended in the first century BCE, the Indo-Greek principalities within the north-west region had themselves come under increasing pressure from the Sakas, reputedly one of a number of nomadic peoples from Central Asia (Puri 1994a). One of their rulers, Maues (r. 85–60 BCE), was established as king at Sirkap in the Taxila Valley of Gandhara by 70 BCE. Although recaptured by the Indo-Greeks shortly after his death, Azes I (c. 48–25 BCE) re-established Indo-Saka hegemony across Gandhara, and his successors extended their authority deeper into the Punjab, Sindh and into the Ganga basin as far as

Figure 12.3. The Temple of the Double-Headed Eagle at Sirkap in the Taxila Valley, Pakistan.

Mathura and as far south as Ujjain (Chakrabarti 1995: 178). Apart from a new series of coinage, the brief Indo-Parthian kingdom of Gondophares (r. 20–46 CE) and his successors appears to have been almost indistinguishable from the preceding Indo-Saka period except for its broader coverage west into Sistan and north to the cities of Kabul, Begram and Kandahar (Puri 1994b: 199).

Successors of the Indo-Greeks both north and south of the Hindu Kush, the Indo-Saka and Indo-Parthian rulers appear to have quickly adopted Hellenistic traditions with Greek legends, titles and gods on their coinage but were also careful to have included Kharosthi and Prakrits as well as lions, elephants and bulls. Indo-Saka and Indo-Parthian rulers also settled within the walls of the established capitals of the region. Indeed, the majority of the street plan exposed in John Marshall's open area trench at Sirkap in the Taxila Valley dates to this period and has demonstrated their adoption of the Hellenistic city-plan (Marshall 1951). His trench measured 595 by 234 metres and revealed a grid-plan street system with the major street lined with shops, shrines and temples, and side-streets leading to courtyard residential complexes, including the notable 43 metre long apsidal shrine within its own courtyard of 3,500 square metres (Coningham and Edwards 1998; Marshall 1951). The city's inhabitants were diverse in their worship, however, as evidenced by the recovery of local terracotta female figurines and statues of the god Hermes, the goddess Hariti and even the Egyptian god-child Harpocrates. Moreover, eastern and western architectural styles were displayed side by side on religious structures within the city, stressing this diversity (Figure 12.3).

Commissioned by Mortimer Wheeler, aerial photographs of Shaikhan Dheri have indicated the presence of a similar rigid grid-iron plan as well as an equally monumental apsidal shrine (1962), confirmed later by the excavations of Ahmed Hassan Dani (1966). Whilst their rulers referred to themselves by the Greek and Sanskrit titles of *Basileus Basileon* and *Maharaja Rajatiraja* (King of Kings), authority beyond the court was entrusted to a loose confederation of semi-independent governors termed *Ksatrapas* and *Mahaksatrapas*, adopting the old Achaemenid and Macedonian titles of Satraps. This legacy was to survive into the third century CE with the adoption of such titles by the Western Satraps (Puri 1994b: 201).

This pattern of loose confederations and multiple principalities, marking a new Era of Regionalisation, was to be integrated by another dynasty with origins in Central Asia by the second century CE. This dynasty, the Kushans, or Yuezhi as they were also recorded, established a minor kingdom in Bactria in the second century BCE, but, under Vima Kadphises (r. 105–127 CE) and his son Kanishka I (r. c. 127–147 CE), extended their hegemony from Central Asia to beyond the Ganga Basin, firmly placing themselves as a trade and exchange conduit between the worlds of the Han and Rome (Puri 1994a). Largely constructed from incomplete references within Chinese textual sources and stray finds of coins, the chronology of the Kushan dynasty was firmly established by the recovery of the Rabatak inscription in Afghanistan in 1993. Written in the Bactrian language in Greek script, the slab recorded the genealogy of Kanishka I and recorded his hegemony over the South Asian cities of Pataliputra, Ujjain, Kausambi and down into the Deccan (Neelis 2007: 85) (Figure 12.4). Whilst a number of the existing cities were reoccupied during Kushan rule, such as the three noted earlier, they also established a number of new centres, such as Begram in Afghanistan, Dalverzin-tepe in Uzbekistan and Sirsukh in Pakistan. Again, some of the clearest evidence has been recovered from the Taxila Valley, where the new city of Sirsukh was laid out at a distance of 1.6 kilometres north-east of Sirkap. Defined by a 5.5 metre thick wall and strengthened by rounded stirrup bastions, the new city measured 1,370 by 1,000 metres (Marshall 1951) (Figure 12.5). The absence of clear residential blocks and deep stratigraphy within Marshall's excavations inside the city have been interpreted as a possible indication that the site might have been used to house a more mobile community, rather like a caravanserai. A successor to Shaikhan Dheri has been searched for in the vicinity of Charsadda, but it now seems more likely that Peshawar formed the Kushan strongpoint, located as it is just south of the Khyber Pass (Durrani et al. 1997). In contrast with the shared style of military architecture, the Kushans appear to have patronised regional and local cults rather than imposing a single imperial *dhamma*. This was exemplified by the example of Kanishka I who is recorded as having dedicated a fire temple at Surkh Kotal in Afghanistan and a Buddhist *stupa* at Shah-ji-ki-Dheri in Peshawar, and also had himself depicted with the Greek Helios, Iranian Adsho,

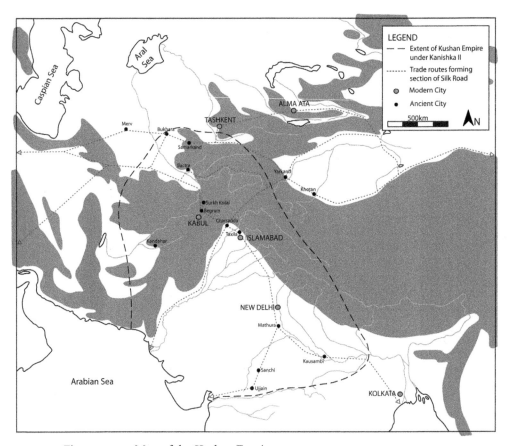

Figure 12.4. Map of the Kushan Empire.

Siva and *Buddha* on his coinage, which retained a Greek script (Coningham and Manuel 2009b).

Kajula Kadphises even depicted himself as Augustus seated on a curule chair, and the dynasty also appears to have patronised a *naga* or snake cult evident through the construction of a major apsidal temple to the south of Mathura at Sonkh (Hartel 1993). Under Kushan hegemony, the major Gandhara and Mathura schools of iconic sculpture became firmly established. Accompanying this plurality of patronage, the Kushans experimented with some of South Asia's first monumental dynastic sculpture in the form of life size depictions of rulers bearing sword and mace. It has also been suggested that the Kushan court was far from stationary and regularly moved across this empire of disparate ethnic, religious and linguistic communities, with a summer capital at Begram and a winter one on the Ganges at Mathura. This sheer breadth of the empire also provided the Kushans with a position to regulate and tax the Silk Routes, and the quantity of Chinese lacquer-work, Roman glass and Indian ivory recovered from the hoard at Begram indicates a fraction of the material which crossed its borders (Hackin and Hackin 1939). It is important also to recognise

Figure 12.5. Stirup bastion at Sirsukh in the Taxila Valley, Pakistan.

that the exchange of goods was accompanied by highly significant exchanges of art, architecture, religion and philosophy. Further south, the break-up of the Mauryan Empire appears to have eventually generated the emergence of a new polity, the Satavahanas, within the Deccan by the first century BCE which thrived on Indian Ocean trade and pilgrimage (Ray 2003; 1994) as did the Anuradhapura kingdom in Sri Lanka to the south (Coningham 2006b). It is interesting to note, however, that the trading ports at Arikamedu and Pattanam appear to have continued to trade independently with the Roman world to the west (Tomber 2008; Cherian 2011), perhaps the former assisted and differentiated by the adoption of a Tamil script rather than early Brahmi. In conclusion, we present Monica Smith's interpretation of this period as "a time of warring, expanding, and contracting political entities.... Archaeological evidence at present sheds little light" but although such "political entities ... did not have the power to control populations and foster shared identities on the basis of shared territories, strong social ties were maintained throughout the subcontinent by other means, including religion (Buddhism and Jainism) and language (Sanskrit and Prakrit)" (2001: 19).

The section just discussed raises a number of challenges facing South Asian archaeology and South Asian archaeologists. The treatment of the post-Mauryan principalities and dynasties remains distinctly historical in approach and there have been few successful attempts to articulate the archaeological and textual narratives despite the publication of a number of multi-disciplinary volumes, such as Doris Meth Srinivasan's 2007 *On the Cusp of an Era: Art in the Pre-Kushana World* and Patrick Olivelle's 2006 *Between the Empires: Society in*

India 300 BCE to 400 CE. These studies, and the review discussed previously, demonstrate that whilst there is considerable potential to extend Shaffer's Tradition terminology to the post-Mauryan period, the archaeological, arte-factual, and textual articulation remain too weak at present for this to be effect-ive. Indeed, the detailed analysis of the end or transformation of the Mauryan Empire also remains weak but should be systematically tackled, and this is one of the numerous challenges that we highlight in the following section.

TRANSFORMATIONS AND CONTINUITIES

At the start of this volume, we set out to analyse and compare the archaeo-logical sequences of South Asia's two major urban-focused developments, the Indus Valley and Early Historic Traditions. Equally importantly, we also set out to assess whether the period between the two could be characterised as a period of continuity and transition rather than the traditional narrative of dis-continuity. We have demonstrated that many scholars are agreed on the general character of the changes and transformations which occurred at the end of the Integration Era and the beginning of the Era of Localisation (Agrawal 2007; Chakrabarti 1995; Kenoyer 1998; Allchin and Allchin 1997; Possehl 2002a). They also mostly agree on the physical characteristics signalling this change, citing the disappearance of the previously shared system of weights and meas-ures, the loss of a uniform script, the loss of integrated towns and cities, the loss of a five-tiered settlement hierarchy, the loss of public buildings, the loss of internal planning, the loss of enclosing walls, and the loss of artefactual stand-ardisation, which included uniform proportions for bricks, as well as disrup-tions to long-established trade networks and a general decline in population (Agrawal 1993: 452). Moreover, as we have noted previously, whilst an earlier generation of scholars were focused on tracing discontinuities and the poten-tial presence of human migrations and invasions, more recently, scholars have changed the focus somewhat in order to explore themes of continuity. In a few instances, this change has occurred in the same individual scholar. For example, in 1971 Professor D. P. Agrawal identified migrations of Aryans and discontinu-ity in his book the *Copper Bronze Age in India* (1971: 240) but then went on to list no fewer than nine areas of continuity between the two urbanisations (the Indus and the Early Historic) in his 2007 book *The Indus Civilization.* Whilst Agrawal's areas of continuity include ovens, circular grain pounding platforms and decorative and symbolic designs (2007: 310), Shaffer had already expanded this to include the presence of large settlements; the construction of large units of public architecture, especially enclosing walls and water tanks; specialised craft industry; long-distance trading networks; a unified system of weights and measures; and the use of a script (Shaffer 1993: 59). Elstov has further advo-cated continuities, commenting that "Harappan religion had a domestic char-acter similar in orthopraxy to that of Early Historic India" (2013: 304) despite the decidedly uncertain "relation of Sanskrit literature to the Harappan culture" (ibid.: 307).

Rather than just focusing on the presence and absence of such traits within both Integrated Eras, this section will now also consider the presence of such elements within the eras which separated the two major urban-focused developments of Integration (Basant 2008; Coningham 1995a). The interpretation which dominated archaeological debate in South Asia for many years posited the presence of a dramatic transition between the Indus cities and the Early Historic urbanisation. This was based on an interpretation of the evidence which was thought to demonstrate clearly the abrupt end of the Indus and the loss of all traits linked to 'civilisation' and the re-appearance of such traits only a millennia later. The greatly improved dating evidence of the last few decades (both relative and scientific, although the latter remains limited), and the vastly extended data set from excavations and explorations of sites of all sizes and in a range of locations, has allowed archaeologists to demonstrate that there was continuity of certain traits during this interregnum, as well as between the two urban-focused developments themselves. However, before commencing this comparison we should also reflect on that fact that not all integrated regions were necessarily subject to urbanisation in antiquity, as illustrated by Supriya Varma's study of the Kathiawar Peninsula in western India (2008: 221).

The first trait to be considered here is that of internal planning, as it is one of the most evident characteristics of the Integrated Era Indus cities with their clear cardinally oriented grid-plans of roads, streets and housing blocks. Similar grid-plans are known from the Early Historic period, and the plans of Sisupalgarh and Bhita are suitable examples (Allchin 1995a; Smith 2001); however, it should also be noted that some Early Historic settlements, such as the Bhir Mound at Taxila (Marshall 1951), did not conform to such regularity. Formal road networks have also been reported at Ujjain and Rajghat (Basant 2008: 203). Whilst we have fewer open area excavations from the 'Chalcolithic' and early Iron Age, where we do have access to horizontal trenches, it is possible to suggest internal planning of settlements did also occur during this period. For example, the 'Chalcolithic' settlement of Ahar comprised cardinally oriented rectangular structures, and associated structures at Balathal appear to have been clearly divided from one another by a distinct street and lane network (Misra 2001: 513). It is interesting to note that even at smaller Malwa Phase sites, such as five hectare Inamgaon, the thirty-two exposed structures appear to have been laid out in rows divided from each other by roads and streets (Dhavalikar et al. 1988: 1002). Sankalia has also commented that such structures were frequently rebuilt one above the other following a similar footprint and plan, suggesting that there was a degree of planning and civic control in place preventing encroachment on the open spaces between structures (Sankalia et al. 1969: 216). Similar rigid planning appears to have been present within Baluchistan at the site of Pirak during Period IIB, where cardinally oriented lanes defined blocks of buildings set around courtyards in the vicinity of Trench PKA (Jarrige and Santoni 1979). It is presumed that this continuity was not merely in the form of physical planning but perhaps of more sym- bolically charged concepts of space and the division of space, even of shared concepts of cosmography and microcosm (Kenoyer 2010).

The presence of large-scale public architecture has also long been identified as a key characteristic of the Indus cities of the Integration Era and the cities of the Early Historic, as noted by archaeologists such as Wright (2010). Examples of such monuments are the monumental great bath at Mohenjo-daro (Mackay 1931a), the storage facilities on the acropolis at Lothal (Rao 1973) and putative storage facilities within Mound F at Harappa (Wheeler 1968). There are also a number of Early Historic examples of monumental architecture such as the pillared hall at Pataliputra (Altekar and Mishra 1959), the 'Jivakarma monastery' at Rajgir or the *stupas* of Sanchi or Dharmarajika (Taxila) (Basant 2008: 203; Allchin 1995a). However, it is also possible to identify evidence of communal investments during the period between the two urban-focused events, such as the Jorwe Phase structure exposed in Trench A1-T at Navdatoli, which contained a large and carefully constructed firepit at its centre. This structure covered 45 square metres, dwarfing the surrounding structures, which only covered an average of 28 square metres (Sankalia et al. 1971: 49). A similarly dis- proportionately large complex with a firepit was uncovered during the Jorwe Phase at Inamgaon, and has been called House 51 and 51A. This structure covered 54.6 square metres whilst the average house at Inamgaon in this phase covered only 15 square metres (Dhavalikar et al. 1988: 1004). The central com- plex of 600 square metres at Balathal is similarly striking for its distinct size and location (Misra 2001: 513), as was the Jorwe Phase apsidal shrine at Daimabad (Ghosh 1989: 114) and the Jorwe phase complex at Gilund (Ghosh 1989: 150). To this ensemble of buildings, we may also add the 10 square metre 'Large Square Building' of Rojdi C in Saurashtra (Possehl and Raval 1989: 171), the storage facility measuring 30 by 24 metres at Gilund (Shinde et al. 2014), the Phase V painted and stepped mud-brick monument on the summit of Mound A at Mundigak (Casal 1961: 88) and the 'Burnt Building' of Period IV at Shahr-i Sokhta (Tosi 1983: 88).

A similar pattern of continuity may be established whilst considering the presence or absence of enclosing and differentiating walls, which are such a striking feature of the individual mounds at Harappa as well as the Integration Era settlements at Kalibangan and Dholavira (Wright 2010). Distinct 'anchors' in the landscape, they were also a core characteristic of the Early Historic city (Basant 2008: 198), as represented by the clay bund at the core of the rampart at Kausambi, which measured 20 metres wide and 9 metres high (Sharma 1960), or by the earliest rampart at Anuradhapura which measured 13 metres wide and at least 3 metres high (Coningham 1999). Whilst not as massive as the examples just cited, there is also clear evidence for enclosing walls at sites occupied between the two urban-focused events, as represented by the Jorwe Phase rampart and ditch at Inamgaon; where the ditch measured 195 metres long and 20 metres wide (Dhavalikar et al. 1988: 237). Further examples have been identified at Sisupalgarh and Mahasthangarh, where Smith has argued that such massive fortification walls were an indication of hierarchical social organisation, and may have been a symbol of authority providing a community focus (Smith 2003: 122, 279–280). A further example is the Malwa Phase 30 metre wide and 6.4 metres high rampart and associated ditch at the site of Eran (Ghosh 1989: 135), and at Rojdi C, the excavators identified the construction of a 2 metre wide wall around the main 7.5 hectare mound (Possehl and Raval 1989: 29). These enclosing walls also contributed to the creation of settlement hierarchies within clusters of sites by distinguishing classes of settlement and their inhabitants. Whilst the five-tiered settlement hierarchies of the preceding Integration Era of the Indus Valley Tradition were absent, there was still evidence of regional hierarchies of at least three tiers as represented in Maharashtra by the primate settlement of Daimabad at 30 hectares, a secondary group with Prakash at 10 hectares and a lower tier of small agricultural settlements (Dhavalikar et al 1988: 1001). Perhaps it is also possible to identify a similar pattern in the Doab, where Lal Qila's 600 square metres was distinctly larger than the more usual 200 to 300 square metre coverage and certainly above the season settlements represented by sites like at Daulatpur. We may attribute this continuity to the influence of shared concepts of social planning and the ordering of space, perhaps again indicative of a shared cosmography. Similarly, such communal constructions require the coordination of labour, building materials and the necessary surplus to support such activities. As noted by Mizoguchi (2002: 200), these activities also encouraged the affirmation of a social affiliation with a specific centre as well as contributing to self-identification. In so doing, such constructions played the role of increasingly differentiating populations into urban and non–urban, and thus instigated the process of ruralisation (Yoffee 1997: 260).

Many scholars have identified a loss of craft specialisation and long-distance trade in the Era of Localisation following the abandonment of the Indus cities, but again, evidence from the intervening period has offered a rather different understanding. For example, there was a formal craft-working focus within the block of buildings in Trench PKA during Period II at Pirak. Rather than hosting a single activity, those working at the locality were engaged in the manufacture of stone blades and bone, ivory and shell objects (Jarrige and Santoni 1979: 374–375). Although depicting a different, dispersed pattern of craft organisation, of the sixty-nine excavated houses within the Late Jorwe village of Inamgaon, 13 percent were engaged in a specialist craft activity ranging from lime making in three, bone tool-making in one, stone blade manufacturers in two and copper or goldsmiths in a further three (Dhavalikar et al. 1988: 216). Further specialism has been suggested by Craddock's identification

of the presence of complex mining activities in Rajasthan in the second millennium BCE (Craddock et al. 1989: 55), and Hooja and Kumar have identified the presence of specialist villages in Rajasthan working on the production
of copper objects (Hooja and Kumar 1997: 330). The standardisation of both
the repertoire of iron objects within the megalithic tombs of Peninsular India
and the 'Copper Hoard Culture', further support the concept of a distinct
continuity in the form of closely bound groups of specialist craftspeople. This
evidence indicates that craft specialisation remained a core element of sedentary settlements and that the social complexity surrounding procurement
and manufacturing remained in place, although the scale of production and
exchange reduced.

Pirak also provided evidence for the continued functioning of long-distance
trade networks through the presence of agate, uncut ivory from the Indus,
and *Xancus pyrum* shell from the Arabian Sea (Jarrige and Santoni 1979: 372).
Finds of lapis lazuli at Ahar (Sankalia et al. 1969: 163) and Navdatoli (Sankalia
et al. 1971: 351) indicated the presence of further extensive networks, and it is
interesting to note that even smaller settlements, such as Inamgaon, appear to
have had access to imported marine shell, gold, ivory and copper (Dhavalikar
et al. 1988: 1006). The presence of large numbers of copper celts marked with
combinations of dots at the manufacturing site of Ganeshwar, as well as scattered examples across Uttar Pradesh, has further suggested to some scholars
that there were focused areas of production and networks of distribution across
this large region (Hooja and Kumar 1997: 330). The presence of more than
100 seal impressions with affinities with Baluchistan and eastern Iran at the
site of Gilund in the Deccan during this timeframe similarly indicates the
functioning of trans-regional networks (Shinde et al. 2014). Finally, reference
should be made to the presence of camel and horses at a number of settlements
during this period, as illustrated by the finds of bones and terracotta figurines at Pirak, as these suggest that very different modes of contact and trade
could now be established with caravans of pack animals. This evidence, when
augmented by the evidence of the introduction of new objects with 'exotic'
styles again stresses the strength of these networks and their expansion as such
objects began to reach populations previously excluded from the Indus Valley
Tradition integration or those who had previously engaged purely on asymmetric lines. Indeed, these 'exotic' imports were critical as they were to play
a role in allowing new and old elites to structure and restructure themselves
following the loss of the agglomerated urban populations of the Indus Valley
Tradition and their walled and differentiated centres. Questions still remain,
however, as to the nature of trading in terms of whether objects were moved
by their manufacturers, specific trading communities or just transferred 'down
the line'.

The question of artefact uniformity is also an important issue to consider
in the light of themes of transformation and continuity as many pioneering

scholars were struck by the standardisation of the metal objects found both within the Indus cities and smaller settlements during the Integration Era of the Indus Valley Tradition (Wright 2010). Indeed it has been implied and stated that such uniformity was lost during this Era of Localisation. Krishnan has also observed that during the Integration Era, Harappan ceramics reached a stage where 'specialised' workshops may have just focused on producing restricted forms but during the Localised Era, ceramic manufacture reverted to a more general production (2002b: 353). As noted earlier, it is still possible to suggest that remarkable groups of uniformity did arise during this period between the two urbanisations by again making reference to the so-called Copper Hoard Culture. As noted earlier, the objects in these hoards were originally identified as the work of "vagabond craftsmen" (Wheeler 1966: 93), but it may be clearly observed that there was a remarkable consistency within the objects' categories of flat celts, barbed harpoons and anthropomorphic figures, which infers a strong degree of standardisation across and far beyond the Ganga basin. Again, it is important to stress that these degrees of standardisation were reached in areas not previously integrated, suggesting that standardisation was not just functional but perhaps related more to stressed and shared concepts of proportion based on ritual and or aesthetic ideals. The loss of the system of Indus weights and measures has also attracted much interest from scholars and, arguably, there was a loss of the very widespread distribution of the distinctive chert cuboid weights. However, as noted by Agrawal, there are also links between the weights system of the Integrated Era and a number of later South Asian fractional systems, such as 16 chattacks forming one seer and 16 annas forming one rupee (Agrawal 1993: 452). Projecting this concept further, Kenoyer has stressed that the basic weight system instigated in the Kot Dijian Phase of the Era of Regionalisation was to be spread across a wider region during the Integration Era of the Indus Valley Tradition and then transferred into the Early Historic Tradition (2010: 120). Reflecting on this striking continuity, Kenoyer has suggested that "merchant communities and traders may have been the primary agents in maintaining weight standardization" (ibid. 117).

Reference may also be made to the continued tradition of the absence of certain key traits across the Eras under consideration, such as the lack of evidence of major public tombs and monumental artwork celebrating war – core traits of both Eras of Integration within the Indus Valley and Early Historic Traditions. It is interesting to recast the monuments and words of Asoka in the light of this observation as there is no imperial tomb for the ruler himself although he had patronised the construction of many monumental imperial foci across South Asia, foci which enshrined the relics of the *Buddha*. Falk has suggested that some rock edicts had been placed to challenge local cults (2006: 57), and other scholars have also noted the appropriation of existing practices and traditions through the construction of other Buddhist monuments (Shaw 2013). Similarly, while he might not have offered patronage for the creation of monumental art works celebrating war and expansion, his reference to the defeat of Kalinga on Rock Edict XIII and Minor Rock Edict I indicates that he was still quite prepared to broadcast the military capability of the Mauryan Empire. This capability had already been amply recorded at a level of individual field armies of more than 20,000 against the Macedonians, and Asoka's grandfather was later able to exchange 500 war elephants to the Seleucids for territorial gain in the north-west (Coningham and Manuel 2008: 236). Furthermore, much focus has been placed on the absence of royal or imperial art in both Eras of Integration. Apart from the various animals or wheels crowning the Asokan pillars, there is little known sculpture and the earliest known sculpture of Asoka himself dates some centuries after his life (Poonacha 2007). In parallel, there are very few human sculptures from the Indus Valley Tradition and few one might term monumental, as they are small and most of the stone examples were recovered from a single site, Mohenjo-daro, and out of context in the upper levels (Ratnagar 1991: 76). Whilst much has been written about the 'Priest-King', (Figure 12.6) one leading scholar concluded that "[i]t is likely that the individuals depicted in these sculptures were influential citizens or even rulers of Mohenjo-daro" (Kenoyer 1998: 102) (Box 12.1).

We also have to face the challenge that until the Indus Script is deciphered there may be other elements of continuity or transformation which we will be unable to identify. For example, the Early Historic Tradition's Era of Integration was attended by both the growth of renunciants as well as newly emerging centres of pilgrimage. For example, the personal pilgrimages of Asoka and the presence of his pillars along trade routes provide evidence of an attempted imperialisation of Buddhism. The complexities of landscapes are also more apparent at this time as illustrated by the heterarchies of settlement surrounding the royal capital of Anuradhapura, where villages appear to be clustered around monasteries rather than towns as might have been anticipated (Coningham and Gunawardhana 2013). The routes thus marked by Asoka's edicts are undoubtedly trade networks, but it is important to stress that some of the nodes were religious and administrative. It would be extremely clear to anyone visiting the great shrines of South Asia today that many shrines serve both religious and economic functions. Our challenge, of course, is whether such a pattern of pilgrimage and trade existed in the Integration Era of the Indus Valley Tradition. With such a lense, perhaps the networks of trade and raw resources so painstaking reconstructed by scholars like Kenoyer (1998) and Lahiri (1992) may also relate to pilgrimage trails, and cities like Mohenjo-daro or even Lothal may have functioned as semi-independent shrines or temple-cities. In this light, it is helpful to consider the pilgrimage and economic roles performed by cities like Varanasi, Anuradhapura and Ayodhya which starkly highlight the presence of heterarchies in contemporary South Asia, as none are polity-level administrative centres. If one or two city-states managed to gain hegemony over a cluster

Box 12.1. Priest-Kings and Dancing Girls

The purpose of this final Box is to again question many of the basic inferences frequently encountered when studying the archaeology of the period between the Indus and Asoka. This we do with reference to two small yet iconic figures, the 'Priest-King' and the 'Dancing Girl'. The former is frequently cited as one of the strongest candidates for a depiction of one of the rulers of the Indus, and the latter as one of the ruled. Both labels owe much to the early excavators at Mohenjo-daro, in particular John Marshall, and it is important to remember the era in which he was working as well as his own sociocultural background, as both may have consciously or unconsciously informed his inferences.

When Marshall described the bronze female sculpture, he wrote that: "The only other sculpture in the round from Mohenjo-daro that claims notice here is the bronze dancing girl. … This is a small figure with disproportionately long arms and legs. Almost, indeed, it is a caricature, but, like a good caricature, it gives a vivid impression of the young aboriginal nautch girl, her hand on hip in half-impudent posture, and legs slightly forward, as she beats time to the music with her feet" (Marshall 1931a: 44–45). In contrast, the steatite sculpture was described by Mackay as "by far the finest piece of statuary that has been found at Mohenjo-daro. It looks like an attempt at portraiture" (1931c: 356).

It is possible to thus distinguish a gender division between these two descriptions, whereby the female sculpture was held to represent youth, leisure pastimes, entertainment as well as an erotic element. The male sculpture, in contrast, was thought to represent maturity, serious pursuits, political and ideological control. Why has it automatically been assumed that only the male sculpture represented leadership? Surely, in the Indus of all Old World Civilisations, we should recognise that we need to be more creative and open-minded concerning attributions of qualities, values and symbolism (Figure 12.6).

Recent researchers have been more circumspect in their discussions and interpretations of these sculptures. For example, Kenoyer referred to the 'Dancing Girl' within his discussion of bangle styles (1998: 144, fig. 7.42) and carefully did not designate her as a dancing girl. Moreover, reflecting on the large corpus of Indus Valley Tradition terracotta figurines depicting women and stone seals depicting female deities, Kenoyer has suggested that "some women of the cities may have had important social and ritual positions and that female deities played an important role" (1998: 133).

Despite these valuable contributions, most general references still follow the accepted trophe of accepting male sculptures as representing

(continued)

representations of rulers and deities. However, as almost all the male stone sculptures from Mohenjo-daro were recovered from the surface of the site or topmost layers (Kenoyer 1998: 100), would they have been likely to have represented rulers? Is it suitable still to draw on either comparative studies with Mesopotamia and Iran or gender norms to interpret these stone sculptures? Why should a "wide mouth with heavy lips … set in a firm line" still equate to an "overall expression of calm authority and power" (Kenoyer 1998: 100).

Upinder Singh (2008: 162) has pointed out that "the 'Dancing Girl' may not have been dancing at all, and even if she was, she may not represent a professional dancer". Singh also has commented on the fact that rulers were commonly portrayed in stone in both Egypt and Mesopotamia and, although she does not make the link explicit, it is clear that she has inferred that this interpretative legacy has resulted in the automatic interpretation that the 'Priest-King' was the only possible candidate for ruler. She also cautions that this interpretation may be far from certain (2008: 178).

Why did archaeologists interpret male stone sculptures as leaders and bronze female sculptures as entertainers (or simply art)? The main reasons behind the early interpretation of the stone sculptures may lie in their scarcity, and the indications that these figures would have been decorated not only with paint but also headbands, arm bands, necklaces, and head-dresses, attached via holes and piercings now visible. Context is often lacking or inconclusive for these artefacts – the 'Priest-King', for example, is thought to be "of the Late Period" (Mackay 1931c: 356) and the other stone statues are from a range of surface or upper levels, thus suggesting they were also late in the sequence at Mohenjo-daro.

The bronze sculptures however, are also very rare – as rare, if not rarer, than the stone sculptures. The use of lost wax casting for their production shows that a very high level of technical skill was required, alongside a very high level of artistic ability. Mackay, the excavator, placed the bronze female sculpture in the Intermediate Period, hundreds of years earlier than the male steatite sculpture (1931c: 345).

Although Marshall dismissed the bronze statue as a caricature, there are similarities between the stone and bronze pieces. Indeed, Mackay described the steatite statue thus: "The eyes are long and half closed, but they are set straight." (1931c: 357), and the bronze statue "[a]s in some of the stone statues, the eyes are half closed, and the expression on the face suggests disdain" (1931c: 345). What seems to be of most importance are the ways in which both Marshall and Mackay interpreted the artists' intentions, whether or not the sculptures represented 'real' sitters or individuals, and how they interpreted the facial expressions of these (actually very small) sculptures. Of the steatite sculpture Marshall stated, "Here the prominent cheekbones, wide, thin-lipped mouth and other features leave no room for doubt that this was a portrait head, and when the nose and eyes were intact, we can well believe that the likeness was a tolerably good one" (1931a: 44). This assertion, with its lack of evidence, should be lightly taken were it not for the gendered caricatures which have permeated understandings of Indus art since.

The bronze statue on the other hand, was never even considered as anything other than a sexualised, frivolous, or even disdainful, piece of art. The sculpture might be "quite realistic" (Mackay 1931c: 345), but it was also damned as a caricature and could not possibly be a contender as a representation of an individual, let alone an individual with power or authority. Yet the bronze sculpture comes from earlier strata than do the stone sculptures and we could reasonably ask why representation/s of leaders and associated deities have only been found in the latest layers; surely if important throughout the Indus there would have been others.

We are not arguing here that the bronze female sculpture is a representation of a leader of the Indus, but we are pointing out that current interpretations of the bronze female and the steatite male sculptures are based on the opinions of two middle-class, middle-aged men, from privileged and particular educational backgrounds, working in the 1930s. These interpretations have become received wisdom and are certainly worth questioning. The genetic skeletal evidence from Cemeteries R37 and H (see Box 7.2) indicates matrilocality among the population, with men seemingly coming to Harappa from diverse areas but "being buried near their wife's ancestors rather than with his own." (Kenoyer 1998: 133). This arguably suggests a strong social focus on female continuity and importance although Schug et al. have also alluded to the presence of interpersonal violence at Harappa (2012). Perhaps it is time for a complete review of the both the material evidence and the theoretical frameworks (and assumptions) around the interpretations of selected artefacts as indicative of leadership purely on the basis of gender and relative scarcity.

of others, would such an influence have been archaeologically visible? Surely the only way one can identify the presence of "hegemonic city-states" (Trigger 2003: 113) is through textual or historic records as with Asoka's Kalinga edict, as apart from certain new urban forms like Sisupalgarh and Bhita, there is little coherent material evidence. Moreover, having acknowledged the dangers of

Figure 12.6. The discovery of the 'Priest King' at Mohenjo-daro (courtesy Marshall Archive, Oriental Museum, Durham University DUROM.1957.1.781).

'inkblot' concepts of imperial boundaries and alternative methods of integrating and articulating territory (Smith 2001), it seems increasingly unlikely that we can use reference to material culture.

Despite this uncertainty and having thus confirmed the presence of a strong degree of transitional continuity between the two Eras of Integration, we will now address the nature of the possible mechanisms responsible for conserving and conveying that continuity for more than half a millennium between the two urban-focused Eras. In so doing, we have to recognise that there is an apparent contradiction within a narrative which supports the presence of continuity through a series of major cultural elements whilst also stressing the loss of a number of shared traits. Indeed, the loss of larger agglomerated and differentiated settlements, and their elites and their recording systems, appears to limit the extent to which broader cultural characteristics may have been shared and preserved between the Eras of Integration.

An equally puzzling contradiction is presented by the apparent uniformity of the material culture of both Eras, despite its spread across a vast diversity of environmental niches, and this is intensified by the apparent lack of individual differentiation within both the Indus Valley and Early Historic Tradition. Moreover, this uniformity was accompanied by an apparent lack of visible elites or clear instruments of coercion through the absence of warfare, elaborate and pre-eminent burials and palaces within both Eras of Integration. This phenomenon appears to raise the presence of a focused levelling narrative, which successfully maintained and reproduced society; certainly this was demonstrated in the Early Historic Tradition by the cremation of all, kings and commoners. We do acknowledge, however, that cremation rituals may have been lavish but that little may survive such practices into the archaeological record. Pioneering archaeologists frequently termed this pattern of uniformity and standardisation as "conservatism that may so easily become stagnation" (Piggott 1950: 139) and even suggested that it reflected the presence of regulating a distinctly hierarchical system of occupational classes (ibid.: 170). It is important to note that these early models were not restricted to those associated with colonial authority, as D. D. Kosambi also referred to "enduring changeless stability" (1965: 64) and "peaceful religious stagnation" (ibid.: 70).

Aspects of these early models have been critiqued on account of their reliance on normative models of ranking and value with Daniel Miller attempting to overcome such an impasse by projecting a model of ascetic subordination (1985) and Paul Rissman developing a more active model of the masking or concealment of wealth through ideology and hoarding (1988). However, the presence of standardisation and uniformity across the periods and regions studied in this volume cannot be avoided; whilst we may question the projection of the caste system into antiquity (Coningham and Young 2007) and agree with Thapar (1995) that such concepts are largely the construct of nineteenth-century colonialism and subaltern responses, reflections on the nature of some of these fundamental relationships are extremely useful for understanding the character of the South Asian past and the methods by which elements of continuity were projected, despite major political discontinuities. For example, fundamental relationships between craft, subsistence and trade were established in the earliest Iron Age settlement at Anuradhapura in the tenth century BCE. At that time, every area of the town sampled by excavation has provided evidence for the presence of metal working and the working of semi-precious materials alongside an understandably wild-biased subsistence strategy (Coningham 2006b; Young et al 2006; Young and Coningham 2006). However, these fundamental relationships continued and survived the emergence of the city of Anuradhapura and its islandwide state so that by the Early Historic period, the 64 hectare settlement still hosted the same pattern of subsistence and the dispersed but co-located organisation of manufacturing. As strikingly, this pattern was still firmly in place when Anuradhapura became the early medieval imperial capital of 100 hectares with a surrounding sacred monastic zone of 30 square kilometres and an ideology of a 'god-king'. Separated by space and time, this pattern is remarkably similar to the spatial pattern at Harappa, where Mark Kenoyer has identified a cluster of almost identical communities on the various walled mounds of the site, none of which enjoyed pre-eminence, which survived the transformation of the settlement from a cluster of 'Chalcolithic' settlements into one of the great conurbations of South Asia (1998). Kenoyer suggested that the urban forms which centred the city-states of both Integrated Eras were themselves dynamic arenas for competition between elite groups (1997b: 69). Perhaps the evidence of remarkably similar activities occurring across both Harappa and Anuradhapura identifies an enduring tradition of the centre as a stage between fairly balanced actors, whether they were royalty or merchants. Such a concept has been used as a capstone for cross-cultural comparisons of the city-state by Norman Yoffee, who stated that they formed "the scene of new struggles for power and authority, the battlegrounds for independence and dominion." (Yoffee 1997: 263). Reflecting on the sacred nature of South Asian urban space (Coningham 2000), we may also reiterate the observation of Bruce Trigger that "urban centres were viewed as exceptionally interesting places in which to live. They were the physical embodiments of political power and human achievement and the places in which humans came into closest contact with the supernatural powers that made the universe function" (2003: 141). These enduring patterns also suggest that many of the social and economic transformations which occurred through the time period covered by this volume were through a slow, stable adaptation and modification of peoples, cityscapes and landscapes – an accretional approach. Having said that, the overall picture is still one of mosaic development as there were still isolated examples of more rapid and radical expansionist approaches, too, as exemplified by the establishment of some of the 'factory forts' of western India or the new Asokan shrine at Lumbini.

It has long been recognised that there are cycles to development, and Algaze has traced a pattern between central alluvial-based and raw resource–rich peripheral communities in Mesopotamia whereby increases in resource procurement were followed by periods of internal coherence and centralisation, which themselves led to expansion in order to control trade routes feeding those resources (2005: 2). To an extent, this is also true for the Regionalisation Eras of both Traditions, identifying that not only was there strong lineal connectivities between the two Traditions but also functional ones as well, all of which were focused on adaptation within South Asia (Gupta 2013). Pursuing this concept of both functional and lineal connectivity, and following Quigley's lead (1993), we would suggest that the relationships between people and their differentiated access to resources represented a powerful mechanism which facilitated and accompanied the development and growth of both rural and urban forms by the replication of simple community units – thus the overwhelming lack of differentiation. Chase and his colleagues have gone as far as to claim that the shared corpus of material culture associated with the "Indus Civilisation is more likely the result of kin-based communities of specialist traders and craftspeople rather than standardization imposed by the centralised political authorities" (2014: 76). Certainly Vidale has suggested "inter-site economic and social patterning of the labour-force employed in craft production" during the Indus Integration Era allowed "well defined socio-economic bonds among the different groups of craftsmen working or living within the cities" (1989: 180), and others have alluded to the presence of multi-generational structures organising space and labour (Chase et al. 2014: 76). The material record of such relationships and their ability to provide continuity have been highlighted by Carla Sinopoli who stated that "Caste organisations and the households that comprised them were units through which knowledge was transmitted – knowledge of technologies and materials, as well as traditions, group histories and origin stories, and religious affiliation and practices. Whilst most producers learned and practiced their crafts in households in which they were born or married, their membership in broader local and pan-regional social groups would have provided both a source of identity and a context for social and political action" (2003: 310). Mark Kenoyer had already widened this discussion from the organisation of craft activities to a broader consideration of a mechanism for regulating purity by drawing attention to the intentional "segregation of living areas, private water sources, drainage and waste disposal and distinct sets of ceramics, specifically those connected with cooking, food preparation and food serving" (1989: 188). Most significantly, this mechanism also enabled South Asian societies to conserve and reproduce themselves in times of instability, integration and conflict. This facet enabled them to survive the emergence and disappearance of states and agglomerated urban populations as well as the ability to generate an extremely strong degree of social and economic continuum or, rather, societal resilience. In this way, we explain the fundamental 'South Asian' nature of the two urban-focused Eras and why, despite 'exotic' contacts, the two archaeological Eras of Integration present more in common with one another than with those contemporary developments in neighbouring regions.

PROSPECT

There are numerous challenges for archaeologists working in South Asia to consider and address, and we will simply raise some of the most significant here at the end of our volume. We do not offer solutions to all these challenges and, of course, other archaeologists will have other challenges that they wish to add to this list. There are very specific tasks which are well known and have been the focus of a great deal of academic endeavour already, such as deciphering the Indus script. There are also particular periods and issues that have been under-researched to date, such as the archaeology of the Kushan Empire, the Mesolithic prelude to Mehrgarh, or the period of Islamic and European colonial contact. The need for many more scientific dating estimates from secure, well-documented contexts from virtually all periods and regions across South Asia is agreed to by many (if not all) archaeologists, and there are other methodological concerns as well. The broader application of archaeological science is needed in order to better understand sites and materials. For example, the use of Gas Chromatography Mass Spectrometry (GCMS) to identify ceramic vessel contents can augment ceramic categories based on ethnographic analogy as well as assist the accurate provenancing of materials. Successful piloting of isotopic analyses of animal and human remains will provide information related to diet, mobility and lifeways during individual lifetimes, while aDNA studies may offer information on ancestry and kinship. South Asia is also acknowledged as an integral field of study within the English-speaking world, and there is the opportunity to engage with the twenty-five grand challenges articulated by a number of leading North American archaeologists in a paper in the *Proceedings of the National Academy of Sciences*, challenges which stretch from 'Why do market systems emerge, persist, evolve and, on occasion, fail?', 'How does ideology structure economic, political and ritual systems?' and 'Why does migration occur and why do migrant groups maintain identities in some circumstances and adopt new ones in others?' to 'How do people form identities, and what are the aggregate long-term and large-scale effects of these processes?' and 'How do humans respond to abrupt environmental change?' (Kintigh et al. 2014: 880).

We are well aware that even the full battery of science-based archaeology will be unable to meet some of the challenges facing us, such as the decipherment of the Indus Script. Approaching some of its associated challenges, such as the social organisation of the Indus Valley Tradition cities, we need to consider alternative theoretical frameworks and reduce our reliance on normative value statements. Developing methodologies to explore social archaeology is critical and can draw on lessons from work in more recent periods (Rizvi 2008; Young and Fazeli 2013). Indeed, whilst uncritical reference to contemporary practice may have fueled narratives of cultural changelessness and cultural continuity (Gupta 2013: 113), it is clear that detailed ethnoarchaeological technical studies have greatly advanced our understanding of manufacturing processes (Allchin 1994; Kenoyer 1997a; Belcher 2003). There is also a distinct need for shared systematic survey recording techniques to be adopted, published and applied across modern geopolitical boundaries if we are more fully to understand the core relationships between urban forms and their hinterlands and neighbours. We also need to invest in additional deep explorations of a number of key Indus and Early Historic cities in order to further question the dynamic nature of these emergent centres and their internal structures and relationships. We also need to focus on artefacts not just as chronological markers but as products of distinct social and economic contexts. How they were conceived, used and discarded will provide invaluable information as to cultural variability and cultural change, and begin to shed light on the people who made and used them as well as shed light on their own artefactual biographies. This use of the term 'people' is shorthand for multiple forms of intra-community differences ranging from households and neighbourhoods to gender, class and age. Such a focus will also allow archaeologists to contemplate questions of scale or, in Susan Pollock's words, to acknowledge that "regional comparisons and large-scale political and economic structures and their implications cannot be adequately comprehended without incorporating the small scale and taking into consideration the dialectical relations between the small scale of daily life and the 'global' level of political, economic and other structures" (2013: 382). Finally, it is critical to note that the archaeological resource of South Asia is non-renewable and that there is enormous pressure on sites and landscapes through agricultural and resource extraction intensification, the spread of modern urbanisation and the investment in mega-infrastructure such as highways and reservoirs. To this, add the concerted pressure from the looting and sale of artefacts and antiquities, and the targeted destruction of heritage, as exemplified by the destruction of the Bamiyan Buddhas, the National Museum of Male and the Babri Mosque and the damage to the Temple of the Tooth and Bodhgaya. Although not as high profile, the damage to other sites such as the Indus Valley Tradition site of Rakhigarhi, which at 130 hectares has been categorised as a city but has never been fully mapped, continues. The resources are not available to protect all archaeological and heritage sites across South Asia, but prioritisation and agenda-setting is more than possible if communities and stakeholders, archaeologists and governments and different religious traditions and genders are involved, but this in itself is a major challenge (Sen et al. 2006).

This preservation and protection agenda need not be one purely fueled by the research needs of practitioners and academicians or by more overt statements of geopolitical identity. Indeed, it also has the potential to provide tens of thousands of people with access to new revenue streams and contribute to the alleviation of poverty through heritage tourism and pilgrimage. Such a potential is not blind faith, particularly at a time during which the Asian Development Bank is actively investing millions of dollars on developing airport, road and visitor centre infrastructure to facilitate international Buddhist pilgrim tourism to South Asia. Their economic projections suggest that there will be some 22 million annual visitors to South Asia by 2020, and that these pilgrims and visitors will have physical demands for the provision of lighting, potable water, sewerage, pathways and access to monuments for worship and veneration. The challenge to archaeologists is how best to assist the realisation of the positive social and economic impacts of tourism and pilgrimage when balanced against the need to preserve and conserve the historic and archaeological fabric and value of individual sites and their landscapes. As archaeologists, we have a responsibility to contribute towards the development guidelines for sustainable physical planning at key sites and to assist the creation of draft criteria against which to test all future developments and alterations at such important cultural sites. At Lumbini, the birthplace of the *Buddha*, this has resulted in the mapping of proposed changes against the criteria of whether the proposals are non-intrusive and reversibility, and whether they will enhance visibility and information at the site and assist focus, access and worship for the visitor, and use authentic materials (Coningham and Tremblay 2013). These guidelines are not only of relevance to site managers and archaeologists but also to stakeholders and faith communities, as illustrated by their recent adoption within the Lumbini Declaration of the International Buddhist Conference on Promotion, Protection and Preservation of Buddhist Culture and Heritage in 2014. Archaeologists worldwide are increasingly committed to dialogue with communities local to the area of research, and this is true of South Asia too (Young et al. 2000; Ali et al. 2012), but it is clear that much more needs to be done. Although engaging local communities in archaeological projects may bring challenge (e.g. Rizvi 2008; Sen et al. 2006), it is an essential agenda.

There is also a very real need to identify the presence or absence of archaeological deposits, often invisible below the surface, so that appropriate placing of pilgrim and other facilities may be made. Moreover, archaeologists can contribute to the high-level definition of sites and their boundaries and an enhanced understanding of site chronologies and sequences, but also that their science-based identifications and categorisations can enhance site interpretation and presentation so that visitors may read sites more fully and more consistently. Reflecting on the interplay between sustainable tourism and sustainable heritage, as a profession we need to pursue an integrated approach in which archaeologists, conservators, planners and economists are all involved with the development of individual management plans for individual sites. The integrated approach also needs to learn of the needs and expectations of the stakeholder communities, whether lay or religious, but equally importantly the protection of the heritage must be stressed as well as the opportunities to enhance knowledge of the site through research and investigation, as development and conservation can only follow archaeological assessments. Moreover, there is a major obligation on archaeologists to contribute to capacity building and training and to contribute to public awareness of scientific discovery through engagement with site custodians, tour guides and tour companies. This is not a quick or easy solution but it is the only way of ensuring that tourism and pilgrimage may be aligned with sustainable heritage.

Finally, we need to reiterate that the purpose of this volume was not to present an encyclopedia of South Asian sites, cultures and sequences within the Indus Valley and Early Historic Traditions. New data will continue to surprise and challenge, which is aptly illustrated by the chance discovery of the site of Mehrgarh following a flash flood on the River Bolan in the early 1970s. Similarly, we may expect the numbers of sites with Asokan edicts to expand as agricultural development and urbanisation intensify or through chance discoveries such as the restoration of the shrine of Kalikamba at Sannathi in Karnataka in 1986, which revealed that the image of Kalikamba had been set into a base slab bearing a previously unknown Asokan edict. Furthermore, careful cleaning of sherds will undoubtedly uncover more evidence of pre-Asokan early Brahmi script to further sever the preoccupation of many textual scholars on the later monumental works of Asoka. What we have achieved is an early staging post of archaeological interpretation where we have aimed to frame and challenge some pervasive and long-held perceptions of South Asian archaeology. As these perceptions have not only become received wisdom in archaeological understanding but have also become embedded in such areas as school curricula and tourist literature, to challenge them is essential. Effective challenges require not only careful analysis and application of the archaeological data, but also the use of appropriate theoretical models and frameworks and technical methodologies, and we hope that this volume will encourage South Asian archaeologists to continue to reconsider and re-evaluate the archaeology of its two major urban-focused Traditions.

REFERENCES

Agrawal, D. P. 1971. *The Copper-Bronze Age in India.* New Delhi: Munshiram Manoharlal.

————. 1982. *The Archaeology of India.* London: Curzon press.

————. 1993. 'The Harappan legacy: break and continuity', in G. L. Possehl (ed.), *Harappan Civilization: A Recent Perspective* (2nd edition), pp. 450–453. New Delhi: American Institute of Indian Studies.

————. 2007. *The Indus Civilisation: An Interdisciplinary Perspective.* New Delhi: Aryan Books International.

Agrawal, D. P., and A. Ghosh. (eds.). 1973. *Radiocarbon and Indian Archaeology.* Bombay: Tata Institute of Fundamental Research.

Agrawal, D. P., J. Kharakwal, S. Kusumgar and M. G. Yadava. 1995. 'Cist burials of the Kumaun Himalayas'. *Antiquity* 69: 550–554.

Agrawal, D. P., and S. Kusumgar. 1974. *Prehistoric Chronology and Radiocarbon Dating in India.* New Delhi: Munshiram Manoharlal.

Agrawala, V. S. 1953. *India as Known to Panini: A Study of the Cultural Material in the Ashta-dhyayi.* Lucknow: University of Lucknow.

Aguado, E., and J. E. Burt. 2007. *Understanding Weather and Climate.* (4th edition). New Jersey: Pearson Prentice Hall.

Ahmad, I. 1978. *Caste and Social Stratification among Muslims in India.* (2nd edition). New Delhi: Manohar.

Ajithprasad, P. 2002. 'The Pre-Harappan Cultures of Gujarat', in S. Settar and Ravi Korisettar (eds.), *Indian Archaeology in Retrospect: Volume II Protohistory*, pp. 129–158. New Delhi: Indian Council for Historical Research.

————. 2004. 'Holocene adaptations of the Mesolithic and Chalcolithic settlements in north Gujarat', in Y. Yasuda and V. S. Shinde (eds.), *Monsoon and Civilization*, pp. 115–132. New Delhi: Lustre Press.

Akkermans, P. M. M. G., and G. M. Schwartz. 2004. *The Archaeology of Syria: From Complex Hunter-Gatherers to Early Urban Societies (c. 16,000–300 BC).* Cambridge: Cambridge University Press.

Alam, M. S., and J-F. Salles. 2001. *France-Bangladesh Joint Venture Excavations at Mahasthangarh: First Interim Report 1993–1999.* Dhaka: Department of Archaeology.

Alcock, S. E., T. N. D'Altroy, K. D. Morrison, and C. M. Sinopoli. (eds.). 2001. *Empire: Perspectives from Archaeology and History.* Cambridge: Cambridge University Press.

Algaze, G. 1993. *The Uruk World System: The Dynamics of Expansion of Early Mesopotamian Civilisation.* Chicago: University of Chicago Press.

————. 2005. *The Uruk World System: The Dynamics of Expansion of Early Mesopotamian Civilisation* (2nd edition). Chicago: University of Chicago Press.

Ali, I. 1994. 'Settlement history of Charsadda District'. *Ancient Pakistan* 9: 1–164.

————. 2003. 'Early settlements, irrigation and trade-routes in Peshawar plain, Pakistan'. *Frontier Archaeology* 1: 1–289.

Ali, I., C. M. Batt, R. A. E. Coningham and R. L. Young. 2002. 'New archaeological exploration in the Chitral Valley, Pakistan: an extension of the Gandharan grave culture' *Antiquity* 76: 647–653.

Ali, I., and R. A. E. Coningham. 2002. 'Recording and preserving Gandhara's cultural heritage', in J. Brodie, J. Doole and C. Renfrew (eds.), *Illicit Antiquities: The Destruction of the World's Archaeological Heritage*, pp. 25–31. Cambridge: McDonald Institute for Archaeological Research.

Ali, I., D. Hamilton, P. Newson, Q. Qasim, R. L. Young, and M. Zahir. 2008. 'New radiocarbon dates from Chitral, NWFP, Pakistan, and their implications for the Gandharan Grave Culture of northern Pakistan'. *Antiquity* 82 (online project gallery).

Ali, I., M. R. Khalil, R. L. Young, and M. Zahir. 2009. 'A Survey of Lower Dir, North West Frontier Province, Pakistan in 2005'. *Man and Environment* 34.1: 30–37.

Ali, I., and L. Rahman. 2005. 'Survey and exploration in Bajaur-Mohmand region, Pakistan'. *Frontier Archaeology* 3: 55–90.

Ali, I., I. Shah, A. Samad, M. Zahir, and R. L. Young. 2012. 'Heritage and archaeology in Chitral, Pakistan: exploring some local views and issues'. *International Journal of Heritage Studies*, DOI:10.1080/13527258.2011.643909.

Ali, I., and M. Zahir. 2005. 'Excavation of Gandharan Graves at Parwak, Chitral, 2003–4'. *Frontier Archaeology* 3: 135–182.

Ali, I., M. Zahir, and M. Qasim. 2005. 'Archaeological Survey of District Chitral, 2004'. *Frontier Archaeology* 3: 91–106.

Ali, T., R. Coningham, M. A. Durrani and G. R. Khan. 1998. 'Preliminary report of two seasons of archaeological investigations at the Bala Hisar of Charsadda, NWFP, Pakistan'. *Ancient Pakistan* 12: 1–34.

Allchin, B. 1994. *Living Traditions: Studies in the Ethnoarchaeology of South Asia*. Oxford: Oxbow Books.

Allchin, B., and F. R. Allchin. 1968. *The Birth of Indian Civilization*. Harmondsworth: Penguin.

———. 1982. *The Rise of Civilisation in India and Pakistan*. Cambridge: Cambridge University Press.

———. 1997. *Origins of a Civilization: The Prehistory and Early Archaeology of South Asia*. New Delhi: Viking.

Allchin, F. R. 1963. *Neolithic Cattle-Keepers of South India: a Study of the Deccan Ashmounds*. Cambridge: Cambridge University Press.

———. 1982. 'How old is the city of Taxila?'. *Antiquity* 56: 8–14.

———. 1993. 'The urban position of Taxila and its place in Northwest India-Pakistan', in H.

Spodek and D. M. Srinivasan (eds.), *Urban Form and Meaning in South Asia: The Shaping of Cities from Prehistoric to Precolonial Times*, pp. 69–81. Washington: National Gallery of Art.

———. (ed.). 1995a. *The Archaeology of Early Historic South Asia. The Emergence of Cities and States*. Cambridge: Cambridge University Press.

———. 1995b. 'The end of Harappan urbanism and its legacy', in F. R. Allchin (ed.), *The Archaeology of Early Historic South Asia: the Emergence of Cities and States*, pp. 26–41. Cambridge: Cambridge University Press.

Allen, C. 2002. *Buddha and the Sahibs: The Men Who Discovered India's Lost Religion*. London: John Murray.

———. 2008. *The Buddha and Dr Fuhrer: An Archaeological Scandal*. London: Haus Publishing.

Altekar, A. S., and V. K. Mishra. 1959. *Report on the Kumrahar Excavations, 1951–55*. Patna: K.P. Jayaswal Institute.

Amore, R., and J. Ching. 1996. 'The Buddhist tradition', in W. G. Oxtoby (ed.), *World Religions. Eastern Traditions*, pp. 214–345. Toronto: Oxford University Press.

Ansari, Z. D., and M. K. Dhavalikar. 1975. *Excavations at Kayatha*. Poona: Deccan College.

Anthony, D. W. 2007. *The Horse, the Wheel, and Language: How Bronze-Age Riders from the Eurasian Steppes Shaped the Modern World*. Princeton: Princeton University Press.

Asher, F. M. 2006. 'Early Indian art reconsidered', in P. Olivelle (ed.), *Between the Empires: Society in India 300 BCE to 400 CE*, pp. 51–66. Oxford: Oxford University Press.

Asthana, S. 1985. *Pre-Harappan Cultures of India and the Borderlands*. New Delhi: Books and Books.

Avanzini, A. (ed.). 2008. *A Port in Arabia between Rome and the Indian Ocean (3rd C. BC–5th C. AD): Khor Rori Report 2*. Rome: Arabia Antica.

Avari, B. 2007. *India: the Ancient Past*. Abingdon: Routledge.

Badian, E. 1987. 'Alexander at Peucelaotis'. *Classical Quarterly* 37: 117–128.

Bandaranayake, S. 1974. *Sinhalese Monastic Architecture: The Viharas of Anuradhapura*. Leiden: E.J. Brill.

———. 1992. 'The settlement patterns of the protohistoric-early historic interface in Sri Lanka', in C. Jarrige (ed.), *South Asian Archaeology 1989*, pp. 15–23. Madison: Prehistory Press.

Bandaranayake, S., and M. Mogren. 1994. *Further Studies in the Settlement Archaeology of the Sigiriya-Dambulla Region*. Colombo: Postgraduate Institute of Archaeology.

Bandaranayake, S., M. Mogren, and S. Epitawatte. 1990. *Studies in the Settlement Archaeology of the Sigriya-Dambula Region*. Colombo: Postgraduate Institute of Archaeology.

Banerjee, N. R. 1960. 'The excavations at Ujjain', in E. Waldschmidt (ed.), *Indologen Tagung 1959*, pp. 74–96. Gottingen: Vandenhoeck-Ruprecht.

———. 1965. *The Iron Age of India*. New Delhi: Munshiram Manoharlal.

Barnes, G. L. 1995. 'An introduction to Buddhist archaeology'. *World Archaeology* 27: 165–182.

Barth, F. 1960. 'The system of social stratification in Swat, North Pakistan', in E. R. Leach (ed.), *Aspects of Caste in South India, Ceylon and North-West Pakistan*, pp. 113–146. Cambridge: Cambridge University Press.

———. 1972. 'Ethnic processes on the Pathan-Baluch boundary', in J. J. Gumperz, and D. Hymes (eds.), *Directions in Socio-linguistics: the Ethnography of Communication*, pp. 454–464. New York: Holt, Rinehart and Winston.

Barthelemy de Saizieu, B., and A. Bouquillon. 1997. 'Evolution of the glazing techniques from the Chalcolithic to the Indus Periods from the data of Mehrgarh and Nausharo', in B. Allchin (ed.), *South Asian Archaeology 1995*, pp. 63–76. New Delhi: Oxford and IBH.

Basak, B. 2008. 'Pataliputra: the changing perceptions of a site', in G. Sengupta and S. Chakraborty (eds.), *Archaeology of Early Historic South Asia*, pp. 39–53. New Delhi: Pragati Publications.

Basant, P. K. 2008. 'Urban centres in North India in the sixth century BC', in G. Sengupta and S. Chakraborty (eds.), *Archaeology of Early Historic South Asia*, pp. 191–212. New Delhi: Pragati Publications.

Basham, A. L. 1971. 'Preface', in T. R. Trautmann (ed.), *Kautilya and the Arthasastra*. Leiden: E.J. Brill.

Begley, V. 1981. 'Excavations of Iron Age burials at Pomparippu, 1970'. *Ancient Ceylon* 4: 49–96.

———. 1996. *Ancient Port of Arikamedu: New Excavations and Researches 1989–1992*. Paris: École Française D'Extreme-Orient.

Belcher, W. R. 2003. 'Fish exploitation of the Indus Valley Tradition', in S. A. Weber and W. R. Belcher (eds.), *Indus Ethnobiology: New Perspectives from the Field*, pp. 95–174. Lanham: Lexington Books.

Bellina, B., and I. Glover. 2004. 'The archaeology of early contact with India and the Mediterranean world, from the fourth century BC to the fourth century AD', in I. Glover and P. Bellwood (eds.), *Southeast Asia from Prehistory to History*, pp. 68–88. London: Routledge Curzon.

Beohar, N. C. 2010. 'The two ancient civilisations', in S. Tiwari (ed.), *Harapan Civilisation and Vedic Culture*, pp. 59–61. New Delhi: Pratibha Prakashan.

Bernard, P. 1994. 'The Greek kingdoms of Central Asia', in J. Harmatta, B. N. Puri and G. F. Etemadi (eds.), *History of Civilizations of Central Asia*, Vol. 2, pp. 99–129. Paris: UNESCO.

Besenval, R. 1994. 'The 1992–1993 field-season at Miri Qalat: new contributions to the chronology of Protohistoric settlement in Pakistan Makran', in A. Parpola and P. Koskikallio (eds.), *South Asian Archaeology 1993*, pp. 81–91. Helsinki: Suomalainen Tiedeakatemia.

Beteille, A. 1965. *Caste, Class and Power: Changing Patterns of Stratification in a Tanjore Village*. Berkeley and Los Angeles: University of California Press.

Bhan, K. K., V. H. Sonawane, P. Ajithprasad, and S. Pratapchandran. 2005. 'A Harappan trading and craft production centre at Gola Dhoro (Bagasra)'. *Antiquity* 75 (online project gallery).

Bhan, S., and J. G. Shaffer. 1978. 'New discoveries in Haryana'. *Man and Environment* 2: 59–68.

Bhandare, S. 2006. 'Numismatics and history: the Maurya-Gupta interlude in the Gangetic plain', in P. Olivelle (ed.), *Between the Empires: Society in India 300 BCE to 400 CE*, pp. 67–112. Oxford: Oxford University Press.

Bhandare, S., and S. Garg. (eds.). 2011. *Felicitas. Essays in Numismatics, Epigraphy and History in Honour of Joe Cribb*. Mumbai: Reesha Books International.

Biagi, P. 2004. 'The Mesolithic settlement of Sindh (Pakistan): a preliminary assessment'. *Praehistoria* 5: 195–220.

Biagi, P., and E. Starnini. 2008. 'The Bronze Age Indus Quarries of the Rohri Hills and Ongar in Sindh (Pakistan)', in R. I. Kostov, B. Gaydarska and M. Gurova (eds.), *Geoarchaeology and Archaeomineralogy*, pp. 77–82. Sofia: Publishing House St Ivan Rilski.

Bibby, G. 1972. *Looking for Dilmun*. Harmondsworth: Pelican Books.

Bidari, B. 2004. *Lumbini: A Haven of Sacred Refuge*. Kathmandu: Hill Side Press.

———. 2007. *Kapilavastu: The World of Siddhartha*. Kathmandu: Hill Side Press.

Bisht, R. S. 1996. 'Excavations at Dholavira, District Kutch'. *Indian Archaeology: A Review 1991–1992*: 26–35.

Bisht, R. S., and S. Asthana. 1979. 'Banawali and some other recently excavated Harappan sites in India', in M. Taddei (ed.), *South Asian Archaeology 1977*, pp. 224–240. Naples: Istituto Universitario Orientale.

Bloom, D. E., and L. Rosenberg. 2011. 'The Future of South Asia: Population Dynamics, Economic Prospects, and Regional Coherence'. *PGDA Working Paper* 68 http://www.hsph.harvard.edu/pgda/working/.

Boivin, N. 2005. 'Orientalism, ideology and agency: examining caste in South Asian archaeology'. *Journal of Social Archaeology* 5.2: 225–252.

———. 2007. 'Anthropological, historical, archaeological and genetic perspectives on the origins of caste in South Asia', in M. Petraglia and B. Allchin (eds.), *The Evolution and History of Human Populations in South Asia*, pp. 341–361. Dordrecht: Springer.

Bopearachchi, O. 2006. 'Coins', in R. A. E. Coningham (ed.), *Anuradhapura. The British-Sri Lankan Excavations at Anuradhapura Salgaha Watta 2. Vol II: The Artefacts*, pp. 7–26. Oxford: Archaeopress.

Brown, P. 1956. *Indian Architecture: Buddhist and Hindu*. Bombay: Taraporevalas.

Brubaker, R. 2008. 'Regional perspectives on Megalithic landscapes: investigating the socio-political dimensions of late prehistoric sites in central Karnataka and west Andhra Pradesh, India'. *Antiquity* 82 (online project gallery)

Brumfiel, E. M., and T. K. Earle (eds.). 1987. *Specialization, Exchange, and Complex Societies*. Cambridge: Cambridge University Press.

Buhler, J. G. 1886. *The Laws of Manu*. Oxford: Oxford University Press.

Cable, C. M., and C. P. Thornton. 2013. 'Monumentality and the third-millennium "towers" of the Oman Peninsula', in S. A. Abraham, P. Gullapalli, T. P. Raczek and U. Z. Rizvi (eds.), *Connections and Complexity: New Approaches to the Archaeology of South Asia*, pp. 375–400. Walnut Creek: Left Coast Press.

Callieri, P. 1992. 'Bir-kot-ghwandai: an Early Historic town in Swat (Pakistan)', in C. Jarrige, (ed.), *South Asian Archaeology 1989*, pp. 339–346. Madison: Prehistory Press.

Callieri, P. F. 1996. 'Seals from Gandhara: foreign imports and local production', in M. F. Boussac and A. Invernizzi (eds.), *Archives et Sceaux di Monde Hellenistique*, pp. 413–422. Athens: Ecole Francaise d'Athenes.

———. 2007. 'Barikot: an Indo-Greek urban centre in Gandhara', in D. M. Srinivasan (ed.), *On the Cusp of an Era: Art in the Pre-Kushan World*, pp. 133–164. Leiden: E.J. Brill.

Caner, L., D. Lo Seen, Y. Gunnell, B. R. Ramesh, and G. Bourgeon. 2007. 'Spatial heterogeneity of land cover response to climatic change in the Nilgiri highlands (Southern India) since the last glacial maximum'. *Holocene* 17.2: 195–205.

Canning, C. J. 1862. *Governor General's Minute on the Antiquities of Upper India of the 22 January 1862*.

Carswell, J., S. U. Deraniyagala and A. Graham. 2013. *Mantai: City by the Sea*. Aichwald: Linden Soft.

Casal, J.-M. 1961. *Fouilles de Mundigak, Volumes I-II*. Paris: Memoires de la Delegation Archeologique Francaise en Afghanistan.

———. 1964. *Fouilles d'Amri*. Paris: Librairie Klincksieck.

———. 1966. 'Nindowari: a Chalcolithic site in South Baluchistan'. *Pakistan Archaeology* 3: 10–21.

Chakrabarti, D. K. 1974. 'The beginning of iron in India: problem reconsidered', in A. K. Ghosh (ed.), *Perspectives in Palaeoanthropology*, pp. 345–356. Calcutta: Firma K.I. Mukhopadhya.

———. 1976. 'Beginning of Iron in India'. *Antiquity* 4: 114–124.

———. 1988a. *History of Indian Archaeology from the Beginning to 1947*. New Delhi: Munshiram Manoharlal.

———. 1988b. *Theoretical Issues in Indian Archaeology*. New Delhi: Munshiram Manoharlal.

———. 1992. *Ancient Bangladesh: A Study of the Archaeological Sources*. New Delhi: Oxford University Press.

———. 1995. *The Archaeology of Ancient Indian Cities*. New Delhi: Oxford University Press.

———. 1999. *India: An Archaeological History: Palaeolithic Beginnings to Early Historic Foundations*. New Delhi: Oxford University Press.

———. 2000. 'The Mahajanapada states of Early Historic India', in M. H. Hansen (ed.), *A Comparative Study of Thirty City-State*

Cultures: An Investigation, pp. 375–392 Copenhagen: Copenhagen Polis Centre.

———. 2001a. *Archaeological Geography of the Ganga Plain: The Lower and the Middle Ganga*. New Delhi: Permanent Black.

———. 2001b. 'The archaeology of Hinduism', in T. Insoll (ed.), *Archaeology and World Religion*, pp. 33–60. London: Routledge.

———. 2003. *Archaeology in the Third World: A History of Indian Archaeology since 1947*. New Delhi: D.K. Printworld Private Limited.

———. 2005. *The Archaeology of the Deccan Routes: the Ancient Routes from the Ganga Plain to the Deccan*. New Delhi: Munshiram Manoharlal.

———. 2010. 'The colonial legacy in the archaeology of South Asia', in J. Lydon and U. Z. Rizvi (eds.), *Handbook of Post-Colonial Archaeology*, pp. 73–80. Walnut Creek: Left Coast Press.

Chakraborty, S. 2008. 'Site function/ site hierarchy / urban or rural: a case study of Bengal Delta', in G. Sengupta and S. Chakraborty (eds.), *Archaeology of Early Historic South Asia*, pp. 113–134. New Delhi: Pragati Publications.

Chapman, R. W. 2003. *Archaeologies of Complexity*. Routledge, London.

Charlton, T. H., and D. L. Nichols. 1997. 'The city-state concept: development and applications', in D. L. Nichols and T. H. Charlton (eds.). *The Archaeology of City-States: Cross Cultural Approaches*, pp. 1–14. Washington: Smithsonian Institution Press.

Chase, B. 2010. 'Social change at the Harappan site of Gola Dhoro: a reading from animal bones'. *Antiquity* 84: 528–543.

Chase, B., P. Aijith Prasad, S. V. Rajesh, A. Patel and B. Sharma. 2014. *Journal of Anthropological; Archaeology* 35: 63–78.

Chattopadhyaya, B. D. 2008. 'Early historical in Indian Archaeology: some definitional problems', in G. Sengupta and S. Chakraborty (eds.), *Archaeology of Early Historic South Asia*, pp. 3–14. New Delhi: Pragati Publications.

Chattopadhyaya, U. C. 2002. 'Researches in Archaeozoology of the Holocene period (Including the Harappan tradition in India and Pakistan)', in S. Settar and R. Korisettar (eds.), *Indian Archaeology in Retrospect: Archaeology and Interactive Disciplines*, pp. 365–422. New Delhi: Manohar Publishers.

Chaubey, G., M., Metspalu, T. Kivisild, and R. Villems 2007. 'Peopling of South Asia: investigating the caste–tribe continuum in India'. *Bioessays* 29: 91–100.

Cherian, P. J. 2011. *Pattanam Excavations: Fifth Season Field Report*. Trivandrum: Kerala Historical Research Council.

Childe, V. G. 1934. *New Light on the Most Ancient Near East*. New York: Routledge.

———. 1936. *Man Makes Himself*. London: Watts.

———. 1939. 'India and the West before Darius'. *Antiquity* 4: 77–85.

———. 1942. *What Happened in History*. London: Penguin.

———. 1950. 'The Urban Revolution'. *The Town Planning Review* 21.1: 3–17.

———. 1954. *New Light on the Most Ancient Near East*. (revised edition) New York: Routledge.

Chowdury, K. A., and G. M. Buth. 1970. '4,500 Year old seeds suggest that true cotton is indigenous to Nubia'. *Nature* 227: 85–86.

Clarke, D. L. 1978. *Analytical Archaeology* (2nd edition). London: Methuen and Co.

Cleuziou. S., and M. Tosi. 1994. 'Black boats of Magan: some thoughts on Bronze Age water transport in Oman and beyond from the impressed bitumen slabs of Ra's al-Junayz', in A. Parpola and P. Koskikallio (eds.), *South Asian Archaeology 1993*, pp. 744–761. Helsinki: Suomalainen Tiedeakatemia.

Compagnoni, B. 1987. 'Faunal Remains', in G. Stacul (ed.), *Prehistoric and Protohistoric Swat, Pakistan (c. 3000-1400 BC)*, pp. 131–154. Rome: Istituto Italiano Per Il Medio Ed Estremo Oriente.

Coningham, R. A. E. 1993. 'Anuradhapura citadel archaeological project: preliminary results of the excavation of the southern rampart 1992'. *South Asian Studies* 9: 111–122.

———. 1995a. 'Dark Age or Continuum? an archaeological analysis of the second emergence of Urbanism in South Asia', in F. R. Allchin (ed.), *The Archaeology of Early Historic South Asia. The Emergence of Cities and States*, pp. 54–72. Cambridge: Cambridge University Press.

———. 1995b. 'Monks, caves and kings: an archaeological assessment of the nature of early Buddhism in Sri Lanka (Ceylon)'. *World Archaeology* 27.2: 224–242.

———. 1997. 'The spatial distribution of craft activities in Early Historic cities and their social implications', in F. R. Allcin and B. Allchin (eds.), *South Asian Archaeology 1995*.

Volume 1, pp. 351–363. New Delhi: Oxford and IBH.

———. 1999. *Anuradhapura. The British-Sri Lankan Excavations at Anuradhapura Salgaha Watta 2. Volume I: The Site.* Oxford: Archaeopress.

———. 2000. 'Contestatory urban texts or were cities in South Asia built as images?'. *Cambridge Archaeological Journal* 10.2: 348–354.

———. 2001. 'The archaeology of Buddhism', in T. Insoll (ed.), *Archaeology and World Religion*, pp. 61–95. London: Routledge.

———. 2002. 'Deciphering the Indus Script', in S. Settar and R. Korrisettar (eds.), *Indian Archaeology in Retrospect*, pp. 81–104. New Delhi: Indian Council of Historical Research.

———. 2006a. 'Conclusion: the nature of the early historic city', in R. A. E. Coningham, (ed.), Anuradhapura. *The British-Sri Lankan Excavations at Anuradhapura Salgaha Watta 2. Vol II: The Artefacts*, pp. 647–650. Oxford: Archaeopress.

———. (ed.). 2006b. *Anuradhapura: The British-Sri Lankan Excavations at Anuradhapura Salgaha Watta 2. Volume II: The Artefacts.* Oxford: Archaeopress.

———. 2007a. 'The Terracotta objects', in R. A. E. Coningham, and I. Ali (eds.), *Charsadda. The British-Pakistani Excavations at the Bala Hisar*, pp. 187–225. Oxford: Archaeopress.

———. 2007b. 'Previous archaeological investigations', in R. A. E. Coningham and I. Ali (eds.), *Charsadda. The British-Pakistani Excavations at the Bala Hisar*, pp. 21–31. Oxford: Archaeopress.

———. 2011. 'Buddhism', in T. Insoll (ed.), *The Oxford Handbook of the Archaeology of Ritual and Religion*, pp. 932–947. Oxford: Oxford University Press.

Coningham, R. A. E., K. P. Acharya, A. Schmidt, and B. Bidari. 2010. 'Searching for Kapilavastu', in P. Gunawardhana, G. Adikari, and R. A. E. Coningham (eds.), *Essays in Archaeology*, pp. 55–66. Colombo: Neptune Publishers.

Coningham, R. A. E., K. P. Acharya, K. M. Strickland, C. E. Davis, M. J. Manuel, I. A. Simpson, K. Gilliland, J. Tremblay, T. C. Kinnaird, and D. C. W. Sanderson. 2013. 'The earliest Buddhist shrine: excavating the birthplace of the Buddha, Lumbini (Nepal)'. *Antiquity* 87: 1104–1123.

Coningham, R. A. E., and I. Ali (eds.). 2007a. *Charsadda: The British-Pakistani Excavations at the Bala Hisar.* Oxford: Archaeopress.

———. 2007b. 'The Habitation levels', in R. A. E. Coningham and I. Ali (eds.), *Charsadda: The British-Pakistani Excavations at the Bala Hisar*, pp. 65–92. Oxford: Archaeopress.

———. 2007c. 'Introduction', in R. A. E. Coningham and I. Ali (eds.), *Charsadda: The British-Pakistani Excavations at the Bala Hisar*, pp. 1–9. Oxford: Archaeopress.

Coningham, R. A. E., and F. R. Allchin. 1995. 'The rise of cities in Sri Lanka' in F. R. Allchin (ed.), *The Archaeology of Early Historic South Asia: The Emergence of Cities and States*, pp. 152–184. Cambridge: Cambridge University Press.

Coningham, R. A. E., F. R. Allchin, C. M. Batt and D. Lucy. 1996. 'Passage to India? Anuradhapura and the early use of the Brahmi Script'. *Cambridge Archaeological Journal* 6: 73–97.

Coningham, R. A. E., and C. M. Batt. 2007. 'Dating the sequence', in R. A. E. Coningham and I. Ali (eds.), *Charsadda: The British-Pakistani Excavations at the Bala Hisar*, pp. 93–98. Oxford: Archaeopress.

Coningham, R. A. E., D. Burroni, R. Donahue, and L. Ford. 2006. 'Stone Objects', in R. A. E. Coningham (ed.), *Anuradhapura. The British-Sri Lankan Excavations at Anuradhapura Salgaha Watta 2. Volume II: the Artefacts*, pp. 377–430. Oxford: Archaeopress.

Coningham, R. A. E., and B. Edwards. 1998. 'Space and society at Sirkap, Taxila: a re-examination of Urban Form and meaning'. *Ancient Pakistan* 12: 47–75.

Coningham, R. A. E., L. Ford, S. Cheshire, and R. L. Young. 2006. 'Unglazed Ceramics', in R. A. E. Coningham (ed.), *Anuradhapura. The British-Sri Lankan Excavations at Anuradhapura Salgaha Watta 2. Volume II: The Artefacts*, pp. 127–332. Oxford: Archaeopress.

Coningham, R. A. E., and P. Gunawardhana. 2012. 'Looting or rededication? Buddhism and the expropriation of relics', in G. Scarre and R. A. E. Coningham (eds.), *Appropriating the Past: Philosophical Perspectives on the Practice of Archaeology*, pp. 281–294. Cambridge: Cambridge University Press.

———. (eds.). 2013. *Anuradhapura Volume 3: The Hinterland.* Oxford: Archaeopress.

Coningham, R. A. E., P. Gunawardhana, M. J. Manuel, G. Adikari, M. Katugampola, R. L Young, A. Schmidt, K. Krishnan, I. Simpson, G. McDonnell, and C. M. Batt. 2007a. 'The state of theocracy: defining an Early Medieval hinterland in Sri Lanka'. *Antiquity* 81: 699–719.

Coningham, R. A. E., I. Ali, and M. Naeem. 2007b. 'The unglazed ceramic objects', in R. A. E. Coningham and I. Ali (eds.), *Charsadda: The British-Pakistani Excavations at the Bala Hisar*, pp. 99–149. Oxford: Archaeopress.

Coningham, R. A. E., R. Young, and I. Ali. 2007c. 'The regional synthesis: a conclusion', in R. A. E. Coningham and I. Ali (eds.), *Charsadda: The British-Pakistani Excavations at the Bala Hisar*, pp. 259–270. Oxford: Archaeopress.

Coningham, R. A. E., M. A. Durrani, T. Ali, and A. Rehman. 2007d. 'The fortifications', in R. A. E. Coningham and I. Ali (eds.), *Charsadda: The British-Pakistani Excavations at the Bala Hisar*, pp. 47–63. Oxford: Archaeopress.

Coningham, R. A. E., and P. Harrison. 2006. 'Metal-working residues', in R. A. E. Coningham (ed.), *Anuradhapura. The British-Sri Lankan Excavations at Anuradhapura Salgaha Watta 2. Volume II: the Artefacts*, pp. 27–76. Oxford: Archaeopress.

Coningham, R. A. E., and N. Lewer. 2000. 'The Vijayan colonisation and the archaeology of identity in Sri Lanka'. *Antiquity* 74: 707–712

Coningham, R. A. E., and M. J. Manuel. 2008. 'Warfare in Ancient South Asia', in de Souza, P. (ed.), *The Ancient World at War*, pp. 229–242. London: Thames and Hudson.

———. 2009a. 'Priest-kings or puritans? Childe and willing subordination in the Indus'. *European Journal of Archaeology* 12: 167–180.

———. 2009b. 'The Early Empires of South Asia', in Harrison, T. (ed.), *The Great Empires of the Ancient World*, pp. 226–249. London: Thames and Hudson.

Coningham, R. A. E., and T. Sutherland. 1998. 'Dwellings or granaries? The pit phenomenon of the Kashmir-Swat Neolithic'. *Ancient Pakistan* 12: 177–187.

Coningham, R. A. E., and F. Swati. 2007. 'The Stone Objects', in R. A. E. Coningham and I. Ali (eds.), *Charsadda: The British-Pakistani Excavations at the Bala Hisar*, pp. 169–186. Oxford: Archaeopress.

Coningham, R. A. E., and J. Tremblay. 2013. 'Re-discovering Lumbini: archaeology and site interpretation', in K. Weise (ed.), *The Sacred Garden of Lumbini: Perceptions of Buddha's Birthplace*, pp. 61–95. Paris: UNESCO.

Coningham, R. A. E., and R. L. Young. 2007. 'The archaeological visibility of caste', in T. Insoll (ed.), *The Archaeology of Identities: A Reader*, pp. 250–264. London: Routledge.

Cooray, P. G. 1984. *An Introduction to the Geology of Sri Lanka (Ceylon)*. Colombo: National Museum of Sri Lanka.

Cork, E. 2004. 'Peaceful Harappans? Reviewing the evidence for the absence of warfare in the Indus civilisation of north-west India and Pakistan (c. 2500–1900 BC)'. *Antiquity* 79: 411–423.

Costantini, L. 1984. 'The beginning of agriculture in the Kachi Plain: the evidence of Merhgarh', in B. Allchin (ed.), *South Asian Archaeology 1981*, pp. 29–33. Cambridge: Cambridge University Press.

Cowgill, G. L. 2004. 'Origins and development of urbanism: archaeological perspectives'. *Annual Review of Anthropology* 33: 525–549.

Craddock, P. T., I. C. Freestone, L. K. Gurjar, A. Middleton, and L. Willies. 1989. 'The production of lead, silver and zinc in early India', in A. Hauptmann, E. Pernicka and G. Wagner (eds.), *Old World Archaeometallurgy. Proceedings of the International Symposium, Heidelberg 1987*, pp. 51–69. Bochum: Selbstverlag des Deutschen Bergbau-Museums.

Crawford, H. E. W. 1998. *Dilmun and Its Gulf Neighbours*. Cambridge: Cambridge University Press.

Cribb, J. 1985. 'Dating India's Earliest Coin', in J. Schotsmans and M. Taddei (eds.), *South Asian Archaeology 1983*, pp. 535–554. Naples: Istituto Universitario Orientale.

Crumley, C. L. 1995. 'Building an historical ecology of Gaulish politics', in B. Arnold and D. B. Gibson (eds.), *Celtic Chiefdom, Celtic State: the Evolution of Complex Social Systems in Prehistoric Europe*, pp. 26–33. Cambridge: Cambridge University Press.

Cunningham, A. 1854. *The Bhilsa Topes; or Buddhist Monuments of Central India*. London: Smith, Elder and Co.

———. 1871. *The Ancient Geography of India*. London: Trubner and Co.

Dahal, J., C. A. Petrie, and D. T. Potts. 2013. 'Chronological parameters of the earliest writing system in Iran', in C. A. Petrie (ed.), *Ancient Iran and its Neighbours: Local Developments and Long-Range Interactions in the Fourth Millennium BC*, pp. 353–378. London: British Institute of Persian Studies.

Dales, G. F. 1962. 'Harappan outposts on the Makran Coast'. *Antiquity* 36: 86–92.

———. 1964. 'The mythical massacre at Mohenjo-daro'. *Expedition* 6.3: 36–43.

———. 1966. 'The decline of the Harappans'. *Scientific American* 214: 92–100.

———. 1974. 'Excavations at Balakot, Pakistan, 1973'. *Journal of Field Archaeology* 1.1–2: 3–22.

———. 1979. 'The Balakot project: summary of four years' excavations in Pakistan', in M. Taddei (ed.), *South Asian Archaeology 1977*, pp. 241–273. Naples: Istituto Universitario Orientale.

———. 1991. 'The phenomenon of the Indus civilisation', in M. Jansen, M. Mulloy and G. Urban (eds.), *Forgotten Cities on the Indus: Early Civilisation in Pakistan from the 8th to the 2nd Millennium BC*, pp. 129–144. Mainz: Philipp von Zabern.

Dales, G. F., and J. M. Kenoyer. 1986. *Excavations at Mohenjo-daro, Pakistan: The Pottery*. Pennsylvania: The University Museum.

———. 1991. 'Summaries of five seasons of research at Harappa 1986–1990', in R. H. Meadow (ed.), *Harappa Excavations 1986–1990: a Multidisciplinary Approach to Third Millennium Urbanism*, pp. 185–262. Madison: Prehistory Press.

Dandamaev, M. A., and G. Lukonin. 1989. *The Culture and Social Institutions of Ancient Iran*. Cambridge: Cambridge University Press.

Dani, A. H. 1966. 'Shaikhan Dheri excavations'. *Ancient Pakistan* 2: 17–120.

———. (ed.) 1967. 'Timargarha and Gandhara grave culture'. *Ancient Pakistan* 3: 1–407.

———. 1968. 'Gandhara grave complex in west Pakistan'. *Asian Perspectives* 11: 99–110.

———. 1971. 'Excavations in the Gomal Valley'. *Ancient Pakistan* 5: 1–177.

———. 1978. 'Gandhara grave culture and the Aryan problem'. *Journal of Central Asia* 1.1: 42–56.

———. 1986. *Taxila*. Lahore: Sang-e-Meel Publications.

———. 1991. *History of the Northern Areas of Pakistan*. Islamabad: National Institute of Historical and Cultural Research.

———. 1992. 'Pastoral-agricultural tribes of Pakistan in the post-Indus period', in A. H. Dani, and V. M. Masson (eds.), *History of Civilizations of Central Asia. Volume I*, pp. 395–419. Paris: UNESCO.

———. 1995. *Human Records on Karakorum Highway*. Lahore; Sang-E-Meel Publications.

Dani, A. H., and P. Bernard. 1994. 'Alexander and his successors in Central Asia', in J. Harmatta (ed.), *History of Civilizations of Central Asia*, pp. 67–97. Paris: UNESCO.

Dani, A. H., and B. K. Thapar. 1992. 'The Indus civilisation', in A. H. Dani and V. M. Masson (eds.), *History of Civilisations of Central Asia: Volume 1. The Dawn of Civilisation: Earliest Times to 700 BC*, pp. 283–318. Paris: UNESCO.

de Cardi, B. 1983. *Archaeological Surveys in Baluchistan 1948 and 1957*. London: Institute of Archaeology.

Deeg, M. 2003. *The Places Where Siddhartha Trod: Lumbini and Kapilavastu*. Lumbini: Lumbini International Research Institute.

Dennell, R. 2009. *The Palaeolithic Settlement of Asia*. Cambridge: Cambridge University Press.

Deo, S. B. 1968. *Archaeological Investigations in the Nepal Terai 1964*. Kathmandu: Department of Archaeology.

Deo, S. B., and Z. D. Ansari. 1965. *Chalcolithic Chandoli*. Poona: Deccan College.

Deraniyagala, S. U. 1972. 'The Citadel of Anuradhapura: excavations in the Gedige area'. *Ancient Ceylon* 2: 48–169.

———. 1986. 'Excavations in the citadel of Anuradhapura: Gedige 1984, a preliminary report'. *Ancient Ceylon* 6: 39–48.

———. 1990. 'Radiocarbon dating of early Brahmi script in Sri Lanka: 600–500 BC'. *Ancient Ceylon* 11: 149–168.

———. 1992. *The Prehistory of Sri Lanka: An Ecological Perspective*. Colombo: Archaeological Survey Department.

Deraniyagala, S. U., and K. A. R. Kennedy. 1972. 'Bellan Bandi Palassa 1970: a Mesolithic burial site in Ceylon'. *Ancient Ceylon* 2: 18–47.

de Silva, K. M. 1981. *A History of Sri Lanka*. Berkeley: University of California Press.

de Terra, H., and T. T. Paterson. 1939. *Studies on the Ice Age in India and Associated Human Cultures*. Washington: Carnegie Institution of Washington.

Dhavalikar, M. K. 1992. 'Kuntasi: a Harappan port in Western India', in C. Jarrige (ed.), *South Asian Archaeology 1989*, pp. 73–82. Madison: Prehistory Press.

———. 1995. *Cultural Imperialism: Indus Civilisation in Western India*. New Delhi: Books and Books.

Dhavalikar, M. K., and S. Atre. 1989. 'The fire cult and virgin sacrifice: some Harappan rituals', in J. M. Kenoyer (ed.), *Old Problems and New Perspectives in the Archaeology of South Asia*, pp. 193–205. Madison: Department of Anthropology.

Dhavalikar, M. K., H. D. Sankalia, and Z. D. Ansari. 1988. *Excavations at Inamgaon*. Pune: Deccan College.

Dichter, D. 1967. *The North-West Frontier Province of West Pakistan. A Study in Regional Geography.* Oxford: Clarendon Press.

Dissanayake, W. 2010. *Ramayana: As Shadows of South Asia's Protohistory.* Colombo: Sooriya Publications.

Dittmann, R. 1984. 'Problems in the identification of an Achaemenian and Mauryan horizon in North Pakistan'. *Archaologische Mitteilungen aus Iran* 17: 155–190.

Dixit, Y., D. A. Hodell and C. A. Petrie. 2014. 'Abrupt weakening of the summer monsoon in northwest India ~4100 yr ago'. *Geology* DOI: 10.1130/ G35236.1.

Dumont, L. 1966. *Homo Hierarchicus. The Caste System and Its Implications.* (transl. 1970). Chicago: University of Chicago Press.

Duncan, J. S. 1990. *The City as Text: The Politics of Landscape Interpretation in the Kandyan Kingdom.* Cambridge: Cambridge University Press.

Dunnell, R. C. 1999. 'The concept of waste in an evolutionary archaeology'. *Journal of Anthropological Archaeology* 18: 243–250.

Dupree, L. 1973. *Afghanistan.* Princeton: Princeton University Press.

Durrani, F.A. 1981. 'Rehman Dheri and the birth of civilization in Pakistan'. *Bulletin of the Institute of Archaeology* 18: 191–207.

———. 1988. 'Excavations in the Gomal Valley: Rehman Dheri excavation report no. 1'. *Ancient Pakistan* 6: 1–232.

———. 1995. 'Excavations in the Gomal Valley: Rehman Dheri excavation report no. 2'. *Ancient Pakistan* 10: 1–232.

Durrani, F. A., I. Ali, and G. Erdosy. 1991. 'Further excavations at Rehman Dheri'. *Ancient Pakistan* 7: 61–151.

Durrani, F. A., I. Ali, and G. Erdosy. 1995. 'New perspectives on Indus Urbanism from Rehman Dheri'. *East and West* 45.1: 81–96.

Durrani, F. A., T. Ali, and I. Rehman. 1997. 'Excavations at Gor Khuttree: a preliminary note'. *Athariyyat (Archaeology): A Research Bulletin of the National Heritage Foundation.* 1: 185–212.

Dutt, B. B. 1925. *Town Planning in Ancient India.* Calcutta: Thacker and Spink.

Earle, T. (ed.). 1991. *Chiefdoms: Power, Economy and Ideology.* Cambridge: Cambridge University Press.

Edwards, D. N. 2005. 'The archaeology of religion', in M. Diaz-Andreu, S. Lucy, S. Babic and D. N. Edwards (eds.), *The Archaeology of Identity: Approaches to Gender, Age, Status, Ethnicity and Religion*, pp. 110–128. London: Routledge.

Eerkens, J. W., and C. Lipo. 2007. 'Cultural transmission theory and the archaeological record: providing context to understanding variation and temporal changes in material culture'. *Journal of Archaeological Research* 15: 239–274.

Ehrich, R. W. (ed.) 1992. *Chronologies in Old World Archaeology* (3rd edition). Chicago: University of Chicago Press.

Eltsov, P. A. 2008. *From Harappa to Hastinapura: A Study of the Earliest South Asian City and Civilization.* Leiden: E. J. Brill.

———. 2013. 'The ghost of the state in deep antiquity: a closer look at the Harappan civilisation from the viewpoint of Sanskrit literature', in S. A. Abraham, P. Gullapalli, T. P. Raczek and U. Z. Rizvi (eds.), *Connections and Complexity: New Approaches to the Archaeology of South Asia*, pp. 299–314. Walnut Creek: Left Coast Press.

Erdosy, G. 1987. 'Early historic cities of Northern India'. *South Asian Studies* 3: 1–23.

———. 1988. *Urbanisation in Early Historic India.* Oxford: BAR.

———. 1995a. 'The prelude to urbanization: Ethnicity and the rise of late Vedic chiefdoms', in F. R. Allchin (ed.), *The Archaeology of Early Historic South Asia: The Emergence of Cities and States*, pp. 75–98. Cambridge: Cambridge University Press.

———. 1995b. 'City states of North India and Pakistan at the time of the Buddha', in F. R. Allchin (ed.), *The Archaeology of Early Historic South Asia: The Emergence of Cities and States*, pp. 99–122. Cambridge: Cambridge University Press.

Faccenna, D. 1980. *Butkara I (Swat, Pakistan) 1956–1962.* Rome: Istituto Italiano per il Medio ed Estremo Oriente.

Fagan, B. M. 2001. *People of the Earth. An Introduction to World Prehistory.* (10th edition). New Jersey: Prentice Hall.

Fairservis, W. A. 1956. 'Excavations in the Quetta valley, west Pakistan'. *Anthropological Papers of the American Museum of Natural History* 45.2: 169–402.

———. 1967. 'The origin, character and decline of an early civilization', in G. L. Possehl (ed.), *Ancient Cities of the Indus*, pp. 66–89 New Delhi: Vikas Publishing House.

———. 1971. *The Roots of Ancient India: The Archaeology of Early Indian Civilisation.* London: George Allen and Unwin.

————. 1986. 'Cattle and the Harappan chiefdoms of the Indus Valley'. *Expedition* 28.2: 43–50.

————. 1989. 'An epigenetic view of the Harappan culture', in C. C. Lamberg-Karlovsky (ed.), *Archaeological Thought in America*, pp. 205–217. Cambridge: Cambridge University Press.

Falk, H. 2006. *Asokan Sites and Artefacts: A Source-Book with Bibliography*. Mainz: Philipp von Zabern.

Farmer, B. H. 1993. *Introduction to South Asia*. London: Routledge.

Fazeli, H., R. A. E. Coningham, A. Marghussian, M. J. Manuel, H. Azizi, and A. M. Pollard. 2013. 'Mapping the Neolithic occupation of the Kashan, Tehran and Qazvin Plains', in R. Matthews and H. Fazeli (eds.), *The Neolithisation of Iran: The Formation of New Societies*, pp. 114–135. Oxford: Oxbow Books.

Fazeli, H., and R. L. Young. 2013 'Animals and people in the Neolithisation of Iran', in R. Matthews and H. Fazeli (eds.), *The Neolithisation of Iran. The Formation of New Societies*, pp. 178–188. Oxford: Oxbow Books.

Fentress, M. A. 1984. 'The Indus "granaries": illusion, imagination and archaeological reconstruction', in K. A. R. Kennedy and G. L. Possehl (eds.), *Studies in the Archaeology and Palaeoanthropology of South Asia*, pp. 89–98. New Delhi: American Institute of Indian Studies.

Flam, L. 1981. *The Paleogeography and Prehistoric Settlement Patterns in Sind, Pakistan (c. 4000–2000 BC)*. PhD Dissertation. Ann Arbor: UMI Dissertation Services.

Flannery, K. V. 2002. 'The origins of the village revisited: from nuclear to extended household'. *American Antiquity* 67 417–433.

Fletcher, R. 2009. 'Low-density, agrarian based urbanism: a comparative view'. *Insights (Durham University)* 2.4: 1–19.

Fogelin, L. 2006. *Archaeology of Early Buddhism*. Lanham: AltaMira.

Foote, R. B. 1887. 'Note on some recent Neolithic and Palaeolithic finds in South India'. *Journal of the Asiatic Society of Bengal* 24: 194–99.

Fox, R. 1969. *Kinship and Marriage: An Anthropological Perspective*. London: Eyre and Spottiswoode.

Francfort, H.-P. 1981. 'The late periods of Shortughai and the problem of the Bishkent culture: middle and late Bronze Age in Bactria', in H. Hartel (ed.), *South Asian Archaeology 1979*, pp. 191–202. Berlin: Dietrich Reimer.

————. 1984. 'The early periods of Shortughai (Harappan) and the western Bactrian culture of Dashly', in B. Allchin (ed.), *South Asian Archaeology 1981*, pp. 170–175. Cambridge: Cambridge University Press.

Franke-Vogt, U. 2005. 'Excavations at Sohr Damb/Nal: results of the 2002 and 2004 seasons', in U. Franke-Vogt and H.-J. Weisshaar (eds.), *South Asian Archaeology 2003*, pp. 63–76. Aachen: Linden Soft.

Fraser, P. M. 1979. 'The son of Aristonax at Kandahar'. *Afghan Studies* 2: 9–21.

————. 1996. *Cities of Alexander the Great*. Oxford: Clarendon Press.

Fuhrer, A. A. 1897. *Monograph on Buddha Sakyamuni's Birthplace in the Nepalese Terai*. Allahabad: Archaeological Survey of India.

Fuller, D. Q. 2006. 'Agricultural origins and frontiers in South Asia: a working synthesis'. *Journal World Prehistory* 20: 1–86.

————. 2008. 'Asia, South: India, Deccan and Central Plateau', in D. Pearsall (ed.), *Encyclopaedia of Archaeology, pp.* 694–705. New York: Springer.

Fuller, D. Q., N. Boivin and R. Korisettar. 2007. 'Dating the Neolithic of South India: new radiometric evidence for key economic, social and ritual transformations'. *Antiquity* 81: 755–778.

Fussman, G. 1988. 'Central and provincial administration in Ancient India: the problem of the Mauryan Empire'. *Indian Historical Review* 14: 43–72.

Gadekar, C., S. V. Rajesh, and P. Ajithprasad. 2014. 'Shikarpur lithic assemblage: new questions regarding Rohri chert blade production'. *Journal of Lithic Studies* 1.1: 1–13.

Gamble, C. 2001. *Archaeology: The Basics*. London: Routledge.

Gates, C. 2003. *Ancient Cities. The Archaeology of Urban Life in the Ancient Near East and Egypt, Greece, and Rome*. London: Routledge.

Gaur, R. C. 1984. *Excavations at Atrijanijhera*. New Delhi: Motilal Banarasidas

————. 1995. *Excavations at Lal Qila*. Jaipur: Publication Scheme.

Genito, B. 2010. 'The Achaemenid Empire as seen as from its Eastern periphery: the case of Dahan-i Ghulaman in Sistan: forty years later, a preliminary revision of data', in P. Matthiae, F. Pinnock, L. Nigro and N. Nicol Marchetti (eds.),

Proceedings of the 6th International Congress of the Archaeology of the Ancient Near East, pp. 77–93. Wiesbaden: Harrassowitz.

Ghosh, A. 1955. 'Editorial notes'. *Ancient India* 10: 1–3.

———. (ed.). 1989. *An Encyclopaedia of Indian Archaeology*. New Delhi: Indian Council of Historical Research.

Ghosh, S. 2008. 'Hellenism in the Indo-Iranian Borderland', in G. Sengupta and S. Chakraborty, (eds.), *Archaeology of Early Historic South Asia*, pp. 69–79. New Delhi: Pragati Publications.

Gilbert, A. S. 1983. 'On the origins of specialized Nomadic Pastoralism in Western Iran'. *World Archaeology* 15.1: 105–119.

Gilliland, K., I. A. Simpson, W. P. Adderley, C. I. Burbidge, A. J. Cresswell, D. C. W. Sanderson, R. A. E. Coningham, M. J. Manuel, K. Strickland, P. Gunawardhana, and G. Adikari. 2013. 'The dry tank: development and disuse of water management infrastructure in the Anuradhapura hinterland, Sri Lanka'. *Journal of Archaeological Sciences* 40: 1012–1028.

Gillmore, G. K., R. A. E. Coningham, H. Fazeli, R. L. Young, M. Magshoudi, C. M. Batt, and G. Rushworth. 2009. 'Irrigation on the Tehran Plain, Iran: Tepe Pardis – the site of a possible Neolithic irrigation feature?'. *Catena* 78.3: 285–300.

Gimbutas, M. 1971. *The Slavs*. London: Thames and Hudson.

———. 1989. *The Language of the Goddess*. San Francisco: Harper Collins.

Gogte, V. D., and A. Kshirsagar. 1988. 'Chalcolithic diet, trace elemental analysis of human bones', in M. K. Dhavalikar, H. D. Sankalia and Z. D. Ansari (eds.), *Excavation at Inamgaon*, Vol. 1(2), pp. 963–990. Pune: Deccan College.

Good, I. 2006. 'Textiles as a medium of exchange in third millennium B.C.E. Western Asia', in V. H. Mair (ed.), *Contact and Exchange in the Ancient World*, pp. 191–214 Honolulu: University of Hawai'i Press.

Good, I. L., J. M. Kenoyer, and R. H. Meadow. 2009. 'New evidence for early silk in the Indus civilisation'. *Archaeometry* 51: 457–466.

Gordon, D. H. 1960. *The Prehistoric Background of Indian Culture*. New Delhi: Munshiram Manoharlal.

Gough, K. 1960. 'Caste in a Tanjore Village', in E. R. Leach (ed.), *Aspects of Caste in South India, Ceylon and North-West Pakistan*, pp. 11–60. Cambridge: Cambridge University Press.

Guha-Thakurta, T. 2004. *Monuments, Objects, Histories: Institutions of Art in Colonial and Post-Colonial India*. Columbia: Columbia University Press.

Gunnell, Y., K., Anupama, and B. Sultan. 2007. 'Response of the South Indian runoff-harvesting civilization to northeast monsoon rainfall variability during the last 2000 years: instrumental records and indirect evidence'. *The Holocene* 17.2: 207–215.

Gupta, A. K., D. M. Anderson, D. N. Pandey, and A. K. Singhvi. 2006. 'Adaptation and human migration, and evidence of agriculture coincident with changes in the Indian summer monsoon during the Holocene'. *Current Science* 90.8: 1082–1090.

Gupta, N. 2013. 'Cultural continuity, identity and archaeological practice in the Indian context', in S. Chrisomalis and A. Costopoulos (eds.), *Human Expeditions: Inspired by Bruce Trigger*, pp. 102–115. Toronto: University of Toronto Press.

Gupta, S. P. 1978. 'Origin of the form of Harappan culture: a new proposition', *Puratattva* 8: 141–146.

———. 1980. *The Roots of Indian Art*. New Delhi: R. B. Publishing Corporation.

———. 2010. Indus, Sarasvati and Aryans in Tiwari, S. (ed.), *Harapan Civilisation and Vedic Culture*, pp. 15–25. Delhi: Pratibha Prakashan.

Hackin, J., and J.-R. Hackin. 1939. *Recherches archéologiques à Bégram*. Paris: Délégation Archéologique Française en Afghanistan.

Halim, M. A. 1972. 'Excavations at Sarai Khola: Part 1'. *Pakistan Archaeology* 7: 23–89.

Haricharan, S., H. Achyuthan, and N. Suresh. 2013. 'Situating megalithic burials in the Iron Age–Early Historic landscape of Southern India'. *Antiquity* 87: 488–502.

Hartel. H. 1993. *Excavations at Sonkh: 2500 years of a town in Mathura District*. Berlin: Dietrich Reimer.

Hawkes, J. 1982. *Mortimer Wheeler: Adventurer in Archaeology*. London: Weidenfeld and Nicolson.

———. 2009. 'The wider archaeological contexts of the Buddhist Stupa site of Bharhut', in J. Hawkes and A. Shimada (eds.), *Buddhist Stupas in South Asia: Recent Archaeological, Art Historical and Historical Perspectives*, pp. 146–174. Delhi: Oxford University Press.

Hegde, K. T. M., K. K. Bhan, V. H. Sonawane, K. Krishnan, and D. R. Shah. 1991. *Excavations at*

Nageshwar: A Shell Working Site on the Gulf of Kutch. Baroda: MS University Press.

Heine-Geldern, R. 1936. 'Archaeological traces of the Vedic Aryans'. *Journal of the Indian Society of Oriental Art* 4: 87–115.

Helms, S. W. 1982. 'Excavations at the 'The city and the famous fortress of Kandahar, the foremost place in all Asia''. *Afghan Studies* 3–4: 1–24.

Hemmy, A. S. 1931. 'System of weights at Mohenjo-daro', in J. H. Marshall (ed.), *Mohenjo-daro and the Indus Civilisation*, pp. 589–598. London: Arthur Probsthain.

Hemphill, B. E., J. R. Lukacs, and K. A. R. Kennedy. 1991. 'Biological adaptations and affinities of Bronze Age Harappans', in R. H Meadow. (ed.), *Harappa Excavations 1986–1990: A Multidisciplinary Approach to Third Millennium Urbanism*, pp. 137–182. Madison: Prehistory Press.

Herman, C. F. 1997. 'The Rangpur sequence of 'Harappan' Gujarat (India): a reassessment', in F. R. Allchin and B. Allchin (eds.), *South Asian Archaeology 1995*, pp. 187–198. New Delhi: Oxford and IBH.

Hodder, I. 1982. *Symbols in Action: Ethnoarchaeological Studies of Material Culture*. Cambridge: Cambridge University Press.

———. 1990. *The Domestication of Europe: Structure and Contingency in Neolithic Societies*. Oxford: Blackwell.

Hodder, I., and S. Hutson. 2003. *Reading the Past: Current Approaches to Interpretation in Archaeology*. Cambridge: Cambridge University Press.

Hodges. H. 1989. *Artifacts: An Introduction to Early Materials and Technology*. London: Duckworth.

Hoffman, B., and H. M.-L. Miller. 2009. 'Production and consumption of copper base metals in the Indus civilization'. *Journal of Worlds Prehistory* 22: 237–264.

Hoffmann, S. A. 1998. 'The international politics of Southern Asia', in J. Sperling, K. Yodendra, K. Malik and D. Louscher (eds.), *Zones of Amity, Zones of Emnity: The Prospects for Economic and Military Security in Asia*, pp. 43–61. E. J. Brill: Leiden.

Hojlund, F. 2007. *The Burial Mounds of Bahrain: Social Complexity in Early Dilmun*. Hojbjerg: Jutland Archaeological Society.

Hooja, R. 1988. *The Ahar Culture*. Oxford: Archaeopress.

Hooja, R., and V. Kumar. 1997. 'Aspects of the early copper age in Rajasthan', in F. R. Allchin and B. Allchin (eds.), *South Asian Archaeology 1995*, pp. 323–339. New Delhi: Oxford and IBH.

Hurcombe, L. 2007. *Archaeological Artefacts as Material Culture*. London: Routledge.

Hutton, J. H. 1946. *Caste in India: Its Nature, Function and Origins*. Bombay: Oxford University Press.

IAR 1957. *Indian Archaeology: A Review* 1957.

———. 1960–1961. *Indian Archaeology: A Review* 1960–1

———. 1962–1963. *Indian Archaeology: A Review* 1962–3.

———. 1973. *Indian Archaeology: A Review* 1973

Iman, A. 1966. *Sir Alexander Cunningham and the Beginnings of Indian Archaeology*. Dhaka: Asiatic Society of Pakistan.

Indrawooth, P. 2004. 'The archaeology of the Early Buddhist kingdoms of Thailand', in I. Glover and P. Bellwood (eds.), *Southeast Asia: From Prehistory to History*, pp. 120–148. New York: Routledge Curzon.

Insoll, T. 2004. *Archaeology, Ritual and Religion*. London: Routledge.

Irwin, J. 1973. 'Asokan Pillars: a reassessment of evidence'. *Burlington Magazine* 115: 706–722.

Janaway, R. C., and R. A. E. Coningham. 1995. 'A review of archaeological textile evidence from South Asia'. *South Asian Studies* 11: 157–174.

Jansen, M. 1985. 'Mohenjo-daro HR-A, House I, a Temple? Analysis of an Architectural Structure', in J. Schotsmans and M. Taddei (eds.), *South Asian Archaeology 1983*, pp. 157–206. Naples: Istituto Universitario Orientale.

———. 1991. 'Mohenjo-daro: a city on the Indus', in M. Jansen, M. Mulloy and G. Urban (eds.), *Forgotten Cities on the Indus: Early Civilisation in Pakistan from the 8th to the 2nd Millennium BC*, pp. 145–166. Mainz: Philipp von Zabern.

Jarrige, C. 1994. 'The Mature Indus phase at Nausharo as seen from a block of Period III', in A. Parpola and P. Koskikallio (eds.), *South Asian Archaeology 1993*, pp. 281–294. Helsinki: Suomalainen Tiedeakatemia.

Jarrige, J-F. 1979. 'Excavations at Mehrgarh, Baluchistan: their significance in the prehistoric context of the Indo-Pakistani borderlands', in M. Taddei (ed.), *South Asian Archaeology 1977*, pp. 463–535. Naples: Istituto Universitario Orientale.

———. 1984. 'Chronology of the earlier periods of the Greater Indus as seen from

Mehrgarh, Pakistan', in B. Allchin (ed.), *South Asian Archaeology 1981*, pp. 21–28. Cambridge: Cambridge University Press.

———. 1991. 'The cultural complex of Mehrgarh (Period VIII) and Sibri', in M. Jansen, M. Mulloy and G. Urban (eds.), *Forgotten Cities on the Indus: Early Civilisation in Pakistan from the 8th to the 2nd Millennium BC*, pp. 94–103. Berlin: Philipp von Zabern.

———. 1993a. 'The early architectural traditions of greater Indus as seen from Mehrgarh, Baluchistan', in H. Spodek and D. M. Srinivasan (eds.), *Urban Form and Meaning in South Asia: The Shaping of Cities from Prehistoric to Precolonial Times*, pp. 25–34. Washington: National Gallery of Art.

———. 1993b. 'Excavations at Mehrgarh: their significance for understanding the background of the Harappan civilisation', in Possehl, G. L. (ed.), *Harappan Civilisation*. New Delhi: American Institute of Indian Studies: 79–84.

Jarrige, J-F., and C. Jarrige. 2006. 'Premiers pasteurs et agriculteurs dans le sous-continent Indo Pakistanais'. *C.R. Palevol* 5: 463–472.

Jarrige, C., J-F. Jarrige, R. H. Meadow, and G. Quivron. 1995. *Mehrgarh: Field Reports 1974–1985, from Neolithic Times to the Indus Civilization*. Karachi: Department of Culture and Tourism of Sindh.

Jarrige, J-F., C. Jarrige, and G. Quivron. 2005. 'Mehrgarh Neolithic: the updated sequence', in C. Jarrige and V. Lefevre. (eds.), *South Asian Archaeology 2001*, pp. 128–141. Paris: Edition Recherche sur les Civilisations.

Jarrige, J-F., and M. Lechevallier. 1979. 'Excavations at Mehrgarh, Baluchistan: their significance in the prehistorical context of the Indo-Pakistani borderlands', in M. Taddei (ed.), *South Asian Archaeology 1977*, pp. 463–535. Naples: Istituto Universitario Orientale.

Jarrige, J-F., and G. Quivron. 2008. 'The Indus Valley and the Indo-Iranian Borderlands at the end of the 3rd millennium and the beginning of the 2nd millennium BC', in E. M. Raven (ed.), *South Asian Archaeology 1999*, pp. 61–83. Leiden: Forsten.

Jarrige, J-F., and M. Santoni. 1979. *Fouilles de Pirak*. Paris: Publications de la Commission des Fouilles Archeologiques.

Jasim, S. A. 2012. *The Necropolis of Jebel al-Buhais*. Shajah: Department of Culture and Information.

Jayaram, N. 1996. 'Caste and hinduism: changing protean relationships', in M. N. Srinivas (ed.), *Caste: Its Twentieth Century Avatar*, pp. 69–86. Delhi: Viking Penguin.

Jayaswal, V. 1998. *From Stone Quarry to Sculpturing Workshop: A report on the Archaeological Investigations around Chunar, Varanasi and Sarnath.* Delhi: Agam Kala Prakashan.

JBF (Japanese Buddhist Federation). 2001. *Archaeological Research at Maya Devi Temple, Lumbini. Volume 1.* Tokyo: Japanese Buddhist Federation.

Johansen, P. G. 2003. 'Recasting the foundations: new approaches to regional understandings of South Asian archaeology and the problem of culture history'. *Asian Perspectives* 42.2: 193–206.

———. 2004. 'Landscape, monumental architecture and ritual: a reconsideration of the South Indian ashmounds'. *Journal of Anthropological Archaeology* 23: 309–330.

———. 2008. 'The production of settlement landscapes and social difference in Iron Age South India: surface collection and documentation at Bukkasagara and Rampuram'. *Antiquity* 82: 317.

Johnson, M. 2010. *Archaeological Theory: An Introduction.* London: Wiley-Blackwell.

Joshi, J. P. 1990. *Excavations at Surkotada and Explorations in Kutch.* New Delhi: Archaeological Survey of India.

Joshi, J. P., M. Bala, and J. Ram. 1984. 'The Indus civilisation: a reconstruction on the basis of distribution maps', in B. B. Lal and S. P. Gupta (eds.), *Frontiers of the Indus Civilisation*, pp. 511–530. New Delhi: Indian Archaeological Society.

Juleff, J. 1990. 'The Samanalawewa archaeological survey'. *Ancient Ceylon* 9: 75–107.

Kalota, N. S. 1978. *India as Described by Megasthenes.* Delhi: Concept.

Kaminsky, A. P., and R. D. Long (eds.). 2011. *India Today: An Encyclopedia of Life in the Republic of India.* Santa Barbara: ABC-CLIO.

Kangle, R. P. 1965. *The Kautilya Arthasastra.* Bombay: University of Bombay.

Karve-Corvinus, G., and K. A. R. Kennedy. 1964. 'Preliminary Report on Langhnaj Excavations'. *Bulletin of the Deccan College Research Institute* 24: 44–57.

Kaw, M. K. 2004. *Kashmir and Its People: Studies in the Evolution of Kashmiri Society.* New Delhi: APH Publishing Co.

Kennedy, K. A. R. 2000. *God-Apes and Fossil Men, Paleoanthropology of South Asia*. Ann Arbor: University of Michigan Press.

Kenoyer, J. M. 1985. 'Shell working at Mohenjo-daro, Pakistan', in J. Schotsmans and M. Taddei (eds.), *South Asian Archaeology 1983*, pp. 297–344. Naples: Istituto Universitario Orientale.

———. 1989. 'Socio-economic structures of Indus civilisation as reflected in specialised crafts and the question of ritual segregation in J. M. Kenoyer (ed.), *Old Problems and New Perspectives in the Archaeology of South Asia*, pp. 183–192. Madison: University of Wisconsin

———. 1991a. 'Urban process in the Indus tradition: a preliminary model from Harappa', in R. H. Meadow (ed.), *Harappa Excavations 1986–1990*, pp. 29–60. Madison, Wisconsin: Prehistory Press.

———. 1991b. 'The Indus Valley tradition of Pakistan and Western India'. *Journal of World Prehistory* 5: 331–385.

———. 1994. 'The Harappan state: was it or wasn't it?', in J. M. Kenoyer (ed.), *From Sumer to Meluhha*, pp. 71–80. Madison: Wisconsin Archaeological Reports.

———. 1997a. 'Trade and technology of the Indus Valley: new insights from Harappa, Pakistan'. *World Archaeology* 29.2: 262–280.

———. 1997b. 'Early city-states in South Asia', in T. H. Charlton and D. L. Nichols (eds.), *The Archaeology of City-States*, pp. 51–70. Washington: Smithsonian Press.

———. 1998. *Ancient Cities of the Indus Valley Civilisation*. Karachi: Oxford University Press.

———. 2004. 'Wheeled vehicles of the Indus Valley civilisation of Pakistan and India', in M. Fansa and S. Burmeister (eds.), *Rad und Wagen: der Ursprung einer Innovation Wagen im Vorderen Orient und Europa*, pp. 87–106. Mainz: Philipp von Zabern.

———. 2006. 'Cultures and societies of the Indus tradition', in R. Thapar, et al. (eds.), *India: Historical Beginnings and the Concept of the Aryan*, pp. 41–97. Delhi: National Book Trust.

———. 2010. 'Measuring the Harappan world: insights into the Indus order and cosmology', in I. Morley and C. Renfrew (eds.), *Comprehending Heaven, Earth and Time in Ancient Societies*, pp. 106–121. Cambridge: Cambridge University Press.

———. 2013. 'Oconography of the Indus Unicorn: origins and legacy', in S.A.Abraham,

P. Gullapalli, T. P. Raczek and U. Z. Rizvi (eds.), *Connections and Complexity: New Approaches to the Archaeology of South Asia*, pp. 107–126. Walnut Creek: Left Coast Press.

Khan, F. A. 1965. 'Excavations at Kot Diji'. *Pakistan Archaeology* 2:11–85.

Khan, F. A., J. R. Knox, P. Magee and K. D. Thomas. 2000. 'Akra: the ancient capital of Bannu'. *Journal of Asian Civilisation* 23.1: 1–202.

Khan, M. A. 1973. 'Excavation at Zarif Karuna, Pakistan'. *Pakistan Archaeology* 9: 1–94.

Khare, R. S. (ed.). 2007. *Caste, Hierarchy and Individualism: Indian Critiques of Louis Dumont's Contributions*. Oxford: Oxford University Press.

Kintigh, K. W., J. H. Altschul, M. C. Beaudry, R. D. Drennan, A. P. Kinzig, T. A. Kohler, W. F. Limp, H. D. G. Maschner, W. K. Michener, T. R. Pauketat, P. Peregrine, J. A. Sabloff, T. J. Wilkinson, H. T. Wright, and M. A. Zeder. 2014. 'Grand challenges for archaeology'. *Proceedings of the National Academy of Sciences* 111: 879–880.

Klein Goldewijk, K., A. Beusen, G. van Drecht, and M. de Vos. 2011. 'The HYDE 3.1 spatially explicit database of human-induced global land-use change over the past 12,000 years'. *Global Ecology and Biogeography*: 20.1: 73–86.

Knox, R. 1681. *An Historical Relation of the Island of Ceylon*. London: Richard Chiswell.

Kohl, P. L. 2007. *The Making of Bronze Age Eurasia*. Cambridge: Cambridge University Press.

Korisettar, R., and M. Petraglia. (eds.). 1999. *Early Human Behaviour in the Global Context: The Rise and Diversity of the Lower Palaeolithic Record*. London: Routledge.

Korisettar, R., and R. Ramesh. 2002. 'The Indian monsoon: roots, relations and relevance', in S. Settar and R. Korisettar (eds.), *Indian Archaeology in Retrospect. Archaeology and Interactive Disciplines*, pp. 23–59. New Delhi: Manohar Publishers.

Korisettar, R., P. C. Venkatasubbaiah, and D. Q. Fuller. 2002. 'Brahmagiri and beyond: the archaeology of the Southern Neolithic', in S. Settar and R. Korisettar (eds.), *Indian Archaeology in Retrospect: Archaeology and Interactive Disciplines*, pp. 151–237. New Delhi: Manohar Publishers.

Kosambi, D. D. 1944. 'Caste and class in India'. *Science and Society* 8.3: 243–249.

———. 1956. *An Introduction to the Study of Indian History*. Bombay: Popular Book Depot.

————. 1965. *The Culture and Civilisation of Ancient India in Historical Outline*. London: Routledge and Kegan Paul.

Kramer, S. N. 1944. 'Dilmun: the land of the living'. *Bulletin of the American Schools of Oriental Research* 96: 18–82.

Krishna, M. H. 1943. *Annual Report of the Mysore Archaeological Department 1942*.

Krishnan, K. 2002a. 'A survey of ceramic analysis with specific reference to pottery', in S. Settar and R. Korisettar (eds.), *Indian Archaeology in Retrospect: Volume II Protohistory*, pp. 376–387. New Delhi: Indian Council for Historical Research.

————. 2002b. 'Studies in Harappan technology: a review', in K. Paddayya (ed.), *Recent Studies in Indian Archaeology*, pp. 350–366. New Delhi: Munshiram Manoharlal.

Krishnan, K, I. C. Freestone, and I. P. Middleton. 2005. 'The technology of "glazed" reserved slipware: a fine ceramic of the Harappan period'. *Archaeometry* 47: 691–703.

Kulke, H., and D. Rothermund. 1990. *A History of India* (1st edition). London: Routledge.

Lahiri, N. 1992. *The Archaeology of Indian Trade Routes (up to c. 200 BC)*. Delhi: Oxford University Press.

————. 2000. 'Archaeology and identity in colonial India'. *Antiquity* 74: 687–692.

Lal, B. B. 1949. 'Sisupalgarh'. *Ancient India* 5: 62–105.

————. 1955. 'Excavations at Hastinapura and other explorations in the Upper Ganga and Sutlej basins'. *Ancient India*: 10–11: 5–151.

————. 1960. 'Megalithic to the Harappa: tracing back the graffiti on pottery'. *Ancient India* 16: 4–24.

————. 1964. *Indian Archaeology since Independence*. New Delhi: Motilal Banarsidass.

————. 1978. 'Did the painted grey ware continue up to the Mauryan times?'. *Puratattva* 9: 64–81.

————. 1979. 'Kalibangan and Indus civilization', in D. P. Agrawal and D. K. Chakrabarti (eds.), *Essays in Indian Protohistory*, pp. 65–97. Delhi: B.R. Publishing Corporation.

————. 1998. *India 1947–1997: New Light on the Indus Civilization*. New Delhi: Aryan Books International.

————. 2002. *The Sarasvatī Flows On: The Continuity of Indian Culture*. New Delhi: Aryan Books International.

————. 2003. *Excavations at Kalibangan, The Early Harappans, 1960–1969*. New Delhi: Archaeological Survey of India.

————. 2005. *The Homeland of the Aryans: Evidence of Rigvedic Flora and Fauna and Archaeology*. Delhi: Aryan Books.

————. 2011. *Piecing Together: Memoirs of an Archaeologist*. New Delhi: Aryan Books International.

Lal, M. 1984a. *Settlement History and Rise of Civilisation in the Ganga-Yamuna Doab*. Delhi: BR Publishing House.

————. 1984b. 'Summary of four seasons of explorations in the Kanpur District'. *Man and Environment* 8: 61–80.

————. 1989. 'Population distribution and its movement during the second and first millennium BC in the Indo-Gangetic divide and Upper Ganga Plain'. *Puratattva* 18: 35–53.

Lamberg-Karlovsky, C. C. 1982. 'Dilmun: gateway to immortality'. *Journal of Near Eastern Studies* 41.1: 45–50.

Lambrick, H. T. 1967. 'The Mohenjo-daro floods'. *Antiquity* 41: 228.

Law, R. 2005. 'Regional interaction in the prehistoric Indus Valley: initial results of rock and mineral sourcing studies at Harappa', in C. Jarrige and V. Lefevre (eds.), *South Asian Archaeology 2001*, pp. 179–190. Paris: Ministere des Affaires Etrangeres.

————. 2006. 'Moving mountains: the trade and transport of rocks and minerals within the Greater Indus Valley region', in E. C. Robertson, J. D. Seibert, D. C. Fernandez and M. U. Zender (eds.), *Space and Spatial Analysis in Archaeology*, pp. 301–313. Calgary: University of Calgary Press.

Leach, E. R. 1960. *Aspects of Caste in South India, Ceylon, and North-West Pakistan*. Cambridge: Cambridge University Press.

————. 1990. 'Aryan Invasions over Four Millennia', in E. Ohnuki-Tierney (ed.), *Culture through Time: Anthropological Approaches*, pp. 227–245. Stanford: Stanford University Press.

Lechevallier, M. 1987. 'Stone-working in Mehrgarh', in M. Jansen, M. Mulloy and G. Urban, (eds.), *Forgotten Cities on the Indus: Early Civilisation in Pakistan from the 8th to the 2nd Millennium BC*, pp. 73–74. Mainz: Philipp von Zabern.

Legge, J., (transl.) 1965. *A Record of Buddhistic Kingdoms*, New York: Paragon Reprint Corp and Dover Publications Inc.

Leshnik, L. S. 1974. *South Indian Megalithic Burials: The Padunkal Complex*. Wiesbaden: Steiner.

————. 1979. 'The Harappan 'port' at Lothal: another view', in G. L. Possehl (ed.),

Ancient Cities of the Indus, pp. 203–211. New Delhi: Vikas.

Lopez, D. S. (ed.). 1995. *Curators of the Buddha: The Study of Buddhism under Colonialism,* Chicago: University of Chicago Press.

Lowe, J., and M. J. C. Walker. 1984. *Reconstructing Quaternary Environments* (1st edition). London: Longman.

Lukacs, J. R. 1983. 'Human dental remains from early Neolithic levels at Mehrgarh, Baluchistan'. *Current Anthropology* 24.3: 390–393.

———. 1989. 'Biological affinities from dental morphology: the evidence from Neolithic Mehrgarh', in J. M. Kenoyer (ed.), *Old Problems and New Perspectives in the Archaeology of South Asia,* pp. 75–88. Wisconsin: University of Wisconsin.

Lukacs, J. R., and B. E. Hemphill. 1991. 'The dental anthropology of prehistoric Baluchistan: a morphometric approach to the peopling of South Asia', in M. A. Kelley and C. Spencer Larsen (eds.), *Advances in Dental Anthropology,* pp. 77–119. New York: Wiley-Liss.

Lukacs, J. R., V. N. Misra and K. A. R. Kennedy. 1983. *Bagor and Tilwa: Late Neolithic Cultures of Northwest India.* Pune: Deccan College.

Lukacs, J. R., and S. R. Walimbe. 1996. *The Physical Anthropology of Human Skeletal Remains. Part 1 – An Osteobiographic Analysis. Excavations at Inamgaon, Vol. II.* Pune: Deccan College Postgraduate and Research.

MacDowall, D. W., and M. Taddei. 1978. 'The early historic period', in F. R. Allchin and N. Hammond (eds.), *The Archaeology of Afghanistan from Earliest Times to the Timurid Period,* pp. 187–232. London: Academic Press.

Mackay, E. 1931a. 'Architecture and masonry', in J. H. Marshall (ed.), *Mohenjo-daro and the Indus Civilisation,* pp. 262–286. London: Arthur Probsthain.

———. 1931b. 'Seals, seal impressions and copper tablets, with tabulation', in J. H. Marshall (ed.), *Mohenjo-daro and the Indus Civilisation,* pp. 370–405. London: Arthur Probsthain.

———. 1931c. 'Statuary', in J. H. Marshall (ed.), *Mohenjo-daro and the Indus Civilisation,* pp. 356–364. London: Arthur Probsthain.

Mackay, E. J. H. 1938a. *Further Excavations at Mohenjo-daro.* Delhi: Government of India.

———. 1938b. *Chanhu-daro.* New Haven: American Oriental Society.

Madella, M. 2003. 'Investigating agriculture and environment in south Asia: present and future contributions of opal phytolithis', in S. A. Weber and W. R. Belcher (eds.), *Indus Ethnobiology: New Perspectives from the Field,* pp. 199–250. Lanham: Lexington Books.

Madella, M., and D. Q. Fuller. 2006. 'Palaeoecology and the Harappan civilisation of South Asia: a reconsideration'. *Quaternary Science Reviews* 25: 1283–1301

Madsen, M., C. Lipo, and M. Cannon. 1999. 'Fitness and reproductive trade-offs in uncertain environments: explaining the evolution of cultural elaboration'. *Journal of Anthropological Archaeology* 18: 251–281.

Magee, P., and C. Petrie. 2010. 'West of the Indus – East of the Empire: the archaeology of the Pre-Achaemenid and Achaemenid periods in Baluchistan and the north-west frontier province, Pakistan', in J. Curtis and St J. Simpson (eds.), *The World of Achaemenid Persia: History, Art and Society in Iran and the Ancient Near East,* pp. 503–522. London: I. B. Tauris.

Magee, P., C. Petrie, R. Knox and F. Khan. 2005. 'The Achaemenid Empire in south Asia and recent excavations at Akra, (NWFP, Pakistan)'. *American Journal of Archaeology* 109: 711–774.

Majumdar, N. G. 1934. *Explorations in Sind. Memoirs of the Archaeological Survey of India No 48.* New Delhi: Archaeological Survey of India.

Malik, S. C. 1968. *Indian Civilization: The Formative Period. A Study of Archaeology as Anthropology.* Simla: Indian Institute of Advanced Study.

———. 1984. 'Harappan social and political life', in B. B. Lal and S. P. Gupta (eds.), *Frontiers of the Indus Civilisation,* pp. 201–209. Delhi: Books and Books.

Mallory, J. P. 1989. *In Search of the Indo-Europeans: Language, Archaeology and Myth.* London: Thames and Hudson.

Mandal, D. 1972. *Radiocarbon Dates and Indian Archaeology.* Allahabad: Vaishali Publishing House.

Manuel, M. J. 2010. 'Chronology and culture-history in the Indus Valley', in P. Gunawardhana, G. Adikari and R. A. E. Coningham (eds.), *Essays in Archaeology: Sirinimal Lakdusinghe Felicitation Volume,* pp. 145–152. Battaramulla: Neptune.

Mariani, L. 1984. 'Craftsmen quarters in the proto-urban settlements of the middle east: the surface analysis', in B. Allchin (ed.), *South Asian Archaeology, 1981.* Cambridge: Cambridge University Press: 118–123.

Marshall, J. 1904. 'Excavations at Charsadda'. *Annual Report of the Archaeological Survey of India 1904*: 141–184.

Marshall, J. H. 1912. 'Excavations at Bhita'. *Annual Report of the Archaeological Survey of India 1911–12*: 29–94.

———. (ed.). 1931a. *Mohenjo-daro and the Indus Civilisation*. London: Arthur Probsthain.

———. 1931b. 'The buildings', in, J. H. Marshall (ed.), *Mohenjo-daro and the Indus Civilisation*, pp. 15–26. London: Arthur Probsthain.

———. 1939. 'The story of the Archaeological Department in India', in J. Cumming (ed.), *Revealing India's Past*, pp. 1–33. London: The India Society.

———. 1951. *Taxila, an Illustrated Account of Archaeological Excavations*. Cambridge: Cambridge University Press.

———. 1960. *A Guide to Taxila*. Cambridge: Cambridge University Press.

Marshall, J. H., A. Foucher, and N. G. Majumdar. 1940. *The Monuments of Sanchi*. Delhi: Archaeological Survey of India.

Matthews, R. 2003. *The Archaeology of Mesopotamia. Theories and Approaches*. London: Routledge.

McCrindle, J. W. 1896. *The Invasion of India by Alexander the Great as Described by Arrian, Q. Curtius, Diodoros, Plutarch and Justin*. London: A. Constable and Co.

McDonnell, J. G., and R. A. E. Coningham. 2007. 'The metal objects and metal-working residues', in R. A. E. Coningham and I. Ali (eds.), *Charsadda: The British-Pakistani Excavations at the Bala Hisar*, pp. 155–159. Oxford: Archaeopress.

McDonnell, J. G., A. Hardy and R. A. E. Coningham. 2006. 'Metal-working residue', in R. A. E. Coningham (ed.), *Anuradhapura: The British-Sri Lankan Excavations at Anuradhapura Salgaha Watta 2. Volume 2: the Artefacts*, pp. 77–85. Oxford: Archaeopress.

McIntosh, J. R. 1981. 'The megalith builders of South India. A historical survey', in H. Hartel (ed.), *South Asian Archaeology 1979*, pp. 459–468. Berlin: Deitrich Reimer.

———. 1985. 'Dating the South Indian megaliths', in J. Schotsmans and M. Taddei (eds.), *South Asian Archaeology 1983*, pp. 467–493. Naples: Istituto Universario Orientale.

———. 2002. *A Peaceful Realm: The Rise and Fall of the Indus Civilization*. Boulder, Colorado: Westview Press.

McIntosh, R. J., and S. K. McIntosh. 2003. 'Early urban configurations on the middle Niger: clustered cities and landscapes of power', in M. L Smith (ed.), *The Social Construction of Ancient Cities*, pp. 103–120. Washington DC: Smithsonian Institution Press.

McNicoll, A. 1978. 'Excavations at Kandahar, 1975: second interim report'. *Afghan Studies* 1: 41–66.

McNicoll, A., and W. Ball. 1996. *Excavations at Kandahar 1974 and 1975*. Oxford: Tempus.

Meadow, R. H. 1979. 'A preliminary note on the faunal remains from Pirak', in J-F. Jarrige and M. Santoni (eds.), *Fouilles de Pirak*, pp. 334. Paris: Publications de la Commission des Fouilles Archeologiques.

———. 1984a. 'Notes on the faunal remains from Mehrgarh, with a focus on cattle (*Bos*)', in B. Allchin (ed.), *South Asian Archaeology 1981*, pp. 34–40. Cambridge: Cambridge University Press.

———. 1984b. 'Animal domestication in the Middle East: a view from the eastern margin', in J. Clutton-Brock and C. Grigson (eds.), *Animals and Archaeology 3. Early Herders and Their Flocks*, pp. 309–337. Oxford: British Archaeological Reports.

———. 1989. 'Osteological evidence for the process of animal domestication', in J. Clutton-Brock (ed.), *The Walking Larder: Patterns of Domestication, Pastoralism, and Predation*, pp. 80–90. London: Unwin Hyman.

———. 1991. 'Faunal remains and urbanism at Harappa', in R. H. Meadow (ed.), *Harappa Excavations 1986–1990. A Multi-Disciplinary Approach to 3rd Millennium Urbanism*, pp. 89–106. Wisconsin: Prehistory Press.

Meadow, R. H., and A. Patel. 2003. 'Prehistoric pastoralism in northwest south Asia from the Neolithic through to the Harappan Period', in S. Weber and W. R. Belcher (eds.), *Indus Ethnobiology*, pp. 65–94. Lanham: Lexington Books.

Mehta, R., and S. Chowdhary. 1966. *Excavations at Devnimori: a Report of the Excavation Conducted from 1960–63*. Baroda: M.S. University of Baroda.

Mehta, R. N. 1969. 'Sudarsana Lake'. *Journal of the Oriental Institute (Baroda)* 18: 20–28.

Menon, J. 2008. 'Archaeology of early historic South Asia: a review', in G. Sengupta and S. Chakraborty (eds.), *Archaeology of Early Historic South Asia*, pp. 15–38. New Delhi: Pragati Publications.

Miller, D. 1985. 'Ideology and the Harappan civilisation'. *Journal of Anthropological Archaeology* 4: 34–71.

Miller, H. M.-L. 2013. 'Weighty matters: evidence for unit and regional diversity from the Indus civilisation weights', in S. A. Abraham, P. Gullapalli, T. P. Raczek and U. Z. Rizvi (eds.), *Connections and Complexity: New Approaches to the Archaeology of South Asia*, pp. 161–176. Walnut Creek: Left Coast Press.

Mishra, S. 1995. 'Chronology of the Indian stone age: the impact of the recent absolute and relative dating attempts'. *Man and Environment* 20: 11–16.

Mishra, S., N. Chauhan, and A. K. Singhvi. 2013. 'Continuity of microblade technology in the Indian Subcontinent since 45 ka: implications for the dispersal of modern humans'. *PLoS ONE* 8.7: e69280

Mishra, T. N. 1978. *The Location of Kapilavastu and Archaeological Excavations, 1967–1972.* Kathmandu: Lumbini Development Committee.

Misra, V. N. 1973. 'Bagor: a Mesolithic settlement in northwest India'. *World Archaeology* 5: 92–110.

———. 1999. 'Agriculture, domestication of animals and ceramic and other industries in prehistoric India: Mesolithic and Neolithic', in G. C. Pande (ed.), *The Dawn of Indian Civilisation (up to c. 600 BC). Volume I*, pp. 233–266. Delhi: Centre for Studies of Civilisation.

———. 2001. 'The prehistoric human colonisation of India'. *Journal of Biosciences* 26: 491–531.

———. 2002. 'The Mesolithic age in India', in S. Settar and R. Korisettar (eds.), *Indian Archaeology in Retrospect. Volume 1: Prehistory*, pp. 111–125. New Delhi: Indian Council of Historical Research.

Misra, V. N., and R. K. Mohanty. 2000. *Excavations at Balathal, District Udaipur, Rajasthan*. Pune: Deccan College Post-Graduate and Research Institute.

———. 2001. 'A rare Chalcolithic pottery cache from Balathal, Rajasthan'. *Man and Environment* 26: 67–74.

Misra, V. N., V. Shinde, R. K. Mohanty, L. Pandey and J. Kharakwal. 1997. 'Excavation at Balathal, Udaipur District, Rajasthan (1995–97), with special reference to Chalcolithic architecture'. *Man and Environment* 22: 35–59.

Mitra, D. 1971. *Buddhist Monuments*. Calcutta: Sahitya Samsad.

———. 1972. *Excavations at Tilaura-Kot and Kodan and the Explorations in the Nepalese Tarai*. Kathmandu: The Department of Archaeology.

Mizoguchi, K. 2002. *An Archaeological History of Japan*. Philadelphia: University of Pennsylvania Press.

Mohan, V. 1998. 'The dynamics of the pre-Harappan phase of the Harappan civilization re-examined'. *Man in India* 78, 3–4: 223–237.

Mohanty, R. K., and M. L. Smith. 2008. *Excavations at Sisupalgarh*. New Delhi: Indian Archaeological Society.

Mohanty, R. K., and V. Selvakumar. 2002. 'The archaeology of the megaliths in India: 1947–1997', in S. Settar and R. Korisettar (eds.), *Indian Archaeology in Retrospect. Prehistory Volume 1*, pp. 313–352. Delhi: Indian Council of Historical Research.

Mohanty, R. K., and S. R. Walimbe. 1993. 'A demographic approach to the Vidarbha megalithic culture'. *Man and Environment* 18.2: 93–103.

Mookherjee, N. 2013. 'Introduction: self in South Asia'. *Journal of Historical Sociology*, 26.1: 1–18.

Moore, E. H. 2007. *Early Landscapes of Myanmar*. Bangkok: River Books.

Moore, P. D., J. A. Webb, and M. E. Collinson. 1991. *Pollen Analysis* (2nd edition). Oxford: Blackwell Scientific Publications.

Moorti, U. S. 1990. 'Evidence of social differentiation and socio-political organisation during the megalithic period in south India'. *Purattava* 20: 1–64.

———. 1994. *Megalithic Culture of South India: Socio-economic Perspectives*. Varanasi: Ganga Kaveri Publishing House.

Morigi, E., and P. Bianchetti. 2005. 'New evidence on the pottery sequence of Ghalegay (Swat, Pakistan)', in U. Franke-Vogt and H.-J. Weisshaar (eds.), *South Asian Archaeology 2003*, pp. 223–230. Aachen: Linden Soft.

Morrill, C., J. T. Overpeck and J. E. Cole. 2003. 'A synthesis of abrupt changes in the Asian summer monsoon since the last deglaciation'. *Holocene* 13.4: 465–476.

Morrison, K. D. 2005. 'Brahmagiri revisted: a re-analysis of the South Indian sequence', in C. Jarrige and V. LeFevre (eds.), *South Asian Archaeology 2001*, pp. 257–261. Paris: Editions Recherche sur les Civilisations ADPF.

———. 2006. 'Historicizing foraging in south Asia: power, history and ecology of Holocene hunting and gathering', in M. Stark (ed.), *The Archaeology of Asia*, pp. 279–302. Oxford: Blackwell.

Moulherat, C., M. Tengberg, J-F. Haquet and B. Mille. 2002. 'First evidence of cotton at

Neolithic Mehrgarh, Pakistan: analysis of mineralised fibres from a copper bead'. *Journal of Archaeological Science* 29: 1393–1401.

Mughal, M. R. 1990. 'Further evidence of the Early Harappan culture in the greater Indus valley'. *South Asian Studies* 6: 175–199.

———. 1992. 'Jhukar and the Late Harappan cultural mosaic of the greater Indus Valley', in C. Jarrige (ed.), *South Asian Archaeology 1989*, pp. 213–221. Madison: Prehistory Press.

———. 1994. 'The Harappan Nomads of Cholistan', in B. Allchin (ed.) *Living Traditions. Studies in the Ethnoarchaeology of South Asia*, pp. 53–68. Oxford and New Delhi: Oxbow Books and Oxford and IBH Publishing Co. PVT. Ltd.

———. 1997. *Ancient Cholistan. Archaeology and Architecture*. Rawalpindi: Ferozsons (Pvt.) Ltd.

Mukherji, P. C. 1901. *A Report on a Tour of Exploration of the Antiquities in the Tarai, Nepal.* Calcutta: Office of the Superintendent of Government Printing.

Mushrif-Tripathy, V., and S. R. Walimbe. 2012. *Human Skeletal Remains from the Medieval Site of Sanjan Osteobiographic Analysis.* Oxford: BAR.

Nagaraja Rao, M. S., and K. C. Malhotra. 1965. *The Stone Age Hill Dwellers of Tekkalakota.* Poona: Deccan College.

Narain, A. K. 1957. *The Indo-Greeks.* Oxford: The Clarendon Press.

Narain, A. K., and T. N. Roy. 1977. *Excavations at Rajghat (1957–1958; 1960–1965): Part II: the Pottery.* Varanasi: Banaras Hindu University.

Narasimhaiah, B. 1980. *Neolithic and Megalithic Cultures in Tamil Nadu.* Delhi: Sundeep Prakashan.

Narayanan, V. 1996a. 'The Hindu tradition', in W. G. Oxtoby (ed.), *World Religions. Eastern Traditions*, pp. 12–133. Toronto: Oxford University Press.

———. 1996b. 'The Jain tradition', in W. G. Oxtoby (ed.), *World Religions. Eastern Traditions*, pp. 134–175. Toronto: Oxford University Press.

National Action Plan on Climate Change. 2008. New Delhi: Government of India.

Nautiyal, K. P., and B. M. Khanduri. 1986. 'New cultural dimensions in the central Himalayan region of Uttarakhand: an archaeological assessment'. *Annali dell'Istituto Universitario Orientale* 46: 77–100.

Neelis, J. 2007. 'Passages to India: Saka and Kusana migrations in historical contexts', in D. M. Srinivasan (ed.), *On the Cusp of an Era: Art in the Pre-Kusāna World*, pp. 55–94. Leiden: E.J. Brill.

Nehru, J. 2010. *Words of Freedom: Ideas of a Nation.* New Delhi: Penguin Books India.

Nichols, D. L., and T. H. Charlton (eds.) 1997. *The Archaeology of City-States: Cross Cultural Approaches.* Washington: Smithsonian Institution

Nimchuk, C. L. 2010. 'Empire encapsulated: the Persepolis Apadana Foundation deposits', in J. Curtis and St J. Simpson (eds.), *The World of Achaemenid Persia: History, Art and Society in Iran and the Ancient Near East*, pp. 221–230. London: I.B. Tauris.

Nolan, K. C., and S. P. Howard. 2010. 'Using evolutionary archaeology and evolutionary ecology to explain cultural elaboration: the case of Middle Ohio Valley Woodland Period ceremonial subsistence'. *North American Archaeologist* 31.2 119–154.

Olivelle, P. (ed.). 2006. *Between the Empires: Society in India 300 BCE to 400 CE.* Oxford: Oxford University Press.

Olivieri, L. M. 1996. 'Notes on the problematical sequence of Alexander's itinerary in Swat. A geo-historical approach'. *East and West* 46.1-2: 45–78.

O'Sullivan, D., and R. L. Young. 2012. 'A world apart? Translating the archaeology of the sacred in the modern world'. *World Archaeology* 44.3: 342–358.

Oxtoby, W. G. 1996. 'The sikh tradition', in W. G. Oxtoby (ed.), *World Religions. Eastern Traditions*, pp. 176–213. Toronto: Oxford University Press.

Paddayya, K. 1973. *Investigations into the Neolithic Culture of the Shorapur Doab, South India.* Leiden: E.J. Brill.

Pant, R. K. 1979. 'Microwear studies on Burzahom'. *Man and environment* 3: 11–18.

Pappu, S. 2008. 'Prehistoric antiquities and personal lives: the untold story of Robert Bruce Foote'. *Man and Environment* 33: 30–50.

Paranavitana, S. 1970. *Inscriptions of Ceylon. Volume I.* Colombo: Archaeological Survey Department.

Parasher-Sen, A. 2008. 'Urban centres: Deccan', in G. Sengupta and S. Chakraborty (eds.), 2008. *Archaeology of Early Historic South Asia*, pp. 313–335. New Delhi: Pragati Publications.

Parpola, A. 1994. *Deciphering the Indus Script.* Cambridge: Cambridge University Press.

Parrinder, E. G. 1957. *An Introduction to Asian Religions.* London: SPCK.

Petrie, C. A., P. Magee, and M. N. Khan. 2008. 'Emulation at the edge of empire: the adoption of non-local vessel forms in the NWFP, Pakistan during the mid–late 1st millennium BC'. *Gandharan Studies* 2: 1–16.

Pettitt, P. B., W. Davies, C. S. Gamble, and M. B. Richards. 2003. 'Palaeolithic radiocarbon chronology: quantifying our confidence beyond two half-lives'. *Journal of Archaeological Science* 30: 1685–1693.

Piggott, S. 1943. 'The earliest Buddhist shrines'. *Antiquity* 17: 2–6.

———. 1950. *Prehistoric India to 1000 BC*. Harmondsworth: Penguin.

Piperno, M. 1983. 'Bead-making and boring techniques in 3rd millennium Indo-Iran', in M. Tosi (ed.), *Prehistoric Sistan*, pp. 319–326. Rome: Istituto Italiano Per Il Medio Ed Estremo Oriente.

Pollock, S. 2013. 'Scales, differences and mobility', in C. A. Petrie (ed.), *Ancient Iran and Its Neighbours: Local Development and Long-Range Interactions in the Fourth Millennium BC*, pp. 279–384. Oxford: Oxbow.

Poonacha, K. P. 2007. *Excavations at Mahastupa, Kanaganahalli, Chitapur Taluk, Gulbarga District, Karnataka (1997–2000)*. New Delhi: Archaeological Survey of India.

Possehl, G. L. 1979. 'Pastoral nomadism in the Indus civilisation: a hypothesis', in M. Taddei (ed.), *South Asian Archaeology 1977*, pp. 539–551. Naples: Istituto Universitario Orientale.

———. 1980. *Indus Civilisation in Saurashtra*. New Delhi: B.R. Publishing Corporation.

———. 1982. 'Harappan civilisation. A contemporary perspective', in G.L. Possehl (ed.), *Harappan Civilisation: A Contemporary Perspective*, pp. 15–28. Warminster: Aria and Phillips.

———. 1986. *Kulli: An Exploration of Ancient Civilisation in South Asia*. Durham: Carolina Academic Press.

———. 1993. 'The Harappan civilisation: a contemporary perspective', in G. L. Possehl, (ed.), *Harappan Civilisation: A Recent Perspective*, pp. 15–28. New Delhi: Oxford and IBH.

———. 1997. 'The transformation of the Indus civilisation'. *Journal of World Prehistory*, 11.4: 425–472.

———. 1998. 'Sociocultural complexity without the state: the Indus civilization', in Feinman, G. M. and Marcus, J. (eds.), *The Archaic States*, pp. 261–291. Santa Fe: School of American Research.

———. (ed.). 2002a. *The Indus Civilization: A Contemporary Perspective*. California: AltaMira.

———. 2002b. 'Harappan and hunters: economic interactions and specialization in prehistoric India', in K. D. Morrison and L. L. Junker (ed.), *Forager-Traders in South and Southeast Asia*, pp. 62–76. Cambridge: Cambridge University Press.

Possehl, G. L., and M. H. Raval. 1989. *Harappan Civilisation and Rojdi*. Leiden: E.J. Brill.

Possehl, G., and P. C. Rissman. 1992. 'The chronology of prehistoric India; from earliest times to the Iron Age', in R. W. Ehrich (ed.), *Chronologies in Old World Archaeology*. (3rd edition.), pp. 465–474. Chicago: University of Chicago Press.

Potts, D. T. 1990. *The Arabian Gulf in Antiquity. Volume 1: From Prehistory to the Fall of the Achaemenid Empire*. Oxford: Clarendon Press.

———. 1993. 'Tell Abraq and the Harappan tradition in southeast Arabia', in G. L. Posshel (ed.), *Harappan Civilisation*, pp. 323–334. New Delhi: American Institute of Indian Studies.

———. 1994a. 'South and Central Asian elements at Tell Abraq', in A. Parpola and P. Koskikallio (eds.), *South Asian Archaeology 1993*, pp. 615–628. Helsinki: Suomalainen Tiedeakatemia.

———. 1994b. *Mesopotamia and the East: An Archaeological and Historical Study of Foreign Relations c. 3400–2000 B.C.* Oxford: Oxbow Books.

———. 1999. *The Archaeology of Elam: Formation and Transformation of an Ancient Iranian State*. Cambridge: Cambridge University Press.

———. (ed.). 2012. *A Companion to the Archaeology of the Ancient Near East*. Oxford: Blackwell.

Pracchia, S., M. Tosi and M. Vidale. 1985. 'On the type, distribution and extent of craft activity areas at Mohenjodaro', in J. Schotsmans and M. Taddei (eds.), *South Asian Archaeology 1983*, pp. 207–247. Naples: Istituto Universitario Orientale.

Premathilake, R. 2006. 'Relationship of environmental changes in Central Sri Lanka to possible prehistoric land-use and climate changes'. *Palaeogeography, Palaeoclimatology, Palaeoecology* 240: 468–496.

Price, T. D., and G. Feinman (eds.). 2010. *Pathways to Power: New Perspectives on the Emergence of Social Inequality*. New York: Springer.

Prinsep, J. 1837. 'Further elucidation of the lat or Silasthambha inscriptions from various sources'. *Proceedings of the Asiatic Society of London*: 790–797.

Puri, B. N. 1994a. 'The Kushans', in J. Harmatta (ed.), *History of Civilisations of Central Asia. Volume II: The Development of Sedentary and Nomadic Civilisations 700 BC to AD 250*, pp. 247–263. Paris: UNESCO.

———. 1994b. 'The Sakas and Indo-Parthians', in J. Harmatta (ed.), *History of Civilisations of Central Asia. Volume II: The Development of Sedentary and Nomadic Civilisations 700 BC to AD 250*, pp. 191–207. Paris: UNESCO.

Quigley, D. 1993. *The Interpretation of Caste*. Oxford: Oxford University Press.

Quivron, G. 1997. 'Incised and painted marks on the Pottery of Mehrgarh and Nausharo-Baluchistan', in F. R. Allchin and B. Allchin (eds.), *South Asian Archaeology 1995*, pp. 45–62. New Delhi: Oxford and IBH.

Raikes, R. 1967. 'The Mohenjo-daro flood: riposte'. *Antiquity* 41: 309–310.

———. 1968. 'Kalibangan: death from natural causes'. *Antiquity* 42: 286–291.

Rajan, K. 1994. *The Archaeology of Tamil Nadu (Kongu Country)*. Noida: Book India Publication Company.

Ramachandran, K. S. 1980. *Archaeology of South India: Tamil Nadu*. New Delhi: Swadesh Prasad Singhal.

Ramaroli, V., J. Hamilton, P. Ditchfield, H. Fazeli, A. Aali, R. A. E. Coningham, and A. M. Pollard. 2010. 'The Chehr Abad "salt men" and the isotopic ecology of humans in ancient Iran'. *American Journal of Physical Anthropology* 143.3: 343–354.

Ramaswamy, S. 2004. *The Lost Land of Lemuria: Fabulous Geographies, Catastrophic Histories*. Berkeley: University of California Press.

Rangarajan, L. N. (ed. and transl.). 1992. *The Arthasastra*. New Delhi: Penguin.

Rao, S. R. 1973. *Lothal and the Indus Civilisation*. London: Asia Publishing House.

Ratnagar, S. 1991. *Enquiries into the Political Organization of the Harappan*. Pune: Ravish.

———. 2000. *The End of the Great Harappan Tradition*. New Delhi: Manohar Publishers.

———. 2002. *Understanding Harappa: Civilization in the Greater Indus Valley*. New Delhi: Tulika.

———. 2004. 'Archaeology at the heart of a political confrontation: the case of Ayodhya'. *Current Anthropology* 45: 239–259.

———. 2006. 'Agro-pastoralists and the migration of the Indo-Iranians', in R. Thapar et al. (ed.), *India: Historical Beginnings and the Concept of the Aryan*, pp. 157–192. New Delhi: National Book Trust.

Ray, H. P. 1994. *The Winds of Change: Buddhism and the Maritime links of Early South Asia*. New Delhi: Oxford University Press.

———. 2003. *The Archaeology of Seafaring in Ancient South Asia*. Cambridge: Cambridge University Press.

———. 2007. *Colonial Archaeology in South Asia: The Legacy of Sir Mortimer Wheeler*. Cambridge: Cambridge University Press.

Reddy, S. 1997. 'If the threshing floor could talk: integration of agriculture and pastoralism during the late Harappan in Gujarat, India'. *Journal of Anthropological Archaeology*, 16.2: 162–187.

———. 2003. 'Food and Fodder: plant usage and changing socio-cultural landscapes during the Harappan phase in Gujarat, India', in S. Weber and W. R. Belcher (eds.), *Indus Ethnobiology*. Lanham: Lexington Books: 327–342.

Renfrew, A. C. 1986. 'Introduction: peer polity interaction and socio-political change', in A. C. Renfrew and J. F. Cherry (eds.), *Peer Polity Interaction and Socio-Political Change*, pp. 1–18. Cambridge: Cambridge University Press.

———. 1987. *Archaeology and Language: The Puzzle of Indo-European Origins*. London: Cape.

Renfrew, A. C., and J. F. Cherry (eds.) 1986. *Peer Polity Interaction and Socio-Political Change*. Cambridge: Cambridge University Press.

Renfrew, C., and P. Bahn. 2010. *Archaeology: Theories, Methods and Practice*. (6th edition) London: Thames and Hudson.

Rhys Davids, T. W. 1903. *Buddhist India*. London: T. Fisher Unwin.

Rijal, B. K. 1979. *Archaeological Remains of Kapilavastu, Lumbini and Devadaha*. Kathmandu: S.K. International Publishing House.

Rissman, P. 1988. 'Public displays and private values – a guide to buried wealth in Harappan Archaeology'. *World Archaeology* 20.2: 209–228.

Rizvi, U. 2008. 'Decolonizing methodologies as strategies of practice: operationalizing the postcolonial technique in the archaeology of Rajasthan', in M. Leibman and U. Rizvi (eds.), *Archaeology and the Postcolonial Critique*, pp. 109–127. Lanham: Altimira Press.

Robb, J. 1991. 'Random causes with directed effects: the Indo-European language spread and the stochastic loss of lineages'. *Antiquity* 65: 287–291.

Robinson, F. 1989. *The Cambridge Encyclopaedia of India, Pakistan, Bangladesh, Sri Lanka, Nepal, Bhutan and the Maldives.* Cambridge: Cambridge University Press.

Rogers, J. D. 2004a. 'Introduction: caste, power and region in colonial South Asia. *Indian Economic and Social History Review* 41.1: 1–6.

———. 2004b. 'Caste as a social category and identity in colonial Lanka'. *Indian Economic and Social History Review* 41.1: 51–77.

Rowland, B. 1953. *The Art and Architecture of India: Buddhist, Hindu and Jain.* London: Penguin.

Roy, S. R. 1989. 'Chirand', in A. Ghosh (ed.), *An Encyclopedia of Indian Archaeology, Volume 2*, pp. 103–105. New Delhi: Indian Council of Historical Research.

Sahni, M. R. 1956. 'Biological evidence bearing on the decline of the Indus Valley civilization'. *Journal of the Palaeontological Society of India* 1: 101–107.

Sahni, R. B. D. R. 1937. *Archaeological Remains and Excavations at Bairat.* Jaipur: Jaipur State Department of Archaeology and Historical Research.

Salgado, M. 2007. *Writing Sri Lanka: Literature, Resistance and the Politics of Place.* Routledge: London.

Sali, S. A. 1984. 'Late Harappan settlement at Daimabad', in B. B. Lal and S. P. Gupta (eds.), *Frontiers of the Indus Civilisation*, pp. 234–242. Delhi: Books and Books.

———. 1986. *Daimabad 1976–79.* New Delhi: Archaeological Survey of India.

Samzun, A. 1991. 'The Early Chalcolithic: Mehrgarh period III', in M. Jansen, M. Mulloy and G. Urban (eds.), *Forgotten Cities on the Indus: Early Civilization in Pakistan from the 8th to the 2nd Millennium BC*, pp. 66–72. Mainz: Philipp Von Zabern.

Sankalia, H. D. 1962. *Prehistory and Protohistory in India and Pakistan.* Bombay: University of Bombay.

———. 1965. *Excavations at Langhnaj.* Pune: Deccan College.

———. 1974. *Prehistory and Protohistory of India and Pakistan.* Poona: Deccan College.

———. 1977. *Prehistory of India.* Bombay: Munshiram Manoharlal Publishers.

Sankalia, H. D., and S. B. Deo. 1955. *Report on the Excavations at Nasik and Jorwe, 1950–51.* Poona: Deccan College.

Sankalia, H. D., S. B. Deo and Z. D. Ansari. 1969. *Excavations at Ahar.* Pune: Deccan College.

———. 1971. *Chalcolithic Navdatoli.* Baroda: MS University of Baroda and Poona: Deccan College.

Sankalia, H. D., S. B. Deo, Z. D. Ansari and S. Ehrhardt. 1960. *From History to Prehistory at Nevasa (1954–56).* Poona: Deccan College.

Santoni, M. 1984. 'Sibri and the south cemetery of Mehrgarh', in B. Allchin (ed.), *South Asian Archaeology 1981*, pp. 52–60. Cambridge: Cambridge University Press.

Sarcina, A. 1979. 'The private house at Mohenjo-daro', in M. Taddei (ed.), *South Asian Archaeology 1977*, pp. 435–462. Naples: Istituto Universitario Orientale.

Sarkar, H., and B. N. Misra 1966. *Nagarjunakonda.* New Delhi: Archaeological Survey of India.

Scarborough, V. L. 2003. *The Flow of Power: Ancient Water Systems and Landscapes.* Santa Fe: School of American Research.

Scarre, C., and B. M. Fagan. 1997. *Ancient Civilizations.* New York: Longman.

Scerrato, U. 1979. 'Evidence of religious life at Dahan-e Ghulaman, Sistan', in M. Taddei (ed.), *South Asian Archaeology 1977*, pp. 709–733. Naples: Istituto Universitario Orientale.

Schopen, G. 1997. *Bones, Stones and Buddhist Monks.* Hawai'i: University of Hawai'I Press.

Schug, G. W., K. E. Blevins, B. Cox, K. Gray, and V. Mushrif-Tripathy. 2014. 'Infection, disease and biosocial processes at the end of the Indus Civilisation'. *PLoS ONE* 8.12: e84814.

Schug, G. W., K. Gray, V. Mushrif-Tripathy, and A. E. Sankhyan. 2012. 'A peaceful realm? Trauma and social differentiation at Harappa'. *American Journal of Physical Anthropology* 143.1: 146–150.

Schuldenrein, J. 2002. 'Geoarchaeological perspectives on the Harappan sites of South Asia', in S. Settar and R. Korisettar (eds.), *Indian Archaeology in Retrospect, Volume II (Protohistory)*, pp. 47–80. New Delhi: Indian Council of Historical Research.

Sen, S. 2002. 'Community boundary, secularized religion and imagined past in Bangladesh: archaeology and historiography of unequal encounter'. *World Archaeology* 34.2: 346–362.

Sen, S., M. Imran, A. Khan, M. Rahman, N. Kabir, S. Rahamn, N. Sakeb, K. M. Islam and A. Rahman. 2006. 'We can protect our past?: re-thinking the dominating paradigm of preservation and conservation with reference to the world heritage site of Somapura Mahavihara, Bangladesh'. *Journal of Social Archaeology* 6.1: 71–99.

Seneviratne, S. 1984. 'The archaeology of the Megalithic Black and Red Ware Complex in Sri Lanka'. *Ancient Ceylon* 5: 237–307.

Sengupta, G., and S. Chakraborty (eds.). 2008. *Archaeology of Early Historic South Asia*. New Delhi: Pragati Publications.

Sengupta, I. 2010. 'Sacred space and the making of monuments in colonial Orissa in the early twentieth century' in H. P. Ray (ed.), *Archaeology and Text: The Temple in South Asia*, pp. 168–188. New Delhi: Oxford.

Service, E. 1971. *Primitive Social Organization: An Evolutionary Perspective* (2nd ed). New York: Random House.

Settar, S., and R. Korisettar (eds.). 2002. *Archaeology and Historiography: History, Theory and Method*. New Delhi: Indian Council of Historical Research.

Sewell, R. B. S., and B. S. Guha 1931. 'Zoological remains', in J. Marshall (ed.), *Mohenjo-Daro and the Indus Civilization*, pp. 649–673. London: Probsthain.

Shaffer, J. G. 1978. *Prehistoric Baluchistan*. New Delhi: B.R. Publishing Corporation.

———. 1986. 'Cultural development in the eastern Punjab', in J. Jacobson (ed.), *Studies in the Archaeology of India and Pakistan*, pp. 195–236. New Delhi: American Institute of Indian Studies.

———. 1992. 'The Indus Valley, Baluchistan and Helmand traditions: Neolithic through Bronze age', in R. W. Ehrich (ed.), *Chronologies in Old World Archaeology*. (2nd edition), pp. 425–446. Chicago: University of Chicago Press. I: 441–464, II.

———. 1993. 'Reurbanization: the eastern Punjab and beyond', in H. Spodek and D. M. Srinivasan (eds.), *Urban Form and Meaning in South Asia: The Shaping of Cities from Prehistoric to Precolonial Times. Studies in the History of Art No. 31*, pp. 53–67. Washington DC: National Gallery of Art.

Shaffer, J. G., and D. A. Lichtenstein. 1989. 'Ethnicity and change in the Indus Valley cultural tradition', in J. M. Kenoyer (ed.), *Old Problems and New Perspectives in the Archaeology of South Asia*, pp. 117–126. Madison, Wisconsin: University of Wisconsin.

Shaffer, J. G., and B. K. Thapar, 1992. 'Pre-Indus and Early Indus cultures of Pakistan and India', in A. H. Dani and V. M. Masson (eds.), *History of Civilizations of Central Asia. Volume 1. The Dawn of Civilization: Earliest Times to 700 BC*, pp. 247–281. Paris: UNESCO.

Sharif, M. 1969. 'Excavation at the Bhir Mound, Taxila'. *Pakistan Archaeology* 6: 6–99.

Sharif, M., and B. K. Thapar. 1992. 'Food-producing communities in Pakistan and Northern India', in A. H. Dani and V. M. Masson (eds.), *History of Civilizations of Central Asia. Volume I: The Dawn of Civilization: Earliest Times to 700 BC*, pp. 127–151. Paris: UNESCO.

Sharma, A. K. 1999. *The Departed Harappans of Kalibangan*. New Delhi: Sundeep Prakashan.

Sharma, B. D. 2010. 'Indus-Sarasvati civilisation: in search of the truth', in S. Tiwari (ed.), 2010. *Harapan Civilisation and Vedic Culture*, pp. 1–9. New Delhi: Pratibha Prakashan.

Sharma, D. P. 2002. *Newly Discovered Copper Hoard: Weapons of South Asia*. New Delhi: Bharatiya Kala Prakashan.

Sharma, G. R. 1960. *The Excavations at Kausambi 1957–59*. Allahabad: University of Allahabad.

———. 1969. *Excavations at Kausambi (1957–59)*. New Delhi: Archaeological Survey of India.

Sharma, G. R., V. D. Misra, D. Mandal, B. B. Misra and J. N. Pal. 1980. *From Hunting and Food Gathering to Domestication of Plants and Animals: Beginnings of Agriculture (Epi- Palaeolithic to Neolithic: Excavations at Chopani- Mando, Mahadaha and Mahagara)*. Allahabad: Abinash Prakasham.

Sharma, R. S. 1983. *Material Culture and Social Formations in Ancient India*. New Delhi: Macmillan.

———. 1999. *Advent of the Aryans in India*. New Delhi: Manohar Publishers.

Sharma, S., M. Joachimski, M. Sharma, H. J. Tobschall, I. B. Singh, C. Sharma, M. S. Chauhan, and G. Morgenroth. 2004. 'Lateglacial and Holocene environmental changes in Ganga plain, Northern India'. *Quaternary Science Reviews*, 23: 145–159.

Sharma, S., M. M. Joachimski, H. J. Tobschall, I. B. Singh, C. Sharma, and M. S. Chauhan. 2006. 'Correlative evidences of monsoon variability, vegetation change and human inhabitation in Sanai lake deposit: Ganga Plain, India'. *Current Science* 90.7: 973–978.

Shaw, J. 2000. 'The sacred landscape', in M. Willis (ed.), *Buddhist Reliquaries from Ancient India*, pp. 27–38. London: British Museum Press.

———. 2013. 'Archaeologies of Buddhist propagation in ancient India: 'ritual' and 'practical' models of religious change'. *World Archaeology* 45.1: 83–108.

Shinde, V. 1998. 'Pre-Harappan Padri culture in Saurashtra: the recent discovery'. *South Asian Studies* 14: 1–10.

Shinde, V., 2000. 'The origin and development of the Chalcolithic in Central India'. *Indo-Pacific Prehistory Association Bulletin* 19: 125–136.

———. 2008. 'Cultural development from Mesolithic to Chalcolithic in the Mewar Region of Rajasthan, India'. *Pragdhara* 18: 201–212.

Shinde, V., T. Osada, A. Uesugi, and M. Kumar. 2009. *Harappan Necropolis at Farmana in the Ghaggar Basin.* New Delhi: Indian Archaeological Society.

Shinde, V., G. L. Possehl, and M. Ameri. 2005. 'Excavations at Gilund 2001–2003: the seal impressions and other finds', in U. Franke-Vogt and H.-J. Weisshaar (eds.), *South Asian Archaeology 2003*, pp. 158–169. Aachen: Linden Soft.

Shinde, V., T. P. Raczek, and G. L. Possehl. 2014. *Excavations at Gilund: The Artifacts and Other Studies.* Philadelphia: University of Pennsylvania Press.

Shrestha, B. B. 1982. *The Prehistoric Archaeology of Nepal with Special Reference to the Beginning of Agriculture.* Unpublished PhD: University of Minnesota.

Shrestha, H. 2008. *Prehistoric Nepal: A Brief Observation.* Pokhara: Yu-Ba Publications.

Shrestha, S. S. 2005. *Excavations at Ramagrama.* Kathmandu: Department of Archaeology.

Simpson, I., N. Kourampas, and H. N. Perera. 2008. 'Bellan-bandi Palassa, Sri Lanka: formation processes of a Mesolithic open-air site identified through thin section micromorphology'. *Archaeologia: Journal of Archaeology* 4: 3–18.

Singh, G. 1964. 'A preliminary survey of the Postglacial vegetational history of the Kashmir Valley'. *Palaeobotanist* 12.1: 73–108.

———. 1971. 'The Indus Valley culture seen in the context of post-glacial climatic and ecological studies in northwest India'. *Archaeology and Physical Anthropology in Oceania* 6: 177–189.

———. 1991. 'Environmental changes in Southern Asia during the Holocene', in S. Chanda (ed.), *Current Perspectives in Palynological Research*, pp. 277–296. New Delhi: Today and Tomorrow's Printers and Publishers.

Singh, G., R. D. Joshi, S. Chopra, and A. B. Singh. 1974. 'Late quaternary history of vegetation and climate in Rajasthan Desert, India'. *Philosophical Transactions of the Royal Society, London* 267: 467–501.

Singh, J. P., and M. Khan. 2002. *Mythical Space, Cosmology, and Landscape: Towards a Cultural Geography of India.* New Delhi: Manak Publications.

Singh, P. 1994. *Excavations at Narhan 1984–1989.* Varanasi: Banaras Hindu University.

———. 2002. 'The Neolithic cultures of northern and eastern India', in S. Settar and R. Korisettar. (eds.), *Indian Archaeology in Retrospect: Volume 1 Prehistory*, pp. 127–150. New Delhi: Indian Council for Historical Research.

Singh, U. 2004. *The Discovery of Ancient India: Early Archaeologists and the Beginning of Archaeology.* Delhi: Permanent Black.

———. 2008. *A History of Ancient and Early Medieval India: From the Stone Age to the 12th Century.* Delhi: Pearson Longman.

Sinopoli, C. M. 1991. *Approaches to Archaeological Ceramics.* New York: Plenum Press.

———. 2001. 'On the edge of empire: form and substance in the Satavahana dynasty', in S. E. Alcock, T. N. D'Altroy, K. D. Morrison and C. M. Sinopoli (eds.), *Empire: Perspectives from Archaeology and History*, pp. 155–178. Cambridge: Cambridge University Press.

———. 2003. *The Political Economy of Craft Production: Crafting Empire in South India, c. 1350–1650.* Cambridge: Cambridge University Press.

Smith, M. E. 2006b. 'How do archaeologists compare early states?'. *Reviews in Anthropology* 35: 5–35.

Smith, M. L. 2001. *The Archaeology of an Early Historic Town in Central India.* Oxford: Archaeopress.

Smith, M. L. (ed.). 2003. *The Social Construction of Ancient Cities.* Washington: Smithsonian Books.

Smith, M. L. 2005. 'Networks, territories and the cartography of ancient states'. *Annals of the Association of American Geographers* 95.4: 832–849.

———. 2006a. 'The archaeology of South Asian cities'. *Journal of Archaeological Research* 14: 97–142.

———. 2008. 'Urban empty spaces. Contentious places for consensus-building'. *Archaeological Dialogues* 15.2: 216–231.

———. 2013. 'The substance and symbolism of long-distance exchange: textiles as desired trade goods in the Bronze Age Middle Asian Interaction sphere', in S. A. Abraham, P. Gullapalli, T. P. Raczek and U. Z. Rizvi (eds.), *Connections and Complexity: New Approaches to the Archaeology of South Asia*, pp. 143–160. Walnut Creek: Left Coast Press.

Smith, V. A. 1901. 'Forward' to *A Report on a Tour of Exploration of the Antiquities in the Tarai, Nepal*. Calcutta: Office of the Superintendent of Government Printing.

Sonawane, V. H. 2002. 'Post-urban Harappan culture of Gujarat', in S. Settar and R. Korisettar (eds.), *Indian Archaeology in Retrospect: Protohistory, Archaeology of the Harappan Civilization Vol. II*, pp. 159–172. New Delhi: ICHR and Manohar.

Spate, O. H. K., and T. A. Learmouth. 1967. *India and Pakistan: A General and Regional Geography*. London: Methuen and Co.

Spencer, C. S. 2010. 'Territorial expansion and primary state formation'. *Proceedings of the National Academy of Sciences* 107: 7119–7126.

Spooner, D. B. 1913. 'Mr Ratan Tata's excavations at Pataliputra'. *Annual Report of the Archaeological Survey of India* 1912–13: 53–86.

———. 1915. 'The Zoroastrian period of Indian History'. *Journal of the Royal Asiatic Society of Great Britain and Ireland*: 63–89.

Srinivasan, D. M. 2007. *On the Cusp of an Era: Art in the Pre-Kushana World*. Leiden: E.J. Brill.

Srinivasan, S., C. M. Sinopoli, K. D. Morrison, R. Gopal and S. Rangunathan. 2009. 'South Indian Megalithic iron and higher carbon steel: with reference to Kadebakele and comparative insights from Mel-Siruvalur', in J. Mei and T. Rehren (eds.), *Metallurgy and Civilisation: Eurasia and Beyond*, pp. 116–122. London: Archetype.

Srivastava, K. M. 1986. *Discovery of Kapilavstu*. New Delhi: Books and Books.

———. 1996. *Excavations at Piprahwa and Ganwaria*. New Delhi: Archaeological Survey of India.

Stacul, G. 1966. 'Preliminary report on the pre-Buddhist Necropolises in Swat (W. Pakistan)'. *East and West* 16: 37–79.

———. 1967. 'Excavations in a Rock Shelter near Ghaligai (Swat, W. Pakistan). Preliminary Report'. *East and West* 17: 185–219.

———. 1969. 'Excavation near Ghaligai (1968) and chronological sequence of protohistorical cultures in the Swat Valley'. *East and West* 19: 44–91.

———. 1973. 'Inhumation and cremation in north-west Pakistan at the end of the second millennium B.C.', in N. Hammond (ed.), *South Asian Archaeology*, pp. 197–201. New Jersey: Noyes Press.

———. 1977. 'Dwelling and Storage-Pits at Loebanr III (Swat, Pakistan) 1976 Excavation Report'. *East and West* 27: 227–253.

———. 1979. 'The black-burnished ware period in the Swat Valley (c. 1700–1500 BC)', in M. Taddei (ed.), *South Asian Archaeology 1977*, pp. 661–673. Naples: Istituto Universitario Orientale.

———. 1984a. 'Cultural change in the Swat Valley and beyond, c. 3000–1400 BC', in B. Allchin (ed.), *South Asian Archaeology 1981*, pp. 205–212. Cambridge: Cambridge University Press.

———. 1984b. 'Harappan post-urban evidence in the Swat Valley', in B. B. Lal and S. P. Gupta (eds.), *Frontiers of the Indus Civilisation*, pp. 271–276. New Delhi: Books and Books.

———. 1987. *Prehistoric and Protohistoric Swat, Pakistan (c. 3000–1400 BC)*. Rome: Istituto Italiano Per Il Medio Ed Estremo Oriente.

———. 1989a. 'Continuity and change in the Swat Valley (18th–15th Centuries BC)', in J. M. Kenoyer (ed.), *Old Problems and New Perspectives in the Archaeology of South Asia*, pp. 249–251. Madison: Wisconsin Archaeological Reports.

———. 1989b. 'Swat, Pirak and connected problems: mid-2nd millennium', in C. Jarrige, (ed.), *South Asian Archaeology 1989*, pp. 267–270. Madison: Prehistory Press.

———. 1994a. 'Neolithic inner Asian traditions in Northern Indo-Pakistani Valleys', in A. Parpol and P. Koskikallio (eds.), *South Asian Archaeology 1993*, pp. 708–714. Helsinki: Suomalainen Tiedeakatemia.

———. 1994b. 'Querns from early Swat', in J. M. Kenoyer (ed.), *From Sumer to Meluhha: Contributions to the Archaeology of South and West Asia in Memory of George F. Dales, Jr*, pp. 235–239. Madison: Wisconsin Archaeological Reports 3.

Stacul, G., and S. Tusa. 1975. 'Report on the excavations at Aligrama (Swat, Pakistan) 1966, 1972'. *East and West* 25: 291–321.

Stargardt, J. 1990. *The Ancient Pyu of Burma. Volume One: Early Pyu Cities in a Man-Made Landscape*. Cambridge: Cambridge University Press.

Stein, A. 1928. *Innermost Asia: Detailed Report of Explorations in Central Asia, Kansu, and Eastern Iran*. Oxford: Oxford University Press.

———. 1929. *On Alexander's Track to the Indus. Personal Narrative of Explorations in the North-West Frontier of India*. London: MacMillan and Co.

Stein, G. 1994. 'Economy, ritual, and power in Ubaid Mesopotamia', in G. Stein and M. Rothman (eds.), *Chiefdoms and Early States in the Near East: The Organizational Dynamics of Complexity*, pp. 35–46. Madison (WI): Prehistory Press.

Stein, G., and M. Rothman. (eds.). 1994. *Chiefdoms and Early States in the Near East: The Organizational Dynamics of Complexity*, pp. 35–46. Madison (WI): Prehistory Press.

Subbarao, B. 1958. *The Personality of India*. Baroda: M. S. University of Baroda.

Sugandhi, N. 2003. 'Context, content, and composition: questions of intended meaning and the Asokan edicts'. *Asian Perspectives* 42: 224–246.

Tainter, J. A. 1988. *The Collapse of Complex Societies*. Cambridge: Cambridge University Press.

———. 2006. 'Archaeology of overshoot and collapse'. *Annual Review of Anthropology* 35: 59–74.

Tambiah, S. 1976. *World Conqueror and World Renouncer*. Cambridge: Cambridge University Press.

Taylor, J. L. 1993. *Forest Monks and the Nation-State: An Anthropological and Historical Study in Northeast Thailand*. Singapore: Institute of Southeast Asian Studies.

Tewari, R. 2003. 'The origins of iron-working in India: new evidence from the Central Ganga Plain and the Eastern Vindhyas'. *Antiquity* 77: 536–545.

Tewari, R., R. K. Srivastava, K. K. Singh, and K. S. Saraswat. 2006. 'Further excavations at Lahuradewa, District Sant Kabir Nagar (U.P.) 2005–06: Preliminary Observations'. *Puratattva* 36: 68–77.

Thapar, B. K. 1973. 'New traits of the Indus civilisation at Kalibangan: an appraisal', in N. Hammond (ed.), *South Asian Archaeology*, pp. 85–104. London: Duckworth.

———. 1975. 'Kalibangan. A Harappan metropolis beyond the Indus Valley'. *Expedition* (Winter): 19–32.

Thapar, R. 1961. *Asoka and the Decline of the Mauryas*. Oxford: Oxford University Press.

———. 1985. *From Lineage to State: Social Formations of the Mid-First Millennium B.C. in the Ganges Valley*. New Delhi: Oxford University Press.

———. 1987. *The Mauryans Revisited*. New Delhi: Centre for Studies in Social Sciences.

———. (ed.). 1995. *Recent Perspectives of Early Indian History*. New Delhi: Popular Prakashan.

———. 1996. *Asoka and the Decline of the Mauryas*. (2nd edition). New Delhi: Oxford University Press.

———. 2002. 'Cyclic and linear time in early India' in K. Ridderbos (ed.), *Time*, pp. 27–45. Cambridge: Cambridge University Press.

———. 2006a. 'The historiography of the concept of 'Aryan'' in R. Thapar et al. (ed.), *India: Historical Beginnings and the Concept of the Aryan*, pp. 1–40. New Delhi: National Book Trust.

———. 2006b. 'The Mauryan Empire in Early India'. *Historical Research* 79.205: 287–305.

Thomas, K. D. 2003. 'Minimizing risk: approaches to pre-Harappan human ecology on the north-west margin of the greater Indus system', in S. A. Weber and W. R. Belcher (eds.), *Indus Ethnobiology*, pp. 397–429. Lanham: Lexington Books.

Thomas, K. D., and F. R. Allchin. 1986. 'Radiocarbon dating of some early sites in N. W. Pakistan'. *South Asian Studies* 2: 37–44.

Thomas, P. K. 2000. 'Animal subsistence in the Chalcolithic culture of western India (with special reference to Balathal)'. *Indo-Pacific Prehistory Association Bulletin* 19: 147–151.

Thornton, C. P. 2013. 'Mesopotamia, Meluhha, and those in between', in H. Crawford (ed.), *The Sumerian World*, pp. 600–619. London: Routledge.

Tieken, H. 2000. Asoka and the Buddhist Samgha: a study of Asoka's schism edict and minor edict 1. *Bulletin of the School of Oriental and African Studies* 63: 1–30.

Tiwari, D. N. 1985. 'Cave burials from Western Nepal, Mustang'. *Ancient Nepal* 85: 1–12.

Tiwari, S. (ed.). 2010. *Harapan Civilisation and Vedic Culture*. New Delhi: Pratibha Prakashan.

Tomber, R. 2008. *Indo-Roman Trade: From Pots to Pepper*. London: Duckworth.

Tosi. M. 1983. *Prehistoric Sistan*. Rome: Istituto Italiano Per Il Medio Ed Estremo Oriente.

Tosi, M. 1984. 'The notion of craft specialisation and its representation in the archaeological record of early states in the Turanian Basin', in M. Spriggs (ed.), *Marxist Perspectives in Archaeology*, pp. 22–55. Cambridge: Cambridge University Press.

———. 1987. 'The Indus civilisation beyond the Indian Subcontinent', in M. Jansen, M. Mulloy and G. Urban (eds.), *Forgotten Cities on the Indus: Early Civilisation in Pakistan from the Eighth to the Second Millennium BC*, pp. 111–128. Mainz: Philipp von Zabern.

Tosi, M., S. M. Shahmirzadi, and M. A. Joyenda. 1992. 'The bronze age in Iran and Afghanistan', in A. H. Dani and V. M. Masson (eds.), *History of Civilisations of Central Asia: Volume 1. The Dawn of Civilisation: Earliest Times to 700 BC*, pp. 191–224. Paris: UNESCO.

Trading Economics 2012. http://www .tradingeconomics.com/bangladesh/ population-density-people-per-sq-km-wb -data.html.

Trautmann, T. R. 1971. *Kautilya and the Arthasastra*. Leiden: E.J. Brill.

——. 1997. *Aryans and British India*. Berkeley: University of California Press.

Trigger, B. G. 2003. *Understanding Early Civilizations: A Comparative Study*. Cambridge: Cambridge University Press.

Tripathi, V. 2008. Genisis and spread of urban process in the Gangetic Plain, in G. Sengupta and S. Chakraborty (eds.), *Archaeology of Early Historic South Asia*, pp. 137–167. New Delhi: Pragati Publications.

Tusa, S. 1979. 'The Swat Valley in the second and first millennium BC: a question of marginality', in M. Taddei (ed.), *South Asian Archaeology 1977*, pp. 675–695. Naples: Istituto Universitario Orientale.

Upadhyay, P. 2008. 'Mineral resource zone around Gangetic Plains: a vital factor for urbanisation in Middle Ganga Plain', in G. Sengupta and S. Chakraborty (eds.), *Archaeology of Early Historic South Asia*, pp. 170–190. New Delhi: Pragati Publications.

Varma, S. 2008. 'The absence of urban centres in Early Historic Kathiawad', in G. Sengupta and S. Chakraborty (eds.), *Archaeology of Early Historic South Asia*, pp. 213–230. New Delhi: Pragati Publications.

Vats, M. S. 1940. *Excavations at Harappa*. Delhi: Government of India.

Verardi, G. 2007. *Excavations at Gotihawa and Pipri, Kapilbastu District, Nepal*. Lumbini: Lumbini International Research Institute.

Vidale, M. 1989. 'Specialised producers and urban elites: on the role of craft industries in Mature Harappan urban contexts', in J. M. Kenoyer (ed.), *Old Problems and New Perspectives in the Archaeology of South Asia*, pp. 171–181. Madison: Department of Anthropology.

——. 2004. 'Growing in a foreign world: for a history of the 'Meluhha villages' in Mesopotamia in the 3rd millennium BC', in A. Panaino and A. Piras (eds.), *Proceedings of the Fourth Annual Symposium of the Assyrian and Babylonian Intellectual Heritage Project*, pp. 261–280. Milan: Universita di Bologna and ISIAO.

——. 2005. 'The short-horned bull on the Indus seals: a symbol of the families in the western trade?', in U. Franke-Vogt and H.-J. Weisshaar (eds.), *South Asian Archaeology 2003*, pp. 147–158. Aachen: Linden Soft.

——. 2010. 'Aspects of palace life at Mohenjo-daro'. *South Asian Studies* 26: 59–76

Vinogradova, N. 2001. 'Towards the question of the relative chronology for proto historic Swat sequence (on the basis of the Swat graveyards)'. *East and West* 51.1–2: 9–36.

Vogelsang, W. J. 1988. 'A period of acculturation in Ancient Gandhara'. *South Asian Studies* 4: 103–113.

——. 1992. *The Rise and Organisation of the Achaemenid Empire: The Eastern Iranian Evidence*. Leiden: E.J. Brill.

Watkins, T. 1992. 'The beginning of the Neolithic: searching for meaning in material culture change'. *Paleorient* 18: 63–75

——. 2004. 'Architecture and "theatres of memory" in the Neolithic of southwest Asia', in E. DeMarrais, C. Gosden and C. Renfrew (eds.), *Rethinking Materiality: The Engagement of Mind with the Material World*, pp. 97–106. Cambridge: McDonald Institute for Archaeological Research.

Wattenmaker, P. 1994. 'Political fluctuations and local exchange systems: evidence from the Early Bronze Age settlements at Kurban Hoyuk', in G. Stein and M. Rothman (eds.), *Chiefdoms and Early States in the Near East: The Organizational Dynamics of Complexity*, pp. 193–208. Madison (WI): Prehistory Press.

Weber, S. A. 1999. 'Seeds of change: palaeoethnobotany and the Indus civilisation'. *Antiquity* 73: 813–826.

——. 2003. 'Archaeobotany at Harappa: indications for change', in S. Weber and W. R. Belcher (eds.), *Indus Ethnobiology*, pp. 175–198. Lanham: Lexington Books.

Wheatley, P. 1971. *The Pivot of the Four Quarters*. Edinburgh: Edinburgh University Press.

Wheeler, R. E. M. 1948. 'Brahmagiri and Chandravalli 1947: megalithic and other culture in Chitaldrug District, Mysore State'. *Ancient India* 4: 181–310.

——. 1949. 'Editorial'. *Ancient India* 5: 1–11.

——. 1950. *Five Thousand Years of Pakistan: An Archaeological Outline*. London: Royal India and Pakistan Society.

———. 1953. *The Indus Civilization. Supplementary Volume of the Cambridge History of India.* Cambridge: Cambridge University Press.

———. 1955. *Still Digging: Interleaves from an Antiquary's Notebook.* London: Michael Joseph.

———. 1959. *Early India and Pakistan to Ashoka.* London: Thames and Hudson.

———. 1962. *Charsada: A Metropolis of the North-West Frontier.* London: Oxford University Press.

———. 1963. *Early India and Pakistan to Ashoka.* London: Thames and Hudson.

Wheeler. R. E. M. 1966. *Civilisations of the Indus Valley and Beyond.* London: Thames and Hudson.

Wheeler, R. E. M. 1968. *The Indus Civilisation.* (3rd edition). Cambridge: Cambridge University Press.

———. 1976. *My Archaeological Mission to India and Pakistan.* London: Thames and Hudson.

Wheeler, R. E. M., M. A. Ghosh and K. Deva. 1946. 'Arikamedu – An Indo-Roman trading station on the east coast of India'. *Ancient India* 2: 17–124.

Whitehouse, D. 1978. 'Excavations at Kandahar 1964: first interim report'. *Afghan Studies* 1: 9–40.

Wickremeratne, A. 1987. 'Shifting metaphors of sacrality: the mythic dimensions of Anuradhapura', in B. Smith and H. B. Reynolds (eds.), *The City as Sacred Centre: Essays on Six Asian Contexts*, pp. 45–59. Leiden: E.J. Brill.

Wilkinson, J. C. 1977. *Water and Tribal Settlement in South-East Arabia: A Study of the Aflaj of Oman.* Oxford: Clarendon Press.

Willis, M. (ed.). 2000. *Buddhist Reliquaries from Ancient India.* London: British Museum Press.

Woolley, L. 1939. *A Report on the Work of the Archaeological Survey of India.* Delhi: Government of India.

Wright, H. T. 2001. 'Cultural action in the Uruk world', in M. S. Rothman (ed.), *Uruk Mesopotamia and Its Neighbours*, pp. 123–127. Santa Fe: School of American Research.

Wright, R. P. 2010. *The Ancient Indus: Urbanism, Economy, and Society.* New York: Cambridge University Press.

———. 2013. 'Commodities and things: the Kulli in context', in S. A. Abraham, P. Gullapalli, T. P. Raczek and U. Z. Rizvi (eds.), *Connections and Complexity: New Approaches to the Archaeology of South Asia*, pp. 107–126. Walnut Creek: Left Coast Press.

Xuanzang, 1996. *The Great Tang Dynasty Record of the Western Regions.* Berkeley: Numata Center for Buddhist Translation and Research.

Yadava, M. G., and R. Ramesh. 2005. 'Monsoon reconstruction from radiocarbon dated tropical Indian speleotherms'. *Holocene* 15.1: 48–59.

Yalman, N. 1960. 'The flexibility of caste principles in a Kandyan Community', in E. R. Leach (ed.), *Aspects of Caste in South India, Ceylon and North-West Pakistan*, pp. 78–112 Cambridge: Cambridge University Press.

Yash Pal, B., R. K. Snood and D. P. Agrawal 1984. 'Remote sensing of the "Lost" Sarasvati River', in B. B. Lal and S. P. Gupta (eds.), *Frontiers of the Indus Civilization. Sir Mortimer Wheeler Commemoration Volume*, pp. 491–497. New Delhi: Books and Books.

Yatoo, M. 2012. *Characterising Material Culture to Determine Settlement Patterns in North West Kashmir.* Unpublished PhD Thesis. University of Leicester.

Yoffee, N. 1995. 'Political economy in early Mesopotamian states'. *Annual Review of Anthropology* 24: 281–311.

———. 1997. 'The obvious and the chimerical: city-states in archaeological perspective', in D. L. Nichols and T. H. Charlton (eds.), *The Archaeology of City-States: Cross Cultural Approaches*, pp. 255–263. Washington: Smithsonian Institution Press.

———. 2005. *Myths of the Archaic State. Evolution of the Earliest Cities, States, and Civilizations.* Cambridge: Cambridge University Press.

Young, R. 2007a. 'The archaeobotanical remains', in R. A. E. Coningham and I. Ali (eds.), *Charsadda: The British-Pakistani Excavations at the Bala Hisar*, pp. 241–245. Oxford: Archaeopress.

———. 2007b. 'The archaeozoological remains', in R. A. E. Coningham and I. Ali (eds.), *Charsadda: The British-Pakistani Excavations at the Bala Hisar*, pp. 247–257. Oxford: Archaeopress.

Young, R. L. 2003. *Agriculture and Pastoralism in the Late Bronze and Iron Age, North West Frontier Province, Pakistan.* Oxford: Archaeopress.

———. 2009. 'Representation within the landscape of northern Pakistan: the meanings of Gandhara'. *South Asian Studies* 25: 29–40.

———. 2010. 'Transhumant groups and subordination in the former north west Frontier Province, Pakistan'. *Ancient Pakistan* 11: 123–138.

Young, R. L., and I. Ali. 2007. 'The environmental setting', in R. A. E. Coningham and I. Ali (eds.), *Charsadda: The British-Pakistani Excavations at the Bala Hisar*, pp. 9–18. Oxford: Archaeopress.

Young, R. L., and R. A. E. Coningham. 2006. 'Botanical remains', in R. A. E. Coningham (ed.), *Anuradhapura: The British-Sri Lankan Excavations at Anuradhapura Salgaha Watta 2. Volume 2: The Artefacts*, pp. 629–646. Oxford: Archaeopress.

———. 2010. 'From village to state: modelling food consumption and ideological change at Anuradhapura, Sri Lanka', in P. Gunawardhana, G. Adikari and R. A. E. Coningham (eds.), *Essays in Archaeology*, pp. 81–92. Colombo: Neptune Publishers.

Young, R. L., R. A. E. Coningham, I. Ali and T. Ali. 2008. 'The archaeological visibility of transhumance tested using faunal material from NWFP, Pakistan', in E. M. Raven and G. L. Possehl (eds.), *South Asian Archaeology 1999*, pp. 203–210. Groningen: Egbert Forsten Publishing.

Young, R. L., R. A. E. Coningham, C. M. Batt and Ali, I. 2000. 'A comparison of Kalasha and Kho subsistence patterns in Chitral, NWFP, Pakistan'. *South Asian Studies* 16: 133–142.

Young, R. L., R. A. E. Coningham, K. Nalinda, J. Perera and H. Khan. 2006. 'Faunal remains', in R. A. E. Coningham (ed.), *Anuradhapura: the British-Sri Lankan Excavations at Anuradhapura Salgaha Watta 2. Volume 2: The Artefacts*, pp. 501–618. Oxford: Archaeopress.

Young, R. L., and H. Fazeli. 2013. 'Women and class in landlord villages of the Tehran Plain, Iran'. *Historical Archaeology* 47.2: 76–98.

Zahir, M. 2012. *The Protohistoric Cemeteries of Northwestern Pakistan: The Deconstruction and Reinterpretations of Archaeological and Burial Traditions*. Unpublished PhD Thesis. University of Leicester.

Zeder, M. L. 2006. 'Central questions in the domestication of plants and animals'. *Evolutionary Anthropology* 15.3: 105–117.

———. 2009. 'The Neolithic Macro-(R)evolution: macroevolutionary theory and the study of culture change'. *Journal of Archaeological Research* 17: 1–63

Zohary, D., and M. Hopf (ed.). 2000. *Domestication of Plants in the Old World: The Origin and Spread of Cultivated Plants in West Asia, Europe, and the Nile Valley*. Oxford: Oxford University Press.

INDEX

Aali, 263

aceramic Neolithic, 110–11, 116, 138, 143

Achaemenid Empire, 10, 88, 290, 332, 350, 357, 360, 373, 404, 414, 454–55

Acharya, K.P., 325

Afghanistan, 10, 28, 32–33, 44, 66, 83, 86, 91, 97, 165, 178, 183, 211, 218, 220, 246, 273, 289, 326, 328, 331, 360–61, 370, 373, 403, 406, 444, 446, 451, 473

agate, 21, 122, 162, 189, 192, 198, 220, 259, 301–2, 336, 386, 447, 480

Agrawal, D.P., 6, 19, 94, 245, 281, 288, 291, 293, 321, 339, 466, 476

Ahar, 300, 477, 480

Ahar-Banas, 281, 302

Ahicchatra, 362, 421

Ai Khanoum, 370–71, 469, 471

Ajatasatru, 358

Ajithprasad, P., 131

Akkermans, P., 171

Akra, 469

Akra Dheri, 324, 331, 351, 372

Alam, M.S., 384

Alamgirpur, 297

Alexander the Great, 71, 87, 329, 355, 360, 370–71, 373–74, 376–77, 399, 404, 410, 424

Algaze, G., 171, 183, 239, 274, 312, 465, 485

Ali, I., 95, 284, 287, 431

Aligrama, 247, 284, 286, 294, 322, 325, 328, 372, 374

Allah Bund, 267–68

Allahabad, 72, 83, 127, 243, 335, 408, 413, 427, 431

Allahdino, 254

Allchin, B. and F.R., 5–6, 25, 109, 127, 256, 272, 319, 328, 335, 343, 466

Allchin, F.R., 7, 281, 328, 401, 413, 437

Allen, C., 67, 438

Altekar, A.S., 478

Altyn-depe, 228

Amaravati, 423

Ambala, 69

Amri, 86, 148–49, 154, 156–57, 167, 174, 255, 257, 265, 268, 465

Amri ware, 149

anchor settlements, 145, 160, 171, 305, 315, 330, 336, 351

Andaman Islands, 33

Andhra Pradesh, 310, 339, 342, 386

animal domestication, 131

animal husbandry, 22, 105, 222

Anthony, D., 56

Anuradhapura, 13, 53, 96, 136, 218, 244, 311, 320, 346, 348, 351, 359–60, 362, 390, 393–95, 403–4, 409, 412, 418–19, 431–32, 444, 447, 456, 475, 478, 482, 484

apsidal shrine, 305, 437, 451, 472–74, 478

Arabian Sea, 6, 32–33, 38, 49, 143, 162, 178, 211, 224, 229, 232–33, 247, 259, 263, 267, 274–75, 326, 333, 449, 464, 480

Arachosia, 332, 397

Aramaic, 371, 378, 401, 406, 444, 453

Aranyakas, 62

Archaeological Survey of India, 74, 77, 80, 83, 93–94, 180, 192, 311, 439

Arikamedu, 80, 83–84, 345–46, 387, 403, 475

Arthashastra, 12, 60, 217, 244, 358, 403, 406–7, 409, 415, 417–19, 427, 431, 451, 465

Aryans, 16, 54, 83, 85, 89–90, 255, 265, 281, 285, 316–17, 342, 476

ash mounds, 77, 131, 133, 135, 266

ASI. *See* Archaeological Survey of India

Asiatic Society of Bengal, 68, 70–71, 408

Asoka, 5, 9, 71–72, 403, 406, 408–12, 414, 424, 426, 436–37, 442, 444–45, 447–48, 450–51, 454, 456–57, 463, 465–68, 481–82, 490

Asokan edicts, 345, 409, 411, 413, 422–23, 436, 439, 452, 467, 490

Astadhyayi, 358, 449

Asthana, S., 160, 194, 336

Athura Veda, 62